Inc.
MAGAZINE'S

DATABASICS
Your Guide to
Online Business Information

Niculae Asciu

Inc.
MAGAZINE'S

DATABASICS
Your Guide to
Online Business Information

by
Doran Howitt and Marvin I. Weinberger
MIW Associates, Inc., Belmont, Massachusetts

Garland Publishing, Inc.
New York & London

15   14   13   12   11   10   9   8   7   6   5   4   3   2   1

Library of Congress Cataloging in Publication Data

Howitt, Doran.
  Inc. magazine's Databasics

  Includes index.
  1. Information storage and retrieval systems—Business.
2. Business—Information services.   I. Weinberger, Marvin.
II. Inc.   III. Title.
IV. Title: Databasics.
HF5548.2.H67   1984   650'.028'5425   84-10305
ISBN 0-8240-7287-1

Cover Photograph: Phillip Holt
Cover Design: Bruce Sanders and Jonathan Billing
Book Design: Jonathan Billing

Distribution to bookstores by Kampmann and Co., Inc.,
New York

Published by Garland Publishing, Inc.
136 Madison Avenue, New York, New York 10016

PRINTED IN THE UNITED STATES OF AMERICA

Contents

PART III
DATABASE VENDORS

PART IV
MAKING THE CONNECTION

PART V
ONLINE INFORMATION IN THE FUTURE

APPENDIXES

DATABASICS Special Offer Section

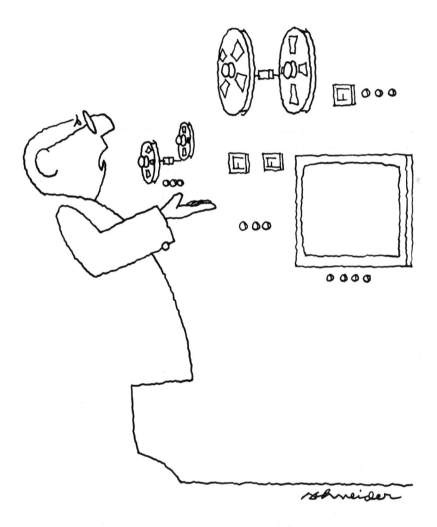

"Be reasonable. I can't credit you as coauthor."

Foreword

As the founder and publisher of *Inc.* magazine, I am always looking for practical ideas to serve the needs of growing companies. This valuable guide is full of such ideas, which is why I am happy to join in bringing it to you.

DATABASICS is both a how-to and a reference book. It teaches you how to profit from the business information contained in online databases. The facts you need can be obtained quickly online, and often at surprisingly low cost. Databases were once the sole province of librarians—but no more. They've become much easier to use. Indeed, the learning curve to master some of the most popular databases is now quite short; and it's worth the effort.

Databases can be used to track stocks and commodities, monitor competitors, identify business opportunities, check credit references, plan trips, investigate acquisition targets, and much more. In sum, it can help you plan for the future and understand events both inside and outside your own field of business. Information like this can provide the crucial difference between success and failure in today's rapidly changing and competitive environment.

In addition to databases, this book explains about peoplebases. That is to say, electronic mail. One of the most powerful emerging opportunities is the use of electronic mail to network groups of businessmen, albeit geographically dispersed, into common interest groups. The members of these electronic conferences leverage off of the knowledge and experiences of one another. We at *Inc.* hope to play an important role in forging these networks.

DATABASICS also contains over a thousand dollars worth of free and discount offers good toward the purchase of modems, software, terminals, database services, and more. Just one or two of these offers can easily pay back your investment in the book.

This is the first book to carry *Inc.'s* name. That is a tribute to the extraordinary energy and perseverance of the staff at MIW Associates: Marvin Weinberger, Doran Howitt, Ellen O'Donnell, Israel Melman, and Steven Fogel.

They spent almost two years on this project, and have made 'business sense' out of a very large and complex field.

Look for future *Inc.* books to help you manage your growing business. Meanwhile, start making *databases* a *basic* part of your business strategy.

Best wishes,
Bernard A. Goldhirsh

Preface

This book is divided into five parts. In Part I we explain what commercial online databases are, where they come from, and how you can use them in your business. We also briefly introduce two related services: information brokers and electronic mail.

In Part II we describe some of the most important business-oriented databases, taking care to point out differences among competing products. This is a selective list; we review about 100 of the approximately 2,000 databases on the market. Our goal in this section is to illustrate the usefulness of databases by going into considerable detail (including sample searches) about a selected number, rather than covering a large number in a superficial manner.

Part III presents several dozen database vendors, the companies that electronically distribute databases. We provide much detail about the more important ones but also introduce a number of new or lesser-known companies. We devote considerable space to the vendors, as we believe this is an area given short shrift in most other books about online databases. Hundreds of databases (including many not covered in Part II) are noted here under the offerings of each vendor.

In Part IV we discuss a number of nuts-and-bolts topics, including the various kinds of hardware and software usable for online communications. In the appendixes we give details of selected terminals, modems, and communications programs. These "smorgasbords," as we call them, illustrate the range of products available as a way of helping the reader to do his own comparison shopping. We do not necessarily recommend these products over others that are not listed.

Part V explores the future of the online industry. It takes a brief look at the kinds of services that today's databases are evolving into, paying particular attention to the applications of artificial intelligence.

No company paid in any way to have its product or service listed in this book. The authors present each database, vendor, broker, terminal, modem, or software package based on editorial considerations only. In most cases, the company concerned was given an opportunity to review the information about it for technical accuracy, but the authors exercised final judgment over what information would and would not be included.

Most of the companies we list use names that are trademarks or service marks. As a matter of style, we have omitted the various trademark insignia, such as ® or ™, that these companies may use. Readers should assume, however, that any name found herein that begins with a capital letter is a protected mark. We have attempted to spell each company's product names the way it does, i.e., using all capital letters, or both capitals and lower case, or spelling "database" as one word or two as the case may be.

As a service to the reader, we invited a number of companies to make discount offers to purchasers of this book. These offers, described in a special section, at the back of the book, provide literally thousands of dollars worth of connect time on database vendors, as well as discounts or rebates on communications software, modems, terminals, periodical subscriptions, and research services. These are not advertisements; the participating companies did not pay to be included, nor do they receive any income from the sale of this book. Our only goal in providing the coupons was to encourage readers to try out the services introduced here.

We have made a considerable effort to insure the accuracy of the data in this book as of fall 1983. The market is changing rapidly, and it is in the nature of a work like this that some of the information becomes outdated quickly. We encourage readers to apprise us of new information, and to contact us with comments or suggestions for future editions. Write to us at:

Databasics
c/o MIW Associates
9 Carleton Road
Belmont, MA 02178
Telephone: 617-484-2361

We can be reached by electronic mail at the following addresses:

The Source: BBW959
ITT/Dialcom: 98:PAC004
CompuServe: 72446, 3140
MCI Mail: 151-6146 (Databasics)

Acknowledgments

This book was written and managed by MIW Associates. Our partners in bringing the book to fruition were Garland Publishing, Inc. and the Goldhirsh Group, publisher of *Inc.* magazine. The authors gratefully acknowledge the assistance of Jeff Conrad and Gavin Borden of Garland; and we also express our thanks to Bernard A. Goldhirsh of the Goldhirsh Group for his support.

Many other individuals also helped bring the book into existence:

Ellen O'Donnell provided a substantial portion of the research, wrote or edited many chapters, and contributed in some measure to almost every section.

Israel J. Melman gave invaluable guidance and editorial criticism. We should have followed his advice more often than we did.

Steven Fogel researched many database vendors and helped supervise the entire project.

Marie Blasko managed a number of vital administrative and clerical chores, all while pursuing full-time law study.

Marie-Christine Allen expertly typed and revised the manuscript under less-than-ideal working conditions.

Steven K. Roberts wrote early drafts of six chapters and contributed a number of valuable ideas.

Shirley Cobert performed copy editing and embarrassed the authors by correcting far too many mistakes.

Others who contributed include: Robert C. Wood, who wrote two chapters; Laurie Rich, who wrote the histories of Management Contents and EIC/Intelligence; Steven Sieck of Link Resources Inc., who wrote the chapter on the future and contributed ideas and suggestions; Bill Bassett, who helped with the editing; Kelly Warnken and Katherine Ackerman, who researched the information brokers listings; Kathleen Long and Kathy Bell, who did the research for several database vendor chapters; and John S. Fine, who lent his technical expertise to our discussions of computer software.

Several organizations were very helpful in providing material used in the book: Data Decisions Inc., which provided much of the material used in the discussion of modems and the modem smorgasbord; GML Corp., which supplied research used in preparing the smorgasbord of terminals; Datapro and The International Software Database, which assisted in preparation of the communications software smorgasbord; and the California Library Agency for Systems and Services, which gave kind permission to reprint material by Janet Bruman in the chapter about communications software. The contributions of these organizations are further noted in the appropriate chapters.

Finally, we express our appreciation to the following people for helping in various ways: Ruth Adams; Jonathan Billing; Geoffrey Braine; John Carlson; Lois, Warren, and Ted Farrelli; Neil Goldhirsh; David U. Greevy; Jessica Harvey; Jean Martinian; Bruce Sanders; Tom Walker; David Weinberger; Ruth Weinstein; Bob Zolnerzak; and Lisa.

About the Authors

Marvin Weinberger has been active in the information industry since 1978 when he founded MIW Associates. He is consultant to major information industry companies on product development and marketing. Weinberger is chairman of the Task Force on Artificial Intelligence for the Information Industry Association. He is also a member of the Massachusetts Bar, with his degree in law from Boston University.

Doran Howitt has written for a variety of business publications, most recently as associate editor at *Inc.* magazine; he is now editorial director for MIW Associates. He holds degrees in economics from the University of California and the Fletcher School of Law and Diplomacy of Tufts University.

PART ONE

ALL ABOUT THE INFORMATION INDUSTRY

"I'm George Prescott. I don't believe I have you in my database yet."

*I*f you're not sure you know what an online database is, Part I will tell you. The first four chapters describe some of the many ways that databases can help you in your business. Chapters 5 through 7 explain in more detail where databases come from. Chapter 8 presents the myriad ways that database vendors charge for information, and Chapter 9 leads you into some more advanced considerations in conducting a successful search. In Chapter 10, we introduce you to people who can conduct a search for you; Chapter 11 illustrates a typical online search session; and Chapter 12 briefly discusses the closely related subject of electronic mail.

1 Databases Come Out of the Closet

Several years ago, the coauthor of this book, then working for a congressional candidate, needed to know the legality of business contributions to political campaigns. At a law library where he went to gather information, a librarian suggested an online database search.

"What does that mean?" he asked. The librarian unlocked a closet, hauled out a device that looked like a portable typewriter, and, connecting it to a telephone, typed in a few words. Seconds later, the machine began printing a list of legal precedents regarding campaign contributions. Then the librarian made a few more keystrokes, and out came printed summaries of dozens of news aricles and scholarly studies on the same subject.

Within ten minutes, our researcher had all he needed to know. The whole session cost $20 and saved him a day's research in the library. He was astonished. Why hadn't anyone told him about databases before? Why was the device kept locked up in a closet? He resolved to learn all he could about online databases.

For a decade, commercially available online databases have been kept literally in the closet. They were developed by a subculture of college professors, scientists, programmers, and librarians who rarely thought to initiate non-specialists into their secret. Who else, indeed, would care enough about bibliographies, statistics, abstracts, thesauri, and indexes? The answer is now becoming clear: business managers, owners, entrepreneurs.

Good information is hard to come by in business. It takes time to gather facts, and time is one of the most precious resources a business manager has. Online databases deliver good information; they save a lot of time; and they cost surprisingly little to use.

In business, there are two basic varieties of "information." One is internal information, such as your company's financial records, sales data, or production reports. The second category is external information—facts about the rest of the business world that affect you, such as: What are the most recent tax rulings on sale leasebacks? What are the top ten retail shoe chains? Is another company using the name that you want to adopt for a new product?

This book is about external information. It will help you answer questions about the business world around you: sale leasebacks, shoe chains, trademarks, or an almost limitless variety of other topics. It will not directly discuss ways to improve your accounting systems. Indirectly, though, it can help improve these systems—by showing you where to gather information about the subject.

To use this book—and to use online databases—you don't need to know how computers work. (Most librarians don't—and they've been using databases for years!) For those of you who do use or own computers, there probably will be much in this book that is new to you. Data-processing experts use computers primarily to keep track of a company's internal information. Most "computer jocks" we meet know little or nothing about commercial online databases.

Something else we ought to mention. You probably have heard about "database management systems" (DBMSs). These lie at the heart of any commercial database—or, for that matter, any internal database you may come across whether on your company's mainframe or your own microcomputer. This book will not say much about DBMSs since you don't need to know how they operate in order to use commercial online databases. The popular DBMS programs sold for microcomputers (which we also will not discuss in this book) are simplified descendants of the large commercial DBMSs. We suggest you FORGET about personal computers and computer programs (until you get to Part IV). You don't even need a computer to take advantage of the databases we're going to tell you about (though if you have one—fine, use it).

To get information from online databases, all you need is an old-fashioned "communicating computer terminal," the kind that has been around for 15 years. You'll also need to follow various instruction manuals, which we'll tell you about. It's NOT computer programming! It's probably EASIER than operating a personal computer. Some online databases can be mastered with 15 minutes of practice. Others demand a few hours. It's worth the effort to learn.

We are so convinced that online databases will help you in your business that we have arranged some inducements to get you to try them—discounts from numerous firms for a number of database systems and related hardware and software products. To take advantage of these offers, all you have to do is send in the coupon found elsewhere in the book. They will help ease your entry into the database world.

2 Information Overload

If you're like most business people today, you probably don't want more information. You already receive more than you can handle. You suffer from "information overload."

In his 1961 book *Science Since Babylon,* historian D. J. Price made the famous observation that "eighty to ninety percent of all the scientists that have ever lived are alive now." It's probably also on the mark to say that 80 to 90 percent of all the information that has ever been printed was created in our lifetime.

This is the information explosion. It occurs, Price explained, through the simple mathematics of exponential growth (something that doubles, triples, or grows by some "power" with each passage of a period of time).

Ironically, Price also observed, man's store of knowledge probably is growing no faster today than it did in centuries past. Suppose that the quantity of knowledge doubles every generation. It's in the nature of exponential growth that, starting from a small base, it may go unnoticed for a long time. At some point, though, when the base has become very large, a doubling becomes much more dramatic, creating the appearance of an explosion. That's the state we've reached today.

In the past few decades, society's response to the information explosion has been marked by the rise of specialization. Most scientists, doctors, or lawyers, for example, now can become expert in only a tiny subfield of their disciplines. They may know little more than a layman about most other branches of science, medicine, or law.

Business, too, has been broken into specialties. One can now spend a career designing employee benefit plans or factoring vacation resort memberships.

But many a business decision-maker, entrepreneur, or risk-taker still must be a generalist. The trucking company owner must follow federal, state, and local regulatory developments; he must keep abreast of activities of organized labor; he must follow developments in banking and vehicle leasing; he must be familiar with trends in the industries whose goods he hauls; he must monitor activities of competitors large and small; he must be knowledgeable about computerized accounting and dispatching systems; he may need expertise in real estate or in a dozen other fields.

How does one stay informed in so many different areas—or keep on top of all the developments in one's specialty—when each field itself may be too complicated for any one person to follow? The traditional business manager's technique of staying informed is the "ear-to-the-ground" method. The manager reads a few trade magazines and general business magazines, attends industry gatherings and conventions to exchange tips with colleagues, talks to customers, bankers, and other business people, and, occasionally, consults a lawyer or other professional for help with a particularly tough question.

An implicit assumption or hope of the ear-to-the-ground method is that if an event or a bit of knowledge is important, one sooner or later will find out about it. One may miss it in this week's news, but an acquaintance or associate surely will point it out next month, or the month after.

Also implicit in the traditional method is a time delay. The news one reads today, or hears from an acquaintance, is not necessarily what one needs today. Perhaps next month or next year it will be useful. A good manager builds up a store of knowledge for the future.

Today, the ear-to-the-ground method is becoming increasingly inadequate. In many industries, there are a dozen—or several dozen—trade journals, newsletters, and related sources of information. For example, in the vending machine industry, there are, among others, *American Automatic Merchandiser*, *Vending Times*, *Canadian Vending*, *Star Tech Journal*, and *Better Vending*, as well as the *Vending Times Buyers' Guide*, the *Vending Times Census*, the *National Automatic Merchandising Association Directory of Members*, and the *International Coin Machine Directory*. Aside from the thousands of specialized publications of this sort, general business publications number in the hundreds. Most of this flood of information either rushes by unnoticed or gets noticed when not needed and then forgotten.

The "grapevine" probably will never be replaced as one of the business world's chief avenues of conveying information. But the grapevine is overloaded. There's too much knowledge in circulation for any individual, or group of individuals, to keep track of.

A new mode of information gathering, one suited to coping with the information explosion, has come to the fore via the computer—the database. It is a systematic approach. One can instruct a computer to search out continually all new data on any subject and deliver it on an ongoing basis; or when knowledge is needed, one can seek out, by computer, the relevant facts.

And unlike the traditional method with its time lag, the new method is instantaneous: when one needs information, one gets it! When one doesn't need it, it doesn't tax one's memory or one's file cabinets.

The new method requires a new set of skills. Just as many a successful businessman's competitive edge is an ability to work the grapevine, the new manager will develop special expertise in *knowing where to find information*.

This book teaches the fundamentals of this new skill. Much information relevant to your business is in place today on databases, ready to be of service to the business manager who seeks to maintain a competitive edge.

Ultimately, you'll find that online databases fill needs you didn't even know you had. Do you, for example, occasionally get ideas for a new gadget? The next time you do, why not search a patent database to discover instantly whether someone else has already invented it? Once you try it, you'll find yourself going to that database to test every new idea you get.

3 Questions and Answers

The business world abounds in unanswered questions. What is the U.S. market for wheelchairs? How many businesses with between 10 and 500 employees are there in Buffalo and Pittsburgh? Has anyone designed a two-way radio that fits in a motorcycle helmet? How many self-service gas stations will be built in the next three years? How does one start a long-distance resale telephone company? What terms have large corporations offered in acquiring small computer software companies?

All of these questions came up in actual cases handled by the authors' research firm, MIW Associates. Let's look at them to see how databases helped answer them. Some details have been changed to protect confidentiality.

PROBLEM: A small U.S. advertising agency has a foreign client that manufactures bicycles. The client tells the advertising firm it is considering making wheelchairs, which use many of the same components as bicycles. It asks the ad agency to gather some data on the U.S. wheelchair market, such as:

◆ How many units are sold yearly?
◆ Who are the major manufacturers?
◆ What models are the most popular?
◆ What new products or innovations are being introduced?

SOLUTION: A search of ten databases, which takes 15 minutes and costs less than $50, turns up more than 100 references about the wheelchair market. Among them:

◆ *A summary of a market study on the medical equipment market, which reports the dollar amount of wheelchairs sold annually to the nation's 19,000 nursing homes.*

♦ *News reports on several new wheelchair designs by Japanese firms, including a plastic one that weighs less than 22 pounds and one with a manually operated device that helps the operator stand up and sit down.*

♦ *A report on a patent awarded for a new wheelchair designed for sports use.*

♦ *A note that a manufacturer of electric wheelchairs ranked 212 on* Inc. *magazine's list of the country's 500 fastest growing private firms in 1981.*

♦ *An article from* American Family Physician *with guidelines for patients on how to evaluate wheelchairs.*

♦ *A note that the magazine* Surgical Business *lists all U.S. manufacturers of home medical equipment, including wheelchairs.*

♦ *A note that a report by the National Center for Health Statistics contains figures on the distribution and use of wheelchairs.*

♦ *An abstract of an article from* The New York Times *about Everest & Jennings International, the dominant wheelchair maker in the United States, which has received many complaints about poor designs.*

PROBLEM: A janitorial contractor from Philadelphia is considering an expansion into several other cities. In order to assess the market there, he wants to know:

♦ The number of business establishments in these cities, by type of business and size.

♦ The number of janitorial services, their locations, and the number of employees.

♦ The names, addresses, and phone numbers of all business establishments with more than 20 employees in selected districts and industries, for test marketing.

SOLUTION: Three databases—EIS, Dun's Market Identifiers, and Electronic Yellow Pages—supplied all of this information.

PROBLEM: An importer notices a couple of motorcyclists on the highway communicating with each other by hand signals. He thinks that a two-way radio mounted in a motorcycle helmet would be an ideal product for a Far Eastern manufacturer of electronics products whom he deals with. Is there something like this on the market? If so, could something better, or less expensive, be made? If not, has such a product ever been designed or tested?

SOLUTION: A database search turns up a publication called Motorcycle Dealernews, *which lists all manufacturers of such products. The importer contacts them, finds that several such products are on the market, and obtains descriptions. Another search of several patent databases identifies three U.S. patents and ten foreign patents for such devices. He contacts the patent holders to inquire whether they've been licensed. His discussions re-*

veal that the potential market is very small, so he decides not to pursue the venture. The database searches have saved him many days of research— and the risks of a bad investment.

PROBLEM: A maker of intercoms thinks that self-service gas station operators may be interested in installing his product in new stations. His idea is that the booth attendant would be able to speak with customers—instructing them on how to operate the pump and making service friendlier and more personal.

Is it worth his time and effort to try to develop this market? He would like to know how many new self-service stations will be built over the next few years, who owns them, and whom he should contact about marketing his product.

SOLUTION: A search of several databases reveals that the most thorough and up-to-date statistics on gasoline stations are found in the Lundberg Letter, *a weekly devoted to "vital statistics and analysis in oil marketing." The database abstracts identify eight issues of the* Lundberg Letter *published over the past year dealing with gas station construction. By giving a few commands through the terminal, the intercom manufacturer orders reprints to be sent to him. The reprints name several petroleum companies that plan to convert a large percentage of stations to self-service.*

PROBLEM: A small group of investors in a midwestern city have been approached about financing a new business that resells long-distance telephone service. This new industry is booming as a result of telephone deregulation and is attracting scores of small, entrepreneurial companies. The investors want all the information they can get about this field. For example, they want to know:

◆ How big an investment do such companies generally need to make?
◆ How much do experts expect the resale industry to grow in the future?
◆ What are possible competitive or regulatory dangers?
◆ What are typical financial and operating ratios of such companies?
◆ What are the most recent trends in this business?

SOLUTION: A search of about ten databases locates more than 30 helpful items. They include:

◆ *The article "Resale—A Case History" in* Telephone Engineer and Management. *In it, the founder of one of the first long-distance resale companies outlines how he got started, what equipment he needed, how he marketed his service, how much he invested, and other details of his business.*
◆ *The article "Developing a Business Plan for Reselling Long Distance Phone Service," by the president of a telecommunications consulting firm, in* Business Communications Review.

PROBLEM: The owner of a small computer software firm is seeking to be acquired by a large company. In order to prepare himself for negotiations, he would like to know as much as possible about other acquisitions of software firms over the past few years, for example:

- What were the specialties of the acquired companies?
- Who were the acquirers?
- What prices were paid?
- What were the circumstances of the acquisition?

SOLUTION: In a search of about 15 databases, the owner finds more than 20 news items about software company acquisitions. Several involve acquisitions of, or by, publicly held companies, in which case the owner retrieves the relevant Securities and Exchange Commission filings from another database. Further searches, giving the name of each acquired company, yield considerable background on their activities. The owner entered negotiations confident that he could justify his valuation of the company. He succeeded in selling the company at a favorable price.

As you can see, the uses of databases are as varied as the business world itself. There's no "typical" application, no standard kind of information. Databases simply offer a fast, effective way to search much of the economy's written information on almost any topic or problem.

4 Getting Started

To start calling up business information online, all you need are:

- ◆ A microcomputer or computer terminal.
- ◆ A modem, which converts digital signals used in computers to analog signals used on phone lines and vice versa (some microcomputers and terminals come with a modem built in).
- ◆ Communications software (terminals don't need it, but for most microcomputers it must be added).
- ◆ An account number and password for an online information vendor. (Often you can get a trial subscription to one or more online services free with the purchase of a modem or communications software; the coupon found in this book can provide free or low-cost access to many of the important services.)

We'll discuss hardware and software in considerable detail later; for now, let's look at what your first online session might be like.

The price for using an information vendor's services can be as low as $5 an hour or as high as $300 an hour. Many useful business databases cost $50 to $100, which really is not expensive, considering that many online searches take only a few minutes. You may, however, want to start with some moderately priced vendors whose services cost $20 to $40 during the day and $5 to $25 at night. These include DIALOG's Knowledge Index, BRS After Dark, The Source, and CompuServe Information Service, all of which are described in other parts of this book.

Going online is like learning to ride a bicycle or run a personal computer: some initial frustration is normal. During your first few experiments online, the system may stall, you may make wrong turns, and you may have to ask for help.

But you'll also enjoy the thrill of exploration, power, and knowledge. Your modem gives you a direct line to a larger share of the world's information than is contained in any but the world's largest libraries. And from the moment you have emerged from the tricky process of signing onto a database and obtaining your first information from it, you will be aware that the process can increase your research efficiency as much as the horse increased the traveling efficiency of humans who previously had to go everywhere on foot. This chapter will describe what it's like to get started, and the rest of the book will provide additional pointers to make your journey more profitable.

Bob, a business consultant, signed onto Dow Jones News/Retrieval and The Source soon after acquiring a Radio Shack Model 100, the leading "lap" computer, a machine small enough to fit in a briefcase yet with both a modem and communications software built in. Bob found his conversations with at least three different computers and four different databases both exhilarating and upsetting.

His first step was to place a local call to Telenet, a national telephone network for computers. Telenet and its competitors carry computer data around the world for far less than the cost of long-distance voice calls. On the Model 100 and many other computers and terminals, calling Telenet is simple: Bob only had to give the command Telecom, push a key designated "call," and type in the appropriate phone number. The Model 100 automatically was supposed to call the number and put itself into communicating mode (often called "terminal mode" or "terminal emulation mode") when Telenet answered with a carrier tone.

On the first try it didn't work. The computer made some sputtering noises, but nothing else happened. Bob decided to try again. He'd been warned that Telenet is sometimes so busy that its telephones don't answer on the first try. Bob again commanded the Model 100 Call. This time, shortly after dialing the number, the computer "beeped" to signal that it had received a computer tone and was converting itself into a terminal.

After that Bob merely had to follow the procedures outlined in the Dow Jones News/Retrieval manual. He entered two carriage returns to tell Telenet's computer that he was there. Soon he saw:

```
TELENET
617 125A
TERMINAL =
```

appear on his screen. Telenet's computer was answering him and asking what kind of computer or terminal he was using.

Bob entered a carriage return and immediately Telenet displayed the symbol @. That's the prompt to enter the code of the database vendor you are calling. The code for Dow Jones is 60942. Bob entered it. The computer answered:

```
60942 CONNECTED
WHAT SERVICE PLEASE?????
```

DJNS, Bob responded, following the directions in the manual.

```
ENTER PASSWORD
```

responded the computer.

Bob started to type in his new Dow Jones News/Retrieval password. But suddenly everything went wrong. Bob noticed that the word WAIT had appeared on the screen. He waited. The message remained for six minutes. He tried typing in his password while the word remained on the screen, but the computer did nothing. He tried disconnecting from Dow Jones using the "break" key on the computer and calling it again through Telenet. He got the same WAIT message.

Bob dialed the customer-service toll-free telephone number listed in the Dow Jones user's manual. The woman who answered didn't seem to know much more about computers than he did, but she had been trained to coach beginners in the process of signing on, and she knew about a peculiarity of the Model 100.

"Did you change the E at the end of the communications parameters of the Model 100 to a D?" she asked. "When you get the machine, your parameters are M7I1E, and I don't remember exactly what the change does, but you have to change the last letter to a D."

She was right. And the computer manual's explanation of how to change communications parameters was easy to follow. Bob merely had to push a key marked "Stat," then enter the new communications parameters: M7I1D.

Bob signed on again and when he typed in the password, the machine responded:

WELCOME TO DOW JONES NEWS/RETRIEVAL COPYRIGHT (C) 1982 DOW JONES & CO., INC.

and then:

ENTER QUERY.

Following the advice in the generally helpful News/Retrieval manual, Bob typed //INTRO, seeking an introduction to the system. He was in "user-friendly" territory now. Rather than requiring him to know a complex series of commands, the computer responded with a menu of choices, each preceded by a number. Bob merely had to enter a number and a carriage return to tell which choice he preferred.

You're not charged for time spent on the INTRO portion of the Dow Jones system, and INTRO informed Bob that this week he could also obtain free time on Dow Jones's online version of the *Academic American Encyclopedia*. But the rest of the material was already explained in the manual, and he had a perfectly good encyclopedia in his office.

Following the advice of the manual, Bob typed in the command //CQ. that quickly took him out of INTRO and into a database containing the latest stock market quotes. The manual told him the stock symbols for his three largest holdings: Long Island Lighting, General Electric, and Digital Equipment Corp. He entered them, and the Dow Jones computer told him their latest prices, volume, the previous day's close, and the current day's opening, high, and low.

Bob now decided to try something more sophisticated. He had a client trying to introduce a new brand of videotape to the U.S. market, so he wanted to ask for news of the video recording industry. The command //DJNEWS put him into a database containing the last 90 days' articles from *The Wall Street Journal*, *Barron's National Business & Financial Weekly*, and the Dow Jones News Service (the latter is the business news wire that used to be called "the broad tape").

The manual hadn't been completely clear about which command Bob would have to use to inquire about videotape, but a bit of study of the manual, and trial and error, led him to the command .I/ELE 01. That meant "industry–electronics, the first (most recent) page of headlines."

The first "page"—actually a list of nine headlines with codes indicating the date and publication where they had appeared and the code Bob would have to type into the computer if he wanted to view them in their entirety—quickly appeared on the screen. Bob immediately saw a *Wall Street Journal* headline he had missed indicating that Matsushita Electric would begin selling digital television in 1984. So Bob ordered the next five pages of headlines, which covered 54 stories on the electronics industry from the past two months. They turned out to be invaluable: Bob found eight articles to print out. From them he learned:

♦ That Japanese videotape recorder exports had risen 135 percent to a record level in the month before.

♦ That the sale of home video components systems had captured 3 to 5 percent of the $11.2 billion home electronics market in the two years since their introduction and that the sale of an RCA television set designed to serve as the centerpiece for a home video component system had risen 293 percent this year.

♦ That Japanese firms manufacturing VHS-format videotape recorders had agreed on a format for high-fidelity VHS sound, something that Beta-format videotape producers insisted would be impossible.

♦ And that Japan Victor Corp. and Sony Corp. were manufacturing videocassettes to be sold by Polaroid under the Polaroid name.

Satisfied with his first experience online, Bob decided to sign off. There was only one problem: he couldn't remember the command he was supposed to use to disconnect from Dow Jones. Several minutes of searching through the Dow Jones manual failed to locate it. As he searched, he was accumulating Dow Jones connect charges at about 20¢ a minute. Finally, Bob simply pushed the button labeled "Bye" on his computer—the equivalent of hanging up the phone on Dow Jones. He would continue to accumulate connect charges for another minute or two until Dow Jones's computer realized there was no one communicating with it anymore. Bob was seething, yet at the same time elated. The entire session after he'd left the INTRO section had taken about 40 minutes at nonprime time rates of $9 to $54 per hour, depending on the database, including the time he'd wasted looking for commands and trying unsuccessfully to sign off. It had definitely been worthwhile.

The next night Bob spent 1 hour and 10 minutes at lower rates with The Source, a general information "utility" with one or two useful business services. He spent 25 fairly frustrating minutes with United Press International's business wire—a widely promoted service that costs only the basic Source price of $20.75 per hour in the daytime and $7.75 at night. It was, unfortunately, confusing to use, and failed to produce much information of value to Bob. But he spent 30 more satisfying minutes with the simplified version of the bibliographic database Management Contents that is available on The Source.

Management Contents provides short summaries, rather than the full text, of news articles. Its full version covers 700 business periodicals and is available for about $80 per hour through such vendors as DIALOG. On The Source a stripped-down version of the database contains summaries of articles from 28 major publications such as *Business Week* and *Forbes*.

Bob entered the key word Video and learned that the database contained abstracts of 59 recent articles on the subject. He printed out the titles of the first 20 and then printed the summaries for 9 of those. One—about price competition in the business—was so interesting that he immediately ordered a copy of the original article. He did that with a series of simple commands, and the article arrived in the mail along with a bill for $10 four days later.

Just as working with Dow Jones News/Retrieval was maddening at times, there were plenty of frustrations in learning to use The Source. But in the evening the total cost of database time was only $13. And Bob suspected that his way of learning about the world had changed forever.

5 The Three Kinds of Databases

Full-text databases and free-text searching

What is a database, anyway? How did all that information get "online"?

It's helpful to divide online databases into three categories. The first we'll call *full-text* databases; the second, *reference* databases; and the third, *fact* databases.

Please note, though, that the terminology in this young industry is still evolving. Some divide the database world into different classes or use different names (we'll note some of the other terms used). Even use of the word "database"—which only recently began to replace "databank," a term from the early days of the computer industry—is still unsettled.

The easiest way to explain what full-text databases are is to show you one. A good example is the online version of *Business Week*.

First, let's look at a page from the familiar paper version of the magazine. We happened to open the July 11, 1983, issue to an article about bus deregulation. It is reproduced on page 20.

Now look at a printout from the electronic *Business Week* database, which is carried on Mead Corporation's database service called NEXIS. We commanded NEXIS to find all articles about bus deregulation. The computer responded with several citations, one of which is reproduced below.

Copyright (c) 1983 McGraw-Hill, Inc.
Business Week

July 11, 1983

SECTION: TRANSPORTATION: Pg. 66

LENGTH: 1362 words

HEADLINE: DEREGULATION WILL TAKE BUS LINES ON A ROUGH RIDE

HIGHLIGHT:
THEY ARE BOUND TO RUN INTO AIRLINE-STYLE FARE WARS AND SHAKEOUTS

DEREGULATION WILL TAKE BUS LINES ON A ROUGH RIDE

THEY ARE BOUND TO RUN INTO AIRLINE-STYLE FARE WARS AND SHAKEOUTS

It's "Greyhound vs. the world," declares Norman R. Sherlock, president of the American Bus Assn. That view reflects the animosities building in the intercity bus industry as it heads down the bumpy road of deregulation. The bus business is the last major segment of the U.S. transportation network to gain a large measure of freedom to go where it wants at the prices it wants. And it is bound to suffer the fare wars, shakeouts, and competition from new low-cost

regulators would not let the carrier abandon them. The ICC is now able to preempt most state authority.

The ICC's handling of Greyhound's application to acquire 2,200 mi. of new routes in 44 states, to add new stops along its current routes, and to drop more than 1,100 points it now serves will indicate how liberally the commission will wield its new power. An administrative law judge has indicated he will recommend that the ICC approve Grey-

hound's. Says Theodore Knappen, senior vice-president: "All of our filings are [for routes served by] Greyhound. But Greyhound has chosen to file against a lot of little guys. That's an unfair fight."

One such smaller carrier is Carolina Coach Co. With 1982 revenues of $30 million and a 2% market share, it is the third-largest company in the highly fragmented U.S. bus industry. Chairman H. Lester Creech complains that in North Carolina, Greyhound "has filed for the only profitable routes we have." And in Massachusetts, Greyhound wants to go from Springfield to Boston, Peter Pan's only route. Picknelly of Peter Pan notes that his company also stops at 89 towns along the way—service that is subsidized by more profitable Boston-Springfield traffic. Greyhound wants only the two terminus cities. Heavy competition there may cut Peter Pan's profits and force the carrier to drop local service or even push it out of business, warns Picknelly. "It's just like the airlines," he says. "Deregulation will only add competition between major cities and hurt small towns." Championing the small carrier in the fight against Greyhound is the industry's trade group, the American Bus Assn.—in which Greyhound dropped its membership last January.

'GOOD MILES.' Greyhound insists the small bus lines' fears are unfounded. "There's more opportunity for small carriers than for Greyhound in deregulation," says Nageotte. For years, he says, small bus companies have complained that "Greyhound has all those good miles. Well, now they can get on them."

And for Greyhound, says Nageotte: "Even if we didn't get one new mile of routes, deregulation would be worth it"—in terms of the new rate and route freedoms deregulation allows. Trailways and Greyhound claim deregulation's big payoff comes from being able to streamline operations. Both are moving aggressively to win so-called open-door rights—the ability to serve towns along their existing routes where states have barred them from taking on passengers. Trailways, for example, has unsuccessfully petitioned California regulators for years to carry traffic between San Francisco and Sacramento on its New York-San Francisco runs. Now the ICC has granted permission.

Many bus-industry experts believe

SMALLER CARRIERS FEAR GREYHOUND AND TRAILWAYS WILL HOG THE MAIN ROUTES

carriers that are buffeting the deregulated airline and trucking industries.

"Sooner or later there'll be some Braniffs in our industry," predicts Peter Picknelly Sr., president of Peter Pan Bus Lines Inc., of Springfield, Mass. Many bus operators think that Phoenix's giant Greyhound Corp., with two-thirds of the scheduled-route market, will be the chief cause of them.

HIGHER AUTHORITY. The act deregulating bus lines took effect last November. But its full impact will begin to be felt only over the next few months, as the Interstate Commerce Commission rules on a flood of bus-company applications to drop profitless routes and to add more attractive ones—changes that intransigent state regulators made difficult in the past. Greyhound, for example, serves many towns where it has not sold a ticket in four years or more, yet state

hound's requests, and most observers think the commission will do so. If it does, Trailways Inc.—Greyhound's archrival and the industry's second-largest carrier—and several smaller operators will probably try to delay Greyhound's victory by suing the ICC and by taking other actions.

Rival bus companies condemn Greyhound for abandoning small towns and for greed in wanting more routes for its vast system. But Greyhound President Frank L. Nageotte points out that half of the proposed abandonments are only stops along a highway. Moreover, he notes that Trailways is no slouch in grabbing for new routes: The Dallas company and its 45 affiliated carriers are filing for more than 5,281 mi. of new routes—more than twice as much as Greyhound. Trailways maintains its action would be less onerous than Grey-

TRANSPORTATION

that the number of bus operators will increase rather than shrink, although some existing companies may go out of business. Already the ICC has applications from 950 aspiring entrants—800 of which are for charter service. Some of these are likely to enter scheduled service later.

Small carriers could well prove tough competitors. Like the fledgling airlines founded since that industry's deregulation five years ago, new bus companies generally enjoy lower costs, especially for labor, than heavily unionized Greyhound. And some smaller, established bus operators are succeeding in winning labor concessions to help their competitive position. Jefferson Lines Inc., of Minneapolis, has persuaded its union to replace a cost-of-living clause with a profit-sharing plan. "I showed them we won't be able to compete with low-cost entrants that are coming in," says Daniel F. Prins, Jefferson's president. "Our labor costs are so low that Greyhound and Trailways will have trouble getting entrenched here."

The bus lines are also moving rapidly to use their new pricing freedoms. Already they can raise fares 10% or cut them 20% without regulatory approval, and they are likely to get full price-setting freedom later. In the interim, the

ICC is promptly granting fare requests. Interstate fares are generally higher than intrastate prices, thanks to stingy state regulators. Bonanza Bus Lines Inc. of Providence, for example, gets 12¢ per seat-mile on its interstate runs but only 7½¢ within Massachusetts. Bus operators say it should be just the reverse, because most passengers dislike bus

> Already the ICC
> has applications from
> 950 aspiring
> new bus companies

travel for longer trips. Bonanza is appealing Massachusetts' niggardliness to the ICC, something deregulation allows for the first time.

The carriers' ability to make fare increases stick, however, will depend on how aggressive the new and smaller bus companies prove as marketers. Fare wars seem likely to erupt on routes that get competition for the first time.

Better marketing, never a hallmark of the bus business, may prove the key to survival for many small carriers. Jeffer-

son Lines has gone into franchising by selling its name, insurance, and other services to drivers, travel agents, and organizations that want to enter the business—principally on the charter side. "The phone is ringing off the hook," says Jefferson's Prins. And to attract teenage passengers, the company has installed Pac-Man video games on four of its buses.

Some carriers may try to develop a market niche by offering specialized services. In mid-July, California charter operator Funbus Systems Inc. will start scheduled service between San Diego, Los Angeles, and San Francisco. It is likely to be the nation's most luxurious bus ride. The carrier's double-deck European buses will feature movies, hostesses, card tables, airline-style seats with tray tables, complimentary wine, a full bar, and a galley preparing hot meals. The one-way fare between Los Angeles and San Francisco is $49, compared with $34.45 for the same trip on Greyhound. That is more than some airlines charge, but Funbus expects to win travelers who hate to fly. Michael L. Valen, president of Funbus, doubts he would have won regulatory approval before deregulation. "Greyhound, with all its power and might, would have buried us in the courts," he believes. □

An article from *Business Week* (reprinted with permission).

BODY:
  "It's Greyhound vs. the world," declares Norman R. Sherlock, president of the American Bus Assn. That view reflects the animosities building in the intercity bus industry as it heads down the bumpy road of deregulation. The bus business is the last major segment of the U.S. transportation network to gain a large measure of freedom to go where it wants at the prices it wants. And it is bound to suffer the fare wars, shakeouts, and competition from new low-cost carriers that are buffeting the deregulated airline and trucking industries.
  "Sooner or later there'll be some Braniffs in our industry," predicts Peter Picknelly Sr., president of Peter Pan Bus Lines Inc., of Springfield, Mass. Many bus operators think that Phoenix's giant Greyhound Corp., with two-thirds of the scheduled-route market, will be the chief cause of them.

HIGHER AUTHORITY. The act deregulating bus lines took effect last November. But its full impact will begin to be felt only over the next few months, as the Interstate Commerce Commission rules on a flood of bus-company applications to drop profit-less routes and to add more attractive ones—changes that intransigent state regulators made difficult in the past. Greyhound, for example, serves many towns where it has not sold a ticket in four years or more, yet state regulators would not let the carrier abandon them. The ICC is now able to preempt most state authority.
  The ICC's handling of Greyhound's application to acquire 2,200 mi. of new routes in 44 states, to add new stops along its current routes, and to drop more than 1,100 points it now serves will indicate how liberally the commission will wield its new power. An administrative law judge has indicated he will recommend that the ICC approve Greyhound's requests, and most observers think the commission will do so. If it does, Trailways Inc.—Greyhound's arch-rival and the industry's second-largest carrier—and several smaller operators will probably try to delay Greyhound's victory by suing the ICC and by taking other actions.
  Rival bus companies condemn Greyhound for abandoning small towns and for greed in wanting more routes for its vast system. But Greyhound President Frank L. Nageotte points out that half of the proposed abandonments are only stops along a highway. Moreover, he notes that Trailways is no slouch in grabbing for new routes: The Dallas company and its 45 affiliated carriers are filing for more than 5,281 mi. of new routes—more than twice as much as Greyhound. Trailways maintains its action would be less onerous than Greyhound's. Says Theodore Knappen, senior vice-president: "All of our filings are [for routes served by] Greyhound. But Greyhound has chosen to file against a lot of little guys. . . ." [*rest of article follows*]

Notice that this is the same article as the one from the magazine, word-for-word! The database contains the *full text* of *Business Week*.

What good does it do to have *Business Week* available from a computer terminal? After all, to find this article, you could have stopped at a library, looked up bus deregulation in the *Business Periodicals Index*, then taken the July 11 issue off the shelf (if it wasn't missing) and photocopied the article.

We needn't emphasize how time-consuming that is. Time is money. If you're like most business managers, you probably wouldn't have made a special trip to the library at all unless the item was very urgent. Rather, you would have gotten along as well as possible without ever knowing what *Business Week* had to say about bus deregulation.

Besides, suppose the topic you were really interested in was the Interstate

Commerce Commission. By looking in a printed index, you may not have come across this bus article at all. You would have missed the article's comments about that subject. In a printed index, only major topic headings are listed.

But by commanding an online database to "find all articles that mention the Interstate Commerce Commission" you have confidence the computer will flag this article for you. How? The computer can search through *every word* in the database looking for those that match the one you give.

This is called a free-text search. Keep this term distinct from full-text databases. Free-text and full-text are two different, though related, concepts. It is unfortunate that two such easily confused phrases have become the industry's accepted terminology. Even people in the database business mix them up.

Let's straighten them out. Full text describes the content of a database. In a full-text database, every word of the original document is included—as opposed to a mere abstract, which appears in a reference database. Free text describes a manner of searching. The alternative is searching by index terms.

Mead's NEXIS has dozens of magazines, newspapers, newsletters, and news wire services online in full text, including all articles from the past five years or so in *Business Week*, the Associated Press news wire, *Congressional Quarterly Weekly Report, Inc.*, *The Economist*, *Aviation Week*, *Chemical Week*, *The Christian Science Monitor*, *The Washington Post*, *Computer World*, *Platt's Oilgram News*, and a number of others. Several of these databases are discussed later in this book, and Mead itself receives lengthy attention separately. Mead, as well as its competitor, Westlaw, also produces databases containing the full texts of every decision by the federal courts and state supreme courts, along with many other legal documents.

Another full-text database service called NewsNet specializes in newsletters and other limited-circulation publications. For example, it carries online the *Real Estate Intelligence Report* and the *Real Estate Investing Letter*. In the field of taxation, it has the daily *Tax Notes Today* and others. In aerospace, it has *Satellite Week*. And it carries about 200 others in several dozen different fields.

The Toronto *Globe and Mail*, Canada's major newspaper, is available on a full-text database known as Info Globe. The U.S. government's *Commerce Business Daily*, the bible of government contractors, is available as a full-text database on DIALOG. And a number of other full-text databases in a variety of subjects are on the market.

Reference databases

Full-text databases, though obvious in their usefulness, are still somewhat uncommon. The majority of databases you're likely to use contain only references to the original information, often with an abstract and key words. This type of database is known as a "reference" or "bibliographic" database.

Why references rather than the full text? Such databases arose because it was expensive to keep information online. Some databases cover hundreds or even thousands of source publications. The ABI/INFORM database, for example (more about it in Chapter 13), abstracts more than 500 business publications, including *Business Week* and most of those that NEXIS has in full text. NEXIS, by comparison, contains only a few dozen full-text publications. Keeping ABI's hundreds of publications online in full text would require hundreds or thousands of times more computer disk capacity than the reference database takes up. It could be done, but it might price ABI out of the market.

Technical advances and market pressures in the computer industry, though, are making online storage cheaper every year. As a result, full-text databases will become more and more the norm in the future.

But there's another reason why reference databases are more common today than full-text databases. References, especially with abstracts, often are *more* useful than the original source.

Suppose you're searching for information on food marketing in the southern United States. A news article about the growth of 7-Eleven convenience stores in Texas might be useful to you. However, if you command a database to search for the term "food," the computer will only retrieve literal uses of that word. In a full-text database, the 7-Eleven article may not even mention the word "food." (Suppose it uses "groceries" instead?)

Now consider a reference database. An indexer or abstractor reads each item before it is entered into the computer, writes a summary, and attaches indexing terms (called "identifiers" or "descriptors"). The abstractor very likely would have used key words such as "food," "retailing," "convenience stores," etc., among the indexing terms. If so, you could conduct a search for the term "food" and you would locate the article.

There are many kinds of indexing terms: controlled vocabulary, ad hoc terms, product codes, SIC codes, trade names, event codes, D-U-N-S numbers, ticker symbols, state names, geographic codes, special features, patent class codes, document types, and dozens of others. What most of these items of information have in common is that they do not necessarily appear in the document being cited; rather, they are added by an indexer.

Each kind of indexing term usually appears in a distinct "field." This means you can search it separately; for instance, if a database holds a field called "state name," you can probably specify in a search something like "state = Washington." This would prevent you from obtaining unwanted references to Washington, D.C., or any of the numerous Washington counties throughout the country.

A controlled vocabulary term, perhaps the most common kind of indexing term, is drawn from a prepared list of relevant words and phrases. ABI/INFORM, for example, uses its own 8,000-term list of business topics; Management Contents Data Base uses a 3,500-term list. A controlled vocabulary list is also known as the database's "thesaurus"; the terms themselves are also known as "descriptors."

Ad hoc indexing terms, also known as "identifiers," often accompany controlled vocabulary terms. An ad hoc term is one that does not appear on the controlled vocabulary list but is one that the indexer considers an important key word for identifying the contents of the particular citation. If an article discusses President Mitterand or F. W. Woolworth Co., for example, the indexer might include these names as identifiers.

Product codes are used in many databases as a way to standardize names for industries and subindustries. The most common product code is the Standard Industrial Classification (SIC) list, which is discussed in more detail in Chapter 9. Some database producers develop their own product codes or else supplement the SIC list with additional proprietary codes.

A few databases, such as ADTRACK, use trade names as an indexing term. This allows an article about the leading beer producer, for example, to be indexed by the brand name Budweiser as well as by the company name Anheuser-Busch.

The Predicasts databases use event codes, which are discussed in Chapter 13.

Several databases that index companies or securities give a D-U-N-S number or ticker symbol for each entry in order to identify positively each company, prevent it from being mixed up with others, and make retrieval of statistics about it swift.

Many databases include index terms for countries, states, cities, Standard Metropolitan Statistical Areas (SMSAs), zip codes, or other geographic divisions. These may be listed by name, abbreviation, code number, or a combination of ways.

Patent databases use several different types of indexing terms, as described in Chapter 23.

If a database includes a variety of kinds of documents, such as magazines, books, movies, broadcast recordings, conference papers, etc., these may be identified as "document-type indexing terms."

The potential pitfall of abstracts and indexing terms lies in their very strength: they're written by human beings, whose accuracy and sophistication can vary widely. Even when they're accurate, bibliographic citations vary in style and completeness from one database to another.

Look, for example, at the citation to an article from the magazine *Byte* in the following printout. This appears in the Magazine Index, a database of more than 370 popular periodicals. The same article is listed in another database, the Microcomputer Index, shown next. And a third citation to the article from INSPEC (Information Services in Physics, Electrotechnology, Computers, and Control) is also shown.

[from Magazine Index]

```
Online information retrieval.
Roberts, Steven K.
Byte  v6  p452(7)  Dec 1981
CODEN: BYTEDJ
SIC CODE: 7374; 8231
DESCRIPTORS: information storage and retrieval systems-evaluation; Magazine
Index (data base)-usage; computer networks-usage; data base management-tech-
nological innovations; Information Access Corp.-services; information services-
innovations.
```

[from Microcomputer Index]

> Online information retrieval: promise and problems
> Roberts, Steven
> BYTE , Dec 1981 , v6 n12 p452-461 , 7 pages   ISSN: 0360-5280
> Languages: English
> Document Type: Article
> Geographic Location: United States
> Describes how an information search is done on the Dialog Information Service. Also includes some comments on the five prerequisites that were needed to develop the Dialog system and comments on future problems in this field.
> Descriptors: *Online Systems; *Online Information
> Identifier: Dialog Information Services, Inc.

[from INSPEC]

> ONLINE INFORMATION RETRIEVAL: PROMISE AND PROBLEMS
> ROBERTS, S.K.
> BYTE (USE) VOL.6, NO.12   452-61   DEC. 1981   Coden: BYTEDJ
> Treatment: GENERAL,REVIEW
> Document Type: JOURNAL PAPER
> Languages: ENGLISH
> THE ONLINE STORAGE CAPABILITIES DESCRIBED IN THE ARTICLE SEEM TO PRE-SAGE ENORMOUS CHANGES IN THE LIBRARY OF THE FUTURE. ONE CAN ONLY AS-SUME THAT MASS STORAGE OF ALL TYPES WILL CONTINUE TO GROW CHEAPER AS HUMAN TIME BECOMES MORE EXPENSIVE: IT FOLLOWS THAT EVER—BETTER TOOLS FOR INFORMATION SEEKERS WILL CONTINUE TO DEVELOP
> Descriptors: INFORMATION RETRIEVAL SYSTEMS; INFORMATION SERVICES
> Identifiers: INFORMATION RETRIEVAL; ONLINE; LIBRARY; FUTURE
> Class Codes: C7210; C7250

From these three descriptions, one would hardly believe that they all refer to the same article! The first seems to be a nuts-and-bolts piece about some specific information storage and retrieval systems. The second tells about searching the DIALOG Infomation Services system. The third consists of philosophical commentary about future libraries. The author, variously referred to as Steven K., Steven, and S. K. Roberts, was interpreted quite differently, based on the training and orientation of the abstractors.

The moral of the story is that reference databases are fallible. Don't, however, let that prejudice you! Reference databases are very useful.

A sophisticated searcher, in reality, rarely looks for information in just one database. In fact, different abstracts for the same source document may complement each other and enhance the search process. If we had been searching for articles about online information, we would have looked at all three of these databases—and a number of others as well. In later chapters, we'll talk at more length about your "search strategy"—that is, deciding which databases to search and what questions to ask them.

The database industry fully realizes the unique strengths and weaknesses of full-text and reference databases. In the future, many databases will carry *both* full text and abstracts of their material. One of these "combination" databases already available is HBR (Harvard Business Review) Online, discussed in Chapter 13. It contains the full text of the well-known journal since 1976, together with an abstract that is unique to the database.

Fact databases

By now, we may have given you a somewhat distorted view of the world of databases—that most databases are just electronic versions of magazines and that the only difference is whether they're full text or reference. This is not so. There is another type of database—the fact database.

Suppose you're interested in how many American turkeys find their way to butcher shops abroad. You can easily locate the following chart in the U.S. Exports Data Base.

TURKEYS, LIVE, IN THE DOWNY STAGE (BC = 1000260)
U.S. Exports to: All Countries (CC = 000)

Year	Quantity in NO	Value in $
1981	1,544,894	1,436,724
1980	634,584	748,976
1979	1,568,258	1,320,039
1978	1,065,754	962,792

Source: U.S. Bureau of the Census   DIALOG File 126

Unlike previous examples, this is not an abstract of an article or even an article itself. Instead, as they say, "It's the facts." Therefore, we call this a fact database (also referred to as a "source" database or a "nonbibliographic" database).

Whatever you call them, fact databases can contain anything you might find in a directory, handbook, reference guide, schedule, statistical report, stock market table—or even information not published in print anywhere, ever.

One new fact database, the Electronic Yellow Pages, is an online version of all the yellow pages directories in the United States—some 4,800 of them—all rolled into one. With the Electronic Yellow Pages, you can instant-ly find all the dry-wall contractors in Topeka, all the plastics fabricators in the country that go by the name A-1, or all the auto-parts supply houses in Oregon. Here's a typical record:

```
0003946
ALL METAL FABRICATORS INC
82 HAYWARD RD/BX 954
ACTON, MA 01720
TELEPHONE: 617-263-3904
COUNTY: MIDDLESEX
SIC: 3444 .(SHEET METAL WORK MFRS.)
CITY POPULATION: 2 .(2,500-4,999)
NET WORTH: F .($125,000 - $199,999)
```

NUMBER OF EMPLOYEES: F .(10-19)
THIS IS A(N) CORPORATION
HEADQUARTERS

There are many other varieties of fact databases. For example, the Producer Price Index, produced by the U.S. Bureau of Labor Statistics, gives wholesale-price inflation rates for about 6,000 primary products. What is the price trend for backhoe attachments? This table is available at your command.

WPU11220125 PRODUCER PRICE INDEX SUBFILE
MACHINERY AND EQUIPMENT; BACKHOE ATTACHMENT
UNADJUSTED DATA

INDEX (1967 = 100)

YEARS	Q1	Q2	Q3	Q4
1980	247.6	256.0	258.7	258.7
1979	220.1	225.8	231.4	231.4
1978	196.4	198.7	202.0	202.0
1977	180.7	182.7	188.9	188.9
1976	NA	NA	176.1	176.1

SOURCE: U.S. BUREAU OF LABOR STATISTICS DIALOG FILE 176
DATES AVAILABLE:(JAN. 1964-1980)

Another Bureau of Labor Statistics database covers consumer prices. How has the cost of medical care in Anchorage, Alaska, risen over the past five years? The following table is also online.

CWU45A42786000 CONSUMER PRICE INDEX FOR URBAN WAGE EARNERS AND CLERICAL WORKERS SUBFILE
MEDICAL CARE;
ANCHORAGE, ALASKA;
UNADJUSTED DATA

INDEX(OCTOBER 1967 = 100)

YEARS	Q1	Q2	Q3	Q4
1983	347.2	346.6	NA	NA
1982	324.6	327.8	335.5	339.4
1981	293.1	303.0	306.3	312.6
1980	266.9	276.3	282.3	283.1
1979	253.7	253.4	254.9	256.5

SOURCE: U.S. BUREAU OF LABOR STATISTICS DIALOG FILE 175
DATES AVAILABLE:(JAN. 1981-MAY 1983)

Data Resources, Inc., a McGraw-Hill subsidiary, and Chase Econometrics/Interactive Data both specialize in fact databases. Data Resources maintains more than 60 fact databases covering a variety of industries and financial markets. For example, its Forest Products database gives statistics on North American production of lumber, plywood, and related products. The database will tell you about prices, imports, exports, production capacity, production costs, housing starts, etc.

Another fact database, Books in Print, corresponds to the constantly changing directories of the same name that occupy about four feet of shelf space. The PAC Directory database records contributions by every political action committee to each candidate for federal office.

This sampling of fact databases is just the tip of the iceberg—other sections of this book will introduce you to hundreds more. The next time you need facts, remember—there's probably a database that can deliver your answer.

6 Where Do Databases Come From?

The "information industry," as those involved in creating and marketing databases have come to call it, arose somewhat to the surprise of many of its participants. Over the course of the past 15 years, scientists, librarians, doctors, educators, bureaucrats, entrepreneurs, computer programmers, aerospace contractors, publishing companies, computer time-sharing companies, and telephone companies all contributed to its birth.

One of the early online database parents was the U.S. National Aeronautics and Space Administration (NASA). In order to keep track of the rapidly growing body of scientific and engineering knowledge that the "space race" was generating during the early 1960s, NASA had developed one of the first bibliographic databases, a list of citations to 200,000 technical reports. The computer NASA used was a "second-generation" machine that employed transistors and diodes, and stored information on punched paper tape or cards.

To conduct a search, a NASA inquirer would enter a batch of instructions on punched cards; then, for the next eight hours or so, the computer would "process" them—compare the inquirer's key words with each stored item by physically scanning through the entire punched-paper databank. At the end of a day (or night) the search results would be waiting.

In 1963, the computer industry's "third-generation" computers, which used integrated circuits and magnetic mass-storage devices, were introduced. Many scientists directed their attention to finding new applications for the powerful machines; among them were several people at Lockheed Missiles and Space Co., a NASA contractor. In 1966, the Lockheed group submitted a proposal to NASA to develop a more efficient aerospace database using these "sophisticated" machines, and NASA awarded Lockheed a $20,000 contract for a prototype. The system was installed at the Ames Research Center in California in 1967. (By then, NASA's database had grown to 260,000 citations.)

It came to be called NASA/RECON, for Remote Console Information Retrieval System, an indication of how novel it was to operate a computer from a control station away from the machine rather than by feeding in stacks of punched cards. Lockheed gave the name DIALOG to the software it developed for the NASA/RECON system, also indicating the novelty of being able to give a command and receive a response right away—that is, being able to "interact" with the computer rather than wait eight hours for output.

NASA/RECON proved popular with NASA scientists. By 1969, terminals were installed at other NASA sites around the country, linked to the computer by telephone lines. Today, the system, still called NASA/RECON, holds records on millions of documents, with 90,000 more added each year. It is used by aerospace researchers throughout the United States and Europe.

At about the same time that NASA was compiling its aerospace database, the U.S. National Library of Medicine was developing the Medical Literature Analysis and Retrieval System, or MEDLARS. Like the early NASA file, MEDLARS initially could only be searched by the cumbersome batch mode.

In 1969, the National Library of Medicine hired System Development Corporation (SDC), a computer software designer, to put its database online as NASA had done. SDC named its online search system ORBIT. MEDLARS operating with ORBIT became MEDLINE (MEDLARS Online). For over a decade it has been one of the most heavily used databases in the world. It now contains more than 4 million records of medical citations.

With the success of these two databases, other organizations approached Lockheed and SDC for similar services. Putting a database online required expensive computer hardware and software, which most organizations did not find economical to acquire for themselves. Thus Lockheed and SDC became database "vendors," also referred to as utilities or wholesalers. They provided and maintained the facilities—central processing units, disk drives, printers, telephone lines, and search software. Through them, a variety of unrelated organizations could sponsor online databases.

Many other early online databases were developed by the federal government. For example, the U.S. Office of Education asked Lockheed to mount a database of 12,000 research citations on the DIALOG system. It became ERIC, the Educational Resources Information Center, now with about half a million records online. The Department of Commerce's National Technical Information Service (NTIS) began its online database with five terminals at various sites. Today it records all reports emanating from federally sponsored or funded research projects. About a million records are online, with about 5,000 added each month.

Private companies and nonprofit organizations soon followed in launching commercial database services. In 1974, the Chemical Abstracts Service and Predicasts (PTS), one of the first bibliographic business databases, converted their widely used printed indexes to database form. Others, such as ABI/INFORM, an important business database founded in 1974, began from scratch as computerized files and never have appeared in print.

As more and more organizations, encouraged by falling computer hardware costs, brought their databases to be added to the DIALOG Information Retrieval Service or to SDC's ORBIT, the two vendors evolved into database "supermarkets." As of mid-1983, DIALOG was "host" to more than 170 databases in fields as diverse as pharmacy and philosophy. SDC was host to more than 70, and a third competitor, which started in 1977, Bibliographic Retrieval Service (BRS), carried about 70.

DIALOG, SDC, and BRS do *not*, with a few exceptions, create the information they sell. Those who create the information form a veritable cottage industry of "information producers." Databases are developed by hundreds of organizations, large and small, across the spectrum of human institutions. Some examples:

♦ A small company called Komp Information Services of Louisville, Kentucky, produces FOODS ADLIBRA, a database covering developments in food technology, packaging, and marketing.

♦ The International Patent Documentation Center in Vienna, Austria, produces INPADOC, a database of 10 million patents filed in 45 countries, with 16,000 patents added every week.

♦ The American Institute of Certified Public Accountants produces Accountants' Index, a bibliographic database covering 300 accounting periodicals, as well as the National Automated Accounting Research System, a full-text database of the accounting industry's regulations and standards.

A variety of other database vendors—besides the three supermarkets—got under way in the early 1970s. Mead Data Central, one of the largest vendors today, began as an experiment funded by the Ohio Bar Association to computerize Ohio case law records. The small time-sharing company that was awarded the contract was acquired in 1970 by the Mead Corporation, a Fortune 500 forest products company. The venture looked promising to Mead executives, so they decided to automate other state and federal case records. Thus was born, in 1973, the LEXIS family of databases, Mead's flagship, used today in most large law firms throughout the country. Over the years it has branched out to meet the needs of various legal specialties, and in 1980 Mead entered the nonlegal market with its NEXIS family. In 1983, Mead Data Central had over 850 employees and sales of well over $100 million in 1983.

Quite a few database producers started from humble, entrepreneurial beginnings. If your own organization has amassed facts or information (whether computerized or not) that might be salable to others, it might be a candidate for becoming a database producer. How is it done? In the next chapter we look at how four database producers got their start.

7 Four Online Entrepreneurs

From indexer to database producer

John Kuranz, president and founder of the Management Contents company, originally wanted to do scientific research. In college he majored in biochemistry; in Vietnam he served as a medic; he next taught high school biology; and, finally, he spent 1972 to 1978 with G. D. Searle, a major pharmaceutical company in Illinois.

Rather than do research, however, Kuranz and several others were assigned to manage Searle's in-house information on pharmaceuticals. "That is, I was an indexer and abstracter," he says. He also searched "by hand" for information requested by other Searle employees.

During this period, Kuranz decided to go to night school to get an MBA. It was in this program that Kuranz became intrigued by the business aspects of information systems. For his class papers, he made a point of trying to find business databases to help him complete his research.

Kuranz put his new skills to work in 1975 by becoming a supervisor in Searle's business information area. He obtained and catalogued information for the marketing/sales force and other nonscience departments. The facts that Kuranz amassed in these years built the databases that he then helped Searle put on its own computers.

One of the services he devised was a compendium of the tables of contents of 120 business magazines. It was circulated within the company, and executives would circle the titles that interested them and return them to Kuranz, who would then deliver copies of the articles to the people requesting them.

Kuranz reasoned that this service would make a good independent business venture; so in 1977 he negotiated to purchase the rights that Searle had obtained from individual publishers to print the tables of contents. Searle essentially financed this original venture by allowing him to pay for the rights over four years. This arrangement, plus about $20,000 in profit-sharing funds that Kuranz had accrued during his years at Searle, was the working capital that got Management Contents off the ground.

Kuranz set up shop with two employees. Unfortunately, it became clear that the table-of-contents business would not generate enough money to keep the company going in the long term. He then made plans for a business information database the way he had done for Searle. He hired 13 part-time free-lancers to index and abstract until he amassed 30,000 records to put into a computer. The work took about a year.

In 1978, Kuranz's new database went online on DIALOG Information Services, with which Kuranz split the revenues fifty-fifty. At that time, a user paid $55 per hour for Management Contents (today the rate is around $80 per hour.) Soon the database was also available online from System Development Corporation, Bibliographic Retrieval Service, Data-Star (a European distributor), and The Source.

For the first two years of operations, Kuranz conducted all of the company's marketing efforts himself. He held training workshops at corporations to familiarize people with his products. "I did a lot of flying in those days," he says.

Going online was just the first part of Kuranz's plan to bring in revenue and make his venture profitable. Another source of income was created by making the abstracts available on microfilm as a low-cost alternative (though, naturally, less easily searchable than the database). Thus, in late 1979, Kuranz introduced Business Index, marketed to public and academic libraries. A printed version of the microfilm product, *Business Publications Index and Abstracts*, was added to the product line in 1983.

In 1980, Kuranz increased his coverage to include legal topics by buying a print product called Legal Contents from a Delaware company. He folded Legal Contents into Management Contents database, adding another 85 to 90 journals to his coverage of business topics. At about the same time, his company was acquired by Ziff-Davis Publishing Co. Kuranz won't reveal the price, but he's still in the driver's seat.

Today Management Contents has over 200,000 records in its database, drawn from 720 journals. Kuranz's staff of indexers and abstracters add 5,000 more records every month.

Kuranz says he hasn't experienced a single lean year since his departure from G. D. Searle. He credits the general online boom for his success and says that the online product has always been his "bread and butter." In 1982-1983, Management Contents saw the least growth since its inception—and the most profit. Kuranz had 18 full-time and 55 part-time employees, and sales had reached over $1 million per year.

For the future, Kuranz is excited about his latest product, The Computer Database, for which plans were unveiled in August 1983. It covers the computer industry the way Management Contents covers business, abstracting over 530 publications cover to cover, adding 5,000 records per month to an initial database of 45,000 records. Kuranz says no competitor covers the entire computer industry as he intends to do. Prospects for this new product look very good, as detailed in Chapter 20.

From speech writer to database producer

EIC/Intelligence, Inc., was born in 1970 out of the frustration of a speech-writing assignment undertaken by its founder, James G. Kollegger. His then employer, the Macmillan Company, gave him two months in which to prepare a speech on the Green Revolution. But when he began his research, he discovered that there were practically no ready sources for facts on environmental topics. He embarked on a time-consuming research effort and managed to finish the speech in the nick of time. He was left with the thought that there had to be a better way.

Several months later, Kolleger founded the Environment Information Center, Inc. His capital was $2,000 in savings and five major credit cards that each had $500 cash advance privileges. The corporate headquarters were Kollegger's one-bedroom apartment. He hired five part-time staffers and began acquiring documents. (They were stored in cardboard boxes under his bed.) The firm's first product was an index titled Ecology Forum (since changed to Environment Abstracts).

Today EIC/Intelligence, Inc., is worth over $5 million, occupies a full floor of offices on 38th Street in New York City, and has 100 employees as well as representatives in Europe, India, China, and other parts of Asia. The company provides over 8,000 clients in more than 50 countries with 27 products and services derived from its four core databases.

At first, virtually everyone Kollegger spoke to about his project told him that the venture would fail. The company did have financial difficulty after its first year of operations in 1971. Kolleger had attracted customers, but the company was undercapitalized. His initial savings and credit were used up. By December 1971, however, he had assembled a group of seven private investors, including his mother, to fund the company with approximately $70,000. At least Kollegger was able to move EIC and his now 13 employees out of his apartment.

Kollegger anticipated EIC's entry into the database field from the very beginning. He had been an operations officer for the U.S. Army with 200 people under him and was thus very familiar with computer communications. According to Kollegger, he knew he would place his products online "from day one." Even the firm's first product was computer typeset, a relatively new method then (and far from perfected). It was a farsighted choice: the process captured all the data on computer tape, allowing easy creation of a database.

The format of Environment Abstracts, 100- to 200-word abstracts covering 21 different categories in the environment field, was the prototype for most EIC products that followed. The idea was to set up a "horizontal" system—one that cuts across the traditional disciplines of a subject to provide information on widely different aspects of a given topic. Coverage included newspapers, press releases, private papers, books, panels, conferences, and conference calendars in addition to more traditional professional journals.

Environment Abstracts was initially available as a twice monthly, softcover journal as well as on microfiche and magnetic tape. Topic areas were indexed through a key-word system, which now comprises nearly 8,000 different terms. Full texts of documents could be delivered to a customer quickly. It took EIC two years, from 1971 through 1973, to compile this first database. Environment Abstracts first went online privately with the Atomic Energy Commission and energy agencies in Europe in 1973. It was made available commercially on DIALOG in 1976.

By the mid-1970s, one area covered by the database—energy—had burgeoned to the point where it was likely to eclipse the other 20 categories. A new product was needed for this one discipline. Thus, Energy Abstracts was added to the EIC product line in 1974.

In April 1976, EIC was acquired by a wealthy Argentinian family, the Graigers, who bought out EIC's private investors and funded the company. Kollegger remained at the helm of EIC. He bought a computer to automate the office and planned several new products.

Then the bottom dropped out. The head of the Graiger family mysteriously disappeared (it was reported that he was killed in a plane crash). The entire family left the country, taking all their capital and thus wreaking financial havoc with their considerable U.S. investments. EIC and Kollegger were left with enormous short-term debts.

Between attrition and layoffs, EIC's personnel ranks shrank by more than 50 percent. Kollegger had no sales force left. The computer system, purchased at great expense, failed and had to be scrapped, leaving even more debts. Then, from 1978 through 1980, as financial woes from the recession hit major academic institutions and other customers, EIC's subscriptions fell.

What kept EIC afloat during this period were a number of government contracts that survived the widespread cutbacks of the late 1970s. By 1981, the worst was over. Kollegger made plans to add a third database, this time in biotechnology. It took EIC only one year to put out the full biotechnology product line called Telegen—paper, fiche, magnetic tape, and online versions. Kollegger points out that it was much easier to do this database because the mechanisms for turning it out were already in place. "The bigger you get," he says, "the faster you move." Much of the information used for the start-up of Telegen in 1978 existed in the other two databases and was easily tapped.

Telegen changed EIC's client base, attracting many more corporate clients. The company found that these new clients were more demanding— they wanted more timely information. EIC responded by creating Telegen/ Alert. Information is keyed into it daily, giving customers immediate online access. Information available on this system includes unpublished and pre-published reports not available elsewhere.

EIC recently created a fourth database, Robomatix, which covers automation and robotics. Robomatix took EIC only six months to pull together. Coverage incudes basic research, applications, markets, regulations, and human factors. It was introduced in March 1983 as a monthly abstract journal, also available on microfiche and magnetic tape. Robomatix is scheduled to go online in early 1984.

Though Kollegger says that EIC's biggest money makers have been its journals, he expects online use to surpass them in profitability within a year or two. EIC unveiled an expanded "alert" system in late 1983, which gives access to EIC's total information base via a user-friendly combination of software and desktop computer. A client merely has to give one of five basic commands to search and retrieve any item in any of EIC's databases. Hardcopy, full-text delivery is available with one additional command.

Kollegger says that he has been approached "repeatedly" with acquisition offers in the past year or two, but he has no current intention of selling. "We're just gearing up," he says.

From chicken coop to database producer

The Institute for Scientific Information (ISI) today offers a broad spectrum of information services used by 300,000 researchers and scholars and by 6,000 libraries worldwide. Its founder and president, Eugene Garfield, directs its operations from the company's $7 million headquarters in Philadelphia. But almost 30 years ago he could not get a bank loan for $500 to finance the publishing operation he had set up in a converted chicken coop on the outskirts of Woodbury, New Jersey.

Garfield, born in New York City in 1925, was first exposed to business in high school when he worked after classes as a clerk in the garment district. After graduation he welded in a shipyard, studied engineering, did construction work, and served in the U.S. Army. After the war he pursued a chemistry degree, supporting himself by driving a cab. But a couple of explosions in the laboratory caused him to reconsider a career as a lab chemist.

At a 1951 American Chemical Society meeting he heard about an army medical indexing project at Johns Hopkins University. It was the first major investigation of machine-based information systems. Since Garfield was looking for a new job, he asked the chairman about openings and became a research assistant on the project. His boss at the chemistry lab recommended him as "a hard but not very original worker."

As Garfield read scientific review articles for indexing, he noticed that nearly every statement was supported by a reference to a previous work. It was an insight that would soon grow, in Garfield's words, into a "personal obsession." In 1953, a glance at *Shepard's Citations*, a reference tool listing case citations for lawyers, was "a eureka experience" for Garfield. By the time his stint at Johns Hopkins was over, he was convinced that citations referenced in scientific material could provide a new and valuable way of indexing scientific literature.

It was also at Johns Hopkins that Garfield hit upon the elegantly simple idea—as did John Kuranz of Management Contents after him—of reproducing in a separate publication the contents pages from a discipline's journals. *Contents in Advance*, as Garfield called his publication, kept him up to date on what was being published in library and information science journals. Though he intended it originally to help himself keep informed, some of his colleagues also found it useful. He continued to publish it while a student at Columbia University, where he went to earn a master's degree in library science.

When he left the university, he went into business as a "free-lance documentation consultant" and began a management-literature version of *Contents in Advance*. In 1956, Bell Labs gave Garfield a $15,000 contract to produce a 500-copy edition of it for the laboratory. Till then, Garfield had done his own printing, binding, and collating from a converted chicken coop in Woodbury. The Bell Labs edition was too large a job for him. He turned to a Camden, New Jersey, printer—who wanted to be paid in advance. But Garfield was broke.

He recalls, "I naively assumed that the Bell Labs purchase order would make it a snap to borrow money from the local bank." But the banks wouldn't accept the piece of paper as collateral. "I could walk out of the bank and be hit by a car or be struck by lightning—then what would the bank do with my purchase order?"

A turning point came when one Woodbury banker suggested that Garfield borrow from a personal finance company. The young entrepreneur walked around the corner to the Household Finance Corporation office. Within five minutes he was signing an agreement for a $500 loan.

When payment for the Bell Labs contract was held up and Garfield needed another $500 for the second issue, he asked the Woodbury HFC for another loan. The manager told him $500 was the legal limit in New Jersey but hinted that Garfield might discreetly inquire at another HFC branch. So Garfield went to the Camden branch and borrowed $500 more. "Without computers," he says, "they couldn't keep track of all their loans those days....The manager there didn't ask me if I had borrowed from another branch, so I didn't tell him."

Garfield was able to repay both loans promptly. He owed the Woodbury HFC about $6.50 in interest. It wasn't even enough for the branch to cover the paperwork. "When I went back to the Camdem HFC, the manager there was even more unhappy. I only owed him about $2.50. I felt sorry for him, so I decided to keep the money a while longer." Thereafter Garfield used the HFC so often that he was awarded a gold Honor Card, which enabled him to borrow from any branch in the country.

By the 1960s, *Contents in Advance* became the well-known *Current Contents*, produced in several editions for different disciplines. He sought help from the American Chemical Society for his idea of a computer-based index that would give organic chemists access to new compounds more easily and quickly. The society turned him down, so Garfield took it upon himself to introduce *Index Chemicus* (now *Current Abstracts of Chemistry & Index Chemicus*). It was his first computerized project, the foundation for a broad line of computer-based chemical information services.

And Garfield had not, since he left Johns Hopkins, stopped thinking about the concept of a citation index for science. Encouraged by a number of scientists, he applied for and received in 1961 a grant from the National Institutes of Health to produce a test index of citations in the genetics literature. Later, when the government turned down his idea to produce a multidisciplinary index, Garfield published the first *Science Citation Index* himself. Despite predictions that it would never "fly," it eventually did well enough to cover Garfield's costs. Garfield next added the *Social Sciences Citation Index* and the *Arts and Humanities Citation Index* to his product list.

Garfield, naturally, used computers to create the indexes. When the online database business began to grow, he was able to join it with ease. In 1976, Garfield engaged DIALOG to put online the tapes containing *Science Citation Index* and so was created the database SCISEARCH. Today SCISEARCH is a bigger money earner for ISI than the original printed edition (which many libraries still receive).

After SCISEARCH came Social SCISEARCH, the online version of the *Social Sciences Citation Index*; ISI/BIOMED, covering the biomedical literature; ISI/GeoSciTech, which indexes petroleum science, oceanography, and related disciplines; ISI/CompuMath, providing access to the literature of mathematics, computer science, and other fields; and ISI/ISTP&B (the Index to Scientific & Technical Proceedings & Books), which provides multidisciplinary coverage of the literature of scientific meetings. ISI's 3-million-compound chemical substructure database is also going online.

Today, ISI's data production work force edits and puts on magnetic tape the bibliographic data from over one million published items a year. The work involves handling over 45,000 issues of 6,700 journals and requires a billion keystrokes a year. ISI employs more than 600 people and maintains sales offices around the world. The company recently entered the microcomputer market with a software system called Sci-Mate. It allows the user to dial up, log on, and search ISI, DIALOG, BRS, SDC, and MEDLINE with a single set of simple commands. It also provides a database management system different from most others on the market in that it is specifically geared for text such as bibliographic references, rather than tabular data.

Garfield looks back with nostalgia on the days when he struggled to finance his shoestring publishing operation. "The banks gladly loan ISI money now," he says. "But I still keep my HFC gold card as a memento of the time when someone was willing to take a chance that I would not be struck by lightning."

Half a million dollars in ten minutes for a new database

In 1979, John Graham and E. Lawrence Price were driving down a British motorway after having looked at some software designed to teach typing. They wondered how they could find similar software on the market. By the end of their drive, they realized that there was no central source for that kind of information, that there should be, and that they would try to provide it.

The first round of financing was easy: Price agreed, on the spot, to invest $500,000. Price had funded projects as diverse as bicycle shops, recording companies, entertainment agencies, magazines, securities companies, and oil exploration. He began his career as an accomplished concert violinist and switched midstream to finance. He currently heads Newcomb, a successful Wall Street securities trading firm.

Had it not been for Price's immediate response, the project probably would never have gotten off the ground. Graham had an excellent job as a publisher exploring the opportunities of new technology. Getting a commitment for $500,000 in ten minutes (the checks started to arrive the next week) sufficiently impressed Graham to go into the venture wholeheartedly. He quit his job and the security of corporate life to start the International Software Database.

Graham knew what he was getting into. Eight years before, he had helped found a printing company named Imprint (now known as the Devon Print Group). He then moved back into corporate life, compiling a database on English literature for Pergamon Press. In 1978, he joined Pitman Books Ltd. to explore electronic publishing; he was in the middle of negotiating a contract with the Chinese government to publish Chinese scientific work in the West when he left for the software venture.

Among the first decisions Graham needed to make about the new software information service were:

♦ Whether to use a manual cataloging system or a database system and, if the latter, whether to use a microcomputer or a more powerful mini-computer.

♦ Whether to limit the data to a certain subset of systems or applications areas or countries.

♦ How to catalog the individual programs.

♦ How to classify the compatible systems (by machine only or also by operating systems and high-level language).

Fortunately, in all of these decisions Graham chose the most difficult short-term solutions, but ones that saved enormous problems in the long term. He decided to structure the information as a database and run it on a large minicomputer. He did not restrict the data, but instead sought out all software (and firmware) worldwide.

After consulting with information scientists, software vendors, users, and librarians, he developed a numbering system for software, the International Standard Program Number (ISPN).

For the system cataloging, after attempting several inadequate methods, he realized it was necessary to build a separate database for the system. This database would interact with the software database.

Offices were established in London and people were hired with whirlwind speed: Graham and Price were determined to be the first to make a software database available.

As the company's product and the raw material are both essentially information, the firm could have located anywhere in the world. After much traveling to investigate possible places, the company set up its headquarters in Fort Collins, Colorado. "Why Fort Collins?" everyone asked.

Graham admits to being slightly puzzled at having ended up in a small frontier town of 70,000 with a rather quiet social life. There was, however, a sound rationale for the decision. In addition to low overhead costs for office space, Fort Collins has an intelligent labor pool available from the local campus of Colorado State University, and the quality of life in the community makes it possible to attract high-level management. The office is located within a few hundred yards of a Cyber 205 installed on the university's campus. The Cyber 205 is the largest supercomputer available; the university's willingness to sell time on it ensures that the International Software Database will never be short of computer power. Information gathered from all over the world is processed in Fort Collins initially on a network of Wang VS 80s and then, if necessary, on the additional online capacity of the Cyber.

Graham admits to having made some bad decisions. For example, he tried to typeset his first catalog on a machine that was inadequate for the vast amount of data the company's computer was producing. Graham and his associates sat up day and night for two and a half weeks feeding photographic paper into a typesetter in order to get the job done.

Another mistake was to invite a large financial firm that expressed an interest in investing in the company to visit the facilities. When the executives toured the building, they seemed to display too much interest in the techniques of the database structure and too little interest in the management and company structure. Shortly afterwards, they announced a competitive product. So far, nothing seems to have come of this competitor.

Originally, Graham expected revenues to finance the total operation. With the benefit of hindsight, he says this was unduly optimistic. At this writing, however, the company was close to concluding a venture-capital deal to finance the American operations. It was negotiating with a private investor in Japan and talking to a Swiss investment bank about financing European operations. The distribution of the printed catalog has now been licensed to Elsevier Science Publishing Co., one of the world's largest technical publishers.

In addition to the original International Software Database, with full information on over 40,000 software packages, there is now the International Systems Database that keeps track of all the available operating systems and their intercompatibility. The database is available online through DIALOG and the Knowledge Index and soon will be available through several other vendors in the United States and Europe. The company's Software Reports services provides customized, up-to-the-minute information on software for as little as $25. In addition to these services, the company now sells virtually any of the software packages in its database.

A continuing problem has been the question of what name to use. The company started life as Imprint Software, became the International Software Database, and for two weeks answered the phone as Access until an international search found too many potential conflicts. Its advertising agency, J. Walter Thompson, has insisted on a shorter name. They looked at Diana (the goddess of the hunt), Axis (shot down because of World War II associations), and Softcore (clearly open to misinterpretation). As we go to press, the firm had changed its name to MENU—The International Software Database.

8 How Much Does It Cost?

If you are a research chemist or an attorney in a large law firm, you may take online databases for granted. Chemists and lawyers are great consumers of information. Science is built on the discoveries of other scientists, and the law is built on legal precedent. Thus the market for chemistry and law databases developed early on.

Business managers, unlike chemists and lawyers, have not had the driving research need for huge quantities of information. Thus the amount of business data available online grew less quickly. It's only since about 1980 that the breadth of online business databases has become significant enough to make the business community pay attention.

In addition to the vast new collection of information available, a number of other attractions are drawing business executives to online databases:

♦ In many cases, it is cheaper today to conduct an online search than previously. Though connect-time rates have stayed about the same, new hardware that delivers information four times faster than earlier models effectively reduces the cost.

♦ The required equipment is cheaper, more versatile, and more widely available. The simplest computer terminals, which used to cost $2,000 to $3,000, now go for $250 to $600. Many businesses and individuals already have acquired terminals or microcomputers that can be used for communicating with online databases.

♦ Search commands are getting easier. Many database systems used to require a day or a couple of days' worth of learning time to be able to use them effectively. Today almost every vendor is hard at work on new "menu-driven" software that will substantially reduce the training time necessary. Within a few years, systems based on "artificial intelligence"—that allow a user to converse with the computer in his natural language—will be marketed.

But how much does using databases cost? Database vendors have dozens of ways of charging money, which can make comparison shopping tough. The same database may be sold for different prices by different vendors. And there's much more involved in wise buying than knowing prices. The contents of different databases may overlap; it's possible to waste money retrieving information that you've already received from another database.

You also have to make sure that you buy the right quality of service. It's no bargain to pay even the rock-bottom price of about $6 an hour for online access if the database doesn't contain the kind of answers you need.

Likewise, there is no point paying for more information than you require. If you're looking for names of pharmaceutical manufacturers in Orange County, California, Dun's Market Identifiers database can supply a list at $100 an hour in online time plus $1.50 per company name. The Electronic Yellow Pages database can do the same for about half the online cost and no additional charge per name. Market Identifiers will tell you each company's approximate annual sales; Electronic Yellow Pages will not.

This chapter provides a general guide to database pricing. You'll find specific prices for each database listed in Part II of this book. Be aware, though, that pricing schemes, like most other aspects of the growing online information industry, are in flux. A price sheet more than a few months old is probably wrong.

Database vendors have dozens of basic kinds of prices. No vendor uses them all, but some do have six or seven different kinds of fees. The main ones are:

♦ Sign-up charges
♦ Monthly minimums
♦ Subscriptions
♦ Consulting fees
♦ Charges for user manuals
♦ Connect time
♦ 1200-baud premiums
♦ Time-of-day discounts
♦ High-volume discounts
♦ Online print charges
♦ Offline print charges
♦ Character stream charges
♦ Telecommunications surcharges
♦ Storage charges
♦ CPU-time charges

Sign-up fees, monthly minimums, subscriptions, user manuals

The first three charges in our list above are the exception rather than the rule. When there is a sign-up fee or minimum, it's usually nominal. For example,

CompuServe Information Service charges a one-time sign-up fee of about $39. NewsNet has a monthly minimum charge of $15.

Some database vendors charge a hefty subscription, minimum, or consulting fee for access to their databases. For example, the economic specialists Data Resources, Inc., and Chase Econometrics gear their services to planners at large corporations and generally have a subscription fee of $5,000 to $10,000 a year for access to their databases. This amount, though, includes the services of economic consultants to help the client understand and use the information.

You'll be happy to know, though, that the majority of vendors operate almost entirely on a pay-as-you-go basis. Except for some modest initial fees for instruction manuals or a training course, there is nothing to pay until you actually conduct a search.

Even Data Resources, realizing that it was missing an important market among smaller companies, has created its "Datakits" service that has no subscription fee. All you need to buy is its VisiLink microcomputer program for $250; with that, you can tap into its databases for preformatted reports that cost between $6 and $125 each, and download them into a VisiCalc template.

Connect time

The biggest chunk of money you spend probably will go for "connect time." This is the amount of time, by the clock, that you're actually in communication by telephone with the vendor's computer. Once you're connected, even if you're just scratching your head and staring at a blank display, the meter keeps ticking.

Connect-time charges vary by database according to how valuable the seller thinks you'll find the information. Rates range from $5 an hour to more than $100 an hour. (The vendor keeps a portion of this, and a portion goes to the producer as a royalty.) Remember that many database searches take only a few minutes, so even $100 an hour may not amount to a lot!

Most vendors give discounts of between 10 percent and 30 percent on connect time for heavy use. Some, such as Bibliographic Retrieval Service, require you to commit in advance to spending a certain amount if you want to receive these discounts, agreeing to spend, say, $750 a year. DIALOG Information Services, on the other hand, offers a discount that kicks in automatically after five hours of usage per month.

Another variety of discount applies to the time of day that you use the service. Dow Jones News/Retrieval, for example, charges between $36 and $72 during the day on weekdays, depending on the database, but only $9 to $54 on nights or weekends. Not all vendors do this, though; for example, System Development Corporation charges the same rate night or day.

A few vendors, such as Dow Jones News/Retrieval, also charge different connect rates depending on how fast your terminal works. In the late 1970s, 300-baud (30 characters per second) terminals became nearly universal for online database access. In the past few years, however, 1200-baud (120 characters per second) terminals, which can retrieve information four times as fast as the older ones, have become increasingly common. (We discuss the merits of these faster terminals in Chapter 26.) Most database vendors still charge only one connect-time rate regardless of the speed. In the future, however, more and more will begin to assess a premium for 1200-baud access.

Print charges

The length of time you are connected does not necessarily indicate how much information you retrieve. You may execute a lengthy, complicated search on an obscure topic and find little information. In some cases, that may be the result you hope for. For example, if you search a patent database to find whether someone else ever patented your idea, you'll be happy to see nothing turn up.

Nevertheless, besides charges based on connect time, you're also likely to pay something extra according to the amount of information you get. A typical charge of this sort in a bibliographic database might be 25¢ per citation retrieved. Note that if your search identifies, say, 500 "hits" (it finds 500 citations on your subject), you don't necessarily pay 500 × 25¢. You have to give a separate command that states how many of those 500 you actually want to look at. You pay the royalty only on those you print out. This is often called a "print" or "type" charge.

In a variation on this, some databases charge a "character-stream" fee. As its name implies, this is based on how many characters of text flow to your terminal from the host computer.

While print charges generally run a dime or quarter, watch out for the exceptions! Dun & Bradstreet charges $1.50 per citation on its Dun's Market Identifiers database (see the listing in Chapter 18). And Arthur D. Little Online, which contains the executive summaries of the famous consulting firm's research reports, costs $100 per executive summary printed.

Telecommunications charges

Aside from connect charges and print charges, there probably will be telephone charges to pay. Unless you happen to be in the same city as your vendor's computer, you'll have to make a long-distance telephone connection. Fortunately, computers can talk to each other over the phone lines via special networks much more cheaply than humans can. We discuss computer telecommunication networks in more detail in Chapter 28; all you need to know here is that the charges average $2 to $8 an hour, regardless of the distance called. And unlike a conventional long-distance call, you typically don't get the bill for the call directly from a telephone company. Rather, the charge is passed through to the database vendor, which adds it to its other charges on its bill to you.

A sample search

Let's look at a simple search and figure out the cost. Suppose you need to know something about the mobile-home industry. You may be a banker considering financing mobile homes for the first time. Or a lawyer or accountant whose client wants to develop a mobile-home park. In any case, you know little about this industry. You want to see recent data on the business: Are mobile-home parks thriving? Are they a good investment? Who are the most successful developers?

We decided to consult the Trade and Industry Index, a database which indexes industry-related news articles from several hundred trade publications, as well as from major newspapers and consumer magazines. We "logged on" to it through DIALOG Information Retrieval Services with our 30-character-per-second terminal and gave it the command SEARCH SC = 2451, which means "search for all records indexed under SIC category 2451 (this is the Standard Industrial Classification for mobile homes; SIC codes are discussed in Chapter 9).

Moments later the system told us it found 90 hits—citations containing our key word. Since we sought only the newest information, we commanded the computer to print out the latest 15 citations; then we logged off. The session took about four minutes. Among the references we found were the following:

```
1177644  DATABASE: NNI File 111
Manufactured housing sales still rising. (column)
Los Angeles Times  v102  Section VII  p22  April 24 1983
col 1  Green, Terence M.  011 col in.
EDITION: Sun
ARTICLE TYPE: column
SIC CODE: 2451
DESCRIPTORS: mobile home industry-finance; Manufactured Housing Institute-statistics
```

```
1161570  DATABASE: NNI File 111
Mobile-home parks break stereotypes
Oser, Alan S.
New York Times  v 132  p45(N)  March 30 1983
CODEN: NYTIA
col 5  028 col in.
EDITION: Wed
SIC CODE: 2451
DESCRIPTORS: mobile home parks-innovations; mobile home industry-finance;
Clearwater Village-management
```

```
1133245  DATABASE: MI File 47
Prospects brighten for manufactured homes. (column)
Wynn, Jack
Barrons  v63  p49(1)  Jan 3 1983
CODEN: BRNSA
illustration; table
```

ARTICLE TYPE: column
SIC CODE: 2451
CAPTIONS: Manufactured housing shipments.
DESCRIPTORS: prefabricated houses-industries; mobile home industry-finance

What was the cost of this search? Well, in mid-1983, DIALOG was charging $85 an hour for connect time on the Trade and Industry Index. Thus, a bill for the session would show the following: $5.67 in connect time ($85 times 4/60 hour), plus 53¢ in telecommunication charges ($8 times 4/60 hour). Total: $6.20.

Since these are not full-text printouts, how do you obtain a copy of the articles cited? One possibility would be to order photocopies through DIALOG's online ordering system. An independent document retrieval firm would actually send you the photocopy. The cost is typically $10 an article. (We say much more about document retrieval in the chapter on information brokers.) Of course, the full text of the last two articles cited—from *The New York Times* and *Barron's*—could be obtained online via NEXIS and Dow Jones News/Retrieval, respectively.

Offline prints

Notice that the most expensive part of the bill in our example was the four minutes of connect time. It is possible to cut that down considerably. Let's look a little more closely at what happens during that time.

The quickest part of the online session was giving the instructions. We just typed a couple of command words that said to search for "mobile homes," and a moment later the computer responded with the number of "hits."

That all happened in *less than a minute*. Then we typed another couple of words, telling the computer to print out 25 citations. The next three of the four minutes were spent watching our printer deliver the information.

We could have eliminated those three minutes of connect time and still gotten the information. But there's a trade-off: We would have had to wait a few days.

The trick is to use "offline printing." That means, rather than seeing your citations while you're online, you order them printed out at the vendor's premises and mailed to you via the old-fashioned U.S. Postal Service.

Let's figure out the savings. In this example we would have been able to log off within about a minute, saving $4.65 in connect time and telecommunications charges. But DIALOG charges 20¢ extra for offline Trade and Industry Index prints, so the total, using offline prints, would have come to $4.55 ($1.55 plus 15 × 20¢), an overall saving of $1.65, or about 27%.

An additional advantage of printing offline is that you may end up with bettter quality printouts. DIALOG's laser printer, for example, yields printouts of almost typeset quality.

Storage and "SDI" charges

Occasionally, you'll want to "store" a command on a vendor's computer. A common purpose for doing so is to use an SDI command. SDI stands for the atrocious phrase "selective dissemination of information." Unfortunately, it has become a standard term in the industry.

SDIs let you get regular updates on a topic of your choice. It works like this: You compose a search strategy for a particular database and command it to be stored in the computer's memory. Each time the producer updates the database, the computer automatically runs your search against the new entries, and all relevant new ones are printed out and mailed to you. You don't have to log on or spend any connect-time money after storing the original command.

As you can imagine, SDIs give you an inexpensive intelligence briefing on the subject of your choice. If you are a recording company executive, for example, you can use an SDI to keep up with popular music reviews that appear in consumer magazines and newspapers. How? Just program Magazine Index and NDEX to search for them. (See descriptions of these databases in Chapter 14.)

How do you pick the appropriate database(s) for your SDI? First, search several for whatever information they presently contain on your subject. When you find a database that is a particularly valuable source, then use an SDI to catch similar items in the future.

Some vendors offer SDI service; some don't. Some offer it only for some of their databases. A typical charge for an SDI on DIALOG is between $5 and $15 per search per update, including 25 records printed and mailed.

You may also find storage charges on vendors who allow you to "manipulate" as well as retrieve data. This usually involves numeric data which you want to save for rearranging or for using in arithmetical calculations.

CPU-based charges

Some vendors figure your bill according to how much work their computer has to do to answer your query. The amount is quoted in CPU time (for "central processing unit") or a similar term. This is a measure of how "hard" a computer works to provide your answer.

Don't confuse CPU time with connect time! It is totally different. In fact, vendors who charge by CPU time may also impose a connect-time charge. The amount of time a central processing unit takes to perform a search is measured in seconds and fractions of seconds. There is no way to tell in advance how much CPU time a search will require.

That's the problem with CPU-based charges: you don't know how big a bill you're running up until you have finished the search. You cannot glance at your watch to tell if you are going over budget.

Why CPU time? The vendors who charge this way generally peddle databases as a sideline to a computer time-sharing business, where CPU-based charges have long been the standard fee basis. Examples are Control Data Corporation, ADP, and General Electric Information Services Company, which are discussed in more detail elsewhere in the book. They use CPU time because they're used to selling not just data, but the capability to "manipulate" the data and store it in customized formats. For example, through one of them you may call up financial statistics on, say, 100 companies in your industry, then compute a set of operating ratios to compare with your own firm. Next you can set aside the whole set of data in your own "private database" on the vendor's computer for use again at some future date.

There are variations on ways to compute CPU time. Mead Data Central, for instance, charges 45¢ for each 25,000 times a search term occurs in the database being used.

In general, CPU-based fees are not any higher than fees based on connect time for the same information. If you become a regular customer of a time-sharing vendor, you'll acquire a "feel" for how much an online session will cost.

One more tip for saving money

When you use a system that charges according to connect time, try to avoid searching during the busy hours of the day—the times when a large number of users are online. The more users, the slower the computer's response time, and the longer and more costly your session will be. At its worst, the system will take pauses lasting expensive minutes or more before responding to a command.

On the East Coast, in general, early morning—when the rest of the country is still asleep or eating breakfast—is the best time to go online. On the West Coast, late afternoon—when the rest of the country has gone home—is good. Evenings are good everywhere in the United States.

9 Tips on Database Searching

In the online database market, thousands of companies sell as many kinds of data through hundreds of online vendors. Almost every producer or vendor distributes a thick instruction manual explaining the finer points of how it arranges the information. It's possible to make a career out of searching databases (some people do—see Chapter 10, Information Brokers, for a list of them).

If the system you want to use is "menu-driven," you may be in luck. In theory, it is simple to use. There are, however, degrees of simplicity, and even menu-driven systems may, at one time or another, confound you.

As likely as not, the system you need to use will not be menu-driven. You will have to learn a set of commands. Unfortunately, as yet there is little standardization in the industry: most vendors have their own command language. For example, the simple command that tells the computer to end the online session may be expressed in any of dozens of ways. For one system, the appropriate word may be QUIT. For others, it may be LOGOFF, END, STOP, BYE, or OFF. Or it may require a symbol such as that for break or escape, control-C, or slash. Other commands have similar variations from vendor to vendor.

Here's the good news: you really can pick up the basics of a particular database very quickly. It doesn't take weeks of practice. With most vendors, a few hours spent reading a manual and getting an hour or two of practice will teach you enough to begin finding practical answers to real questions.

We suggest you begin by familiarizing yourself with at least two vendors. Pick one menu-driven system, such as BRS After Dark, and one command-driven system, such as Dow Jones News/Retrieval or DIALOG. Many vendors provide new users with free time to get acquainted with the system (some have made a special offer in the coupon section at the back of this book). Take advantage of the offer and spend a couple of hours hunting for information.

As you become comfortable going online, you'll gradually want to branch out and try other services and other databases. Each new one you use will be easier to master because you'll know how to "think database." Going online will soon become second nature, and a whole new world of business knowledge will open up. As a matter of fact, you may soon tire of wading through the simple but time-consuming menu-driven systems and opt for the more direct and sophisticated command-driven options.

Despite the differences among vendor systems, many rules of database searching apply almost universally. In the rest of this chapter, we summarize the most important tips and tricks that experienced online searchers have discovered.

Learn to play the trade-off between quantity and precision

You search databases to find answers to questions. Ideally, you'll find exactly what you need. Usually, your search will fall short of the ideal.

Suppose you're studying the market for paint. It's an easy matter to gather great quantities of irrelevant data. In broad-coverage databases there may be hundreds or thousands of references to trade press reports about paint products. In other databases you find listings of companies that make or sell paint. In yet others there are technical reports about developments and discoveries in paint chemistry. There is even an entire database devoted to the subject Surface Coatings Abstracts (available on DIALOG).

But you don't want great quantities of data. That just contributes to information overload. Rather, you need precise facts—perhaps a list of new products introduced in the past year, sales figures for the ten largest producers, or a detailed analysis of one company's experience in the business.

We don't promise you'll find exactly what you need waiting for you in a database. For example, you will not necessarily find a definitive list of new products. You may, however, search 5 databases, retrieve 50 citations to trade magazine articles, and find 8 items in 5 journals that together describe 12 products introduced recently. Each article may carry a different amount of detail, and you cannot be sure that something important is not missing. But you surely can use them to assemble a very useful list—and remember, it only took you a few minutes and a few dollars to find!

In other words, databases can lead you quite a distance toward your answer. Sometimes you can raise the precision of your search (that is, the degree to which it exactly fulfills your need) by increasing the quantity of data you retrieve. By searching ten databases rather than five, you may find a couple of additional trade reports on new paint products.

As with so many investments in business, at some point you start getting decreasing returns: searching another ten databases may not yield much more than the first ten did. That assumes, of course, that you chose the first ten wisely; there's always the possiblility that an obscure database turns out to contain the gold mine you seek. As you become "infowise," you'll learn to play the trade-off between quantity and precision effectively.

Decide what kind of information you seek

To pick the database or databases most likely to answer your question, your problem should be well defined. Do you want a simple introduction to your topic or a comprehensive review of all available information? Will reviews and trade press articles suffice, or do you need original research reports, government documents, or corporate records? Do you need a simple fact— the name of a manufacturer of fondu cement or of the country's leading expert on employee stock ownership plans—or do you need a wide-ranging review of, say, the distribution process in the photo-finishing industry?

If you have a clear goal in mind, you'll be able to pick the most likely databases to find the answer. Use the database descriptions in this book to help you make your selection.

Ask for help

Communicating with a large computer over phone lines can be a finicky process. Online searching takes a bit of getting used to. The tiny snags are the ones that will give you headaches. You'll forget to press "return" at the end of a command and sit wondering why the computer doesn't respond. You'll unwittingly type REAL ESTATE APPRIASAL rather than APPRAISAL and fail to get any information. You'll enter what you think are proper directions and be greeted on your computer screen with the response ILLEGAL COMMAND with no further hint as to what's wrong.

These are the times when we urge you to take advantage of the toll-free telephone numbers provided by most database vendors. When your search doesn't work as expected, or whenever you get confused, call up and ask! Most vendors maintain a customer-assistance staff just waiting to help you out. (Even if there's no toll-free number, spend a few dollars on a call. It's probably the fastest way to solve your problem.) Usually, you'll be surprised at how simple the solution to your problem is. Also, try calling the database producer (many of them maintain toll-free phone numbers). They usually are ready to talk you through a difficult search.

While online, whenever you get stuck, don't hesitate to hang up the phone for a few minutes to think about what to do next. Some of the more expensive services cost a dollar or two a minute; you don't want to use up online time while you sit scratching your head. Soon you'll learn to think through your entire search before you get online. You'll plan out the commands you need to use—looking them up if you don't remember them—and make a few notes to have at your fingertips.

Map out your search strategy in advance

No matter how experienced you are as a database searcher, the process usually brings surprises. For example, in looking for data on the mobile-home industry, we logged onto a database called American Statistics Index (ASI), a master guide to U.S. government statistical publications, produced by Congressional Information Service Inc. (A similar search about mobile homes on the Trade and Industry Index was described in Chapter 8.) Imagine our surprise when the computer responded that ASI carried 1,661 entries mentioning mobile homes!

Why so many? It seems that many government statistical reports about cities and regions carry figures on how many people live in various types of housing, including mobile homes. To us, though, most of those reports were of limited interest; we wanted only reports dealing directly with the mobile-home market.

The moral of the story: always have in mind (even better, have on paper) some refinement of your initial search strategy. What will you do if your search turns up too many references? What if it turns up zero? You'll have to narrow or broaden your request.

In the example above, we could have limited our search just to items that mention mobile homes as an indexing term (indicating this to be a major topic of the report). We might also have combined the search term with another word, such as park or manufacturing, in order to retrieve only reports on mobile-home parks or mobile-home manufacturing.

You should try to anticipate even the most mundane commands. This will save you considerable time fumbling around online with the meter ticking. Will you use online or offline prints? Do you know the correct command to order them? Do you want to print out full records or only partial ones (such as title and source without the abstract)? Do you know the command for that?

Think in Boolean (and other) connectors

Most database vendors use a set of "connectors"—commands to link search terms together—named after the nineteenth-century English mathematician George Boole. A Boolean connector, in the database industry, is simply one of the three words AND, OR, or NOT.

AND, as in *rich and famous*, refers to what mathematicians call an intersection. It means the set of records in which the words rich and famous both occur. *Rich or famous*, on the other hand, refers to the mathematical union of the two terms: all records containing either one word or the other (or both). *Rich not famous*, as you can guess, refers to records with rich but excludes those that also have famous.

Here's a typical application of Boolean connectors. Suppose you're looking in a database for a roundup of the latest marketing trends in the pharmaceutical industry. You might first search for "marketing or sales," then for "pharmaceuticals or drugs," and then combine the two resulting sets of records with an AND command. To exclude information about drug abuse, you might use a NOT connector on records that have "abuse or addiction" in them.

Though Boolean connectors are fundamental, you'll also encounter other logical connectors. For example, many vendors give you the option of an "adjacency" connector, which is more restrictive than AND. Suppose you need information on direct marketing. Though "direct marketing" contains two words, it is logically one thought; the words, when adjacent in this phrase, refer to a well-defined business concept. If you were searching a database on the SDC system, you could give it the search term DIRECT ADJ MARKETING. The computer would select only records in which this entire two-word string appeared intact; it would pass up records that contain "direct" and "marketing" in two different places.

Think of word roots and alternate search terms

Computers are not very smart. If you command one to search for the word "bankrupt" in a free-text search, it will not necessarily find references that contain "bankrupted" or "bankruptcy." Most vendor systems, however, let you truncate a search term; for example, on SDC's system you can enter BANKRUPT:, which tells the computer to pick out occurrences of the term with or without suffixes.

That's an improvement. How about records that do not mention bankruptcy in any form but instead contain one of these terms—Chapter 11, default, insolvency, liquidation, failure, crashed, went broke, folded, out of business, delinquent, receivership, or collapsed? If you're interested in the topic bankruptcy, would you want to see records containing these ideas?

The first imperative in conducting a database search, then, is to think of all possible synonyms and variations on your search term. Do this *before* you go online. It takes only a minute or two to give the computer a list of alternate terms connected by an OR statement—*if* you have the list ready. A good thesaurus can be an invaluable aid to a brainstorming session. Also, look through any published information you already have on your topic to pick out the various terms it uses.

Pay attention to abbreviations

Is the Securities and Exchange Commission abbreviated S.E.C. or SEC? Is it known as the Department of the Treasury or the Treasury Dept.? Is the state that shares Virginia's southern border known as N.C. or NC or N. Carolina or North Carolina? Most computers care about the difference. If you ask for SEC when a database uses S.E.C., you often won't find what you're looking for.

You'll even find inconsistencies within individual databases. One might use the abbreviation SEC, without periods, but abbreviate the Department of Energy D.O.E. Another database might do the opposite.

The solution? Just try all the variations you can think of. Never be content with only one spelling of an abbreviation.

Learn to use the controlled vocabulary

Before you begin to search any database, it is a good idea to see whether it has controlled vocabulary terms that pertain to your subject. Controlled vocabulary terms and codes provide you with one of the most useful database search tools. If you're searching ABI/INFORM for information about, for example, stock option plans for employees, you probably can conduct a more successful search by first consulting the ABI/INFORM user's guide. It will tell you that its indexers use the terms "ESOP," "ESOT," and "fringe benefit plans," in addition to "stock options." By specifying some or all of these terms, you may pick up items that "stock options" alone misses.

For the databases that you use most often, it's worth keeping the complete controlled vocabulary list—often called a thesaurus—on your bookshelf (you may have to pay the producer a nominal fee for it). If you don't have the thesaurus, some vendors permit you to examine the controlled vocabulary online, paying standard connect-time rates while you're doing so. On DIALOG, for example, you would apply the EXPAND command to the descriptor field; on SDC, the NEIGHBOR command; or on BRS, the ROOT command.

Some database vendors develop their own, unique controlled vocabulary; others adopt a set of terms already used elsewhere; others do both. One controlled vocabulary list, the SIC codes, is so widely used that we devote the following section to it.

Be familiar with SIC codes

Get used to seeing the federal government's Standard Industrial Classification (SIC) codes. Their numbers pop up everywhere; they are the most common controlled vocabulary used in business databases.

SIC codes have seven digits; each digit contributes a degree of specificity. For example, numbers beginning with 2 or 3 stand for manufacturing industries. The number 31 stands for leather and leather products. Number 2772 stands for greeting card publishing. At the seven-digit level, greeting cards are broken down into such categories as:

- ◆ 2771113 Christmas cards sold at counters
- ◆ 2771115 Chrismas cards, packaged or boxed
- ◆ 2771122 Valentine cards, sold at counters
- ◆ 2771124 Valentine cards, packaged or boxed
- ◆ 2771126 Mother's Day cards
- ◆ 2771128 Other seasonal cards
- ◆ 2771133 Other greeting cards sold at counters
- ◆ 2771135 Other greeting cards, packaged or boxed

The majority of databases that have SIC codes use only the first four of the seven digits. If you need information, for example, on billboard advertising, you can narrow in on the subject by searching for items indexed under SIC number 7312, outdoor advertising services. If you're interested in insured mutual savings banks that are not members of the Federal Reserve System, you can use SIC number 6033.

Unfortunately, four-digit SIC codes aren't always so nicely on target. If you're searching for data on computer printers, the closest you can get with a four-digit SIC code is number 3573, electronic computing equipment, which covers almost the entire computer industry. If you seek a list of shopping centers, you would have to use number 6512, operators of nonresidential buildings, which includes office buildings as well as shopping centers. Don't let that discourage you, however; from there, you can probably home in on computer printers or shopping centers by using a free-text search.

Even the full seven-digit codes can be inadequate, especially for the newest technologies. The last major revision to the SIC codes was made in 1972, though the government makes minor changes and additions on an ongoing basis. Thus if your topic is one that entered the business world only in the last few years, such as insulin synthesis or automated bank teller machines, don't count on finding an SIC number devoted to it. The next major overhaul of the SIC system isn't expected for another five years.

Several database producers compensate for this by modifying the SIC codes themselves. Predicasts, for example, producer of four databases described elsewhere in this book (F&S Indexes, PROMT, Time Series, and Forecasts), uses seven-digit "product codes" that look like SIC codes. The first four digits, by and large, correspond to the SIC list, but at the seven-digit level some of them are very different. Some codes it uses for the chemical industry don't even correspond to SIC at four digits.

Some of the databases described in this book whose controlled vocabulary is based on SIC codes include:

♦ PTS's F&S Indexes, PROMT, Times Series, and Forecasts

♦ HARFAX Industry Data Sources

♦ Trade and Industry Index

♦ Standard & Poor's Corporation Records

♦ Economic Information Systems (EIS)

♦ Dun's Market Identifiers and Million Dollar Directory

♦ ADTRACK

How do you find out what code numbers to use for your topic? Each database producer that uses SIC-based codes publishes its own list. You'll find it in the database manual. If you don't have the producer's manual handy, another producer's manual *may* tell you the code you need. (You'll have to test the number online.)

For the official four-digit SIC list, you can buy a copy of the federal government's 1972 *Standard Industrial Classification Manual* (stock number 041-001-00066-6) for $15 from the Superintendent of Documents, Washington, D.C. 20402, or from any Government Printing Office bookstore (many large cities have one; check the phone book). This lists many of the subindustries under each category, though it doesn't give the corresponding seven-digit codes. A supplement published in 1977 is also available for $2.75 (stock number 003-005-00176-0). For manufacturing industries, you'll find the 1977 seven-digit SIC codes in the Census Bureau's Numerical List of Manufactured Products (GPO stock number 003-024-01644-3), which costs $6.

Be careful when using British databases that show SIC codes. The United Kingdom has its own very different set of four-digit Standard Industrial Classification Codes, also called SIC. The United Nations has yet another code used primarily for international trade statistics; fortunately, it carries a slightly different name: Standard Industrial Trade Classification, or SITC.

Learn to search interactively

Many experienced searchers become complacent about their search skills. They know how to formulate a relatively successful search strategy on their first try—so they log on, give a few commands, retrieve a few records, log off, and that's it.

That is not necessarily the best way to proceed. An effective search session resembles detective work.

Suppose you are looking for guidelines on how to structure the board of directors for a civic improvement organization. You log on to the ABI/INFORM database and search for records containing the terms "boards of directors" and "nonprofit." The first citation you find isn't what you need. But look at the citation's controlled vocabulary terms. It's indexed under "boards of trustees" and "foundations." Aha! Why not see what you can find under those terms?

The point is to let your first, tentative search lead you to others. This is interactive searching. You gradually home in on the information you need.

Pay attention to searchable fields

In most databases each record is divided into "fields." In a bibliographic database, for example, there might be seven fields: title, author, publication, date, abstract, descriptors, and identifiers.

Get in the habit of examining which fields the database you're using contains. You'll find them described in the literature supplied by the vendor or producer (or both). Knowing the fields will help you seach more effectively.

For example, you'll notice that the Predicasts (PTS) databases have a field called "event code." Each record is assigned a number that defines what kind of news is being reported—such as license sought, license available, license sold. This can help you narrow down a search with great precision.

Be skeptical of failed searches

Suppose you give the term "pickup truck" in a free-text search to a broad-coverage business database like Predicasts' F&S Indexes, and the system replies by telling you it found nothing on the subject. Don't believe it. Ask yourself:

♦ Did you incorrectly put a hyphen in the word ("pick-up" rather than "pickup")? Predicasts uses no hyphen in its spelling of this word.

♦ Did you also try the terms "utility vehicle," "small truck," "light-duty truck," or related terms?

♦ Did you insert the proper connector for two-word terms? On the DIA-LOG system, for example, you must say "pickup(w)truck" in order to look for a two-word phrase in free text.

Small oversights like these can make your search go awry. Don't give up on your first try, or even on your second try. Call the vendor or producer and discuss your results. Consult the manual. Formulate the search in different terms. Be skeptical of failed searches—there are very few business topics that aren't covered by some database.

Don't get stuck in a rut with one vendor

Several of the large "supermarket" vendors would have you believe that their service is the only one you need. We know professional researchers and librarians who learn to use only one or two systems and never bother to learn about others. Thus they remain ignorant of many worthwhile databases.

It's easy to fall into this rut since each of the major vendors offers numerous valuable databases. But don't be lulled into a feeling that your favorite vendor has all you need. Many of the best databases are available exclusively from one vendor and have no direct competitor elsewhere. The industry is fragmented; it's easy to lose sight of some significant products. Some examples:

♦ The Society of Automotive Engineers' database of meeting and conference papers is available only on SDC's ORBIT.

♦ Dun's Market Identifiers, with data on most U.S. companies with more than ten employees, is available only on DIALOG.

♦ Advertising and Marketing Intelligence, which abstracts 65 marketing journals, is available only from Mead Data Central.

♦ The Military and Federal Specifications and Standards database, which indexes all documents that set standards for products bought by the U.S. government, is available only on BRS or through its sister company, Information Handling Service.

♦ NewsNet is the only place where you'll find online 16 newsletters about the publishing and broadcasting business, as well as similar coverage of newsletters in a score of other industries.

♦ Pergamon InfoLine is exclusive vendor of Pira, a database devoted to the paper, board, printing, and packaging industries.

We encourage you to obtain literature from many vendors and examine all of the material to see whether they offer databases you might want to use. Subscribing to only one vendor is like watching only one television station: you miss out on a lot of good "programming."

There's a similar danger in relying too much on a single database. This leads to our next suggestion.

Be skeptical of databases that claim to offer complete coverage

Online databases in general contain a far greater range of information than you normally could find using other resources. But most still have a considerable distance to go before they are truly complete.

In venerable marketing spirit, though, database producers tend to create an overly optimistic impression of how much information they have online. In brochures describing Management Contents, for example, you'll read that the database covers business and management literature published since 1974 and that it abstracts more than 700 periodicals. Does that mean it has abstracted 700 periodicals, all going back to 1974? You might get that idea, but it's not correct.

When Management Contents began abstracting in 1974, it covered only a fraction of the sources it indexes now. Gradually, over the years, it added new publications. Each time it did so, it began its indexing with the current issue—not with those from 1974. For example, it began covering the journal *Medical Economics* in 1981; thus the database contains references from it only since the January 1981 issue.

We don't wish to embarrass Management Contents on this score. Its competitors lean toward the same kind of inference. Perhaps it would complicate their marketing literature to say "Coverage starts sometime between 1974 and the present." And we certainly don't want to discourage you from using Management Contents or other databases. If you seek only the most recent information about, say, hospital accounting systems, then you wouldn't care that the majority of the references date only from the past few years rather than from the past decade. We simply want you to be aware of what's in a particular database and what's not.

In a similar vein, be wary of "cover-to-cover" or "complete" indexing. When a producer states that its database holds the full text of a journal or that it indexes a journal cover to cover, this means you'll find online *most* of the publication. You, however, will not find any number of items, such as brief articles, editorials, letters to the editor, corrections to previous stories, charts, illustrations, announcements, calendars, and, of course, the advertisements. In other words, cover to cover generally refers to the major stories in the publication, not to absolutely everything between the two covers.

If a source *doesn't* get cover-to-cover indexing in a database, then it may be indexed "selectively." Again, be careful about assuming too great a degree of thoroughness. The producer may list hundreds of source publications, but it may draw one article a year from some of them.

Keep up with database moves

The online database industry is still in its formative stage. Databases hop around from vendor to vendor. Today's vendor catalog may be wrong six months from now.

For example, in September 1982, the RAPRA database of the Rubber and Plastics Research Association of Great Britain disappeared from DIALOG and the PATSEARCH patent database disappeared from BRS. Where did they go? To Pergamon Corporation's new service, Pergamon InfoLine.

New databases continue to come on the market almost weekly. In the fall of 1982, Cuadra's *Directory of Online Databases* listed 1,350 databases and 213 vendors; a year later, there were 1,800 databases and 270 vendors. In general, the market is probably growing at about 30 percent to 35 percent a year.

As you become an experienced user, you'll learn to keep track of moves that affect you by skimming the newsletters published by many of these companies. Which brings us to another suggestion.

Set up a filing system for database manuals, brochures, and newsletters

Most database vendors and producers put out stacks of glossy brochures, newsletters, announcements, updates, price schedules, and the like. And almost every one publishes its own user's manual.

Collect all this material and file it neatly away. Sooner or later, you'll be glad to have it around. These are your road maps to a vast frontier of information that will help you do your job more effectively.

User's manuals form the core of your collection. Clear a shelf and start filling it up with manuals from each major vendor (many are listed in Part III) and from the database producers that interest you (Part II). You may have to lay out $20 or $30 for some of them, but they're worth it. At first, some of this literature may not make very good reading. As you become more familiar with the information industry, however, it all will start to look quite elementary.

Vendors' manuals tell you the basics—what commands to use, what databases are available. You can't go online without them.

Manuals put out by individual database producers help you get the most out of your search. If you're looking for information on how to raise equity capital for a small business, the Management Contents manual can tell you that the database also indexes articles under the terms "cost of capital" and "capital structure." If you're looking for data on the probable payback for converting residential heating systems from oil to gas, the Energyline manual can tell you that it uses the index term "boiler convertability."

Probably the most interesting and enjoyable reading you'll encounter are the vendor and producer newsletters. Any company that publishes one would love to start sending it to you. Get yourself on five or ten mailing lists. In the newsletters you'll learn about how other people use databases to solve information problems. You'll find out about the slew of new services constantly coming on the market, one of which might be just the one to help you. You'll make yourself knowledgeable about the most sophisticated ways to find out what's going on in the business world.

As for books and periodicals, we suggest some you may want to acquire in Appendix A.

Learn to hunt for information in unlikely databases

On first impression, you might think social science databases like Sociological Abstracts and PsycINFO are meant only for professors of sociology or psychology. But they can be valuable sources if you're researching consumer behavior or personnel management.

Likewise, you might ordinarily bypass Pira, a database about the paper, board, printing, and packaging industries—but this database also contains abstracts from more than 100 internationally known general management periodicals.

The National Technical Information Service database, despite its name, contains references to many government-funded reports on management techniques.

The Institute for Scientific Information's CompuMath database, intended mainly for mathematicians, also indexes articles from many computer industry trade journals.

How do you find out about such "hidden" information sources? By being a bit adventuresome, by using your intuition, and by becoming familiar with the database world. It really doesn't cost much to try looking for the same information in 10 or 20 different databases. For a couple of dollars, you can find out whether PsycINFO or CompuMath has anything about your topic. If they do, a few more dollars gets the information printed out for you.

Several major vendors offer a particularly easy way to find out whether a topic is covered in unexpected databases. The generic name for this procedure is "cross-database searching." DIALOG calls its version the DIALINDEX. The SDC name is Data Base Index. BRS's is called CROSS.

If you're searching for advice on, say, truck leasing, you might be tempted to search only the major bibliographic management databases, ignoring, perhaps, the *American Banker* database on SDC, which carries the full text of the daily American Banker newspaper. But if you first use SDC's Data Base Index, you can give the key words "truck" and "lease," and the computer will respond by telling you how many records with those two terms each of its 70 databases contains. That way, you won't miss any database with something on trucks and leasing.

Take note of how timely a database is

If you need very recent, timely information, you have to pay attention to how up-to-date the databases that you use are. Those we introduce in this book range in timeliness from up-to-the-minute to many months delayed.

For reference databases, timeliness has two components. First, there's the question of how long it takes to index and abstract the source material. Second, there is the question of how frequently the vendor "reloads" or adds new records to the online database. Typically, reference databases have a lag of a couple of weeks before new records are written, and the database is reloaded once, twice, or four times a month.

Full-text databases generally get online faster than reference databases. For a full-text database, this simply involves taking computerized typesetting tapes from the publisher and transferring them to the database tape, a process that can be accomplished in days or even hours. But if the producer adds controlled vocabulary terms, then a human being must scrutinize each article, and the process will take longer.

Suppose your boss needs to make a speech, and he asks you to find out everything you can about an important bill pending in Congress. You'd like to collect news reports, analyses, editorials, etc., on the bill. The NDEX database might seem to be a good source to search. It indexes most major articles from eight important regional newspapers. Unfortunately, though, its indexers usually have about a six-week backlog of newspapers piled up. In addition, since a new batch of records is added to the database only monthly, your search could miss articles that have appeared within the last ten weeks. From a legislative point of view, your database search could be hopelessly out of date. You'd do better to consult, among others, the New York Times Information Bank or NEWSEARCH, which have a time lag of only about 24 hours.

Take note of how big a database is

Most databases we introduce in this book are best measured by the number of records they contain. As a rule of thumb, you can consider a database with less than 100,000 records "small"; one with between 100,000 and 1 million, "medium"; and with more than 1 million, "large."

Whether it's a reference, full-text, or fact database, the number indicates how many individual articles or similar items the database lists. (This measure doesn't apply to some statistical databases, such as the demographic ones described in Chapter 16, because that information isn't broken down into such distinct units.)

Bigger isn't necessarily better, though a database's size does give some indication of its character. Small databases usually are small for a reason: because the database is highly selective about what information it carries, or because it concentrates on a relatively narrow area, or because it is a new database that eventually will grow much larger.

A good example of the first case is Energyline (see Chapter 22). Though other energy industry databases index millions of documents, Energyline in eight years has grown to hold only about 40,000 records. Why? Because the producer selects only major items that make a "useful contribution" to the accumulated knowledge about the industry. Thus, despite its relatively small size, Energyline may, from a user's point of view, be packed with valuable information.

The FIND/SVP Reports and Studies Index (see Chapter 16) exemplifies the second kind of small database. It is devoted to indexing a very special class of information: reports and studies sold by market research and consulting firms. It has about 10,000 records.

The Computer Database (see Chapter 20), which indexes computer journals, is an example of the third case. Begun in 1983, it was expected to have about 50,000 records online at the end of the year. But at an expected increase of about 60,000 records a year, it will not remain small for long.

Most general reference databases fall into the medium category. Management Contents, for example, has accumulated close to 200,000 records. The National Newspaper Index holds 600,000 records.

Though we call these "medium," they contain incredible amounts of data. How else can you search records of half a million news articles for any group of words you wish? With National Newspaper Index you can accomplish this feat in seconds, and for a few dollars.

Then there are the databases of mind-boggling size. INSPEC, the Information Services in Physics, Electrotechnology, Communications, and Control, contains references to more than two million technical articles, reports, books, theses, and the like. World Patents Index has records on 6 million patents from 28 countries. Usually, a database must have collected information for quite a few years to attain such size. INSPEC, for example, goes back to 1969. World Patents Index's records go back at least a decade for most of the countries it covers. If you're looking mainly for recent data, then don't be impressed by these colossal files—they're not necessarily more thorough than some medium-sized databases.

10 The Information Brokers

Online databases might seem to diminish the need for libraries and librarians. To the contrary, as information awareness on the part of business has grown, business librarianship has boomed. More and more companies are establishing in-house libraries, and at the same time fee-based "information brokers" are proliferating. Anyone seeking to master the information explosion should be aware of the services available from these organizations.

There are several important reasons why you may need the help of an information broker even if you're a regular database user:

♦ Some databases require specialized knowledge of a field in order to use them effectively. You cannot search the LEXIS legal databases effectively, for example, unless you're a lawyer or a trained legal researcher.

♦ Some databases have restricted access or high subscription fees. NASA's valuable technology database NASA/RECON, for example, is directly available only to certified NASA subcontractors. You can, however, ask a NASA-affiliated information broker to perform a search for you.

♦ Command languages vary from database to database, and it's difficult for one person to become proficient in all. You should try to learn the systems that would be most useful to you, but sometimes it is advisable to entrust an important or complicated search to a specialist familiar with the quirks of the particular database.

♦ Brokers specialize in obtaining hard-to-find documents, whether they be government reports, obscure publications, or information from abroad. The majority of databases on the market today are the bibliographic type: they'll tell you about the information on your topic that exists but not necessarily deliver all that information to you. Brokers, in their role as document suppliers, can find and photocopy almost any published item.

♦ Perhaps most importantly, significant quantities of information still are not recorded or indexed in databases! The information explosion outpaces even the database industry. The most up-to-date knowledge does not appear in print—it still exists only in the minds of particular individuals, whether they be government officials, technology experts, consultants, trade association directors, scholars, researchers, or even your competitors. A qualified broker will conduct a manual literature search involving government and university libraries, newspaper morgues, and other significant archives to dig out the relevant material for you. The best information brokers act almost as detectives, seeking out the person who has the answer to your question. They will conduct interviews, perform market surveys, gather product specifications, investigate industry distribution patterns, and do many other kinds of useful work.

Information brokers come in many varieties, with many names: information specialists, information consultants, free-lance librarians, information retailers, information-on-demand companies, free-lance researchers, and others. No firm dominates the market; rather, many small organizations, most with a particular specialty or strength, vie for your business.

In Appendix B, you'll find details on some of the country's major information brokers and selected smaller organizations, along with their typical prices and specialties. We have attempted to select the most important companies, though some good firms may not be represented on the list. Two major firms, InfoSource in Pittsburgh and Control Data Fact Finders in Minneapolis, declined to be listed.

In selecting an information broker (whether from this list or another) here are some suggestions to keep in mind:

♦ Be as detailed as possible in explaining your assignment. Many a database search has produced useless results because the seeker was vague or even unsure about what was needed. Spend some time discussing your problem with the searcher, and ask the searcher questions about the topic to see if you both have the same understanding. What's most helpful is to give your searcher samples of any information you already have that most closely approximates what you seek. Try to think of all the possible synonyms or terms related to your topic, and list them all for the searcher. Ask to review the search strategy before it is conducted. Keep in mind the search hints outlined in Chapter 9.

♦ If at all possible, be present during an online search. You can then give the information specialist immediate feedback on whether the results are useful or not. If the specialist gets onto a wrong tack, you can suggest a change. And you'll be able to monitor the cost of the search as it takes place, to decide if additional expense is warranted.

♦ Be clear as to the type of report that you want. A simple database printout may be adequate for your purposes—and relatively inexpensive. On the other hand, if your search is complicated, involving both database and manual research as well as interviews with experts, you should select a broker who will compile a summary (or even analysis) of the findings. Though more expensive, this type of service is often well worth it if you need concise, organized facts and not a "data dump."

♦ To find a skilled searcher in your own area, contact the library of any large university. Often libraries offer search services to the public on a cost-plus basis. If the library does not offer the service, it may be able to refer you to a qualified free-lancer. Be sure to ask which databases and which vendors the searcher plans to tap; compare them to those listed in this book. The best searchers are skilled at using many vendors' systems, not just one.

♦ In ordering document photocopies, try to use a supplier that specializes in the kind of documents you need. Many database producers supply copies of the documents indexed in their database; for example, Management Contents will provide a copy of most items it lists, and several patent database producers sell photocopies of patents. Check the database listings elsewhere in this book to find out whether a database producer offers this service. An inexpensive but less reliable source for hard-to-find journals or reports is the interlibrary loan department of a nearby university library. The waiting time, however, is likely to be considerable.

♦ For federal government documents, check with a federal document depository; many large community and university libraries have been so designated. Their services are available to the public, even at the universities. A government documents librarian can often dig up information for you at no charge, though you'll have to make a trip to the library to read or copy it.

♦ Be sure to obtain a price estimate from the broker you contact. Online searching as well as document retrieval can become expensive. It's wise to specify a maximum amount to be spent.

♦ To obtain documents that you identify through your own online search, several database vendors, including DIALOG and SDC, offer a quick way to give your order to a broker. You just transmit your instructions to the broker while online. But unless you have a long list of items or are transmitting the order overseas, this may not be any more economical than a phone call because you incur connect-time charges while you're ordering online.

♦ Many information brokers provide a "watch" service similar to the SDI service described in Chapter 8. They will search for data on your topic regularly and send you a periodic update. They may also undertake in-depth studies that border on management consulting work, though usually at rates lower than traditional management consultants. A number of information brokers specialize in developing and maintaining libraries tailored to specific organizational requirements.

11 A Typical Database Search Session

Every business has competitors. It's a must to keep a keen eye on their products, sales, marketing techniques, personnel changes, financing arrangements, lawsuits, and so forth. It is reasonably easy to follow these events with traditional methods, especially with publicly held companies, but the time and the legwork required usually prevent people from paying as much attention as they should to this critical part of doing business. (Until it's too late, of course.)

Consider the case of Cybertronic Systems, a real company whose name has been changed to protect confidentiality. Cybertronic, run by Cy, Bert, Ron, and Nick, makes color-graphic display terminals. Recently, a consultant taught Cy, the vice president of marketing, how to search online databases.

One of the first things that Cy did with his new-found online capability was to spend a morning researching the competition. About an hour and a half of that time was spent online, searching for references to Ramtek, one of the firm's competitors. Let's see how he went about it and what he managed to find.

Cy's first step was the establishment of a search strategy. In this case, the strategy was trivial—he was simply looking for all records that happened to contain the word Ramtek. After leafing through the DIALOG manual, he made a preliminary list of the databases that he wanted to try:

Database and DIALOG File Number

Business Bibliographic:
    ABI/INFORM 15
    Management Contents 75
    HARFAX 189
Business News:
    Trade and Industry Index 148
    Standard & Poor's News 132

Standard & Poor's News Daily 133
NEWSEARCH 211
PTS PROMT 16
Company Information:
  EIS Industrial Plants 22
  EIS Nonmanufacturing Establishments 92
  PTS Annual Reports Abstracts 17
  Disclosure 100
  Electronic Yellow Pages—Mfrs. 510
Science and Technology:
  INSPEC 13
  COMPENDEX 8
  SCISEARCH 34
  NTIS 6
  Conference Papers Index 77
Patents:
  CLAIMS 24, 25, 125

Rather than perform a search for Ramtek in these files one at a time, he decided he would use the system's master directory known as DIALINDEX (discussed in Chapter 9). For a relatively modest $35 per hour, this directory allows you to search through every single database on the system at once. Unfortunately, it doesn't let you retrieve the information; it just tells you how many "hits" can be found in each of the databases specified. You can then go through the specific databases one at a time to perform the true searches, skipping the ones that yielded no results in the DIALINDEX search. Here's the way it worked for Cy:

After initially logging on, entering his password, and reading DIALOG's news of the day (new databases, changes, and so on), Cy issued the command to begin searching in DIALINDEX by saying BEGIN 411 (this is DIALOG's file number for DIALINDEX).

At this point, Cy entered his list of databases in response to DIALOG's ? prompt. (For convenient identification, we will show Cy's commands in lower-case letters. He could have used either upper or lower case, or both—DIALOG's computer treats them the same.)

```
? select files 15, 75, 189, 148, 132, 133, 211, 16, 260, 22, 92, 17,
  100, 510, 13, 8, 34, 6, 77, 24, 25, 125
```

DIALOG responded:

```
File6:NTIS - 64-83/Iss11
File8:COMPENDEX - 70-83/Mar
File13:INSPEC - 77-83/Iss08
File15:ABI/INFORM - 71-83/Mar
File16:PROMT - 72-83/Jun (UD = 8306W1)
File17:PTS Annual Reports Abstracts - 83/Apr
File22:EIS Plants - Mar/83 Data (Types $0.50 each)
File24:CLAIMS/US Patent Abstracts 1971-1981
```

File25:CLAIMS/US Patent Abstracts Jan 1982 - Jan 1983
File34:SCISEARCH - 81-83/Wk10
File75:Management Contents - 74-83/Mar
File77:Conference Papers Index - 73-83/Mar
File92:EIS Nonmanufac. - Mar/83 Data (Types $0.50 each)
File100:DISCLOSURE II Apr 20 83
File125:CLAIMS/US Patent Abstracts Weekly - Feb 1 1983 TO Apr 5 1983
File132:Standard & Poors News - 79-83/WK17
File133:Standard & Poors Daily News
File148:Trade and Industry Index - 81-83/Apr
File189:HARFAX Industry Data Sources 79-83/Apr
File211:NEWSEARCH
File510:Electronic Yellow Pages - Manufacturers

Note that DIALOG responded to his select files command by displaying a nicely sorted list of the databases that he was interested in. At this point, the system issued another ? and politely waited for Cy's command. Since he was only interested in the simple occurrence of the name Ramtek in each database, his response was straightforward:

? select ramtek

DIALOG's response:

(6)	11 RAMTEK
(8)	8 RAMTEK
(13)	17 RAMTEK
(15)	7 RAMTEK
(16)	41 RAMTEK
(17)	1 RAMTEK
(22)	1 RAMTEK
(24)	0 RAMTEK
(25)	0 RAMTEK
(34)	0 RAMTEK
(75)	0 RAMTEK
(77)	0 RAMTEK
(92)	1 RAMTEK
(100)	1 RAMTEK
(125)	0 RAMTEK
(132)	51 RAMTEK
(133)	1 RAMTEK
(148)	16 RAMTEK
(189)	0 RAMTEK
(211)	0 RAMTEK
(510)	5 RAMTEK

In one quick search, Cy discovered that scattered throughout those 21 files, there were 161 hits on Ramtek. He also found out that eight of the specified files yielded nothing. Thus, he had already more than paid for his $35 per hour DIALINDEX search by avoiding the need to explore databases that carry price tags of $73 to $165 per hour.

At this point, he smelled fresh coffee brewing; so instead of switching to one of the databases and starting his investigation, he temporarily logged off.

It had cost Cy $2.84 for the service. Of course, Cy had no information yet, but now he knew exactly where and how to get it.

After refilling his cup, Cy logged on again and quickly switched to the ABI/INFORM database to look at the seven bibliographic records it contained. The first step, once he arrived in "file 15," was to select the search term:

? select ramtek

DIALOG's response:

1 7 RAMTEK

In response to the select command, the system quite briskly created set number 1 consisting of seven records, matching the number predicted by the DIALINDEX search Cy had done a few minutes earlier. Each one of the seven hits corresponded to an article or other bibliographic item, and it was a simple matter to print a list of their titles to see if any looked interesting enough to investigate further. With the type 1/6/1-7 command, Cy requested that DIALOG display all seven items of set 1 in format 6, which consists of only the title and the accession number (basically the article's serial number in the database):

? type 1/6/1-7

DIALOG's response:

1/6/1
82023172
Process-Control Market Expects More from Graphics Vendors than Low Price

1/6/2
82022219
General-Purpose Graphic Terminals Unburden Hosts

1/6/3
82005842
Graphic Capabilities for the Small Business

1/6/4
81023952
Making Color Affordable

1/6/5
81003534
Language Aids in Computer Designing

1/6/6
80017378
New Small Printers Increase Forms Need

1/6/7
79000387
Some Firms Postpone Stock Offerings

?

The computer automatically ranked the citations in order from the most recent to the oldest, and although number 7 looked potentially interesting from a business standpoint, it turned out to be written in 1978. Cy saw no reason to print out the full abstract of each one; he could always go back later and call each up directly via its accession number without having to repeat the search. Type 81023952/5, for example, would display the full bibliographic record and abstract (format 5) of Making Color Affordable.

Cy proceeded to repeat his search in INSPEC, COMPENDEX, and NTIS, in each case printing a list of titles and occasionally a full abstract. While in the INSPEC engineering database, he did a quick search on the term cs = ramtek. (The "cs" stands for "corporate source.") The result indicated that, of the 17 articles mentioning Ramtek, 12 were written by Ramtek personnel. He decided to have a look at one of those:

1/5/4
957623 C82042691
COPROCESSING TO EASE THE GRAPHICS BURDEN
GORDON, M.F.; COPE, S.V.
RAMTEK CORP., SANTA CLARA, CA, USA
COMPU. DES. (USA) VOL.21, NO.7 147-52 JULY 1982 Coden: CMPDAM
Treatment: PRACTICAL
Document Type: JOURNAL PAPER
Languages: ENGLISH
ARCHITECTURES EMPLOYING MULTIPLE MICROPROCESSORS ENHANCE GRAPHICS AND IMAGE PROCESSING WITHOUT SACRIFICING SPEED. THE AUTHORS LOOK AT THIS TYPE OF SYSTEM FOR GRAPHICS AND IMAGE PROCESSING APPLICATIONS. IN PARTICULAR THEY LOOK AT RAMTEK'S RM-9460 MODULAR DISPLAY SYSTEM
 Descriptors: COMPUTER GRAPHIC EQUIPMENT; MULTIPROCESSING SYSTEMS; COMPUTERISED PICTURE PROCESSING
 Identifiers: MULTIPLE MICROPROCESSORS; GRAPHICS; IMAGE PROCESSING; RAMTEK; RM-9460; MODULAR DISPLAY SYSTEM
 Class codes: C5410

This information was not particularly exciting to Cy, who was much more eager to dig up news about the company, merger/acquisition activity, marketing ploys, etc. Noting that there were, according to DIALINDEX, 16 articles mentioning Ramtek in file 148 (the Trade and Industry Index), he switched databases again, performed the basic select command on the company name, and printed the list of articles. Here are a few of them:

1/5/1
1145753 DATABASE: NNI File 111
 Ramtek, holders offering 851,249 shares at $28 each.
 Wall Street Journal Section 2 p26(W) p30(E) Feb 7 1983

CODEN: WSJOAF
col 3   002 col in.
EDITION: Mon
SIC CODE: 3573
DESCRIPTORS: Rametk Corp. - securities; computer industry-securities

1/5/3
1077815 DATABASE: TI File 148
   Color graphics printers emulating CRT terminals will cut network loading.
   McLeod, Jonah
   Electronic Design   v30   pss59(2)   June 10 1983
   illustration; portrait
   SIC CODE: 3674; 7372
   NAMED PEOPLE: McEwan, Charles-interviews
   DESCRIPTORS: Ramtek Corp.-officials and employees; printers (data processing
systems)-technological innovations

1/5/7
0486636 DATABASE: NNI File 111
   Digital Equipment Corp. (business brief - to market computer graphics system with
Ramtek Corp.)
   New York Times   v131   p34(N)   July 28 1982
   CODEN: NYTIA
   col 4   001 col in.
   EDITION: Wed
   DESCRIPTORS: Digital Equipment Corp.-contracts and specifications; Ramtek
Corp.-contracts and specifications

1/5/8
0369229 DATABASE: NNI File 111
   Ramtek to guarantee loans in return for debentures.
   Wall Street Journal   v106   p10(W)   March 26 1982
   CODEN: WSJOAF
   col 6   002 col in.
   EDITION: Fri
   SIC CODE: 3573
   DESCRIPTORS: Ramtek Corp.-finance; computer industry-finance

1/5/10
0266214 DATABASE: TI File 148
   Ramtek pulls out as Loral lowers bid by $10 million.
   Moad, Jeff
   Electronic News   v27   p1(2)   May 18 1981
   SIC CODE: 3600
   DESCRIPTORS: Ramtek Corp.-mergers and consolidations; Loral Corp.-mergers
and consolidations; electronic industries-mergers and consolidations

Cy circled a number of articles on the listing as it emerged from the printer
and made a note to have his secretary track down the full articles. His other
option, of course, was online ordering. For instance, he could have typed the
command keep 1, followed by .order info Ship to Attention of Cy Rigsby, and Infor-

mation on Demand in Berkeley, California, would have put photocopies of all 16 articles in the mail within a few days (along with a bill for about $160).

Warming to the task, Cy rubbed his hands together and hopped to file 16, PROMT. DIALINDEX had noted 41 postings in this file, and he knew that the database was detailed and timely. He quickly discovered a few recent articles of great relevance:

1/5/1
1097799 Bus Week 83/03/21 P126,127
High-tech and new-issue enthusiasm on Wall Street: Will it continue? Some market analysts warn that speculation is high and is nearing a peak that could lead to a shakeout, while others, such as Prudential-Bache's GA Smith, say higher multiples could be in store, since many emerging growth companies' earnings are growing at more than double the 6-8% return projected for the S&P 500. The long-awaited stock market correction could fall inordinately hard on high tech stocks, which have led this rally—the likes of Analogic, E-Systems, GenRad, Intel, Ramtek, Prime Computer, Rolm and Teradyne are selling at P.E multiples of 25-35 and up. Net sales of aggressive growth mutual funds were $433 mil in Jan 1983—higher than the 1970's total. Merrill Lynch may have already received up to $1 bil in orders for SCI/TECH Holdings, a high-tech mutual fund to be offered in late March 1983. This offering in itself—the largest ever—could help buoy the prices of high-tech issues.

*1USA *United States *8510000 *Research & Development *751 *stock price

1/5/2
846260 #ComputrwlX 82/11/17 P49-56
Business computer graphics has emerged as a cost-effective solution to generating reports and presentations, according to R Varga, Ramtek Corp (Santa Clara, Calif). Unfortunately, growth rate in the market may be limited by those that have acquired hardware and developed software on their own. In these instances, end-user acquisitions may be technically intensive and time-consuming. In regard to expansion, users are purchasing turnkey systems and relying entirely on one source for all parts of the graphics system. Many believe a volume market will emerge when such turnkey vendors can successfully target their products to have broad appeal to the non-technical end user.

*1USA *United States *3573091 *Computer Graphics Systems *337 *applications

1/5/4
809462 Elec News 82/08/02 P24
Digital Equipment signed a joint agreement with Ramtek to market a redesigned version of Ramtek's high-end graphics CRT terminal. The marketing agreement, under which the 2 firms will 'collaborate' in sales of DEC's VAX computers and the redesigned version of Ramtek's RS-9400 graphics terminal, is not exclusive. DEC chose Ramtek in part because of the large number of software packages in existence that run on the Ramtek graphic terminals. The agreement comes soon after Ramtek and Lexidata—the 2 finalists for a potential OEM contract worth up to $100 mil—were told that DEC no longer wanted to sign an OEM agreement.

*1USA *United States *3753288 *Graphics Display Terminals *388
    *mfr sales agreemnt *Ramtek
1USA United States 3573288 Graphics Display Terminals 388 mfr sales
    agreemnt Ramtek

1USA United States 3573288 Graphics Display Terminals 389 distrib
agreement Digital Equipment

1/5/10
712284 #Mini-Micro 81/12 P95-98
Raster scan is finding an increasing number of applications with its high resolution
and color capability for 3-D representation, according to H Okamoto, dir of business
development at Ramtek Corp (Santa Clara, Calif). Article details the advantages and
disadvantages of each of the display technologies--storage tube, stroke writer, plasma panel and raster scan.

*1USA *United States *3573288 *Graphics Display Terminals *337
  *applications
1USA United States 3573288 Graphics Display Terminals 337
  applications
1USA United States 2679580 Display Devices 340 product specs

 ˙It was quickly becoming a productive morning. There was clearly quite a
bit of published information that would help Cy assemble a comprehensive
competitive report on Ramtek. He decided to start looking for "hard" data—
sales figures, addresses of branch offices, and so on.

His first stop was the Electronic Yellow Pages—Manufacturers. DIALIN-
DEX had noted five hits—probably a headquarters location and four field
offices. He did the search and received the following on his terminal:

1/5/1
0449127
RAMTEK CORPORATION
2211 LAWSON LN
SANTA CLARA, CA 95050
TELEPHONE: 408-988-2211
COUNTY: SANTA CLARA
SIC: 3573 .(ELECTRONIC COMPUTING EQUIPMENT MFRS.)
CITY POPULATION: 6 .(50,000-99,999)
NET WORTH: A .($1,000,000 AND OVER)
NUMBER OF EMPLOYEES: C .(100 - 499)
THIS IS A(N) CORPORATION
            HEADQUARTERS

1/5/2
0353544
RAMTEK INC
2211 HURFUS
HOUSTON, TX 77092
TELEPHONE: 713-774-2233
COUNTY: HARRIS
SIC: 3069 .(RUBBER PRODUCTS MFRS. (FABRICATED), N.E.C.)
CITY POPULATION: 2 .(2,500-4,999)
NET WORTH: M .($0-$9,999)
NUMBER OF EMPLOYEES: G .(1 - 9)
THIS IS A(N) CORPORATION
            HEADQUARTERS

1/5/3
0336761
RAMTEK CORPORATION
520 CENTRAL PKY
PLANO, TX 75074
TELEPHONE: 214-422-2200
COUNTY: COLLIN
SIC: 3573 .(ELECTRONIC COMPUTING EQUIPMENT MFRS.)
CITY POPULATION: 1 .(1,000-2,499)
NET WORTH: A .($1,000,000 AND OVER)
NUMBER OF EMPLOYEES: G .(1 - 9)
THIS IS A(N) CORPORATION
          BRANCH

1/5/4
0283017
RAMTEK CORPORATION
2050 ALGONQUIN ROAD
ROSELLE, IL 60172
TELEPHONE: 312-397-2279
COUNTY: DUPAGE
SIC: 3523 .(MACHINERY & EQUIPMENT MFRS. - FARM)
CITY POPULATION: 4 .(10,000-24,999)
NET WORTH: A .($1,000,000 AND OVER)
NUMBER OF EMPLOYEES: G .(1 - 9)
THIS IS A(N) CORPORATION
          BRANCH

1/5/5
0122198
RAMTEK CORPORATION
8260 GREENSBORO DR
MC LEAN, VA 22102
TELEPHONE: 703-893-2020
COUNTY: FAIRFAX
SIC: 3573 .(ELECTRONIC COMPUTING EQUIPMENT MFRS.)
CITY POPULATION: 4 .(10,000-24,999)
NET WORTH: A .($1,000,000 AND OVER)
NUMBER OF EMPLOYEES: F .(10 - 19)
THIS IS A(N) CORPORATION
          BRANCH

"Hm," Cy mused, "other Ramteks?" There was apparently a little one in Houston, Texas, that made fabricated rubber products as well as a big one in Illinois that made farm machinery. Cy examined the listings and noticed that the SIC code for electronic computing equipment manufacturers was 3573 and that of farm equipment manufacturers was 3523. A typo? What about the other one? Being naturally curious—and because it would affect his subsequent research efforts—he logged off DIALOG for a few minutes to call the two mysterious Ramteks. It turned out that they were, in fact, both part of the graphics company.

That just goes to show: you can't believe everything you read—even if it's on a CRT screen. EYP wasn't alone in Ramtek-related database errors. One Trade and Industry Index citation spelled the name "Ramteck"; the EIS Industrial Plants Data Base showed the American Gear and Supply Company as a subsidiary; and Disclosure's entry was peppered with spelling errors.

Cy logged back on. Now he was interested in financial information. In the PTS Annual Reports Abstracts, he found his quarry mentioned in the management discussion of Intelligent Systems Corporation's 10K report:

```
1/5/1
0109672
Intelligent Systems                                        10-K Report
Corporate ID: 012074                           Year Ending March 31, 1981
COMPETITION
```

The Company competes in both the color graphic terminal and desktop computer systems markets. In the terminal market, Aydin Corporation, Hewlett-Packard, IBM, Ramtek and Tektronix are all color display manufacturers, but offer primarily high-resolution displays, most of which are priced substantially higher than the Company's products. Intelligent Systems has concentrated on that part of the market where color is desirable but higher resolution displays are not required. In this segment, the Company believes it does not at the present time have significant competition in its price range from other color graphic display manufacturers. However, the Company's products do compete with lower priced black-and-white graphic products which are produced by a number of large companies including Hewlett Packard and Tektronix. The company recently introduced a new line of products that will compete in a portion of the higher resolution market . . .

Cy interrupted the printout and switched to the Disclosure database for extracts from Ramtek's 10K and other SEC Filings. This would give a thorough summary of the company's financial position, key personnel, plans, borrowings, recent history, and more. Since it is a lengthy document, he ordered it printed offline and mailed to him ($10) rather than pay connect fees plus $6 for an online printout.

Cy then checked the Conference Papers Index. Finding only an old 1973 paper, he switched to Commerce Business Daily to see what Ramtek products were being acquired or sought by the government. Among others, he found:

```
0161207
```

RAMTEK 9460 COLOR GRAPHICS SUBSYSTEM for a DEC VAX 11-780 with necessary interface hardware and software. The acquisition will include all documentation training and maintenance support for the systems life of 8 years. The system will be delivered and installed at the U.S. Army Concepts Analysis Agency, 8120 Woodmont Ave, Bethesda, MD-All personnel participating in installation and maintenance will be required to have secret clearance. Sol MDA903-83-R-0026 will be available approx 15 Dec 1982. See note 64. (330)

Sponsor: Defense Supply Service-Washington, Rm 1D245, The Pentagon, Washington, DC 20310 (Attn: Ms Ann M Kumbar, 202/697-6021)

Subfile: PSU .(U.S. GOVERNMENT PROCUREMENTS, SUPPLIES)

Section Heading: 70 General Purpose ADP Equipment Software, Supplies and Support Eq.

CBD Date: DECEMBER 1, 1982

Cy made mental notes to get on bid lists and keep the appropriate procurement offices well supplied with Cybertronic Systems spec sheets.

Cy stretched and checked his watch—he had been on almost 30 minutes. There were a few other long shots, but he wanted a chance to dig through the existing listings first. He logged off the DIALOG system, having spent less than $50.

But there was one other thing he wanted to do before turning his attention to other tasks: obtain Ramtek stock and earnings information from Dow Jones. So without even hanging up the phone, he issued the command C 60942 on the terminal, responded to the system's WHAT SERVICE PLEASE??? message with the acronym DJNS, and then entered his password. Within about ten minutes, he had completed the following exchange with Dow Jones News/Retrieval:

//medgen   [*Cy's command*]

MEDIA GENERAL-FINANCIAL
    SERVICES, INC.
MARKET AND FUNDAMENTAL DATA ON
COMMON STOCKS AND RELATED
SUMMARY MATERIAL ON INDUSTRY
GROUPS, COPYRIGHT (C) 1983.

ENTER QUERY
rmtk/p   [*Cy's command*]

RAMTEK CORPORATION

-PRICE & VOLUME- 04/22/83   (113)

PRICE CHANGE   (1)
-LAST TRDNG WK 4.7%
-LAST 4 WKS -3.3%
-LAST 13 WKS 18.7%
-LAST 52 WKS 30.9%
-YR TO DATE 45.9%

CHANGE VS. S & P 500
-LAST TRDNG WK 104%
-LAST 4 WKS 92%
-LAST 13 WKS 106%
-LAST 52 WKS 97%
-YR TO DATE 128%

PRICE RANGE   (2)
-LAST CLOSE $22.25
-52 WEEK HIGH $26.25
-52 WEEK LOW $11.75
-5 YEAR HIGH $26.25
-5 YEAR LOW $7.50

RELATIVE PRICE
-P/E RATIO CURRENT 25.6
-P/E RATIO 5 YR AVG HI 25.0
-P/E RATIO 5 YR AVG LOW 12.6

-PRICE TO COMMON EQUITY 287%
-PRICE TO REV PER SHARE 128%
-RELATIVE PRICE INDEX 296%

PRICE ACTION (3)
-BETAS UP 2.14
-BETAS DOWN 1.41

VOLUME
-THIS WK SHRS 66,000
-THIS WK DOLLAR $1,451,000
-THIS WK % SHRS OUTSTND 2.47%
-LIQUIDITY RATIO 221,000
-ON BALANCE INDEX 48

rmtk/f   [*Cy's command*]

RAMTEK CORPORATION
-FUNDMNTL DATA- 04/22/83   (113)

REVENUE (1)
-LAST 12 MOS $46 MIL
-LAST FISCAL YEAR $46 MIL
-PCT CHANGE LAST QTR 3.8%
-PCT CHANGE YR TO DATE 0.5%
EARNGS 12MOS $2.4S MIL

EARNINGS PER SHARE
-LAST 12 MONTHS $0.87
-LAST FISCAL YEAR $1.00
-PCT CHANGE LAST QTR -12.0%
-PCT CHANGE FY TO DATE -28.9%
-PCT CHANGE LAST 12MOS 20.8%
-FIVE YR GROWTH RATE 0.0%

DIVIDENDS (2)
-CURRENT RATE $0.00
-CURRENT RATE YIELD 0.0%
-5 YR GROWTH RATE 0.0%
-PAYOUT LAST FY 0%
-PAYOUT LAST 5 YEARS 0%
-LAST X-DVD DATE 00-00-00

RATIOS
-PROFIT MARGIN 5.2%
-RETURN ON COMMON EQUITY 11.2%
-RETURN ON TOTAL ASSETS   NA
-REVENUE TO ASSETS   NA
-DEBT TO EQUITY 13%
-INTEREST COVERAGE   NA
-CURRENT RATIO 1.9

SHAREHOLDINGS (3)
-MARKET VALUE $59 MIL
-LTST SHR OUTSTND 2,651,000
-INSIDER NET TRADING 0

-SHORT INTEREST RATIO 0.0 DYS
-FISCAL YEAR ENDS 6 MOS

//earn   [*Cy's command*]

CORPORATE EARNINGS ESTIMATOR
ZACKS INVESTMENT RESEARCH INC.
CHICAGO, ILL.

THIS WEEKLY DATABASE PROVIDES
CONSENSUS FORECASTS OF EARNINGS
PER SHARE FOR 2,400 COMPANIES
BASED ON ESTIMATES PROVIDED BY
1,000 RESEARCH ANALYSTS AT MORE
THAN 50 MAJOR BROKERAGE FIRMS.
FOR CONSISTENCY, ESTIMATES ARE
CONVERTED TO PRIMARY EARNINGS
BEFORE EXTRAORDINARY ITEMS.

PLEASE ENTER DESIRED STOCK
SYMBOL AND PRESS RETURN rmtk   [*Cy's command*]

RAMTEK
--FISCAL YEAR ENDS 6/83

EARNINGS PER SHARE ESTIMATES
--MEAN 1.31
--HIGH 1.51
--LOW 1.10
NUMBER OF ANALYSTS 2
P/E RATIO (ESTIMATED EPS) 17.12

PAST EARN PR SH ESTIMATED (MEAN)
--WEEK AGO 1.31
--13 WEEKS AGO 1.45
--26 WEEKS AGO 1.63

RAMTEK
--FISCAL YEAR ENDS 6/84

EARNINGS PER SHARE ESTIMATES
--MEAN 1.99
--HIGH 2.27
--LOW 1.70
NUMBER OF ANALYSTS 2
P/E RATIO (ESTIMATED EPS) 11.27

PAST EARN PR SH ESTIMATED (MEAN)
--WEEK AGO 1.99
--13 WEEKS AGO N/A
--26 WEEKS AGO N/A

Before finishing, Cy decided to check the Standard & Poor's News file on CompuServe. Easily done—he issued yet another network address to the local Telenet node, signed on to the system in Columbus, Ohio, got past the welcome messages, and deftly commanded spdisp. The response:

Welcome to S&P's General Information File which contains the business summary, important developments, product/service line contributions to revenues/profits, corporate officers and selected financial items on over 3,000 companies.

For only $0.25 per company lookup (plus connect charges), you have access to the S&P file. You can look at information for Tandy Corp. (TAN) and H&R Block (HRB) without additional charge.

S&P's General Information File

1 Instructions/Information
2 Select company by name
3 Select company by ticker
4 Select company by industry
5 Data definitions
    (CR) to exit

Last menu page, key digit   !3

Please enter ticker
    (ENTER) returns to MENU   !rmtk   [*Cy's command*]

Standard & Poor's   RMTK

RMTK
RAMTEK CORP.
Cusip# 75187410
Last updated 04/04/83
S&P Industry 1702

Information has been obtained from sources believed to be reliable, but its accuracy is not guaranteed.

Key YES or Y to display   !y   [*Cy's command*]
Standard & Poor's   RMTK

SP RANK: NR	EXCHANGE: OTC
SALES($M)	46.02
NET($M)	2.67
1982 EPS EST($)	1.00 (A)
12 MONTH EPS($)	0.87
1981 EPS($)	0.62
1980 EPS($)	0.57
1979 EPS($)	0.56
EPS 5-YR GROWTH(%)	- 2.00

YEAR END MONTH: JE

Summary
This company designs, manufactures and markets computer graphics display systems for a wide variety of applications, including CAT scanners. In fiscal 1983's first quarter, results were impaired by below-target sales and the company's large investment in developing a new graphics display product, the MARQUIS, to be marketed jointly with Digital Equipment Corp.

Business Summary
Formed in 1971 to enter the emerging market for low- and medium-cost computer graphic displays, Ramtek Corporation designs, develops, manufactures, markets and services computer graphic displays and intelligent terminals. Foreign sales, in west-

ern Europe and Canada, and the Middle East, accounted for about 25% of the total in fiscal 1982. Sales to General Electric, primarily for CAT scanners (sophisticated medical x-ray diagnostic devices), accounted for 23% of fiscal 1982 sales.

Important Developments
Feb. '83-
The company sold 650,000 common shares and Exxon Corp. sold 201,249 shares at $20 each in a public offering which eliminated Exxon's holdings of Ramtek common. Proceeds to Ramtek of $12,082,500 were earmarked to repay short-term bank borrowings and for working capital.

Nov. '82-
Ramtek reduced its workforce by 41 employees, or 7% of its operations staff. Management attributed the cutbacks to "sluggish sales." It added that its field sales force remained intact and that product development efforts continued as planned.

Office-2211 Lawson Lane, Santa Clara, Calif. 95050. Tel-(408)988-2211. Chrmn & Pres-C. E. McEwan. Exec UP, Secy & Treas-T. J. Adams. Dirs-T. J. Adams, J. R. Andrews Jr., R. Eliassen, C. E. McEwan, W. C. Mills. Transfer Agent & Registrar-Bank of America, San Francisco. Incorporated in California in 1971.

Cy hung up the phone, leaned back in his chair, and contemplated the pile of paper that had accumulated behind the printer. In one hour, he had completed the basic groundwork for an extensive investigation of Ramtek's technical and financial activities—and he still hadn't performed the patent searches that he had intended. (Although he had turned up 0 in the patent databases during the DIALINDEX search, he had made a mistake: it is necessary to specify the company name as a "patent assignee" with the search prefix PA= in order to find patent listings.)

But this was a good start. By lunchtime, Cy had sent his assistant to a university library for copies of the technical articles, sketched some curves representing Ramtek's financial progress and likely future, spotted an apparent weakness in their CAT scanner display marketing that could prove interesting, and generally acquired a healthy understanding of Cybertronic's number-one competitor.

12 Electronic Mail[1]

Once you have the equipment necessary for database searching, you also have a potential electronic mailbox. The two technologies work the same way. Dozens of electronic mail vendors are already competing for your business, and dozens more will soon, including many of the database vendors listed in this book.

Every company depends upon communications to conduct its day-to-day business. In fast-paced business situations, it is vital that a company be confident that the necessary information is being directed to the appropriate individuals as efficiently as possible. Messages that are delayed or not delivered can mean lost business or result in incorrect actions in delicate situations. Further, a message delivered late can often cause someone to act upon information that is no longer valid.

Electronic mail offers an extremely attractive solution to the problem of providing timely and cost-effective communication, both within a company and outside it. The concept of sending messages as impulses along a wire has been in operation since 1844, when the United States government completed the first telegraph line from Washington to Baltimore. The first message transmitted over this telegraph line was, "What hath God wrought?" Now, 140 years later, people planning and directing modern offices are asking themselves the same question.

During the last decade, three factors emerged that together have become the driving forces behind electronic mail. First, the reliability and scope of telecommunications links have increased enormously. This means that a user may now communicate with a central computer or another user over a much expanded range. Second, large-scale integration technology has made it economical to build low-cost intelligent terminals and communica-

[1]Adapted from a longer work by Leslie H. Goldsmith of I. P. Sharp Associates, Ltd. (reprinted with permission).

tions interfaces. Third, large organizations, or those with geographically dispersed personnel, have increasingly recognized the need for better communication mechanisms to manage themselves effectively and to disseminate information in a controlled fashion. This ability to communicate efficiently has had an increasingly high value in our highly competitive business environment.

Traditional communication methods

Why are the two most common forms of dispersed corporate communication, the telephone and the postal service, so inadequate? In the United States alone, almost 75 billion pieces of mail are moved annually by the Postal Service; of this figure, four out of five pieces are business letters. No data are readily available concerning the number of pieces that are lost, damaged, or pilfered. But that aside, the United States Postal Service is hard-pressed to cope with the current level of postal traffic.

Mail service difficulties are by no means relegated to the government postal services. Many companies are experiencing similar problems with their own intracompany mail service. Research into one large organization, Exxon Corp., reveals that in-house mail spends 1 percent of its time being originated, 1 percent being copied, 3 percent being typed, 21 percent sitting in incoming or outgoing bins at various points during its journey, and 74 percent in the delivery system. A full 45 percent of the internal Exxon mail spends three days getting to its destination—days that could be critical to decision making. These figures are typical for large corporations, and almost certainly indicate what the future might hold for smaller corporations that are expanding at a rapid rate.

In contrast to the postal system, the inefficiency of the telephone stems mainly from its inherent requirement that individuals be simultaneously in a position to converse with each other. The most striking cases of this occur with people attempting to communicate across time zones, but the fundamental problem is much more general and is one most everyone has encountered. For example: Mr. Allen needs to discuss a problem with Mr. Burger. Allen calls Burger, who is out of the office, so someone takes a message. When Burger returns the call, Allen is tied up on another line, and so Burger leaves a message. Allen calls again, but now Burger is in a meeting. When the meeting ends, it's almost five o'clock. Burger pessimistically calls back and is not surprised to learn that Allen has already left for the day. This exercise in "telephone tag" has become one of the most frustrating games in business. Studies have shown that, on the average, the caller fails to reach the person being called on the first attempt in 28 percent of all business telephone calls. The same type of thing can occur when trying to get together for a face-to-face meeting. Communication merry-go-rounds can cost valuable time in crucial situations.

The telephone has other serious inefficiencies as well. Phone calls often come at inconvenient times or interrupt a train of thought. The recipient of the call might be tired or otherwise in an unreceptive frame of mind when he receives the call. This can result in pretentious displays, where the recipient feigns interest, or even in misunderstandings.

Telephone communication also has the disadvantage of being verbal and impermanent. At the end of the call, there is no record of what conclusions or decisions were reached or of those that were not. And, of course, no telephone call would be complete without the social amenities and convivialities that accompany verbal exchanges.

The inefficiencies of the telephone are supported by a report published in the November 1978 *Fortune* magazine, in which managers consistently cited the telephone as the highest time waster. The situation is indeed ironic, for the telephone is undoubtedly the most widespread method of communication in use today.

How electronic mail works

Each electronic mail user has access to a terminal. Since the terminal serves only as a link to the computer, the same terminal needn't be used all the time. For example, while traveling, it is often convenient to carry a portable terminal to stay in touch. That the location of the terminal is irrelevant is one of the reasons why electronic mail is unique.

Each user has a unique address code, often simply called an address. It serves to identify the senders and recipients of messages and often is the person's initials or a short form of his name. William Shakespeare might have the address WMS or BILL, for example. It should be stressed, however, that to read the mail in an electronic mailbox, you must use a confidential personal ID.

Any number of individuals can be assembled into an electronic mail group. A group contains the address codes of each of its members, who usually share a common interest or are associated with the same company or organization. For example, a group might contain all people involved in marketing. A message addressed to a group usually may be sent to everyone in the group, as if each address code had been typed explicitly. Thus, it is as easy to send a message to a single individual as it is to address a large distribution list.

A message can be sent to one or more individuals or groups, and also "carbon-copied" (CC'd) to others. A message usually can also be sent URGENT or REGISTERED by its sender. Urgent messages appear before nonurgent ones when the recipient reads his mail. Registered messages cause a confirmation of receipt to be reported back to the sender each time the message is received.

The following is a sample electronic mail message as it appears on the I.P. Sharp Associates system called Mailbox. When a message is sent, Mailbox automatically assigns a unique message number to it and records the time and date it was filed. The text of the message follows and may be anything from a simple memo to an elaborately formatted document or report.

URGENT CONFIDENTIAL FROM JBC
NO. 1235813 FILED 11.08.56 MON 6 OCT 1980
FROM JBC
TO   TAM
CC   DEB GEOFF

On your design and implementation timetable for the financial planning system, everything looks satisfactory with the possible exception of the completion date of the final phase. It seems to me that targeting for the middle of April is getting dangerously close to the mandatory deadline of 27 April. I think it might be preferable to shorten the preliminary design and qualification test phases by several days, to allow more of a buffer zone for any unanticipated problems in the other stages.
JIM

Learning to use electronic mail usually is simple. In fact, most users become comfortable with it in a matter of hours. I.P. Sharp's Mailbox commands, for instance, are generally English words that are easy to remember because of their suggestive meanings. For example, to ask for information about incoming messages that have not yet been read, the Mailbox command is UNREAD. Mailbox responds by listing each pending message, including its sender, privacy level, and an indication of whether the user was included in the TO or CC category. UNREAD also tells the user whether messages he has sent have been received. To read some or all pending messages, Mailbox's command is PRINT. Further, because Mailbox messages can be manipulated as data, it is possible to involve them in auxiliary operations such as filing, cross-referencing, or retrieving.

Sending mail is also easy. The user types the word SEND, and Mailbox responds by prompting for the address codes of the recipients. When this information has been entered, the Mailbox prompts for the text of the message, which can be of any length. After the user signals the end of the text, he simply gives the command to send the message. The message is filed, and its message number and time stamp are printed: it is then immediately available to all of its recipients, regardless of geographic locations.

Before sending the message, the user can also choose to alter any aspect of it, such as the distribution list or the text itself. Another simple command will cancel the message and start over. Even after it has been sent, the sender can still retract the message before it has been read (at once making it unavailable to its recipients) and then either modify and resend it or else discard it.

Mailbox also provides a forwarding facility, so that messages received may be passed on to another person with one simple command. The user may extend the message he is forwarding by adding his own commentary or preface to it. Another Mailbox command lets an individual perform a variety of inquiries, such as ascertaining the address code of another user, the identity of a user with a particular address code, the composition of a group, or the groups to which any individual belongs.

If the user is on vacation, or otherwise expects not to be reading his mail regularly, he can just send a special Mailbox message to that effect (possibly including who to contact in case of difficulty). Then, anyone who sends the person a message will be automatically notified of his unavailability. When he returns, the accumulated messages will provide an account of the activities that transpired during his absence.

The electronic mail user who is away from the office on business can enjoy its benefits wherever he happens to be. Consider, for example, the case of the corporate professional who begins a hectic week-long business trip. To him, being out of town is synonymous with being out of touch, and he has no recourse but to attempt to contact his office at least once a day. Even as his plane leaves the runway, calls begin pouring in for him, and message slips begin piling up. But what follows is a series of frustrating attempts by him to reach his office. He may, for instance, try to escape temporarily from one of his many scheduled meetings to call in. However, this can be awkward, or even impolite. He may instead try to call the office during lunch—but where is his secretary? Out at lunch also, of course. At the hotel room that evening, our traveler has a lot of time on his hands, but everyone has long since left the office.

With electronic mail, experiences like this can be avoided. Today's lightweight portable terminals and lap computers make it possible to extend the realm of office communication to just about anyplace, be it home, a hotel room, or even a customer's office. As long as there is a telephone, efficient communication can occur at any time with people who needn't know where you are or where you will be—and vice versa.

Additional benefits

Electronic mail also accelerates the collaboration of groups of people. Conversations can proceed more effectively, and with a multiplicity of contributions, without the need for colocation. Electronic mail and its companion, electronic conferencing, make it feasible to increase meetings from the classical limit of 8 to 10 participants to upward of 50 or 100. Further, regardless of the size of the group, electronic mail reduces the inability or reticence of certain members to participate in a discussion because of personality differences or shyness.

There is also a lessened need to use conventional mail or costly express delivery services. The decrease in interruptions from telephone calls that results from the use of electronic mail has the positive effect that working days are no longer "interrupt driven."

The potential working day and week are both extended due to the portability of terminals, which can be used wherever there is a telephone. This allows people to work creatively when they feel creative. Indeed, one survey conducted by the Yankee Group of Boston showed that 20 percent of electronic mail usage occurred outside normal business hours. The computer can be used to drive a retrieval system that can store messages (or other documents) for an unlimited period of time. Typical systems permit retrieval based on any number of criteria, including sender, recipients, date sent, key words, text searching, and so on.

People read about six times faster than they can talk, and thus they are able to get the point across much more quickly with written communication. Electronic messages also tend to be more succinct, since there is usually less non-task-oriented information in them than a verbal conversation would graciously permit.

Managerial and professional personnel spend most of their time communicating with others, either verbally or in writing. As a result, even small improvements in their modes of communication can have a large economic benefit. While electronic mail is by no means a replacement for all other forms of communication (some tasks certainly require verbal engagement), it does have a profound positive impact on corporate communication patterns, often opening channels that did not previously exist.

Electronic mail vendors

Many of the database vendors listed in Part III of this book either offer electronic mail services or plan to do so in the future. These include:

- ◆ ADP Network Services, Inc.
- ◆ Bibliographic Retrieval Service
- ◆ CompuServe, Inc.
- ◆ Dialcom, Inc.
- ◆ DIALOG Information Services, Inc.
- ◆ General Electric Information Services Company
- ◆ General Videotex
- ◆ InnerLine
- ◆ I. P. Sharp Associates, Ltd.
- ◆ MCI Mail
- ◆ Source Telecomputing Corporation
- ◆ System Development Corporation
- ◆ Tymshare, Inc.

Three others important electronic mail companies not mentioned in that section are:

- ◆ GTE Telenet Communications Corporation, 8829 Boone Blvd., Vienna, Virginia 22180 (703-442-1000)
- ◆ Computer Corp. of America, 4 Cambridge Center, Cambridge, Massachusetts 02142 (617-492-8860)
- ◆ Computer Sciences Corp., 2100 East Grand Ave., El Segundo, California 90245 (213-615-0311)

PART TWO

A GUIDE TO
SELECTED
BUSINESS
DATABASES

"Just ask it. 'How many burgers can the Free World eat?'"

*T*his section presents in considerable detail the major business-oriented databases—those that we feel a manager is most likely to use. It also introduces some more specialized databases in a few narrower fields as a way of illustrating the depth of knowledge available in databases.

Each database is first described in a general manner and contrasted with its competitors. Each is also given a "profile" in which we list basic data about it such as producer, cost, vendor, etc.

For selected databases, we give a sample problem and then reproduce one record from the database search that would help solve it. It should be kept in mind that a typical search produces dozens of such records, not just the one we reprint.

For a few databases we also present a list of publications abstracted, a list of the database's indexing terms, or other illustrative material. While we would have liked to give such thorough coverage to every database, space considerations allowed us to do so for only a few. We hope, however, that these lists demonstrate the vast range of information contained in most of the databases we discuss.

A longer selection of databases is available in our vendor listings, where we briefly note most of the databases offered by each vendor. The reader may also wish to consult one of the directories listed in Appendix A for more comprehensive listings.

13 Broad-Coverage Business Databases

The broad-coverage databases are your initial weapon for attacking the information explosion. They contain a staggering range of information, touching on almost every possible business topic. When an unfamiliar business problem arises, or a question about a new field occurs to you, you can often make quick headway toward an answer by searching these databases.

The first six that we discuss—ABI/INFORM, Management Contents, Trade and Industry Index, PTS F&S, PTS PROMT, and HARFAX Industry Data Sources—are all bibliographic databases with many features in common. The next three—NEXIS, Dow Jones News, and HBR/Online—are full-text databases and very different in character from one another.

The six bibliographic databases each index and abstract hundreds of business and trade periodicals. Surprisingly, though, there is very little duplication of each other's coverage. Each database occupies a niche in this market; each catches articles or sources of information that the others miss. ABI/INFORM, for example, indexes the magazine *Advertising Age* but not *Advertising World*; Management Contents does the reverse. If your subject is worth searching in one of these databases, it's very likely worth searching in several of them.

ABI/INFORM

Data Courier Inc.'s ABI/INFORM (the awkward name comes from "abstracted business information") has a core of more than 300 journals from which almost every item is indexed and abstracted. Only items of "short-term interest," such as advertisements, letters to the editor, daily or weekly news, or editorials, are excluded. (In the industry this degree of thoroughness often, though somewhat misleadingly, is called "cover-to-cover" indexing.) For example, every article in *Health Care Management Review* is listed and abstracted. See the ABI/INFORM Core Journals listing following the Sample Record below.

ABI/INFORM selectively indexes another 300 or so journals. That means articles are chosen for inclusion in the database if they are relevant in some way to "management ideas or concepts." According to ABI/INFORM, an item from a noncore periodical must be of "lasting rather than passing value" in order to merit an entry in the database. For example, articles from *Arizona Business* magazine are cited if they're relevant to management; about 200 articles from this magazine since 1971 have been included in the database.

ABI/INFORM has the lengthiest and most informative abstracts of any database discussed in this group. It uses a detailed, 8,000-word controlled vocabulary, which can be a great aid to searching. A portion of the vocabulary listing is reproduced in our Example of ABI/INFORM Controlled Vocabulary.

ABI/INFORM also is notable for its dedication to quality control. Misspellings, incorrect dates, and other errors plague some databases and cause searchers to miss relevant records; ABI/INFORM probably has fewer mistakes than most.

Sample record

PROBLEM: I'd like some practical ideas for getting more customer feedback about my product.

(1) The '800' Formula for Launch, Growth and Feedback
(2) McKean, Aldyn
(3) Marketing Communications v8n5 pp: 38-44,50 May 1983 ISSN: 0164-4343
  JRNL CODE: MCO
  DOC TYPE: Journal Paper LANGUAGE: English LENGTH: 6 pages
  AVAILABILITY: Marketing Communications, 475 Park Avenue S., New York, NY 10016
(4) Three examples of telephone marketing using toll-free "800" numbers testify to the power and benefits to consumers in advertisements carrying these numbers. In 1980, Brown and Williamson Tobacco Co. launched Barclay, a low-tar cigarette, by establishing an 800 number consumers could call to receive a coupon for a free carton. Barclay gained a 3% share of the market, worth $375 million a year. Cap'n Crunch cereal sales rose by more than 30% when Quaker Oats Co. ran a sweepstakes in which children called an 800 number to find out whether they had won a bicycle. Procter and Gamble (P&G) tested an 800 number customer service operation by putting toll-free numbers on Duncan Hines Brownie Mixes in 1974. By June 1981, every P&G product displayed such a number. Customers offer ways to improve products, help expedite quality control, and generate new product and advertising ideas. Research shows that over 90% of the people who contact P&G are satisfied by the response given.
  DESCRIPTORS: Telephone selling; Advertising campaigns; Tests; Markets; Cigarette industry; Quaker Oats-Chicago; Procter & Gamble-Cincinnati; Case studies
  CLASSIFICATION CODES: 9110 (CN = Company specific); 7300 (CN = Sales & selling); 7200 (CN = Advertising); 8600 (CN = Manufacturing industries not elsewhere classified)

Notes: (1) title (2) author (3) source (4) abstract

ABI/INFORM core journals

AACE Transactions
ABA Banking Journal
Abacus (Australia)
Academy of Management Journal
Academy of Management Review
Accounting, Organizations & Society (UK)
Accounting Review
ACES Bulletin (Association for Comparative
   Economic Studies)
Administrative Science Quarterly
Advanced Management Journal
AIIE Transactions
Akron Business & Economic Review
American Business Law Journal
American Demographics
American Economic Review
American Economist
American Journal of Small Business
Antitrust Bulletin
Appraisal Journal
Arbitration Journal
AREUEA Journal (American Real Estate &
   Urban Economics Association)
ARMA Records Management Quarterly
ASCI Journal of Management (India)
ASEAN Business Quarterly (Singapore)
Atlantic Economic Journal
Australian Business Law Review
Australian Journal of Management
Ball State Business Review
Banker (UK)
Bankers Magazine
Bankers Monthly
Banking Law Journal
Bank Marketing
Barclays Review (UK)
Baylor Business Studies
Bell Journal of Economics
Bell Laboratories Record
Benefits International (UK)
Best's Review (Life/Health)
Best's Review (Prop/Casualty)
British Journal of Industrial Relations
   (UK)
Business
Business & Society
Business & Society Review
Business Economics
Business Horizons
Business Law Review
Business Quarterly (Can.)
Business Review (Federal Reserve Bank of
   Philadelphia)
Business Review (Wells Fargo Bank)
California Management Review
Canadian Business Law Journal

Canadian Business Review
Canadian Chartered Accountant
Canadian Journal of Economics
Cash Flow
Chase Economic Observer
Chicago MBA
Citibank Monthly Economic Letter
CLU Journal
Columbia Journal of World Business
Computer Decisions
Computer Networks (Neth.)
Computers & Industrial Engineering
Computers & Operations Research (UK)
Computers in Industry
Corporation Law Review
Cost & Management (Can.)
Cost Engineering
CPA Journal
CPCU Journal
Credit Union Executive
Data Communications
Datamation
Decision Sciences
Directors & Boards
Economic Development & Cultural
   Change
Economic Journal (UK)
Economic Perspectives (Federal Reserve
   Bank of Chicago)
Economic Review (Federal Reserve Bank of
   Atlanta)
Economic Review (Federal Reserve Bank of
   Richmond)
EEO Today
Employee Benefits Journal
Employee Relations Law Journal
Energy Communications
Energy Policy (UK)
Energy Systems & Policy
Engineering Costs & Production Economics
   (Neth.)
Engineering Economist
Estate Planning
European Economic Review (Neth.)
European Journal of Marketing (UK)
European Journal of Operational Research
   (UK)
Federal Home Loan Bank Board Journal
Federal Reserve Bank of Minneapolis
   Quarterly Review
Federal Reserve Bank of New York
   Quarterly Review
Federal Reserve Bank of St. Louis Review
Finance & Development
Financial Analysts Journal
Financial Executive

Financial Management
Financial Planning Today
Financial World
Fortune
Government Accountants Journal
Governmental Finance
Group & Organization Studies
Growth & Change
GTE Automatic Electric Worldwide
　Communications Journal
Harvard Business Review
Health Care Management Review
Hospital Financial Management
Hospital Material Management Quarterly
Human Resource Management
IBM Systems Journal
IEEE Transactions on Engineering
　Management
IEEE Transactions on Professional
　Communication
IEEE Transactions on Software
　Engineeering
Industrial & Labor Relations Review
Industrial Engineering
Industrial Marketing Management
Industrial Management
Industrial Relations
Industrial Relations Law Journal
Information Processing & Management
　(UK)
Information Processing Letters (Neth.)
Infosystems
Institutional Investor
Internal Auditor
International Economic Review
International Journal of Computer &
　Information Sciences
International Journal of Manpower (UK)
International Journal of Operations &
　Production Management (UK)
International Journal of Physical
　Distribution & Materials Management
　(UK)
International Journal of Public
　Administration
International Journal of Social Economics
　(UK)
International Labour Review (Switz.)
International Management (UK)
International Studies of Management &
　Organization
International Tax Journal
Issues in Bank Regulation
J. of Accountancy
J. of Accounting & Economics (Neth.)
J. of Accounting, Auditing & Finance
J. of Accounting Research

J. of Advertising
J. of Advertising Research
J. of Applied Behavioral Science
J. of Applied Management
J. of Applied Psychology
J. of Bank Research
J. of Banking & Finance (Neth.)
J. of Business (Univ. of Chicago)
J. of Business Administration (Can.)
J. of Business Finance & Accounting (UK)
J. of Business Research
J. of Business Strategy
J. of Collective Negotiations in the Public
　Sector
J. of Commercial Bank Lending
J. of Consumer Affairs
J. of Consumer Research
J. of Contemporary Business
J. of Corporate Taxation
J. of Developing Areas
J. of Development Economics (Neth.)
J. of Economic Dynamics & Control (Neth.)
J. of Economics & Business (Temple Univ.)
J. of Enterprise Management
J. of Environmental Economics &
　Management
J. of Finance
J. of Financial & Quantitative Analysis
J. of Financial Economics (Neth.)
J. of General Management (UK)
J. of Housing
J. of Human Resources
J. of Industrial Economics (UK)
J. of Information Science Principles &
　Practice (Neth.)
J. of International Business Studies
J. of International Economics (Neth.)
J. of International Law & Economics
J. of Labor Research
J. of Macroeconomics
J. of Management
J. of Management Studies (UK)
J. of Marketing
J. of Marketing Research
J. of Micrographics
J. of Monetary Economics (Neth.)
J. of Money, Credit & Banking
J. of Occupational Psychology (UK)
J. of Operations Management
J. of Pension Planning & Compliance
J. of Policy Modeling
J. of Political Economy
J. of Portfolio Management
J. of Products Liability
J. of Property Management
J. of Purchasing & Materials Management
J. of Real Estate Taxation

J. of Retail Banking
J. of Retailing
J. of Risk & Insurance
J. of Small Business Management
J. of Systems & Software (Neth.)
J. of Systems Management
J. of the Academy of Marketing Science
J. of the American Planning Association
J. of the Market Research Society (UK)
J. of the Operational Research Society (UK)
J. of the Society of Research Administrators
J. of Transport Economics & Policy (UK)
J. of World Trade Law (UK)
Labor Law Journal
Land Economics
Life Association News
Lloyds Bank Review (UK)
Logistics & Transportation Review (Can.)
Long Range Planning (UK)
Los Angeles Business & Economics
Magazine of Bank Administration
Manage
Management Accounting
Management Decision (UK)
Management Focus
Management International Review (W. Ger.)
Management Science
Management Today (UK)
Management World
Managerial Finance (UK)
Managerial Planning
Manufacturers Hanover Economic Report
Marketing & Media Decisions
Mathematics of Operations Research
Mergers & Acquisitions
Michigan Business Review
Microprocessing & Microprogramming (Neth.)
Mid-Atlantic Journal of Business
Midland Bank (UK)
Mid-South Business Journal
Mini-Micro Systems
Monthly Labor Review
Mortgage Banking
MSU Business Topics
National Institute Economic Review (UK)
National Public Accountant
National Real Estate Investor
National Tax Journal
Nebraska Journal of Economics & Business
New England Economic Review
New England Journal of Business & Economics
NFIB Quarterly Economic Report for Small Business
Operations Research

Organizational Behavior & Human Performance
Organizational Dynamics
Organization Studies
Oxford Bulletin of Economics & Statistics (UK)
Pension World
Personnel
Personnel Administrator
Personnel Journal
Personnel Management (UK)
Personnel Psychology
Personnel Review (UK)
Planning Review
Practical Accountant
Public Administration Review
Public Finance Quarterly
Public Personnel Management
Public Productivity Review
Public Relations Journal
Public Utilities Fortnightly
Quarterly Review of Economics & Business
Quarterly Review of Marketing (UK)
R & D Management (UK)
Real Estate Appraiser & Analyst
Real Estate Law Journal
Real Estate Review
Regional Science & Urban Economics (Neth.)
Regulation
Research Management
Research Policy (Neth.)
Retail Control
Review of Business
Review of Business & Economic Research
Review of Economics & Statistics (Neth.)
Review of Taxation of Individuals
Risk Management
Savings & Loan News
Sloan Management Review
Small Business Report
Small Systems World
Southern Economic Journal
Southern Review of Public Administration
Southwest Business & Economic Review
Strategic Management Journal
Studies in Economic Analysis
Supervisory Management
Systems & Software Review
Taxation for Accountants
Taxes
Tax Executive
Tax Law Review
Tax Review
Texas Business Executive
Texas Business Review

Traffic Management
Training
Training & Development Journal
Trusts & Estates

U.S. Economic Outlook
Uniform Commercial Code Law Journal
Wharton Magazine
Woman CPA

Example of ABI/INFORM controlled vocabulary

u = Use (The term you have chosen is not an authorized term; use this one instead.)

uf = Used for (The term following uf is not an authorized term but may be useful in free-text searches.)

rt = Related term (Broader, narrower, or synonymous authorized terms.)

sn = Scope note (Additional information about usage, dates of usage, or authorized form of term.)

Auction market
Auctions
  sn See also Quick Scan SIC list
Audience profile
  rt Profiles
Audiences
  rt Hooper ratings
Audio
  sn Used as combining term
Audiovisual
  sn Used from 1979 forward
  sn Used as combining term
Audit administration techniques
  sn Used only before 1979
Audit bureaus
  rt BPA
Audit committees
  rt Auditing policies
  rt Boards of directors
  rt Committees
Audit cycles
Audit departments
  sn Used from 1979 forward
  sn Use Audit depts before 1979
Audit engagements
  rt Proposals for new engagements (ACC)
Audit evidence
Audit guides
  u Auditing procedures
Audit objectives
Audit requirements
  sn Used form 1979 forward
Audit trails
Audited financial statements
  rt Financial statements
  rt Unaudited financial statements
Auditing
  sn Broad general term. Use more specific term or use as combining term
  sn See also Quick Scan SIC list

  rt Audits
  rt Compliance auditing
  rt Directors examinations
  rt Disciplinary proceedings
  rt Internal auditing
  rt Preliminary audit survey
  rt Recomputation
Auditing of computer systems
  uf Test decking
  rt Computer audits
Auditing policies
  uf Auditing principles
  rt Audit committees
Auditing principles
  u Auditing policies
Auditing procedures
  uf Audit guides
  rt Alternative auditing procedures
  rt Limited review (ACC)
Auditing profession
Auditing standards
  rt Due professional care
Auditors
  sn See also Quick Scan SIC list
Auditors obligations
  u Client relationships
Auditors opinions
  uf Qualified opinions
  rt Accountants reports
  rt Adverse opinions (ACC)
  rt Significant auditor disagreement
Auditors reports
  u Accountants reports
Auditors responsibilities
  u Client relationships
Audits
  sn See also Quick Scan SIC list
  rt Auditing
  rt Computer audits
  rt Continuous audits

rt Defense contract audits
rt Energy audits
rt Information audits
rt Interim audits
rt Management audits
rt Operation audits
rt Social audit
rt Tax audits
rt Test audits
Authority
Authority lines
u Organizational plans
Authorizations
Authorized capital
u Capital stock
Authors
sn See also Quick Scan SIC list
Automated
sn Used from 1979 forward
sn Used as combining term
Automated accounting systems
uf Computerized accounting systems
rt Data processing
Automated auditing systems
uf Computerized auditing systems
rt Computer audits
rt Data processing
Automated Clearing Houses
sn See also Quick Scan SIC list
uf ACH
rt Clearinghouses
Automated teller machines
sn Used with field code (BNK) before 1979
sn See also Quick Scan SIC list
uf ATM
rt Bank automation
Automatic
sn Used as combining term
Automatic control
Automatic data processing
u Data processing
Automatic transfer of funds
rt EFTS
rt Transfer of funds

Automatic typing equipment
u Word processing equipment
Automation
rt Bank automation
rt CAM
rt Office automation
Automobile dealers
sn See also Quick Scan SIC list
rt Dealers
Automobile fleets
uf Fleets
rt Automobile leasing
rt Motor vehicle fleets
Automobile garages
u Automotive repair services
Automobile industry
rt Motor vehicle industry
Automobile insurance
sn See also Quick Scan SIC list
uf Collision insurance
rt Insurance
rt No fault automobile insurance
rt Property insurance
rt Uninsured motorist coverage
Automobile leasing
sn See also Quick Scan SIC list
uf Car leasing
rt Automobile fleets
rt Leasing companies
Automobile service
sn See also Quick Scan SIC list
rt Service stations
Automobiles
sn See also Quick Scan SIC list
uf Cars
rt CAFE
rt EPA mileage ratings
rt Gas guzzlers
rt Motor vehicles
Automotive repair services
sn See also Quick Scan SIC list
uf Automobile garages
rt Service stations
Automotive supplies

Profile

Database: ABI/INFORM
Producer: Data Courier, Inc., 620 South Fifth St., Louisville, Kentucky 40202, 502-582-4111
Toll-Free Telephone: 800-626-2823
Vendor: DIALOG, SDC, ESA-IRS, Data-Star, BRS, Dialcom, InnerLine.
Cost: $73 per hour on DIALOG. Online prints are 20¢ per record, offline prints are 30¢ per record. Available on DIALOG's Knowledge Index for $24 per hour including telecommunications.

Date Began Online: 1973
Source of Information: All articles from 304 core journals; selected articles from about 250 other journals. Coverage starts as early as 1971, depending on journal.
Type of Coverage: Bibliographic with abstracts.
Size: Approximately 220,000 records.
Updating: Monthly with 3,000 records added per update.
Indexing Terms: Controlled vocabulary of 11,000 terms.
User Aids: *Search INFORM*, user's guide, $47.50. *LOG/ON*, bimonthly newsletter, free.
Printed Equivalent: None.
Document Retrieval: $7.95 per article plus $2 surcharge per article for international orders. Orders received by 2 P.M. are shipped the following day.
Notes: A five-month segment of the database called ONTAP ABI/INFORM for "online training and practice" is available on DIALOG at $15 per hour.

Management Contents

The Management Contents database aims to cover roughly the same subject area as ABI/INFORM. It indexes more than 500 business periodicals, about the same as ABI/INFORM. Indexing is all "cover to cover" rather than sometimes being selective as in ABI/INFORM. But the abstracts in Management Contents are shorter and less informative than those of ABI/INFORM. Its controlled vocabulary of 3,500 terms is less than one-half the size of ABI/INFORM's; thus the terms are more general and possibly less useful.

Despite the similarity in what both ABI/INFORM and Management Contents say about their goals, differences in indexing and abstracting policies make overlap between the two astonishingly small. In an identical search on both databases, it's possible to find that only 10 percent of the citations are included in both databases.

Management Contents recently branched out by indexing other sources of business information besides periodicals. For example, it now includes abstracts of American Management Associations' courses, new books about business, various conference proceedings, and 100 law journals.

Sample record

PROBLEM: I'd like to find articles on successful entrepreneurs and their new products.

(1) FBR83C28&2
(2) Of Baseball and Bubble Gum.
(3) Byrne, J.A.
(4) Forbes, Vol. 131, No. 7, March 28, 1983, p. 102, Journal.
(5) A former pitcher for the New York Yankees, Jim Bouton, is trying to get into the bubble gum card business. After appearing on the cards himself, his idea is to sell personalized bubble gum cards. Although he has had mixed successes in business— his Baseball Brain calculators failed but his shredded bubble gum in a pouch had

over eighteen million dollars in sales in its first year—he feels the timing is right for his new idea to succeed.

(6) Descriptors: Entrepreneur; Product Introduction; Market Entry; Innovation; 0310; 0455; 2410; 0926

Notes: (1) journal code (2) title (3) author (4) source (5) abstract (6) indexing terms and codes

Management Contents journal list

JOURNALS
ABA Banking Journal (Formerly Banking
  Journal)
ABACUS (Aust.)
ABCA Bulletin
Academy of Management Journal
Academy of Management Proceedings
Academy of Management Review
Accountancy (UK)
Accountant, The (UK)
Accountant's Magazine (UK)
Accounting and Business Research (UK)
Accounting and Finance (Aust.)
Accounting Forum
Accounting Journal
Accounting, Organizations & Society (UK)
Accounting Review
Across the Board (Formerly Conference
  Board Record)
Adherent
Administration and Society
Administrative Law Review
Administrative Science Quarterly
Advances in Consumer Research
  Proceedings
Advertising World
Agricultural Law Journal
Aids Proceedings
AIIE Industrial Management
AIIE Proceedings
AIIE Transactions
Air Force Comptroller
Akron Business & Economic Review
All-Aba Course Materials Journal
American Business Law Journal
American Council on Consumer Interest
  Proceedings
American Demographics
American Economic Review and
  Proceedings
American Journal of Agricultural Economics
American Journal of Small Business
American Marketing Association
  Proceedings
American Review of Public Administration
  (Formerly Midwest Review of Public
  Administration)

American Salesman
Antitrust Bulletin
Antitrust Law & Economics Review
Applied Economics (UK)
Appraisal Journal
Arbitration Journal
Arizona Business
Arkansas Business and Economic Review
Armed Forces Comptroller
ASCI J. of Management (India)
Association Management
Atlantic Economic Journal
Au Courant (Can.)
Australian J. of Management
Balance Sheet
Banca Nazionale Del Lavoro Review (Italy)
Banker, The (UK)
Bankers Magazine
Bankers Monthly
Banking Law Journal
Bank Marketing
Barron's
Baylor Business Studies
Bell Journal of Economics
Benefits International (UK)
Best's Review Life/Health Insurance Edition
Best's Review Property/Casualty Insurance
  Edition
Boston College Law Review
Boston University Law Review
British J. of Industrial Relations
Bulletin of Economic Research (UK)
Bureaucrat
Business (Formerly Atlanta Economic
  Review)
Business and Society
Business and Society Review
Business Economics
Business Horizons
Business Law Review
Business Lawyer
Business Owner
Business Quarterly (Can.)
Business Week (Industrial Ed.)
CA Magazine (Can.)
California Management Review
Cambridge Law Journal

Canadian Banker & ICB Review
Canadian Business
Canadian Business Law Journal
Canadian Business Review
Canadian J. of Economics
Canadian Labour
Canadian Manager
Canadian Public Administration
Canadian Taxation (Ceased publication Vol. 3 1981)
Cashflow Magazine
Challenge (Magazine of Economic Affairs)
Chief Executive (UK)
Chief Executive (US)
China Business Review
CLU Journal
Collegiate News & Views
Columbia J. of World Business
Columbia Law Review
Commercial Law Journal
Commodities: Magazine of Future Trading
Compensation Planning Journal
Compensation Review
Computer Law Journal
Computers & Operations Research
Concepts (Ceased publication Vol. 5 1982)
Conference of Actuaries in Public Practice Proceedings
Contract Management
Cornell Executive
Cornell Law Review
Corporate Director
Corporate Planning (UK)
Corporation Law Review
Cost and Management (Can.)
CPA Journal
Credit
Credit & Financial Management
Credit World
Decision Sciences
Delaware Journal of Corporate Law
Direct Marketing
Director, The (UK)
Directors & Boards
Distribution
Dun & Bradstreet Reports
Dun's Business Month
Economic and Industrial Democracy (UK)
Economic and Social Review (Ire.)
Economic Bulletin for Europe
Economic Development & Cultural Change
Economic Geography
Economic Inquiry
Economic Journal (UK)
Economic Review (Pak.)
Economist (UK)
EEO Today
EFTA Bulletin (Switz.)

Employee Benefit Plan Review
Employee Benefits Journal
Employee Relations (UK)
Employee Relations Law Journal
Employment Review
Engineering Costs & Production Economics (Neth.)
Engineering Economist
Engineering Management International (Neth.)
Engineering News-Record
Estates & Trusts Quarterly (Can.)
Estates, Gifts & Trusts Journal
Euromoney (UK)
European Economic Review (Neth.)
European J. of Marketing (UK)
European J. of Operational Research (Neth.)
Executive (Can.)
Executive (Formerly *Credit Union Executive*)
Executive Skills
Federal Communications Law Journal
Federal Reserve Bank of N.Y. Quarterly Review
Federal Reserve Bulletin
Finance & Development
Financial Analysts Journal
Financial Executive
Financial Management
Financial Planning Today
Financial Review
Financial World
Forbes
Fortune
Fund Raising Management
Futures (UK)
Futurist
GAO Review
George Washington J. of International Law & Economics (Formerly *J. of International Law & Economics*)
Golden Gate University Law Review
Government Accountants Journal
Government Executive
Governmental Finance
Group & Organization Studies
Growth and Change
Handling & Shipping Management
Harvard Business Review
Harvard J. on Legislation
Harvard Law Review
Health & Society (Milbank Memorial Fund Quarterly)
Healthcare Financial Management
Health Care Management Review
Health Services Research
Hospital & Health Services Administration

Housing Finance Review
Human Relations
Human Resource Management
Human Resource Planning
Human Systems Management (Neth.)
Idea: The J. of Law & Technology
IEEE Transactions Proceedings
Illinois Business Review
In Business
Inc.
Industrial and Commercial Training (UK)
Industrial and Labor Relations Review
Industrial Development
Industrial Distribution
Industrial Engineering
Industrial Management
Industrial Marketing
Industrial Marketing Management
Industrial Organization Review (Ceased
    publication)
Industrial Relations
Industrial Relations (Can.)
Industrial Relations Journal (UK)
Industrial Relations Law Journal
*Industrial Relations Research Association
    Proceedings*
Industrial Society (UK)
Industry Week
Information & Management (Neth.)
Information & Management (Formerly
    Information & Records Management)
Information Processing & Management (UK)
Information Services & Use
Inquiry
Institutional Investor
Institutional Investor International Edition
Insurance Counsel Journal
Insurance Liability Reporter
Insurance Mathematics & Economics
    (Neth.)
Interfaces
Internal Auditor
International Economic Review
International J. of Advertising (UK)
    (Formerly *J. of Advertising*)
International J. of Government Auditing
International J. of Manpower (UK)
*International J. of Operations and
    Production Management* (UK)
*International J. of Physical Distribution &
    Materials Management* (UK)
International J. of Social Economies (UK)
International Labour Review (Switz.)
International Management (UK)
*International Review of Administrative
    Sciences* (Belg.)
*International Studies of Management &
    Organization*

International Tax Journal
International Trade Forum (Switz.)
IPRA Review
J. of Accountancy
J. of Accountanting, Auditing & Finance
J. of Accounting & Economics (Neth.)
J. of Accounting Research
J. of Administration Overseas (Ceased
    publication 1980, replaced by *Public
    Administration and Development*)
J. of Advertising
J. of Advertising Research
J. of American Insurance
J. of Applied Behavioral Science
J. of Applied Psychology
J. of Bank Research
J. of Banking & Finance (Neth.)
J. of Behavioral Economics
J. of Business (Univ. of Chicago)
J. of Business Administration (Can.)
J. of Business Communication
J. of Business Finance and Accounting (UK)
J. of Business Law (UK)
J. of Business Research
J. of Business Strategy
*J. of Collective Negotiations in the Public
    Sector*
J. of Commercial Bank Lending
J. of Common Market Studies (UK)
J. of Communication Management
    (Formerly *J. of Organizational
    Communication*)
J. of Consumer Affairs
J. of Consumer Research
J. of Contemporary Business
J. of Corporate Taxation
J. of Corporation Law
J. of Developing Areas
J. of Development Economics (Neth.)
J. of Development Studies (UK)
J. of Econometrics (Neth.)
J. of Economic Behavior & Organization
    (Neth.)
J. of Economic Dynamics & Control (Neth.)
J. of Economic Issues
J. of Economic Literature
J. of Economic Psychology (Neth.)
J. of Economic Theory
J. of Economics and Business
J. of Energy Law & Policy
*J. of Environmental Economics and
    Management*
J. of European Industrial Training (UK)
J. of Finance
J. of Financial & Quantitative Analysis
J. of Financial Economics (Neth.)
J. of Forecasting
J. of Futures Markets

J. of General Management (UK)
J. of Housing
J. of Human Resources
J. of Industrial Economics (UK)
J. of Information Science (Neth.)
J. of Insurance
J. of International Business Studies
J. of International Economics (Neth.)
J. of Labor Research
J. of Law & Economics
J. of Management
J. of Management Development
J. of Management Studies (UK)
J. of Marketing
J. of Marketing Research
J. of Mathematical Economics (Switz.)
J. of Monetary Economics (Switz.)
J. of Money, Credit & Banking
J. of Occupational Behavior (UK)
J. of Occupational Psychology (UK)
J. of Organizational Behvaior Management
J. of Pension Planning & Compliance
J. of Personal Selling & Sales Management
J. of Policy Analysis & Management
J. of Policy Modeling
J. of Political Economy
J. of Portfolio Management
J. of Post-Keynesian Economics
J. of Products Liability (UK)
J. of Property Management
J. of Public Economics (Switz.)
J. of Purchasing and Materials Management
J. of Real Estate Taxation
J. of Regional Science
J. of Retail Banking
J. of Retailing
J. of Risk & Insurance
J. of Small Business Management
J. of State Taxation
J. of Statistical Planning and Inference (Neth.)
J. of Systems Management
J. of Taxation
J. of the Academy of Marketing Science
J. of the American Planning Association
J. of the American Society for Information Science
J. of the Market Research Society (UK)
J. of the Operational Research Society (Formerly the *Operational Research Quarterly*)
J. of the Society of Research Administrators
J. of Urban Economics
J. of World Trade Law (UK)
Labor Law Journal
Land Economics
Law & Policy in International Business

Leadership & Organization Development Journal (UK) (Formerly *Leadership & Organization Development Control*)
Lloyds Bank Review (UK)
Local Finance (Neth.) (Ceased publication with December 1982 issue)
Logistics & Transportation Review (Can.)
Long Range Planning (UK)
Magazine of Bank Administration
Maintenance Management International (Neth.)
Manage
Management Accounting
Management Accounting (UK)
Management Decision (UK)
Management Focus
Management in Government (UK) (Formerly *Management Services in Government*)
Management International Review (W. Ger.)
Management Quarterly
Management Review
Management Science
Management Today (UK)
Management World
Managerial Finance (UK)
Managerial Planning
Managers Magazine
Managing
Marketing (UK)
Marketing and Media Decisions
Marketing Times
Massachusetts CPA Review
Mathematics of Operations Research
Medical Economics
Mergers & Acquisitions
Metropolitan Life Insurance Statistical Bulletin
Michigan CPA
Michigan Law Review
Mid Atlantic J. of Business (Formerly *J. of Business*)
Mid South Business Journal (Formerly *Mid South Quarterly Business Review*)
Modern Healthcare
Modern Office Procedures
Money
Montana Business Quarterly
Monthly Labor Review
Mortgage Banking
MTM J. of Methods—Time Management
Municipal Finance Journal
Multinational Business
Nation's Business
National Contract Management Journal
National Forum: Phi Kappa Phi Journal

National Institute Economic Review (UK)
National Productivity Review
National Public Accountant
National Real Estate Investor
National Tax Journal
National Underwriter - Life & Health
  Insurance
National Underwriter - Property & Casualty
  Insurance
NBER Reporter
Nebraska J. of Economics and Business
New England Business
Northwestern University Law Review
Occupational Hazards
Office
Office Administration and Automation
  (Formerly Administrative Management)
Ohio CPA Journal
Omega (UK)
Operations Research
Optimum (Can.)
Organization Studies
Organizational Behavior and Human
  Performance
Organizational Dynamics
Outlook (Formerly California CPA
  Quarterly)
Pension World
Personnel
Personnel Administrator
Personnel Journal
Personnel Management (UK)
Personnel Psychology
Personnel Review
Perspective
Planned Innovation (UK)
Planning (Formerly Practicing Planner)
Planning Review
Practical Accountant, The
Production
Professional Report, The
Public Administration (UK)
Public Administration and Development
Public Administration Review
Public Finance and Accountancy (UK)
Public Finance Quarterly
Public Personnel Management
Public Relations Journal
Public Relations Quarterly
Public Relations Review
Public Utilities Fortnightly
Purchasing
Quarterly J. of Economics
Quarterly Review of Economics and
  Business
Quarterly Review of Marketing (UK)
R & D Management (UK)

Real Estate Law Journal
Real Estate Review
Real Property, Probate & Trust Journal
Records Management Quarterly
Regional Science & Urban Economics
Regulation
Research Management
Retail and Distribution Management
Review of Business
Review of Business & Economic Research
  (Formerly Mississippi Valley J. of
  Business & Economics)
Review of Economics & Statistics (Neth.)
Review of Social Economy
Review of Taxation of Individuals
Review of World Economics (W. Ger.)
Risk Management
SAM Advanced Management Journal
Sales & Marketing Management
Savings Bank Journal
Securities Regulation Law Journal
Security Management
Site Selection Handbook
Sloan Management Review
Small Business Report
SOCIO Economic Planning Sciences (UK)
South Dakota Business Review
Southern California Law Review
Southern Economic Journal
Southern Marketing Association
  Proceedings
Stamford Law Review
State Government
Strategic Management Journal (UK)
Successful Meetings
Supervision
Supervisory Management
Tax Advisor, The
Tax Executive
Tax Law Review
Tax Lawyer
Tax Management International Journal
  (Formerly International Journal)
Tax Review
Taxation for Accountants
Taxation for Lawyers
Taxes, The Tax Magazine
Technological Forecasting & Social Change
Three Banks Review (UK)
Thrust: J. for Employment & Training
  Professionals
Topics in Health Care Financing
Topics in Health Care Materials
  Management
Topics in Health Records Management
Toxic Substances Journal
Traffic Management

Training
Training & Development Journal
Transportation Law Journal (Can.)
Transportation Research (UK)
Trusts & Estates
UCLA Law Review
Uniform Commercial Code Law Journal
United States Banker
University of California Davis Law Review
University of Chicago Law Review
Valuation
Vanderbilt Law Review
Venture
Viewpoint
Virginia Law Review
Vision
Vital Speeches of the Day
Wharton Magazine, The (Suspended
   publication with Fall 1982 issue)
Wisconsin Law Review
Woman CPA
World Development (UK)
World Economy (UK)
Yale Law Journal

AMERICAN MANAGEMENT ASSOCIATIONS
COURSES
Accounting for Managers, 2nd ed.
Advertising: Strategy and Design, 4th ed.
Automating Your Office: A How-to Guide
Basics of Cost Accounting
Basic Systems and Procedures, 2nd ed.
Budgeting by Departments & Functional
   Areas, 3rd ed.
Capital Structures and Long-Term
   Objectives, 3rd ed.
Commercial Banking, 2nd ed.
Communication Skills for Managers
Computer Basics for Management, 6th ed.
Contingency Planning
Cost Accounting for Profit Improvement
Data Base Concepts and Design
Developing Computer-Based Accounts
   Receivable Systems
Developing Computer-Based General
   Ledger Systems
EDP and Accounting
EDP Feasibility Study, The, 2nd ed.
Efficient Reading for Managers
Executive's Guide to Office Space Planning,
   The
Executive's Guide to Wage and Salary
   Administration, The, 2nd ed.
Financial Goals and Strategic Planning
First-Line Management
Fundamentals of Finance & Accounting for
   Nonfinancial Managers plus Supplement

Fundamentals of Modern Marketing
Fundamentals of Modern Personnel
   Management
Fundamentals of Traffic Management
Getting Results Through MBO
Getting Results with Matrix Management
Getting Results with Time Management
How Successful Women Manage
How to Be an Effective Secretary in the
   Modern Office
How to Be a Successful Product Manager
How to Be a Successful Project Manager
How to Budget a Service Organization
How to Build Effective Investor Relations
How to Build Memory Skills
How to Build a Power Vocabulary
How to Manage Administrative Operations
How to Manage a Data Processing
   Department
How to Manage Maintenance
How to Manage the New Product
   Development Process
How to Manage Paperwork
How to Plan and Manage Warehouse
   Operations
How to Sell Effectively
How to Write a Business Plan
How to Write Technical Reports
How to Write Winning Reports
Human Resource Development: A
   Manager's Guide
Job of the Corporate Controller, The
Leadership Skills for Executives
Leasing for Profit
Long-Range Planning
Macroeconomics and Company Planning
   Management Information Systems
Management Strategies for the Small Firm
Management of Personal Selling, 3rd ed.
Managerial Economics
Manager's Guide to Human Behavior, A
Manager's Guide to Financial Analysis, A
Managing Commercial Credit
Managing Corporate Credit
Managing Employee Benefits
Manufacturing Management
MBO for the Public Agency
Mergers and Acquisitions: A Financial
   Approach
Performing the Operations Audit, 2nd ed.
Personal Financial Planning, 1982 ed.
   Company, 3rd ed.
Planning Cash Flow
Planning for Control Managers
Principles of Finance
Principles of Investment Management
Purchasing Management
Quantitative Aids to Decision Making, 3rd ed.

*Quality Control: Meeting the New
    Competition*
*Reading and Interpreting Financial
    Statements*
Return on Investment, 2nd ed.
Role of the Internal Auditor, The
Strategic Marketing Planning
Strategies in Marketing Research
Success Through Assertiveness
*Successful Marketing for Service
    Organizations*
*Theory and Practical Management Control,
    The*, 2nd ed.
Training for Productivity
Trainsactional Analysis for Managers
Using the Computer as a Marketing Tool
Using Mathematics as a Business Tool
What Accounting Managers Do
What Managers Do
Writing for Management Success
Zero-Based Planning and Budgeting

Audiocassette Courses with Workbooks

Achieving Computer Security
*Assertiveness for Career and Personal
    Basic Business Psychology*
Communication Skills for Secretaries
Computer Fundamentals for Managers, 2nd
    ed.
Constructive Discipline for Supervisors
Creative Problem Solving
Effective Team Building
*Executive Writing, Speaking, & Listening
    Skills*
*Finance and Accounting for Non-Financial
    Managers*
Fundamentals of Budgeting

*Guide for Executive Secretaries and
    Administrative Assistants*
Guide to Operational Auditing, A
How to Be an Effective Middle Manager
How to Be an Effective Supervisor
How to Be a Successful Public Speaker
*How to Evaluate Performance and Assess
    Potential*
How to Improve Customer Service
How to Improve Your Memory
How to Interpret Financial Statements
How to Interview Effectively
How to Make Better Decisions
How to Market by Telephone
How to Plan for Profits
How to Run Effective Meetings
How Successful Managers Manage
Listen and Be Listened To
Management of Field Sales, The
*Managerial Skills for New and Prospective
    Managers*
Managing by Objectives
Managing Cash Flow
Managing Conflict
Orientation and the Hiring Process
Personal Selling Skills
*Planning and Implementing a Personal
    Fitness Program*
Practical TA for Managers
Setting and Achieving Personal Goals
Strategic Planning
Successful Delegation
*Supervisors Guide to Boosting Productivity,
    The*
Total Time Management
Understanding and Managing Stress
Using Managerial Authority
Winning With Leadership Skills

Profile

Database: Management Contents
Producer: Management Contents, 2265 Carlson Dr., Suite 5000, Northbrook, Illinois 60062, 312-564-1006
Toll-Free Telephone: 800-323-5354
Vendor: DIALOG, SDC, BRS, Data-Star (Europe), The Source.
Cost: Price varies by system but is between $40 and $80 per hour. Online prints cost about 15¢ and offline prints are about 25¢.
Date Began Online: 1976
Source of Information: More than 500 regional, national, and international business journals and periodicals. Also includes books, proceedings and transactions, and professional study courses from the American Management Associations, American Institute of Certified Public Accountants, and Employee Benefit Research Institute. Coverage back to 1974 for some periodicals.

Type of Coverage: Cover-to-cover indexing with abstracts.
Size: 180,000 records in August 1983.
Updating: Daily on NEWSEARCH on DIALOG (see Chapter 14); otherwise monthly, approximately 4,000 records added per month.
Indexing Terms: Controlled vocabulary of 3,500 descriptors, each with code numbers.
User Aids: *Management Contents Data Base Thesaurus*, with *Indexer's Manual and Dictionary*, $100.
Printed Equivalent: None.
Document Retrieval: $10 per article, sent in next business day's mail.

Trade and Industry Index

Information Access Corporation's Trade and Industry Index sees its mission somewhat differently from the preceding two databases. Whereas Management Contents, for example, defines its goal as covering the "basic functions of business [such as] accounting, finance, marketing, production, and personnel," the Trade and Industry Index aims for industry-specific coverage. Thus its 340 core publications, indexed cover to cover, are made up primarily of major trade journals. They are listed below after the Sample Record.

Trade and Industry Index is much newer than the previous two databases; its references go back only to the beginning of 1981. Many sources covered in ABI/INFORM and Management Contents begin in the mid-1970s. A unique feature of the Trade and Industry Index is its inclusion of industry-related articles from many nonbusiness, general-interest periodicals. These records are simply copied from the company's other databases—the Magazine Index and the National Newspaper Index (both of these are discussed in Chapter 14) as well as the Legal Resource Index.

Most bibliographic databases are updated (or "reloaded" in the industry terminology) one to four times a month. In order to be as current as possible, the producer of Trade and Industry Index maintains a separate database called NEWSEARCH, which is reloaded daily. It contains each day's new entries for all of the company's databases. Once a month, the contents of NEWSEARCH are "dumped" into the Trade and Industry Index or one of the company's other three databases.

(Note, Management Contents puts its daily updates into NEWSEARCH; in return, "industry-related" records from Management Contents appear in Trade and Industry Index. Thus, the records in Trade and Industry Index duplicate some of those in Management Contents.)

Trade and Industry Index's abstracts are unpredictable. Some of its records contain no abstract at all; some have only a sentence or two; and some have several paragraphs. Its controlled vocabulary uses SIC codes (see Chapter 9 for a discussion of SIC codes), as well as generic product names, brand names, and geographical areas. For general topic headings, Trade and Industry relies chiefly on Library of Congress subject headings, which are not particularly useful for business purposes.

Sample record

PROBLEM: Can you find me an article that takes a sober look at the health of the beer industry?

(1) Survival is priority for beer wholesalers, breweries. (with maps, tables, graphs)
(2) Katz, Philip C.
(3) Beverage Industry v 74 p10(5) Jan 28 1983
    illustration; table; table; table; graph; graph
(4) State beer wholesaler associations assessed problems and priorities of the industry, including excise taxes, transshipment, alcohol abuse, mandatory deposits, and threats to the tier system. Overall market growth is also analyzed.
     SIC CODE: 2082
(5) CAPTIONS: U.S. alcohol beverage consumption 18 & over.; Increase in U.S. beer market 1972-1981.; Changes in alcohol beverage market 1972-1981.; Beer per capita consumption. (Michigan, Maine); Beer per capita consumption (Vermont, Oregon).
(6) DESCRIPTORS: wholesale trade—statistics; brewing industry—statistics; beer—marketing

Notes: (1) title (2) author (3) source (4) abstract (5) captions to tables and graphs (6) indexing terms

Journals indexed in Trade and Industry Index

Coverage beginning in January 1981 unless otherwise indicated.
[1]Coverage beginning in January 1982.
[2]Coverage beginning in January 1983.
Trade and Industry Index also includes selective indexing coverage from Magazine Index (400 journals) and Legal Resource Index (700 journals).

ABA Banking Journal
Administrative Management
Advertising Age
Agrichemical Age
Air Conditioning, Heating & Refrigeration News
Air Progress
Air Transport World
American Banker
American Business Law Journal
American City and County
American Druggist
American Economic Review
American Family Physician
American Federationist
American Forests
American Import-Export Bulletin (name changed to *American Import-Export Management*)
American Import-Export Management (formerly *American Import-Export Bulletin*)
American Metal Market
American Paint & Coatings Journal

American Printer (formerly *American Printer & Lithographer*)
American Printer & Lithographer (name changed to *American Printer*)
American Statistical Association Journal
Amusement Business
Antitrust Bulletin
Antitrust Law Journal
Appliance Manufacturer
Arbitration Journal
Audio-Visual Communications
Automotive Industries
Automotive Marketing
Automotive News
Aviation Week
Backstage
Backstage-Business Screen
The Banker
Bankers Magazine
Bankers Monthly
Banking Journal
Barron's
Best's Review—Life-Health Insurance Edition

*Best's Review—Property-Casualty
   Insurance Edition*
Beverage Industry
Beverage World
Billboard
Black Enterprise
Boating Industry
Body Fashions—Intimate Apparel
Brick & Clay Record
Broadcasting
Building Design & Construction
Building Supply News
*Buildings: The Construction & Building
   Management Journal*
Business America
Business and Society Review
Business & Commercial Aviation
Business Economics
Business History Review
Business Horizons
Business Insurance
Business Week
Canadian Business Review
Candy & Snack Industry
Chain Store Age—Executive's Edition
*Chain Store Age—General Merchandising
   Edition*
Chain Store Age—Supermarkets
Challenge: Magazine of Economic Affairs
Chemical & Engineering News
Chemical Marketing Reporter
*Chemical Marketing Reporter—Chemical
   Business*
Chemical Week
Christian Science Monitor (Business
   Section and selected articles)
Citibank Monthly Economic Letter (ceased
   publication)
CLU Journal
Coal Age
Colorado Business
Commodities
Communications News
Computer Decisions
Computerworld
Computing Surveys
Construction Equipment
Construction Review
Consultant
Contractor
Control Engineering[1]
*Cornell Hotel & Restaurant Administration
   Quarterly*
Corporation Law Review
Creative Computing
Credit & Financial Management
Daily News Record

Dairy Record
Data Communications
Data Management
Datamation
Defense Electronics
Design News
Diesel & Gas Turbine Progress (name
   changed to *Diesel Progress*)
Diesel Progress (formerly *Diesel & Gas
   Turbine Progress*)
Directors and Boards
The Director
Discount Store News[2]
Distribution Worldwide
Drug & Cosmetic Industry
Drug Topics
Dun's Business Month (formerly *Dun's
   Review*)
Dun's Review (name changed to *Dun's
   Business Month*)
Economic Indicators
Economic Record
The Economist
Editor & Publisher
EDN
EDP Industry Report
Electric Light & Power
Electrical Construction & Maintenance
Electrical World
Electronic Design
Electronic News
Electronics
Employee Relations Law Journal
Energy User News
Engineering & Mining Journal
Engineering Economist
Estate Planning
European Chemical News
European Chemical News—Chemscope
Farm Journal
Fast Service (ceased publication)
Federal Home Loan Bank Board Journal
Feedstuffs
Financial World
Fleet Owner
Folio
Food Development (formerly *Food Product
   Development*, now included in *Processed
   Prepared Foods*)
Food Processing
Food Product Development (name changed
   to *Food Development*)
Food Service Marketing
Footwear News
Footwear News Magazine
Forbes
Forest Industries

Fortune
Foundry Management & Technology
Fueloil & Oilheat
Fusion
Gift & Decorative Accessories
Government & Product News
Graphic Arts Monthly
Handling & Shipping Management
Hardware Age
Hardware Retailing
Harvard Business Review
Healthcare Financial Management
  (formerly Hospital Financial
  Management)
Highway & Heavy Construction
Home & Auto
Hospital Financial Management (name
  changed to Healthcare Financial
  Management)
Hospitals: Journal of American Hospital
  Association
Hotel & Motel Management
Hotels & Restaurants International
  (formerly Service World International)
Housewares
Housing
Hydraulics & Pneumatics
Implement & Tractor
Inc.
Industrial & Labor Relations Review
Industrial Development
Industrial Equipment News
Industrial Finishing
Industrial Relations
Industrial Research and Development
Industry Week
Infosystems
Insider's Chronicle
Institutional Distribution
Instructor
Interavia
Interior Design
International Monetary Fund Staff Papers
International Tax Journal
International Trade Forum
Iron Age
Jewelers Circular Keystone
Jobber Topics
J. of Accountancy
J. of American Real Estate & Urban
  Economics
J. of Corporate Taxation
J. of Commerce
J. of Developing Areas
J. of Occupational Medicine
J. of Occupational Psychology
J. of Pension Planning and Compliance

J. of Products Liability
J. of Property Management
J. of Purchasing & Materials Management
J. of Small Business Management
J. of Systems Management
J. of Taxation
J. of Urban Economics
J. of World Trade Law
Kilobaud Microcomputing (name changed
  to Microcomputing)[1]
Labor Law Journal
Labor Today
Land Economics
Lawn & Garden Marketing
Library Journal
Lodging Hospitality
Los Angeles Times (Business Section and
  selected articles)
Machine Design
Management Today
Marine Fisheries Review
Marketing & Media Decisions
Mass Transit
Medical Economics
Medical Laboratory Observer
Medical News
Meetings & Conventions
Merchandising
Mergers and Acquisitions
Microcomputing (formerly Kilobaud
  Microcomputing)[1]
Mini-Micro Systems
Mobile-Manufactured Home Merchandiser
Modern Floor Coverings
Modern Machine Shop
Modern Materials Handling
Modern Office Procedures
Modern Plastics
Modern Power Systems
Modern Tire Dealer
Money
Monthly Labor Review
Monthly Review
Mortgage Banking
Motor Age
Motor Ship
Motorcycle Dealer News
Nation's Business
Nation's Cities Weekly
Nation's Restaurant News
National Fisherman
National Institute Economic Review
National Petroleum News
National Real Estate Investor
National Tax Journal
National Underwriter—Life & Health
  Edition

National Underwriter—Property & Casualty
    Edition
New York Times (Business Section and
    selected articles)
Newsweek (Business Section and selected
    articles)
Nursing
Nursing Homes
Occupational Outlook
OECD Observer
Oil & Gas Journal
Oil Daily
Online
Overdrive
Package Engineering
Packaging Digest
Paper Trade Journal
Paperboard Packaging
Patient Care
Personnel Administrator
Petroleum Economist
Pets-Supplies-Marketing
Photographic Society of America Bulletin
    (also known as PSA Journal)
Physician & Sports Medicine
Pipeline & Gas Journal
Pit & Quarry
Plant Engineering
Plastics World
Platt's Oilgram
Playthings
Power
PR Newswire[2] (records include full text)
Processed Prepared Foods (incorporating
    Food Development)
Production Engineering
Product Marketing
Professional Builder
Progressive Architecture
Progressive Grocer
PSA Journal (also known as Photographic
    Society of America Bulletin)
Public Administration Review
Public Utilities Fortnightly
Public Works
Publishers Weekly
Pulp & Paper
Purchasing
Quick Frozen Foods
Quick Frozen Foods International
Railway Age
Real Estate Appraiser & Analyst
Real Estate Today
Restaurant Business Magazine
Restaurant Design
Restaurant Hospitality
Restaurants & Institutions (ceased
    publication)

Retailing Home Furnishings
Review of Black Political Economy
Review of Economics and Statistics
Review of Taxation of Individuals
RN
Rubber World
Sales & Marketing Management
Savings & Loan News
School Arts
School Library Journal
School Product News
Securities Regulation Law Journal
Service World International (name
    changed to Hotels & Restaurants
    International)
Shooting Industry
Site Selection Handbook
Skiing Trade Monthly News
Soap-Cosmetics-Chemical Specialties
Social Security Bulletin
Solar Age
Special Libraries
Stores Magazine
Successful Farming
Super Service Station
Supermarket Business
Supermarket News
Survey of Current Business
Tax Advisor
Tax Notes
Taxes
Telecommunications
Telephone
Telephone Engineer & Management
Television Digest
Textile Industries
Textile World
Time (Business Section and selected
    articles)
Today's Education
Tooling & Production
Travel Weekly
Trusts and Estates
Uniform Commercial Code Law Journal
U.S. Tobacco Journal
U.S. News & World Report (Business
    Section and selected articles)
Variety
Vending Times
Wall Street Journal
Ward's Auto World
Washington Post (Business Section and
    selected articles)
Womens Wear Daily
Wood & Wood Products
Woodworking & Furniture Digest
World Mining
World Oil

Profile

Database: Trade and Industry Index
Producer: Information Access Corporation, 404 Sixth Ave., Menlo Park, California 94025, 415-367-7171
Toll-Free Telephone: 800-227-8431
Vendor: DIALOG.
Cost: $85 per hour. Offline prints 20¢ per record. Database will be added to DIALOG's Knowledge Index.
Date Began Online: January 1981
Source of Information: Comprehensive indexing and selective abstracting of 340 core trade journals and business journals. Selective indexing of articles from other Information Access databases: National Newspaper Index, Legal Resource Index, Magazine Index. Also full text of PR Newswire. Information from January 1981 on.
Type of Coverage: Bibliographic with selective abstracting, except for PR Newswire, which is full text.
Size: 425,000 records as of July 1983.
Updating: 16,000 records per month are added with daily updates on NEWSEARCH. Current to within a week to ten days of receipt.
Indexing Terms: Library of Congress subject headings and SIC codes.
User Aids: *Access to Access*, user's guide for all Information Access databases, $24. *Subject Guide* to IAC databases, $45. *IAC News*, monthly newsletter, free.
Printed Equivalent: None.
Document Retrieval: Not offered.

PTS F&S Indexes

Predicasts, Inc., produces a range of databases (it refers to them collectively as Predicasts Terminal System or PTS), two of which fall within our broad-coverage business information category—F&S Indexes and PROMT. The first, F&S Indexes, is more thorough than the others that we consider in this chapter in its coverage of news about individual companies. F&S takes care to include even minor news articles announcing corporate expansions, acquisitions, or new products. Among U.S. databases, F&S Indexes has the strongest coverage of foreign company and product news. The name F&S comes from the *Funk & Scott Indexes*, a set of books that Predicasts has published for many years. The database claims to carry references to general business and management topics, but the coverage here is spotty compared to ABI/INFORM and Management Contents.

F&S draws on 1,200 business publications around the world—many in foreign languages—as well as news releases, annual reports, government documents, etc. The database contains all the information from *PTS F&S Index of Corporate Change*, *PTS F&S Index International*, and *PTS F&S Index Europe*.

Records in F&S Indexes have only one- or two-sentence abstracts (omitting article titles entirely), and the company chooses articles selectively rather than indexing periodicals cover to cover. The Predicasts databases use several controlled vocabularies. One is a unique list of several hundred "event codes." If you seek news on acquisitions and mergers in an industry, for example, Predicasts gives you this set of index terms to specify exactly what kind of news you need:

acquirer seeks
acquirer seeks assets
acquirer buys assets
acquirer completes purchase
acquisition off (acquirer)
acquires minority interest
acquisition sought
divestiture
subsidiary sold
asset spin-off
assets (partial) to be sold
assets (partial) sold
acquired—completes sale
acquisition off (acquired)
minority interest sold

In addition to the event codes, Predicasts databases also index all articles by SIC codes.

Sample record

PROBLEM: I want some ideas on merchandising strategies used by successful sporting goods shops.

(1)   Mens Wear 83/02/21 P48 SRCE:003630   (1usa)
(2)   Abercrombie & Fitch Sporting goods merchandising strategy discussed
(3)   1usa United States   5941000 Sporting Goods, Bicycle Stores   240
       Marketing Procedures

Notes: (1) journal, date, page, code (2) brief abstract (3) country code and name, product code and name, event code and name

Profile

Database: PTS F&S Indexes
Producer: Predicasts, Inc., 200 University Circle Research Center, 11001 Cedar Ave., Cleveland, Ohio 44106, 216-795-3000
Toll-Free Telephone: 800-321-6388
Vendor: DIALOG, BRS, Data-Star.
Cost: Approximately $95 per connect hour, plus 20¢ per online print, 25¢ per offline print.
Date Began Online: 1972
Source of Information: 2,500 publications from around the world including business magazines, trade journals, management science publications, company news releases, and government reports. Coverage is selective and concentrates on corporate activities, technological developments, market data and trends, international economics, and sociopolitical events.
Type of Coverage: Bibliographic, with one- or two-line descriptions. Information is added within two to four weeks of publication.

Size: More than 2 million records as of January 1983.

Updating: Monthly, approximately 250,000 added per year.

Indexing Terms: Country codes, SIC-based product codes, event codes, company name, journal name.

User Aids: PTS User's Manual, $25, contains description of databases and all retrieval codes. *The Predicasts Company Thesaurus*, $225, contains 100,000 company names, cross-indexed for subsidiaries and joint ventures, organized by country and SIC-based product codes. *The PTS Online News*, free newsletter.

Printed Equivalent: F&S United States, monthly, cumulative quarterly, cumulative annually, $600 (with weekly supplements, $710). *F&S Europe*, monthly, cumulative quarterly, cumulative annually, $600. *F&S International*, monthly, cumulative quarterly, cumulative annually, $600.

Document Retrieval: $8.50 by mail, $10 by phone or Dialorder. Shipped within 48 hours of receipt of order.

Other Services: Predicasts prepares custom market reports based on Predicasts databases for $375. The company also has a market research arm that prepares studies that the company sells. These are listed in FIND/SVP Reports and Studies Index.

PTS PROMT

Predicasts' other broad-coverage business database is PROMT, which stands for Predicasts Overviews of Marketing and Technology. Like F&S Indexes, its emphasis is on marketing and product-related information rather than general information about management.

Everything cited in PROMT also appears in F&S Indexes. The difference is that rather than a sentence or two of description, PROMT contains lengthy abstracts taken from only about 500 periodicals plus selected other sources. The abstracts are generally long and informative, second in quality only to ABI/INFORM.

Thus, PROMT is a smaller database than F&S Indexes. It cites primarily the more important items, giving a much more thorough reference than F&S.

Sample record

PROBLEM: I'd like some information on the new cable sports networks. Who are the largest investors? Who's selling ad time on them?

(1)   Ad Age 83/06/27   P1,82

(2)   Anheuser-Busch will feed programming into a cable sports network it will launch within the next 2 yrs. In its first step toward this goal, the brewer has entered into a partnership with Katz Sports on the worldwide broadcast and cable rights to the Big 8 college basketball games. The A-B deal would give the brewery exclusive beer sponsorship of the Big 8 games, comprised of colleges from 6 midwestern states. Other advertisers would buy additional ad time from A-B through Katz Sports, although it is not expected that other breweries will have access to the games. A-B will use the Big 8 games to fill part of the programming schedule of a cable network to be assembled by L Albus, former commissioner of the Metro college sports conference and A-B's dir of sports programming. The move of A-B to become a sports syndicator is the latest escalation of what one source called 'the mano a mano strategies of the breweries to lay claim to exclusive turfs.'

(3) *1USA *United States *4834000 *Cable Television Systems *361
    *services R&D
(4) 1USA United States 7816000 Services for Movie, TV Production 148
    parents-jt venture Anheuser-Busch
    1USA United States 7816000 Services for Movie, TV Production 148
    parents-jt venture Katz Sports

Notes: (1) source (2) abstract (3) indexing codes and terms (asterisk indicates major category) (4) other indexing codes and terms

Profile

Database: PTS PROMT

Producer: Predicasts, Inc., 200 University Circle Research Center, 11001 Cedar Ave., Cleveland, Ohio 44106, 216-795-3000

Toll-Free Telephone: 800-321-6388

Vendor: DIALOG, BRS, Data-Star.

Cost: Roughly $95 per connect hour, plus 35¢ per online print, 40¢ per offline print.

Date Began Online: 1972

Source of Information: 1,000 publications from around the world including trade journals, general business periodicals, management science publications, company news releases, and government reports. Coverage is selective and concentrates on corporate activities, technological developments, market data and trends, and management science articles.

Type of Coverage: Bibliographic with abstracts (150-word average with 500-word maximum). Information is added within two to four weeks of publication.

Size: 600,000 records as of January 1983.

Updating: Monthly, approximately 120,000 added per year.

Indexing Terms: Country codes, SIC-based products codes, event codes, company name, journal name.

User Aids: *PTS User's Manual*, $25, contains description of databases and all retrieval codes. *The Predicasts Company Thesaurus*, $225, contains 100,000 company names, cross-indexed for subsidiaries and joint ventures, organized by country and SIC-based product codes. *The PTS Online News*, free newsletter.

Printed Equivalent: *PROMT*, monthly, $800 per year.

Document Retrieval: $8.50 by mail, $10 by phone or Dialorder. Shipped within 48 hours of receipt of order.

Other Services: Predicasts prepares custom market reports based on Predicasts databases for $375. The company also has a market research arm that prepares studies that the company sells. These are listed in FIND/SVP Reports and Studies Index.

HARFAX Industry Data Sources

Harper & Row's HARFAX Industry Data Sources has a much narrower focus than the previous databases. It lists sources containing "hard," numeric data on industries. HARFAX covers 2,100 business and trade journals very selectively; only the most significant articles containing extensive data are included. It also draws heavily on trade association reports, industry studies by brokerage firms, government publications, and the like.

HARFAX's abstracts do not give the numerical data itself; rather, they just inform the user as to what figures or kind of information the source document contains. The controlled vocabulary relies primarily on SIC codes. HARFAX is a relatively new database and aims to achieve worldwide coverage by the end of 1984.

(Another source for industry numeric data is Predicasts' databases PTS Forecasts and PTS Annual Time Series. Since these actually contain the numeric data itself, the databases are discussed in Chapter 16 on marketing research and advertising.)

Sample record

PROBLEM: Is there a forecast of consumption of major molded plastics?

(1) CN = 82-021664
(2) Polystryrene Clearly Rules Transparent Grades.
(3) Plastics World
(4) July 1982   pg.14-15
PUBLISHER: Cahners Publishing Company 221 Columbus Ave. Boston MA 02116 United States of America
TELEPHONE: (617) 536-7780
DOCUMENT TYPE: Journal Article (jnal)
RECORD STATUS: Primary Source
LANGUAGE: English
GEOGRAPHIC COVERAGE: United States of America (usa)
(5) Reviews a study by Business Communications Co. on the market dominance of PS in transparent molded plastics sector. Table gives consumption (1981, 1986) and average annual growth (1981-1986) of PS, acrylic, polycarbonate, butadiene styrene, cellulosics, ABS, PVC, SAN, and others.
(6) DATA DESCRIPTORS: Consumption, 1981-1986; Forecasts, 1981-1986; Market Analysis; Average Annual Production Growth, 1981-1986
SIC CODES: 2821, Plastics materials and resins
INDUSTRY DESCRIPTORS: Plastics

Notes: (1) control number (2) title (3) journal (4) date and page (5) abstract (6) indexing terms

Profile

Database: HARFAX Industry Data Sources
Producer: Harfax Database Publishing, 54 Church St., Cambridge, Massachusetts 02138, 617-492-0670
Toll-Free Telephone: None.
Vendor: BRS, DIALOG, NEXIS, Data-Star (Europe).
Cost: Approximately $75 per hour. Offline printing charges are 20¢ to 30¢ per record.
Date Began Online: March 1981
Source of Information: 2,100 business and trade journals as well as industry studies, government publications, etc. Only items containing numeric data are selected. Information covers 1979 to present and country coverage varies by year. United States and Canada start 1979, Western Europe 1981, Asia and South America 1979. Worldwide coverage scheduled for 1984.

Type of Coverage: Bibliographic with a detailed abstract. There is approximately a three- to six-month delay between publication time and appearance in database.
Size: 52,000 records in October 1983.
Updating: Monthly with 2,400 added per update.
Indexing Terms: SIC codes plus geographic terms, statistical data descriptors, industry terms, document-type descriptors, language terms.
User Aids: *Industry Data Sources Database User Guide and Thesaurus*, $50.
Printed Equivalent: *Harfax Directory of Industry Data Sources, U.S. and Canada* (3 volumes), $225. *Harfax Directory of Industry Data Sources, Western Europe*, $125. *Harfax Guide to the Energy Industries*, $60. *Harfax Guide to the High-Technology Industries*, $65. *Harfax Guide to Industry Special Issues*, $65.
Document Retrieval: Not offered.
Other Services: Harfax performs custom searches; cost is approximately $60 per hour including online time and telecommunications.

NEXIS

Mead Data Central's NEXIS is both a database and a family of databases. The original NEXIS service, the part of its services that concerns us here, is the first full-text database we discuss in this chapter.

NEXIS contains the full texts of about 100 newspapers, newsletters, and journals. They are mostly, though not all, business-related. Though this represents a much smaller set of sources than the databases described previously in this chapter, the fact that the information is full text makes NEXIS one of the largest online databases as measured by the number of words.

[In 1982, Mead Data Central took over distribution of all the New York Times Information Service's databases and began marketing them also under the NEXIS label. The two main databases produced by the New York Times Co.—both bibliographic, not full text—are the Information Bank (Infobank) and Advertising and Marketing Intelligence. The former is described in Chapter 14 and the latter in Chapter 16.]

The full-text NEXIS delivers an eclectic group of business publications. To carry the full text of a copyrighted publication requires a publisher's permission; NEXIS is limited to those publications that agree to be included. (Producers of reference databases, on the other hand, generally index and summarize any article without regard to copyright laws.) The entire list of NEXIS's periodicals is given following this discussion.

NEXIS's full-text character, however, is very attractive to some users. One advantage, of course, is the convenience of finding an entire article online—rather than having to go to a library to find something cited in a reference database or waiting for a document retrieval firm to deliver a photocopy of it. Printing full-text records can be expensive at NEXIS's connect-time rate, but document retrieval services and trips to the library can be even more costly.

There are no controlled vocabulary terms in NEXIS. In a reference database that could be a fatal limitation. But with a full-text database, a searcher has a good chance of locating relevant records by a free-text search. In addition, a full-text database enables the user to catch information that the abstractor missed. A typical NEXIS printout is reproduced in Chapter 5.

NEXIS source list

Typically, materials published daily are available the following day; materials published weekly are available one week after publication; materials published monthly are available three weeks after publication. Wire services are available 12 to 48 hours after they are carried over the wire. The date of availability depends on the agreement with each publication and wire service.

NEWSPAPERS

American Banker (Beginning on January 2, 1979)

BBC Summary of World Broadcasts and Monitoring Report (Beginning on January 1, 1979)

The Bond Buyer (Beginning in January 1981)

The Christian Science Monitor (Beginning on January 2, 1980)

ComputerWorld and ComputerWorld Extra (Beginning in January 1982)

Facts on File World News Digest (Beginning in January 1975)

Harfax Database of Industry Data Sources (Current Version)

The Japan Economic Journal (Beginning in June 1980)

Legal Times (Beginning in January 1982)

Manchester Guardian Weekly (Beginning in January 1981)

The New York Times (Beginning in June 1980)

The Washington Post (Beginning on January 1, 1977)

MAGAZINES

ABA Banking Journal (Beginning in January 1980)

Aviation Week & Space Technology (Beginning in January 1975)

Business Week (Beginning in January 1975)

Byte (Beginning in January 1982)

Chemical Engineering (Beginning in January 1981)

Chemical Week (Beginning in January 1975)

Coal Age (Beginning in January 1981)

Congressional Quarterly Weekly Report and Editorial Research Reports (Beginning in January 1975)

Data Communications (Beginning in January 1982)

Defense and Foreign Affairs (Beginning in January 1981)

Dun's Business Month (Dun's Review) (Beginning in January 1975)

The Economist (Beginning in January 1975)

Electronics (Beginning in January 1981)

Engineering and Mining Journal (Beginning in January 1981)

Engineering News-Record (Beginning in January 1981)

High Technology (Beginning in June 1981)

Inc. (Beginning in June 1981)

Industry Week (Beginning in January 1981)

Issues in Bank Regulation (Beginning in Winter 1981)

J. of Bank Research (Beginning in Winter 1981)

Mining Annual Review (Beginning in June 1981)

Mining Journal (Beginning in January 1981)

Mining Magazine (Beginning in January 1981)

National Journal (Beginning in January 1977)

Newsweek (Beginning in January 1975)

Offshore (Beginning in January 1981)

Oil & Gas Journal (Beginning in January 1978)

The Magazine of Bank Administration (Beginning in January 1981)

U.S. News & World Report (Beginning in January 1975)

WIRE SERVICES

The Associated Press world, national and business wires (Beginning on January 1, 1977)

Jiji Press Ticker Service (Beginning on January 4, 1980)

Kyodo English Language News Service (Beginning on December 1, 1980)

PR Newswire (Beginning on January 22, 1980)

Reuters North European News Service (Beginning on December 1, 1981)

Reuters General News Report (Beginning on April 15, 1979)

United Press International world, national, business and sports wires (Beginning on September 26, 1980)

United Press International states wires (Beginning on November 1, 1980)

Xinhua (New China) News Agency (Beginning on January 1, 1977)

NEWSLETTERS

Advertising Compliance Service (Beginning in September 1981)

Banking Expansion Reporter (Beginning in January 1982)

Coal Outlook (Beginning in January 1975)

Coal Week (Beginning on January 1, 1981)

Defense & Foreign Affairs Daily (Beginning on January 1, 1981)

Defense & Foreign Affairs Weekly (Beginning in December 1981)

The Dorvillier News Letter (Beginning in January 1981)

East Asian Executive Reports (Beginning in September 1979)

Economic Week (Beginning on January 1, 1981)

Electric Utility Week (Beginning on January 1, 1981)

Enhanced Recovery Week (Beginning on August 1980)

Inside Energy/with Federal Lands (Beginning on January 5, 1981)

Inside FERC (Beginning on January 1, 1981)

Latin America Commodities Report (Beginning on December 3, 1976)

Latin America Regional Reports (Beginning in November, 1979)

Latin America Weekly Report (Beginning on October 12, 1979)

Metals Week (Beginning on January 1, 1981)

Middle East Executive Reports (Beginning in September 1978)

The Morgan Guaranty Survey (Beginning in January 1982)

Nuclear Fuel (Beginning on January 1, 1981)

Nucleonics Week (Beginning in January 1981)

Platt's Oilgram News (Beginning in January 1981)

The RayLux Financial Service Newsletter (Beginning in September 1981)

Securities Week (Beginning in January 1981)

Synfuels Week (Beginning in August 1979)

Update/The American States (Beginning in January 1981)

World Financial Markets (Beginning in January 1982)

TO BE ADDED

Financial Times (Beginning in January 1982)

Forbes (Beginning in January 1975)

Legal Times of Washington (Beginning in January 1981)

McGraw-Hill Newsletters (Beginning in January 1981):
    Coal Week International
    Inside NRC
    McGraw-Hill's Biotechnology Newswatch
    Platt's Energy Litigation Report
    Platt's Oil Policy Letter
    Synfuels

Washington Quarterly (Beginning in January 1982)

Wharton News Perspectives (Beginning in January 1983)

GOVERNMENT DOCUMENTS

The Federal Register (Beginning in July 1980)

The Code of Federal Regulations

Federal Reserve Bulletin (Beginning in January 1980)

Profile

Database: NEXIS

Producer: Mead Data Central, 9333 Springboro Pike, Dayton, Ohio 45401, 513-865-6800

Toll-Free Telephone: 800-227-9597

Vendor: Mead Data Central.

Cost: $90 per hour, base rate, or as low as $30 per hour, depending on amount of usage, plus 45¢ for each 25,000 times a search term appears in the database.

Date Began Online: 1980

Source of Information: Approximately 100 periodicals, newspapers, newsletters, and other publications.

Type of Coverage: Full text.

Size: Information not available at time of publication.

Updating: Typically, materials published daily are available the following day; materials published weekly are available one week after publication; materials published

monthly are available three weeks after publication; wire services are available l2 to 48 hours after they are carried over the wire.
Indexing Terms: None used.
User Aids: Information not available at time of publication.
Printed Equivalent: Corresponds to the full text of each publication carried.
Document Retrieval: Not offered.

Dow Jones News

The Dow Jones News database is easy to describe. It contains only the full text (back to June 1979) of *The Wall Street Journal*, *Barron's*, and the Dow Jones News Service (a news wire). Thus, compared to some of the databases described above, it constitutes a somewhat limited information source. (Don't confuse the Dow Jones News database with Dow Jones News/Retrieval. The latter is a database *vendor*; it encompasses both this database and a number of others. Dow Jones News/Retrieval is discussed in Chapter 24.)

The Wall Street Journal and *Barron's*, of course, are indexed and abstracted in number of databases, including the Predicasts group and the Trade and Industry Index. But for the full-text, cover-to-cover *Journal* and *Barron's*, Dow Jones News is the only source.

The Dow Jones News controlled vocabulary consists of a very small list of industry and news categories—only a couple of hundred general terms—as well as stock ticker symbols. The previous observations regarding NEXIS apply here: a free-text search on this database can make for very effective information retrieval.

An important technical note: when signing onto Dow Jones News, keep in mind the difference between the commands &FTS and //DJNEWS. The former lets you use free-text search on the entire database. This service is called Dow Jones News Free Text Search. The latter limits you to the most recent 90 days and allows you to search only by stock and bond ticker symbols or by one of the few dozen news category terms.

Sample record

PROBLEM: I manage the warehouse for a growing consumer electronics firm. Have there been attempts to unionize workers in other young companies in this field?

(1) 080303-1046
(2) ONTARIO COURT RULES TANDY CORP. MUST BARGAIN WITH STEELWORKERS
(3) 03/03/80
     WALL STREET JOURNAL (J)
(4) TAN   LABOR
(5)   RS
(6)   TANDY CORP. LOST AN APPEAL BEFORE THE ONTARIO SUPREME COURT IN ITS PROTRACTED BATTLE IN CANADA WITH THE UNITED STEELWORKERS.
     THE APPEAL WAS OF AN ONTARIO LABOR RELATIONS BOARD RULING THAT CONDEMNED THE COMPANY FOR ITS "PERSISTENT AND FLAGRANT UNFAIR LA-

BOR PRACTICES" AND ORDERED TANDY TO CONCLUDE A COLLECTIVE BARGAIN-
ING AGREEMENT WITH THE STEELWORKERS.

IF THE STEELWORKERS NEGOTIATE AN AGREEMENT WITH TANDY, IT WILL BE
THE FIRST UNION TO DO SO IN THE U.S. OR CANADA, UNION AND COMPANY OFFI-
CIALS SAID.

THE DISPUTE, WHICH HAS BEEN BITTER AND OCCASIONALLY VIOLENT, CON-
CERNS 200 EMPLOYES AT THE CANADIAN WAREHOUSE OF RADIO SHACK, A MAN-
UFACTURER AND MERCHANDISER OF CONSUMER ELECTRONICS THAT IS
CONTROLLED BY TANDY.

THE STEELWORKERS, WHO HAVE BEEN RECOGNIZED AS BARGAINING AGENT
FOR THE WAREHOUSE, CALLED A STRIKE LAST AUGUST AT THE FACILITY WHICH IS
AT BARRIE IN SOUTHERN ONTARIO. THE STRIKE WAS SET AFTER CONTRACT NE-
GOTIATIONS BECAME DEADLOCKED OVER A UNION DEMAND FOR MANDATORY
DEDUCTION OF UNION DUES FROM ALL EMPLOYE PAYCHECKS.

Notes: (1) accession number (2) headline (3) date of article (4) company code, industry category (5) company code (6) text of story

Profile

Database: Dow Jones News
Producer: Dow Jones & Co., Inc., P.O. Box 300, Princeton, New Jersey 08540, 609-
452-2000
Toll-Free Telephone: 800-257-5114
Vendor: Dow Jones News/Retrieval.
Cost: $72 per hour prime and $36 per hour nonprime.
Date Began Online: March 1981
Source of Information: Dow Jones News Service, *The Wall Street Journal*, and *Bar-
ron's*. All stories are added within five days of publication and go back to June 1979.
Type of Coverage: Full text.
Size: More than 200,000 articles.
Updating: Daily.
Indexing Terms: Approximately 50 subject codes, 55 industry codes, and company
codes.
User Aids: *Dow Jones News/Retrieval Fact Finder*, $10; *An Introduction to Free-Text
Search of Dow Jones News Database*, free.
Printed Equivalent: *The Wall Street Journal* and *Barron's*.
Document Retrieval: Not offered.

HBR/Online

John Wiley & Sons, Inc.'s HBR/Online, like Dow Jones News, is a full-text
database. Its sole content is the text of the *Harvard Business Review* dating
from 1976, with abstracts alone for a number of years earlier. Like Dow Jones
News, we consider HBR/Online a very narrow information source compared
to other databases discussed in this chapter.

And like *The Wall Street Journal*, the magazine *Harvard Business Review*
is well indexed and abstracted elsewhere, notably in ABI/INFORM and Management Contents, among other databases. Thus a search of HBR/Online
may be superfluous to some users.

But Wiley has gone to considerable effort to make this one of the most versatile business databases on the market. Unlike NEXIS and Dow Jones News, HBR/Online contains abstracts of each magazine article right along with the full text, as well as five sets of controlled vocabulary terms: subject, geographic, company, industry, and product/brand name. If *Harvard Business Review* has something to say on your topic, you're quite certain to locate the article. To some people, of course, the presence of full text is very attractive for convenience reasons.

At present, then, this database is an anomaly. Next to other databases that carry hundreds or even thousands of journals, this full-text database of one magazine has limited scope. In the future, however, we expect more and more databases to parallel the type of full coverage of HBR/Online. Eventually, this kind of database may be the norm, not the exception.

Sample record

PROBLEM: I'd like to take a look at some recent views by consultants on competitive strategy at the global level.

(1) 825040
(2) How Global Companies Win Out
(3) Hout, Thomas - Boston Consulting Group ; Porter, Michael E. - Harvard Univ. Graduate School of Business Administration ; Rudden, Eileen - Boston Consulting Group
HARVARD BUSINESS REVIEW, Sep/Oct 1982, p. 98
DOCUMENT TYPE: HBR Article
CORPORATE FUNCTIONS: Marketing management; Product management; International management; International marketing.

ABSTRACT:
Some manufacturers hold and even increase profitability against international competitors because they change from a multidomestic strategy, which allows individual subsidiaries to compete independently in different domestic markets, to a global one, which pits a company's entire worldwide system of product and market position against the competition. Before forging a global strategy, a company that recognizes its business as potentially global should consider the following: what kind of strategic innovation might trigger global competition, what is the best position among all competitors to establish to defend the advantages of global strategy, and what kind of long-term resources will be required to establish the leading position.

The examples of three companies (Caterpillar, L.M. Ericsson, and Honda) that successfully forged global strategies illustrate how companies can change the rules of international competition to their favor.

Global competition forces top management to change the way it thinks about and operates its businesses, and in some cases global strategy requires unconventional actions. The successful global competitor manages its business in various countries as a single system, not a portfolio of independent positions, and focuses on its ability to leverage positions in one country's market against those in other markets. No one organizational structure applies to all of a company's international businesses, and organizational reporting lines and structures should change as the nature of the international business changes. Adherence to conventional financial management and practices may constrain a good competitive response. A global strategy goes against the traditional tests for capital allocation, and debt and dividend policies should vary with the requirement of the integrated investment program of the whole company.

GRAPHS AND EXHIBITS:
Financial comparison of Caterpillar and Komatsu.
Ericsson's technology lever: reduction of software cost through modular design.
The effect of volume on manufacturing approaches in motorcycle production.
Honda Motor Company's financial policy from 1954 to 1980.

SUBJECT DESCRIPTORS: *International marketing; *Product management; *Corporate strategy; *Marketing strategies; *Competition.
GEOGRAPHIC DESCRIPTORS: *International;
COMPANY/ORGANIZATION DESCRIPTORS: *Caterpillar Tractor; *Ericsson (L.M.) Telephone (Sweden); *Honda Motor (Japan); Kawasaki Heavy Industries (Japan); BSR (United Kingdom); Garrand Engineering Ltd. (United Kingdom); Sears Roebuck; Texas Instruments; IBM; Matsushita Electric Industrial (Japan); Hattori (K.) Co. Ltd. (Japan); Michelin (France); Ford Motor; Toyota Motor (Japan); Komatsu (Japan); Zenith Radio; Hewlett-Packard (United Kingdom); Tektronix; Dow Chemical; Du Pont; Mitsubishi Motor; Harley-Davidson; BMW (West Germany); BSA (United Kingdom); Yamaha Motor (Japan); Navy.
INDUSTRY DESCRIPTORS: Machinery industry; Motor vehicles industry; Electrical and electronic industries; Chemicals industry; Pharmaceuticals industry; Aerospace industry.
PRODUCT/BRAND NAME DESCRIPTORS: *Construction machinery; *Telephone systems; *Sodertalje; *Abo; *Motorcycles; Optical instruments; Electrical equipment; Communications equipment;

CITED REFERENCES:
Counter-Competition Abroad to Protect Home Markets, Watson, Craig M., Harvard Business Review, 1982/Jan, p. 40.
A Framework for Swedish Industrial Policy, Boston Consulting Group, Stockholm: Uberforlag, 1978.
Strategy Alternatives for the British Motorcycle Industry, Boston Consulting Group, British Secretary of State for Industry, 1975/Jul/30.
Competitive Strategy: Techniques for Analyzing Industries and Competitors, Porter, Michael E., Free Press, 1980.

(full text follows)

Notes: (1) control number (2) title (3) author and affiliations

Profile

Database: HBR/Online
Producer: John Wiley & Sons, Inc., Electronic Publishing, 605 Third Ave., New York, New York 10158, 212-850-6178
Toll-Free Telephone: None.
Vendor: DIALOG, BRS, Data-Star, may be added to NEXIS.
Cost: $75 per hour plus 10¢ per citation for offline prints.
Date Began Online: 1983
Source of Information: Harvard Business Review from 1971 to date, with some earlier coverage.
Type of Coverage: Full text plus abstracts since 1976; abstracts since 1971; elective coverage before 1971.
Size: 2,000 records in August 1983.
Updating: Bimonthly, concurrent with publication of *Harvard Business Review*.

Indexing Terms: Subject terms, company names, industries, geographical terms, product/brand names.
User Aids: *HBR Online Thesaurus*, $50. *Wiley Search Update*, free newsletter.
Printed Equivalent: *Harvard Business Review*.
Document Retrieval: Available from *Harvard Business Review*.

14 General News Databases

Business managers may need to stay abreast of many diverse subjects, for example, political issues, social controversies, international affairs, popular culture, sports, music, television shows, health news. The possible topics are endless. If you manage a chain of grocery stores, you may want to keep track of recipes and diet advice that appear in the popular press. If you employ single mothers, you may want to review what the nation's popular magazines have to say about this group's unique needs and problems in the work force. If you want to participate in a local political debate about condominium conversion legislation, you may want to review similar contests that have occurred throughout the country.

General news databases can help bring you up to date on these topics and countless others quickly, thoroughly, and inexpensively. They afford you a very easy way to find almost any information that has appeared in popular American magazines and major newspapers. The general news databases we consider in this chapter are Infobank, The New York Times, Magazine Index, National Newspaper Index, NEWSEARCH, NDEX, Info Globe, and TEXTLINE.

Infobank

Infobank is a good source for national and international news. It indexes and abstracts 10 major U.S. newspapers, 7 international affairs journals, 4 science magazines, 20 business news magazines, and 15 news and public affairs magazines.

The database is large—more than 2 million records—and coverage extends as far back as 1969 for some of the publications. Articles are chosen from each magazine or newspaper selectively; thus the database lists primarily the longer, more substantive articles in these publications and omits items of lesser importance. A controlled vocabulary of about 5,000 terms aids searching.

One businessman wanted to leave his skull to the Royal Shakespeare Theatre. He wondered if there was any precedent for doing that; a search of Infobank turned up five stories about people who willed their skulls to theaters.

Sample record

PROBLEM: I'm interested in reading about Greyhound Corp.'s corporate strategy. What are its prospects in 1984?

SOURCE: BUSINESS WEEK (BW)

DATE: July 25, 1983, Monday

SECTION: Page 88, Column 1

ABSTRACT:
Article on financial prospects for Greyhound Corp in wake of its decision to sell its subsidiary Armour Food Co to ConAgra Inc. Although Greyhound's revenues will drop from $5 billion in 1982 to $3 billion in 1984, sale gives chairman John W Teets a chance to put company into better shape than it has been in for years. Armour contributed just $13 million of company's net income of $103 million in 1982. Graphs. Photo (L).

GRAPHIC: Illustrations: Combination

SUBJECT: COMPANY AND ORGANIZATION PROFILES; MERGERS, ACQUISITIONS AND DIVESTITURES

ORGANIZATION: CONAGRA INC; GREYHOUND CORP; ARMOUR FOOD CO

NAME: TEETS, JOHN W

Publications selectively abstracted for Infobank

GENERAL CIRCULATION NEWSPAPERS
Atlanta Constitution
Chicago Tribune
Christian Science Monitor
Houston Chronicle
Los Angeles Times
Miami Herald
The New York Times
San Francisco Chronicle
The Seattle Times
Washington Post

BUSINESS PUBLICATIONS
Advertising Age
American Banker
Automotive News
Aviation Week and Space Technology
Barron's
Business Week

Dun's Business Month
Editor and Publisher
Financial Times (Canada)
Financial Times (London)
Forbes
Fortune
Harvard Business Review
Japan Economic Journal
Journal of Commerce
Oil and Gas Journal
Oil Daily
Platt's Oilgram
Wall Street Journal
Women's Wear Daily

INTERNATIONAL AFFAIRS
Economist of London
Far Eastern Economic Review
Foreign Affairs

Foreign Policy
Latin American Weekly
Middle East
World Press Review

SCIENCE PUBLICATIONS
Astronautics
Industrial Research
Science
Scientific American

OTHER PERIODICALS
Atlantic
California Journal

Consumer Reports
Current Biography
Current News
National Journal
National Review
New Yorker
Newsweek
Saturday Review
Sports Illustrated
Time
U.S. News & World Report
Variety
Washington Monthly

Profile

Database: Infobank (The Information Bank)
Producer: The New York Times Co., Indexing Services, 229 West 43rd St., New York, New York 10036
For information call Mead Data Central.
Toll-Free Telephone: Mead Data Central: 800-227-4908
Vendor: Mead Data Central (NEXIS).
Cost: $90 per hour, base rate, or as low as $30 per hour depending on use, plus 45¢ for each 25,000 times a search term appears in database.
Date Began Online: 1975
Source of Information: 60 newspapers, magazines, scientific and financial periodicals. Covers *The New York Times* from 1969 to the present. Other coverage varies by publication.
Type of Coverage: Bibliographic, with abstracts. Lag of 24 hours for *The New York Times*, with others on a priority schedule.
Size: More than 2 million records.
Updating: Updates daily, with 15,000 records added per month.
Indexing Terms: 5,000 subject terms, along with personal, organization, and geographic names. Also includes names of foods, drugs, animals, chemicals, books, movies, and play titles.
User Aids: *Infobank Thesaurus and Directory*, free.
Printed Equivalent: None.
Document Retrieval: Not offered.

The New York Times

This database is just what its name says: the full text of *The New York Times*. It is a companion database to Infobank (also produced by the New York Times Co.) and uses the same controlled vocabulary.

The database contains all articles, features, columns, editorials, and letters from the final Late Edition of the weekday, Saturday, and voluminous Sunday editions of *The New York Times*, back to June 1, 1980. That's the full text—not abstracts! Each new edition is online within 48 hours of publication; controlled vocabulary terms are added within about a week.

Profile

Database: The New York Times
Producer: The New York Times Co., 229 West 43rd St., New York, New York 10036
For information call Mead Data Central.
Toll-Free Telephone: Mead Data Central: 800-227-4908
Vendor: Mead Data Central (NEXIS).
Cost: $90 per hour base rate, or as low as $30 per hour for high-volume use, plus 45¢ for each 25,000 times a search term appears in database.
Date Began Online: June 1980
Source of Information: All articles, features, columns, editorials, and letters from final Late Edition of the weekday, Saturday, and Sunday *New York Times.*
Type of Coverage: Full text with index terms. Current as of 24 to 48 hours after publication. Controlled vocabulary added within five to seven working days.
Size: 240,000 records.
Updating: Daily with 1,800 records added per week.
Indexing Terms: Roughly 4,500 subject terms plus personal, organizational, and geographic names as well as names of foods, drugs, animals, chemicals, books, movies, and plays.
User Aids: *Infobank Thesaurus and Directory* containing current controlled vocabulary (January 1983 on) and earlier controlled vocabulary for June 1980 to December 1982.
Printed Equivalent: *The New York Times*.
Document Retrieval: Not offered.

Magazine Index

Information Access Co.'s Magazine Index provides cover-to-cover indexing (except for advertisements and ephemeral items) of more than 435 popular American magazines. It includes all magazines indexed by the popular directory *Readers' Guide to Periodical Literature*, and more. You can use it to track down consumer product reviews, stories or editorials on major issues, biographical pieces about newsworthy people, or popular articles about science, travel, sports, arts, and many other subjects.

Many of the publications are indexed back to 1959. However, for technical reasons the two years 1971-1972 are missing; the company plans to add these in the future. Although the records do not have abstracts, extensive controlled vocabulary terms and other key words help the user evaluate listed articles.

Sample record

PROBLEM: For a speech before local business people, I'd like to find popular magazine articles containing the views of some prominent economists on inflation.

```
(1)     Roadblocks to recovery. (deficits & interest alarm economists)
(2)     Alexander, Charles
        Time  v119  p36(3)  Feb 22 1982
        CODEN: TYMEA
```

illustration; table
SIC CODE: 9311
CAPTIONS: Inflation, % change in C.P.I., Dec. to Dec., 1981, forecast 1982.; Unemployment, % of civilian labor force, forecast 1982.; Growth, % change in real G.N.P. quarterly at annual rates (with 1982 forecast).
NAMED PEOPLE: Greenspan, Alan-forecasts; Feldstein, Martin-forecasts; Eckstein, Otto-forecasts
DESCRIPTORS: finance, public-economic aspects; inflation (finance)-statistics; unemployed-forecasts; prime rate-economic aspects; gross national product-forecasts

---

Notes: (1) title and subtitle (2) author

Journals indexed in Magazine Index

Coverage beginning in January 1977 unless otherwise indicated.
[1]Coverage beginning January 1978.
[2]Coverage beginning January 1979.
[3]Coverage beginning January 1980.
[4]Coverage beginning January 1981.
[5]Coverage beginning January 1982.
[6]Coverage beginning January 1983.

Action Now (formerly *Skateboarder's Action Now*, ceased publication)[4]
Administrative Management
The AFL-CIO American Federationist (formerly *American Federationist*, ceased publication)
Aging
Air Progress
Alaska
Alternatives[6]
America
American Art Review
American Artist
American Baby
American City and County
American Craft (formerly *Craft Horizons*)[2]
American Economic Review
American Education
American Federationist (name changed to *The AFL-CIO American Federationist*)
American Film
American Forests
American Girl (ceased publication)[2]
American Heritage
American Historical Review
American History Illustrated
American Home (ceased publication)[1]
American Image
American Legion
American Libraries
American Photographer[3]
American Record Guide
American Rifleman

The American Scholar
American School and University
American West
Americana
Americas
Analog
Annals of the American Academy of Political and Social Science
Antiques (name changed to *The Magazine Antiques*)
The Antiques Journal (ceased publication)
Apartment Life (name changed to *Metropolitan Home*)[4]
Archery World
Architectural Digest
Architectural Record
Art in America
Art News
Artscanada[6]
ASIS Bulletin (name changed to *Bulletin of the American Society for Information Science*)[1]
Astronomy
Atlantic (also known as *Atlantic Monthly*)
Atlas World Press Review (name changed to *World Press Review*)[3]
Audio
Audubon
Aviation Week & Space Technology
Backpacker
Barron's
Beaver[6]
Better Homes & Gardens

Bicycling
Bike World (combined with *Bicycling*)
Bioscience
Black Enterprise[1]
Blair & Ketchum's Country Journal
Boating
Boston Magazine
Boy's Life
Bulletin of the American Society for Information Science (formerly *ASIS Bulletin,* name changed to *Journal of the American Society for Information Science*)[1]
The Bulletin of the Atomic Scientists
Business America (formerly *Commerce America*)[1]
Business Economics
Business Horizons
Business Week
Byte
California Magazine (formerly *New West*)
Camera 35 (ceased publication)
Camping Magazine[1]
Canadian Business Magazine[6]
Canadian Composer[6]
Canadian Consumer[6]
Canadian Dimension[6]
Canadian Forum[6]
Canadian Geographic[6]
Canadian Historical Review[6]
Car and Driver
Center Magazine
Ceramics Monthly
Challenge
Change
Changing Times
Chatelaine[6]
Chemistry (name changed to *SciQuest*)
Chicago
Children Today[1]
The Christian Century
Christian Herald
Christianity Today
Cinema Canada[6]
The Clearing House
Co-Ed
CoEvolution Quarterly
Colorado Business
Commentary
Commerce America (name changed to *Business America*)[1]
Commonweal
Congressional Digest
Computers & Electronics (formerly *Popular Electronics*)
The Conservationist
Consumer Guide

Consumer News (ceased publication)
Consumer Reports
Consumer's Digest
Consumers' Research Magazine
Cosmopolitan
Country Gentleman
Country Music
Countryside
Craft Horizons (name changed to *American Craft*)[2]
Crawdaddy (name changed to *Feature*)[1]
Creative Computing
Creative Crafts
Cruising World
Cuisine (formerly *Sphere*)
Current
Current Biography
Current Health (high school level)
Current History
Cycle
Cycle Guide
Cycle World
Daedalus
Dallas Magazine
Dance Magazine
Datamation
Department of State Bulletin
Desert (ceased publication)
Design
Design News
Design Quarterly
Down Beat
The Drama Review[2]
Dun's Business Monthly (formerly *Dun's Review*)
Dun's Review (name changed to *Dun's Business Monthly*)
Dynamic Years
Early American Life
Earth Science
Ebony
Economic Indicators
The Education Digest
Electrical World
Electronics
Encore (ceased publication)
The English Journal
Environment
Esquire
Essence
Family Handyman
Family Health (name changed to *Health*)
Fantasy and Science Fiction (also known as *Magazine of Fantasy and Science Fiction*)
Farm Journal
Fate

FDA Consumer[1]
Feature (formerly *Crawdaddy*, ceased
    publication)[1]
Federationist (name changed to *The AFL-
    CIO American Federationist*)
Field & Stream
Film Comment
Film Quarterly
Financial World
First World
Flower and Garden
Flying
Focus
Food and Nutrition
Forbes
Forecast for Home Economics[2]
Foreign Affairs[1]
Foreign Policy
Fortune
Futurist
GEO[3]
Glamour
Golf Magazine
Good Housekeeping
Gourmet
Guitar Player
Guns & Ammo
Harper's Bazaar
Harper's
Harvard Business Review
The Harvard Medical School Health Letter
    (formerly *Health Letter*)
Health (formerly *Family Health*)
Health Letter (name changed to *The
    Harvard Medical School Health Letter*)
High Fidelity
History Today[1]
Hobbies
Holiday (name changed to *Travel-Holiday*)
Horizon
Horn Book
Horticulture
Hot Rod
House & Garden
House Beautiful
Human Behavior (ceased publication)
The Humanist
Inc.[5]
The Indian Historian (suspended
    publication during 1981; name changed
    to *Wassaja Indian Historian*)
Industrial Research & Development
Industry Week
Information Technology & Libraries[5]
Instructor
Intellect (name changed to *USA Today*)
International Wildlife

Interview
Jet
The J. of American History
J. of Small Business Management
*J. of the American Society for Information
    Science* (formerly *Bulletin of the
    American Society for Information
    Science*)[1]
Kilobaud Microcomputing (name changed
    to *Microcomputing*)[5]
Labor Today
Ladies' Home Journal
Lapidary Journal
Library Journal
The Library Quarterly[1]
Library Technology Reports[1]
Library Trends[1]
Life[1]
The Living Wilderness
Look Magazine (ceased publication)[2]
Los Angeles[1]
Macleans
Mademoiselle
The Magazine Antiques
*The Magazine of Fantasy and Science
    Fiction* (also known as *Fantasy and
    Science Fiction*)
Management Today
Mankind (ceased publication)[1]
McCall's
Mechanix Illustrated
Meet The Press
Metropolitan Home (formerly *Apartment
    Life*)[4]
Microcomputing (formerly *Kilobaud
    Microcomputing*)[5]
Model Airplane News
Model Railroader
Modern Bride
Modern Maturity
Modern Office Procedures
Modern Photography
Money
Moneysworth
Monthly Labor Review
Monthly Review
The Mother Earth News
Mother Jones
Motor Boating & Sailing
Motor Trend
Minneapolis-St. Paul[1]
Ms.
The Mufon UFO Journal
The Musical Quarterly
The Nation
National Catholic Reporter
National Geographic

National Geographic World
National Parks & Conservation
National Review
National Wildlife
Nation's Business
Nation's Cities Weekly
Natural History
Nature Canada[6]
Negro History Bulletin
New Catholic World
The New Leader
New Orleans
New Realities
The New Republic
New Stateman
New Times (ceased publication)
New West (name changed to California Magazine)
New York
New York Review of Books
The New York Times Book Review
New York Times Magazine
The New Yorker
Newsweek
Nuestro[3]
Occupational Outlook Quarterly
Oceans
Off-Road
Omni[1]
Online
Opera News
Organic Gardening
Oui
Our Public Lands (name changed to Your Public Lands)
Outdoor Life
Parents' Magazine
Parks and Recreation
Penthouse[1]
People
Performing Arts in Canada[6]
Petersen's Photographic Magazine[1]
Phi Delta Kappan
Philadelphia Magazine
Photographic Society of America Journal (also known as PSA Journal)
Physics Today
Playboy
Playboy Guide to Electronic Entertainment[4]
Playboy Guide to Fashions for Men[4]
Plays
Poetry
Politics Today (ceased publicaton)[1]
Popular Electronics (name changed to Computers & Electronics)
Popular Mechanics
Popular Photography
Popular Science

Present Tense
Prevention
The Progressive
PSA Journal (also known as Photographic Society of America Journal)
Psychology Today
Public Management
Public Opinion Quarterly
Publishers Weekly
Quest
Radio Electronics
Railway Age
Reader's Digest
Reader's Digest (Canada)[6]
Real Estate Today
Redbook
Retirement Living (name changed to 50 Plus)
Review of Economics and Statistics
Road & Track
Rolling Stone
RQ[1]
Runner's World
Sail
Sales & Marketing Management
San Francisco
The Saturday Evening Post
Saturday Night[6]
Saturday Review (ceased publication)
Savvy[5]
School Arts
School Library Journal
Science
Science 80 (name changed to Science 81)[3]
Science 81 (name changed to Science 82)[4]
Science 82 (name changed to Science 83)[5]
Science 83[6]
Science Digest
Science News
Scientific American
SciQuest (formerly Chemistry, ceased publication)
Scouting
Sea Frontiers
Sea Secrets
Senior Scholastic
Sepla
Seventeen
Sierra Club Bulletin
Sing Out
Skateboarder's Action Now (name changed to Action Now)[4]
Skiing
Skin Diver
Sky and Telescope
Smithsonian
Soaring
Soccer (ceased publication)

Society
Southern Living[1]
Soviet Life
Space World
Special Libraries
Sphere (name changed to *Cuisine*)
Spinning Wheel
Sport
The Sporting News
Sports Afield
Sports Illustrated
Stamps
Stereo Review
Successful Farming
Sunset
Surfer[1]
Technology Review
Teen
Tennis Magazine
Texas Monthly (ceased indexing in 1979)
Theatre Crafts
Time
Today's Education
Town and Country
Trailer Boats
Trailer Life
Trains
Travel-Holiday (formerly *Holiday*)
TV Guide
UN Chronicle
The UNESCO Courier
US Catholic
U.S. News & World Report
USA Today[1]
Variety

Vintage
Vital Speeches
Viva (ceased publication)
Vogue
The Washington Monthly
The Washingtonian
Wassaja (formerly *Wassaja Indian Historian*)
Wassaja Indian Historian (formerly *The Indian Historian,* name changed to *Wassaja*)
The Water Skier
Weatherwise
Weight Watchers
Wilson Library Bulletin
Wine World
Woman's Day
WomenSports
The Workbasket and Home Arts Magazine
Workbench
Working Woman[1]
World Health
World Press Review (formerly *Atlas World Press Review*)[3]
World Tennis
Writer[1]
Writer's Digest[1]
Yachting
Yale Review[1]
Yankee
Your Public Lands (formerly *Our Public Lands*)
35mm Photography (ceased publication)
50 Plus (formerly Retirement Living)

Profile

Database: Magazine Index
Producer: Information Access Co., 404 Sixth Ave., Menlo Park, California 94025, 415-367-7171
Toll-Free Telephone: 800-227-8431
Vendor: DIALOG.
Cost: $85 per hour plus 20¢ for offline prints. Knowledge Index, $24 per hour.
Date Began Online: 1977
Source of Information: Cover-to-cover indexing of 435 popular magazines from the United States and Canada. Includes all magazines indexed by *Readers' Guide to Periodical Literature*. Covers 1959-1970, 1973-present.
Type of Coverage: Bibliographic without abstracts. Updated within a week after receipt of material.
Size: 1.3 million articles.
Updating: Daily on NEWSEARCH; 400 items added per day.
Indexing Terms: Library of Congress subject headings plus other terms when Library of Congress has not kept up with new terminology. SIC codes also.
User Aids: *IAC News*, six times yearly, free. *Access to Access: An Online User's Guide to IAC Databases*, $24. *Subject Guide to IAC Databases*, $45.

Printed Equivalent: Microfilm version. No data prior to 1977.
Document Retrieval: Not offered.
Notes: A smaller version of the database, ONTAP Magazine Index, for "online training and practice" is available on DIALOG at $15 per hour.

National Newspaper Index

Information Access Co. also produces the National Newspaper Index (NNI), which uses the same controlled vocabulary as its Magazine Index. NNI indexes five newspapers: *The New York Times*, *The Wall Street Journal*, *The Christian Science Monitor*, *The Washington Post*, and *The Los Angeles Times*. Like Magazine Index it doesn't contain abstracts—only a controlled vocabulary and other key words.

Infobank, of course, also covers these five newspapers and includes abstracts, but Infobank picks stories selectively, whereas NNI indexes the five publications cover to cover. Thus, it may be a better bet for tracking down short articles. The only items not included are weather charts, stock market tables, crossword puzzles, horoscopes, and advertisements.

Sample record

PROBLEM: I'm on a Democratic campaign committee. What were President Reagan's 1980 campaign promises about inflation?

(1)   Politics, promises and three plans for tax relief.
(2)   Hershey, Robert D., Jr.
      New York Times   v129   Section 3   pFl   Aug 31 1980   CODEN: NYTIA
      col 5   040 col in.   illustration; photograph
      EDITION: Sun
      DATELINE: Washington
      NAMED PEOPLE: Carter, Jimmy, Pres., U.S.-economic policy; Reagan, Ronald-economic policy; Long, Russell-economic policy
(3)   DESCRIPTORS: presidents-campaigns; taxation-political aspects; United States Congress-economic policy
(4)   IDENTIFIERS: tax reform-political aspects

Notes: (1) title (2) author (3) controlled vocabulary terms (4) ad hoc indexing terms

Profile

Database: National Newspaper Index
Producer: Information Access Co., 404 Sixth Ave., Menlo Park, California 94025, 415-367-7171
Toll-Free Telephone: 800-227-8431
Vendor: DIALOG.
Cost: $85 per hour, plus 20¢ per full record printed offline. Knowledge Index, $24 per hour.
Date Began Online: 1979
Source of Information: *The New York Times* (1/79-), *The Wall Street Journal* (1/79-), *The Christian Science Monitor* (1/79-), *The Washington Post* (9/82-), *The Los Angeles Times* (11/82-).

Type of Coverage: Cover-to-cover bibliographic, no abstracts.
Size: 640,000 records.
Updating: Daily on NEWSEARCH, 14,000 added per month.
Indexing Terms: Library of Congress subject headings plus other terms when Library of Congress has not kept up with new terminology. Also SIC codes.
User Aids: *IAC News*, six times yearly, free. *Access to Access*: *An Online User's Guide to IAC Databases*, 1982, $24. *Subject Guide to IAC Databases*, 1982, $45.
Printed Equivalent: National Newspaper Index (microfilm). Does not include *The Washington Post* or *The Los Angeles Times*.
Document Retrieval: Not offered.

NEWSEARCH

NEWSEARCH holds the daily updates to Magazine Index and National Newspaper Index as well as several other databases, such as Trade and Industry Index and Management Contents, which were described in Chapter 13. The contents of NEWSEARCH are transferred to the appropriate database monthly.

Profile

Database: NEWSEARCH
Producer: Information Access Co., 404 Sixth Ave., Menlo Park, California 94025, 415-367-7171
Toll-Free Telephone: 800-227-8431
Vendor: DIALOG.
Cost: $95 per hour, plus 20¢ for offline prints. Available on Knowledge Index, $24/hour.
Date Began Online: 1979
Source of Information: Daily updates for five databases: National Newspaper Index, Magazine Index, Trade and Industry Index, Legal Index, and Management Contents. Latest two to six weeks only; then records are transferred into these databases.
Type of Coverage: Bibliographic, with abstracting in some databases. Size: Approximately 50,000 records.
Updating: Daily, with 1,700 records added per day.
Indexing Terms: Library of Congress subject headings plus SIC codes for Information Access Co. databases. Management Contents uses a separate controlled vocabulary (see Chapter 13).
User Aids: *IAC News*, six times yearly, free. *Access to Access*: *An Online User's Guide to IAC Databases*, $24. *Subject Guide to IAC Databases*, $45.
Printed Equivalent: None.
Document Retrieval: Not offered.

NDEX

Bell & Howell's NDEX (Newspaper Index) provides a more regional perspective on the news than does the National Newspaper Index. It indexes eight metropolitan newspapers plus ten newspapers for black readers. (Three additional metropolitan papers were indexed in past years but are no longer included.) The database omits certain news categories, such as sports and travel, but it does index most other articles longer than three column-inches.

NDEX records do not contain abstracts. For searching and evaluating its records it uses a large, 13,000-word controlled vocabulary, with additional identifying terms, such as proper names, added to each citation.

Sample record

PROBLEM: My stockbroker told me about a theory correlating the prices of precious metals with Middle Eastern events. To check it, I need historic data on the Middle East in 1978.

(1)	SPECIAL MAGAZINE ISSUE ON THE MIDDLE EAST SITUATION
	CHICAGO TRIBUNE (CT), 78/10/08, SEC 9, PG 1, COL 1
(2)	PHOTO
(3)	12381; 13761; 13731; 13877; 15401; 16705; 23401; 17543
(4)	ARAB REPUBLIC OF EGYPT (1971-); ISRAEL; IRAN; JORDAN; MIDDLE EAST; PE-TROLEUM; PALESTINE LIBERATION ORGANIZATION; SAUDI ARABIA
(5)	ARAFAT YASSER; BEGIN MENACHEM; FAHD PRINCE; HUSSEIN KING; MOHAM-MED REZA PAHLAVI; SADAT ANWAR; ZAYED SHEIK

Notes: (1) title (2) indicates accompanying photo (3) category codes (4) indexing terms (5) supplementary indexing terms

NDEX newspaper coverage

Starting dates are given in parentheses.

METROPOLITAN NEWSPAPERS
Detroit News (1979)
Denver Post (1979)
Houston Post (1976)
Los Angeles Times (1976)
New Orleans Times Picayune/States-Item
  (1976)
San Francisco Chronicle (1976)
St. Louis Post-Dispatch (1981)
U.S.A. Today (1983)
Chicago Tribune (1976-1981 only)
Washington Post (1979-1981 only)
Chicago Sun-Times (1979-1982)

BLACK NEWSPAPERS (all start 1977)
Afro-American (Baltimore)
Amsterdam News (New York)
St. Louis Argus
Atlanta Daily World
New Pittsburgh Courier
Cleveland Call and Post
Chicago Defender
Michigan Chronicle
Los Angeles Sentinel
Norfolk Journal & Guide

Profile

Database: NDEX
Producer: Bell & Howell Co., Micro Photo Division, Old Mansfield Rd., Wooster, Ohio 44691, 216-264-6666
Toll-Free Telephone: None.
Vendor: SDC.
Cost: $90 per hour.
Date Began Online: 1976
Source of Information: Index to all news articles longer than three column inches. Covers eight regional papers and ten newspapers for black readers. Entries are delayed until about six weeks after publication.

Type of Coverage: Bibliographic with index terms, no abstracts.
Size: 7 million records.
Updating: Monthly.
Indexing Terms: 13,000 terms.
User Aids: Bell & Howell's Guide to Subject Headings, $15. *SDC Guide*.
Printed Equivalent: Bell & Howell's Index for each separate newspaper.
Document Retrieval: Not offered.

Info Globe

For general or business news about Canada, the publishers of the country's national newspaper, *The Globe and Mail*, have put the newspaper online in the full text Info Globe database. Info Globe includes more than 300,000 articles published since 1977; stories are available online the day of publication. General subject terms are added to each story to assist in searching.

Sample record

PROBLEM: I'd like to know more about Canadian research projects in oil production and recovery.

(1) 1. 822930167 WED. Oct. 20, 1983 PAGE: B3
    2. BYLINE: ANTHONY McCALLUM
(2) 4. CLASS: ROB
    5. DATELINE: Calgary AB   WORDS: 418
(3) 6. * * * Research * group funds project * *
    By ANTHONY McCALLUM
    Globe and Mail Reporter
(4) 7. CALGARY -- The Alberta Government's * oil * sands * research * group has agreed to put up 75 per cent of the cost of a $24.5 million experimental enhanced * oil * recovery project in central Alberta.
    If successful, the project could increase * oil * production from the Joffre pool by 14 million barrels, said C. W. Bowman, chairman of the Alberta * Oil * Sands * Technology and * Research * Authority.
    AOSTRA is a provincial Crown corporation formed in 1975 to encourage * research * on new ways to produce * oil * from * oil * sands * and * heavy * oil * deposits. Two years ago, the Government expanded its mandate to include * research * of enhanced recovery from conventional * oil * pools.
    The project, operated by Vikor Resources Ltd. of Calgary, is the first agreement researched between AOSTRA and the industry since the change was made. AOSTRA has set aside $75 million to fund enhanced recovery projects.
    As existing reservoirs are depleted, the * oil * becomes more difficult to extract. Companies flood the pools with water and force more * oil * to the surface, but flooding leaves some * oil * in the ground.
    Enhanced recovery techniques are intended to increase production after flooding through the addition of chemicals.
    The AOSTRA-Vikor project will inject carbon dioxide into a portion of the Joffre Viking sandstone pool in central Alberta that was flooded with water and produced to its economic limit in the mid-1960s.
    After flooding, the field produced 35.6 million barrels of * oil * from estimated reserves of 93.1 million barrels. If the test is applied to the entire pool, an additional 14 million barrels of * oil * could be recovered.

It will take about five years to complete the test. If the initial results are successful, Vikor intends to begin commercial operations in 1985.

Field operations will begin as soon as regulatory approval is received and contractual arrangements are completed, said R. K. Craig, Vikor president.

Vikor is a private company specializing in enhanced recovery projects. It is owned by Highfield Corp. Ltd., Intercomp Resource Development and Engineering Ltd., Roxy Petroleum Ltd., Tiverton Petroleums Ltd. and San Antonio Exploration Ltd., all of Calgary.

The project is the first to be confirmed since the Alberta Government announced changes to its incentive package for enhanced recovery schemes earlier this week, although Esso Canada Resources Ltd. of Calgary plans to re-examine its proposed carbon dioxide project at the Judy Creek * oil * field.

Alberta Energy Minister Mervin Leitch said the improved incentives are expected to improve the economics of such projects and persuade the industry to go ahead.

8. ADDED SEARCH TERMS: Alberta * oil *

Notes: (1) document number, date (2) section of newspaper (ROB = "Report on Business") (3) headline (set off by asterisks) (4) text of story (search terms used for this search are set off by single asterisks)

Profile

Database: Info Globe
Producer: Info Globe, Division of The Globe and Mail, 444 Front St., West, Toronto, Ontario M5V 2S9 Canada, 416-585-5250
Toll-Free Telephone: Numbers available for Canada only.
Vendor: Info Globe.
Cost: $159 per hour, which includes telecommunications. No monthly minimum. Offline prints are $5 per 1,000 lines. (All prices are in Canadian dollars.)
Date Began Online: 1977
Source of Information: *The Globe and Mail*.
Type of Coverage: Full text, cover-to-cover treatment of all articles in the newspaper.
Size: More than 300,000 articles.
Updating: Daily by 6 A.M. EST of publication date.
Indexing Terms: Information not available at time of publication.
User Aids: *Info Globe Manual*, $30. *Info Globe News*, free newsletter.
Printed Equivalent: *The Globe and Mail*.
Document Retrieval: Not offered.
Other Services: Custom searches $80 per hour; $25 minimum plus online and offline charges.

Textline

For current business and political news from abroad, Textline carries abstracts of major articles from many important European newspapers. It concentrates on news stories about companies and industries, and it also draws on press releases, corporate financial reports, broker's surveys, and the like. Based in the United Kingdom, Textline covers 41 British journals as well as 37 publications from other countries.

Each article is abstracted very thoroughly in English. If you want to know what the world's press is saying the same day the news appears, a companion database called Newsline carries headlines (but only headlines) of major articles the day they appear in print.

Textline uses a large controlled vocabulary carefully devised to emphasize financial terms. The database operates on a menu-driven system available in the United States.

Sample record

PROBLEM: I heard about a company in England call Executrade. Is there any recent material in the British press on this firm?

8TH MAY 1983.

(1) THE SUNDAY TELEGRAPH HAS LOOKED AT THE PROVIDERS OF COMPUTER BASED SERVICES TO BUSINESS, FOCUSING UPON FINSBURY DATA SERVICES AND EXECUTRADE.

(2) Executrade Centres, Inter Commodities' ICV Information Systems - a joint venture with British Telecom - and Finsbury Data Services are just 3 of the UK companies competing in a market which is dominated by the likes of Dow-Jones, Telerate and Reuters. Executrade, which is 12.5% owned by Gerrard and National, and which is run by Paul and Nicholas de Savary, is offering telephone answering, telex and dictation services through video terminals in client offices.

ICV is marketing existing Prestel services under the umbrella of Citiservice, including chart analysis, LIFFE, and services from Datastream and the Economist.

Finsbury Data Services, founded by Graham Blease, and backed by Scottish and Northern Investments (47.4% stake), Scottish Amicable (35.1%), and British and Commonwealth Shipping, provides a database called Textline, which covers business and financial news from 80 sources. A current turnover of 1M pounds is expected to translate into profits in the year to 30/6/84, and there are major expansion plans afoot. The paper believes that the savings offered by these services will get larger in the coming year, and competition in the market will increase.

SOURCES
STEL 8/5/83 P24 [Sunday Telegraph]

Notes: (1) descriptive title (not original headline) (2) abstract

Textline sources

AUSTRIA
Die Presse

BELGIUM
Le Soir
Courier de la Bourse et de la Banque
De Standaard
Financieel Ekonomische Tijd

DENMARK
Berlingske Tidende
Borsen

EIRE
Irish Independent
Irish Times

FRANCE
AGEFI
Le Figaro
Le Monde
Les Echos

GERMANY
Blick durch die Wirtschaft
Borsen Zeitung
Die Welt
Frankfurter Allgemeine Zeitung
Handelsblatt

HOLLAND
Financieel Dagblad
NRC Handelsblad
Volkskrant

INTERNATIONAL
Agence Europe
European Report
International Herald Tribune

ITALY
Corriere della Sera
24 Ore

JAPAN
JIJI Press

SOUTH AMERICA
Latin America Newsletters:
Andean Group Regional Report
Brazil Regional Report
Caribbean Regional Report
Mexico & Central America Regional Report
Southern Cone Regional Report
Weekly Report

SPAIN
El Pais
La Vanguardia

SWITZERLAND
Le Journal de Geneve
Neue Zurcher Zeitung

UNITED KINGDOM
Aberdeen Press & Journal
Belfast Telegraph
Birmingham Post
Campaign
Cornishman

Corporate Reports
County Press (IOW)
Daily Express
Daily Mail
Daily Telegraph
East Anglia Daily Times
Eastern Daily Press
Economist
Financial Times (Frankfurt)
Financial Times (London)
Financial Times Supplements
Financial Weekly
Glasgow Herald
Guardian
Investors Chronicle
Liverpool Echo
Lloyds List
Mail on Sunday
Manchester Evening News
Marketing
Marketing Week
Observer
Portsmouth News
Press Releases
Scotsman
Sheffield Morning Telegraph
Shetland Times
Standard
Sunday Express
Sunday Standard
Sunday Telegraph
Sunday Times
Times
Western Mail
Western Morning News
Yorkshire Post

Profile

Database: Textline
Producer: Finsbury Data Services Limited, 68/74 Carter Lane, London EC4V 5EA England, 01-248-9828
Toll-Free Telephone: None.
Vendor: Finsbury Data Services.
Cost: $120 per hour including telecommunications.
Date Began Online: 1980
Source of Information: Company, industry, product, economic, and public affairs articles from over 80 non-U.S. newspapers and journals. About half of the sources are from the United Kingdom. Time coverage starts January 1980 for major U.K. metropolitan publications; others added later. (Newsline covers several days' headlines from 27 daily and 11 weekly U.K., French, and German publications and is current by 8 A.M. EST the day of publication.)
Type of Coverage: Menu-driven bibliographic with detailed abstracts. All information is translated into English. Information is current within five to seven days of publication.
Size: More than 380,000 abstracts.

Updating: Daily.
Indexing Terms: Codes for companies, industries, countries, sources, business topics, and key words.
User Aids: *Textline Operating Manual* (includes topic codes, industry codes, country codes, source codes, and thesaurus). Company code book.
Printed Equivalent: None.
Document Retrieval: Not offered.

15 The Latest News: News Wires Online

Some people need to know the news fast. Perhaps they trade stocks, bonds, commodities, or foreign exchange. Perhaps they are public relations executives who need to stay constantly abreast of major controversies. Or perhaps they are lobbyists looking for opportunities to advance their views to legislators and politicians. These and other people may not want to wait for tomorrow's newspaper to find out what's going on. They want to read "today's news today."

Four major news wire services—United Press International (UPI), Associated Press (AP), Dow Jones News Service, and PR Newswire—provide literally up-to-the-minute news through online vendors. The government's latest economic reports, the latest happenings in Congress, news from all of the nation's state legislatures, and reports on the political leanings of the generals who carried out the latest coup d'etat in Latin America are all instantly available online.

These databases let you receive news as fast as your local newspaper or radio station gets it. Indeed, three of them give you access to the exact same wire stories that come clattering over the Teletype machine in almost every newsroom in the country.

One word of caution, though—the news wire services are run for editors, not for readers. Depending on which service you use, you might get the news in bits and pieces the way editors do.

Each time a wire service reporter finds out a new fact about a breaking story, he sends an update or correction over the wire. On UPI, for example, you might find a series of news snippets correcting a story that ran 12 hours ago; to understand them, you have to go back and search the wire for the original story. It takes some practice to learn how to read the news wire.

Another cautionary note—AP and UPI provide the raw material for mid-sized and small-town newspapers. If the news you're looking for probably wouldn't be used in the *Hartford Courant* or the *Anaheim Bulletin*, then don't expect to find it on the wires. Even such a leading financial wire as Dow

Jones News Service tends to offer primarily market prices, government statistics, and rewritten information from press releases.

Dow Jones News Service

Dow Jones News Service has always been one of the movers of U.S. stock markets. In the days before the electronic revolution, brokerage offices had two Dow Jones "tapes": the narrow "ticker tape," which reported stock prices, and "the broad tape," the Dow Jones News Service machine that reported the latest financial news.

Dow Jones News Service printers are still common in brokerage offices, while the ticker has been totally replaced by electronics.

But you needn't take a trip to a broker's office to read this news wire. Every news report also enters the Dow Jones News database only 90 seconds after it runs on the wire. For more information on it, see the Dow Jones News database discussion in Chapter 13.

United Press International

"The world's largest news-gathering organization" is the way that United Press International (UPI) sometimes describes itself in database service brochures. That's perhaps stretching things a bit. UPI has more clients than any other news service, but that is because it is often cheaper than its competitors. It can be said to have more journalists if you count such affiliates as the national news service of Hungary, which UPI officials say has a news exchange agreement with UPI. But the Associated Press has a significantly larger budget and a larger staff. UPI, however, has been more aggressive about putting its wire online for database users.

United Press International stories are readily accessible on The Source, Dialcom, and Dow Jones News/Retrieval the moment that they are transmitted to newspapers. Moreover, it is possible to search for stories containing a particular word or words of your choosing. Vendors offering UPI allow you to search not only UPI's main news wires, but also its 50 state news services. The Associated Press on CompuServe offers much more limited search possibilities.

On Dialcom, when you punch the command NEWS, you get a complete menu of some 15 news services (including 9 UPI services and news agencies of West Germany, OPEC, and the U.S. Department of Agriculture). When you choose the service you desire, the system simply asks you for a key word to search for, then automatically begins printing the first paragraphs of all stories containing that word, starting with the most recent.

The Source offers some unique features. The command BIZDATE will give you an electronic "daily business tabloid" based on UPI—a summary of the latest business news and an assortment of current analytical articles. The command DATA DANEWS will give you key words to access such general UPI features as the daily news summary supplied to newspaper editors.

Dialcom is planning to introduce a system called Profile, which would allow users to order all stories on any UPI wire containing a particular key word or words to be placed in a personal file that users can call up at their leisure. An item on the Dialcom "News" menu enables you to call up all recent stories slugged urgent on UPI's national wire. But what is urgent to an editor trying to get the most up-to-date news into his newspaper at press time may not be particularly urgent to you. Calling up a file of "urgent" stories will probably provide you with information about tornadoes in Kansas and the latest shooting in Belfast.

UPI stories, along with stories from the AP, Reuters, and the PR Newswire, are also available on the NEXIS database of Mead Data Central. However, the news is available on NEXIS only after it has ceased to be news—generally with a delay of about 48 hours.

Sample record

PROBLEM: I run a lumberyard. Before I place another order with one of my suppliers, Louisiana-Pacific, what are the latest developments in the strike against them?

12-16-83 04:20 pes =

Carpenters launch boycott of L-P
    PORTLAND, Ore. (UPI) - The United Brotherhood of Carpenters announced an "unprecedented" campaign to boycott products of Louisiana-Pacific Corp. Friday, accusing the company of failing to pay fair wages to striking lumber workers.
    The consumer and labor boycott was requested by the Western Council of Lumber, Production and Industrial Workers, an affiliate of the Carpenters. The LPIW represents most of the 1,500 workers at nearly a score of Western lumber mills who have been on strike against L-P since June 24.
    "There is absolutely no economic justification for Louisiana-Pacific's refusal to pay decent wages to its employees," said Carpenters president Patrick J. Campbell. "L-P is carrying out a campaign of economic coercion against our striking members and their families."
    The AFL-CIO executive council, at the request of the 750,000-member Carpenters union, voted to support the boycott. The AFL-CIO and its Union Label & Services Trades Department have begun an appeal to its nearly 14 million members and the general public, asking that they not buy L-P wood products.
    The call for a national boycott against a giant wood-products and building-supply company is "unprecedented in the 102-year history of the union," Campbell said, and "the action reflects the UBC's grave concern over L-P's total disdain for their employees' economic welfare."

Profile

Database: United Press International Online
Producer: United Press International, 220 East 42nd St., New York, New York 10017, 212-850-8600
Toll-Free Telephone: None.
Vendor: The Source, Dialcom, Dow Jones, NewsNet. (UPI articles are also available for historical searches on NEXIS and DIALOG.)

Cost: Included in the basic cost of access on The Source. Extra cost on Dialcom brings total cost of using UPI on Dialcom to $26 per hour. On Dow Jones, $12 to $36 per hour, depending on time of day and contractual arrangements; double for 1200 baud.

Date Began Online: 1978

Source of Information: News bureaus worldwide. Regional, national, and international stories are supplied on The Source and Dialcom; national and international stories only on Dow Jones.

Type of Coverage: Full text.

Size: The full contents of UPI's national, international, and regional wires for approximately the past week. (The historical databases go back much further: NEXIS to 1980, DIALOG to April 1983.)

Updating: Continuous on The Source, Dialcom, and Dow Jones. Daily update with a 48-hour delay on NEXIS and DIALOG.

Indexing Terms: None. Free text searchable.

User Aids: See user manuals for each vendor; help available online on The Source and Dialcom.

Printed Equivalent: The national, international, and regional sections of most daily newspapers are largely produced with wire service news.

Document Retrieval: Not applicable.

The Associated Press

A better claim than UPI to the title "world's largest news-gathering organization" can be made by the Associated Press. It is a cooperative of newspapers, broadcasting companies, and other news outlets. Newspaper editors find that UPI is the quickest source of crime news but that AP is the most thorough of the wire services.

At this writing, CompuServe is the only major online vendor to offer Associated Press stories immediately as they are transmitted to newspapers. It does not, however, permit users to search for occurrences of a particular key word, nor does it carry the full text of original wire stories. Instead, perhaps in recognition of the difficulty of using the original wire online, AP provides a special service designed for online and videotex users. The service offers special news summaries and menus, with wire stories reedited and shortened to lengths easy to digest from a video display. This can be helpful, but it is an inadequate substitute for an efficient method of searching for the particular topic you are interested in.

CompuServe plans to introduce a profile service similar to Dialcom's, providing searches of all AP wires including regional wires for topics specified in advance. But it has announced no plans to allow users to search stories that had already run on the wire.

Profile

Database: The Associated Press Videotex Wire

Producer: The Associated Press, 50 Rockefeller Plaza, New York, New York 10020, 212-621-1500

Toll-Free Telephone: None.

Vendor: CompuServe, also several small regional videotex services on an experimental basis. Plans have been made to offer the database through The Source and Dialcom. (AP news is also available for historical searches on NEXIS.)
Cost: Included in the basic cost of accessing CompuServe.
Date Began Online: 1980
Source of Information: AP reports from a worldwide network of correspondents.
Type of Coverage: Reports from AP national and international wires are specially edited for this service.
Size: 300 articles available per day, generally kept online for 48 hours or less.
Updating: Continuous.
Indexing Terms: None. Searchable by menu only.
User Aids: Help available online.
Printed Equivalent: None.
Document Retrieval: Not applicable.

PR Newswire Association

A large proportion of the business news about specific companies that appears in newspapers consists of press releases that a journalist has rewritten. Frequently, the journalist knows virtually nothing about the company beyond what is stated in the press release. Thus you may want to go directly to the sources the journalists use.

For business news, the single most important provider of press releases to the media is the PR Newswire Association, a cooperative with 7,500 members. Of these, 75 percent are corporations, including public relations firms; the rest are government agencies and nonprofit organizations, including universities and labor unions.

Members can disseminate public announcements quickly by sending them out to newspapers over the cooperative's wire service (newspapers receive free hookups). NewsNet carries the full text of the news wire updated hourly. (Several other vendors have PR Newswire on a 24-hour delay.) If you have the appropriate hardware, you can command NewsNet to watch for specific topics and, when they appear, to print them out on your terminal without your even having to be around.

Profile

Database: PR Newswire
Producer: PR Newswire Association, 150 East 58th St., New York, New York 10155, 212-832-9400
Toll-Free Telephone: None.
Vendor: NewsNet. (Also available with daily updating on NEXIS, NEWSEARCH, and with monthly updating on Trade and Industry Index.)
Cost: $24 per hour on NewsNet.
Date Began Online: 1981
Source of Information: Press releases supplied by some 7,500 corporations and other organizations.
Type of Coverage: Full text.
Size: Approximately 37,000 releases on NewsNet. 150 to 300 filed per day and kept online for one year.

Updating: Hourly on NewsNet.
Indexing Terms: None. Free text searchable.
User Aids: See manuals of databases carrying the wire.
Printed Equivalent: None.
Document Retrieval: Not applicable.

16 Advertising and Marketing Research

The databases that we shall consider in the fields of advertising and marketing research can aid you with the sine qua non of your business: selling your product. The group includes two advertising databases, Advertising and Marketing Intelligence and ADTRACK; two guides to market research studies, FIND/SVP Reports and Studies Index and Arthur D. Little/Online; two marketing statistics databases, PTS Forecasts and PTS Time Series; and a consumer credit database, TRW's Updated Credit Profile.

Advertising and Marketing Intelligence

The bibliographic database Advertising and Marketing Intelligence (AMI) offers the most general perspective on this entire field. Produced by The New York Times Information Service and J. Walter Thompson Co., it indexes and abstracts 65 trade and professional publications devoted to advertising or marketing (see the list following the Sample Record).

An advertising executive can tap this database to find:

- ♦ Who has won or lost clients in Texas?
- ♦ Who has won or lost insurance company clients?
- ♦ What are the advertising developments in the fast-food industry?
- ♦ What are the most successful new advertising campaigns?
- ♦ What has a particular ad firm been doing?
- ♦ What is a particular company's advertising strategy?

Advertising and Marketing Intelligence is reasonably current, as far as bibliographic databases go: references get online within about three weeks of publication, and the database is updated daily with new items. The coverage is very thorough, omitting only minor news items (and advertisements!).

Sample record

PROBLEM: Are there any recent market surveys of fast-food restaurant chains?

SOURCE: Nation's Restaurant News (NRN)

DATE: March 14, 1983

SECTION: Page 50, Column 1

ABSTRACT:
Survey of second-tier restaurant chains highlights Chicken George, eight-restaurant, fast-food chicken chain, C A Muer Corp, which has $66 million in total annual sales, Garcia's of Scottsdale, which has 22 Mexican-style dinnerhouses, Bob Evans Farms' restaurant division, which earned $4.6 million on net sales of $53 million in first half of fiscal 1983, and Shari's, 25-unit chain.

TYPE: Survey

SUBJECT: BARS AND RESTAURANTS; CHICKEN GEORGE; FAST FOOD; C A MUER; GARCIA'S; BOB EVANS; SHARI'S; CORPORATE FINANCES

Publications abstracted in *Advertising and Marketing Intelligence*

Ad Day
Ad East
Advertising Age
Advertising Techniques
Adweek East
Adweek Midwest
Adweek Southeast
Adweek Southwest
Adweek Western Advertising News
Air Transport World
American Demographics
Art Directions
Automotive News
Beverage Industry
Billboard
Box Office
Broadcasting
Cablevision
Chain Store Age Supermarkets
Chicago Tribune (Ad Column)
Direct Marketing
Drug Store News
Editor and Publisher
Folio
Food Engineering
Food Service Marketing
Friday Report
Harvard Business Review
HFD Retailing Home Furnishings
Industrial Marketing
J. of Advertising
J. of Advertising Research
J. of Communications
J. of Consumer Research

J. of Marketing
J. of Marketing Research
J. of Retailing
Madison Avenue
Marketing Communications
Marketing News
Media Decisions
Media Industry Newsletter
Medical Marketing and Media
Merchandising
Nation's Restaurant News
National Petroleum News
O'Dwyer's PR Newsletter
Photo Marketing
Product Marketing
Progressive Grocer
Public Opinion
Public Opinion Quarterly
Public Relations Journal
Public Relations Review
Quick Frozen Foods
Retail Week
Sales & Marketing Management
Stores
Television Radio Age
The New York Times (Ad Column)
Travel Weekly
U.S. Tobacco Journal
Variety
Video News
Wall Street Journal (Who's News Column)
Ward's Auto World
Women's Wear Daily

Subject and product terms to use in searching AMI

Account Changes
Acne Aids
Ad Awards
Ad Billings
Ad Budgets
Ad Campaigns
Ad Effectiveness
Ad Expenditures
Ad Industry
Ad Media
Ad Method
Ad Rates
Ad Revenues
Advocacy Ads
Agency Income
Agency Profiles
Agency Solicitations
Agency Structure
Air Conditioning
Airlines
Airplanes
Alarms (Use Protective Devices)
Apparel—Children
Apparel—Men
Apparel—Women
Association Ads
Audience Research
Auto Maintenance
Automobiles
Babies' and Children's Apparel (Use
    Apparel—Children)
Baby Foods
Baby Toiletries
Bait Ads
Baked Foods
Banking
Bathroom Fixtures
Beer and Ale
Beverages
Bicycles
Boating
Books and Publishing (Use Books)
Branded Products
Breath Fresheners
Broadcast Industry
Cable Television and Pay Television
Calculators
Camping Equipment
Car Accessories
Car Leasing
Car Rentals
Catalogs
Catalog Showrooms
Cereals
Charity
Chart
Chemicals

Chewing Gum
Children's Ads
Children's Programs
Chocolate Based Beverages (Use Chocolate
    Based)
Classified Ads
Cleaning Equipment
Cleaning Services
Cleansers (For Household and Industrial)
Client Relations
Column
Comparative Ads
Condiments
Confectionary
Consumer Behavior
Consumer Electronics
Contraceptives
Convenience Foods
Convenience Stores
Cookware
Cooperative Ads
Copyright
Corporate Finances
Corporate Structure
Corrective Ads
Cough and Cold Remedies (Use Cough and
    Colds)
Coupons
Creams and Lotions
Credit Cards
Cruises
Dairy Products
Dentifrices
Demographics
Deodorants
Deodorizers
Department Stores
Desserts
Detergents
Dietetic
Direct Mail
Directories
Dishwashers
Disinfectants
Disposables
Do-It-Yourself Products (Use Do-It-Yourself)
Domestic Cars
Drink Mixes
Drug Products
Drug Stores
Dryers
Economic Trends
Education
Eggs and Egg Products (Use Eggs)
Electronic Marketing
Employment and Employment Services
    (Use Employment)

Energy Conservation
Endorsements
Equipment Leasing (For Other Than Cars)
Ethic Ads
Ethic Cosmetics
Ethics
Executive Changes
Executive Changes—Ad (Includes Public Relations)
Executive Changes—TV (Includes Radio and Cable)
Executive Profiles
Farm Machinery and Supplies (Use Farm Machinery)
Fast Food
Feminine Hygiene
First Aid
Floor Coverings
Foods
Foot Care
Footwear
Forecast
Foreign Cars
Franchising
Freight and Delivery Services (Use Freight)
Freezers
Frozen Foods
Fruit
Funeral Services
Furniture
Gambling
Garden Supplies
Gasoline
Gas Stations
Gourmet Foods
Greeting Cards
Guns
Hair Dryers
Hair Preparations
Hair Salons
Health Care Services
Health Clubs
Health Foods
Hearing Aids
Heaters
Heating Fuel
Hobbies
Home Appliances
Home Building
Home Furnishing
Hotels and Motels
Household Supplies
Ice Cream
Industrial Ads
Industrial Machinery
Industry Sales
Information Systems
Insecticides
Inserts (Supplements)

Institutional Ads
Insurance
Investments
Jams and Jellies
Jewelry
Juices
Kitchen Fixtures
Labels and Labeling
Laundry Aids
Law and Regulation
Laxatives
Leather Goods
Legal Services
Lighting
Linen
Liquor
Loan Companies
Luggage
Magazines
Makeup and Cosmetics (Use Makeup)
Manicure Products
Marketing
Marketing Rights
Market Segment
Market Share
Meat
Media Access
Media Buying
Medical Equipment and Supplies (Use Medical Equipment)
Medicine and Drugs
Men's Apparel (Use Apparel—Men)
Men's Toiletries
Mergers (Acquisitions and Divestitures)
Misleading Ads
Mobile Homes
Motion Pictures
Motorcycles
Motor Oil
Mouthwash
Musical Instruments
Name Changes
Nationality Foods
Network Television
New Agencies
New Products
New Publications
Newspapers
Office Machinery
Ointments
Olympic Games
Optical Goods
Outdoor Advertising (Billboards)
Outdoor Cooking
Packaging
Pain Relievers
Paints
Paper Products
Pasta

Perfume, Toilet Water, and Cologne (Use
  Perfume)
Petroleum Products
Pets and Pet Foods
Photographic Equipment (Use Photo
  Equipment)
Point of Purchase
Political Ads
Political Research
Press Relations
Pressure Groups
Pricing
Product Failures
Product Safety
Product Testing
Professional Ads
Program Trends (TV and Radio)
Promotions
Psychographics
Public Opinion
Public Relations
Public Service Ads
Public Television
Public Utilities
Publishing Industry
Radio
Radio Sets
Ranges and Ovens
Ratings
Real Estate
Recordings
Recordings, Tapes, and Cassettes (Use
  Recordings)
Recreation
Recreation Vehicles
Refrigeration
Research
Research Methods
Restaurants
Retail Ads
Salad Dressings
Sampling
Satellites
Seafood and Fish (Use Seafood)
Seasonings
Self-Promotion (Agency)
Self-Regulation
Sewing
Shaving and Accessories (Use Shaving)
Shopping Centers
Shortening and Oils (Use Shortening)
Skin Cleansers
Small Appliances
Snacks
Special Section
Specialized Media
Specialty Ads
Spices
Sponsorship

Sporting Events
Sporting Goods
Spot Television and Radio
Spreads
Stationery Supplies
Statistics
Stereo Sets
Subliminal Ads
Sugar
Suits and Litigation
Suntan Preparations
Supermarkets
Supplement
Survey
Sweeteners
Swimming Pools
Syrups
Tableware
Tape Recorders
Tea
Telegrams
Telephones
Television
Television Sets
Textiles
Theaters
Theme Parks
Tires
Tobacco Products
Toilet Goods
Toiletries—Children
Tools and Home Workshop (Use Tools)
Toys
Trademarks
Trade Publications
Trading Stamps
Transit
Transportation
Travel
Travelers Checks
Trucks
Vacuum Cleaners
Vegetables
Video Recorders
Video Recordings
Vitamins
Wall Coverings
Washers
Watches and Time Pieces (Use Watches)
Water Conditioning
Waters
Waxes and Polishes
Wearing Apparel
Wine
Women's Apparel (Use Apparel—Women)
World Events
World's Fair
Yellow Pages

Profile

Database: Advertising and Marketing Intelligence (AMI)
Producer: The New York Times Co., 229 West 43rd St., New York, New York 10036, in conjunction with The J. Walter Thompson Co.
Toll-Free Telephone: Mead Data Central 800-227-4908
Vendor: Mead Data Central.
Cost: $90 per hour or less depending on use plus 45¢ per 25,000 times a search word appears in the file. Off-peak charges are $45 per hour or less.
Date Began Online: September 1979
Source of Information: 65 major trade and professional publications dealing with the advertising world. Coverage starts in September 1979 and is current within 20 days for weeklies and monthlies, within 10 days for dailies.
Type of Coverage: Bibliographic with abstracts.
Size: 145,000 records in August 1983.
Updating: Daily with 3,000 records added per week.
Indexing Terms: Several hundred subject terms.
User Aids: NEXIS User Guide and *Infobank Thesaurus and Directory*, both free.
Printed Equivalent: None.
Document Retrieval: Not offered.

ADTRACK

The ADTRACK database offers a very precise way to follow specific advertising campaigns. It lists exclusively the items that Advertising and Marketing Intelligence and almost all other bibliographic databases omit—the advertisements!

ADTRACK keeps track of all the advertisements of one-quarter page or larger that appear in any of approximately 160 popular magazines (see the journal list following the Sample Record). About 13,000 advertisements are recorded every month. The company plans to add more publications to the database, including *The Wall Street Journal* and a number of trade publications.

ADTRACK can help you:

♦ Find advertisements for new food and beverage products introduced in April 1982.

♦ Find out where Prudential placed insurance advertisements during the first quarter of 1983.

♦ Find out where manufacturers of portable typewriters placed their advertisements last Christmas season.

♦ Identify all the advertisements placed by a men's outerwear producer.

ADTRACK's controlled vocabulary is based on the SIC codes. Many other ad features are indexed by controlled terms, such as:

♦ Offers of brochures, pamphlets, or catalogs in the ad.

♦ Notation in the ad of credit cards accepted.

♦ Ad size.

◆ Color or black and white.

◆ Co-op ads.

◆ Gatefold ads.

◆ Toll-free telephone number given.

Be warned, though, that ADTRACK usually takes about ten weeks to get references online after the ads appear. The database thus may be of limited application if you need to track up-to-date information.

ADTRACK magazine list

All publications on this list have been indexed since October 1980 unless otherwise noted. Every ad of one-quarter page or larger has been indexed.

1001 Decorating Ideas (to *1001 Home Ideas* 1/81)
1001 Home Ideas (from *1001 Decorating Ideas* 12/80)
Airborne
Air Cal (from *Air California* 3/80)
Air California (to *Air Cal* 4/80)
American Baby
American Rifleman
American Way
Apartment Life (to *Metropolitan Home* 4/81)
Architectural Digest
Atlantic
Audubon
Baby Talk
Barron's
Bassmaster
Better Homes & Gardens
Black Enterprise
Bon Appetit
Book Digest
Bride's
Business Week
Car & Driver
Car Craft
Changing Times
Co-ed
Cosmopolitan
Cuisine
Delta Sky
Discover
Dun's Business Month (from *Dun's Review* 8/81)
Dun's Review (to *Dun's Business Month* 9/81)
Eastern Review
Ebony
Esquire
Essence
Expecting
Extra (acquired *Texas Flyer* 1/83)

Families (begin 10/81)
Family Circle
Family Handyman
Family Weekly (begin 1/82)
Field & Stream
Financial World
Flying Colors
Forbes
Fortune
Frontier
Gentlemen's Quarterly
GEO
Glamour
Globe
Golf Digest
Golf Magazine
Good Housekeeping
Gourmet
Grit
Guns & Ammo
Harper's
Harper's Bazaar
Harvard Business Review
High Fidelity
Hot Rod
House & Garden
House Beautiful
Houston Home/Garden
Inc. (begin 1/82)
Industry Week
Inside Sports (begin 1/82)
Jet
Ladies' Home Journal
Life
Mademoiselle
McCall's
Mechanix Illustrated
Metropolitan Home (from *Apartment Life* 3/81)
Modern Bride
Modern Photography

Money
Moneysworth
Mother Earth News
Mothers' Manual
Motor Trend
Ms.
Nation's Business
National Enquirer
National Geographic
National Lampoon
National History
New Woman
New York Magazine
New York Times Magazine (begin 1/82)
New Yorker (The)
Newsweek
Next (end 9/81)
Omni
Organic Gardening (begin 1/82)
Oui
Outdoor Life
Ozark
Pace
Pan Am Clipper
Parade
Parents
Passages
Penthouse
People
Pickup/Van & 4WD
Playboy
Playgirl
Popular Electronics (begin 1/82)
Popular Hot Rodding
Popular Mechanics
Popular Photography
Popular Science
Prevention
PSA California
Psychology Today
Quest 80
Quest 81
Reader's Digest
Redbook
Republic Scene
Road & Track

Rolling Stone (begin 1/82)
Runner's World
Saturday Evening Post
Saturday Review
Science 80
Science 81
Science 82
Scientific American
Self
Seventeen
Sierra
Ski
Skiing
Smithsonian
Southern Living
Southwest
Sport
Sporting News
Sports Afield
Sports Illustrated
Star
Stereo Review
Sunset
Tailwinds
Teen
Tennis
Texas Flyer (to Extra 1/83)
Time
Town & Country
Travel & Leisure (begin 1/82)
True Story
TV Guide
TWA Ambassador
U.S. News & World Report
United Mainliner
Us
Usair
Vogue
W
Western's World
Woman's Day
Working Mother
Working Woman
World Tennis
Yankee

Sample record

Let's request ADTRACK to search for advertisements indexed under the special feature "new or improved product," combined with the product code 20 (food and beverages) and with a publication date of 82/04 (April 1982). The command would look like this:

    SELECT SF = NEW AND PC = 20 and PD = 8204

Our search found 68 ads that fit this description. Here are three of the listings:

(1) 226940
(2) LEROUX
(3) PEPPERMINT SCHNAPPS
     PLAYBOY, 8204, ISSN 0032-1478
     04/82 PAGE: 213 1 PAGE
     FULL COLOR
     NEW OR IMPROVED
(4) LIQUEURS .(20853255)

     226749
     FOOD AND WINES FROM FRANCE
     FRENCH CHEESES--CHEVRE, FRENCH CHEESES
     CUISINE, 8204, ISSN 0164-6117
     04/82 PAGE: 15 1 PAGE
     FULL COLOR
     EXTRA MERCHANDISE OFFER; NEW OR IMPROVED
     CHEESE EX COTTAGE CHEESE .(20220000)

     226639
     PILLSBURY
     HEAT'N EAT--BIG PREMIUM HEAT'N EAT, BISCUITS
     FAMILY CIRCLE, 8204, ISSN 0014-7206
     04/27/82 PAGE: 121 1 PAGE
     FULL COLOR
     COUPON; NEW OR IMPROVED
     ROLLS NEC .(20512919)

Notes: (1) DIALOG accession number (2) company (3) brand number (4) product and product code

Profile

Database: ADTRACK
Producer: Corporate Intelligence, Inc., 1337 St. Clair, P.O. Box 16129, St. Paul, Minnesota 55116, 612-698-3543
Toll-Free Telephone: None.
Vendor: DIALOG.
Cost: $95 per hour. Offline and online prints are 25¢ per record printed.
Date Began Online: November 1981
Source of Information: All advertisements of one-fourth page or larger from approximately 160 consumer magazines. Most magazines have more than $2 million ad sales per year. Time lag of ten weeks, with information back to October 1980.
Type of Coverage: Bibliographic.
Size: Approximately 350,000 records.
Updating: About every six weeks, with 13,000 added per month.
Indexing Terms: Product names and codes (based on SIC codes).
User Aids: ADTRACK Training Manual; ADTRACK User's Manual.
Printed Equivalent: None.

Document Retrieval: Copies of ads cited in the database supplied for $1.50 per ad plus $10 per order ($10 charge waived if customer keeps a deposit account of $150 initially and $25 minimum). Color photocopies or transparencies available—call for quote.

FIND/SVP Reports and Studies Index

By listing individually published market research reports, the FIND/SVP Reports and Studies Index complements Advertising and Marketing Intelligence. Such reports do not appear in any magazine or journal; most of them are "multiclient studies" sold by research and consulting firms for prices ranging from several hundred to several thousand dollars. Other documents such as trade journal annuals, directories, and newsletters may be included as well. FIND/SVP also lists many Wall Street investment firm research reports on individual companies or industries.

In addition to producing this database, the FIND/SVP company performs custom searches on many databases, offers other information services, and conducts its own multiclient studies. These services are described in the listing of information brokers (see Appendix B).

Sample record

PROBLEM: My restaurant makes terrific pasta, and customers tell me I should go into the pasta-making business. Are there any market studies on the pasta industry to help me with my decision?

(1) THE PASTA MARKET
SEP 1981 165 p. $895 ONE-TIME
(2) Publ: FIND/SVP, NEW YORK, NY
Availability: PUBLISHER
Document Type: MARKET/INDUSTRY STUDY
Report No.: AA37
Covers market size and projections; demographics of major new market segments such as dieters and sports enthusiasts; new products; advertising copy strategies; profiles of major food companies and independents; and retail and food service outlets. Examines reasons behind the mergers and acquisitions trend that's shaking up the pasta industry.
Descriptors: FOOD; PASTA; MACARONI PRODUCTS

Notes: (1) title (2) publisher

Profile

Database: FIND/SVP Reports and Studies Index (FIND/SVP)
Producer: FIND/SVP, 500 Fifth Ave., New York, New York 10110, 212-354-2424
Toll-Free Telephone: 800-223-2054
Vendor: DIALOG.
Cost: $65 per hour plus telecommunications; 25¢ per record for offline prints.
Date Began Online: April 1982

Source of Information: Market and industry reports and surveys available from over 400 publishers in 75 countries. Includes investment research, industry, and company reports from major Wall Street investment firms. Reports date from 1977 to present.
Type of Coverage: Bibliographic with abstracts.
Size: 10,000 records.
Updating: Quarterly with 800 records added and prices updated.
Indexing Terms: 55 broad industry descriptors and several hundred subject descriptors. Also indexed by country.
User Aids: *FINDEX User Guide and Manual*, $25.
Printed Equivalent: *FINDEX: The Directory of Market Research Reports, Studies and Surveys*, printed once a year with one update, $165.
Document Retrieval: FIND/SVP sells most reports for prices quoted in the database.
Other Services: FIND/SVP offers a variety of customer research services.

Arthur D. Little/Online

Arthur D. Little, Inc., one of the research companies whose reports are indexed in FIND/SVP database (discussed above), also produces its own database. Arthur D. Little/Online covers Arthur D. Little's publications much more thoroughly than FIND/SVP. For example, in 1983 FIND/SVP listed 15 studies by Arthur D. Little, whereas Arthur D. Little/Online has 325 of its own studies on file. Another 10 to 20 are added to the company's own database monthly; FIND/SVP is updated quarterly only.

Arthur D. Little/Online has an unusual feature: aside from an abstract, some records carry the report's entire executive summary. The executive summary, part of the original document that sets forth the major findings in the author's own words, is usually longer and more detailed than an abstract written by someone else. But watch out: there is an extra $100 charge for these executive summaries.

Sample record

PROBLEM: Are there any detailed studies available on the market for clinical laboratory test instruments?

(1) Outlook for the Clinical Laboratory as a Marketplace
(2) Wood, Alyce
     January 31, 1977   1-10
     PUBLISHER: Arthur D. Little Decision Resources
     AVAILABILITY: Arthur D. Little Decision Resources, Dept. V,17
     Acorn Park, Cambridge, MA 02140   Tel: (617) 864-5770 x4461
     DOCUMENT TYPE: Research Letter
     CONTENTS:
     Types of Clinical Laboratory Tests
     Characteristics of the Clinical Laboratory Business
     The Market for In Vitro Diagnostic Products
     Regulatory and Review Trends
     Impact on the Market

TABLES AND FIGURES:
Table 1. Most Frequently Performed Clinical Laboratory Tests,
1976 (excluding tests performed in doctors' offices)
Table 2. Market for Clinical Laboratory Diagnostic Products,
1975-1981 (millions of 1975 dollars)
Table 3. Selected Manufacturers of Specialized Instrumentation
Table 4. Selected Acquisition Activity in Clinical Diagnostics,
1974-76

For full summary ($100) type Format 9

DESCRIPTORS: Health care; Scientific and technical instruments; Markets; Regulation; Acquisitions; Growth rates; Health organizations management

Notes: (1) title (2) author

Profile

Database: Arthur D. Little/Online
Producer: Arthur D. Little, Inc., Acorn Park, Cambridge, Massachusetts 02140, 617-864-5770
Toll-Free Telephone: None.
Vendor: DIALOG.
Cost: $90 per hour. Offline prints are 20¢. For some of the records there is a $100 surcharge to display or print the executive summary.
Date Began Online: February 1983
Source of Information: Arthur D. Little publications including industry outlook reports, research letters, newsletters, conference reports, management reports, public opinion index and marketing index reports from Opinion Research Corp. About 350 publications are included dating from 1977. The database is current to the last month or two.
Type of Coverage: All have table of contents. About 75 percent have extensive abstracts. The remainder have executive summaries that may be accessed for $100 per record. Executive summaries include specific forecasts and projections.
Size: 350 records.
Updating: Monthly with 10 to 20 records added.
Indexing Terms: Information not available at time of publication.
User Aids: Information not available at time of publication.
Printed Equivalent: None.
Document Retrieval: Arthur D. Little Decision Resources has the documents in the database available for purchase.

PTS Time Series and PTS Forecasts

What if you need facts and figures for your market research, but don't want to spend hundreds or thousands of dollars on a multiclient study? Be sure to refer to Chapter 13, Broad-Coverage Business Databases; HARFAX Industry Data Sources, in particular, may contain references to less expensive market studies not found in FIND/SVP. HARFAX lists many items available at nominal cost from trade associations. Two other databases in that chapter, PTS F&S Indexes and PTS PROMT, also may contain valuable market research sources. Predicasts, indeed, emphasizes that PROMT is designed for this purpose; we included it in Chapter 13 because, as a bibliographic database, it resembles the broad-coverage databases more than it does the ones in this chapter.

Predicasts produces two other databases intended for marketing research: PTS Time Series and PTS Forecasts. Each can be described as a cross between a fact database and a bibliographic database. They draw on many of the same sources as PROMT and F&S—namely, hundreds of business periodicals as well as annual reports, government documents, etc. But rather than just referring you to the source, Time Series and Forecasts actually extract the relevant facts and figures from the sources and enter them in the database.

For example, a search using Predicasts product code 242 (lumber) combined with the key word "shipments" calls forth the following entry, among others, from the U.S. Time Series database. It shows shipments of southern pine lumber in the United States since 1957. The figures come from the Department of Commerce publication *Current Business*.

(1) 206413   Curr Bus   81/06/00   PS-27   Bus Stat   80/10/00   P132
    United States
    Southern pine lumber. shipments.

YEAR	MIL brd ft
1957	6641.
1958	6545.
1959	6734.
1960	5303.
1961	5683.
1962	5704.
1963	6106.
1964	6389.
1965	6903.
1966	6466.
1967	6444.
1968	7061.
1969	7032.
1970	7035.
1971	7894.
1972	8072.
1973	7775.
1974	6760.
1975	7142.
1976	7500.
1977	8305.
1978	8264.
1979	7932.
1980	6663.

    GROWTH RATE= 0.7%
(2) CC=1USA   PC=2421202   EC=631

Notes: (1) journals and dates (2) country code, product code, event code

This entry shows annual data for past years. To look into the future, the Forecasts database summarizes published projections about many of the same industries listed in the Time Series. For example, how much can we expect the use of plastics to grow in the auto industry? A search of Forecasts might turn up this record:

```
Chem Week   80/02/20   P54   United States
Plastic materials. used in. automobiles.

     YEAR      MIL lbs.

     1979      1490.
     1985      1630.
     1990      2100.

     GROWTH RATE = 3.2%
(1)  Best, J   Market Search
     CC = 1USA      PC = 2821000,3711100      EC = 691
```

Notes: (1) author of forecast

This entry tells you that in *Chemical Week*, February 20, 1980, an article projected how much plastic material would be used in automobiles in 1985 and 1990. The projected growth rate is 3.2 percent per year.

These Predicasts databases use the same controlled vocabulary as PROMT and F&S Indexes. Thus you can perform a search on all Predicasts databases almost as easily as doing so on one.

Profile

Database: PTS Time Series
Producer: Predicasts, Inc., 200 University Circle Research Center, 11001 Cedar Ave., Cleveland, Ohio 44106, 216-795-3000
Toll-Free Telephone: 800-321-6388
Vendor: DIALOG, BRS, Data-Star.
Cost: Approximately $95 per connect hour plus 35¢ per online print, 40¢ per offline print.
Date Began Online: 1972
Source of Information: Annual statistical information, current and back to 1957. Among the sources are trade publications, government and agency reports, industry association reports. Covers production, consumption, foreign trade, general demographic, and national income data.
Type of Coverage: Factual time series tables assembled from annual statistical sources, with bibliographic references.
Size: 177,000 records as of January 1973.
Updating: Quarterly.
Indexing Terms: Country codes, SIC-based product codes, event codes, company name, journal name.
User Aids: *PTS User's Manual*, $25, contains description of databases and all retrieval codes. *The Predicasts Company Thesaurus*, $225, contains 100,000 company names, cross-indexed for subsidiaries and joint ventures, organized by country and SIC-based product codes. *The PTS Online News*, free newsletter.

Printed Equivalent: *Predicasts U.S. Basebook*, annual, $425. No international print equivalent.
Document Retrieval: $8.50 by mail, $10 by phone or Dialorder. Shipped within 48 hours of receipt of order.
Other Services: Predicasts prepares custom market reports based on Predicasts data-bases for $375. The company also has a market research arm that prepares studies that the company sells. These are listed in FIND/SVP.

Profile

Database: PTS Forecasts
Producer: Predicasts, Inc., 200 University Circle Research Center, 11001 Cedar Ave., Cleveland, Ohio 44106, 216-795-3000
Toll-Free Telephone: 800-321-6388
Vendor: DIALOG, BRS, Data-Star.
Cost: Roughly $95 per connect hour, plus telecommunications, plus 20¢ per online print, 25¢ per offline print of full record.
Date Began Online: 1972
Source of Information: 2,500 publications from around the world, including news-papers, special studies, trade journals, general business publications, company news releases, and government reports. Includes only articles containing statistical information.
Type of Coverage: Bibliographic with statistical abstracts. Information is added within two to four weeks of publication.
Size: 600,000 records as of January 1983.
Updating: Quarterly, with 30,000 records added per update.
Indexing Terms: Country codes, SIC-based product codes, event codes, journal name, years of forecast, growth rate, author of forecast.
User Aids: *PTS User's Manual*, $25, contains description of databases and all retrieval codes. *The Predicasts Company Thesaurus*, $225, contains 100,000 company names, cross-indexed for subsidiaries and joint ventures, organized by country and SIC-based product codes. *The PTS Online News*, free newsletter.
Printed Equivalent: *Predicasts Forecasts (U.S.)*, quarterly, $650 per year; *Worldcasts*, forecasts by region or product, quarterly, $900 per year. Both *Worldcasts* editions $1,300 per year.
Document Retrieval: $8.50 by mail, $10 by phone or Dialorder. Shipped within 48 hours of receipt of order.
Other Services: Predicasts prepares custom market reports based on Predicasts data-bases for $375. The company also has a market research arm that prepares studies that the company sells. These are listed in FIND/SVP.

TRW's Updated Credit Profile

Our last class of marketing databases is probably the one you're most famil-iar with: consumer credit reporting services. This group actually makes up one of the most widely used online databases. (Note that business credit ratings are mentioned in Chapter 18.)

There are five major computerized consumer credit reporting agencies in the United States. The largest is TRW Information Services Division; others are Transunion, Credit Bureau Inc., Chilton, and Pinger. While you probably know that subscribers can obtain credit reports from them by telephone or mail, did you also know that reports are online, available through computer terminals? In fact, it's cheaper to obtain the information by terminal: TRW charges $3.00 for a consumer credit check delivered verbally, but only $1.50 if you obtain it online.

Don't plan on subscribing to one of these services if you're not a retailer. The Federal Fair Credit Reporting Act limits access to "bona fide credit grantors . . . with a legitimate business need for the information . . . in relation to a credit transaction."

Profile

Database: TRW's Updated Credit Profile
Producer: TRW—Information Services Division, 505 City Parkway West, Orange, California 92668, 714-937-2000
Toll-Free Telephone: None.
Vendor: TRW.
Cost: $8 per report, $5 in state of Maryland. For subscribers, $1.25 to $3.50 depending on volume and method of access.
Date Began Online: 1969
Source of Information: Credit information on consumers gathered by subscribers to the service (banks, department stores, some insurance companies, etc.).
Type of Coverage: Factual; credit information "available only to those with a genuine need to know." Menu-driven system.
Size: 90 million consumers.
Updating: Daily. Negative information kept seven years and bankruptcy information kept ten years.
Indexing Terms: Need consumer's name, address, social security number, year of birth to search.
User Aids: *Information Spectrum*, a quarterly magazine. Subscriber directories.
Printed Equivalent: None.
Document Retrieval: Not applicable.
Other Services: Corporate credit information available.

17 Demographics Databases

Often a question about marketing information is really a question concerning demographics. If you ask, "Where do I find customers like so and so," then you're asking about demographics. There are numerous databases concerned only with demographic information. With them you can:

♦ Find areas dense with your prime customers.
♦ Analyze the sales potential of different sites.
♦ Find out how much people in an area earn, how old they are, how well-educated they are, or how much their homes are worth.
♦ Cross-tabulate this kind of information, so that you find whether an area has well-educated homeowners who are between the ages of 21 and 35 years old and earn more than $30,000.

Don't think you have to manage a consumer products company with a multimillion dollar advertising budget to make use of such data. If you are a fast-food entrepreneur, demographics can help you pick a location for a new franchise—or avoid opening one in an unpromising location. If you are a sales manager, demographic data can help you divide up your market into sales territories of equal potential.

We will discuss the products of three of the leading producers of online demographic databases: CACI, Inc., Donnelley Marketing Information Services, and Urban Decision Systems, Inc. All three gather their information from the same basic sources—U.S. Census Bureau data, supplemented by other federal government reports. But each adds to the data, revises it, updates it, and rearranges it in a unique way.

If you seek demographic information on a single town, the least expensive source may be to go directly to a city or county government or chamber of commerce, not to a database. But if you're searching a five-county area to find the best location for a new auto-parts outlet, that could be unwieldy. The easiest source of answers is probably a database of one of the firms.

The best way to find out whether one can supply the information you seek is to phone and ask. We suggest you call all three and do some comparison shopping. All will be glad to discuss their systems. For a fee, they will conduct a search for you and probably will try to sell you additional services as well. Custom reports on a specific area can be had for under $50. However, it is cheaper for you to learn to use the online databases yourself if you expect to need demographic data on a continuing basis.

In the demographics marketplace, there are two basic varieties of online data: (1) basic census figures, including trends and site demographics, and (2) sales-potential studies.

Basic census figures

Basic census figures can tell you about population, incomes, races, ages, housing, etc., according to one of the standard geographical slices of the United States: census tract, town, county, standard metropolitan statistical area, zip code area. The database producers extract this information from 1970 and 1980 census figures (the earlier numbers help in identifying trends), updated annually from public and proprietary data. We suggest you inquire when each company's data was updated last. Sometimes, one may fall several months behind in updating. Check to see if census information for the current year has been updated; it becomes available in April.

Site demographics involves the same kind of figures but differs in how it slices up the territory. Suppose you're considering a retail location, and you know from experience that 40 percent of your clients will come from one mile or closer, 20 percent will come from one to three miles, and 20 percent from three to five miles. You require a demographic report on three circular areas with a one-, three-, and five-mile radius. The perimeters probably cut across census tracts, town borders, zip code areas, and every other geographic subdivision.

But site demographic databases can supply your figures. You can specify the center of your circle by an address (you need latitude and longitude). And you can specify any shape of area—triangle, octagon, oval, etc.

SITE II and DORIS databases

CACI, Inc., offers two basic demographic databases, SITE II and DORIS (Demographic Online Retrieval Information System). SITE II is menu-driven and easier to use than DORIS; for any geographical area, you have a choice of 19 preformatted reports covering the basic census figures. One report costs $45 to $80. DORIS requires a more complicated set of instructions, but you can order the information printed in almost any format that you designate. And once you learn how to use it, it's faster than going through SITE II's menu.

```
                    1980 CENSUS PROFILE REPORT          PAGE 1 OF 2

SEVEN CORNERS SH. CTR.     AREA REFERENCE:        RADIUS: INNER    0.00
ROUTE 7 & ROUTE 50         LATITUDE:   38 52  8           OUTER    3.00
0-3 MILE CIRCLE            LONGITUDE:  77  9 20  WEIGHTING:      100.0%
**********************************************************************
*                         1980 CENSUS  1983 UPDATE  ANNUAL CHANGE   *
*     POPULATION             144296       144862       0.13%        *
*     HOUSEHOLDS              59418        61888       1.37%        *
*     MEDIAN HSHLD INCOME  $ 24082      $ 29439        6.92%        *
**********************************************************************
POPULATION:                     AGE BY:       MALE         FEMALE       TOTAL
  WHITE      121290  84.1%    0- 4    4109  6.0%    3994   5.3%   5.6%
  BLACK        9543   6.6%    5- 9    4074  5.9%    3885   5.1%   5.5%
  OTHER       13463   9.3%   10-13    3641  5.3%    3405   4.5%   4.9%
  TOTAL      144296 100.0%   14-17    4388  6.4%    3902   5.2%   5.7%
                             18-20    2759  4.0%    2878   3.8%   3.9%
  SPANISH      8192   5.7%   21-24    5124  7.4%    5748   7.6%   7.5%
  ASIAN        8511   5.9%   25-29    7491 10.9%    7817  10.4%  10.6%
  GRP QTRS      986   0.7%   30-34    7269 10.6%    7335   9.7%  10.1%
  FAM POP    115686  80.2%   35-44    9341 13.6%    9605  12.7%  13.1%
  HH POP     143310  99.3%   45-54    7430 10.8%    7978  10.6%  10.7%
                             55-64    7431 10.8%    9213  12.2%  11.5%
HOME VALUE (NON-CONDO'S):    65-74    4215  6.1%    5917   7.8%   7.0%
$   0- 20K      50   0.2%    75-84    1316  1.9%    2781   3.7%   2.8%
$  20- 30K      91   0.3%    85+       260  0.4%     996   1.3%   0.9%
$  30- 40K     147   0.6%    TOTAL   68848 100.0%  75454 100.0%
$  40- 50K     395   1.5%    AVERAGE 34.67         37.75          36.28
$  50- 80K    8400  31.8%    MEDIAN  31.95         34.16          33.06
$  80-100K    8463  32.0%
$100-150K     6997  26.5%    MARITAL STATUS (POP > 14 YRS):
$150-200K     1346   5.1%    SINGLE                34525          28.9%
$200+          526   2.0%    MARRIED               64475          54.0%
TOTAL        26415 100.0%    DIVORCED/SEPARATED    12066          10.1%
AVERAGE   $  97583           WIDOWED                8303           7.0%
MEDIAN    $  89747
% OWNED      52.1%           OCCUPIED HSG UNITS     59418          95.8%
                            VACANT HSG UNITS:
GROSS RENT (INCL UTIL):      FOR SALE OR RENT       1825           2.9%
NO $ RENT      427   1.5%    SEASONAL/MIGRATORY       10           0.0%
$  < 100       311   1.1%    OCCASIONAL USE/OTHER    761           1.2%
$100-149       181   0.7%    TOTAL HSG UNITS        62013         100.0%
$150-199       676   2.4%
$200-249      3136  11.3%    SINGLE PERSON HOUSEHOLDS  17192       28.9%
$250-299      7051  25.3%    MALE                    6511          11.0%
$300-399      8961  32.2%    FEMALE                 10681          18.0%
$400-499      3801  13.7%
$500+         3285  11.8%    FAMILY HOUSEHOLDS       37827          63.7%
TOTAL        27829 100.0%    MARRIED COUPLE          30882          52.0%
AVERAGE   $    345           SINGLE MALE HEAD OF HH   1574           2.6%
MEDIAN    $    326           SINGLE FEMALE HEAD OF HH 5371           9.0%
% RENTED     47.9%
                            NON-FAMILY HOUSEHOLD      4399           7.4%
CONDOMINIUM HOUSING:         MALE HEAD OF HH          2569           4.3%
RENTED         946  24.6%    FEMALE HEAD OF HH        1830           3.1%
OWNED         2558  66.4%
VACANT         347   9.0%    TOTAL HOUSEHOLDS        59418         100.0%
TOTAL         3851 100.0%    AVERAGE SIZE             2.41
AVERAGE VALUE:              TOTAL FAMILIES          37828
(OCCUP'D)  $  50363         AVERAGE SIZE             3.06
--------------------------------------------------------------------
SOURCE:  CACI, ARLINGTON, VA  (800) 336-6600    COPYRIGHT 1983 CACI
              LOS ANGELES, CA (213) 824-5656
```

Typical census data from CACI's SITE II database (reprinted with permission).

170 / A Guide to Selected Business Databases

```
                    1980 CENSUS PROFILE REPORT            PAGE 2 OF 2

OCCUPATION:                 INCOME LEVEL: NO. OF HSHLDS   NO. OF FAMILIES
  EXEC      14426  18.7%  $   0- 2.4K    1472   2.5%        664   1.8%
  PROF      15643  20.3%  $ 2.5- 4.9K    2017   3.4%        710   1.9%
  TECH       3767   4.9%  $ 5.0- 7.4K    2595   4.4%       1011   2.7%
  SALES      6735   8.7%  $ 7.5- 9.9K    2962   5.0%       1446   3.8%
  CLERICAL  17572  22.8%  $10.0-12.4K    3604   6.1%       1544   4.1%
  PRIVATE     645   0.8%  $12.5-14.9K    3542   6.0%       1733   4.6%
  SERVICE    7555   9.8%  $15.0-17.4K    4142   7.0%       2116   5.6%
  FARMING     440   0.6%  $17.5-19.9K    3526   5.9%       1845   4.9%
  CRAFT      5659   7.3%  $20.0-22.4K    3853   6.5%       2281   6.0%
  OPER       2939   3.8%  $22.5-24.9K    3155   5.3%       1959   5.2%
  LABORER    1631   2.1%  $25.0-27.4K    3353   5.6%       2314   6.1%
                          $27.5-29.9K    2560   4.3%       1801   4.8%
INDUSTRY:                 $30.0-34.9K    5401   9.1%       3915  10.3%
  AGRIC       557   0.7%  $35.0-39.9K    4158   7.0%       3326   8.8%
  CONST      3982   5.2%  $40.0-49.9K    6310  10.6%       5230  13.8%
  MANUF      4147   5.4%  $50.0-74.9K    5186   8.7%       4575  12.1%
  TRANS      2505   3.3%  $75K+          1582   2.7%       1363   3.6%
  COMMUN     2211   2.9%  TOTAL         59418 100.0%      37833 100.0%
  WHOLESL    1457   1.9%  AVERAGE      $ 27916           $ 32312
  RETAIL    10857  14.1%  MEDIAN       $ 24082           $ 29296
  FINANCE    5981   7.8%
  SERVICE    6305   8.2%  WKS UNEMP (POP>15):    POP BELOW POVERTY:
  RECRE      3690   4.8%  1- 4      4905  40.3%  WHITE    6755  70.9%
  HEALTH     4104   5.3%  5-14      4066  33.4%  BLACK    1830  19.2%
  EDUC       5474   7.1%  15+       3197  26.3%  OTHER     946   9.9%
  GOVT      18114  23.5%                         TOTAL    9531 100.0%
  OTHER      7634   9.9%                                        % OF
                          SOURCE OF HSHLD INCOME:              TOT. HH
EDUCATION COMPLETED:      WAGE OR SALARY            50467      84.9%
(POP > 24 YRS)            NONFARM SELF-EMPLOYED      5313       8.9%
  ELEMENT.   7101   7.4%  FARM SELF-EMPLOYED          615       1.0%
  SOME HS    7375   7.7%  INTEREST/DIVIDEND/RENT    34094      57.4%
  HS GRAD   26115  27.1%  SOCIAL SECURITY           10665      17.9%
  SOME COL  18952  19.7%  PUBLIC ASSISTANCE          2083       3.5%
  COL GRAD  36854  38.2%  OTHER                     15629      26.3%
  AVERAGE   13.61
  MEDIAN    13.61         GROUP QUARTERS POP BY TYPE:
                          COLLEGE                       1       0.1%
VEHICLES AVAILABLE:       INMATE/MENTAL                43       4.4%
  NONE       5665   9.5%  INMATE/NURSING              710      72.0%
  1         26553  44.7%  INMATE/OTHER                  0       0.0%
  2         19796  33.3%  OTHER (INC MILITARY)        232      23.5%
  3+         7403  12.5%  TOTAL                       986     100.0%

YEAR STRUCTURE BUILT:    UNITS IN STRUCTURE:     STORIES IN STRUCTURE:
(OCCUPIED HSG UNITS)     (YR-ROUND HSG UNITS)    (YR-ROUND HSG UNITS)
  1975-80    3977   6.7%  1 DET.   31157  50.2%  1- 3  49261  79.4%
  1970-74    4865   8.2%  1 ATT.    3568   5.8%  4- 6   4878   7.9%
  1960-69   13726  23.1%  2          412   0.7%  7-12   5227   8.4%
  1950-59   18151  30.5%  3-4       2578   4.2%  13+    2639   4.3%
  1940-49   13273  22.3%  5+       24251  39.1%
  < 1940     5427   9.1%  MOBILE      39   0.1%
-------------------------------------------------------------------
SOURCE:  CACI, ARLINGTON, VA   (800) 336-6600    COPYRIGHT 1983 CACI
         LOS ANGELES, CA (213) 824-5656
```

Typical census data from CACI's SITE II database (*continued*) (reprinted with permission).

DEMOGRAPHIC FORECAST REPORT

```
SEVEN CORNERS SH. CTR.              LATITUDE:        38 52  8
ROUTE 7 & ROUTE 50                  LONGITUDE:       77  9 20
0-3 MILE CIRCLE                     CIRCLE: INNER RADIUS   0.0
                                            OUTER RADIUS   3.0
                                            WEIGHTING    100.0
```

	1980 CENSUS	1983 UPDATE	1988 FORECAST	1983-1988 CHANGE	ANNUAL GROWTH
POPULATION	144296	144862	146050	1188	0.2%
HOUSEHOLDS	59418	61888	64638	2750	0.9%
FAMILIES	37831	37483	37951	468	0.2%
AVG HH SIZE	2.4	2.3	2.2	-0.1	-0.7%
AVG FAM SIZE	3.1	2.9	2.8	-0.1	-0.7%
TOT INC (MIL$)	1663.1	2009.2	2491.8	482.6	4.4%
PER CAPITA INC $	11525 $	13870 $	17061 $	3191	4.2%
AVG FAM INC $	32344 $	37336 $	43861 $	6525	3.3%
MEDIAN FAM INC $	29493 $	33901 $	39965 $	6064	3.3%
AVG HH INC $	27989 $	32465 $	38550 $	6085	3.5%
MEDIAN HH INC $	24210 $	29439 $	33577 $	4138	2.7%

	1980 CENSUS	%	1983 UPDATE	%	1988 FORECAST	%
TOTAL POP	144296	100.0	144862	100.0	146050	100.0
RACE DISTRIBUTION						
WHITE	121290	84.1	119064	82.2	116933	80.1
BLACK	9543	6.6	10120	7.0	10775	7.4
OTHER	13463	9.3	15678	10.8	18342	12.6
HISPANIC	8192	5.7				
AGE DISTRIBUTION						
0- 4	8101	5.6	7582	5.2	7124	4.9
5-11	11498	8.0	10890	7.5	10183	7.0
12-16	9636	6.7	9033	6.2	8537	5.8
17-21	10056	7.0	10483	7.2	10367	7.1
22-29	23953	16.6	23697	16.4	24167	16.5
30-44	33520	23.2	33698	23.3	34844	23.9
45-54	15410	10.7	16500	11.4	16328	11.2
55-64	16644	11.5	16219	11.2	16258	11.1
65+	15482	10.7	16760	11.6	18342	12.5
AVERAGE AGE	35.9		36.6		37.2	
MEDIAN AGE	34.0		34.8		35.4	

ALL INCOME FIGURES ARE EXPRESSED IN CURRENT DOLLARS FOR 1980, 1983, AND 1988. THE AVERAGE ANNUAL INFLATION FOR THE U.S. FROM 1970-1980 WAS 8%.

SOURCE: CACI, ARLINGTON, VA   (800) 336-6600   COPYRIGHT 1983 CACI
        LOS ANGELES, CA (213) 824-5656

Typical demographic forecast from CACI's SITE II database (reprinted with permission).

Profile

Database: SITE II/DORIS
Producer: CACI, Inc., 1815 N. Fort Meyer Dr., Arlington, Virginia 22209, 203-841-7800
Toll-Free Telephone: 800-336-6600
Vendor: CompuServe, Control Data (Business Information Services), Chase Econometrics/Interactive Data, COMSHARE, General Electric Information Services Co., United Information Services, Tymshare.
Cost: Average site report costs $45 to $80, depending on vendor.

Date Began Online: 1973
Source of Information: U.S. Census Bureau information combined with proprietary formulas.
Type of Coverage: Preformatted reports on SITE II; command-driven reports on DORIS.
Size: Information not available at time of publication.
Updating: Annually.
Indexing Terms: Zip code area, county, census tract, or any geometric area.
User Aids: User manual, $9.50. Each vendor also publishes its own documentation.
Printed Equivalent: Not applicable.
Other Services: CACI offers a variety of custom demographics-related reporting services.

American Profile

Donnelley's American Profile database is very similar to SITE II and DORIS. (Donnelley was founded by a former CACI employee.) As a division of Dun & Bradstreet Corp., Donnelley has access to D&B's vast set of credit records on almost every U.S. company. Thus Donnelley augments some of its demographic databases with data taken from the D&B files, such as statistics on employment in each area. (The business data also finds its way into D&B's Dun's Market Identifiers and Million Dollar Directory databases, described in the next chapter.)

Profile

Database: American Profile
Producer: Donnelley Marketing Information Services, 1351 Washington Blvd., Stamford, Connecticut 06902, 203-965-5465
Toll-Free Telephone: 800-243-9500
Vendor: Control Data Business Information Services, Dun & Bradstreet Computing Services.
Cost: Varies by report—approximately $35 to $40 per report.
Date Began Online: 1980
Source of Information: 1970 and 1980 U.S. Census; information and current year estimates of the U.S. Census Bureau; proprietary information on five-year trends, automobile ownership characteristics, mobility factors, economic data, and private sector employment from Dun & Bradstreet commercial database.
Type of Coverage: Eight menu-driven demographic reports: Trend Report; Update Report; Profile Report; Census Household Details; Census Population Details; Census Change Report; Geographic Report; and Economic Report.
Size: Information not available at time of publication.
Updating: Annually.
Indexing Terms: States, Standard Metropolitan Statistical Areas (SMSA), zip codes, SMSA components, counties, census tracts, minor civil divisions, marketing area codes (ADI, DMA, Metromarket, and SAMI), census-defined places, Donnelley location reference-point codes.
User Aids: *American Profile User's Manual*, free; Maptool—protractor for reading maps to obtain displacement from reference points.
Printed Equivalent: None.
Document Retrieval: Not applicable.
Notes: The company offers a phone-in service for ordering these reports.

ONSITE

Our third major online demographic database, ONSITE, comes from the smallest of the companies that we are considering—Urban Decision Systems, Inc., a 50-employee firm devoted exclusively to the demographics business. ONSITE isn't menu-driven like the databases previously reviewed. Consequently, it is somewhat more complicated for an occasional user. But its system would be more convenient for a frequent user.

Urban Decision Systems contends that it is the only one of the three producers that updates its databases entirely with publicly available information. If you should question the accuracy of the data, the company will show you how the numbers were derived; the others use both public and proprietary data.

Profile

Database: ONSITE
Producer: Urban Decision Systems, Inc., 2032 Armacost Ave., P.O. Box 25953, Los Angeles, California 90025, 213-820-8931; in Connecticut, 203-226-7367
Toll-Free Telephone: None.
Vendor: STSC.
Cost: Averages $25 per report. Color graphics price to be announced.
Date Began Online: 1973
Source of Information: U.S. Census data from 1970 and 1980, with Census Bureau updates and updates from other publicly available sources.
Type of Coverage: Analysis of demographic charateristics according to user-selected criteria and geographic areas.
Size: Information not available at time of publication.
Updating: Annually.
Indexing Terms: Codes of counties, zip codes, minor civil divisions, states, metropolitan areas, census tracts, "Areas of Dominant Influence," designated market areas, and codes for locations of 15,000 places.
User Aids: *ONSITE User's Manual*, free; Help and Info commands online; regular mailings to users; *Reference Location Directory*—codes for 15,000 locations for which ONSITE contains proper longitude and latitude information.
Printed Equivalent: None.
Document Retrieval: Not applicable.
Notes: Custom reports available through phone-in service, including color graphics and maps.

Sales-potential studies

Very often census data alone may not do you much good. Suppose a demographic report tells you that a particular town or neighborhood has an average family income of $27,000 and a median age of 38. What good does that do you if you own an auto-parts store and want to open another outlet? How do you interpret the information? That's where sales-potential studies come in.

A sales-potential report combines census data with figures on the population's retail spending habits in order to estimate how much people in any

```
              DONNELLEY MARKETING INFORMATION SERVICES
            A COMPANY OF THE DUN & BRADSTREET CORPORATION

DONNELLEY MARKETING                          MARKET POTENTIAL 12/16/83
BALTIMORE, MD  SMSA                      1983 ANNUAL FAST FOOD RESTAURANT
                    DONNELLEY EXPENDITURE POTENTIAL INDEX
                        REGIONAL        U.S.
                         100.4          102.8
-------------------------------------------------------------------------
    EXPENDITURE POTENTIAL:   THIS STORE TYPE        ALL OTHERS
      PER HOUSEHOLD             $    492           $    920
      TOTAL ($000)             $  390123           $  727920
-------------------------------------------------------------------------
    EXPENDITURE POTENTIAL GROWTH             RETAIL SUPPORT POTENTIAL
      RATE (1970-83):   AREA    REGION     USA
      PER HOUSEHOLD     6.13%    6.29%    6.06%    1983:    1271 STORES
      TOTAL            8.08%    8.68%    8.43%    1970:    1185 STORES
-------------------------------------------------------------------------
               TOTAL        TOTAL      HOUSEHOLD    AVERAGE     MEDIAN HH.
  YEAR      POPULATION    HOUSEHOLDS   POPULATION   HH. SIZE     INCOME
  1980       2174023       756980      2121958       2.80       $19094
  1983       2218961       792422      2166896       2.73       $22557
-------------------------------------------------------------------------

                      ANNUAL   ANNUAL   ANNUALIZED GROWTH     EXPENDITURE
                      TOTAL    $ PER    RATE (1970-1983)   POTENTIAL INDEX
                      ($000)   HSHLD    TOTAL  PER HSHLD    REGION   U.S.

BREAKFAST             102204    129     8.25%    6.27%       97.4    102.8
LUNCH                 324042    409     7.83%    5.87%      100.6    110.5
DINNER                456298    576     8.37%    6.39%      101.7    103.3
SCHOOL MEALS           29395     37     6.21%    4.28%      102.6     98.2
BOARD & OTHER MEALS    12511     16     5.75%    3.83%       92.5    113.0
CANDY & GUM             5193      7     8.02%    6.05%       96.2     80.3
ICE CREAM PRODUCTS     13630     17     7.68%    5.72%      101.4     92.8
CRACKERS,CHIPS, ETC.    2949      4     6.94%    4.99%       91.1     88.8
PIES,NUTS & MISC. SNACKS 96060  121     8.50%    6.52%      100.6    109.8
MILK & CHOCOLATE DRINKS  2439     3     6.88%    4.93%       93.7     79.8
COFFEE, TEA            13041     16     7.37%    5.41%       91.0     72.8
COLAS, JUICES & SODAS  21034     27     8.47%    6.49%       94.3    128.3
ALCOHOLIC BEVERAGES    24242     31     8.52%    6.55%       91.6     50.2
ALL OTHER ITEMS        15005     19
                     --------- ----
MARKET POTENTIAL     1118043   1412
```

+   EXPENDITURE POTENTIAL INDEX - SHOWS THE AMOUNT BY WHICH AREA PER HOUSEHOLD
    EXPENDITURES DIFFER FROM THAT WITHIN THE REGION & THE NATION. VALUES BELOW
    100 SIGNIFY THAT AREA IS BELOW REGIONAL OR NATIONAL PER HSHLD EXPENDITURES.
+   RETAIL SUPPORT POTENTIAL - PROVIDES THE NUMBER OF AVERAGE SIZE STORES WHICH
    THE AREA SHOULD BE CAPABLE OF SUPPORTING.   AREA ID: 1. 0. 0

Donnelly's Market Potential report for fast-food restaurants in Baltimore, Md. (reprinted with permission).

given area are likely to spend on a particular product or service. CACI's SITE POTENTIAL database, for example, can analyze a territory's fitness for any of 19 broad types of retail businesses: shopping centers, groceries, drugs, apparel, footwear, department stores, automotive aftermarket, home improvement, optical, hair salon, bakeries, dry cleaners, photographic, appliances, ice cream, restaurants, commercial banks, savings and loans, consumer finance companies.

A. WEALTHY AREAS
1. Established suburbs
2. Newer suburbs
3. Central city areas

B. MIDDLE INCOME, POST-WAR SUBURBS, OLDER POPULATION
4. Upper middle income
5. Older families and retirees
6. Families with older children
7. Blue collar

C. YOUNG, MIDDLE INCOME POPULATION, HIGH VALUE HOUSING
8. Newer suburbs, upper-middle income
9. Young families, suburban housing
10. Middle income, high rent
11. Upper-middle income, very high rent

D. HIGH DENSITY RENTAL HOUSING
12. Highly educated, professionals
13. Older, less educated, white collar

E. COLLEGE AREAS
14. Urban with young professionals
15. Suburban and rural colleges

F. IMMIGRANT AND ETHNIC URBAN AREAS
16. Older hispanic immigrants
17. Middle income Europeans
18. Poor families, very old housing
19. Blue collar, East Europeans

G. MINORITY AREAS
20. Young hispanics, southwestern states
21. Hispanics and blacks, low rent housing
22. Poor urban blacks, high unemployment
23. Lower-middle income blacks, low value houses and apartments
24. Blacks, blue collar, older rental housing

H. LOWER-MIDDLE INCOME, YOUNG FAMILIES, POST-1940 HOUSES
25. Young families, whites and hispanics
26. Blue collar, middle income
27. Mobile homes
28. Mobile homes and seasonal housing

I. OLDER HOUSING, BLUE COLLAR, LOWER-MIDDLE INCOME
29. Young families with children
30. Middle income
31. Low income, older population

J. SMALL TOWNS, OLDER POPULATION, OLD HOUSING
32. White collar service workers
33. Retirees
34. Seasonal housing, retirees

K. AGRICULTURAL AREAS
35. Large farms, wealthy farm owners, poor laborers
36. Self-employed farmers
37. Rural small towns

L. DEPRESSED RURAL TOWNS, BLUE COLLAR
38. Rural industrial areas
39. Low income blacks and whites
40. Poor families, high unemployment
41. Small farms
42. Young families, blacks and whites, farm laborers

M. SPECIAL POPULATIONS
43. Military areas
44. Institutions

The 44 types of neighborhoods according to CACI's ACORN ("a classification of residential neighborhoods") (reprinted with permission).

In the auto aftermarket, for example, SITE POTENTIAL gives a set of projected spending figures and "market-potential indexes" for each of 13 different business subcategories. It may say, for example, that the weekly total expenditure on tires and tubes is $15,000. By dividing that figure among the existing competitors in the district, you can see whether there's room for another tire outlet. SITE POTENTIAL also compares the district to the surrounding economic region. If the market potential index for tires and tubes is 132, that means that tire sales per capita are likely to be 32 percent greater than the average sales potential of the surrounding economic region.

Donnelley's Market Potential database is very similar to SITE POTENTIAL, covering the same business types. Its own twist on the data is to show the number of stores an area could support, though that information may not be too helpful because it doesn't say how large the stores are assumed to be.

Urban Decision Systems' Retail Potential also is similar to these two databases; its twist is to estimate the square footage of a particular type of store that the area will support. You can compare the square footage of existing stores to see if there is room for another.

Enhancements

Two recent developments in packaging of demographic data should be noted—"cluster analysis" and color graphics. At this writing all three companies were planning to put cluster analysis products online. CACI's product, called ACORN (for "a classification of residential neighborhoods") dispenses with most of the barrage of numbers you get in other demographic reports. It classifies every one of 300,000 neighborhoods in the country under one of 44 types (see list on page 175). You can then use its database in various ways to home in on the groups who make your best customers.

Sophisticated color graphics is the other development. Demographic data lends itself well to presentation in maps and charts. Urban Decision Systems offers color printouts that display any of its data in a mile-grid map of any location in the country. Five 16-by-16-mile maps showing population, household count, aggregate income, per capita income, and 1970 to 1980 population change cost $99. The company calls the service COLORSITE. CACI offers a similar service, though not in full color. It calls its service SITE-MAP. Donnelley offers color maps for about $200, depending on the number of census tracts included. Prices, quality, and options are changing quickly at all three companies.

18 Databases About Companies

According to Walter E. Heller International Corp.'s Institute for Small Business, there are about 4 million businesses in the United States, not counting shell corporations. Only about ll,000 of them, or $\frac{1}{4}$ percent, are publicly owned and must by law publish detailed financial data on their operations. The other 99-3/4 percent of American firms barely have to tell the world a syllable about their business. This chapter reviews online data sources about both public and private companies.

The data furnished by public corporations is gathered, analyzed, and republished by dozens of organizations, including, of course, database producers. The ll,000 public corporations account for about 70 percent of all domestic production; naturally, following their activities is extremely important to many people in business. In this chapter, we discuss six of the leading databases that specialize in financial data on publicly held firms. They are Disclosure II Online, COMPUSTAT II, PTS Annual Reports Abstracts, Standard & Poor's News Online, Value Line Data Base II, and Spectrum Ownership Profiles Online. Though the six gather their basic data largely from the same sources, each has a unique perspective and offers some information that the others do not.

If you seek facts about any of the rest of the 4 million American businesses, you may have a tougher time. Nevertheless, this 30 percent of the U.S. economy is big enough to warrant the attention of information gatherers, analysts, and database producers. We consider six other databases that, while they also cover public companies, can tell you a surprising lot about most of the country's privately held businesses. They are Dun's Market Identifiers, Million Dollar Directory, Economic Information Systems Business Data Base, Electronic Yellow Pages, DunSprint, and TRW Business Credit Profile. Each of these databases is much different from the six that report just on public companies. By and large, they have far less detail on any individual company, but the huge number of companies they cover makes them very impressive indeed.

Finally, if you're investigating companies abroad, there are a number of database sources that might help you. We present the database most accessible in the United States: Dun's Principal International Businesses.

Disclosure II Online

We start with Disclosure II (the II is commonly dropped). Disclosure has a contract with the Securities and Exchange Commission to act as the public supplier of documents filed at the commission. Daily, a Disclosure messenger picks up newly released filings; almost immediately you can, for $10 and up, ask Disclosure for a microfiche copy to be put in the mail to you (copies on paper are more expensive). The information is extracted from the document and incorporated into the database within about three weeks.

Disclosure contains records on every "operating" company that files with the SEC, or about 9,000 in all. It excludes about 2,000 "nonoperating" public companies, such as mutual funds or real estate investment trusts, that do not directly produce goods or services. Of the 9,000, about 1,500 are traded on the New York Stock Exchange and about 770 on the American Stock Exchange. The rest, about 6,500, are traded over-the-counter or on one of the regional exchanges. About half of these 6,500 are traded actively; the other half thinly. Disclosure Online records, at $2 to $10 per, may sound expensive. But the typical record is several pages long—quite an extensive citation compared to many bibliographic databases.

Searchable Fields: Disclosure II on DIALOG (as summarized in the DIALOG manual)

BASIC INDEX
Company Name
Description of Business
Directors/Nominees Names
Officers Names
Subsidiaries
Ownership
Management Discussion Text

ADDITIONAL INDEXES
Auditor Change
Auditor
Accrued Expenses
Accounts Payable
Auditor's Report
Total Current Assets
Current Long-Term Debt
Cost of Goods
Cash
Current Portion of Capital Leases
Disclosure Company Number
Company Name

Current Outstanding Shares
Comments
Convertible Debt
City
Depreciation & Amortization
Deferred Charges
Deferred Charges (Taxes/Income)
Directors/Nominees
Accumulated Depreciation
Deposits & Other Assets
Extraordinary Items & Discontinued
   Operations
Number of Employees
Exhibits
Exchange
Finished Goods
Fortune Number
Fiscal Year End
Gross Profit
Investment & Advances to Subsidiaries
Income Before Tax
Income Taxes

Income Before Depreciation & Amortization
Interest Expense
Investment Gains/Losses
Incorporation
Intangibles
Inventories
Net Income Before Extraordinary Items
Long-Term Debt
Total Current Liabilities
Other Long-Term Liabilities
Total Liabilities & Net Worth
Mortgages
Minority Interest (Income)
Minority Interest (Liabilities)
Marketable Securities
Officers
Other Noncurrent Assets
Net Income
Noncurrent Capital Leases
Nonoperating Income/Expense
Notes Payable
Notes Receivable
Net Sales
Other Current Assets & Prepaid Expenses
Other Income
Other Liabilities
Outstanding Shares
Other Corporate Events

Primary SIC Code
Net Property, Plant, & Equipment
Property, Plant, & Equipment
Preferred Stock
Provision for Income Taxes
R & D Expenditures
Receivables
Other Current Liabilities
Raw Materials
Retained Earnings
Subsidiaries
SIC Codes
Shareholders' Equity
Sell, Gen. & Admin. Expenses
Ownership
Common Stock Net
Shares, Held by Officers & Directors
Capital Surplus
Number of Shareholders
State
Total Assets
Telephone Number
Total Liabilities
Treasury Stock
Ticker Symbol
Work in Progress
Cross Reference
Zip Code

Profile

Database: Disclosure II Online
Producer: Disclosure, 5161 River Rd., Bethesda, Maryland 20816, 301-951-1300
Toll-Free Telephone: 800-628-8076
Vendor: DIALOG, Dow Jones News/Retrieval, Control Data Business Information Systems, I. P. Sharp, InnerLine, ADP Network Services. Others probably will be added in the future.
Cost: Varies by vendor. On Dow Jones, $36 to $72 per hour (double at 1200 baud), plus $2 per company record (nonprime time) or $5 (prime time). On DIALOG and InnerLine, $60 per hour, plus $6 per company record (printed online) or $10 per company record (printed offline). The remaining three charge according to the more complicated time-sharing company algorithms (see Chapter 8 on the cost of database searching).
Date Began Online: 1979
Source of Information: Taken primarily from official forms filed with the Securities and Exchange Commission by U.S. publicly held companies. Data is from 10-K (annual), 10-Q (quarterly), and 8-K (unscheduled event) reports, registration statements, prospectuses, and other sources.
Type of Coverage: Data is extracted from the filings and reorganized according to Disclosure's own format; the filings are not reproduced in their entirety. The data can be displayed only (not manipulated) on DIALOG, Dow Jones, and InnerLine. On Control Data, ADP, and I. P. Sharp, software is available for analyzing, comparing, and manipulating the data and for creating customized reports. A microcomputer software package, MicroDisclosure, is available for personal computers for download-

ing data from DIALOG and analyzing it offline. The latest three years of line items on each company (along with a five-year summary) are maintained online.

Size: Coverage of approximately 9,000 companies. These are all companies that file with the SEC except approximately 2,000 investment companies, real estate investment trusts, etc.

Updating: New filings are added to the database tapes within about three weeks of when they are received by the SEC; the updated tapes are then reloaded weekly on DIALOG, Dow Jones, ADP, I. P. Sharp; biweekly on Control Data; monthly on Inner-Line.

Indexing Terms: Approximately 100 fields can be searched individually. (See Searchable Fields list.)

User Aids: *Disclosure II User's Manual*, $25. *Disclosure Online News*, free newsletter. *Guide to SEC Corporate Filings*, free. *Guide to SEC Filing Companies*, free.

Printed Equivalent: None.

Document Retrieval: Disclosure Inc. converts to microfiche most documents filed with the SEC by publicly held companies. All documents are available for purchase. The cost is $10 per document (on microfiche) or 37¢ per page (photocopied from microfiche onto paper—$10 minimum). For copies of documents made immediately from the original: 45¢ per page, $25 minimum. A 5 percent discount is given for deposit account customers. Disclosure also offers a subscription service by which you may receive automatically all reports of a certain kind that you specify (examples: all filings by companies in a certain SIC code; all prospectuses; or all 10-Ks for NYSE companies).

COMPUSTAT II

COMPUSTAT II covers about 6,000 companies, rather than the 9,000 on Disclosure. It excludes the thinly traded stocks. Unlike Disclosure, it does not carry the text of the management's discussion from the 10-K (annual) SEC filing, nor officers and directors, salaries, and stockholdings from the proxy statement.

But COMPUSTAT's financial listings tend to be more thorough than Disclosure's. Where Disclosure lists only "depreciation and amortization" as one line item, for example, COMPUSTAT may separate "depreciation expense," "depletion expense," and "amortization of intangibles" as three line items.

COMPUSTAT's new Business Information file breaks down operating results of its companies into industry segments by SIC code. Companies are required to report data from all industry segments in which sales, operating profits, or identifiable assets represent 10 percent or more of the company's consolidated figures. This is valuable for analyzing the results of an industry across companies that engage in several lines of business.

COMPUSTAT is more suited for historical analysis than Disclosure. It goes back as far as 20 years; Disclosure keeps only the latest three years of line items, with a five-year income summary.

Most of the COMPUSTAT vendors require a hefty subscription fee. DRI, however, makes some data items available inexpensively through its Datakits system for analysis using VisiCalc on a personal computer.

COMPUSTAT—*Annual Industrial Data Items*

INCOME STATEMENT (HISTORICAL)
Sales
Cost of Goods Sold
  Rental Expense
  Pension Expense
  Labor and Related Expense
Selling, General and Administrative
  Expenses
  Advertising Expense
  Research and Development Expense
Operating Income Before Depreciation
Depreciation, Depletion, Amortization of
  Intangibles
  Depreciation Expense
  Depletion Expense
  Amortization of Intangibles
Interest Expense (Total)
  Interest Expense on Long-Term Debt
Nonoperating Income/Expense
  Interest Income
  Rental Income
  Equity in Earnings (Unconsolidated
    Subsidiaries)
Special Items
Pretax Income
Income Taxes (Total)
  Federal Taxes
  State Taxes
  Foreign Taxes
  Deferred Taxes
  Investment Tax Credit
Minority Interest
Income Before Extraordinary Items and
  Discontinued Operations
  Extraordinary Items
  Discontinued Operations
Net Income (Loss)

Earnings Per Share Information

Preferred Dividends Available for Common
  Savings due to Common Stock
  Equivalents
Earnings Per Share (Primary)—Excluding
  Extraordinary Items and Discontinued
  Earnings
Earnings Per Share (Primary)—Including
  Extraordinary Items and Discontinued
  Operations
Earnings Per Share (Fully Diluted)—
  Excluding Extraordinary Items and
  Discontinued Operations
Earnings Per Share (Fully Diluted)—
  Including Extraordinary Items and
  Discontinued Operations
Shares Used to Calculate Primary Earnings
  Per Share

Shares Used to Calculate Fully Diluted
  Earnings Per Share

INCOME STATEMENT (RESTATED)
Sales
Cost of Goods Sold
Selling, General and Administrative
  Expenses
Operating Income Before Depreciation
Depreciation, Depletion, Amortization of
  Intangibles
Interest Expense
Nonoperating Income/Expense
Pretax Income
Income Taxes (Total)
Minority Interest
Income Before Extraordinary Items and
  Dicontinued Operations
Extraordinary Items and Discontinued
  Operations
Net Income (Loss)

Earnings Per Share Information

Earnings Per Share (Primary)—Excluding
  Extraordinary Items and Discontinued
  Operations
Earnings Per Share (Primary)—Including
  Extraordinary Items and Discontinued
  Operations
Earnings Per Share (Fully Diluted)—
  Excluding Extraordinary Items and
  Discontinued Operations
Earnings Per Share (Fully Diluted)—
  Including Extraordinary Items and
  Discontinued Operations
Shares Used to Calculate Primary Earnings
  Per Share

STATEMENT OF CHANGES IN FINANCIAL
POSITION (HISTORICAL)

Sources of Funds

Income Before Extraordinary Items and
  Discontinued Operations
Extraordinary Items and Discontinued
  Operations
Depreciation, Depletion, Amortization
Deferred Taxes
Unremitted Earnings (Loss of
  Unconsolidated Subsidiaries)
Other Funds from Operations
Total Funds from Operations
Sale of Property, Plant, Equipment
Issuance of Long-Term Debt
Sales of Common and Preferred Stock
Decrease in Investments

Other Sources of Funds
Total Sources of Funds

Uses of Funds

Cash Dividends
Common Dividends
Capital Expenditures
Reduction of Long-Term Debt
Purchase of Common and Preferred Stock
Increase in Investments
Acquisitions
Other Uses of Funds
Total Uses of Funds

MARKET INFORMATION
Price—High
Price—Low
Price—Close
Dividends Per Share
Common Shares Outstanding
Number of Common Shareholders
Common Shares Traded
Stock Splits/Dividends

SUPPLEMENTARY INFORMATION

Income Statement Related

Excise Taxes
Foreign Currency Adjustment
Tax Loss Carryforward
Minimum Rental Commitment in the First,
    Second, Third, Fourth and Fifth Year
    After the Balance Sheet Date

Balance Sheet Related

Inventory Valuation Method
Average Short-Term Debt
Average Interest Rate on Short-Term Debt
Long-Term Debt Tied to Prime Debt
Long-Term Debt Maturing in the Second,
    Third, Fourth and Fifth Year After the
    Balance Sheet Date
Preferred Stock—Liquidating Value
Preferred Stock—Redemption Value
Convertible Debt and Preferred Stock
Common Equity (Tangible)
Unrestricted Retained Earnings
Treasury Stock (Number of Common
    Shares)
Total Invested Capital
Present Value of Noncapitalized Leases
Unfunded Pension Costs—Vested Benefits
Unfunded Pension Costs—Past/Prior
    Service
Compensating Balances

Other

Employees (Historical and Restated)
Capital Expenditures (Historical and
    Restated)
Order Backlog
Auditor/Auditor's Opinion
Common Shares Reserved for Conversion

BALANCE SHEET (HISTORICAL)

Assets

Cash and Short-Term Investments
    Cash
Receivables
    Trade Receivables
    Income Tax Refund
    Estimated Doubtful Receivables
Inventories
    Raw Materials
    Work in Progress
    Finished Goods
Other Current Assets
    Prepaid Expenses
Total Current Assets
Property, Plant, Equipment (Gross)
    Accumulated Depreciation
Property, Plant, Equipment (Net)
    Land
    Natural Resources (Net)
    Buildings (Net)
    Machinery and Equipment (Net)
    Leases (Net)
    Construction in Progress
Investments in and Advances to
    Unconsolidated Subsidiaries
Investments in and Advances to Others
Intangibles
Other Assets
    Deferred Charges
Total Assets

Liabilities

Short-Term Debt
    Notes Payable
    Long-Term Debt Due in One Year
Accounts Payable
Income Taxes Payable
Other Current Liabilities
    Accrued Expenses
Total Current Liabilities
Long-Term Debt
    Convertible Debt
    Convertible Subordinated Debt
    Subordinated Debt
    Notes
    Debentures

Capitalized Lease Obligations
Other Long-Term Debt
Deferred Taxes
Investment Tax Credit
Minority Interest
Other Liabilities
Total Liabilities

Stockholders Equity

Preferred Stock
Common Equity
  Common Stock

Capital Surplus
Retained Earnings
Treasury Stock
Stockholders Equity

BALANCE SHEET (RESTATED)
Property, Plant, Equipment (Net)
Long-Term Debt
Retained Earnings
Working Capital
Stockholders Equity
Total Assets

Profile

Database: COMPUSTAT II
Producer: Standard & Poor's Corp., COMPUSTAT Services, Inc., 7400 S. Alton Court, Englewood, Colorado 80110
Toll-Free Telephone: 800-525-8640
Vendor: ADP Network Services, Boeing Computer Services, Chase Econometrics/Interactive Data, Citishare, CompuServe, Data Resources, Fact Set Data Systems, Management Decision Systems (MDS), Warner Computer Systems.
Cost: $5,000 to $50,000 annual subscription fee.
Date Began Online: 1962
Source of Information: Quarterly and annual reports, 10-K reports, Uniform Statistical Reports on Utilities, news releases.
Type of Coverage: Up to 175 annual line items and 70 quarterly items for industrial companies, as far back as 20 years. Up to 220 annual items and 143 quarterly items for banks. Up to 400 annual items and 185 quarterly items for utilities.

Also included are a Price-Dividend-Earning File for 4,200 companies and approximately 120 indexes, including the S&P 400, S&P 500, the Dow Jones 30 Industrials, the American Stock Exchange and New York Stock Exchange indexes.

The Business Information File breaks out operating results by SIC code for about 6,000 companies. A company may be identified by up to 90 SIC codes.
Size: Over 6,000 companies.
Updating: Weekly.
Indexing Terms: CUSIP, ticker symbols, SIC codes. Most data items shown in chart are searchable.
User Aids: *COMPUSTAT II User Manuals*, free with subscription; *Weekly Status Reports*.
Printed Equivalent: None.
Document Retrieval: Not offered.
Other Services: COMPUSTAT's Research Department will do custom work; contact the company for price information.

PTS Annual Reports Abstracts

Unlike Disclosure and COMPUSTAT, which extract their data from SEC filings, PTS Annual Reports Abstracts devotes its attention to the annual reports that companies distribute to their shareholders. Some companies' 10-Ks are virtually identical to their annual shareholders' reports, but in many cases the two documents are quite different. The larger public companies often put extensive narratives about the company's activities in the annual report; these may not appear at all in the 10-K for the SEC.

Thus Predicasts' (PTS) goal was to complement databases like Disclosure by providing access to the material in annual reports. If an annual report makes significant mention of different product lines, Annual Reports Abstracts will enter an individual abstract in the database for each one. On average, the database contains 11 abstracts from each annual report. This makes it a good source to learn the circumstances behind the statistics, including information on new products and technologies, acquisitions, corporate goals, etc. But, bear in mind, this is all from management's point of view.

Annual Reports Abstracts covers 4,500 companies, or only about half as many as Disclosure. It has all NYSE and ASE companies, along with some of the most actively traded OTCs. Unlike most other databases in this chapter, it also covers annual reports of selected companies from Japan, Canada, and Western Europe.

All product information it carries is assigned as definitive a code as possible, enabling users to narrow in on even casual textual references. The database is indexed according to the same useful controlled vocabularies as the other Predicasts databases, including seven-digit SIC codes whenever possible and event codes. Other searchable fields include corporate sales, number of employees, stock exchange, D-U-N-S number, ticker symbol, and a corporate identification code linking all records pertaining to a specific organization. Annual Reports Abstracts does provide some of the same information as Disclosure, including some fiscal year-end data and a five-year income summary.

Sample record

PROBLEM: I'm researching companies that make membrane keyboards. I need information on Honeywell's activities in this field.

Honeywell	Annual Report
Corporate ID: 004841-00000	Year Ending December 31, 1981

INDUSTRIAL SYSTEMS

Honeywell's industrial components business grew during the year, and investment in new products and facilities continued. Micro Switch established a plant in Las Cruces, New Mexico, to produce low-cost membrane keyboards. New solid-state products included a linear Hall-effect device for current and position sensing, and a flow-through pressure sensor for rapidly expanding medical electronics market. The photoelectric controls business expanded in Europe with the acquisition of Cometa in Grenoble, France. Synertek, which manufactures microprocessor, memory, and custom VLSI components serving computer, telecommunications, and consumer markets, had an excellent year. Early in 1982 wafer production began at Synertek's new plant in Santa Cruz, California.

The industrial components business entered 1982 with good backlogs. Order rates should remain level for the first half, with improvements in the last half. The success of membrane keyboard will contribute to a growing share of computer terminal markets: membrane-keyboard production will begin in Europe and Japan. Synertek's Santa Cruz plant will provide the capacity to respond to increased demand for semiconductor products expected later in the year. Expanded marketing efforts in Europe for semicondcutor and optoelectronic components should increase business there substantially.

835	New Mexico
1USA	United States
1USA	United States
4FRA	France
010	Free World
010	Free World
010	Free World
4F	Europe ex USSR
4F	Europe ex USSR
3679520	Keyboards
3674850	Hall-effect devices
3823520	Electronic flow & level sensors
3622035	Pilot circuit devices
3670000	Electrical components
3679520	Keyboards
3674000	Semiconductor devices
3674000	Semiconductor devices
3674400	Optoelectronic devices
443	New capacity
336	Product introduction
336	Product introduction
157	Acquirer completes purchase
222	Management policies and goals
222	Management policies and goals
222	Management policies and goals
246	International marketing
246	International marketing

Profile

Database: PTS Annual Reports Abstracts
Producer: Predicasts, Inc., 11001 Cedar Ave., Cleveland, Ohio 44106, 216-795-3000
Toll-Free Telephone: 800-321-6388 (outside Ohio)
Vendor: BRS, DIALOG.
Cost: DIALOG: $120 per hour, 85¢ offline prints, 80¢ online prints. BRS: $90 per hour, 40¢ offline prints, 63¢ online prints, plus 18¢ per page.
Date Began Online: February 1983
Source of Information: Corporation annual reports and 10-K reports filed with the Securities and Exchange Commission.
Type of Coverage: Abstracts of text and financial statistics.
Size: 4500 companies by end of 1983; NYSE, ASE, and most active 800 OTC; selected international reports. Most utilities and financial corporations excluded. 50,000 records.
Updating: Each month approximately 350 companies are added or updated. Financial or basic corporate data is replaced annually; text material is kept for three years.

Indexing Terms: Product code, company name, ticker symbol, D-U-N-S number, and others.
User Aids: *PTS User's Manual*, $15. (Annual Reports Abstracts insert from manual is free.)
Printed Equivalent: None.
Document Retrieval: Full document delivery service available: 35¢ per page, $10 minimum for foreign annual reports.
Other Services: Seminars are available for instruction on use of the database.

Standard & Poor's News Online

Standard & Poor's Corporation Records, a well-known seven-volume set (with daily loose-leaf updates) can be found in most libraries, stock brokerage firms, and the offices of many corporations. Like Disclosure, it supplies summary data on most of the country's publicly held corporations (about 10,000 of them). But S&P takes a somewhat different approach to gathering its data.

Disclosure takes data almost exclusively from SEC filings, such as the 10-K. PTS Annual Report Abstracts casts its net a little wider by tapping annual reports as well. COMPUSTAT collects some information from news releases. Standard & Poor's News Online draws on these sources, plus reports filed with regulatory bodies, newspaper articles, and any public legal documents relating to the corporation.

Standard & Poor's assembles its data with the investor in mind. Its full records include detailed descriptions of each of a company's bond issues, S&P bond ratings, and dividend information on its stock. The corporate background is written by S&P rather than taken from management's discussion in the 10-K or annual report. The financial figures, however, are less detailed than those in Disclosure or COMPUSTAT.

As this book is being written, only the daily updates volume (back to 1979) is online. S&P was planning to put the full *Corporation Records* online by the beginning of 1984.

The daily update, Standard & Poor's News Online, reports on the latest announcements concerning a company, whether they be interim earnings, changes in dividend, sale of securities, changes in line of business, etc. Indexing is only by company name; unlike most other databases in this chapter, it is not possible to search by SIC code, sales figures, D-U-N-S number, or line item.

Profile

Database: Standard & Poor's News Online
Producer: Standard & Poor's Corporation, 25 Broadway, New York, New York 10004, 212-208-8622
Toll-Free Telephone: None.
Vendor: DIALOG and DIALOG's Knowledge Index.

Cost: On DIALOG, $85 per hour, plus 15¢/record for offline prints. On Knowledge Index, $24 per hour, including telecommunications charges.

Date Began Online: 1980

Source of Information: Wire services, press releases from company, all reports filed with regulatory bodies to which company reports, leading newspapers, releases from stock exchanges, etc.

Type of Coverage: Factual data abstracted and written in S&P's format. This is the full text of the printed equivalent.

Size: Approximately 300,000 records covering 10,000 companies.

Updating: Daily, 300 to 400 news items added each day.

Indexing Terms: Indexing is only by company name.

User Aids: *Standard & Poor's Corporation Records Online User's Manual*, $15 plus postage

Printed Equivalent: *S&P Corporation Records Current News* (Volume 7 of *Corporation Records*), $615 per year.

Document Retrieval: Not applicable.

Notes: First six volumes of *Corporation Records*, available online in 1984, will provide more complete company description.

Value Line Data Base II

The Value Line database, an online version of the well-known *Value Line Investment Survey*, contains detailed financial data similar to COMPUSTAT but for a much smaller group of companies. It covers only about 1,650 firms—those, according to Value Line, that account for 95 percent of the trading volume on the major U.S. exchanges.

Unlike the other databases in this chapter, Value Line includes projections of a number of variables for each company, including sales, earnings, book value, and cash flow, for three to five years ahead. The database, however, does not contain the timeliness or safety ranks present in the printed version.

The database is available for a $5,500 annual subscription fee or, on several vendors, on a per use basis of 8¢ per data item retrieved. The company has also announced a new microcomputer package called VALUE/SCREEN to be used in analyzing the data. The price was set at $495 a year. Other information on the new offering was not available at the time of publication.

Profile

Database: Value Line Data Base II

Producer: Value Line Data Services, Value Line, Inc., 711 Third Ave., New York, New York 10017, 212-687-3965

Toll-Free Telephone: None.

Vendor: ADP Network Services, CompuServe, COMSHARE, Data Resources, General Electric Information Services, Chase Econometrics/Interactive Data, Shaw Data Services, Sligos (France), Tymshare.

Cost: Annual subscription, $5,500; quarterly subscription, $1,700. Available on a per use basis of 8¢ for each data item retrieved (from Chase, CompuServe, and Data Resources).

Date Began Online: 1973
Source of Information: Corporate financial reports and Value Line analysts.
Type of Coverage: Financial data abstracted from original source and reformatted; also original projections by Value Line analysts. Each vendor offers different software for manipulating and analyzing the data. Data goes as far back as 1955, but the number of years carried depends on each vendor. No textual information.
Size: 1,650 companies.
Updating: 30 times a year.
Indexing Terms: Value Line industrial codes, ticker symbols, SIC codes. Most data items are searchable.
User Aids: Each vendor supplies a manual based on its own software capabilities.
Printed Equivalent: *Value Line Investment Survey*, $365.
Document Retrieval: Not applicable.

Spectrum Ownership Profiles Online

There is only one database that keeps track of who owns the stock of the major publicly held corporations in the United States, based on all pertinent information filed with the Securities and Exchange Commission—Spectrum Ownership Profiles Online. Other databases carry some ownership information from SEC filings, but Spectrum is the only one that carries all eight relevant SEC filings, providing one authoritative source for the information.

The database includes company ownership information reported in the following SEC filings: 13D and 13G regarding ownership of 5 percent or more of a company's stock; 14D-1 regarding tender offers; 13(f) regarding institutional common stock holdings and convertible holdings; N1Q regarding investment company holdings; and Forms 3 and 4 regarding insider ownership. A contract to compile and make commercially available many of these filings has been specifically awarded to the database producer, Computer Directions Advisors, Inc., by the SEC. With the exception of insider ownership information, data is updated daily.

The system covers more than 6,000 publicly held companies and includes common stocks and convertibles. A complete profile of a firm can be ordered with a single command, or particular reports may be selected. The ownership summary provides the user with an overview of current holdings and is supplemented by a series of reports that are organized by type of filing.

Investment company funds are required to file their common stock holdings and transactions with the SEC on Form N1Q. Reports are filed each quarter by individual funds, even when they are part of a larger investment management group. More than 550 open- and closed-end investment company funds with combined assets exceeding $40 billion are currently filing N1Q reports. Holdings may be sorted by size or alphabetically by fund.

Institutions managing equity assets exceeding $100 million are required to file their holdings with the SEC on Form 13(f) on a quarterly basis. More than 500 major institutions with assets greater than $400 billion are currently filing 13(f) reports. These include banks, insurance companies, investment companies, universities, and foundations. Spectrum allows a user to learn the holdings of a particular portfolio or to learn which portfolios hold specific securities. New positions and changes in ownership are identified.

Any stockholder owning more than 5 percent of a publicly held U.S. corporation must file Form 13G with the SEC within 45 days following the end of each calendar year. Any change in the 13G information or new 5 percent position must be reported to the SEC on Form 13D within 10 days of the purchase or sale. More than 10,000 Forms 13D and 13G are filed annually. Ownership positions related to tender offers are reported to the SEC on Form 14D-1 within 10 days of the event date.

Insider information is provided on SEC Forms 3 and 4. Every officer, director, or 10 percent principal stockholder must file a Form 3 with the SEC within 10 days of establishing an initial position in any of the firm's registered securities. A change in the number of shares held is filed on Form 4. Approximately 150,000 Forms 3 and 4 are filed annually. The information provided on these forms is updated monthly by CDA.

The most commonly used method of accessing Spectrum is by CUSIP (Commission on Uniform Securities Identification Procedures) number, ticker symbol, or company name. The database can also be accessed by owner's portfolio. Spectrum is currently available directly from CDA or through GTE Telenet Communications Corporation. The database will probably also be available from DIALOG in 1984.

Spectrum allows great flexibility in sorting information. Data may be sorted according to alphabetical listing, value (high, low), quarterly change, holdings (high, low), type of manager, geographic location by owner (for example, all owners in Chicago), filing date (for example, all new filings from IBM since November 1983) and numerous other methods.

Profile

Database: Spectrum Ownership Profiles Online
Producer: Computer Directions Advisors, Inc., 11501 Georgia Ave., Silver Spring, Maryland 20902-1975, 301-942-1700
Toll-Free Telephone: None.
Vendor: GTE Telenet Communications and Computer Directions Advisors. Will be available on DIALOG in 1984.
Cost: $15,000 per year subscription plus $45 hour for unlimited reports, or $95 per report plus $45 hour. Parts of reports can be obtained for a lower cost. $100 one-time sign-up charge.
Date Began Online: 1980
Source of Information: SEC filings, as well as 375 of the largest European investment company shareholder reports.
Type of Coverage: Factual data is extracted from SEC filings and reformatted.
Size: Over 150,00 filings per year.
Updating: Daily.
Indexing Terms: CUSIP numbers, ticker symbols, company name. Information can also be accessed by individual portfolio.
User Aids: *Spectrum Ownership Profiles Users Manual*.
Printed Equivalent: *Investment Company Stock Holdings Survey*, quarterly, $150 per year; *Investment Company Portfolios*; *13(f) Institutional Stock Holdings Survey*; *13(f) Institutional Portfolios*; *Five Percent Ownership based on 13G, 13D, and 14D-1 Filings*;

Insider Ownership Based on Forms 3 and 4; *13(f) Holdings Survey of Convertible Bonds and Convertible Preferred Stocks.*
Document Retrieval: Not offered.

Dun's Market Identifiers

The distinction we drew at the beginning of this chapter—between databases that cover publicly held companies and those that cover private companies—is perhaps artificial. All of the databases in the latter category also list public companies. For example, among the 1.5 million establishments in Dun's Market Identifiers, about 10 percent are branches or affiliates of public firms. Nevertheless, since Dun's, and the databases to follow, include primarily privately owned firms, that is the feature about them that we consider most important.

Dun & Bradstreet Corporation (D&B) dominates the "private" market. You may be familiar with D&B as the country's largest credit rating bureau for businesses; it has 75 percent of that market.

D&B employs an army of credit analysts who gather information about the credit worthiness of American businesses. Many companies contribute financial data on themselves in order to establish a good standing in D&B's records. Creditors also contribute data on how fast they get paid by companies to whom they have extended credit. D&B gathers what additional information it can from third-party sources.

All of this information goes into a master database containing records on more than 5 million business "establishments." An establishment may be a company or a branch or subsidiary of another company. Almost any establishment that pays its own bills—and thus accumulates a credit history—will find itself listed.

This master database is the foundation of DunSprint, D&B's original on-line database. This online source for credit reports is available by subscription only (more on DunSprint later).

Even without the credit information, D&B's records constitute a valuable database. Dun's Marketing Services exists just to sell this noncredit information on American firms—who they are, where they are, what is their line of business, how big they are, who the president is, etc.

The centerpiece of Dun's Marketing Services is the database Dun's Market Identifiers (MI). It is available through DIALOG without a subscription. (Compared to most of the databases in this book, though, it's expensive: $100 per hour plus $1.00 to $1.50 per company record.) It consists of all the establishments in D&B's master database that have at least $1 million in sales or 10 employees (branches or subsidiaries of each listed company are included even if they don't meet the size requirement). That adds up to about 1.5 million companies.

D&B drops from the database any establishment whose record has not been updated for 18 months, for it figures the information is out of date by that time. D&B logs about 500,000 new businesses each year, with an equal number of failures or dissolutions.

Each establishment receives a nine-digit D-U-N-S number (Dun's Universal Numbering System), a system that has become accepted as the equivalent of a Social Security number throughout much of American industry (and is present in other business databases). For every establishment that is a branch or subsidiary of another, the database gives the D-U-N-S number for as many as three levels of corporate "parents," which D&B refers to as the headquarters location, parent, and ultimate company.

D&B suggests some of the following applications as typical uses of its Market Identifiers database:

♦ Market Analysis—to identify and qualify the market for company products and services (geographically, by industry, by company size).

♦ Sales Prospecting Programs—to identify firms that represent potential customers for sales calls.

♦ Precall Planning—to give company information to the salesperson (executive names, locations, business activities) to take the "cold" out of "cold calling."

♦ Sales Executive Decision Making—to restructure sales territories for greater efficiency based on the distribution of clients (actual or potential). To develop realistic sales goals and quotas.

♦ National Account Identification—to locate new prospects in a unique way by looking at the corporate family of related companies (parents, subsidiaries, headquarters, or branch locations) within the current customer base.

♦ Territory Alignment—to segment markets or territories by their potential for new sales or marketing opportunities.

♦ New Product Development—to measure the market size and potential for a proposed new product or service.

♦ Market Research—to determine the scope of the market being analyzed, select sample calls by predetermined parameters, and print a list of the companies to be interviewed.

♦ Competitive Analysis—to find out about the competition by identifying the companies currently serving a specific market.

♦ Mergers/Acquisitions/Divestitures—to locate candidate companies for acquisitions and monitor the rapidly changing corporate ownership and affiliation applications.

♦ Vendor Qualifications—to select and evaluate vendors based on special requirements (location, size, line of business).

♦ Accounting—to find out company name, address, and other business information for ongoing administrative activities. To identify customers and vendors using the D-U-N-S number.

Sample record (fictitious data)

```
FEDERAL PACIFIC ELECTRIC CO
CARTER CONTROLS
150 AVENUE L
```

425 RIVER ST STN
NEWARK, NJ 07101
PHONE: 201-589-7500
ESSEX COUNTY   SMSA: 409 (NEWARK, NJ)
BUSINESS: CIRCUIT BREAKERS
PRIMARY SIC: 3613 SWITCHGEAR, SWITCHBOARD APPARATUS
SECONDARY SIC: 3612 TRANSFORMERS
SECONDARY SIC: 3675 ELECTRONIC CAPACITORS
SECONDARY SIC: 3679 ELECTRONIC COMPONENTS, NEC
YEAR STARTED: 1979
SALES: $402,000,000
EMPLOYEES HERE: 1,700
EMPLOYEES TOTAL: 11,000
THIS IS:
   A MANUFACTURING LOCATION
   A HEADQUARTERS LOCATION (OR A SINGLE LOCATION OR A BRANCH)
   A SUBSIDIARY
   A CORPORATION (OR A PARTNERSHIP OR A PROPRIETORSHIP)
   A PUBLIC COMPANY
DUNS NUMBER: 00-214-6272
HEADQUARTERS DUNS: 00-214-6272
PARENT DUNS: 00-419-7646 RELIANCE ELECTRIC CO
CORPORATE FAMILY DUNS: 00-121-3214 EXXON CORPORATION
CHIEF EXECUTIVE: H.E. KNUDSON, JR., VP

Profile

Database: Dun's Market Identifiers (MI)
Producer: Dun's Marketing Services, 3 Century Drive, Parsippany, New Jersey 07054, 201-455-0900
Toll-Free Telephone: 800-526-9018
Vendor: DIALOG.
Cost: $100 per hour plus $1.00 to $1.50 per company record, depending on format.
Date Began Online: 1982
Source of Information: Taken from the files of Dun & Bradstreet's credit reporting service. Data is collectd by 1,500 analysts throughout the United States. Information may be supplied by cited companies themselves or derived from third-party sources. This database does not contain financial reports or Dun & Bradstreet's credit ratings (those are obtainable by qualified users through the DunSprint database).
Type of Coverage: Criteria for inclusion: establishments with at least $1 million in sales or at least 10 employees, and that have had a D&B credit update within the previous 18 months. For details of individual data items, see Summary of Information section (pages 194–195).
Size: Approximately 1.5 million business establishments.
Updating: Quarterly, approximately 450,000 records are changed each update.
Indexing Terms: All fields listed in Summary of Information section (pages 194–195).
User Aids: *Dun's Online User's Guide*, $50. DIALOG database chapter on Market Identifiers, $5.
Printed Equivalent: Dun's Marketing Services also sells the database contents in printed form on index cards.

Document Retrieval: Not applicable.
Other Services: Dun's Marketing Services also sells a variety of sales and marketing information services, including market analysis, market research, and direct-mail lists.

Million Dollar Directory

The Million Dollar Directory (MDD), also by D&B, is primarily a subset of Dun's Market Identifiers, with somewhat more thorough listings. This database is mainly a spin-off of the printed reference books of the same name.

To create this database, D&B selects all the companies in Dun's Market Identifiers that have a net worth (not sales) of $500,000 or more. Thus D&B eliminates about 90 percent of the establishments, leaving about 120,000. D&B sends each of these firms a questionnaire requesting further information, such as the names of as many as 20 top executives, and the company's own description of its lines of business. If a company does not specifically respond to the questionnaire, it's probably not listed in the database (or in the printed version). Thus, it is possible that a large company would be missing from the Million Dollar Directory but still appear in Dun's Market Identifiers.

Sample record

PROBLEM: My company has produced a management application software package appropriate for pharmaceutical companies. I need to identify drug companies with over $50 million in sales.

```
0098114
ADRIA LABORATORIES INC.
5000 POST ROAD
DUBLIN, OH 43017
PHONE: 614-764-8100
FRANKLIN COUNTY   SMSA: 136 (COLUMBUS, OHIO)
BUSINESS: Research & Development Laboratories Pharmaceutical Mnfr & Whl
Drugs Drug Proprietaries & Druggists Sundries
PRIMARY SIC:      7391    RESEARCH & DUPT LABS
SECONDARY SIC:    2834    PHARMACEUTICAL PREPS
SECONDARY SIC:    5122    DRUGS/PROPRIETARIES
YEAR STARTED:     1974
SALES: $87,700,000
EMPLOYEES HERE: 90
EMPLOYEES TOTAL: 650
THIS IS:
A HEADQUARTERS LOCATION
A CORPORATION
AN IMPORTER & EXPORTER
```

DUNS NUMBER: 07-374-8907
PARENT DUNS: 07-374-8907
CORPORATE FAMILY DUNS: 07-374-8907
MARKETING: McCormick, James / VP
OPERATIONS: Fleming, Robert L. / VP
CONTROLLER: Tramontana, Giovanni / Comp

Summary of information in Dun's Market Identifiers (MI) and Million Dollar Directory (MDD)

These items are present in both databases except those marked thusly: * = in MDD only, not in MI; ** = in MI only, not in MDD.

Company Name
Secondary Trade Name
Line of Business Information
  Business Description
  Standard Industrial Classification (SIC)
  Primary Code for the Primary Line of
    Business
  Other Code(s) Describing Additional
    Lines of Business (up to 5)
  Description of SIC
  Importer* and/or
  Exporter*
  Manufacturing Operations at This
    Location
Relationships with Other Establishments
  Headquarters Company or
  Branch Location** or
  Single Location
  Subsidiary of Another Company
Geographic Information
  Address (Physical and Mailing Address)
  County Name
  City
  State
  Zip Code
  Standard Metropolitan Statistical Area
    (SMSA)
    Code
    Name
  Telephone Area Code
D-U-N-S Numbers
  D-U-N-S Number of the Establishment
  D-U-N-S Number of the Headquarters
    Company
  D-U-N-S Number of the Parent Company
  D-U-N-S Number of the Ultimate
    Company of the Corporate Family
Company Size Information
  Annual Sales Volume
  Number of Employees
    At This Establishment (Employees
      Here)

For the Organization Headed by This
  Establishment (Employees Total)
Company Executives
  Chief Executive Officer (CEO)
  Other Executives*
    Advertising
    Chairman
    Controller
    Corporate Secretary
    Counsel
    Data Processing
    Director
    Engineering
    Executive Vice President
    Finance
    International
    Manufacturing
    Marketing
    Operations
    Other Directors
    Owner
    Partner
    Personnel
    President
    Public Relations
    Purchasing
    Research & Development
    Senior Vice President
Other Company Information
  Year the Company Established
  Stock Exchange(s) Where Shares
    Traded*
  Ticker Symbol on the Stock Exchange(s)*
  Bank Employed by Company*
  Accounting Firm Employed by Company*
  Law Firm Employed by Company*
  Legal Status
    Corporation or
    Partnership or
    Proprietorship
  Public or
  Privately Held

Profile

Database: Million Dollar Directory (MDD)
Producer: Dun's Marketing Services, 3 Century Drive, Parsippany, N.J. 07054, 201-455-0900
Toll-Free Telephone: 800-526-9018
Vendor: DIALOG.
Cost: $100 per hour, plus $1.00 to $1.50 per company record, depending on format.
Date Began Online: 1982
Source of Information: The listings originate in Dun's Market Identifiers, from which the largest companies—those having net worth of $500,000 or more—are taken. These companies are sent a separate questionnaire for the purpose of gathering additional details not in the MI database.
Type of Coverage: Criteria for inclusion: companies with $500,000 or more in net worth who respond to a Dun's questionnaire. Those who do not respond are not listed. The MDD listing may include as many as 20 top executives' names and titles; the business descriptions are provided by the company itself, not by D&B's analysts as in MI.
Size: Approximately 120,000 establishments.
Updating: Annually.
Indexing Terms: All fields listed in Summary of Information section (above) are searchable.
User Aids: *Dun's Online User's Guide*, $50. DIALOG database chapter on Million Dollar Directory, $5.
Printed Equivalent: The annual *Million Dollar Directory*, three volumes, $795 a year for complete set or $275 a year for first volume only (companies with $1 million or more in net worth).
Document Retrieval: Not applicable.
Other Services: (See MI listing).

Economic Information Systems Business Data Base

Economic Information Systems (EIS) produces the main competitor to Dun's Market Identifiers. Its database lacks a single official name; it is known variously as the EIS Establishment/Company File, EIS Business Data Base, or just EIS, though DIALOG and Control Data, the two vendors, have their own names for it (see Notes below in Profile). We shall use EIS.

The EIS database depends more heavily than D&B on third-party sources for its data, which can be both an advantage and a disadvantage. EIS gathers its facts from a wide variety of published sources, including industrial directories, annual reports, and clipping services, as well as telephone research. The lists are then compared to the U.S. Census Bureau's statistics on business establishments and employment by region and by SIC code; if there are discrepancies between EIS and the Census Bureau, then EIS investigates and reconciles them.

An advantage of this approach is that EIS catches some establishments that D&B might ignore. D&B lists an establishment only if it accumulates a credit history; thus a branch location whose bills are all paid by a headquarters would not appear in the database. EIS, on the other hand, seeks to find all such establishments and to list them in its database.

Another advantage to using EIS is its price: the charge for each company record on DIALOG is only one-third what D&B charges. The listings, though, are somewhat less detailed; for example, EIS doesn't give executives' names. Though it does list the headquarters that corresponds to a branch location, it doesn't indicate two higher levels of corporate ownership as do D&B's databases.

EIS cuts off its list of establishments at those with 20 or more employees, as opposed to 10 or more in Dun's Market Identifiers. This gives EIS 475,000 establishments versus 1.5 million for Dun's. EIS contends that these 475,000 establishments account for approximately 90 percent of the U.S. economy's sales in manufacturing firms and 85 percent in nonmanufacturing.

EIS is unique in including a rough indication of each company's market share in its primary SIC area of business. The percentage figure is calculated from EIS's sophisticated econometric formulas. Sometimes, however, these figures are not very reliable.

Sample record

PROBLEM: I am distribution manager for a small "boutique" brewery. I have heard that Springfield, Massachusetts, is a good test market. Who are some prospective distributors?

> 219863
> COUNTRY CLUB SODA CO.
>   180 Avocado Street
>   Springfield, Massachusetts 01104
>   County: Hampden
>   413-736-6394
>
> (1)   5181   BEER AND ALE WHOLESALING
>
> (2)   SALES MIL $: 012.9   INDUSTRY %: 0.08
> (3)   employment; 3 (50-99)

Notes: (1) four digit SIC code and name of category (2) sales and market share (3) employment category 3 (between 50 and 99 employees)

Profile

Database: Economic Information Systems (EIS) Business Data Base
Producer: Economic Information Systems Inc. (a division of Control Data), 310 Madison Ave., New York, New York 10017, 212-697-6080
Toll-Free Telephone: None at time of publication. The company plans to add an 800 line in the future.
Vendor: DIALOG, Control Data Business Information Services.
Cost: On DIALOG, $90 per hour plus 50¢ per company record retrieved (online or offline). On Control Data, $2,500 per year plus various computer use charges.
Date Began Online: 1976
Source of Information: Gathered from a wide variety of publicly available sources, including news clippings, industrial directories, telephone research and reports

from any company that publishes data on its sales or the location of its establishments. As a check, records are compared against the Census Bureau's County Business Patterns, which lists the number of establishments in each county by number of employees and a four-digit SIC code. When discrepancies are noted, they are investigated and corrected.

Type of Coverage: Criteria for inclusion are 20 or more employees and annual sales of approximately $500,000.

Size: Approximately 475,000 establishments.

Updating: Revised quarterly.

Indexing Terms: For each establishment, the following data elements are included: name, address, city, state, telephone, zip code (and all the above elements for the headquarters location, if different); SIC category (code and name); number of employees; sales in millions of dollars; market share in its primary SIC code; indication of foreign ownership or public ownership; a seven-digit code indicating census district and county (DIALOG only); and a code identifying the parent company.

User Aids: *EIS Information Retrieval User's Manual* (for DIALOG), $25. DIALOG EIS database chapter, $5. *Control Data X/Market Reference Manual*, free to customers of Control Data Business Information Services.

Printed Equivalent: Several printed directories are derived from this database, including *The Top 1,500 Companies, The Second 1,500 Companies, The Top 1,500 Private Companies, Zip Code Business Patterns*, and *The Structure of U.S. Business*. Brochures about these publications are available on request.

Other Services: Control Data representatives are available to help customers use the database effectively. A number of custom printed reports based on the database are available at prices from $75 to $1,000, including: "Shipment" and "Share of Market" reports on any four-digit SIC code, which analyze the industry in terms of key producers and ownership structure; "Line of Business Reports," which analyze individual companies in terms of sales, market share, and diversity of operations; and "Historical Market Share Reports," which rank the market shares of the top 25 companies in any four-digit manufacturing industry. Several of these reports are also available online.

Notes: On Control Data, the database can be analyzed and manipulated to create a variety of custom reports. No analysis is possible on DIALOG—only display of company data according to one of six pre-formatted reports. On DIALOG, the database is divided into two files, EIS Industrial Plants and EIS Nonmanufacturing Establishments. On Control Data, the entire database is named X/MARKET.

Electronic Yellow Pages

The Electronic Yellow Pages (EYP) offers the widest possible list of U.S. businesses—more than 11 million of them. That, in fact, points to a problem, for the list is about twice the number of operating businesses identified by the Census Bureau!

The solution to the riddle is that the database, like the ordinary yellow pages themselves, contains many duplicate entries. To assemble it, Market Data Retrieval obtains computer tapes of most of the yellow pages directories in the country. Each company is listed under the headings (connected to SIC codes) under which it chose to advertise.

EYP is the only online source for listings of the nation's smallest businesses—the father-and-son construction companies, small accounting firms, and especially small retailers. If you want to find all of the pizza shops in the country named Bob's, an EYP search can turn up your answer in a minute.

Sample record

PROBLEM: I am distribution manager for a small "boutique" brewery. I have heard that Springfield, Massachusetts, is a good test market. Who are some prospective distributors? (Compare to EIS Sample Record, above.)

```
0001307
    COUNTRY CLUB SODA CO. INC.
    AVOCADO
    SPRINGFIELD, MA 01104
    TELEPHONE: 413-736-6394
    COUNTY: HAMPDEN
SIC:
5182    .(WINES & DISTILLED ALCOHOLIC BEVERAGE WHLS.)
5181    .(BEER & ALE WHLS.)
ADVERTISING CLASS: BOLD FACE
CITY POPULATION: 7 .(100,000-249,999)

THIS IS A(N) CORPORATION
```

Profile

Database: Electronic Yellow Pages
Producer: Market Data Retrieval, Ketchum Place, Westport, Connecticut 06880, 203-226-8941
Toll-Free Telephone: 800-243-5538
Vendor: DIALOG.
Cost: $60 per hour plus 20¢ per record.
Date Began Online: 1982
Source of Information: The data is taken from 4,800 U.S. yellow pages directories, which represent virtually all yellow pages listings in the country. Some special compilations from other sources are done on sections of the database, such as schools and libraries, for which the company has more complete information.
Type of Coverage: Each entry contains the basic yellow pages information (name, address, telephone), plus county, SIC code, type of yellow pages listing (ordinary, display, etc.), city population by size category, and several other items depending on the type of business, such as size of office and whether it is a proprietorship, corporation, or headquarters.

The database is divided into ten files: construction, financial, manufacturers, professional, three retail files, two services files, and wholesalers. An eleventh file is an online index to the SIC classifications to help the user determine which SIC code to use in searching.
Size: Approximately 11 million records.
Updating: Twice yearly. Only current listings are kept online.
Indexing Terms: Based on SIC codes. Most items listed above at Type of Coverage are also searchable.
User Aids: DIALOG EYP database chapter, available free.
Printed Equivalent: The database is available as mailing lists, galley listings, and 3 × 5 telemarketing cards. Mailing labels are normally $40 per thousand.
Document Retrieval: Not applicable.

DunSprint

DunSprint is D&B's master database, referred to earlier. The basic service, the online equivalent of what D&B calls the Business Information Report, supplies a credit and financial profile on a company, requested by name, address, or phone number. A variety of related online services based on this database offer many more ways to use the data. For example, Dunsquest allows a user to search across companies by key financial ratio, etc. This database is much more detailed than Dun's Market Identifiers, and is correspondingly more expensive.

Business credit reporting is a major business. In 1980, approximately $270 million was spent for business credit information; by 1985, this is expected to grow to almost $400 million.

Profile

Database: DunSprint
Producer: Dun & Bradstreet, 99 Church St., New York, New York 10007, 212-285-7134
Toll-Free Telephone: None, but local offices are located in many cities.
Vendor: Dun & Bradstreet.
Cost: Each company report costs about $9; an annual minimum of $1,000 to $1,500 is required.
Date Began Online: Information not available at time of publication.
Source of Information: Responses from listed companies as well as creditors and public sources.
Type of Coverage: Factual—credit experiences of creditors, with basic company data and financial profile.
Size: Approximately 5.5 million establishments.
Updating: Daily.
Indexing Terms: Basic reports are retrievable by company name, address, D-U-N-S number.
User Aids: User manuals supplied free to subscribers.
Printed Equivalent: The same reports are available in printed form, delivered by mail.
Other Services: D&B offers several other online services based on this master database. They include Dunsquest (Dun's Financial Profiles), which supplies balance sheets, income statements, and key ratios for 1.2 million companies, searchable by over 70 parameters; and Payment Analysis Report (PAR), which assigns numerical scores that rate the payment history of companies in the master database. D&B also offers a variety of other customized services.

TRW Business Credit Profile

A relatively new competitor to D&B, TRW Inc. has one of the largest consumer credit agencies in the United States. In 1975, it decided to challenge D&B's dominance in business credit, and it went online with a new computerized system in 1976. The Business Credit Profile was developed in cooperation with the National Association of Credit Management, a confederation of more than 60 independent trade groups.

TRW limits access to bona fide credit executives; D&B has no such policy. TRW's subscriber agreement specifies that information will be used only for credit purposes—not to compile lists of sales leads.

Profile

Database: TRW Business Credit Profile
Producer: TRW Information Services Division, 1 City Blvd. West, Suite 920, Orange, California 92668, 716-937-2666
Toll-Free Telephone: None.
Vendor: TRW Information Services Division.
Cost: 100 to 499 reports: $8.45 (for noncontributor of information to database); $7.85 (for contributor of information).
Date Began Online: 1976
Source of Information: Credit information from the companies that subscribe to the service. Public record information—tax liens, judgments, and bankruptcies—as they appear in court records are also included in the database.
Type of Coverage: Trade payment information on nearly 8 million business locations representing all major industries. Key business facts on over 400,000 companies and comprehensive business and financial data on public companies supplied by Standard & Poor's Corporation are also available.
Size: Eight million business locations.
Updating: New information added when received.
Indexing Terms: Searchable by company name, address, state, and zip code.
User Aids: Information not available at time of publication.
Printed Equivalent: The same reports are available in printed form, delivered by mail.
Document Retrieval: Not applicable.
Other Services: Asset Control Techniques (ACT) services provide credit executives with the ability to have their accounts receivable information continually monitored according to criteria the credit executive chooses.

Dun's Principal International Businesses

Dun's Principal International Businesses is derived from D&B's international credit reporting service in the same manner that Market Identifiers is derived from the domestic credit service. Its coverage is very selective, however—only the 56,000 leading companies from 133 countries are included. Like Market Identifiers and the Million Dollar Directory, it also can be expensive to retrieve records for a large group of companies; they cost $1 to $2 each.

Sample record

PROBLEM: I believe the Philips electronics company of the Netherlands makes telephone equipment. Is this correct? Where do I contact the division?

```
0036246
PHILIPS TELECOMMUNICATIE INDUSTRIE BV
JAN V/D HEYDENSTRAA" j#PB 32
HILVERSUM, NETHERLANDS 100 JD
43712
NH
```

```
BUSINESS:          TEL,TELG APPARATUS
PRIMARY SIC:       3661        TEL,TELG APPARTUS
SECONDARY SIC:     3662        RADIO & TV COMM'N EQP
YEAR STARTED:      1918
EMPLOYEES TOTAL:               64,000
SALES (LOCAL CURRENCY):        NA
SALES (U.S. CURRENCY):         NA
THIS IS:
A SUBSIDIARY
A PUBLICLY HELD COMPANY
DUNS NUMBER: 40-200-8783
PARENT NAME: PHILIPS GLOEILAMPENFABRIEKEN NV
PARENT DUNS: 40-200-9138
PARENT CITY: EINDHOVEN
PARENT STATE/PROVINCE: N BRABANT
PARENT COUNTRY: NETHERLANDS
CHIEF EXECUTIVE: D. C. GEEST, ALG DIRECTEUR
```

Profile

Database: Dun's Principal International Businesses
Producer: International Marketing Services, Dun & Bradstreet International, 1 World Trade Center, Suite 9069, New York, New York 10007, 212-938-8400
Toll-Free Telephone: 800-526-9018
Vendor: DIALOG.
Cost: $100/hour, plus $1 to $2 per record.
Date Began Online: 1983
Source of Information: Interviews conducted by D&B International analysts located worldwide. Companies selected according to size, international prominence, and potential for business activity outside their own country.
Type of Coverage: Factual. Coverage of public, private, and government-controlled companies.
Size: 56,000 records.
Updating: Annually.
Indexing Terms: D-U-N-S number, SIC code, parent name, parent city, parent country, name of chief executive officer, sales (U.S.), sales (own currency).
User Aids: Not available at time of publication.
Printed Equivalent: *Principal International Businesses* (abridged version of the database).
Document Retrieval: Not applicable.

19 Stock Market Databases

Most securities transactions these days are recorded electronically as they occur. They create, in effect, ready-made databases. Dozens of vendors stand ready to deliver the figures to your computer terminal. Each personalizes the data in some way—such as by calculating key performance ratios, collecting historical data, offering analysis software, creating charts, adding fundamental data, etc. But all the information comes from the same public sources—the major exchanges or market makers where the trading occurs.

There are databases covering stocks, bonds, money markets, commodities, options, investment funds, foreign exchange, and foreign securities. To describe all of these is beyond the scope of this book. We shall deal exclusively with stock market databases, though most of the vendors we introduce also offer databases of other securities.

This market is evolving rapidly, and more services will undoubtedly come onto the market soon after this book appears. In evaluating these services and others, here are some of the crucial points of comparison:

♦ How frequently is the data updated? The freshest possible stock information is delivered on a continuous or "real-time" basis, which means you receive it as it happens, or as fast as your stockbroker would. At present, only a few vendors offer real-time data to individual users, though more are expected to join them soon. The next fastest speed available lags 15 to 20 minutes behind the ticker, such as the New York and American exchange prices on Dow Jones Quotes. Others update "periodically throughout the day." This applies to OTC (Over-the-Counter) on Dow Jones or the major exchanges on UNI-STOX. Other vendors update their figures once a day or even less often, such as once a week.

♦ Which stocks do they carry? All vendors have the New York and American stock exchanges. Most carry NASDAQ's (National Association of Securities Dealers Automated Quotations) most active over-the-counter stocks and stocks that trade on regional exchanges, but none carries all the lesser issues. The most thinly traded issues appear nowhere online; they are quoted only in the "pink sheets" published by the National Quotation Bureau in New York (available through most stockbrokers).

♦ Is it a user-friendly system? Some vendors design their service with the individual investor in mind. They make it easy to sign up and easy to learn how to use. Others are geared to corporate clients accustomed to time-sharing computer services; they may be too complicated (or expensive) for an individual or occasional user.

♦ What does it cost? Pricing schemes may be simple (straight connect time) or complicated (central processing units, minimums, subscription fees, charges based on amount of data retrieved, etc.). It's not always easy to comparison shop, but keep in mind that prices charged by two vendors for similar data may be drastically different.

♦ What are the software options? There are three basic kinds of service. The simplest supplies you with information according to a predetermined format, such as a stock's high, low, close, and volume. A more complicated option, from some online vendors, lets you create charts, combine figures from stocks you select, or perform various kinds of mathematical analysis. The newest kind of service involves buying special microcomputer software programs on disk that let you download data and then analyze it offline.

Quotdial

Quotron Systems, Inc., is the major real-time financial information vendor in the United States. Quotron introduced the first electronic system to provide stock market quotations to brokers through custom desk-top terminals in 1960. The firm has grown considerably in size and sophistication and currently offers a vast array of securities data to the financial community. Its terminals sit on more than 50,000 brokers' desks. That translates into about a 65 percent share of the market; two main competitors, Bunker-Ramo Information Systems and ADP Financial Information Services, split what's left.

Quotron's main offerings are available only through its own dedicated terminals. Some of the data available on a real-time basis include last price, bid/ask spread, volume, news affecting the stock, year's high/low, dividend and earnings reports, a variety of stock indices, continuous monitoring for specified changes (for limit orders), graphics displays, and many other specialized services.

The standard terminal offered to brokers carries a minimum billing of $1,300 a month. Quotron also offers a terminal called VuSet for nonprofessionals for a rent of 260 a month, exclusive of usage charges. Both are custom terminals, incompatible with other vendors.

In an effort to attract an even larger segment of the casual-user market, Quotron has recently begun offering another service called Quotdial. The service is "after market," meaning that it is available only when trading on the major New York exchanges has ceased. On days when trading takes place, the service is available from 4:15 P.M. to 7:30 A.M. Eastern Time. On weekends and holidays, the service normally operates 24 hours.

Quotdial is intended for use on personal computers using 300- or 1200-baud modems. No dedicated software is required.

Quotdial will probably offer real-time data in 1984, particularly if exchange subscription charges levied by exchanges themselves for casual users are substantially reduced. The service is so new that a price structure has not yet been established, but it is anticipated that the service will be priced very competitively.

Profile

Database: Quotdial
Producer: Quotron Systems, Inc., 5454 Beethoven St., Los Angeles, California 90066, 213-827-4600
Toll-Free Telephone: 800-624-9522
Vendor: Quotron Systems.
Cost: Not available at time of publication. Will be priced "very competitively" relative to similar systems.
Date Began Online: 1983
Source of Information: Major exchanges, NASDAQ, etc.
Type of Coverage: Data available for individual stocks include exchange identifier, last sale price, net change, best bid and ask, size of bid and ask, volume, time of last trade, dividends, percentage yield, earnings, P/E ratio, ex-dividend date, earnings forecasts, and notification of Dow Jones or Reuters news stories (but Quotdial does not carry the stories themselves). Data also is available for market indicators and statistics, options, bonds, commodities, and futures indices. Hours of operation for the service are normally 4:15 P.M. to 7:30 A.M. Eastern Time on days when the stock markets are open and normally 24 hours per day on other days.
Updating: Continuous (effectively once a day for after-hours service).
Indexing Terms: Securities are indexed by ticker symbol.
User Aids: Information not available at time of publication.

Bridge Information System

As we go to press, Bridge Data Company offers the least expensive true real-time quote service, the Bridge Information System. The price is steep—$200 minimum usage per month and another $200 a month in exchange fees on top of that. But for an investor who wants quotes the instant they appear on the ticker, this is an excellent source. The exchanges are considering relaxing their fees for real-time access, so prices may come down in the future, and other vendors surely will offer competing real-time services.

Bridge also offers an after-hours service at a much reduced cost. This is competitive with many of the other daily-update stock quote databases.

Bridge covers the major listed stocks, including all 4,000 NASDAQ issues. It also carries quotes for options and commodities. A variety of technical data is available including price-volume charts, moving averages, historic data, volatility charts, and probability charts. A simple terminal is all that's necessary to receive the charts; no computer or special software is needed. Bridge also allows the user to track portfolio performance. It has more than 100 industry portfolios and more than 50 special portfolios assembled according to ranking techniques, such as price performance, market value, etc. Bridge can also track any customer-designed portfolio. Bridge is the firm that calculates and disseminates many familiar stock indexes including the Value Line Index, the Standard & Poor's indexes, and the Dow Jones indexes.

Prospective users may connect their terminals to Bridge's system for a free demonstration. Call Bridge to obtain the local dial-in number.

Profile

Database: Bridge Information System
Producer: Bridge Data Company, 10050 Manchester Rd., St. Louis, Missouri 63122, 314-821-5660
Toll-Free Telephone: 800-325-3986
Vendor: ADP Network Services, Bridge Data Company, Market Data Systems, CompuServe.
Cost: Bridge Data Company, Dial-in Costs:
   Real-Time Service (during market hours): cost per hour, $60; monthly minimum usage cost, $200; one-time start-up cost, $50; minimum advance deposit, $600; exchange fees—use of Bridge Information System during market hours requires the approval of the various exchanges. The monthly fees charged by the exchanges for access to real-time data—currently about $200 per month—are usually billed directly to customers.
   After Market Hours Service (weekdays between 5:30 P.M. and 9 A.M. Eastern Time, weekends, and holidays): cost per hour (three-minute minimum), $12; monthly minimum usage cost, $50; one-time start-up cost, $50; minimum advance deposit, $150.
Date Began Online: 1968
Source of Information: Major exchanges, NASDAQ, etc.
Type of Coverage: Listed and OTC stocks from most U.S. or Canadian exchanges. Data includes high, low, close, and volume. Other information available from Bridge includes price information concerning financial futures, commodities, foreign securities, and all listed options. Much of the data available can be viewed in a variety of chart and tabular formats.
Updating: Continuous (real time).
Indexing Terms: Securities are indexed by ticker symbol.
User Aids: The Bridge Information System: An Introduction, 35 pp. (available only online at the time of publication). Other Bridge documentation available online and in print form to hard-wired customers, or for $100 in print form to other customers.
Printed Equivalent: None.
Document Retrieval: Not applicable.

Dow Jones Quotes

If you can't afford Bridge's rates for real-time quotes, you could turn to one of the services that offer the same data with a lag of 15 or 20 minutes. The most popular one—indeed, one of the most popular online databases in the country—is Dow Jones Quotes/Current. Its companion database is Dow Jones Quotes/Historical.

These two databases cover all of the exchange-listed and NASDAQ companies. They also carry current data on bonds and options (though not commodities). The historical figures cover only stocks.

The Dow Jones databases give only the bare-bones basics: close and open (or bid and asked), high, low, and last prices, and volume. The historical data is aggregated by quarter, by month, or by day for 12-day intervals. The *Fact Finder* manual contains a handy list of stock symbols.

For any further analysis, you'll need to buy one of the Dow Jones microcomputer software packages. These include:

♦ Market Analyzer ($349), which collects and stores quotes and constructs charts for technical analysis.

♦ Market Manager ($299), which collects prices for selected stocks and computes the value of a portfolio. It includes a Tax Lot accounting system to help match sales within existing positions to minimize tax liability from capital gains.

♦ Market Microscope ($699), which is discussed below in connection with the Media General database.

Profile

Database: Dow Jones Quotes/Current; Dow Jones Quotes/Historical
Producer: Dow Jones News/Retrieval, P.O. Box 300, Princeton, New Jersey 08540, 609-452-1511
Toll-Free Telephone: 800-257-5114 (except New Jersey, Alaska, Hawaii)
Vendor: Dow Jones News/Retrieval.
Cost: $50 one-time connect fee. Prime time: $36 to $54 per hour. Nonprime time: $6 to $9 per hour. Double for 1200 baud.
Date Began Online: 1979
Source of Information: Major exchanges, NASDAQ, etc.
Type of Coverage: Data available includes quotes for common and preferred stocks, bonds and options traded on major U.S. exchanges, including OTC. Quarterly summaries begin in 1978, with quarterly and monthly summaries available from 1979 to the present. Daily prices are available beginning in 1979. Data include high, low, close, and volume for quarterly, monthly, and daily summaries.
Updating: Daily for historical quotes; continuous for current quotes, with delays of 15 to 30 minutes.
Indexing Terms: Data on each security is retrievable only by its exchange symbol. A complete symbol directory is offered online.
User Aids: Dow Jones News/Retrieval Fact Finder, $10.
Printed Equivalent: None.
Document Retrieval: Not applicable.

MicroQuote

Dow Jones's closest competitor in stock quotes databases is CompuServe Information Service's MicroQuote. CompuServe says its quotes run 20-30 minutes behind the ticker, and it covers most of the same securities that Dow Jones does.

CompuServe, however, carries much more historical data on each stock than Dow Jones. For many years the firm has been in the business of providing these kinds of financial databases to corporations and financial institutions, and it has developed a very comprehensive set of statistics. MicroQuote also carries online 200 market indexes, such as the NYSE composite, Standard & Poor's 500, etc.

Even for current quotes, which are basically the same on any system, MicroQuote offers additional capabilities, such as storing a list of stocks, instead of having to type them in again each time you use the system. It calculates the change from the last quote, indicates a new high or low, flags a stock that has any special event associated with it, and allows the user to vary the display format. Of course, to use these extra capabilities, you must learn the appropriate commands.

MicroQuote database items (for equities)

MASTER
CUSIP number (current)
CUSIP number (previous)
Dividend history dates
Price history dates
Exchange
Issue type
Issue status
Issuer name
Latest pricing date
Security class
S&P quality rating
SIC code
Ticker symbol
Beta factor and percentile
Earnings per share (12 month)
EPS footnote
Indicated annual dividend
IAD footnote
Marginability code
Shares outstanding
Shares outstanding footnote
12-month ending date

PRICE
Closing price
High or asking price
Low or bid price
Trading volume
Holiday status code
Pricing status code
Adjustment factor

DIVIDEND
Entry/revision date
Lateness/revision code
Record date
Payment method
Tax base code
Transfer code
Dividend type
Dividend amount or rate
Ex-dividend date
Payable date
Payment order code
Bearer code

Profile

Database: MicroQuote
Producer: CompuServe Information Service, MicroQuote, 5000 Arlington Centre Blvd., P.O. Box 20212, Columbus, Ohio 43220, 614-457-0802
Toll-Free Telephone: 800-848-8199
Vendor: CompuServe.
Cost: At 300 baud, $12.50 per hour during prime time or $6 nonprime time. At 1200 baud, $15 during prime time or $12.50 nonprime.
Date Began Online: 1981
Source of Information: Major exchanges and NASDAQ.

Type of Coverage: Price, earnings per share, marginability, beta, dividend information. Prices available on a daily basis back to December 31, 1973.
Size: 50,000 securities including stocks, bonds, options, mutual funds. Also 200 market indices.
Updating: Stocks and options updated continuously, about 20 minutes behind the market.
Indexing Terms: CUSIP number or ticker symbol.
User Aids: *MicroQuote User's Guide*, $6.95.
Printed Equivalent: None.
Document Retrieval: Not applicable.

UNISTOX

At the time this is written, UNISTOX, produced by United Press International, provides closing prices for individual stocks 30 minutes after the end of trading each day. UPI, however, has plans to revamp UNISTOX considerably. Current stock quotes will be provided with only a 20-minute delay, in competition with Dow Jones and CompuServe. Eventually UPI seeks to carry real-time data.

UNISTOX is organized by menu-driven, numbered reports. The most commonly used are NYSE, AMEX, and OTC stock closings; mutual fund prices, Dow Jones average closings, money market futures, markets at a glance, gold and silver spot prices, and money fund prices.

Selection of specific securities is by abbreviations called "stubs." Unfortunately, UPI stock abbreviations are not necessarily the same as the ticker symbol, and they can be changed without notice (UNISTOX provides a weekly update on changes, additions, and deletions of stubs). The stub symbols were adopted by UNISTOX because they proved easier for newspaper editors to use, a factor of obvious importance. There is a somewhat cumbersome method for finding out stubs online. Users who wish to track a wide variety of securities may find the stub symbols a bit frustrating.

Recognizing that a larger market exists for securities data, UPI has ambitious plans for modernizing and expanding service in this area, including the development of at least one new database called StoxQuote. This will provide price data for NYSE, AMEX, and OTC issues transmitted by satellite. Each client will receive a two-foot diameter receiving disk and a decoding device. UPI expects that StoxQuote clients will include brokers, hotels, and business restaurants. There are currently no plans to market the service to home users, and UPI has yet to determine the price structure for StoxQuote.

Profile

Database: UNISTOX
Producer: United Press International, 1400 I St., N.W., Washington, D.C. 20005, 202-289-0909
Toll-Free Telephone: None.
Vendor: The Source, Dialcom.
Cost: On Dialcom, $26 per hour prime time, $22 per hour off-prime. On The Source, $20.75 per hour prime time, $7.75 per hour off-prime (300 baud).

Date Began Online: 1979
Source of Information: Major exchanges and NASDAQ.
Type of Coverage: Daily data reports on stocks and other securities. Among data available are prices, dividends, volume, price/earnings ratios, major indices. Accessible through more than 140 types of formats.
Updating: Periodically throughout the day for some items; daily for other items. (Continuous with 15-minute delay to be available.)
Indexing Terms: UPI "stub" (not the same as ticker symbols).
User Aids: UNISTOX Manual, $5.
Printed Equivalent: Corresponds to daily data published by many newspapers.
Document Retrieval: Not applicable.

MARKETSCAN

Info Globe, a Canadian company, is attempting to give American stock quote vendors some competition by offering its MARKETSCAN database in the United States. This has daily quotes for the NYSE, AMEX, and Canadian exchanges, but no over-the-counter quotes. It is updated only once a day and its historical figures go back about one year. MARKETSCAN gives only the basic price and volume data.

Profile

Database: MARKETSCAN
Producer: Info Globe, 444 Front St. West, Toronto, Ontario M5V 259, Canada, 416-585-5250
Toll-Free Telephone: Not available in U.S.A.
Vendor: Info Globe.
Cost: Prime time, $120 per hour; nonprime, $30 per hour; plus 1¢ per data line. Prices quoted in Canadian dollars.
Date Began Online: 1981
Source of Information: New York and American exchanges plus four Canadian exchanges. No over-the-counter stocks.
Type of Coverage: Price and volume information only. Daily quotations available back 250 trading days.
Updating: Daily.
Indexing Terms: Ticker symbol only.
User Aids: MARKETSCAN Manual, $10.
Printed Equivalent: None.
Document Retrieval: Not available.

Media General Data Base

The Media General Data Base is somewhat different from the databases discussed previously. It is updated only weekly, and it covers only about 4,000 stocks, or the most important issues only. Its strong point is that it provides a large variety of statistics on these stocks. It is available through Dow Jones News/Retrieval and The Source, among others, which makes it a very popular service.

Media General (it is called Stockvue on The Source) has a slightly different selection of data on the two vendors. The company's master database has some 200 data items; Dow Jones and The Source each select about 50 of them for their systems. The Source carries the data organized into 12 selectable formats or "screens," while Dow Jones breaks the information down into just 4 formats.

Media General "screens" on The Source

Screen 1: "LOCATOR"—Shows the stock's name and symbol, its industry group and description of that group, and the exchange where it is traded.

Screen 2: "INDUSTRY GROUPS"—Stocks are categorized by 175 subindustry groups within 60 overall groups. Screen 2 shows these groups and the number to use to call up information that includes stock name, symbol, exchange, current price, and percent of change in price for the current week.

Screen 3: "PRICE CHANGE & RANGE"—For any given stock(s), shows the weekly high, low, and closing prices, and percentages of change; the 200-day moving average, and the 52-week high and low.

Screen 4: "PERIODIC PRICE CHANGE (%)"—Illustrates the percentage of change in price over the last trading week, the last 4, 13 and 52 weeks, and for the year-to-date.

Screen 5: "PRICE EARNINGS RATIOS"—Shows the current and five-year average high and low price earnings ratios, and the five-year high, low, and current price.

Screen 6: "RELATIVE PRICE/ACTION"—Shows the market value of each stock as percentages of revenue, market norm, and industry norm; shows the price-equity ratio, relative price index, earnings yield, up Beta and down Beta.

Screen 7: "TRADING VOLUME"—Shows number of shares traded in the past week; that volume as a percentage of outstanding shares; the weekly dollar value of shares; and the liquid ratio and on-balance index.

Screen 8: "TREND TO MARKET"—Shows the 200-day price index vs market and vs industry; the price trend vs market for the last 5 and 30 days; and the volume trend vs market for the last 5 and 30 days.

Screen 9: "EARNINGS PER SHARE"—Shows the earnings per share for the last 12 months and for the last fiscal year; the percentage of change in earnings from the last year and for the year to date and last 12 months; and the five-year growth rate for earnings.

Screen 10: "REVENUES AND RATIOS"—Shows the revenues and earnings for the last fiscal year, profit margin, return on equity, debt-to-equity ratio and current debt-to-equity ratio.

Screen 11: "SHAREHOLDINGS"—Here is the market value of shares; last-out shares; insider transactions; short interest; short-interest ratio; and market value at fiscal year ending date.

Screen 12: "DIVIDENDS"—Shows the current dividend rate and yield; the current and five-year average payout, and the latest ex-dividend date.

Profile

Database: Media General Data Base
Producer: Media General Financial Services, Inc., 301 East Grace St., Richmond, Virginia 23219, 804-649-6736
Toll-Free Telephone: 800-446-7922
Vendor: Dow Jones News/Retrieval, The Source, Business Information Systems, National Computer Network of Chicago.
Cost: On The Source, $20.75 per hour prime time, $7.75 per hour nonprime. On Dow Jones, $48 to $72 per hour prime time, $36 to $54 per hour nonprime. All prices are for 300 baud.
Date Began Online: 1980
Source of Information: Prices and volumes from Associated Press; corporate data from companies and press reports.
Type of Coverage: Prices and volumes, annual and quarterly income statements, and annual balance sheets for individual stocks and more than 170 industry groups. Other data available include P/E ratio, current; P/E ratio, five-year average high (low); price to common stock equity; beta coefficients; total share volume (weekly); total dollar volume; percent of shares outstanding; revenue and earnings; dividend rates; debt-to-equity ratios; and insider net trading. Coverage includes 4,000 companies (NYSE, AMEX, and selected OTC) and 170 industry groups. Data items vary by vendor.
Updating: Weekly.
Indexing Terms: Retrievable by stock symbol or industry group.
User Aids: Pamphlets available from each vendor.
Printed Equivalent: Media General financial tables appear in a variety of formats in several publications, principally the *Media General Financial Weekly and Industrial Scope*.
Document Retrieval: Not applicable.

More sophisticated services

The four stock databases covered below are in somewhat of a different class from the ones described thus far. The four all offer extensive manipulation and analysis capabilities through proprietary software that each company has developed. You don't need a microcomputer to use them; most of the analysis is done on the company's mainframe, with a dumb communicating terminal all that is really required to use the software (though several now offer microcomputer programs to enhance their capabilities). These databases are each updated daily at the end of trading.

ANALYTICS

Chase Econometrics/Interactive Data Corp. offers the ANALYTICS databases, one of the largest selections of stocks. It is one of the few to carry price data on most of the smaller issues, including non-NASDAQ stocks traded through the pink sheets.

ANALYTICS, however, is intended primarily for more sophisticated users. The manuals are well written and organized, but they demand some study and practice to use them effectively. Chase charges a $250 monthly subscription fee, making this service economical primarily for corporate clients.

With ANALYSTICS, it is possible to select stock price data for a company and combine it with data from many other databases carried by Chase such as Value Line or COMPUSTAT. For example, you could use this capability to analyze the sales performance of all high-technology companies with a price/earnings ratio of greater than 15.

Profile

Database: ANALYSTICS
Producer: Chase Econometrics/Interactive Data Corp., 486 Totten Pond Rd., Waltham, Massachusetts 02154, 617-890-1234
Toll-Free Telephone: 800-225-8452
Vendor: Chase Econometrics/Interactive Data.
Cost: Subscription fee of $250 per month, plus decreasing charges that depend on the amount of data used.
Date Began Online: Information not available at time of publication.
Source of Information: Major exchanges, NASDAQ, Associated Press.
Type of Coverage: The PRICES database (subfile of ANALYSTICS) contains daily prices, earnings, and dividend information for stocks, bonds, options, and other securities, back to 1968 for major stocks and 1971 for NASDAQ stocks. Other stock information carried in other ANALYSTICS subfiles includes stock-split and dividend information, quarterly earnings per share, monthly shares outstanding, short interest, insider transactions, and many indices and averages.
Updating: Daily for PRICES subfile.
Indexing Terms: CUSIP number, ticker symbol, Interactive Data Corp. symbol.
User Aids: *Analytics User's Manual—Data Base Guide* and *System Guide*, $50 per set.
Printed Equivalent: None.
Document Retrieval: Not applicable.

FASTOCK II

ADP's FASTOCK II database carries a selection of stocks similar to ANALYSTICS. The main applications emphasized by ADP involve using the market data by itself rather than in combination with fundamental data from other sources. Examples of such uses are creating a portfolio and monitoring its performance, or charting the daily price movements of securities.

FASTOCK's software is partially menu-driven and seems relatively easy to use (FORTRAN can also be used). There is no minimum or subscription charge. As this goes to press, ADP had just introduced a microcomputer software package called Datapath for downloading into a Lotus 1-2-3 spreadsheet program. This could reduce the cost of FASTOCK as well as allow Lotus 1-2-3 owners to use the data without having to master FASTOCK's own repertoire of commands.

Profile

Database: FASTOCK II
Producer: ADP Network Services, Inc., 175 Jackson Plaza, Ann Arbor, Michigan 48106, 313-769-6800
Toll-Free Telephone: 800-237-3282 (800-ADP-DATA)
Vendor: ADP Network Services.
Cost: $15 per hour at 300 baud, plus 2¢ per data item retrieved, plus a charge for computer resource units. There is a one-time sign-up fee of $100 and monthly minimum billing of $100. The price for downloading data is 2¢ per data point.
Date Began Online: 1978
Source of Information: Major exchanges, NASDAQ, etc.
Type of Coverage: The most basic data is available on 20,000 common stock issues, plus 77,000 other securities. Data includes dividend, yearly high/low, beta, shares outstanding. Software allows a variety of analysis procedures including portfolio evaluations and plotting. Data concerning NYSE and AMEX issues begin in January 1968. OTC stocks and mutual funds have data available from January 1972 to the present. Regional and Canadian exchange data begin in 1974. A microcomputer program for the IBM PC called Datapath ($235) is available for downloading data into a Lotus 1-2-3 spreadsheet.
Updating: Daily.
Indexing Terms: Data retrievable by CUSIP number, ticker symbol, exchange code, issue type code, issuer name, SIC code, etc.
User Aids: *FASTOCK II User's Guide* and *FASTOCK II Securities Directory*, prices available on request.
Printed Equivalent: None.
Document Retrieval: Not applicable.

NASTOCK

I. P. Sharp's North American Stock Market (NASTOCK) database is geared to the same sorts of uses as ADP's FASTOCK, such as portfolio management, charting, or technical analysis. NASTOCK differs in several important ways, though. One, it doesn't cover the OTC companies—only the NYSE, AMEX, and Canadian exchanges. Also, NASTOCK's coverage begins in 1981 rather than in the early 1970s.

NASTOCK is available through a relatively easy-to-learn language called INFOMAGIC as well as through Sharp's standard language Retrieve, which requires knowledge of the APL programming language.

I. P. Sharp offers a sophisticated color plotting system called Superplot. The plots are printed out at a local I. P. Sharp office (for offices, see the list in the I. P. Sharp discussion in Chapter 24).

Profile

Database: North American Stock Market (NASTOCK)
Producer: I. P. Sharp Associates, Ltd., 2 First Canadian Place, Suite 1900, Toronto, Ontario M5X 1E3, Canada, 416-364-5361
Toll-Free Telephone: None.
Vendor: I. P. Sharp Associates.

Cost: Using SHARP APL, $1 per connect hour, plus 70¢ per 1,000 characters transmitted or received, plus 45¢ per CPU used. Using INFOMAGIC, $60 per hour (double at 1200 baud).

Date Began Online: 1981

Source of Information: Major exchanges and NASDAQ.

Type of Coverage: Contains current and historical prices, volumes, and indices for major U.S. and Canadian exchanges. Coverage begins May 22, 1981, for most exchanges. Data provided includes bid price, ask price, open price, high price, low price, close price, previous close, volume symbol, and description. Custom analysis and formatting, such as moving averages, can be performed.

Updating: Daily.

Indexing Terms: Exchange symbol.

User Aids: *NASTOCK Database, MAGIC User's Manual, RETRIEVE—Sharp APL Database Retrieval System.*

Printed Equivalent: None.

Document Retrieval: Not applicable.

DataKits

Data Resources, Inc. (DRI), a competitor of Chase Econometrics/Interactive Data, has supplied a wide variety of economic and business data to institutional customers since its founding in 1969. (The company is described more fully in Chapter 24.)

In the past, DRI's clients have had to pay subscriptions of several thousand dollars a year and up. It has recently attempted to broaden its customer base by providing access to simplified collections of data at lower rates.

To accomplish this, DRI and VisiCorp embarked on a joint venture to produce DataKits and VisiLink. DataKits are frames of information organized as VisiCalc worksheets. VisiLink ($250) consists of software that allows personal computers to gain access to DRI DataKits and then transfer the information to a VisiCalc template. (At this writing, DataKits can be used only with Apple and IBM personal computers.) The VisiTrend/Plot ($300) program allows a user to display data in graph form.

The securities data provided by DataKits is drawn from DRI's enormous DRI-SEC database. DRI-SEC is used by institutional clients as a research source for investigating securities markets. DRI-SEC provides data only up to the previous trading day. Pricing information on more than 45,000 securities issues and 200 market indices are available. Data from 1968 is available for all listed issues on the NYSE, AMEX, OTC, and regional and Canadian exchanges. Types of securities for which a variety of information is available include equity and debt issues, convertibles, options, and government bonds, as well as dividends and interest payments.

Stock market data represents just part of the information obtainable through DataKits. S&P's COMPUSTAT Financial and Money and Credit Markets data are also available for investment analysis. More than 30 DataKits are also available for business and economic analysis. Among these are the Dodge Construction Reporter, Health Care Planner, State Economic Forecaster, and European Country Reporter.

Obtaining a DataKit involves a number of simple steps. The VisiLink program is first loaded into a compatible personal computer with a compatible modem. The program automatically phones and connects to DRI. The user then types in a valid identification using either a charge card or a current DRI account.

The user selects DataKits from the DataKits catalog that is stored on a utility diskette and displayed by the VisiLink program. Then the user fills in an "order form" to customize the contents of the worksheet according to the user's needs.

Catalogs are updated periodically and are automatically received when communicating with DRI. More than 60 DataKits are currently available, and DRI is periodically adding new ones. (The catalog is updated automatically when online to DRI.) The cost for a DataKit can be anywhere from $10 to $125, depending on the amount and type of data delivered. DRI expects a typical DataKits user to spend about $1,000 a year, though there's no minimum required. DRI's S&P COMPUSTAT Supplement gives ticker symbols and aggregate industry codes needed to complete order forms for some of the DataKits. The Supplement is provided free with the purchase of VisiLink.

DataKits list

There are currently eight DataKits that furnish data on the stock market. STOCK UPDATE REPORTER provides closing price, change from day before, high, low, and volume. Up to 100 tickets or CUSIP numbers can be entered for the companies desired. For $10 plus 25¢ for each company requested, one day's data is supplied, either for the previous trading day or any prior day chosen. The files are updated only once a day.

DAILY STOCK RETRIEVER gives data on 30 consecutive days of trading activity. Each day the high, low, and closing prices and volume are reported. Up to five stocks can be retrieved. The ending data for reporting purposes can be the most recent day available or a prior date. Any of the following composites may also be tracked for the 30-day period: Dow Jones Average (30 industrials), New York Stock Exchange (composite), Standard & Poor's 500 (common), Standard & Poor's 400 (industrials), Value Line (composite). The cost is $10 plus 50¢ for each company requested.

The WEEKLY STOCK RETRIEVER, MONTHLY STOCK RETRIEVER, and QUARTERLY STOCK RETRIEVER DataKits operate in much the same fashion as the DAILY STOCK RETRIEVER, providing data for 30 consecutive weeks, months, or quarters, respectively. The cost of the WEEKLY STOCK RETRIEVER is $20 plus 75¢ per company.

Data for up to 100 stocks can be retrieved using STOCK PRICE REPORTER. The closing price for the date requested will be reported as well as the following data: price and percent change for 1, 4, 12, and 24 weeks ago; high and low price over the past year; price-earnings ratio; earnings per share. The cost is $10 plus 50¢ per company.

Investors can monitor a portfolio position using PORTFOLIO VALUE ANALYZER. Up to 100 stocks can be tracked. Individual issues and total portfolio performance can be monitored and updated. Dividend data is provided and actual profit or loss and simple and compound annual rates of reform are shown. The cost is $10 plus $1 per company.

Using modern portfolio theory, PORTFOLIO RISK ANALYZER calculates the expected return and the risk of holding a portfolio of up to 25 selected stocks in the proportions specified by the user. The VisiCalc program permits the user to change the number of shares per security to maximize the return or minimize the risk, for each security in the portfolio; the following items are calculated: current value, weight in the portfolio, weighted return.

The use of VisiCalc in data manipulation is essential.

Profile

Database: DataKits—stock market databases
Producer: Data Resources, Inc., 24 Hartwell Ave., Lexington, Massachusetts 02173, 617-861-0165
Toll-Free Telephone: None.
Vendor: Data Resources.
Cost: $6 to $125, depending on the DataKit requested. Median price is about $35. Higher priced DataKits generally include forecasted data from DRI. The user must purchase VisiLink software ($250).
Date Began Online: 1982
Source of Information: Major exchanges and NASDAQ.
Type of Coverage: Information on equity issues includes high, low, and closing prices through the previous day, percent change, volume, and dividends. Data is available back to 1972.
Updating: Daily.
Indexing Terms: CUSIP number, exchange code, ticker symbol.
User Aids: *DataKits Bulletin*, $65, credited toward DataKits ordered during initial 30 days.
Printed Equivalent: None.
Document Retrieval: Not applicable.

20 Computer and Electronics Databases

As you might expect, news and data about the fast-paced computer and electronics industries have found their way into a number of databases. Curiously, though, these industries are not as well indexed on databases as some other fields are—medicine, for example. You'll find plenty of gaps in the information about them. Nevertheless, whatever your role in the computer or electronics industry—whether as engineer, programmer, manager, or just a potential microcomputer buyer—you may find the databases described in this chapter valuable. And you can expect scores of new databases covering this field to emerge in the next few years.

INSPEC

The granddaddy of computer industry databases is INSPEC, which stands for Information Services in Physics, Electrotechnology, Computers, and Control. Covering literature published since 1969, it holds a massive collection of technical references—more than 2 million records. Each has an abstract and is indexed according to a 10,000-word controlled vocabulary. The editors scan 2,350 journals for relevant articles; more than 350 of them are abstracted completely. Approximately 15,000 new records are added every month.

Though INSPEC is intended primarily for engineers and scientists, it contains references to many nontechnical articles about new products, etc. The business staff may want to use it to track technical developments, follow competitors' technical activities, or just find out who is working in particular areas. It does not, however, provide much coverage of the computer industry trade press.

If you find it valuable to search INSPEC for technical literature, in all probability COMPENDEX, the major engineering index, will also carry some references to your topic. We describe COMPENDEX in Chapter 21.

Sample record

PROBLEM: I'm working on the business plan for a young software company. Should we plan to write software that takes advantage of new speech synthesis capabilities? I need a concise, technical review of the recent developments in this area.

(1) 469476   B80005754, C80006904
(2) THE COMPUTER SPEAKS
(3) SHERWOOD, B.A.
     UNIV. OF ILLINOIS, URBANA, IL, USA
(4) IEEE SPECTRUM (USA)   VOL.16, NO. 8   18-25   Aug. 1979   CODEN: IEESAM
     Treatment: APPLIC; GENERAL,REVIEW
     Document Type: JOURNAL PAPER
     Languages: ENGLISH
     REVIEWS THE TECHNIQUES FOR PRODUCING SYNTHETIC SPEECH FROM A COM-
     PUTER. THE AUTHOR EXPECTS SUCH METHODS TO BE AVAILABLE TO THE BUSI-
     NESS WORLD BEFORE TOO LONG INCLUDING RAPID SPEECH SYNTHESIS FROM
     PRINTED TEST INPUTS ABLE TO ACCOMMODATE AN UNLIMITED VOCABULARY.
     TOPICS INCLUDE: ANALOGUE RECORDING; HUMAN SPEECH; COMPRESSED DIGI-
     TAL SPEECH; SPEECH SYNTHESIS FROM TEXT; SOFTWARE; CONVERSION TO
     SOUND; SYNTHETIC SPEECH FOR BUSINESS
(5) Descriptors: SPEECH SYNTHESIS
(6) Identifiers: SYNTHETIC SPEECH; SPEECH SYNTHESIS; ANALOGUE RECORDING;
     HUMAN SPEECH; COMPRESSED DIGITAL SPEECH; SOFTWARE
     Class codes: B6130; C7890; C5590

Notes: (1) DIALOG accession number and abstract number (2) title (3) author (4) journal reference (5) controlled vocabulary terms (6) ad hoc indexing terms

Profile

Database: Information Services in Physics, Electrotechnology, Computers, and Control (INSPEC)
Producer: The Institution of Electrical Engineers, Station House, Nightingale Rd., Hitchin Hertfordshire SG5 1RJ England, 0462-53331. In U.S.A., INSPEC Dept., IEEE Service Center, 445 Hoes Lane, Piscataway, New Jersey 08854, 201-981-0060
Toll-Free Telephone: None.
Vendor: DIALOG, BRS, SDC, CAN-OLE (Canada), Data-Star (Europe), SEARCH/J (Japan), ESA-IRS.
Cost: Approximately $90 per hour, depending on vendor. Offline prints 35¢ and online prints 25¢. Knowledge Index, $24 per hour.
Date Began Online: 1969
Source of Information: Cover-to-cover contents of 350 journals and scanning of 2,000 additional journals. Also includes conference proceedings, technical reports, books, patents, and university theses.
Type of Coverage: Bibliographic, with abstracts.
Size: More than 2 million records.
Updating: Every two weeks, with approximately 7,500 records per update.
Indexing Terms: Controlled vocabulary of 10,000 words and scientific terms.
User Aids: *INSPEC Matters*, quarterly newsletter, free. *INSPEC User Manual*, $70. *INSPEC Thesaurus*, $70.
Printed Equivalent: Four separate publications: *Physics Abstracts*, $1,460 yearly;

Electrotechnology Abstracts, $1,080 yearly; *Computers and Control Abstracts*, $660 yearly; *IT Focus*, $95 yearly.
Document Retrieval: Not offered.

TELECOM

Telecommunications, a major science field under our broad category of computers and electronics, has a valuable new database of its own. Called TELECOM, it has been compiled for many years as a private marketing research database by the Philips electronics company of the Netherlands. Recently, Philips decided to make the database public through the Dutch database vendor Samsom Data Systemen, which is accessible from the United States.

TELECOM contains bibliographic references (some contain abstracts, some don't) from more than 250 periodicals, reports, and conference papers. The database holds an impressive 65,000 records and is updated with more than 1,250 new references a month.

At this writing, the database had just gone online and full documentation was not available. According to Samsom, the database contains information about 25,000 products, 7,000 systems, and 18,000 companies. The controlled vocabulary holds these general headings:

- Product or product group (commercial and technical)
- Economic sector
- Country or continent
- Manufacturer, subdivided into:
  General information
  New products
  Contracts
  Agreements
  Mergers and joint ventures
- Types of products and/or systems

Sample record

PROBLEM: What kind of new developments in fiber-optics have been taking place in Japan?

(1) 306585
     Japan
(2) Modulation and multiplexing systems and repeaters for optical communication
(3) Electronics, 11-08-1982, 55: p. 83,84
(4) Nippon Telegraph & Telephone public corp. (N.T.T.)
(5) Researchers at N.T.T.'s Ausashino electrical communication laboratory have developed simple and cheap optical amplifiers that eliminate conventional baseband regenerative repeaters in fibre-optic communication systems. According to Tatsuya Kimura, director of the third research section at the laboratory, a system using an optical-fibre cable with a loss of 0.6 to 0.3 db per kilometre and two 20 db amplifiers in

cascade will provide common-carrier quality transmission over a distance of between 140 and 280 km. He also estimates that optical amplifiers could be used in cascade for a distance of 400 to 800 km before a regenerative repeater would be needed (for fibre cables with losses of 0.6 to 0.3 db/km).

Notes: (1) document number (2) title (3) journal (4) firm description (5) abstract

Profile

Database: TELECOM
Producer: Philips Telecommunicatie Industrie BV (for information contact Samsom Data Systemen BV, P.O. Box 180, 2400 AD Alphen aan den Rijn, The Netherlands)
Toll-Free Telephone: None.
Vendor: Samsom Datanet.
Cost: 250 guilders per hour.
Date Began Online: 1983
Source of Information: 250 periodicals, newspapers, report-series, and congressional proceedings are scanned for information that deals with the field of telecommunications. Information covers 1977 to present.
Type of Coverage: Bibliographic with controlled terms and selective abstracts (30 percent of references contain abstracts).
Size: Approximately 115,000 records as of December 1983.
Updating: Approximately monthly with 1,250 records added per update.
Indexing Terms: Country numbers, country names, document numbers, and controlled terms.
User Aids: Online thesaurus to be added; *Samsom Datanet C.C.L. User Manual.*
Printed Equivalent: None.
Document Retrieval: Not Offered.

International Software Database

Quite likely, your only involvement in the computer industry is as a computer user. If you're a data-processing manager or even a microcomputer owner, you might find it handy to consult International Software Database for help in finding computer programs.

This is a "fact" database, not one that refers you to magazines or other publications. It lists 55,000 products currently on the market for all kinds of computers—micros, minis, mainframes. This database can help you:

♦ Locate software that performs a particular function.

♦ Find hardware compatible with the software programs you're interested in.

♦ Keep up-to-date on new programs in any category.

The database contains the manufacturer's own description of the product, along with hardware requirements, related programs, price, and a variety of other information such as references to published reviews of software. It is accessible for the flat rate of $24 an hour on DIALOG's Knowledge Index.

The producer also can sell you any computer program listed in the database. You can order by phone or through DIALOG's Dialorder.

Sample record

PROBLEM: I'm looking for a data communications program for my Apple II. I'd like it to be fairly elementary and cost under $150.

(1) TRANSEND 2
(2) SSM MICROCOMPUTER PRODUCTS
2190 PARAGON DR
SAN JOSE, CA 95131
(408)946-7400
Terms: COD, TERMS AVAILABLE
(3) APPLE II/48K/149.00$/149.00$
APPLE II/IMPLIED
APPLE II + /IMPLIED
CAPPLE II + /48K/149.00$/149.00$
DOS 3.3 (APPLE)/48K/149.00$/149.00$
Country of Currency: USA
Source Code Available: NO
Integrated Packaging: NO
Updates: NO
Special Configuration: Disk II with controller. Serial interface and modem.
Warranty: YES
(4) Transend 2 is a systems approach to data communications. This software provides three levels of sophistication. You may start in either lower level and update to more advanced levels without purchasing an entirely new software package. The first level turns the Apple into an intelligent terminal, enabling it to communicate with other micros, bulletin-board systems, timesharing services, information utilities and a variety of mini- and mainframe computers. The second level program adds "verified file transfer" to its capabilities. Level three adds a more complete text editor, password file protection and calendar scheduling.
(5) 825 SYSTEMS/COMMUNICATIONS

Notes: (1) title of program (2) vendor or distributor (3) system listings (4) abstract (5) indexing code

Profile

Database: International Software Database
Producer: MENU, International Software Database Corp., 1520 College Ave., Fort Collins, Colorado 80524, 303-482-5000
Toll-Free Telephone: 800-843-6368 (800-THE-MENU)
Vendor: DIALOG.
Cost: $60 per hour plus 15¢ for offline prints. Knowledge Index, $24 per hour.
Date Began Online: December 1982
Source of Information: Producers of currently available software.
Type of Coverage: Factual, includes product descriptions supplied by the producers. Some records include a list of published reviews of the software.
Size: 55,000 products.
Updating: Monthly, approximately 500 added each update.
Indexing Terms: 75 descriptor terms. Also includes machine, operating systems, applications, vendor, price, and International Standard Program Number.
User Aids: *International Software User's Guide*, $10.

Printed Equivalent: *The Software Catalog—Microcomputers*, twice yearly with two updates, $142.50. *The Software Catalog—Minicomputers*, twice yearly with two updates, $191.50.

Document Retrieval: All listed software is available for sale by Imprint Software Ltd.

Other Services: Software reports can be obtained directly from Menu for $25 for the first 10 programs, $1 for each additional report up to 50, and 50¢ for each report thereafter.

Microcomputer Index

As a microcomputer owner or potential owner, you probably find keeping up with news about these machines a dizzying task. Scores of new magazines and newspapers review products, describe new applications, and recount the experiences of users. For every useful article you see, you may miss ten others.

Several companies are trying to lend some help by compiling databases of microcomputer periodicals. The databases are geared to a nontechnical audience and are relatively inexpensive to use. Their main use is in helping you figure out what to buy.

The oldest, Microcomputer Index, started in 1981. It abstracts 50 popular microcomputer periodicals cover to cover and another 10 selectively (omitting, of course, ads and minor announcements).

Try searching this database to locate:

♦ Software reviews

♦ Hardware reviews

♦ Book reviews

♦ New product announcements

♦ Feature articles on specific applications

A controlled vocabulary of 700 terms aids in searching. It includes both names of products and general terms. About 850 articles are added each month. Like International Software Database, this is available on DIALOG's Knowledge Index.

Sample record

PROBLEM: I plan to purchase a tax preparation program for my microcomputer. Are there any published reviews of some popular programs of this type?

(1)	8147169
(2)	Tax preparation for CP/M systems
(3)	Heintz, Carl
(4)	Interface Age , Dec 1981 , v6 n12 p46-49 , 3 pages ISSN 0147-2992
	Languages: English

Document Type: Software Review
Geographic Location: United States
(5) A favorable review for the Federal and State Tax Preparation System by Microcomputer Tax Systems. Review describes a set of programs that allows the accountant to prepare federal and state returns for individuals and partnerships.
(6) Descriptors: *Software Review; *Business; *Taxes; *CP/M
(7) Identifiers: Federal and State Tax Preparation System; Microcomputer Tax Systems

Notes: (1) accession number (2) title (3) author (4) journal (5) abstract (6) controlled vocabulary terms (7) ad hoc indexing terms

Microcomputer Index—magazines covered as of June 1983

COMPLETE COVERAGE:
Access: Microcomputers in Libraries
ANTIC
Apple Orchard
Byte
Call A.P.P.L.E.
Classroom Computer News
Compute!
Computing Teacher
Creative Computing
Desktop Computing
Dr. Dobb's Journal
Educational Computer
Electronic Learning
InfoWorld
Interface Age
Micro: The 6502/6809 Journal
Microcomputing
Microsystems
Nibble
*PC: The Independent Guide to IBM Personal
    Computers*

Peelings II
Personal Computing
Popular Computing
Softside
Small Business Computers
Sync
T.H.E. Journal
80 Microcomputing

PARTIAL COVERAGE
Business Week
Educational Technology
Instructional Innovator
Media & Methods
MUMPS Users' Group Quarterly
Nation's Business
Popular Electronics
Radio-Electronics
Softalk
80-U.S. Journal

Profile

Database: Microcomputer Index
Producer: Microcomputer Information Services, 2464 El Camino Real, Suite 247, Santa Clara, California 95051, 408-984-1097
Toll-Free Telephone: None.
Vendor: DIALOG.
Cost: $45 per hour plus 15¢ for offline prints. Knowledge Index, $24 per hour.
Date Began Online: December 1982
Source of Information: All articles, product reviews, new product announcements, and book reviews from 50 popular computer periodicals. Scanning of 10 additional periodicals. Earliest coverage is January 1981; starting date varies by publication.
Type of Coverage: Bibliographic, with abstracts. Lag of 45 days or more from the time items are published.
Size: 20,000 records.
Updating: Monthly, approximately 850 added per month.

Indexing Terms: Controlled vocabulary of 700 descriptive terms.
User Aids: DIALOG chapter on Microcomputer Index, $4.
Printed Equivalent: *Microcomputer Index*, printed bimonthly, $45 per year.
Document Retrieval: Not offered.
Other Services: The company offers to refer customers who need searches to qualified searchers.

DISC and Periodical Guide for Computerists

Both Applegate Computer Enterprises and Bibliographic Retrieval Service (BRS)—the latter better known as a database vendor, not as a producer—have jumped on the microcomputer database bandwagon. Applegate has started the Periodical Guide for Computerists on CompuServe, and a similar database called DISC (Data Processing and Information Science Contents) is on BRS. They're very similar.

The former scans about 35 microcomputer periodicals; DISC scans about 20. Neither of them includes abstracts, which may limit their usefulness compared to Microcomputer Index. But both are very cheap to use: DISC is available on BRS After Dark at $15 an hour; Periodical Guide for Computerists on CompuServe at $5 an hour.

As this is written, Applegate is updating Periodical Guide for Computerists only quarterly, which means it may be significantly behind the news for the fast-changing microcomputer business. DISC and Microcomputer Index, by contrast, are updated twice monthly.

Both DISC and Periodical Guide for Computerists use a very small controlled vocabulary: the former has 60 terms and the latter 14 terms. This can make for imprecise searching, since without abstracts you have to rely on just the index terms and the title to catch an article you're interested in. (By contrast, the Microcomputer Index uses 700 terms in addition to abstracts.) If, however, your topic is general—such as, perhaps, "how-to articles about telecommunications" (these are DISC terms)—then you might find these two databases useful.

Sample record

PROBLEM: I need a beginning article about modems to distribute in my office.

(1) AN POP8212012. 82121.
(2) AU MIASTKOWSKI-S
(3) TI MODEMS: HOOKING YOUR COMPUTER TO THE WORLD.
(4) SO POPULAR COMPUTING. VOL. 2, NO. 2. DECEMBER 1982.
     PG 111.
(5) PT 0: ORIGINAL ARTICLES.
(6) CC TL: TELECOMMUNICATIONS. PE: PERIPHERALS.

Notes: (1) accession number (2) author (3) title (4) source (5) publication type (6) classification codes

Profile

Database: DISC
Producer: Bibliographic Retrieval Service, Inc., 1200 Route 7, Latham, New York 12110, 518-783-1161
Toll-Free Telephone: 800-833-4707
Vendor: BRS.
Cost: Regular base rate of $35 per hour. $15 per hour on After Dark service.
Date Began Online: January 1982
Source of Information: All articles in 20 popular computer magazines. Also a table of contents of the magazines. Coverage starts January 1982.
Type of Coverage: Bibliographic, no abstracts. No more than a one-month lag.
Size: 6,000 records as of July 1983.
Updating: Biweekly, approximately 100 records per update.
Indexing Terms: 60 classification codes.
User Aids: *BRS—DISC Database Guide*, 16 pages, $3.
Printed Equivalent: None.
Document Retrieval: Not offered.

Periodical Guide for Computerists journal list

80 Microcomputing
68 Micro Journal
Business Computer Systems
Byte
Call A.P.P.L.E.
Classroom Computer News
Compute
Computer Decisions
*Computers in Mathematics & Science
 Teaching*
Creative Computing
Dr. Dobb's Journal
Desktop Computing
Educational Computer
InfoWorld

Interface Age
Lifelines
Mechanix Illustrated
Microcomputing
Microsystems
Nibble
PC
Personal Computer Age
Personal Computing
Popular Computing
Popular Electronics
Popular Mechanics
Popular Science
Small Business Computers

Periodical Guide for Computerists major subject headings

Communications
Computers
Education
Games
General
Graphics
Hardware
Languages

Microcomputers
Microprocessors
Networks
Programming
Robotics
Software
Software Word Processors

Profile

Database: Periodical Guide for Computerists
Producer: Applegate Computer Enterprises, 470 Slagle Creek Rd., Grants Pass, Oregon 97527, 503-846-6742
Toll-Free Telephone: None.

Vendor: CompuServe.
Cost: $22.50 per hour, $5 per hour during nonprime hours.
Date Began Online: 1982
Source of Information: Most articles in 28 monthly and weekly microcomputer periodicals. Software reviews back to January 1981.
Type of Coverage: Bibliographic, no abstracts. Lag of up to three months after publication.
Size: 5,000 records as of August 1983.
Updating: 3,500 records added per quarter.
Indexing Terms: 15 subject categories.
User Aids: None.
Printed Equivalent: Periodical Guide for Computerists, annual, $15.95.
Document Retrieval: Not offered.

The Computer Database

Finally, the producer of the Management Contents database (see Chapter 13) plans a giant leap into this field with its new offering called simply The Computer Database. This database fills a large gap in the market between INSPEC, the huge technical database, and the tiny microcomputer databases oriented toward the general computer user. The Computer Database will provide very broad bibliographic coverage of the computer field from the perspectives of business people, computer users, and computer professionals.

The Management Contents company began abstracting materials for this database in January 1983. The database indexes and abstracts 500 computer-related publications cover to cover (except for editorials, book reviews, calendars, and the like); in addition, it includes selected materials from books, courses, and research reports. The database started its life online with 45,000 citations—larger than any in this chapter except INSPEC and TELECOM—and will grow at the rate of 60,000 a year after that. A controlled vocabulary of 3,500 words is used to enhance searching.

Major subject headings

Business & Industry Applications
Company Names, Locations, Types
Computer Games
Computer Graphics
Computer Systems and Equipment
Consumer Information
Database Management
Electronics
Financial Information
Hardware Design, Development, Review
Home Computers

Interfaces
Letters to the Editor
Microprocessors
New Products
Operating Systems
Performance Evaluation
Programming Languages
Prototyping
Software Design, Development, Review
Telecommunications
Word Processing

Profile

Database: The Computer Database
Producer: Management Contents, 2265 Carlson Dr., Suite 5000, Northbrook, Illinois 60062, 312-564-1006

Toll-Free Telephone: 800-323-5354
Vendor: DIALOG.
Cost: $85 per hour.
Date Began Online: December 1983
Source of Information: Most articles in 530 computer-related periodicals, journals, and newsletters. Also coverage of computer-related books, professional courses, conference proceedings, etc. Significant coverage of telecommunications and electronics.
Type of Coverage: Bibliographic with abstracts.
Size: Approximately 45,000 records in December 1983.
Updating: Monthly, approximately 5,000 records added per update.
Indexing Terms: Controlled vocabulary of 3,500 terms.
User Aids: *The Computer Database Thesaurus & Dictionary*, $120.
Printed Equivalent: None.
Document Retrieval: $10 per article; sent in next business day's mail.

21 Other Science and Technology Databases

The information explosion can nowhere be better seen than in the fields of science and engineering. Whatever the discovery, chances are that there will be a conference for presenting it, journals to analyze it, and, perhaps, a new field to take off from it.

A look at one of the most prominent university libraries will give some clues to the extent of this scientific information explosion and the challenge of managing it. The Massachusetts Institute of Technology library subscribes to over 20,000 scientific magazines and periodicals. Even so, the library director says budget constraints and an inflation rate of l5 percent limit subscriptions to only half the desired number of publications in certain fields. He cites a report that 3.4 new publications were started between l976 and l980 for every one that ceased being published.

Online databases offer a better way for individuals to keep track of scientific information. All of the databases in this chapter draw on hundreds of thousands of worldwide sources; Chemical Abstracts, for example, includes material published in 75 countries. We shall present here databases devoted to chemistry, agriculture, engineering, technical standards and specifications, the rubber and plastics industries, the paper/board, printing, and packaging industries, as well as pertinent government publications and conference papers from numerous disciplines.

COMPENDEX

Covering new developments in every field of engineering, COMPENDEX is one of the most widely used technology databases. It is a convenient source for references to articles in hundreds of journals (professional, technical, and trade), reports, conference proceedings, and monographs from all over the world. In addition to engineering, there is some coverage of related topics in science, energy, and management.

COMPENDEX is very well indexed, using a large controlled vocabulary (over 12,000 terms) developed by the producer. You can also search by the producer's classification codes—hundreds of numbers assigned to subjects—or use free-text searching.

While the database includes material in 26 languages, there is always an English-language abstract. Much important engineering literature originates in Japan, Germany, and the Soviet Union, so we consider the English abstract an important asset.

Sample record

PROBLEM: I am research and development manager for a small electronics company. We are investigating digital telephone equipment as a possible new product area. I need some background on the current market for such products.

(1) 82-096449
(2) NEW DIGITAL TRANSMISSION SERVICES FOR THE BUSINESS COMMUNITY
(3) BOWSHER BRIAN
(4) Marconi Co, Engl
(5) Commun Broadcast v 7 n 2 Feb 1982 p 3-10 (COBRDB)
(6) 716
(7) *DIGITAL COMMUNICATION SYSTEMS—United Kingdom; DATA TRANSMISSION—Multiplexing; TELEPHONE SYSTEMS
(8) DIGITAL TELEPHONY
For many years digital transmission equipment has been installed in telephone networks, yet has not been extended to customers' premises to provide improved data services. Marconi equipment is described that has been designed in conjunction with British Telecom to bring all the advantages of digital transmission to the customer with data transmission needs. This equipment is used to provide a digital leased-line service in the UK called 'Kilostream', which will be of particular benefit to the business community. The demand for such a service is discussed, together with the availability of suitable transmission plant. Also the customer interface is described, and the method of routing and of synchronization, as well as the powerful supervisory and alarm system. Lastly, the scope for further development is explored.

Notes: (1) accession number (2) title (3) author (4) organization and country (5) source (6) category codes (7) controlled vocabulary terms (8) ad hoc indexing terms

Profile

Database: COMPENDEX
Producer: Engineering Information, Inc., 345 E. 47th St., New York, New York 10017, 212-705-7615
Toll-Free Telephone: 800-221-1044 (outside New York State)
Vendor: DIALOG, SDC, BRS, ESA-IRS, Pergamon.
Cost: $98 per hour connect charge on DIALOG, plus 30¢ per citation (printed online or offline).
Date Began Online: 1969
Source of Information: Worldwide literature on all fields of engineering, including professional and industrial journals, reports, conference proceedings, monographs, and other technical material. Coverage is from 1969 to the present.
Type of Coverage: Bibliographic, with abstract.

Size: 1.5 million records.

Updating: Monthly, approximately 9,500 records added per update.

Indexing Terms: Up to six controlled vocabulary terms per item are selected from *Subject Headings for Engineering* (SHE)—over 12,000 terms. Ad hoc language terms are also assigned. Classification codes are selected from SHE and CAL Classification Codes.

User Aids: *The Compendex Search Manual*, $75. *Subject Heading Guide to Engineering Categories*, $15. *Publications Indexed for Engineering* (with supplements), $30. *CAL Classification Codes*, free.

Printed Equivalent: *Engineering Index*, published monthly, price $1,180 (the annual is $680; price for both, $1,425).

Document Retrieval: All documents listed in COMPENDEX are available from the Engineering Societies Library, 345 East 47 St., New York, New York 10017, 212-705-7611. Cost for orders placed by mail is 40¢ per page, plus $4 for handling and $1 for billing per document (billing charge is waived for holders of deposit accounts, minimum $50). "Priority service" costs an additional $5 per document.

Other Services: No custom searches, but referrals given to archives and libraries, particularly Engineering Societies Library.

Notes: Fields of engineering covered: civil, environmental, geological, bioengineering, mining, metals, petroleum, fuel, mechanical, automotive, nuclear, aerospace, electrical, electronics, control, chemical, agricultural, food, industrial; other material on management, mathematics, physics, instruments, training, and the engineering profession.

NTIS

It's apparent from the success of the NTIS database that someone besides U.S. Senator William Proxmire (issuer of the famed Golden Fleece awards) is interested in how the federal government is spending your research dollars. The NTIS (for National Technical Information Service) database is where to go for virtually any publicly available report on government-sponsored research, development, and engineering projects.

The preparers are federal agencies, their grantees or contractors, and special technology groups. (NTIS is also the exclusive outlet for sales of many of the reports contained in the database.) Hundreds of subjects are included; ten years ago the focus was almost exclusively on physical sciences, but source material today is from dozens of agencies and covers "nearly every topic of practical importance."

NTIS is especially useful for engineers and technical information specialists, but it includes topics of interest to anyone in business. You'll find material on energy, environmental issues, computer science, physics, chemistry, materials science, health, production control, robotics, artificial intelligence, and management science (note that most of the management studies are theoretical in approach). Also included are reports on foreign research and development (many received through exchange programs with the United States) and patent information on government-owned inventions that are available for public licensing.

An individual record on NTIS will give you a lot of information about the document, though the abstracts are not particularly long or consistent. If the title is in a foreign language, an English title is also given. You can see whether NTIS sells the document; if so, for what price, and if not, other availability information. You'll be given both the name of the organization sponsoring the work and the one performing it. The abstract can be either "informative," summarizing the scope and content, or "indicative," summarizing the kind of document. Abstracts may be written by the author(s), NTIS, or the sponsoring agency.

Searching by subject can be tricky; some of the major agency suppliers, such as the Department of Energy, do their own cataloging and abstracting, so the key words are assigned from different controlled vocabularies. Reports on electric power generation, for example, may be indexed differently by the National Aeronautics and Space Administration, the Department of Defense, and the Department of Energy. NTIS has these thesauri for sale, however. For its own indexing, NTIS uses two "subject category codes" and its *Thesaurus of Engineering and Scientific Terms*.

NTIS is carried by all three major U.S. vendors (DIALOG, SDC, and BRS) as well as by ESA-IRS.

Sample record

PROBLEM: I sell pollution control equipment. Is there an EPA study showing the levels of various toxic substances monitored in a number of states?

> Accession No. PB-248 660/3SL
> Title: Compilation of State Data for Eight Selected Toxic Substances. Volume 1.
> Title Report: Final Report
> Authors: Roberts, Elisabeth; Spewak, R.,; Stryker, S.; Tracey, S.
> Corporate Source: Mitre Corp., McLean, Va. Environmental Protection Agency, Washington, D.C. Office of Toxic Substances
> Pagination/Date: Sept. 75, 165p*
> NTIS PRICES: NTIS PRICES: PC A08/MF A01
> Availability: Paper copy also available in set of 5 reports as PB-248 659-SET, PC $36.00
> Category Codes: 06T; 06F; 57Y*; 57H; 68*
> Descriptors: *Environmental surveys; States (United States); Monitors; Toxicology; Arsenic; Beryllium; Cadmium; Cyanides; Lead (Metal); Mercury (Metal); Chlorine aromatic compounds; Data acquisition; Data processing; Water pollution; Air pollution; Chemical compounds
> Identifiers: *Toxic agents; Biphenyl/chloro; State agencies; NTISEPAOTS
> Spons Ag Acronym/No. EPA-560/7-75-52-Vol-1
> Announcement Publication: U7606
> Report Nos. MITRE-75-52-Vol-1
> Contract/Grant Nos. EPA-68-01-2933
> Abstract: In June 1974, toxic substances data in the U.S. was collected and analyzed in 20 key States. This report describes that effort and discusses the amount, type and usefulness of the data and the toxic substances monitoring capabilities of the State agencies contacted.

Profile

Database: NTIS
Producer: U.S. National Technical Information Center, 5285 Port Royal Rd., Springfield, Virginia 22161, 703-487-4807

Toll-Free Telephone: None.
Vendor: DIALOG, SDC, BRS, ESA-IRS.
Cost: On DIALOG: $45 per hour connect charge, plus 15¢ per record printed offline.
Date Began Online: 1972
Source of Information: The majority of documents are research, development, and engineering reports and other analyses prepared by the U.S. government, especially the Departments of Defense and Energy and the National Aeronautics and Space Administration. Also included in this category are reports from grantees and contractors and by special technology groups. Other materials include foreign reports, patents and patent applications issued to federal agencies and available for public licensing, environmental impact statements, special health care section, and translations.
Type of Coverage: Bibliographic. Most citations contain abstracts (the two exceptions are NASA reports announced prior to 1973 and Atomic Energy Commission reports announced prior to 1975).
Size: Over 1 million records.
Updating: Biweekly, with 2,500 to 3,000 records added per update.
Indexing Terms: About one-quarter of the sources are given descriptive cataloging and abstracting by NTIS using the *Thesaurus of Engineering and Scientific Terms* (TEST). Remaining documents are indexed at originating agency using its controlled vocabulary.
User Aids: *A Reference Guide to the NTIS Bibliographic Data Base*, 1980 ed., free. Thesauri in use by NTIS and contributing agencies, $20 to $40 each: *Thesaurus of Engineering and Scientific Terms; DDC Retrieval and Indexing Terminology; Energy Information Data Base—Subject Thesaurus; NASA Thesaurus, Vol. 1—Alphabetical Listing; NASA Thesaurus, Vol. 2—Access Vocabulary*.
Printed Equivalent: Database is source for the following NTIS journals and newsletters: *Government Reports Announcements and Index*, biweekly, and 26 different biweekly abstract newsletters.
Document Retrieval: Over 1 million titles are for sale. Most reports are available in hard copy or microfiche; some on magnetic tape or microfilm.
Other Services: Occasional custom searching. Other products: current awareness service on microfiche; over 2,500 special bibliographies; directories of computer software applications; custom-designed publications; computer products; *NTIS Tech Notes* (providing selections of latest information on federal technological advances).
Notes: NTIS, a self-supporting government agency, is part of the U.S. Department of Commerce.

CAS databases

If your business is active in one or more fields of science and technology, chances are that you require information about chemicals from time to time. You may be curious to know, for example, if anyone else has discovered that new substance that your chief chemist came up with; if there are any patents on applications for it; or if there have been any studies of its safety or effectiveness. You may be looking for an alternative (safer or cheaper, perhaps) to a chemical that you use in manufacturing one of your products.

There is a convenient and widely available source of chemical information that you can access from your terminal—the Chemical Abstracts Service (CAS) group of databases. CAS's large staff indexes and writes abstracts for every significant piece of information about chemicals collected from sources around the world. The results of their labor, over 6 million references since 1967, appear in various forms in CAS's publications and online databases.

A few cautionary comments are in order for the new user. Chemistry searching is a unique undertaking. The databases have variations with which the user should become familiar. For example, the files may change in content and arrangement every few years; the CA Search bibliographic file varies in form and name between vendors; and substances tend to be known by different names (such as generic, trade, and common). CAS publishes dozens of user-aid books, many of which you will need to become familiar with. You will probably need a background in chemistry or help from someone who has in order to figure out the citations, which are full of technical terminology (much of it abbreviated). If all this doesn't daunt you, then we urge you to forge ahead. Chemistry searching is rewarding, and its potential for enhancing pertinent research and development activities of your business is great.

The CAS registry number is the easiest and most direct way to search CAS's databases, as well as many others in the chemistry field. Each new substance mentioned in the world's literature since 1965 has been given a unique number that serves as its "address." If you don't know this number at the start of your search, you can obtain it by several means, including printed indexes and online "chemical dictionary" files. Two examples of such online files are CHEMNAME on DIALOG and CHEMDEX on SDC.

The CAS Online database can give you a prompt answer to the query, "Is this a known substance? If so, what are its vital statistics?" You can also search for bibliographic references with abstracts as far back as 1967.

With the proper terminal, the searcher of CAS Online simply enters structural or substructural information into the system. He gets back the following answers about his substance.

♦ CAS registry number
♦ Molecular formula
♦ Structural diagram
♦ CA index name (the "official" name selected by CAS)
♦ Other names
♦ Up to ten bibliographic citations and/or abstracts (optional)

You can construct your diagram in either of two ways, depending on your terminal. One is to type commands on the keyboard of any text or standard graphics terminal. Or, if you have access to an intelligent graphics terminal, you can be an artist and "draw" the features by selecting them from a menu and positioning them on the screen, using a tablet and stylus.

A typical search on CAS Online is estimated to cost about $100 to $125. The hourly connect charge is kept low ($35) to encourage thinking time (though there are other charges). You may choose a novice or expert version of the command language and store your searches for periodic updates.

A subset of the producer's database, which contains bibliographic records from *Chemical Abstracts*, is available as CA Search from many major vendors (though the files may be implemented in different ways and be under different names). Unlike CAS Online, CA Search citations do not contain abstracts. They do contain an abstract number and information for finding the abstract in the print journal in an appropriate library. The citations are heavily indexed, so you should be able to get a good idea of the subject from the title and indexing terms.

Sample record

PROBLEM: In order to solve a manufacturing problem, I need information on bonding agents for polyvinyl chloride (a synthetic rubber).

```
95220960     CA: 95(26)220960q     JOURNAL
     Study of types of sole materials in order to optimize the adhesion conditions. Part
II.   AUTHOR: Spasova, M.; Zlateva, P.   LOCATION: Inst. Obuvn. Kozhukharskata,
Kozharskata Galanteriinata Prom., Sofia, Bulg.
JOURNAL: Kozh. Obuvna Prom-st.   DATE: 1981   VOLUME: 22   NUMBER: 8
PAGES: 7-9   CODEN: KZOPAS   ISSN: 0368-7295   LANGUAGE: Bulgarian
SECTION:
CA037003 Plastics Fabrications and Uses
     IDENTIFIERS: rubber shoe sole adhesion, polyurethane adhesive rubber sole-
neoprene rubber adhesive sole
     DESCRIPTORS: Urethane polymers, uses and miscellaneous...
adhesives, for synthetic rubber soles...
Shoes, soles...
     materials and adhesives for, optimization of
Adhesives...
     neoprene rubber, for synthetic rubber soles
Rubber, natural, uses and miscellaneous... Rubber, butadiene, uses and miscella-
neous... Rubber, butadiene-styrene, uses and miscellaneous...
     shoe soles from, optimization of adhesion of
Rubber, synthetic...
     thermoplastic, shoe soles from, optimization of adhesion of
     CAS REGISTRY NUMBERS:
9002-86-2   24937-78-8   shoe soles from, optimization of adhesion of
```

Profile

Database: CA Search
Producer: Chemical Abstracts Service, 2540 Olentangy River Rd., P.O. Box 3012, Columbus, Ohio 43210, 614-421-3600
Toll-Free Telephone: 800-848-6533 (Search Assistance Desk, outside Ohio only); in Ohio or outside the United States, 614-421-3698
Vendor: BRS, DIALOG, SDC, Pergamon InfoLine, ESA-IRS, Questel.
Cost: On DIALOG, $68 per connect hour, plus 12¢ per record typed online and 25¢ per record printed offline.
Date Began Online: 1979
Source of Information: CAS reviews nearly 2 million documents per year relating to chemistry, chemical engineering, and related sciences of which over 450,000 are selected for inclusion in this database. Criteria for including documents are described as "rigorous...only new and significant research findings." Scientific and

technical journals, patent documents, government reports, dissertations, and books are indexed. The file is available back through 1967 on most vendors.

Type of Coverage: Bibliographic citations only (no abstracts; abstracts are carried on the CAS Online database).

Size: Approximately 6 million records as of August 1983.

Updating: Every two weeks, with over 17,000 records added per update.

Indexing Terms: A combination of controlled vocabularies and natural language, including (1) key-word phrases, which usually consist of one to five words reflecting the main scientific findings in the document; (2) CA index name, molecular formula, registry number, and type of information about the substance; (3) general subject index entries, consisting of concept headings.

User Aids: *CA Index Guide*, $50; *How to Use CA Search*, $20; *Subject Coverage and Arrangement of Abstracts by Sections in Chemical Abstracts* (and supplements), $20; *1000 Journals Most Frequently Cited in Chemical Abstracts*, free; *Registry Handbook: Common Names*, $600; other documentation available from vendors.

Printed Equivalent: *Chemical Abstracts*, published weekly, $7,500 per year including semiannual *Volume Index*; weekly issues alone cost $5,000, *Volume Index* alone costs $6,000. Rates discounted to colleges and universities.

Document Retrieval: Many of the cited documents are available through CAS Document Delivery Service. If CAS is not permitted by law to copy the document, it will lend it instead. Price is $14 per document, $12 if CA abstract number is included with order.

Other Services: Custom searches. Fee for a single search on any CAS file is $250, which includes up to 100 retrievals. Additional retrievals are 30¢ each. An exact structure search or family search on CAS Online is $100. The company also produces Chemical Industry Notes database, which indexes approximately 80 business-oriented periodicals.

Profile

Database: CAS Online

Producer: Chemical Abstracts Service, 2540 Olentangy River Rd., P.O. Box 3012, Columbus Ohio, 43210, 614-421-3600

Toll-Free Telephone: 800-848-6533 (Search Assistance Desk, outside Ohio only); in Ohio or outside the United States, 614-421-3698

Vendor: Chemical Abstracts Service.

Cost: Fee for setting up account, $50; charge per connect hour, $35; telecommunications, $10 per hour. Additional fee charged for type of search as follows: full file, $80; current awareness, $10; sample search, free; full file, completely defined structure search, $12. Charge for answers displayed or printed online is 8¢ to $1 each; offline prints are an additional 10¢ each.

Date Began Online: 1980

Source of Information: Registry File: indexes new substances found since 1965 in the literature cited in *Chemical Abstracts*. New substances prior to 1965 may be added during 1984. CA File: CAS reviews nearly 2 million documents per year relating to chemistry, chemical engineering, and related sciences of which over 450,000 are selected for inclusion. Criteria for included documents are described as "rigorous ... only new and significant research findings." Scientific and technical journals, patent documents, government reports, dissertations, and books are indexed and abstracted.

Type of Coverage: Registry File: facts about chemicals and their structures. CA File: bibliographic information with abstracts going back to 1967 to be added by 1984.

Size: Registry File: over 6.3 million unique substances registered with CAS from 1965 to the present. CA File: about 6.2 million bibliographic records from 1967 to the present.

Updating: Registry File: 7,000 new substances added per week. CA File: 17,000 new documents added every two weeks.

Indexing Terms: CA File: a combination of controlled vocabularies and natural language, including (1) key-word phrases, which usually consist of one to five words reflecting the main scientific findings in the document; (2) CA index name, molecular formula, registry number, and type of information about the substance; (3) general subject index entries, consisting of concept headings.

User Aids: *CA Index Guide*, $50; *Using CAS Online, The Registry File*, $35; *Using CAS Online, The CA File*, $15; *CAS Online Workbook*, $20; *Guide to Commands*, $10; *Graphic Structure Input Manual and Tape*, $30; *Screen Dictionary,* $20; booklet and manual on searching polymers by structure, $15; workshops available.

Printed Equivalent: Registry File: none. CA File: *Chemical Abstracts*, published weekly, $7,500 per year (includes semiannual *Volume Index*). Weekly issues alone cost $5,000, *Volume Index* alone costs $6,000.

Document Retrieval: Many of the cited documents are available through CAS Document Delivery Service. If CAS is not permitted by law to copy the document, it will lend it instead. Price is $14 per document, $12 if CA abstract number is included with order.

Other Services: Customer searches. Fee for a single search on any CAS file is $250, which includes up to 100 retrievals. Additional retrievals are 30¢ each. An exact structure search or family search on CAS Online is $100. The company also produces Chemical Industry Notes database, which indexes about 80 business-oriented periodicals.

Information Handling Services databases

In November 1965, a power blackout covered the U.S. Northeast during rush hour. Thousands of people were trapped in elevators. Contrary to what many of them feared, not one elevator fell during the blackout. No one was injured in an elevator accident. Why?

The elevators held fast because of a section on safety devices in the elevator code of the American Society of Mechanical Engineers. This standard is voluntary, but it is an example of standards that most states and municipal codes routinely require the builders of elevators to meet.

Standards and specifications are important in numerous industries, such as utilities, electronics, construction, transportation, communications, textiles, and packaging. They are most often written by trade associations and technical commissions.

There is also a huge number of standards and specifications originating from the U.S. government, particularly the Department of Defense. If you are a government contractor or interested in becoming one, you'll need to have access to them, whether the item is for an F-16 fighter plane or the music stands of the marching band.

You'll also need to be sure that you have the most current edition of the standard.

Three databases produced by Information Handling Services (IHS) of Englewood, Colorado—MLSS, STDS, and ISMS—form an online system of citations to important standards literature in the United States and abroad. Over 400 public and private standardizing bodies are represented. The full text of documents may be found in the company's microfilm storage system or may be ordered from a supplier online.

A companion database, VEND, contains references to the catalogs of over 26,000 vendors who perform 80 percent of the manufacturing of industrial products today. You can obtain copies of complete catalogs either in their original format or, for select sections, with similar products from different vendors grouped together.

IHS has developed over 6,500 locator codes to classify standards by subject. Descriptors are assigned from a controlled vocabulary of 60,000 terms.

Sample record

PROBLEM: Is there an ANSI approved standard for fixed carbon resistors?

(1) EIA RS-172-B. 8207.
(2) FIXED COMPOSITION RESISTORS (R 1980)
(3) ELECTRONIC INDUSTRIES ASSOCIATION (EIA)
(4) INDUSTRY STANDARDS (ISTD)
(5) 75
      22 PAGES
(6) A-19-03 - RESISTOR, FIXED, CARBON COMPOSITION.
(7) YES.
(8) EN.
      DOCUMENT NUMBER: RS-172-B, 2177-A-05
      FILM LOCATION: 2I09-0252
      STATUS

Notes: (l) accession number (2) title (3) organization (4) type of document (5) issue date (1975) (6) locator code (7) ANSI approval (8) language (English)

Profile

Databases: Military & Federal Specifications & Standards (MLSS); Industry & International Standards (STDS); ISMS (MLSS and STDS combined)
Producer: Information Handling Services, l5 Inverness Way East, Englewood, Colorado 80150, 301-790-0600
Toll-Free Telephone: 800-525-7052
Vendor: BRS.
Cost: MLSS and STDS may be searched separately or as a combined file, ISMS. Royalty fees are as follows: MLSS, $20 per hour; STDS, $20 per hour; ISMS, $30 per hour. Each citation printed online is 3¢, and each offline citation costs l0¢. These charges are in addition to regular BRS fees of $16 to $35 per connect hour.
Date Began Online: October l982
Source of Information: MLSS cites the active and historical standards and specifications of the U.S. government, especially the Department of Defense. Military standard drawings and qualified products lists are included. STDS cites standards and specifications originating from over 400 standardizing bodies in the United States and abroad. Included are the National Bureau of Standard's Voluntary Engineering Standards.

Type of Coverage: Bibliographic, without abstracts.
Size: More than 73,000 standards.
Updating: MLSS, weekly; ISMS, weekly; STDS, every two months.
Indexing Terms: Each citation is assigned one or more locator codes (from a group of over 6,500), plus words or phrases that correspond to the codes. Government documents are classified by the Federal Supply Classification Code.
User Aids: *MLSS—VSMF Subject Index*, $150; *STDS—VSMF Subject Index*, $100.
Printed Equivalent: Printed indexes to IHS's microfilm and microfiche holdings.
Document Retrieval: Documents may be ordered from Global Engineering Documents, 2625 Hickory St., Santa Ana, California 92707, 714-540-9870, 213-624-1216, and 800-624-7179 (toll free—not available in California). Fees usually consist of a document charge ($3 and up) and possible charges (depending on document) for handling and reproduction and for older, hard-to-find materials. Microfilm or microfiche full-text subscriptions available from producer.
Notes: New societies are continually added to source list.

PIRA

The Research Association for the Paper and Board, Printing and Packaging Industries, located in England, produces the PIRA database. Each month, relevant articles are selected from over 1,000 journals on virtually every aspect of these industries. Some of the main areas are raw materials, processing, technology, disposal of waste, marketing, and safety. PIRA includes other documents as well, many of which are hard-to-find: government publications, standards and specifications, directories, reports, dissertations, directories, manufacturers' catalogs, and translations.

A recent search of PIRA yielded the following items: how to make a scratch-off lottery ticket (pay attention to security precautions and "obliterating inks"); what makes a successful cigarette package (use crack-proof varnish, odor-free ink, moisture-proof film, and a catchy design); and how the Ministry of Oman wants you to label your exported foodstuffs (freshness dates must be given in Arabic or the items will be returned).

You don't have to be a printer or paper manufacturer to benefit from PIRA. Anyone who has questions about his product's packaging (its effectiveness or safety, for example), produces printed matter, stores packaged items in a retail environment or ships them, or has questions about using waste print materials will find information here.

PIRA contains a more general business subfile of carefully selected articles on management and marketing. (It is also available as a separate database, but it is much smaller than most other business databases discussed in this book.) Its intent is to "inform management and marketing executives of the theoretical and practical areas of their activities." *Harvard Business Review*, *Computerworld*, and *The Economist* are among the publications included.

PIRA's indexing terms are taken from a large controlled vocabulary. You may purchase the thesaurus, which will make your searching easier and help you remember that the British and American spellings of many words vary. Though the source material is in over 20 languages, the title is always translated into English. PIRA's abstracts are informative and well written.

Sample record

PROBLEM: What are the merits of various competing kinds of milk packaging materials?

(1) AN:03-81-01629 JA: 8106 UP: 8201
(2) Alternative Packaging for Milk
(3) Nunn DW
(4) Emballering, vol 11 no 6 1980 pp 5-9
(5) ISSN: 0017-8012
(6) DT:J
(7) SN:03
     CL:3033
(8) MH: Packaging Special Products - food and beverages - dairy products, fats and edible oils
(9) CT: cost; water; board; economic; consumer; energy; milk; consumption; container; electricity; glass; investment; laminate; transport; trade; returnable; waste, agent; material; retail; benefit; organisation; cleaning; consumer; attitude
(10) TN:PC
(11) When comparing milk containers of glass, PC or laminated board, no economic advantage for returnable containers of any material is evident. Cost benefits due to the smaller energy consumption of returnable packages are absorbed by the investment made by dairies and the retail trade as well as by transport cost. The higher consumption of electricity, water, and cleaning agents also supports the conclusion. No real reduction of waste material can be achieved. Consumer organisations therefore favour board packages (II V abstr.)

Notes: (1) accession number (2) title (3) author (4) journal (5) International Standard Serial Number (6) document type (journal) (7) classification codes (8) main headings (9) controlled vocabulary terms (10) trade name (11) abstract

Profile

Database: PIRA

Producer: Research Association for the Paper and Board, Printing and Packaging Industries, Randalls Rd., Leatherhead, Surrey, KT22 7RU, England; Tel.: Leatherhead 76161

Toll-Free Telephone: Pergamon InfoLine, Marketing Department, 800-336-7575

Vendor: Pergamon InfoLine.

Cost: $70 per connect hour, plus 15¢ per offline print.

Date Began Online: 1977

Source of Information: About 1,000 journals that regularly carry information on packaging, paper and board technology, printing (including machinery, inking, and paper technology), management, and marketing. Material also includes standards and specifications, market reports, technical reports, theses, directories, books, government publications, national press, manufacturers' catalogs, and translations.

Type of Coverage: Bibliographic, with abstracts.

Size: 75,000 records.

Updating: Updated monthly, with 800 records added per update.

Indexing Terms: *PIRA Thesaurus* used for major topics and concepts in document.

User Aids: *InfoLine User Guide*, $50; PIRA chapter from *User Guide*, $8; *PIRA Thesaurus* may be purchased from PIRA (contact producer for further information).

Printed Equivalent: *International Packaging Abstracts*, *Paper and Board Abstracts*, *Printing Abstracts*, *Management and Marketing Abstracts*. Database contains additional peripheral material.

Document Retrieval: Photocopies available from producer in England. As of August 1983, converted U.S. prices are $2.67 per article for PIRA members and $3.06 per article for nonmembers. Requestor must use order form.

Other Services: Customer search service; two types of selective updating service in printed format; translation service; service offering abstracts four weeks prior to publication in journals. Company has two other databases available: Management and Marketing Abstracts (a subset of PIRA) and PAKLEGIS (a new, small database covering international packaging legislation).

RAPRA

Produced by the Rubber and Plastics Research Association of Great Britain, RAPRA contains references to journals of these two industries on a world-wide basis, as well as the usual variety of other printed documents. Theses, specifications, and patents (from 1978 to 1980) are also included.

Some examples of subjects related to rubber and plastics you'll find in RAPRA are chemistry, applications, technology, toxicity, hazards, environmental effects, tests, product information, marketing information, factory activity, and company news.

RAPRA's citations include abstracts. They are indexed according to an extensive subject classification scheme that especially facilitates searching for information about compounds and polymers.

Sample record

PROBLEM: Where can I find information on the properties of polymeric film when stressed?

(1) AN: 7710386L JA: 8206
(2) UP: 8201
(3) Modelling of polymeric film-blowing process.
(4) AU: Gupta R.K.; Metzner A.B.; Wissbrun K.F.
(5) Polym.Engng.Sci., 22, No.3, Feb. 1982, p. 172-81
(6) CL: 42021-9(10)2; 42C21-832
(7) DT: Journal
(8) CT: Viscoelastic; Isothermal; Plastic; Extrusion Blow Mold; Deformation; Stress; Stretch; Model; Rheology; Temperature; PS; Melt Flow; Non-Isothermal: Analysis
(9) TN: STYRON 666
(10) A pilot scale film-blowing process was set up to simulate the variables of deformation rate, temperature changes and stress levels and use made of the White-Metzner Rheological constitutive equation modified to take into account the non-isothermal nature of the process to describe the viscoelastic nature of the melt. Experiments were carried out on Styron 66, a broad molec. weight distribution PS. It was found that when the deforming film was subjected to stretching but to little or no blowing, the axial stresses in the film were predicted excellently by the model under both

isothermal and non-isothermal conditions. It was, however, impossible to predict accurately the circumferential stresses. (52nd Annual Meetings, Society of Rheology, Feb. 1982). 22 Refs.

Notes: (1) accession number and journal announcement (2) update code (3) title (4) authors (5) journal (6) classification codes (7) document type (8) controlled vocabulary terms (9) trade names (10) abstract

Profile

Database: RAPRA (Rubber and Plastics Abstracts)
Producer: Rubber and Plastics Research Association of Great Britain, RAPRA Information Centre, Shawsbury, Shrewsbury, Shrops. SY4 4NR England, Tel.: 0939 250383
Toll-Free Telephone: Pergamon InfoLine, Marketing Department, 800-336-7575
Vendor: Pergamon InfoLine.
Cost: $80 per hour connect charge, plus 15¢ per offline print.
Date Began Online: 1972
Source of Information: Over 500 journals and periodicals, in addition to books, reports, conference proceedings, patents, and dissertations. Coverage is from 1972 to the present, except for patents (1978 to 1980 only).
Type of Coverage: Bibliographic, with abstracts. Coverage of periodicals is selective.
Indexing Terms: Both controlled vocabulary and free-language terms are used for indexing. Material is also classified according to a system for diverse types of information on polymers.
User Aids: *Pergamon InfoLine User Guide*, $50. Chapter from *User Guide* on RAPRA, $8; list of controlled descriptors, $75; *RAPRA Classification Code*, $15; trade name and company name list, $130; list of journals covered, free.
Printed Equivalent: *RAPRA Abstracts.*
Document Retrieval: Available directly from producer.
Other Services: Manual literature searching; consulting; translation (including Japanese and Russian); inquiry answering service.

AGRICOLA

For those whose business requires them to seek information about farming, food, plants, pesticides, natural resource management, and other agricultural topics, AGRICOLA is a valuable database to know about. It is a comprehensive source of scientific and technical information from around the world, and it is relatively inexpensive (an average search is estimated to cost less than $10). However, it has quirks and fluctuations that the user should be aware of.

AGRICOLA is a large database, with over 2 million records, covering everything from aphids to zebrawood. The citations you'll find are to the usual variety of printed documents, most carried by the National Agricultural Library (producer of the database) including serials, government publications and reports, and books. Only a small percentage of records contain abstracts. There are a few surprises, such as a collection of over 700 environmental impact statements, over 3,000 translations, and a changing array of subfiles on such specialties as livestock diseases, tropical soils, and land use.

AGRICOLA's emphasis is on scientific and technical information. Pages and pages in the user's manual list the kinds of items that may or may not be selected; newspapers, "monthly hints," and "success stories," for example, are excluded. As for citations about bugs, "Selection in the classes Insecta, Myriapoda, and Arachnida is exhaustive. Only the terrestrial members of the class Isopoda (sowbugs, pillbugs) are selected for indexing."

On more general subjects, you're likely to find plenty of material on the following:

- Agricultural engineering
- Agricultural products
- Agricultural economics
- Food production, packaging, distribution
- Food service
- Forest products
- Chemical fertilizers, pesticides, herbicides
- Forest products
- Environmental management
- Natural resource management
- Textiles
- Farming
- Horticulture
- Ranching

The records in AGRICOLA are prepared by at least four different indexing groups. Some provide abstracts, while others do not. Indexing policies and the extent to which a controlled vocabulary is used vary among the groups, as do the vocabularies. Even the standardizing subject codes the National Agricultural Library put together have changed over time. You'll need to obtain and study various user aid materials to keep track of all this. The National Agricultural Library admits the difficulty of maintaining consistent coverage, with these and other variables such as the tendency of federal and state governments to reorganize agencies, changing their names and those of their publications.

Sample record

PROBLEM: What is the vitamin E content of various edible oils?

(1) ID # -75-9429064
(2) VITAMIN E ADEQUACY OF VEGETABLE OILS
(3) BIERI, J G; EVARTS, R POUKKA
(4) J AM DIET ASSOC 66 (2): 134-139 FEB1975
(5) DESCRIPTORS- VITAMIN E, VEGETABLE OILS, UNSATURATED FATS, CORN OIL, SAFFLOWER OIL, SOYBEAN OIL, HYDROGENATED FATS, NUTRIENT REQUIRE-MENTS

(6) CAT CODE- 1510
SEARCH- 19750200

(7) DOC TYPE- ARTICLE LOCATION- FNC
EXTRACT: IN THIS STUDY, YOUNG MALE RATS WERE FED DIETS CONTAINING 20 PERCENT FAT IN THE FORM OF SOYBEAN, CORN, OR SAFFLOWER OIL OR HYDRO-GENATED SHORTENING, AND THEIR VITAMIN E STATUS WAS ASSESSED FOR TWENTY-SEVEN WEEKS. ON THE BASIS OF GROWTH RATE, RED CELL HEMOLYSIS, PLASMA CREATING PHOSPHOKINASE ACTIVITY AND TESTICULAR DEVELOP-MENT, SOYBEAN AND CORN OILS AND SHORTENING PROVIDED ADEQUATE VITA-MIN E. WITH SAFFLOWER OILS, THERE WAS SLIGHT RED CELL HEMOLYSIS. WHEN TOCOPHEROLS IN CORN OIL WERE REDUCED BY HALF, VITAMIN E STATUS STILL APPEARED NORMAL.

Notes: (1) accession number (2) title (3) author (4) publication (5) controlled vocabulary terms (6) category code (7) document type and location

Profile

Database: AGRICOLA (Agriculture On-Line Access)
Producer: National Agricultural Library, Beltsville, Maryland 20705, 301-344-3813
Toll-Free Telephone: None.
Vendor: DIALOG, BRS.
Cost: On DIALOG, the connect charge is $35 per hour, plus 10¢ per citation printed offline.
Date Began Online: 1973
Source of Information: About 6,000 serials are reviewed for indexing; 500 are covered in depth, others selectively. Other documents include books, government documents, reports, conference proceedings, university research papers and theses, major speeches, and some nonprint media. Material must contain information on agriculture, nutrition, or related disciplines. About one-third of the sources are in languages other than English. Coverage goes back to 1970.
Type of Coverage: Bibliographic. Less than half of the records contain abstracts.
Size: Approximately 2 million records as of August 1983
Updating: Monthly, about 10,000 records added per update.
Indexing Terms: Material in AGRICOLA is indexed according to four major controlled vocabularies, as well as other minor ones: National Agricultural Library Subject Category Codes, Library of Congress Subject Headings, Food and Nutrition Information Center terms, and American Agricultural Economic Documentation Center terms.
User Aids: AGRICOLA *User's Guide* and supplemental inserts. Controlled vocabulary lists available from various sources. Check *User's Guide* for details.
Printed Equivalent: *Bibliography of Agriculture*, Oryx Press, monthly. *National Agricultural Library Catalog* (no abstracts), Rowman and Littlefield Publishers.
Document Retrieval: User may request interlibrary loan through local library or photocopies may be ordered from AGRICOLA.

Conference proceedings

Have you attended conferences in your professional field lately? Chances are you had to put up with a lot of bad food to hear a few good ideas.

There's no getting around the importance of conferences in virtually every field. It is at these meetings that most of the new, "hot" ideas and findings in science and technology make their initial appearance. (It's a much faster process than getting published in a journal.)

But people can't usually attend all the conferences of professional interest; and even at a given conference, it is difficult to attend all of the scheduled meetings. One good solution for busy professionals who need to keep up with conference proceedings is to get the information from online databases. (Of course, there is a wait of a few months after the meeting for the papers to be received and indexed by the database service.)

Many databases list titles of official conference volumes. That's fine if, for example, knowing that there was a meeting of the International Solar Energy Society in May 1979 in Atlanta is sufficient for your purposes. If, however, you need to know about individual papers, such as "A Solar Hen House" or "Industrial Solar-Energy Activity in Monaco," then you'll probably want to consider using a specialized conference paper database such as Ei Engineering Meetings or Index to Scientific & Technical Proceedings & Books.

Ei Engineering Meetings

Ei Engineering Meetings is a relatively new database begun in July 1982. Engineering Information, Inc., is keeping its acquisitions staff busy tracking down "every technical and professional paper from approximately 2,000 published national and international conference proceedings each year" on the subjects of engineering and technology. The database contains several useful features, including a short review record describing the overall scope of each conference where the paper was presented, a "code" belonging to this review that you can put to several search uses, search compatibility with COMPENDEX (see separate listing in this chapter), and extensive subject indexing. There are no abstracts for individual papers. The fact that papers must have been published to be included can save you a lot of running around and disappointment (this selection is not always made on other databases); publication information is given. Ei takes a few months longer than several other services to get citations online after material is first received.

Sample record

PROBLEM: I heard there was a good paper on managing software development at last year's National Aerospace and Electronics Conference. Where can I get a copy?

ACCESSION NUMBER: 83-015988
CONFERENCE NUMBER: 01321
TITLE: LARGE-SCALE SOFTWARE DEVELOPMENT - MANAGEMENT TECHNIQUES
AUTHORS: EVANS, M. W; PIAZZA, P; SONNENBLICK, P
ORGANIZATIONAL SOURCE: FORD AEROSP & COMMON CORP, PALO ALTO, CALIF, USA
SOURCE: IEEE PROCEEDINGS OF THE NATIONAL AEROSPACE AND ELECTRONICS CONFERENCE 1982 V 1. PUBL BY IEEE, NEW YORK, NY, USA. AVAILABLE FROM IEEE SERV CENT (CAT N 82CH1765-7 NAECON), PISCATAWAY, NJ, USA P 496-504; 1982

LANGUAGE: ENGLISH
JOURNAL CODEN: NASEA9
CONFERENCE INFORMATION: PROCEEDINGS OF THE IEEE 1982 NATIONAL AERO-
SPACE AND ELECTRONICS CONFERENCE, NAECON 1982, DAYTON, OHIO, USA 1982
MAY 18-20
SPONSOR: IEEE, DAYTON SECT, OHIO, USA; IEEE AEROSP AND ELECTRON SYST
SOC, NEW YORK, NY, USA
INDEX TERMS: COMPUTER SOFTWARE
SUPPLEMENTARY TERMS: SOFTWARE DEVELOPMENT PROCESSES; MANAGE-
MENT TECHNIQUES; PROGRAM EVALUATION REVIEW TECHNIQUE
CATEGORY CODES: 723; 901

Profile

Database: Ei Engineering Meetings
Producer: Engineering Information, Inc., 345 E. 47th St., New York, New York 10017,
212-705-7615
Toll-Free Telephone: 800-221-1044
Vendor: DIALOG, SDC, ESA-IRS, Data-Star.
Cost: On DIALOG, the connect charge is $65 per hour, plus 20¢ per offline print.
Date Began Online: July 1982
Source of Information: Cites all papers from the published proceedings of about
2,000 engineering and technical conferences worldwide. These are taken from jour-
nals, books, and volumes of conference proceedings. Consistent coverage since July
1982 (selective coverage prior to then).
Type of Coverage: Bibliographic. Two types of records: (1) individual record of each
paper, without abstract, and (2) record describing overall focus of conference, with
short review. Indexing is at the article level.
Size: Approximately 165,000 records as of December 1983.
Updating: Monthly, with about 7,500 records added per update.
Indexing Terms: Indexing for each citation includes (1) controlled vocabulary terms
taken from Ei's *Subject Headings for Engineering* (over 12,000 terms), (2) subject
classification code from Ei's own system, (3) reference to conference review record
and (4) free-language terms.
User Aids: *Subject Headings for Engineering*, $35; *Subject Heading Guide to Engi-
neering Categories*, $15; *Publications Indexed for Engineering*, annual with quarterly
supplements, $30; *CAL Classification Codes*, free.
Printed Equivalent: Review records for conferences are added to the producer's
COMPENDEX database and its printed counterpart, *Engineering Index*, monthly and
annual.
Document Retrieval: All documents listed in Ei Engineering Meetings are available
from the Engineering Societies Library, 345 East 47th St., New York, New York 10017,
212-705-7611. Cost for orders placed by mail is 40¢ per page, plus $4 for handling and
$1 for billing per document (billing charge is waived for holders of deposit accounts,
minimum $50). "Priority service" costs an additional $5 per document.

Index to Scientific & Technical Proceedings & Books

The Institute for Scientific Information's Index to Scientific & Technical Proceedings & Books (ISTP&B) is similar to Ei Engineering Meetings in that
published proceedings are indexed at the chapter or article level, but it is

bigger and goes back a few years further, to 1978. ISTP&B includes all major scientific disciplines (engineering, technology, and applied science account for 34 percent of the coverage). It contains not just conference literature but also scientific books by more than one author. The user cannot search by subject since no subject indexing is done, though the company feels that searching by title alone will yield good results. ISI claims that it covers 3,300 conferences a year as opposed to Ei's 2,000. The company's policy is to get items online within about two months of receipt.

The ISI/ISTP&B hourly rate is high ($150); however, it is drastically cut (to $50) if the user also subscribes to the print version of the information, an arrangement most suitable for libraries.

Sample record

PROBLEM: The R&D department of a large pharmaceutical company needs information on an aspect of a neurological process called myelination. The staff has exhausted the resources available in books and journals. Have there been any conferences on this subject during the past few years?

(1) ST0001234
(2) MECHANISMS OF ASSEMBLY OF MYELIN IN MICE - A NEW APPROACH TO THE PROBLEM
    ENGLISH
    ARTICLE
(3) BRUN PE; PEREYRA PM; GREENFIELD S
(4) McGILL UNIV, DEPT BIOCHEM, MONTREAL H3G 1Y6 QUEBEC, CANADA
(5) INTERNATIONAL SYMP ON NEUROLOGICAL MUTATIONS AFFECTING MYELINA-TION: RESEARCH TOOLS IN NEUROBIOLOGY-CORRELATIONS TO HUMAN NEURO-LOGICAL DISEASES
(6) SEILLAC, FRANCE
(7) 80/4/13-17
(8) INSERM/EUROPEAN MOLEC BIOL ORG/EUROPEAN SOC NEUROCHEM/PACKARD INSTRUMENTS CO/MERIEUX
    FDN
(9) INSERN SYMPOSIUM SERIS, NO 14
    NEUROLOGICAL MUTATIONS AFFECTING MYELINATION: RESEARCH TOOLS IN NEUROBIOLOGY - CORRELATIONS TO HUMAN NEUROLOGICAL DISEASES; PP413-422
(10) 80
(11) BAUMANN N
(12) ELSEVIER NORTH-HOLLAND BIOMED PRESS (AMSTERDAM): 565PP, 62CHAPS; $85.75 HB; LC #80-23369; ISBN 0-444-80270-3 AVAILABLE FROM ELSEVIER NORTH-HOLLAND INC, 52 VANDERBILT AVE, NEW YORK, NY 10017
(13) B223J
(14) P08055
(15) RU CQ

Notes: (1) accession number (2) title (3) authors (4) organization source (5) conference title (6) conference location (7) conference date (8) conference sponsors (9) series title (10) year (11) editor (12) publishing information (13) ISI book number (14) ISI proceedings number (15) category code

Profile

Database: Index to Scientific & Technical Proceedings & Books (ISTP&B)

Producer: Institute for Scientific Information (ISI), 3501 Market St., University City Science Center, Philadelphia, Pennsylvania 19104, 215-386-0100

Toll-Free Telephone: 800-523-1850

Vendor: Information Consultants. (Users sign up through ISI.)

Cost: $150 per connect hour, reduced to $50 if user subscribes to corresponding printed product. Offline printing is 20¢ per citation.

Date Began Online: 1978

Source of Information: Conference proceedings (published in journals, journal supplements, serials, and monographs) and multiauthored books in fields of science and technology. About 3,300 proceedings and 1,600 books are covered annually. Coverage is from 1978 to the present. Scope is international.

Type of Coverage: Bibliographic, without abstract. Indexing is at the chapter or article level. Indexing of journals is selective.

Size: Approximately 500,000 records as of August 1983.

Updating: Monthly, 8,000 items per update.

Indexing Terms: No subject indexing is performed; therefore, no controlled vocabulary is used. Producer encourages searching by title as it considers titles to be specific and descriptive.

User Aids: *ISI Online Database Guide*, $25. Training workshop available.

Printed Equivalent: *Index to Scientific & Technical Proceedings*, published monthly with year-end annual. Print version does not include multiauthored books.

Document Retrieval: Original Article Text Service (OATS), pricing as follows: for materials after 1981, price is $7 each for up to 10 pages; each additional 10 pages is $2. For materials from 1979 and 1980, cost is $10 for the first 10 pages. Book Order Referral Service is also offered, by which ISI directs customer orders and checks to appropriate publishers.

Other Services: Custom searches; prices quoted individually.

Databases About
22 Energy and the Environment

The energy industry, and a field with which it is closely linked—the environment—are particularly well covered by databases. In this chapter we introduce you to some of these energy databases: Energyline, DOE Energy, P/E News, Tulsa, and Energynet. We also discuss the following databases concerning the environment: Enviroline, Environmental Bibliography, Pollution Abstracts, TOXLINE, and AQUALINE.

Energyline

EIC/Intelligence offers in Energyline a carefully chosen set of references to energy information. The database's "interdisciplinary" approach makes it a valuable source for managerial, economic, and political information on the industry.

EIC/Intelligence has a unique vision for this database. It takes care to try to represent all sides of an issue and will cite speeches, television programs, or films when these offer a new view. Energyline also draws on thousands of sources, such as periodicals, government documents, industry reports, books, conference proceedings, federal rulings, and patents. It seeks to list only "major" items that make a "useful contribution" to the accumulated knowledge about this industry. Put another way, Energyline specifies that "a document's shelf life must be years rather than months or weeks" to be included in the database. The database uses a large controlled vocabulary and has informative abstracts. Thus, though Energyline is smaller than some of the databases that follow, if you find any references in it at all about your topic, you can rely on their being helpful.

Sample record

PROBLEM: I'm a trustee for a retirement fund that has investments in nuclear power utilities. I'd like to read some evaluations of the prospects for such companies under the Reagan administration.

(1) 82-20808
(2) THE NOW AND FUTURE ILLS OF THE NUCLEAR GIANT
(3) MARTIN, DOUGLAS
(4) NEW YORK TIMES, NOV 22, 81, SEC4, P10
(5) COMMENTARY
(6) 15-76 (NUCLEAR RESOURCES & POWER)
(7) NUCLEAR POWER PLANT CANCELLATIONS/1; PRIVATE ELECTRIC UTILITIES/1; RADIOACTIVE WASTE DISPOSAL/2; NUCLEAR FUEL SAFETY/2; POLICY-PLANNING, FED/2; REGULATIONS, ENV-FED/3; (S.I.C.) 491/1; NUCLEAR UTILITIES/1
(8) THE NUCLEAR INDUSTRY IS IN A STATE OF DECLINE AND DISRUPTION. A DEARTH OF NEW PLANT ORDERS COMBINED WITH THE PROBLEMS OF NUCLEAR FUEL DISPOSAL AND SAFETY HAVE MADE NUCLEAR POWER UNATTRACTIVE FOR UTILITIES, THE PUBLIC, AND CONGRESS. THE REAGAN ADMINISTRATION HAS COMMITTED ITSELF TO HELPING THE NUCLEAR INDUSTRY, BUT HIGH COSTS, COMPLICATED REGULATION, AND RADIOACTIVE WASTE CONTINUE TO PROMISE MORE PROBLEMS FOR THE INDUSTRY.

Notes (1) accession number (2) title (3) author (4) source (5) document type (6) category (7) indexing terms (8) abstract

Profile

Database: Energyline
Producer: EIC/Intelligence, Inc., 48 West 38th St., New York, New York 10018, 212-944-8500
Toll-Free Telephone: 800-223-6275
Vendor: DIALOG, SDC, and ESA-IRS.
Cost: The hourly connect charge is $90 on all three systems. Costs for prints are also uniform, at 25¢ per citation offline and 15¢ per citation online.
Date Began Online: 1975
Source of Information: Over 3,500 periodicals, thousands of conference proceedings and government and institutional reports, newspapers, and books. Starting date is 1971.
Type of Coverage: Bibliographic, with abstracts. About 35 periodicals are abstracted completely; in most cases, however, coverage is selective.
Size: Over 40,000 as of July 1983.
Updating: File is updated ten times per year, with approximately 500 records per update.
Indexing Terms: Each document is indexed by up to 14 descriptors drawn from a controlled vocabulary of over 5,000 items. Each descriptor is assigned one of three weight levels of importance. Material is assigned to 21 review classifications: U.S. economics, U.S. policy and planning, international, research and development, general, resources and reserves, petroleum and natural gas resources, coal resources, unconventional resources, solar energy, fuel processing, fuel transport and storage, electric power generation, electric power storage and transmission, nuclear resources and power, thermonuclear power, consumption and conservation, industri-

al consumption, transportation consumption, residential consumption, environmental impact.

User Aids: *Energyline User's Manual*, $45. *Online Search Aid*, free.

Printed Equivalent: Energy Index (annual, 1975–1981). *Energy Information Abstracts* (1976-present).

Document Retrieval: Microfiche ($7.50 per fiche, which holds up to 98 pages), paper photocopies ($7.50 up to 10 pages, 40¢ per page thereafter). Users must open a deposit retrieval account of $50 to $100.

Notes: Criteria for inclusion of a document is highly selective. Attention is paid to the quality of the contribution, avoidance of unneccessary duplication of information, inclusion of useful sections only, length of shelf life, and newness.

DOE Energy

The U.S. Department of Energy's DOE Energy is a very different database from Energyline. Whereas the latter carefully culls its material down to the most pertinent, DOE Energy includes almost everything that comes its way. And it has been doing this for a long time—it was founded in 1945 as an arm of the Atomic Energy Commission (it became computerized in 1975). Since then, it has catalogued vast quantities of documents, and now holds about 1.1 million, more than 20 times the 40,000 in Energyline. But the databases complement each other—you'll find items in Energyline that aren't in DOE Energy and vice versa.

About one-half of DOE Energy's records refer to journals; most of the other half consists of government R&D reports and other documents collected by the Department of Energy's Technical Information Center. Though the majority of the information cited takes an engineering or scientific view, DOE Energy does include items dealing with domestic and foreign energy policy (including some hard-to-find foreign reports sent to the U.S. government on exchange) and with economic and environmental aspects of the energy industry. The database's controlled vocabulary contains 25,000 terms, so a user's manual probably will help you find your subjects of interest, if listed. Most of the federal documents and some others listed in the database can be obtained through the National Technical Information Service.

Sample record

PROBLEM: My bank is considering financing a new housing development that incorporates some costly energy-conservation features. How do I determine the payback of these features?

(1)   002111 ERA-06:000958, EPA-07:000228, EDB-80:128399
(2)   Analysis of single-family-dwelling thermal performance
(3)   Hutchins, P.F. Jr.; Hirst, E.
(4)   Oak Ridge National Lab., TN

(5)   Resour. Energy (Netherlands)   2:1   75-96   Sep 1979   Coden: RESND
Document Type: Journal Article;
Languages: English
Subfile: EPA .(Energy Abstracts for Policy Analysis)ERA .(Energy Research Abstracts)
Contract No.: W-7405-ENG-26
Various levels of investment in energy-efficient designs are analyzed for new single-family dwellings to develop relationships between initial cost and annual energy savings in space heating and cooling. The analysis is performed for a 1200 ft ranch-style home in nine US locations using natural gas or electricity for space heating. The results define relationships between annual energy savings in space heating and cooling versus additional initial costs, which demonstrate the law of diminishing marginal returns. Potential reductions in annual energy use range from 30 to 60% when compared to the present Housing and Urban Development Minimum property Standards (HUD-MPS). Optimum levels of investment in energy-conserving design were computed for each location. When compared to the HUD-MPS, major differences were noted for all but the natural gas-heated homes in areas with less than 5200 heating degree days. Paybacks for additional investment above the current standard range from 15 to 20 years for natural gas users and four to six years for electrically-heated homes based on 1975 average fuel prices. 22 references, 10 figures.
Descriptors: CAPITALIZED COST; ECONOMICS; ENERGY CONSERVATION; *HOUSES--ENERGY EFFICIENCY; INVESTMENT; OPERATING COST; PAYBACK PERIOD; PERFORMANCE
Special Terms: BUILDINGS; COST; EFFICIENCY; RESIDENTIAL BUILDINGS
Class Codes: 320101*; 291000

Notes: (1) accession numbers (2) title (3) authors (4) organizational source (5) journal and country

Profile

Database: DOE Energy
Producer: U.S. Department of Energy, Technical Information Center, P.O. Box 62, Oak Ridge, Tennessee 37831, 615-576-1155
Toll-Free Telephone: None.
Vendor: SDC, DIALOG.
Cost: On DIALOG, $40 per hour standard connect charge, plus 15¢ per citation printed offline.
Date Began Online: 1981
Source of Information: DOE Energy covers the worldwide journal literature on all aspects of energy, including scientific and technical information, social and economic impacts and environmental effects of energy-related activities, and supporting research in chemistry, physics, biology, and engineering. This literature accounts for approximately 50 percent of the database. The remaining source documents consist of other unclassified information processed by the TIC: many technical reports on research and development projects sponsored by the U.S. government, materials received by federal agencies on an exchange basis from foreign governments, patents, theses, books, and translations. Starting date of information varies by subject.
Type of Coverage: Bibliographic, with abstracts from 1976 to the present. Inclusion is selective, according to predetermined subject scope.
Size: 1.1 million records as of July 1983.

Updating: Twice per month, with 9,000 records per update.
Indexing Terms: Thesaurus of 25,000 terms used, updated twice monthly.
User Aids: *Thesaurus*, may be purchased from the National Technical Information Service, Springfield, Virginia 22l6l, $40.
Printed Equivalent: The database is used to generate a semimonthly abstract journal, monthly update journals, current awareness bulletins, and selected bibliographies.
Document Retrieval: None. Most U.S. government-sponsored reports are available for direct purchase from NTIS (see User Aids above). Citations indicate the price and availability of each document.
Other Services: Other services are available to the Department of Energy and its contractors and selected agencies.

American Petroleum Institute's databases

The petroleum business probably accounts for more published data than any other segment of the energy industry. Several organizations have started large, successful databases devoted exclusively to petroleum.

The American Petroleum Institute's Petroleum/Energy Business News Index, or just P/E News, deals with business and marketing, not the technical side of the petroleum industry. It has been indexing petroleum literature since 1954 and began using computer indexing in 1964. It indexes 16 major petroleum business publications (see list that follows Sample Record), the most notable being *Petroleum Intelligence Weekly* and *Platt's Oilgram News*. The latter appears in full text. In addition, business-related short news items from another 150 technical journals are taken from the APILIT database (described below).

P/E News is fast, as far as bibliographic databases go; it puts some references online within about a week of when material is published. The database went online in 1975, and in l983 it had grown to cover about 300,000 records, adding about 700 items weekly. The database does not contain abstracts or text, although it makes extensive use of controlled vocabulary terms and other index terms.

The American Petroleum Institute also produces a more technically oriented APILIT database. Its records are selected from 200 journals, as well as other sources such as conference papers. In APILIT you'll find references that don't show up in DOE Energy, such as information about engineering for a refinery or references to developments in the petrochemical industry. APILIT's 300,000 records make it one of the major sources for this kind of literature. The abstracts are generally long and detailed. The controlled vocabulary comprises a large number of technical terms. APILIT also has an eclectic focus on people in the petroleum industry. It lists interviews, photo captions, and even obituaries.

For still more specialized technical information, the institute produces APIPAT, a database covering patents related to petroleum technology. Since we consider more comprehensive patent databases in a separate chapter, we will not detail APIPAT here; if you are interested in it, you can obtain information about it from the same sources shown for APILIT.

Sample record (P/E News)

PROBLEM: My oilfield supply company seeks new opportunities in West Africa. What new fields are being developed there?

(1) BD29481
(2) SAGA PETROLEUM, KVAERNER ENGINEERING SIGN LETTER OF INTENT WITH BENIN TO DEVELOP SEME OILFIELD
(3) OIL GAS J.   V76   N.45   P38   (11/6/78)
(4) OGJ
(5) *BENIN, *CONTRACT: *KVAERNER ENGINEERING; OIL AND GAS FIELDS; RESEARCH AND DEVELOPMENT; *SAGE PETROLEUM A/S &CO; SEME OILFIELD

Notes: (1) accession number (2) title (3) journal (4) journal code (5) indexing terms

P/E News list of source publications

Indexed from 1975
Middle East Economic Survey
The Oil Daily
The Petroleum Economist
Petroleum Intelligence Weekly
Platt's Oilgram News

Oil and Energy Trends (discontinued 1982)
Petroleum Times
Energy Asia
Petroleum News—Southeast Asia
Bulletin de l'Industrie Petroliere

Indexed from 1978
The Oil & Gas Journal

Indexed from 1979
National Petroleum News
(Also added in 1979 were selected short news items from about 150 journals.)

Indexed from 1981
Lundberg Letter

Indexed from 1982
Synfuels (discontinued 1983)
Nickle's Daily Oil Bulletin (discontinued 1982)

Indexed from 1983
International Petroleum Finance
Petroleum Outlook
Platt's Oil Marketing Bulletin
U.S. Oil Week

Profile

Database: P/E News (Petroleum/Energy Business News Index)
Producer: American Petroleum Institute, Central Abstracting and Indexing Service, 156 William St., New York, New York 10038, 212-587-9660
Toll-Free Telephone: None.
Vendor: SDC.
Cost: $95 per hour connect time, plus 20¢ per citation printed online and 30¢ per citation printed offline. Subscribers to API Technical Index receive a 10¢ discount on each citation printed.
Date Began Online: 1975
Source of Information: P/E News indexes 16 publications in depth and short news items from over 150 journals. Other source documents are eclectic and include book reviews, announcements, interviews, statistics, obituaries, and photo captions. Five journals begin in 1975, with others added from 1978 to date.
Type of Coverage: Bibliographic, no abstracts. Coverage dates from 1975.
Size: Approximately 300,000 records.
Updating: Weekly, 800 pieces added per update.

Indexing Terms: An average of ten index terms are assigned per document. Nonstandardized language is used, with some standardized terms.
User Aids: *Index Guide and Keyword Frequency List*, $33.
Printed Equivalent: *Petroleum/Energy Business News Index* (monthly).
Document Retrieval: Photocopying is available from eight periodicals at $9 per item ($12 for *Lundberg Letter*).
Other Services: Searches performed ($195 each, plus 20¢ per citation in excess of 100); phone consultation on search strategy (free).
Notes: Company also produces two other petroleum-related databases: APILIT, which indexes scientific journals, trade magazines, and conference papers dealing with petroleum technology, science, and engineering; APIPAT, which contains petroleum- and petrochemical-related patents from the United States and about 12 other countries. P/E News is updated more frequently (weekly) than print version (monthly). Company expects to increase coverage of marketing literature.

Tulsa

The Tulsa database, produced by the University of Tulsa, holds about 350,000 references on technical aspects of the petroleum industry, from exploration until the oil gets into the pipeline or other mode of transportation; thus Tulsa complements APILIT, which covers transportation through refining.

There are extensive controlled vocabulary terms and abstracts, making the database very useful both for searching and for evaluating individual records.

Sample record

PROBLEM: I've heard that injecting carbon dioxide into a well can improve extraction. Is there any evidence for this?

(1) 330542
(2) NUMERICAL EVALUATION OF THE EFFECT OF SIMULTANEOUS STEAM AND CO2 INJECTION ON THE RECOVERY OF HEAVY OIL
(3) LEUNG L C
(4)   AIME GOLDEN GATE SECT CALIF REG MTG (SAN FRANCISCO, 82, 03,24-25) PP 613-622, 1982 (SPE-10776)
    ENGLISH
(5) *VISCOUS OIL RECOVERY; *CARBON DIOXIDE INJECTION; *DESIGN; *ENGINEERING; *FACTOR; *GAS INJECTION; *INJECTION; *MATHEMATICAL MODEL; *MATHEMATICS; *MODEL; *OIL RECOVERY; *PROCESS DESIGN; *RECOVERY FACTOR; *STEAM INJECTION; ALBERTA; APPROXIMATION; ATHABASCA OIL FIELD; ATHABASCA SANDSTONE; BOILER; BREAKTHROUGH; BUSINESS OPERATION; CALIFORNIA; CANADA; CARBON DIOXIDE; CASE HISTORY; CHANGE; CHARACTERISTIC; CHART; COMBINATION FLOODING; COMPARISON; COMPOSITION; COMPRESSIBILITY; CRUDE OIL; DATA; DESIGN CRITERIA; DISPLACEMENT; DOWNHOLE STEAM GENERATOR; ECONOMIC FACTOR; EFFICIENCY; ENHANCED RECOVERY; EVALUATION; EXAMPLE; EXPANSION; FEASIBILITY; FIELD DATA; FIELD TESTING; FLOW PROPERTY; FLUID; GAS COMPRESSIBILITY; GAS DRIVE; GEOLOGIC STRUCTURE; GRAPH; HEATING EQUIPMENT; IMMISCIBLE FLUID; KERN

CO. CALIF; KERN RIVER OIL FIELD; LIQUID VISCOSITY; MANUFACTURED CRUDE OIL; MATHEMATICAL ANALYSIS; MECHANICAL PROPERTY; NORTH AMERICA; OIL AND GAS FIELDS; OIL FIELD; OIL PRODUCING; OIL RESERVOIR; OIL SATURATION; OIL SOLUBILITY; OIL SWELLING; OXIDE; PERFORMANCE; PERMEABILITY; PERMEABILITY (ROCK); PETROLEUM; PHYSICAL PROPERTY; SEPARATION; POROSITY; POROSITY (ROCK); PRODUCING; RECOVERY MECHANISM; RESERVOIR; RESERVOIR CHARACTERISTIC; SATURATION; SECONDARY RECOVERY; SIMULATION; SIMULTANEOUS; SOLUBILITY; SOLUTION GAS DRIVE; SOLVENT; SPECIFICATION; STACK GAS; STEAM SOAKING; STRIPPING; SWEEP EFFICIENCY; TABLE (DATA); TAR SAND OIL; TAR SAND OIL RECOVERY; TERTIARY RECOVERY; TESTING; THERMAL RECOVERY; UNITED STATES; VISCOSITY; VISCOSITY REDUCING; VISCOUS CRUDE OIL; WASTE MATERIAL; WATER OIL RATIO; WATER SATURATION; WATER SOLUBILITY; WESTERN US
*VISCOUS OIL RECOVERY
RESERVOIR ENG & REC METHOD
(6) THE IMMISCIBLE DISPLACEMENT MECHANISM OF CO2 IN A SIMULTANEOUS INJECTION OF CO2 AND STEAM IN A HEAVY OIL RESERVIOR IS EVALUATED BY USING A NUMERIC SIMULATION MODEL. IN A HUF-N-PUF PROCESS, THE VISCOSITY REDUCTION EFFECT OF CO2 ON HEAVY OIL IS THE MAJOR CONTRIBUTOR TO INCREASED RECOVERY IN A HIGH COMPRESSIBILITY RESERVOIR. IN A NORMAL COMPRESSIBILITY RESERVOIR, THE MAJOR BENEFIT IS DERIVED FROM THE SOLUTION GAS EFFECT OF THE INJECTED CO2. IGNORING THE SOLUBILITY OF CO2 IN WATER CAN INTRODUCE AN OPTIMISTIC INCREMENTAL RECOVERY OVER STEAMONLY INJECTION. IN A STEAM DRIVE PROCESS, THE ADDITION OF CO2 TO THE INJECTED STEAM DOES NOT IMPROVE THE RECOVERY SIGNIFICANTLY IF THE STRIPPING EFFECT OF STEAM IS THE MAJOR RECOVERY MECHANISM. SWELLING EFFECT OF CO2 DOES NOT APPEAR TO PLAY ANY ROLE IN THE INCREMENTAL RECOVERY. (12 REFS.)
(7) 82

Notes: (1) accession number (2) title (3) author (4) source (5) indexing terms (6) abstract (7) year of publication

Profile

Database: Tulsa
Producer: University of Tulsa, Information Services Division, Harwell Hall, Room 101, 600 S. College, Tulsa, Oklahoma 74104, 918-592-6000, ext. 3005
Toll-Free Telephone: None.
Vendor: SDC.
Cost: A search license must be purchased from the University of Tulsa, at a charge ranging from $70 to $125 per hour. As part of the license arrangement, user pays up to $1.50 per citation for online prints and up to $2.00 per citation for offline prints.
Date Began Online: 1978
Source of Information: Coverage of over 650 U.S. and foreign periodicals, patent journals, government reports, conference papers, and other publications, from January 1965 to the present.
Type of Coverage: Bibliographic, with abstracts. Indexing is selective by article.
Size: 350,000 as of July 1983.
Updating: 300 to 400 records added per weekly update.
Indexing Terms: Descriptors are assigned by professional geologists and engineers and selected from a controlled vocabulary of approximately 55,000 terms.

User Aids: *The Exploration and Production Thesaurus*, $50. *The Geographic Thesaurus*, $50. Supplementary descriptor lists $6. List of publications, no charge.
Printed Equivalent: *Petroleum Abstracts*, published weekly, varying subscription rate.
Document Retrieval: Available from the Sidney Born Duplicating Service, University of Tulsa, 40¢ per page plus copyright royalties.
Other Services: Custom literature and patent searching is available to customers and noncustomers. Computerized searches are charged on a per-search basis, and manual searching of the file prior to 1965 is priced hourly. The University of Tulsa collection contains a card file of over 200,000 technical abstracts dating between 1930 and 1960.
Notes: The subject is defined by the producer as exploration, production, and transportation in the petroleum industry, with an emphasis on technical information. There is some inclusion of materials on ecology, pollution, alternate fuels, and mineral commodities. The source list is periodically revised. The abstracting service is nonprofit, supported by the petroleum industry.

Energynet

If your energy question calls for more help than references to an article or report might supply, try consulting EIC/Intelligence's small Energynet database. It simply holds a list of about 3,000 organizations and 8,000 experts active in energy-related fields. The listings may be governmental bodies, trade associations, corporations, consulting firms, publishing companies, etc. Many of them can supply various kinds of assistance and information services.

You can consult this database to find out which organizations or companies are involved with wind generation of electrical power. Or, if you have invented an efficiency enhancer for domestic boilers, you can find out where in the government to go for marketing or technical assistance.

Sample record

PROBLEM: I understand that cogeneration can help reduce energy costs in my factory. How do I track down an expert on this?

(1)   03-13500 Trade and Professional Associations 9/81
(2)   ELECTRIC POWER RESEARCH INST.
      3412 Hillview Ave.
      Palo Alto, CA 94304
      (415) 855-2000
(3)   Conducts research on all phases and methods of electric power generation and transmission to meet future demand, considering economic and environmental factors; investigates methods of nuclear, solar fusion, hydroelectric, and geothermal. Founded 1973: 625 organizational members; annual budget: $250 million.
      Descriptors: *ELECTRIC; *ELECTRIC POWER ASSNS; *ENERGY R & D, INST; *RESEARCH ENV; *ENERGY STORAGE R & D; *FUSION R & D' *NUCLEAR POWER R & D; *SOLAR ENERGY R & D; *GEOTHERMAL ENERGY R & D; *HYDROELECTRIC POWER;

*MAGNETOHYDRODYNAMICS; *FOSSIL FUEL R & D; *ENERGY CONVERSION R & D; *ENERGY TRANSMISSION R & D; TRADE ASSNS; RESEARCH ASSNS
   Executive: Culler, Floyd; President
   Public Information Contact: Schuster, Ray; Director, Communications Div. (415) 855-2251
   Public Information Contact: Van Atta, Dan; Manager, Public Information (415) 855-2262
   Activities:
   Publications & Products
   Journals
   EPRI Journal

(4)   Subject areas cover all aspects of new electricity-related developments. Also reports on R & D progress of six EPRI divisions: Electrical Systems, Energy Analysis & Environment, Fossil Fuel & Advanced Systems, and Nuclear Power.
   Updated: 9/81
   Subject Category: *ELECTRIC

(5)   *JOURNALS - ELECTRIC; *ENERGY R & D, INST; *RESEARCH PROJECTS INFORMATION; monthly, free.

Notes: (1) accession number, organization type (2) organization title (3) description of organization (4) description of journal (5) journal indexing terms

Profile

Database: Energynet
Producer: EIC/Intelligence, Inc., 48 West 38th St., New York, New York 10018, 212-944-8500
Toll-Free Telephone: 800-223-6275
Vendor: DIALOG.
Cost: Connect charge is $90 per hour, plus 15¢ per record printed online and 50¢ per record printed offline.
Date Began Online: 1975
Source of Information: Questionnaires and telephone interviews.
Type of Coverage: For each item, title, address, telephone number, and key contacts are given. Citation also contains abstract of mission or goal and up to ten descriptors. Current year only is online.
Size: 3,000 organizations and 8,000 experts.
Updating: Database is updated annually.
Indexing Terms: Each citation has up to ten descriptors chosen from a 2,000-term controlled vocabulary.
User Aids: *Energynet User's Manual* available in late 1984, approximately $45. *User's Guide*, free.
Printed Equivalent: *The Energy Directory*, a hard-bound reference volume, price $250 (including twice yearly updates).
Document Retrieval: Not offered.

Enviroline

If you are involved in a manufacturing business, you may well need to address environmental questions. Quite a few databases can keep you informed about such issues.

EIC/Intelligence's Enviroline offers the broadest bibliographic coverage of environmental topics from the point of view of management, planning, economics, and law. Enviroline, like its sister database Energyline, draws on thousands of sources, selecting only "major" items for inclusion. It also takes the same approach of trying to find the best expressions of each point of view.

Enviroline records include abstracts from 1975 onward. There is a 7,000-term controlled vocabulary, including terms that correspond to the SIC codes. Enviroline has a particularly short lag between publication of source material and the time when references appear online, making it useful for up-to-date or topical information.

Sample record

PROBLEM: My company, in the mining industry, needs to be prepared to speak out on natural resources issues. In particular, we'd like to know about changes in resource management policies that have been proposed by federal officials themselves rather than by industry spokesmen.

(1) 82-02956
(2) THE FEDERAL REGULATORY OUTLOOK: THE JUSTICE DEPARTMENT PERSPECTIVE
(3) MOORMAN, JAMES W.
(4) US DEPT OF JUSTICE
(5) NATURAL RESOURCES LAWYER, 1981, V13, N4, P639 (4)
    COMMENTARY
    GENERAL
(6) *REGULATIONS, ENV-FED; *US DEPT JUSTICE; RESOURCE MANAGEMENT; FED GOVT PROGRAMS; POLITICS, ENV-FED
(7) OVERREGULATION OF NATURAL RESOURCE DEVELOPMENT IS EXAMINED. AS A RESULT, A BACKLASH SIMILAR TO THAT AGAINST THE STRINGENCY OF ENVIRONMENTAL LAWS AND THE CLEAN AIR AND WATER ACTS HAS OCCURRED. LAWS GOVERNING NATURAL RESOURCE DEVELOPMENT SHOULD NOT BE LIFTED; RATHER, NEW LEGISLATION AND REGULATIONS SHOULD BE CURBED SO THAT LAWS CURRENTLY IN EXISTENCE CAN BE IMPLEMENTED AND ENFORCED IN SOLVING CURRENT PROBLEMS. SOME LAWS DATING FROM THE 70'S MAY BE OBSOLETE.

Notes: (1) accession number (2) title (3) author (4) organization (5) journal (6) indexing terms (7) abstract

Profile

Database: Enviroline
Producer: EIC/Intelligence, Inc., 48 West 38th St., New York, New York 10018, 212-944-8500
Toll-Free Telephone: 800-223-6275
Vendor: DIALOG, SDC, ESA-IRS.
Cost: $90 per hour connect time, plus 15¢ per citation printed online and 25¢ per citation printed offline.
Date Began Online: 1975
Source of Information: Over 5,000 sources from around the world, including periodi-

cals, reports from the private and public sectors, conference proceedings, newspapers, congressional hearings, speeches, books, and films. Starting date: 1971.

Type of Coverage: Bibliographic, with abstracts (beginning in 1975). EIC is highly selective in its choice of documents. An aggressive effort is made to represent all aspects of an issue—research, legal, economic, etc.

Size: 92,000 records as of May 1983.

Updating: Ten times per year. 700 records per update.

Indexing Terms: 7,000 terms. Up to 14 descriptors per document are drawn from this vocabulary. Subject has been divided into 21 broad review classifications: air pollution, chemical and biological contamination, energy, environmental education, environmental design and urban ecology, food and drugs, general, international, land use and misuse, noise pollution, nonrenewable resources, oceans and estuaries, population planning and control, radiological contamination, renewable resources—terrestrial, renewable resources—water, solid waste, transportation, water pollution, weather modification and geophysical change, and wildlife.

User Aids: *Enviroline Online User's Manual*, $45. Free telephone consulting on file content.

Printed Equivalent: *Environment Abstracts*, frequency ten times per year, $845 (includes hard-bound *Environment Index/Abstracts Annual*, issued yearly).

Document Retrieval: Microfiche ($7.50 per fiche, which holds up to 98 pages), paper photocopies ($7.50 up to 10 pages, 40¢ per page thereafter).

Environmental Bibliography

The sources for Environmental Bibliography are narrower than for Enviroline. Environmental Bibliography covers 360 journals related to the environment or nature; thus it doesn't draw on the many other types of documents that Enviroline does. Since it also lacks abstracts, you'll have to judge whether you want to retrieve an article just from the title and indexing terms.

But its coverage of these journals is more comprehensive than that of other databases. Environmental Bibliography indexes specialized environmental publications very thoroughly; the database will list many articles that Enviroline leaves out. Managers may be especially interested in its attention to energy policy, energy management, and energy conservation.

Sample record

PROBLEM: Our company, a solid-waste disposal firm, dumps garbage from barges into the ocean. What potential environmental objections are there to this practice?

(1) Environmental aspects of ocean dumping in the western Gulf of Mexico
     Features
(2) Meyer, E. R.; Giam, C. S.; Trefry, J.; Sauer, T.; Schwab, C.; Schofield, J.; Atlas, E.; Brooks, J.; Bernard, E.
     Journal Water Pollution Control Federation, 1980 VOL. 52, NO. 2 (February), p. 329
     Descriptors: Gulf of Mexico; Waste disposal (ocean dumping); Phytoplankton

Notes: (1) title (2) authors

Profile

Database: Environmental Bibliography
Producer: International Academy at Santa Barbara, 2074 Alameda Padre Serra, Santa Barbara, California 93103, 805-965-5010
Toll-Free Telephone: None.
Vendor: DIALOG.
Cost: $60 per hour, plus 15¢ per record printed offline.
Date Began Online: 1973
Source of Information: Over 360 journals, covering all aspects of the environment from general to specialized and technical.
Type of Coverage: Bibliographic, without abstracts. Coverage of periodicals varies from selective to complete.
Size: 250,000 as of September 1983.
Updating: 4,300 records are added every two months.
Indexing Terms: Descriptors are drawn from a small controlled list or from natural language, according to the indexer's judgment in each case. Vocabulary help is given in the manual, and the user is also urged to consult the Annual Index (supplied with manual) for other ideas.
User Aids: The manual, *EPB Online Vocabulary Aid*, includes search hints and a selective list of vocabulary terms and comes with a print copy of the journal's *Annual Index*.
Printed Equivalent: *Environmental Periodicals Bibliography* is issued five times a year along with an *Annual Index*. Price $650 per year.
Document Retrieval: Not offered.

Pollution Abstracts

Cambridge Scientific Abstracts, in its Pollution Abstracts, concentrates on pollution topics. The database does not delve into the broader environmental issues covered in Enviroline and Environmental Bibliography, such as land use, nonrenewable resources, population planning, etc.

Pollution Abstract's orientation is somewhat more technical. Its sources, however, are as wide and varied as Enviroline—5,000 sources, including very thorough coverage of 300 core journals. It has abstracts for records since 1978.

In addition, Cambridge Scientific Abstracts produces three specialized bibliographic databases of interest to individuals seeking information on energy or the environment: Oceanic Abstracts, Aquatic Sciences and Fisheries Abstracts, and the Life Sciences Collection.

Sample record

PROBLEM: My real estate development company plans to build condominiums near a railway spur. What design guidelines should we be aware of?

(1)   Railway traffic: Environmental noise controls for new housing sites.
(2)   Clegg, J.D.
(3)   Bolton Metropolitan Borough, Environmental Health Dept., Civic Centre, Bolton BL1 1SA, England

(4)   Second workshop on railway and tracked transit system noise Lyon, France Oct 17-19, 1978

(5)   JOURNAL OF SOUND AND VIBRATION 66(3), 363-467, Coden: JSVIAG Publ.Yr: 1979

illus. refs.

ISSN: 0022-460X

Sum.

Journal Announcement: V11N2

Languages: ENGLISH

Doc Type: JOURNAL PAPER CONFERENCE PAPER

TREATMENT CODES: M .(METHODOLOGICAL) ; D .(DESCRIPTIVE) ; C .(CASE STUDY) ; A .(APPLICATIONS)

(6)   New housing should not be constructed within 30 m of a railway line, on a site where the 24-hr Leq is .60 dBA, or on a site where the peak sound level is .80 dBA. A physical sound barrier will also often be required. The need for additional sound insulation of windows should also be considered. A housing development in Bolton, England, has been occupied for 1 yr without complaints of noise from the railway 30-40 m away. A 3-m-high continuous earth-mound with trees and pathways serves as a physical barrier. (MS.FT)

(7)   Descriptors: Engineering; Buildings; Noise reduction; Trains; Transportation noises; Noise standards; England

(8)   Identifiers: housing development; Bolton; noise barriers

Notes: (1) title (2) author (3) organization source (4) conference (5) journal (6) abstract (7) controlled vocabulary terms (8) ad hoc indexing terms

Profile

Database: Pollution Abstracts

Producer: Cambridge Scientific Abstracts, 5161 River Rd., Bethesda, Maryland 20816, 301-951-1400

Toll-Free Telephone: 800-638-8076

Vendor: DIALOG, BRS, ESA-IRS.

Cost: On DIALOG, $58 per hour connect time, plus 15¢ per online print and 20¢ per offline print.

Date Began Online: Information not available at time of publication.

Source of Information: 5,000 sources from around the world are screened, including periodicals, conference proceedings, research reports, technical reports, etc. 300 "core" journals are heavily covered.

Type of Coverage: Bibliographic, with abstracts. Some sources are covered completely, some selectively.

Size: 96,000 records as of July 1983.

Updating: Bimonthly, 1,500 records added per update.

Indexing Terms: Information not available at time of publication.

User Aids: *User Manual*, for all CSA products, $50.

Printed Equivalent: *Pollution Abstracts*, bimonthly.

Document Retrieval: Not offered.

TOXLINE

Its 1.6 million records back to 1965 make TOXLINE a large and very comprehensive database. Actually, it is a collection of 11 databases on diverse aspects of toxicology. You can find out just about anything pertaining to the effect of environmental chemicals or substances on human beings, animals, plants, and the environment.

The database is produced by the National Library of Medicine, and most of its information is intended for a scientific audience. But any business that uses, manufactures, or otherwise handles potentially toxic substances may find it worthwhile to have access to this database. It is important to the chemical, pharmaceutical, pesticide/herbicide, bioengineering, and public health fields.

Sample record

PROBLEM: I'm an insurance plan administrator. A new herbal tea company has inquired about a group plan. What are the risks associated with this work?

(1) HEEP/80/11116
(2) URAGODA CG
(3) CENT.CHEST CLIN., DEANS RD., COLOMBO 10, SRI LANKA
(4) RESPIRATORY DISEASE IN TEA WORKERS IN SRI LANKA
(5) THORAX; 35 (2). 1980. 114-117.
(6) ENG
(7) THORA
(8) HEEP COPYRIGHT; BIOL ABS. BLENDING OF DIFFERENT GRADES OF TEA IS A VERY DUSTY PROCESS WHICH EXPOSES WORKERS TO A FINE FLUFF. TEA BLENDERS (125) WITH AN AVERAGE SERVICE OF 22.9 YEARS IN THE INDUSTRY WERE INTER-VIEWED ACCORDING TO A STANDARD QUESTIONNAIRE, AND SUBMITTED TO A CLINICAL AND RADIOGRAPHICAL EXAMINATION. THE EXAMINATION WAS RE-PEATED 8 AND 31 MO. LATER. FORTY-SIX WORKERS (36%) HAD RESPIRATORY ILL-NESS, 31 HAD CHRONIC BRONCHITIS (24.8%), 8 HAD ASTHMA (6.4%), AND 7 HAD ACTIVE OR INACTIVE PULMONARY TUBERCULOSIS (5.6%). THE PREVALENCE OF CHRONIC BRONCHITIS AND ASTHMA WAS MORE THAN THAT EXPECTED IN THE GENERAL POPULATION. APPARENTLY THESE 2 CONDITIONS ARE ETIOLOGICALLY RELATED TO LONG-TERM EXPOSURE TO TEA FLUFF.
(9) **8009**

Notes: (1) secondary source i.d. (2) author (3) author's address (4) title (5) source (6) language (7) journal code (CODEN) (8) abstract (9) entry year and month

Major topics covered in TOXLINE

Toxicity Bibliography
Chemical-Biological Activities
Pesticides Abstracts
International Pharmaceutical Abstracts
Abstracts on Health Effects of
  Environmental Pollutants
Environmental Mutagen Information Center
  File

Environmental Teratology Information
  Center File
Toxicology/Epidemiology Research
  Projects
Toxicology Document and Data
  Depository
Toxic Materials Information Center File
Hayes File on Pesticides

Profile

Database: TOXLINE
Producer: National Library of Medicine, Toxicology Information Program, 8600 Rockville Pike, Bethesda, Maryland 20209, 301-496-6193

Toll-Free Telephone: None.

Vendor: National Library of Medicine (in the United States).

Cost: $55 per connect hour weekday rate, $48 per connect hour offpeak. Offline prints are 41¢ per page. Connect charge may vary slightly due to a pricing structure that takes into account CPU time and characters printed.

Date Began Online: 1972

Source of Information: TOXLINE consists of 11 distinct files and contains citations to the worldwide literature on toxicology. Virtually every type of document is represented, including articles from periodicals (general to the most technical), reports from government and institutional sources, research projects, directories, books, and conference proceedings. Most information dates from 1965.

Type of Coverage: Bibliographic. Most citations contain abstracts and CAS registry numbers.

Size: 1.5 million records as of October 1983.

Updating: Updates monthly. Approximately 10,000 records are added every month.

Indexing Terms: There is no controlled vocabulary for the entire TOXLINE database; however, some of the 11 separate subfiles share individual ones.

User Aids: The organization requests that users attend a training session of three to five days, given in various regional locations. Experienced searchers may request a waiver. TOXLINE manual, $7. Guide to all four NLM Toxicology Files including TOXLINE, $14.

Printed Equivalent: Subfiles correspond to dozens of periodicals on chemistry, biology, pharmaceuticals, toxicology, and related subjects.

Document Retrieval: NLM offers extensive interlibrary loan services; it is recommended that the user inquire at the local library.

Other Services: NLM does not offer custom searches. It recommends contacting the Toxicology Information Response Center at Oak Ridge, Tennessee, 615-576-1743, which does perform searches.

Notes: The U.S. National Library of Medicine is part of the National Institutes of Health at the U.S. Public Health Service, U.S. Department of Health and Human Services. Other databases produced by NLM in the toxicology field include Registry of Toxic Effects of Chemical Substances and the Toxicology Data Bank.

AQUALINE

AQUALINE, produced in Great Britain, does a very good job of indexing and abstracting worldwide sources of information on such topics as:

♦ Water resource development and management
♦ Water treatment
♦ Water distribution systems
♦ Sewage systems
♦ Waste water treatment
♦ Sludge disposal

(For further online information about the water industry, the National Water Well Association produces WATERLINE, which is aimed at individual water-well owners as well as water professionals. To a limited extent, it is a bibliographic service; but it carries primarily information that originates in the Water Well Association, such as consumer tips, legislative updates, a parts and equipment clearinghouse, and newsletters on ground-water topics.)

Sample record

PROBLEM: Our firm is bidding on a contract to clean sediment from a reservoir. Are there any risks to our workers in this kind of project?

77-52086 AQUALINE 75008256
The depositional environment of zinc, lead and cadmium in reservoir sediments.
HYNE N.J.; PITA F.W.
KIER INTERNATIONAL
Water Research, 1975, 9, No. 8, 701-706.
Despite the presence of several intervening reservoirs, reservoirs on the Grand river system downstream from the mining area around Joplin, Miss., have been found to contain higher concentrations of zinc, lead, and cadmium than reservoirs in other areas, and these metals tend to be concentrated in the bottom deposits. Both zinc and lead appear to be correlated with depth of water, organic content, and percentage of clay-sized sediments. It is postulated that zinc and lead are transported by ionic and/or organo-metallic solution into the reservoirs, and because of the relatively long retention period in the reservoirs the metals are then removed from the water by the clay minerals. On average 0.3 p.p.m. zinc and 0.04 p.p.m. lead are removed from the water passing through Fort Gibson reservoir.
Classification Codes: 8, Effects of pollution
Trade Names: KOCH STATIC MIXERS
Geo-Location: JOPLIN/GRAND RIVER/FORT GIBSON
Controlled Terms: RESERVOIRS / SEDIMENT / WATER / ZINC (-SEE ALSO HEAVY METALS-) / AREA / CONCENTRATION / CONTENTS / MINES AND MINING / PERIOD OF TIME (SEE ALSO TIME) / PRESENCE / REMOVAL / RETENTION/ SYSTEMS / CORRELATION / DOWNSTREAM / IONS / TRANSPORT / AVERAGE / LENGTH / BOTTOM / DEPTH / CADMIUM / CLAYS / DEPOSITION (SEE ALSO SEDIMENTATION) / ENVIRONMENT / METALS (SEE ALSO HEAVY METALS, INDIVIDUAL METALS) / ORGANIC

Profile

Database: AQUALINE
Producer: Water Research Centre, Mendmenham Laboratory, P.O. Box 16, Mendmenham, Marlow, Buckinghamshire, SL7 2HD, England, 049-166-531
Toll-Free Telephone: None.
Vendor: DIALOG, ESA-IRS.
Cost: On DIALOG, cost is $35 per connect hour, 30¢ per record printed offline, and 25¢ per record printed online. On ESA-IRS, connect charge is $54 per hour, and each record is 20¢ printed offline and 10¢ printed online.
Date Began Online: November 1979, ESA-IRS; February 1981, DIALOG.
Source of Information: Over 600 journals, in addition to books, reports, conference proceedings, theses, and publications from water-related institutions. Coverage dates from 1969, and the company plans to add files dating back to 1960. Many engineering and environmental topics, such as waste-water treatment and disposal, and water pollution.
Type of Coverage: Bibliographic with abstracts. Coverage is selective.
Size: Approximately 30,000 records.

Updating: 4,500 records added per month, including about 300 supplementary abstracts that do not appear in the printed index *WRC Information*.

Indexing Terms: Thesaurus of over 70,000 towns.

User Aids: *Thesaurus*, $70. *Online User Guide*, free. List of source journals, free.

Printed Equivalent: *WRC Information*, published weekly.

Document Retrieval: Must make a deposit arrangement.

Other Services: Custom searches, translation service, current awareness service ($60 per year), technical inquiry service.

Notes: Abstracts are arranged under eight subject categories: water resources and supplies, water quality, monitoring and analysis of water and wastes, water treatment, underground services and water use, sewage, industrial effluents, and effects of pollution.

Patent and
23 Trademark Databases

For more than half of the inventions patented in the United States, no announcement or description appears anywhere except in the patent document. Thus patents afford a unique resource for monitoring new technological developments. In particular, patent databases can help a company:

- Track competitors' activities—Where is their research heading? What patents are they claiming?
- Avoid duplication of effort—Can I buy an idea rather than reinventing it?
- Get ideas for research and development—What new products and new applications of technologies are other inventors thinking about?
- Locate licensing opportunities for existing but unused technologies—Is there an invention that complements our line of products?
- Find appropriate companies for potential business ventures—Who might need my technology or vice versa?
- Track the work of specific scientists or inventors—Who's working on what types of inventions? Can we hire the people ourselves?

Of course, if you have invented something, these databases can help you determine whether your idea is "novel" and thus patentable. A successful patent must pass two levels of novelty: it must not infringe on an existing patented invention (patents are valid for 17 years), and it must not duplicate any other "prior art," patented or not, expired or not.

The databases we discuss help mainly in verifying the first level of novelty. They only go back a few decades at most. In addition, we must emphasize that a do-it-yourself novelty search can give you only a preliminary indication of the patentability of your idea. If you really intend to apply for the patent, hire a patent lawyer. He will engage a professional patent searcher to conduct a more thorough novelty investigation.

Professional searchers use these same databases, but they don't completely trust them, even for recent records. None of the databases includes all of the drawings contained in the patent document, which may be an important part of the record. Professional searchers worry about misspellings and missing documents, and they supplement the databases with manual searches. Also, they will investigate whether an invention is patented in countries not covered in a particular database; a patent is protected in all countries in which an application is filed within a year of the first application.

For these and additional reasons, you should regard a do-it-yourself pat-

---

United States Patent [19]

Byrne

[11] **4,184,335**

[45] **Jan. 22, 1980**

[54] **WAVE MOTOR TANK**

[76] Inventor: **Irvin J. Byrne**, 3200 NW. 79th St., Apt. H811, Miami, Fla. 33147

[21] Appl. No.: **885,531**

[22] Filed: **Mar. 13, 1978**

[51] **Int. Cl.²** **F03B 13/12**
[52] **U.S. Cl.** **60/496; 60/507**
[58] **Field of Search** 60/495, 496, 497, 507; 417/331, 333, 337; 290/53

[56] **References Cited**

U.S. PATENT DOCUMENTS

2,470,313	5/1949	Levin	60/496
2,935,024	5/1960	Kofahl	60/496

Primary Examiner—Allen M. Ostrager
Attorney, Agent, or Firm—Robert D. Farkas

[57] **ABSTRACT**

An improved wave motor tank utilizes a tank having an open mouth portion disposed in a downwardmost position when residing in a body of water experiencing the effects of waves and tides. The tank is coupled to a mechanical apparatus, well known in the art, utilized in extracting energy due to the fall and rise of the tank. The interior of the tank is subjected to a negative pressure so as to tightly couple the tank to the water in which it is caused to reside. The tank is provided with a flotation chamber which contains a gas thereon, offsetting the weight of the tank and any ballast attached thereto, maintaining such tank at a near weightless condition yet effectively "clamped" to the surrounding water.

8 Claims, 3 Drawing Figures

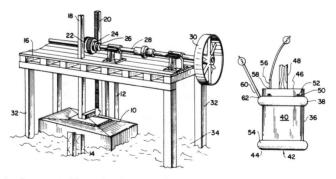

A typical patent. Note the basic information, drawings, and an abstract on the first page, and further drawings on the second page. The main narrative starts on the third page. The claims are listed starting in the middle of column 6; the claim preceded by a "1" is the main claim.

U.S. Patent   Jan. 22, 1980   **4,184,335**

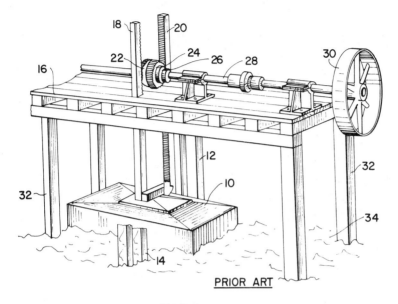

PRIOR ART

FIG.1

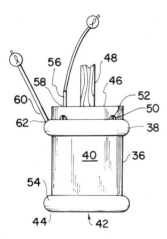

FIG. 2

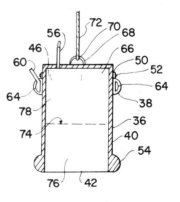

FIG.3

A typical patent (*continued*).

4,184,335

1

WAVE MOTOR TANK

BACKGROUND OF THE INVENTION

1. The Field of the Invention

This invention relates to improvements in wave motor tanks and more particularly to that class of wave motor tank which is useful at extracting energy from tidal and wave motion of large bodies of water due to the rise and fall thereof.

2. Description of the Prior Art

The prior art abounds with wave motor apparatuses, a major class of which utilizing reciprocally operating tanks which are buoyantly supported by a body of water. Such tanks frequently require vertical guidance and utilize cables, chains or rigid members, which when coupled to the tank, transmit a force therealong due to the displacement of such tank when the tank shifts its position in response to wave motion and the tides. Typical of such a wave motor, is the apparatus taught in U.S. Pat. No. 884,080 issued Apr. 7, 1908, to G. T. Fallis. Fallis discloses a buoyant sealed tank having a pair of racks upstanding therefrom, which is vertically guided and allowed to rest in and on a body of water. A platform is provided, having supporting columns anchored in the soil beneath the body of water. The columns pass through openings in the platform and each engage a pair of pinion gears, carried on a common shaft, each pinion is mounted on a separate one-way clutch such that the shaft is caused to rotate in one direction at all times, responsive to the buoyant forces directing the tank in an upward direction as the tide comes in, for example, and responsive to the weight of the tank when the tide goes out. Similarly, swells and wave motion further cause the output shaft to rotate in the same direction due to the waves' effect upon the tank. The output shaft is provided with a pulley for purposes of coupling such shaft to an electric generator or the like. Unfortunately, the forces transmitted to the output shaft, when the tank is moving in an upward direction, are limited to a force equivalent to the net buoyancy of the tank. When the tank descends, as when the tide or waves permit same, the only force transmitted to the pair of racks thereof is a downward force of the same magnitude as the upward force. This is so because the weight of the tank must always be slightly less than the buoyant forces exerted thereon. Since it is presumed that the tank is always in contact with the water, the buoyant forces are always at work. Thus, the torque transmitted to the output shaft, regardless of direction taken by the Fallis tank is proportional to the difference between the buoyant forces exerted on the tank less the weight thereof. Friction, induced by the vertical posts providing vertical guidance for the tank, further diminishes the efficiency of the system. Such vertical posts are required because the Fallis tank is susceptible to horizontal motion of the water about the tank which tends not only to displace the tank laterally but tends, more importantly, to shift the line of motion of the tank away from the vertical.

U.S. Pat. No. 3,894,241 issued July 8, 1975 to S. Kaplan discloses a power source which is powered by the energy in water waves that has a frame which supports a shaft above the waves. A large number of floats are constrained by the frame to be moved up and down under the shaft by the waves. Above each float a first pulley having a first releasable ratchet and a non-releasable ratchet has a chain pass over it to hold a first

2

weight at one end. On each float there is mounted a second pulley which engages the other end of the chain, the second pulley having a second releasable ratchet. Each chain passes through a passage in the float to terminate a second lighter weight. As waves move each float up, a second releasable ratchet allows its second pulley to turn. As each float moves down, it pulls a chain about a first pulley raising a first weight, a first releasable ratchet allowing its first pulley to turn and a non-releasable ratchet allowing it to turn without rotating the shaft. As each first weight reaches a desired height, a means releases both releasable ratchets to drop each first weight to turn the shaft by means of the first pulley and the non-releasable ratchet. Sufficient floats and associated weights and apparatus insure that the shaft will be constantly turning by falling weights to provide a power source. Each of the floats are maintained in a vertical guidance system and each provides a turning force to the shaft utilizing the chains therefor. The Kaplan apparatus requires that the total weight of the float must be greater than the difference between the individual weights associated therewith. In this manner, when a large number of floats are employed, at least one of the weights will always be falling so as to provide a constant power output to the shaft. The Kaplan apparatus teaches a mechanism which is effective in providing a turning force to the output shaft which is best suited for use with a float which cannot descend as rapidly as the water in the region adjacent thereto. Obviously, when the floats utilized by Kaplan are made sufficiently large, such floats will respond to wave and tide actions and reside in the water at all times. This effectively removes the advantage of the Kaplan apparatus such that the net force applied to the Kaplan chain when the float operating such chain moves in the downward direction is equivalent to the difference between the weight of the float and the buoyant forces of the water always contacting same.

SUMMARY OF THE INVENTION

A primary object of the present invention is to provide an improved wave motor tank which is effectively locked to a body of water regardless of the size of the tank employed.

Another object of the present invention is to provide an improved tank for use in wave motors which tends to maintain itself in an upright position at all times.

Still another object of the present invention is to provide a wave motor tank which couples a greater force to a rotating shaft thereabove when such tank is moving in a downward direction than tanks of a conventional construction.

Yet another object of the present invention is to provide an improved wave motor tank which has an effective specific gravity of zero when disposed in a "floating" position in a body of water.

A further object of the present invention is to provide an improved floatation tank which may be easily and effectively transported from place to place, ossessing a low weight.

Another object of the present invention is to provide a floatation tank for wave motors which increases the efficiency of converting water motion to a suitable form of energy derived therefrom over existing floatation tanks.

Prior art floatation tanks, of any size, had to be constructed such that the tank possesses sufficient strength

A typical patent (*continued*).

4,184,335

3

to maintain the tank in floatable condition whilst allowing the tank to be buffeted by the action of waves and tides of the water supporting same. Forgetting the mechanical constraints requiring such tanks to maintain their physical integrity during the buffeting that they receive in such environment, the tank efficiency is measured in terms of, in the main, the weight of the tank, an important consideration for manufacturing and transportation, the buoyancy of the tank, an important consideration in terms of the forces generated by such tank when rising and falling with the water supporting same and the overall size and form factor of the tank, an important consideration when designing a tank so as to optimize its use in varying locations responsive to local tide and wave conditions thereat. Also of importance is the need to provide vertical support columns so as to guide the tank in a constrained area whilst allowing such tanks to rise and fall in place. The present invention recognizes these parameters and provides a ready solution thereto in a most effective manner. A tank, of any size, may be constructed as an effective weight much greater than the actual weight thus allowing the improved tank to more nearly follow the undulations of the water supporting it. Yet, the improved tank is permitted to move upwardly as if its net buoyancy is much greater than the actual buoyant forces exerted thereon, tending to maintain the improved tank in a floated condition. Since the improved tank is "clamped" to a given body of water and since the improved tank experiences the effective weight of a much heavier tank, the improved tank tends to require less vertical guidance than prior art tanks. This is accomplished by utilizing an inverted open mount container, of any convenient size or shape, having a rigid or flexible member affixed to the uppermost regions thereof for use in communicating the force generated by the tank motion in an upward and downward position. A negative pressure is caused to be experienced in the upper closed end region of the tank, utilizing a flexible hose coupled to a vacuum pump, if desired therefor. A floatation collar or sealed chamber of any desired type is secured to, or made integral with, the container at a location adjacent the uppermost regions thereof. If desired, additional weighted portions may be secured to the lowermost regions further tending to maintain the improved tank in an upright position. The negative pressure within the tank, causes water to enter the tank in the lowermost regions thereof across the open mouth portion and to be maintained therein so as to effectively "clamp" the tank to the water. A judicial balance between the size of the floatation chamber and the weight of the tank and its added supplemental weights, if used, can be struck so as to maintain the tank in an almost weightless condition if desired. Thus, the tank may be adjusted so as to move upwardly and downwardly, expressing moderate forces on the shaft or cable coupled thereto, or, if desired, may communicate great forces upon increasing the negative pressure so as to exert a great downward force, much greater than the actual weight of the tank, when the water level descends. Since the force of the negative pressure is exerted on a broad area, equivalent to the open mouth portion of say, a cylindrical tank, such downward force may be massive indeed. As long as the tank is maintained in a near upright condition, this force is directed downwardly in a vertical line. The floatation collar or buoyancy void or compartment must be of sufficient size so as to provide a buoyant force to the improved tank, maintaining same in a floating condi-

4

tion. As long a such buoyant force is slightly greater than the weight of the improved tank and the force exerted by the negative pressure or vacuum therewithin, the improved tank will float. However, any attempt to move the improved tank upwardly relative to the surface of the water contained within the tank will be resisted by the product of the negative pressure times the surface area of the cross section of the interior tank at the intersection of the surface of the water therein and the vacuumized interior thereover. Thus, the tank, if effectively "clamped" in a most efficient manner to the water supporting same, will result in increased efficiency in a wave motor operation. If desired, the floatation collar or floatation chamber may be coupled to a source of compressed air, utilizing a flexible hose therefor.

These objects as well as other objects of the present invention will become more readily apparent after reading the following description of the accompanying drawings.

BRIEF DESCRIPTION OF THE DRAWINGS

FIG. 1 is a perspective view of an apparatus, well known in the prior art, utilizing a floatation tank.

FIG. 2 is a side elevation view of the present invention.

FIG. 3 is a side elevation, cross-sectional view of the present invention shown having an alternate means of supporting same thereon.

DESCRIPTION OF THE PREFERRED EMBODIMENT

The structure and method of fabrication of the present invention is applicable to a hollow container, preferably fabricated from a plastic or metallic rugged material, such as polypropylene or steel, having an open mouth portion disposed in a lowermost position. Such container may be a hollow cylindrical tank having a cap at the uppermost end and an open mouth portion at the lowermost end. A first pipe communicates to the interior of the tank by passing through the cap portion thereof. Such pipe may be coupled to a source of negative pressure, such as a vacuum pump. Alternatively, if desired, a valve may be interposed at the top of the tank such that when negative pressure is induced in the tank after having the open mouth portion thereof immersed in a body of water, the pipe may be removed, maintaining the negative pressure in the uppermost regions of the tank. A floatation collar or compartment may be secured to the tank. In the preferred embodiment, a unitary waterproof floatation collar, resembling a donut-shaped hollow ring is secured, by any convenient means, to the exterior portions of the tank, preferably in the uppermost regions thereof. Such sealed donut-like shaped floatation collar may be positioned at preferred locations along the height of the tank or, may be supplanted by a plurality of rib-like compartments extending in annular-like fashion about the exterior surface of the tank. If desired, any and all of the floatation compartments or the floatation collar may be coupled to a source of compressed air which is used to maintain such collars full of air, providing buoyancy for the tank. Alternatively, a permanently sealed floatation collar may be employed. If additional weight is desired to maintain the tank in a more upright condition, weights may be secured within or without the tank, adjacent the lowermost regions thereof, so as to position the longitudinal axis of the tank along a vertical line, having the

A typical patent (*continued*).

4,184,335

5

open mouth regions thereof residing in a horizontal plane when the tank is disposed in an operative condition within a body of water. A rigid post, rod or other member may be secured to the exterior of the tank for purposes of transmitting the forces exerted on the tank by the body of water supporting same, when such tank moves upwardly and downwardly. Alternatively, a flexible chain, rope or the like may be employed, having the lowermost regions thereof secured to an eye-bolt-like device, fastened to the exterior surface of the cap portion of the tank. The rigid member or the flexible rope-like member is coupled to any wave motor device useful in translating reciprocal motion into convenient forms of energy, well known in the art. Such device includes hydraulic pumps which in turn operate hydraulic motors driving electric generators, rotating shafts which in turn drive electric generators and the like.

Now referring to the figures, and more particularly to the prior art embodiment illustrated in FIG. **1** showing a floatation tank **10** shown guided by vertical posts **12** and **14**. Such vertical posts are secured to platform **16**. Racks **18** and **20** engage gears **22** and **24** respectively. Each of the gears utilize a one-way clutch, typified by clutch **26**, in driving output shaft **28**. Pulley **30** is utilized in providing output power to a belt, not shown. Vertical columns **32** provide vertical support to platform **16**, when positioned over a body of water **34**. Such prior art apparatus is disclosed in U.S. Pat. No. 884,080 issued Apr. 7, 1908 to G. T. Fallis. Floatation wave motor tank **10** moves upwardly and downwardly depending upon the height of water **34**.

FIG. **2** illustrates a cylindrical tank **36**, being an embodiment of the present invention. Floatation collar **38** is secured to the exterior surface **40** of cylindrical hollow tank **36**. Open mouth portion **42** of the tank is disposed adjacent end **44** thereof, shown opposite to cap end **46**. Rigid post or beam **48**, shown attached to cap end **46**, is the equivalent of one of the racks **18** or **20**, shown in FIG. **1**. Tab ears **50**, secured to collar **38**, utilize bolts **52** to secure collar **38** to surface **40**. Bulbous portion **54** of tank **36**, is shown located adjacent end **44** thereof. Hollow pipe **56** is secured to cap end **46** and has end **58** thereof communicating to the interior of tank **36**. Hollow flexible pipe **60** is shown having end **62** thereof engaging collar **38**, and communicates to the interior thereof.

FIG. **3** illustrates tank **36**, shown having bulbous portion **54** thereof in a solid construction disposed adjacent open mouth portion **42**. Interior **64**, of floatation collar **38**, is shown communicating to pipe **60** which is communicated to a source of compressed air, if desired. Alternatively, collar **64** may be sealed off, containing air therein for floatation purposes. Pipe **56** is shown communicating into the interior region **66** of tank **36**. Eye-bolt-like device **68** is shown secured to cap end **46**, having the lowermost end **70**, of flexible line **72**, secured thereto. Flexible line **72** is useful in coupling tank **36**, shown in FIG. **3** to a wave motor apparatus, similar to the device shown in FIG. **1**, by having the other end of flexible line **72** wrapped about output shaft **28**, shown in FIG. **1**. Dotted lines **74** simulate the uppermost level of water contained in region **76**, in the interior of tank **36** when region **78** thereof experiences negative pressure. The cross-section of tank **36**, at the location of dotted lines **74**, determines the downward thrust due to the negative pressure of region **78**. Obviously, the greater

6

the negative pressure, or vacuum level, the greater such downward thrust.

One of the advantages of the present invention is an improved wave motor tank which is effectively locked to a body of water regardless of the size of the tank employed.

Another advantage of the present invention is an improved tank for use in wave motors which tends to maintain itself in an upright position at all times.

Still another advantage of the present invention is a wave motor tank which couples a greater force to a rotating shaft thereabove when such tank is moving in a downward direction than tanks of a conventional construction.

Yet another advantage of the present invention is an improved wave motor tank which has an effective specific gravity of zero when disposed in a "floating" position in a body of water.

A further advantage of the present invention is an improved floatation tank which may be easily and effectively transported from place to place, possessing a low weight.

Another advantage of the present invention is a floatation tank for wave motors which increases the efficiency of converting water motion to a suitable form of energy derived therefrom over existing floatation tanks.

Thus, there is disclosed in the above description and in the drawings, an embodiment of the invention which fully and effectively accomplishes the objects thereof. However, it will become apparent to those skilled in the art, how to make variations and modifications to the instant invention. Therefor, this invention is to be limited, not by the specific disclosure herein, but only by the appending claims.

The embodiment of the invention in which an exclusive privilege or property is claimed are defined as follows:

1. A wave motor apparatus comprising a floatation tank, means to couple the elevation of said tank to an energy gathering apparatus responsive to said elevation of said tank, the improvement comprising a hollow tank having an open mouth portion disposed only at one end thereof, the other end of said tank being closed, said means to couple being affixed to said other end of said tank, means to induce a negative pressure in the interior of said tank when said open mouth portion thereof is disposed below the surface of a body of water, means to provide a buoyant force to said tank when said tank is disposed residing in said body of water.

2. The apparatus as claimed in claim **1** further comprising means to maintain said other end of said tank above said open mouth portion thereof.

3. The apparatus as claimed in claim **2** wherein said means to maintain said other end of said tank comprises said one end of said tank having a region adjacent thereto having a greater mass than another region of said tank disposed intermediate said one end of said tank and said other end of said tank.

4. The apparatus as claimed in claim **1** wherein said means to induce said negative pressure comprises a first hollow pipe communicating to the interior of said tank, said first pipe being located adjacent said other end of said tank, the other end of said tank communicating with a source of negative pressure.

5. The apparatus as claimed in claim **1** whe. .in said means to provide a buoyant force to said tank comprises a hollow collar, said hollow collar secured to said tank,

A typical patent (*continued*).

ent search only as a trial run before entrusting your patent application to a specialist. For any of the other purposes noted above, however, the databases probably are as accurate and as recent as you'll need.

We consider seven patent databases. The first five, PATDATA, LEXPAT, PATSEARCH, CLAIMS, and USP, cover U.S. patents only. The last two, INPADOC and World Patents Index, cover patents from many countries. In addition, we will discuss TECHNOTEC, a sort of "computer-dating" service for inventors and licensees, and TRADEMARKSCAN, the only online trademark database.

Before we begin comparing the patent databases, let's look at an actual patent in the accompanying illustration (pages 270–275) to see what kind of information it contains.

Patent databases differ in how much of the original patent they reproduce. Currently, they all deliver online only part of the original document. A database can help you find existing patents; but then, to get the complete story on each one, there may be no substitute for obtaining a photocopy of the original.

A number of the companies cited in this chapter also offer a patent photocopying service; those that do are noted. You can also order patent copies through an independent document retrieval firm, Rapid Patent Service, which is the largest firm specializing in patent delivery. Its address and phone numbers follow: P.O. Box 2527, Eades Station, Arlington, Virginia 22202, 703-920-5050 or, toll free, 800-336-5010.

PATDATA

BRS's PATDATA is probably the least sophisticated U.S. patent database we consider. It is also the cheapest to use—BRS has put PATDATA on its After-Dark service, which means it's searchable for the astonishing price of $6 an hour (including the telephone connection) during evenings and weekends. (See Chapter 24 for more on BRS After Dark. BRS is both the producer and vendor of this database.) Compare that to the typical charge of around $100 an hour for most of the databases listed in this chapter! It's definitely a good buy for limited applications—probably the best one to use for learning about patent databases without running up much of a bill.

In using patent databases, though, it is sometimes important to be able to call the producer or vendor with a question. You may have trouble finding help in searching PATDATA; we didn't find anyone at BRS who was particularly knowledgeable about the database.

PATDATA simply contains, for each patent, the first-page information that appears in our patent illustration. It has the abstract and other basic information but not the summary, claims, or other detailed explanations. The database goes back to 1975, meaning it contains about 600,000 patent records. Like most U.S. patent databases, it gets new records online within about two weeks of when they're published by the Patent Office.

Profile

Database: PATDATA
Producer: Bibliographic Retrieval Service, 1200 Route 7, Latham, New York 12110, 518-783-1161
Toll-Free Telephone: 800-833-4707; in New York, 800-553-5566
Vendor: BRS, BRS After Dark.
Cost: Connect charge based on use, $36 to $55 per connect hour. Online print charge for patent name or abstract is 3¢ per citation. Offline charges are 18¢ per page plus $1 for mailing. On BRS After Dark, $6 per hour including telecommunications.
Date Began Online: June 1, 1982
Source of Information: All U.S. patents since January 1, 1975.
Type of Coverage: Full text of front page of patents, except that examiner and attorney are not listed. No summary or claims.
Size: 600,000 patent records.
Updating: Weekly, with 1,500 added per update.
Indexing Terms: Not applicable.
User Aids: BRS PATDATA Database Guide, $3, 25 pages.
Printed Equivalent: None.
Document Retrieval: Not offered.

LEXPAT

Mead's LEXPAT also goes back to 1975, but it has the *full written text* of every patent. Thus, its entries are many pages longer than those on PATDATA. It contains essentially the same material that appears in PATDATA, plus the summary, all the claims, and any other written information that may appear in the patent document.

The summary and claims can be valuable for two reasons: they help make the search more thorough because your search term may appear in a claim but not in the abstract, and once you find a patent, the claims help you understand and evaluate it.

But even the full text of a patent doesn't tell a complete story. That's because the most valuable information in some patents may be in the diagrams, not in the text. LEXPAT, being a "textual-numeric" database (as are all except VIDEO PATSEARCH, discussed below), cannot store illustrations. Thus, even though LEXPAT is a full-text database, you still need to obtain a photocopy of a patent if you really want to know everything that is in it.

Despite this limitation, LEXPAT represents a bold new trend in patent databases. It's the only database with the full text online. That also makes it by far the largest database, measured by amount of online computer storage devoted to the database.

Profile

Database: LEXPAT
Producer: Mead Data Central, 9333 Springboro Dr., Dayton, Ohio 45401, 513-865-6800

Toll-Free Telephone: 800-227-9597
Vendor: Mead Data Central.
Cost: $90 per hour base rate, less depending on usage, plus a search charge of 55¢ per 25,000 occurrences of search term.
Date Began Online: April 1983
Source of Information: All U.S. patents issued since January 1, 1975; current within six days of publication.
Type of Coverage: Full text (no drawings).
Size: 600,000 patents.
Updating: Weekly, with 1,500 added per update.
Indexing Terms: Not applicable.
User Aids: None.
Printed Equivalent: None.
Document Retrieval: Not offered.
Notes: Assignment and classification information updated bimonthly. Index and manual of classifications are available online.

PATSEARCH and VIDEO PATSEARCH

Pergamon International Information Corporation is the only patent database company that has tried to solve the problem of illustrations. It offers for rent a videodisk system called VIDEO PATSEARCH containing photos of the front page of each patent listed in its PATSEARCH database. After finding a patent number through a conventional database search, you can examine its first-page diagram by viewing it on a videodisk player. But even VIDEO PAT-SEARCH is only a partial solution; it doesn't show diagrams that appear after the first page.

Currently, PATSEARCH goes back to 1971. This means it contains five years more than PATDATA and LEXPAT, or close to a million patents. The company has announced plans to add patents back to 1966, which will give it full coverage of all active patents. PATSEARCH reproduces the main claim in addition to the first-page information, which gives it a little more than PATDATA but still far less of the full patent than LEXPAT.

Profile

Database: PATSEARCH
Producer: Pergamon International Information Corporation, 1340 Old Chain Bridge Rd., McLean, Virginia 22101, 703-442-0900
Toll-Free Telephone: 800-336-7575
Vendor: Pergamon InfoLine.
Cost: $80 per hour plus telecommunications. Prints with abstract cost 20¢ per record online or 40¢ per record offline. No charge for prints without abstract.
Date Began Online: 1980
Source of Information: All U.S. patents issued after January 1, 1971. Current to last two weeks.
Type of Coverage: Cover pages plus main claim from *Patent Gazette*. Examiner and attorney not listed. No summary or subsidiary claims.
Size: 900,000 records.

Updating: Weekly, with approximately 1,500 records added per update.
Indexing Terms: Not applicable.
User Aids: PATSEARCH database chapter, $8. *InfoLine User's Guide*, including chapter on PATSEARCH, $50. *Update*, monthly InfoLine newsletter.
Printed Equivalent: None.
Document Retrieval: $3 per copy, usually within a week; $7 per copy, in next day's mail.
Other Services: VIDEO PATSEARCH, videodisks with photos of front-page drawing of each patent. The company also offers custom searching on the database.

CLAIMS

IFI/Plenum's CLAIMS is actually a family of patent databases. It goes much farther back in time than its U.S. competitors, covering chemical patents since 1950 and mechanical and electrical patents since 1963. (These three categories account for almost all U.S. patents. There are two other minor kinds of patents: botanical plants and fabric designs.) Depending on when it was issued, a patent listed in CLAIMS may have an abstract only; main claim only; or, since 1979, the abstract and main claim. There are no summaries or subsidiary claims.

Unlike most of its competitors, CLAIMS doesn't list citations to previous or later patents in this database. Instead, IFI/Plenum puts all citations in a separate database called CLAIMS/Citation, which is relatively expensive to use—besides search time fees, it adds $50 for the list of citations to a single patent.

CLAIMS is especially well indexed for chemical patents, which make up the majority of issued patents. But using the special UNITERM chemistry-related controlled vocabulary also is more expensive: $300 an hour, versus $95 an hour to search without the special controlled vocabulary.

Profile

Database: CLAIMS
Producer: IFI/Plenum Data Company, 302 Swann Ave., Alexandria, Virginia 22301, 703-683-1085
Toll-Free Telephone: 800-368-3093
Vendor: DIALOG.
Cost: $95 per hour; offline prints cost 25¢ for bibliographic material and 50¢ for text. Online prints cost half as much as offline prints. Files containing UNITERM codes for chemical searching (files 223, 224, 225) cost $300 per hour. A reference file for UNITERM codes (242) costs $95 per hour.
Date Began Online: 1975
Source of Information: U.S. chemical patents since 1950; mechanical and electrical patents since 1963.
Type of Coverage: Front page of U.S. patents with abstract and main claim depending on time period. Attorney and examiner are not listed.
Size: Approximately 1.5 million records.
Updating: Weekly, 1,500 records added per update.

Indexing Terms: UNITERM descriptors available for chemical patents under separate database.
User Aids: DIALOG chapter for CLAIMS, $5. *CLAIMS Biblio/Abstract Search Manual*, $10. A variety of other user aids are available.
Printed Equivalent: None.
Document Retrieval: U.S. Patents, $4, plus 30¢ per page. Rush rate (one day) $10 per patent, plus 30¢ per page.
Other Services: The company performs patent searches.

USP

Derwent's USP databases (USPA, USP70, and USP77), like PATSEARCH, go back to 1970. They have abstracts, all claims, and citations, which gives them more information on each patent than PATSEARCH or CLAIMS. Derwent notes that there are some missing records between 1970 and 1975, though it is working on completing the coverage.

Profile

Databases: U.S. Patents Alert (USPA), U.S. Patents 1970-1976 (USP70), U.S. Patents 1977-1982 (USP77)
Producer: Derwent, Inc., Suite 500, 6845 Elm St., McLean, Virginia 22101, 703-790-0400
Toll-Free Telephone: None.
Vendor: SDC.
Cost: $100 per hour, plus $1 for offline prints of whole record, 50¢ per record with main claim and abstract, 25¢ for bibliographic information.
Date Began Online: 1981
Source of Information: U.S. patents since August 1970.
Type of Coverage: Full front-page information and all claims.
Size: Combined size 900,000 patents.
Updating: USPA contains current records since 1982. Updating is weekly for USPA with 1,500 added per update.
Indexing Terms: Not applicable.
User Aids: *SDC User Guide*, cost $7.50. *Online Patents News*, free.
Printed Equivalent: None.
Document Retrieval: $4.30 for four-day service; $8.80 for rush service; $3.40 per page for facsimile within 24 hours.
Other Services: Searches performed on request.

International patent searching

Limiting your search to U.S. patent databases is probably shortsighted. Obviously, if you're interested in developments in a specific field of technology, you certainly shouldn't care where an invention was patented.

Even if you're interested in following a U.S. company, it's important to search foreign patent literature. The company probably applies for patents in other countries, and many countries grant approvals much more quickly than the United States does. If a U.S. firm applies for a patent in several countries at once, it's likely to receive its first approval overseas. Consequently, its patent will be listed in the foreign patent literature but still be unpublished in the United States.

Just as importantly, some countries make patent *applications* public, and these are entered into the international patent databases. Nations following this practice include Belgium, Germany, Britain, and the Scandinavian countries. Other countries make applications public 18 months after filing. In the United States, a patent application is secret until it is approved. You may learn more about a U.S. company by searching foreign patent databases than by searching American databases.

World Patents Index

Derwent's World Patents Index contains patents granted in 28 countries, which account for the majority of patents issued in the world (the United States is included). Coverage goes back to the mid-1960s for certain subclasses of patents, such as pharmaceutical, agricultural, veterinary, chemical, and polymer patents. But complete coverage of all kinds of technologies began only in 1974. Not all countries are included since 1974, however; some were added to the database in later years.

For patents granted prior to 1981, the World Patents Index does not contain claims or abstracts. Titles serve as miniabstracts; Derwent translates them and changes short titles into 17- or 18-word descriptions.

Since 1981, Derwent has been writing its own abstracts, in English, for each patent, and it plans to add abstracts for selected earlier patents. Derwent is the only company that goes to the effort and expense of writing new abstracts for each patent; this probably gives its database an extra measure of consistency and objectivity. Since writing abstracts takes time, there is a delay of about 10 to 12 weeks before newly issued patents appear online.

Derwent goes to considerable lengths to add other indexing information to facilitate searching. It includes its own classification terms and codes to supplement the international codes. Because patent examiners in various countries don't always apply the international codes in the same manner, Derwent adds the international classification codes that it thinks are appropriate. The company also uses standardized names for corporate families around the world to help in searching by company assignees.

World Patents Index, like CLAIMS, also applies special codes for chemistry-related patents. Use of these codes is restricted to Derwent "subscribers"—those who spend at least $2,000 a year on Derwent services.

Profile

Database: World Patents Index (WPI and WPIL)
Producer: Derwent Publications, Ltd., Patents Documentation Services, Rochdale House, 128 Theobolds Rd., London WC1X 8RP, England, 01-242-5823. U.S. Office: Derwent, Inc., Suite 500, 6845 Elm St., McLean, Virginia 22101, 703-790-0400

Toll-Free Telephone: None.
Vendor: SDC.
Cost: Non-Derwent subscribers: $150 per hour for WPI and $160 per hour for WPIL, plus 25¢ for offline prints without abstracts and 45¢ with abstracts. Discounts are given to Derwent subscribers spending $2,000 per year.
Date Began Online: 1976
Source of Information: Patents from 28 countries. Current to 10 or 12 weeks. Coverage starts as early as 1963 for some countries and technologies. Most begin in the mid-1970s.
Type of Coverage: Bibliographic information prior to 1981 (WPI); with abstracts written by Derwent for patents issued since 1981 (WPIL). Titles are recomposed as mini-abstracts. All in English.
Size: More than 6 million patents.
Updating: 11,000 patents per week.
Indexing Terms: International Classification Codes, "Manual" codes and Derwent Classification Codes added. Manual codes are only searchable by Derwent subscribers.
User Aids: Online instruction manual and numerous other manuals.
Printed Equivalent: None.
Document Retrieval: Document cost plus small handling fee.
Other Services: The company will perform custom searches.
Notes: Derwent plans to add abstracts for pre-1981 patents during 1984.

INPADOC

INPADOC gives the broadest international coverage: 57 countries. But INPADOC has no abstracts, no claims, and no added indexing information (other than the classification codes contained in the original patent). Most titles are in the original language, except that if the original is in a non-Roman alphabet, then it is translated into English. The starting dates for each country vary, from the 1960s to 1970s.

All in all, INPADOC probably is less useful than World Patents Index. Two exceptions would be to locate patents issued in minor countries not contained in the World Patents Index or to search for the most recent patents. Without writing abstracts, INPADOC can put new patents online faster than World Patents Index.

Profile

Database: INPADOC
Producer: International Patent Documentation Center, A-1040, Vienna, Austria, Tel. 0222-658784. In the United States call Pergamon InfoLine, 703-442-0900
Toll-Free Telephone: 800-336-7575 (Pergamon InfoLine)
Vendor: Pergamon InfoLine.
Cost: $120 per hour plus telecommunications. Offline prints cost 25¢ per record.
Date Began Online: June 1983
Source of Information: Patents from 51 countries. Coverage time varies by country from 1964, for most Western countries since 1968. All patents from these patent offices current within days.
Type of Coverage: Bibliographic information includes title, patent numbers, Interna-

tional Classification codes, application numbers, filing dates, priority patent dates, priority country, priority application number, assignee, inventor.
Size: 10 million records.
Updating: Weekly, with 16,000 added per update.
Indexing Terms: Not applicable.
User Aids: *InfoLine User Guide*, including chapter on INPADOC, $50; chapter alone, $8. (Obtain manuals through Pergamon.)
Printed Equivalent: Available on microfiche.
Document Retrieval: Non-U.S. patents, $10; overnight, $14. Documents over ten pages are charged 75¢ per page.

Patent classification codes

If you plan to do a lot of patent searching, a key to finding specific kinds of inventions in most of these databases is to become familiar with one of the classification codes they use (United States, International, or the Derwent codes used in World Patents Index). You should get a copy of either the *Index to U.S. Patent Classification* ($7, Government Printing Office stock number 003-004-90031-8) or the more comprehensive *Manual of Classification* ($44 per year, including update bulletins, Government Printing Office stock number 003-004-81001-7). There are also five special databases that just list classification codes: IFI Plenum's CLAIMS/CLASS, which accompanies CLAIMS; Pergamon's PATCLASS, which accompanies PATSEARCH; Derwent's USCLASS, which accompanies USP; and Mead's INDEX, which accompanies LEXPAT. Questel's INPI-4 database lists the International Classification Codes.

For help in searching these databases effectively, the producers of CLAIMS, World Patents Index, and PATSEARCH all are in the business of performing patent searches themselves. We suggest you talk to one of the three.

You may want to look into several related databases—PATLAW, produced by the Bureau of National Affairs, for U.S. rulings and decisions regarding patents and trademarks (vendor: Pergamon InfoLine); APIPAT, produced by the American Petroleum Institute, for petroleum-related patents from nine countries (vendor: SDC); and CA Search, produced by Chemical Abstracts Service, for chemical-related patents from 15 countries (vendors: SDC, BRS, DIALOG).

TECHNOTEC

Control Data's TECHNOTEC database can serve some of the purposes listed at the beginning of the chapter, even though it is not a patent database. As a matter of fact, perhaps it shouldn't be classified as a database at all. TECHNOTEC, called a Technology Exchange Service, functions much like classified advertisements. Participants "create" the database by entering announcements either of technology available for sale or licensing or of a needed technology. Users of the service (it is open to anyone) search the database by key word, looking for an announcement of interest. In 1983, TECHNOTEC held about 17,000 announcements.

Profile

Database: TECHNOTEC
Producer: Control Data Corporation, 8100 34th Ave. South, Minneapolis, Minnesota 55440, 612-853-8100
Toll-Free Telephone: 800-328-1870
Vendor: Control Data Corporation—CYBERNET.
Cost: $150 per listing or $150 per hour to search, with discounts available for heavy usage for listing, searching, or a combination of the two.
Date Began Online: 1974
Source of Information: Current listings of products available for licensing and of parties seeking products to license.
Type of Coverage: Announcements placed by participating companies.
Size: 17,000 records.
Updating: Every two weeks.
Indexing Terms: Not applicable.
User Aids: *Database User Information Manual* for TECHNOTEC & TRADEOPS, free. *Newsline*, bimonthly newsletter about technology and information services.
Printed Equivalent: None.
Document Retrieval: Not offered.
Other Services: Custom searching, consulting, reports, private technology databases.

TRADEMARKSCAN

Our last database, TRADEMARKSCAN, is one of the most exciting online databases to become available to the business community. Thomson and Thomson, Inc., the producer, has been cataloging trademarks since 1920 and has the most comprehensive collection in the country—1.4 million marks. TRADEMARKSCAN holds about 600,000 textual-numeric trademarks from its files. (Graphic marks won't be online, but Thomson and Thomson can search for those for customers on an individual basis.) The company expects to update the database twice monthly with about 7,000 changes or additions.

If your business plans to introduce a new product, you probably will need to register a name. TRADEMARKSCAN can help you determine whether the name you have selected is already in use. This can save the time and expense of having it formally checked by trademark counsel.

TRADEMARKSCAN can also help you select a potential product name in the first place. Start by searching for all other names used for your particular kind of product. Then, for ideas, you might check names used in other classes of products. Legally, you can adopt an unrelated product name already in use—for example, using an automobile name for a restaurant.

Are your competitors planning to introduce new products? You might find out very promptly if you search TRADEMARKSCAN regularly for the names of those companies. Trademark applications, unlike patents, are public from the day they're filed; thus scanning the database can alert you to their plans and their competitive strategies.

Many American trademarks are simply misspelled English words. TRADEMARKSCAN can help you find them through its unique ability to search for homonyms. The term "10SNE1" can mean "tennis anyone," but TRADEMARKSCAN would locate it for you.

At the beginning of this chapter we warned you to hire a professional if you're applying for a patent. A similar warning applies here. If you fail to find a word in this database, that doesn't give you sufficient assurance to go ahead and adopt it as your new mark. Your attorney should have a professional trademark search performed. This includes searching common-law, unregistered, and state-registered marks. (Thomson and Thomson is the leading company in the country that performs such searches for the legal profession.) But the database can help you with your "initial cut" by alerting you to many marks already claimed.

TRADEMARKSCAN, available on DIALOG, has a number of search features not used in other DIALOG databases. To learn how to search TRADEMARKSCAN without spending too much money, Thomson and Thomson will offer a companion ONTAP (Online Training and Practice) database at reduced cost on DIALOG.

Sample record

```
0457700
KELLOGG'S CORN FLAKES
CLASS: 046 .(Foods and Ingredients of Foods)
GOODS/SERVICES: CEREAL BREAKFAST FOODS
SERIES CODE: 1    SERIAL NO.: 211533   REG. NO.: 0207268
STATUS: Renewed
STATUS DATE: January 05, 1968   DATE OF USE: May 01, 1907
OWNER: KELLOGG CO BATTLE CREEK MI
```

Profile

Database: TRADEMARKSCAN
Producer: Thomson and Thomson, Inc., 120 Fulton St., Boston, Massachusetts 02109, 617-367-3110
Toll-Free Telephone: None.
Vendor: DIALOG.
Cost: $85 per hour.
Date Began Online: October 1983
Source of Information: Trademark applications and approvals from the U.S. Patent and Trademark Office.
Type of Coverage: Contains text (no pictures) of all active applications and registrations: mark, goods or services, classification, owners and their addresses, status, status date, first use date, etc. Current to six or seven weeks of filing.
Size: More than 600,000 trademarks.
Updating: Biweekly, with 2,400 added and 4,500 changed or amended per update.

Indexing Terms: None. Free-text searching by word or by beginning, ending, or embedded letter string.

User Aids: DIALOG chapter on TRADEMARKSCAN, $5.

Printed Equivalent: None.

Document Retrieval: Plans for document retrieval are being developed.

Other Services: Thomson and Thomson performs trademark and company name searches for clients for a fee; it also supplies related trademark information from trademark files.

PART THREE
DATABASE VENDORS

"Software! Software!"

*P*art III introduces most of the major database vendors, along with some of the newer or lesser known firms. Aside from the information you might expect—such as address, services offered, and pricing structure—we attempt to give you, the reader, an idea of each company's place in the database industry: its background, competitors, main market, and plans for the future.

Some companies are also mentioned elsewhere in the book as, among other things, database producers, information brokers, and software publishers. The Institute for Scientific Information, for example, is noted in this book as producer of the SCISEARCH database, creator of the SciMate Software package, and here as a database vendor. We decided not to try to group all of such a company's activities in just one place. Rather, since the firm is active in three distinct aspects of the information industry, we describe each activity with its competitors in that area.

The vendors in Part III probably represent most of those that a beginning (or even experienced) general business user would be interested in. There are actually hundreds more specialized vendors. Depending on your field, you may wish to acquaint yourself with some of them through one of the reference books listed in Appendix A.

A title marked with an asterisk (*) indicates a company that offers a discount described in the coupon section at the back of this book.

24 Vendors in Depth

ADP Network Services

ADP Network Services, Division of Automatic Data Processing, Inc., 175 Jackson Plaza, Ann Arbor, Michigan 48106, 313-769-6800, 800-521-3166

Other offices

Europe: Belgium—Antwerp, Brussels; England—Birmingham, Leicester, London (5 Offices), Luton, Manchester, Middlesex, Newcastle-upon-Tyne; France—Courbevoie; Italy—Milan, Rome; The Netherlands—Amstelveen, Delft, Eindhoven; Scotland—Edinburgh; West Germany—Essen, Frankfurt.

United States: California—Culver City, San Francisco; Colorado—Aurora; Connecticut—Hartford, Stamford; District of Columbia; Florida—Miami Springs; Hawaii—Honolulu; Illinois—Chicago; Indiana—Indianapolis; Maryland—Baltimore; Massachusetts—Boston, Waltham (computer facility); Michigan—Ann Arbor, Dearborn, Grand Rapids, Kalamazoo, Lansing; Minnesota—Minneapolis; Missouri—St. Louis; New Jersey—Princeton, Roseland; New York—New York (commercial and brokerage; banking); Ohio—Cincinnati, Cleveland, Columbus, Dayton, Toledo; Oregon—Portland; Pennsylvania—Philadelphia, Pittsburgh; Texas—Dallas, Houston; Washington—Seattle; Wisconsin—Milwaukee.

Hours of operation

24 hours a day, 365 days a year.

Customer assistance

ADP provides three sources of customer assistance.

800-ADP-DATA This telephone number is for questions about a database (updating, availability, cost, accuracy, application, etc.). It is available 8:30 A.M. to 5:30 P.M. EST.

313-769-6800 This office can handle questions regarding system operations, user file restorations, mounting of user magnetic tapes, status of print jobs, etc., 24 hours a day.

Local offices Each of nearly 60 local offices has technical and marketing staff to support the applications of local clients. They are backed up by a specialized field support staff and by product specialists at the Ann Arbor facility.

Position in database industry

ADP Network Services specializes in customized solutions to client problems. Solutions are formulated using applications software, developed by ADP or by proprietary vendors, and database information.

ADP offers 35 databases, both numeric and textual, in the following categories: economic data (United States and international), banking data, corporate financial data, investment data, and other.

ADP's typical customers include larger corporations, banks, investment banking and brokerage firms, insurance companies, and government agencies. Its main competitors are CompuServe, Interactive Data Corporation, Data Resources, and I. P. Sharp Associates. ADP has emphasized furnishing fixed-price solutions to information problems; the integration of multiple computers into information systems that are relatively easy to access and use; and local support.

ADP Network Services provides several services to assist users in finding data appropriate to their needs, such as the Data Advisory Service and advanced online searching.

Company background

ADP is the largest independent computing services company in the world. It provides over 100,000 clients with a wide range of computing services, including payroll and related employee reporting services, bookkeeping, time sharing on an international teleprocessing network, and comprehensive databases. ADP has also been a leader in the videotext field.

Since its beginning in 1949, ADP's thrust has been to furnish computing services that are low cost, fully developed, and flexible to business, government, and other organizations. The company's growth has been rapid and continuous, both internally and through strategic acquisitions. For years ADP averaged 15 percent annual growth. ADP employs over 15,000 people and has annual revenues of over $750 million.

The Network Services Division grew out of Cybernetics Corporation, an independent company founded in 1969 which introduced its first public database in 1972. Cybernetics was purchased by ADP in 1974, whereupon it became the Network Services Division.

Initially, Network Services was quite independent. Over time, its marketing has begun to focus on areas where other ADP divisions have a high market share, such as financial and corporate services. Today, as the supplier of network and time-sharing services, it is one of ADP's largest and fastest growing divisions.

Computer facilities

ADP Network Services maintains three operations centers. Principal computers consist of 36 DEC10s, 100 DEC20s, and 2 VAXs. Over 10,000 simultaneous users can be supported.

Summary of database services

In its database applications, ADP specializes in financial information—corporate and banking financials, securities prices, etc. Major categories of databases include economic data (United States and international), banking data, corporate financial data, and investment data. Some of the information is exclusive to ADP, such as Townsend-Greenspan & Co.'s forecasts.

ADP's databases may be accessed from mainframe, mini-, or micro-computer operating environments. The company sells interactive software to help users simplify and standardize their searches. A wide range of software is also available for analyzing and displaying information as well as for creating statistical and financial models. ADP designs custom software applications.

Some of its databases require payment of a subscription fee, but thereafter a customer may use as much data as needed. Transaction pricing has been introduced as an alternative to fixed fees.

Most of ADP's products require significant time and applications expertise on the user's part to achieve proficiency. But the new, easy-to-use SCAN system provides four types of graphs and three types of reports to help the user display data found in any of the company's time-series databases. SCAN is self-documented, and most users can gain proficiency on it in three hours or less.

Telecommunications access

ADP is accessible at 300 or 1200 baud via Telex, TWX, Telenet, Tymnet, and Datapac commercial carriers. ADP Network Services also operates its own value-added network, AutoNet, which can be reached by a local call in about 200 U.S. cities or by WATS (at 300 or 1200 baud). AutoNet is accessible in over 50 countries throughout the world.

Hardware and software requirements

ADP can be accessed from most terminals.

The DATAPATH software package for the IBM PC with LOTUS 1-2-3 enables users to download from ADP's databases and analyze the information offline.

Fee structure and sign-up

Clients sign a standard ADP contract. Monthly billings are for a minimum of $100, and charges include connect time, computer resource units, amount of online storage used, and database subscription charges (if any). Some databases are priced by time-series use. Reports sold through databases such as Disclosure II are fixed price.

Customers should consult ADP regarding prices for specific services.

Offline printing and remote capabilities

Offline printing and plotting are available at marginal extra cost.

Documentation available

There is documentation for all products at varying prices. Many ADP services are self-documenting, with extensive online help messages.

Customer training

All local ADP offices are equipped to serve as client training facilities. Classes are usually held for individual clients or groups at no charge.

Document retrieval

Not applicable.

Other services

ADP Network Services assists in the development of private databases that incorporate private data with information from ADP databases. ADP offers consulting services and is equipped to help clients find solutions that may require more than computing.

The Data Advisory Service will search ADP's own databases and produce reports at a cost of $50 for two-week service or $150 for three-day service. Custom Data Services will find and supply any publicly available data not in ADP's online databases; the fees for this service start at $100.

Cash management and project management assistance is available. So is electronic mail. ADP is a growing electronic mail supplier to industry.

In order to provide sophisticated modeling and consulting services, ADP has affiliated with several companies. A joint venture with Townsend-Greenspan & Co. offers planners and economists a wide range of services, including model building, forecasting, system implementation, and access to material from the Townsend-Greenspan model of the U.S. economy. A venture with Alcar Associates makes financial models available.

Public database offerings

Customers should consult ADP regarding royalty charges for databases.

U.S. economic data

Short-Term Projections/Long-Term Projections 1,300 short-term and 900 long-term forecasts of principal U.S. macroeconomic variables, extending eight quarters (STP) and ten years (LTP) into the future. Forecasts are produced by Townsend-Greenspan & Co., Inc. STP's are updated quarterly and LTP's semiannually.

U.S. Economic Heterogeneous collection of over 23,000 historical time series on major sectors of the U.S. economy, covering major economic and financial data; 1947 to date. Source information is from government agencies and private organizations; updating is daily, within hours of release.

SCAN 200 200 time series of the most popular business indicators of the U.S. economy; 1947 to date. Information is from government agencies and private organizations and is updated daily. The database is equipped with a graphics and reporting package.

Conference Board 1,000 exclusive business-related time series from 1951 to date, produced by The Conference Board. The file, updated daily, covers capital appropriations and expenditures, consumer buying attitudes and plans, auto sales by ten-day periods, business executives' expectations, capital market activity, etc.

Consumer Price Indexes 9,000 indexes for the cost of living for wage earners, clerical workers, and all urban consumers; 1947 to date. The information, provided by the Bureau of Labor Statistics, is updated monthly. Inflation is measured in terms of costs to consumers on national, regional, and metropolitan levels.

Producer Price Indexes 5,900 indexes for the cost of wholesale goods; 1967 to date. The Bureau of Labor Statistics produces the information, which is updated monthly.

Flow of Funds 4,300 major series describing the sources and uses of funds in the U.S. economy; 1952 to date. The series measure flows between economic sectors. Source of the information is the Federal Reserve Board, and updating is quarterly.

Business Conditions Digest 500 indicators of general economic activity that serve as a source of business cycle and lead/lag indicators. Information originates from the Bureau of Economic Analysis and is updated monthly.

International economic data

International Financial Statistics 49,500 time series of international financial statistics on over 160 world economies: 1948 to date—annually; 1957 to date—quarterly; 1965 to date—monthly. The producer is the International Monetary Fund, and updating is monthly.

European Economic Indicators 1,480 times series of general economic indicators for Belgium, France, Germany, Italy, the Netherlands, and the U.K.; 1970 to date. Information is provided by central banks, government agencies, and the international press. Files are updated daily.

Main Economic Indicators/Quarterly National Accounts 6,775 (MEI) and 1,700 (QNA) time series of general economic indicators for 25 OECD member countries; 1960 to date. OECD provides the information. MEI is updated monthly, while QNA is updated quarterly.

Corporate financial data

Note: All COMPUSTAT databases are produced by S&P COMPUSTAT, and new information is inserted weekly.

COMPUSTAT Industrial Data on industrial firms for which stock is traded in the United States (annual information for 7,000 firms, quarterly for 2,500) and on key Canadian firms.

COMPUSTAT Geographic Summary of financial data on 3,000 companies by region of U.S. activity and by foreign country.

COMPUSTAT Utility Annual and quarterly financial data for 250 of the largest U.S. utilities and their subsidiaries.

COMPUSTAT Telecommunications Annual and quarterly financial data for the 100 largest U.S. telecommunications firms and their subsidiaries.

COMPUSTAT Line of Business Summary financial data on 6,000 top U.S. corporations by line of business. Up to 30 lines of business are identified for each company.

Disclosure II Access to 10-K forms, 8-K forms, proxy statements, registrations, and annual reports filed with the SEC. Information is supplemented by weekly stock market price reports. Access is either programmable or by preformatted reports.

EXSTAT Financial information on more than 2,500 British, European, Australian, and Japanese companies with up to 11 years of historical data. Source of the database is Extel Statistical Services, Ltd. The database is updated weekly.

Value Line Essential market and financial data, projections, and 11 years' historical data for over 1,600 industrial, retail, utility, transportation, and financial firms. Weekly stock price information is added by ADP. Information comes from Value Line Data Services and is updated biweekly.

Banking data

BANCALL Financial information on over 14,000 FDIC commercial banks with more than 500 items per bank, gathered by Stratford Main Corporation from Federal Reserve Call Reports. Information is updated semiannually and goes back five years.

BANCOMPARE Ten years of annual data on 280 banks and bankholding companies, with over 800 items reported for each. User-defined peer groups can be screened and analyzed. Information is gathered by Cates Consulting from annual reports and 10-K, 10-Q, and call reports and is updated annually.

COMPUSTAT Banking Balance sheet, income statement, and market information for the 146 largest U.S. bank holding companies, with 222 annual and 141 quarterly items. Information, provided by S&P COMPUSTAT from a variety of sources, is updated weekly.

Savings and Loan Information on over 4,000 federally chartered savings and loan institutions, with 200 items on each. The data, which comes from the Federal Home Loan Bank Board, is updated semi-annually.

Investment data

Foreign Exchange (FX) 1,225 time series with up to six years' coverage of daily exchange rates for 33 major currencies. Rates include spot, one-, three-, and six-month forward, bid and asked. Files are updated daily at the close of the New York interbank market.

FASTOCK Up to 12 years' daily history of prices, dividends, and volumes for 97,000 stocks, options, mutual funds, and bonds traded in U.S. markets. Merrill Lynch supplies dealer-priced bond information, and Muller Data Corporation supplies the remaining data collected from wire services and exchanges. Files are updated daily.

Other

Bridge Data Real-time, intra-day trading stock and option prices for the United States, with preformatted displays from Bridge Data Corporation, St. Louis.

Prognos Five- and ten-year forecasts of key economic variables for developed and developing countries from Prognos, A.G., the European Center for Applied Economic Research, consulting arm of the Swiss Bank Corporation, Basel.

Bank of England Over 4,000 financial variables on the U.K., updated quarterly, from the Bank of England, London.

Central Statistical Office Over 2,000 economic variables on the United Kingdom, updated monthly, from the U.K. Central Statistical Office, London.

Bibliographic Retrieval Service (BRS)

Bibliographic Retrieval Service, 1200 Route 7, Latham, New York 12110, 518-783-1161, 800-833-4707, 800-553-5566 (in New York State)

Other offices

Marketing Office: 3 South Bryn Mawr, Bryn Mawr, Pennsylvania 19010, 215-527-4116.

Hours of operation

8:00 A.M. to 6:00 P.M. EST, Monday through Friday, for BRS/Search, or 6:00 P.M. to 3:00 A.M. EST for After Dark.

Customer assistance

For assistance, call 800-833-4707. The customer-service staff answers questions about searching, sign-on protocols, equipment compatibility, and training and can provide general information about the company and documentation.

Position in database industry

Like DIALOG and SDC, BRS is a "supermarket" vendor offering a wide range of files. Its major subject strengths are medicine, education, and reference sources. It offers some full-text files, including that of the Harvard Business Review, certain journals of the American Chemical Society, and the Kirk-Othmer Encyclopedia of Chemical Technology. A unique feature is BRS's User Advisory Board, which monitors all system activity and provides feedback from users to BRS management.

The majority of BRS customers are academic or corporate libraries, with hospital libraries making up another 10 to 15 percent of the market. In January 1983, BRS also entered the market of individuals doing their own searching with two user-friendly, menu-driven systems, After Dark and Colleague/Medical.

Company background

BRS was founded in 1977 to provide an economical searching alternative to academic libraries. Its founders, Ron Quake and Janet Egeland, were employed by the Biomedical Communication Network of the State University of New York at Albany. They began with a line of credit from the Schenectady Trust Company and $25,000 in advance commitments from prospective customers. At first, ten databases were offered on a subscription basis.

The firm grew rapidly, and in 1980 it was purchased by Thyssen-Bornemisza, a diversified Dutch company with annual sales of over $1 billion. BRS now forms the centerpiece of the company's Information Technology Group along with such other acquisitions as Information Handling Services and Predicasts.

Computer facilities

Information not available at time of publication.

Summary of database services

BRS provides three types of service. BRS/Search has a full range of databases, with Boolean search and free-text functions. BRS After Dark, for generalists, is menu-driven and offers a more limited range of databases. Colleague, also menu-driven, is targeted at the user who specializes in medicine, education, engineering, or business.

Proficiency on After Dark and Colleague can be achieved after a few online sessions; BRS/Search may require attending a training session, reading all documentation, and some hours of practice.

BRS produces six databases of its own: PRE-MED, DISC, PATDATA, SPIF, TERM, and FILE.

There is available a complete private file or customized database service that includes database design, program loading, storage, updating and editing, online searching of private files, and consulting services.

The BRS/Search system software, a modification of the IBM STAIRS package, is a powerful, command-driven system. It features full Boolean logic and truncation, and it can perform complex search strategies with nested logic and positional searching. The command language is simple and easy to learn. All the subject fields in BRS, including abstracts, are directly searchable. Bibliographic fields are standardized across all the files. There is no graphics capability on this system.

A unique feature of BRS is that results from several databases can be merged, duplicated, or eliminated, and output sorted into one display.

BRS has a limited electronic mail capability that allows a subscriber to send a message of up to 12 lines to another subscriber. Full MCI mail is scheduled for availability in the future.

BRS/CROSS is an online index to BRS's databases. This file will display the number of postings for any set of search terms run on one or more BRS databases.

SDIs (automatic searches whenever a database is updated) are available from most of BRS's files. The charge is $3.30 per profile per database monthly, plus royalties and print charges.

Telecommunications access

BRS can be accessed through Tymnet, Telenet, Uninet, and Datapac commercial common carriers at 300 and 1200 baud. The system can also be accessed through direct dial. There is no differential charge for 1200 baud access.

Hardware and software requirements

No special terminals are needed to search the BRS system.

BRS offers for sale mainframe, mini-, and microcomputer versions of the BRS/SEARCH software. It provides consulting and assistance to purchasers.

Fee structure and sign-up

BRS provides both subscription and hourly access rates. Its Hourly Access Plan permits users to pay for searching on an as-needed basis. The basic connect hour rate is $35 plus database royalties and telecommunications. An initial password fee of $50 is applicable to searching done within the first three months.

The Subscription Access Plan is available at four price levels. A user makes an annual subscription payment based on the number of hours of searching for one year. If more hours are used, the subscriber is charged at the same hourly subscription fee.

BRS Subscription Access Rates

Annual Subscription Payment	Number of Annual Connect Hours	Basic Connect Hour Rate
$ 750	25	$30
$1500	60	$25
$2400	120	$20
$3800	240	$16

The basic connect hour rates listed cover the cost of connect time to the BRS system only. A royalty fee is additional for the use of some databases. Royalty fees and telecommunications charges are assessed monthly. Royalty fees range up to $75 per hour. (Current rate sheets, updated quarterly, are available from BRS.)

After Dark costs $50 to sign up and $6 per connect hour, plus database royalties. There is a $12 monthly minimum. Royalties cost up to $15 per hour and are not applicable to the minimum.

Colleague has a $50 sign-up fee and a $100 monthly minimum. Separate services are available for information on medicine, education, engineering, and business. Check with BRS for the latest price information.

Offline printing and remote capabilities

Offline prints are produced the same day as ordered and are mailed first class the following morning. A packet charge of $1 is assessed for each off-line order. BRS also charges per page of citations printed. (The number of citations included on a page differs among databases.)

Special offline services that merge and sort the results of up to seven database searches are available.

Documentation available

The following BRS publications are available. Check with BRS for latest price information.

- *BRS System Reference Manual for BRS/Search Online System Users*
- *BRS Bulletin*, monthly newsletter, free to each password holder; notifies of system changes, new databases, etc.
- *BRS Training Workbook*, by Sally Knapp, based on the ERIC database
- *Searching the MEDLARS Database*, by Dr. Linn Kelner
- *Brief System Guide* (flip book), free to subscribers
- *After Dark Datalines*, bimonthly newsletter free to After Dark users
- *After Dark User's Manual*, free to subscribers
- Database guides for each database

Software manuals:

- *BRS/Search User's Guide: Micro/Mini Version*
- *BRS/Search System Administrator Guide: Micro/Mini Version*
- *BRS/Search System Reference Manual: Mainframe Version*
- *BRS/Search User's Guide: Mainframe Version*
- *BRS/Search System Administrator Guide: Mainframe Version*
- *BRS/Search Online Data Collection Manual: Mainframe Version*

Customer training

BRS offers the following training for the BRS/Search system:

Introductory training   A seven-hour session geared to the novice searcher who has no experience using BRS, the course offers an introduction to the BRS/Search system, basic searching procedures and commands, and a brief review of databases available. The emphasis is on how search requests are actually processed by the computer and how best to apply this for cost-effective searching. Registration fees: users, $35 per person; nonusers, $55 per person.

Half Intro   A half-day session introduces the BRS system to searchers with experience on other systems. The session covers databases available, basic commands, and system features in an accelerated, condensed format. Registration fees: users, $25 per person; nonusers, $40 per person.

BRS MEDLARS training   This six-hour session focuses on the construction and content of the MEDLINE database and how it is loaded for searching on BRS. The emphasis is on the producer's indexing policies and the structure of the medical subject-heading vocabulary. Registration fees: users, $50 per person; nonusers, $70 per person.

Document retrieval

At this time BRS has no online ordering of documents.

Public database offerings

Royalty charges and connect hour prices unavailable for publication. Contact BRS Customer Service for current catalog and rate sheet.

Science/medicine

AGRICOLA   Coverage of the report and journal literature in agriculture and related fields.

BIOSIS Previews   Coverage of journals and monographs, research communications, and government reports in the biosciences.

CA Search   The major source for information on all aspects of chemistry. It is the online version of *Chemical Abstracts*.

COMPENDEX   Abstracted information from engineering and technological literature.

DISC   Index of microcomputing literature.

EPILEPSYLINE   Information on epilepsy and related diseases.

Health Planning and Administration   The National Library of Medicine's database of information on health economics, administration, and planning.

INSPEC   Worldwide literature indexed in the fields of physics, engineering, and computer science.

IPA (International Pharmaceutical Abstracts)   A major source of pharmaceutical and drug-related information.

MATHFILE   Coverage of the worldwide literature on mathematical research.

MEDLARS Online   The major source of information on medicine, nursing, dentistry, and related fields.

MEDOC   Index of government documents in the health sciences.

NTIS   Index of reports of research and development projects sponsored by U.S. and non-U.S. governments.

Pollution Abstracts   Citations to literature on air, water, and noise pollution and related topics.

PRE-MED   Coverage of current clinical medicine.

Business/financial

ABI/INFORM   Abstracts of journal literature on management and administration that is applicable to many businesses and industries.

Fintel Newsbase   Index of the *Financial Times of London*.

HARFAX Industry Data Sources   Online version of a directory to numeric information on 65 major industries.

Index to Frost & Sullivan   Market research reports and multiclient studies cited.

Industry & International Standards   Engineering standards from industry sources.

Management Contents   Abstracts and citations to literature on accounting, finance, industrial relations, marketing, and operations research.

Military & Federal Specifications & Standards   An exhaustive online registry of these important government documents.

PATDATA   Abstracts of all patents registered with the U.S. Patent Office.

Predicasts's (PTS) ten databases   Coverage of business and economics including journal literature and statistical time series.

Reference

Academic American Encyclopedia   A multidisciplinary encyclopedia accessible by subject.

American Men and Women of Science   A biographical register of professionals active in science and technology.

BOOKSINFO   Bibliographic data on over 800,000 books.

Books in Print   Same as the printed publications of the same name.

California Union List of Periodicals   Lists of the periodical holdings of most libraries in California, including many hard-to-find titles.

Dissertation Abstracts   Online index to all dissertations from accredited American institutions.

GPO Monthly Catalog   Online version of the monthly catalog of the U.S. Government Printing Office.

Ulrich's International Periodicals Directory   References to more than 100,000 serials.

Universal Serials and Book Exchange   10,000 serial titles available for distribution.

Education

Bilingual Education Bibliographic Abstracts   The literature of bilingual and bicultural education.

ERIC (Educational Resources Information Center)   The major bibliographic source of educational information in the United States.

Exceptional Child Education Resources   Index of published and unpublished literature on the education of handicapped and gifted children.

NIMIS   Instructional materials for the education of the handicapped.

Resources in Computer Education   Information on computer applications in education.

Resources in Vocational Education   Coverage of vocational education.

School Practices Information File   References to information on school practices in the United States.

Social sciences/humanities

Alcohol Use and Abuse   Coverage of the literature on alcoholism.

Catalyst Resources for Women   Current information on women and careers.

DRUGINFO   The literature on the various aspects of drug abuse.

Family Resources   Produced by the National Council on Family Relations, index of marriage and family literature.

Journal of the Society of Architectural Historians   Online guide to materials on architectural history.

NARIC   Index of print and audiovisual materials useful in the rehabilitation field.

National Information Sources on the Handicapped   Comprehensive coverage of information on physical disabilities and related areas.

NIMH   Indexes by the National Institute of Mental Health of the literature on mental health and related areas.

PRE-PSYC   Information on topics in current clinical psychology.

PsycINFO   Indexes the world's literature in psychology and related disciplines in the behavioral sciences.

Public Affairs Information Service   The literature of the social sciences, including foreign affairs and international relations.

Religion Index   Coverage of literature on church history, biblical literature, theology, and related areas.

Social Sciences Citation Index   Index of the major literature of the social sciences.

Sociological Abstracts   Coverage of the world's literature on sociology and related disciplines.

BRS special files

BRS Bulletin Online   Online monthly newsletter.

CROSS   Index to all BRS files.

FILE   The BRS database directory that lists current prices.

MESSAGES   An electronic message-switching file.

NEWS   The system update file.

TERM   An online social sciences thesaurus.

Citishare

Citishare Corp., subsidiary of Citicorp, 850 Third Ave., Box 1127, New York, New York 10043, 212-572-9600

Other offices

Not applicable.

Hours of operation

24 hours a day, seven days a week.

Customer assistance

The service desk is available 24 hours a day, seven days a week, at 212-559-4636.

Position in database industry

Citishare is a distributor of databases serving the business and financial community. Information provided by its databases includes securities, financial, and economic data, and information on many public and private companies.

Company background

Citishare Corp. is a subsidiary of Citicorp, the parent company of Citibank, N.A. Citibank is one of the largest national banks in the United States. Citishare provides computer time sharing of services that include databases, financial modeling and analysis, graphics, information (database) management, and statistical analysis.

Citishare, which began as an in-house computer services provider to Citibank and its affiliates, has evolved into a full-service computer time sharer serving the entire business and financial community. New databases are being added on a regular basis.

Computer facilities

Three DECsystem 2060s can accommodate large numbers of multiple users simultaneously. A TOPS-20 operating system is used. Two Honeywell DPS 852s (with a DTSS-20 operating system) can also accommodate large numbers of multiple users simultaneously.

Summary of database services

A wide range of economic-, financial-, and banking-related data and services are furnished. Some of the databases are available only to subscribers of the database producers. Some have graphics capability.

Databases are accessed through conversational or command-driven software. In addition, many can be accessed via Fortran and APL programs designed and written by users, which allows them to manipulate the data.

Telecommunications access

Citishare's DEC computers are accessible by Tymnet. Telenet and Uninet are used to access the Honeywell computers. Direct dial-in is available to customers in the New York City area. Baud rates supported are 300 and 1200.

Hardware and software requirements

Any industry-standard ASCII terminal may be used for access to Citishare's systems, as can any microcomputer with communications capability.

Fee structure and sign-up

Prospective customers sign up using the company's standard contract for remote computing services.

Prime time on the system is from 8:00 A.M. to 6:00 P.M. EST, Monday through Friday, and during certain holiday periods. Nonprime time is all other hours. Nonprime-time use offers substantially lower rates. Jobs must be initiated and completed within the nonprime-time period in order to qualify.

Online connect-time charges are $7.50 (prime) and $3.50 (nonprime) for up to 300 baud, and $12 (prime) and $5 (nonprime) for 1200 baud and over. Specific fees depend on subscription arrangements. Certain databases require an extra subscription or per report charge. Other charged services are Citishare Resource Units (CRUs) consumed (1¢ each prime, 4/10¢ each nonprime); batch processing; disk storage; peripheral use of magnetic tape, line printers, or card readers; file restorations; special handling of input/output; and special operator coverage. Discounts are available for volume users. Any applicable taxes are additional. There is a monthly minimum of $250.

Offline printing and remote capabilities
Not applicable.

Documentation available
Documentation includes:

- Manuals describing the database and the associated software
- System use manuals made available by the hardware manufacturer and operating system developer
- Periodic newsletters

Customer training
Training through classes or on an individual basis is available on general system use and on certain products. Classes are taught by Citishare product managers and other personnel.

Document retrieval
Not applicable.

Other services
Not applicable.

Public database offerings

CITIBASE   A series of 4,000 U.S. economics time series maintained by Citibank's economics department. The database is updated daily and can be used to analyze economic activity and construct graphs.

CITIDATA   Produced by Citibank, historical information on key financial indicators for 31 currencies including interest rates, exchange rates, European Monetary System, official SDR rates, and gold prices. The database is updated daily and may be used to analyze and plot trends.

CITIQUOTE   Produced by Citishare, current and historical financial, trading, and descriptive information for thousands of securities of all types. A five-year history of pricing and dividend information is maintained. The database is updated daily.

CITIRATE   Produced by Citibank, the current day's key financial indicators for the 31 currencies contained in CITIDATA. Rates are available as of 9:30 A.M. EST and can be used to construct nine standard reports on interbank and other interest rates, exchange rates, cross rates, European Monetary System, official SDR rates, and gold prices.

COMPMARK   Produced by Standard and Poor's, information on over 39,000 public and private companies, including sales, number of employees, etc. Companies can be screened by user-defined criteria, including market regions and SIC codes. COMPMARK is updated quarterly.

COMPUSTAT II   Produced by Standard and Poor's Computer Services, Inc. and available only to COMPUSTAT subscribers, financial information (10-K and 10-Q) based on the COMPUSTAT database of 6,000 public companies. The data can be manipulated and analyzed according to user specifications, and it is updated weekly.

CONSENSUS   Produced by Citishare with data from the Institutional Brokers Estimate System (I/B/E/S) from Lynch, Jones & Ryan, the consensus annual and quarterly earnings estimated for over 2,400 publicly traded corporations based on estimates of over 1,200 contributing analysts representing over 70 prestigious institutional research firms. The database covers over 240 industry groups and contains historical information back to January 1976. It is updated weekly.

INSURE   Produced by A. M. Best and available only to A. M. Best subscribers, insurance data. The database was developed for the property/casualty industry and contains annual statement data, reserve data, and business information by line and state on over 3,000 property/casualty and life/health insurers. The database, with five years of data in 5 million time series, is updated annually.

STOCKPORT   Produced by H.F. Pearson & Co., a database of institutional stock portfolios concerning stock ownership information. It includes buys and sells of institutionally owned stocks. Portfolios are evaluated with current stock prices. It is updated weekly.

*Comp-U-Card International

Comp-U-Card International, Inc., 777 Summer St., Stamford, Connecticut 06901, 203-324-9261, 800-843-7777

Other offices

Not applicable.

Hours of operation

24 hours a day, seven days a week.

Customer assistance

Assistance is available from 9:00 A.M. to midnight EST, seven days a week, at 800-843-7777. The service department answers operational questions as well as any questions that arise after a user has purchased merchandise via Comp-U-Card.

Position in database industry

Comp-U-Card International provides Comp-U-Store, the first electronic shop-at-home service available to home computer users nationwide. Comp-U-Store consists of information and prices on over 50,000 brand-name products that may be purchased at up to 40 percent discount from list prices. Customers order goods online. Delivery takes two to three weeks.

Competition in this market is growing. Experiments with videotext services have shown there is a large market for stop-at-home services. Comp-U-

Store is a leader in reaching this market. Although the typical users are home computer owners, business use is growing.

Comp-U-Card is considering adding new product lines to Comp-U-Store. New individual items appear constantly.

Company background

Comp-U-Card was founded in 1973 as a private company. It became a public company in September 1983. From the beginning, its objective was to apply computer database technology to the merchandising of consumer products. Comp-U-Store was begun as an online service in 1980. Today there are over 150 employees.

Computer facilities

Comp-U-Store runs on a large DEC mainframe.

Summary of database services

Comp-U-Card provides one database—Comp-U-Store. It allows users to shop electronically for over 50,000 brand-name products. Users can compare prices and features online and can browse for different types of goods.

All prices are calculated by Comp-U-Card to reflect taxes and delivery costs. Users order online and arrange payment either by Mastercard, Visa, or personal check.

Other features include monthly specials on selected goods and Comp-U-Stakes, an online auction where members bid for popular products. New products are placed on the electronic auction block several times a week.

A sample of Comp-U-Store's 50,000 name-brand products follows:

- Appliances—Amana, General Electric, Whirlpool, Maytag, Litton, Jenn-air
- Home entertainment equipment—Panasonic, Sony, RCA, Zenith, Marantz, Hitachi
- Cameras—Kodak, Nikon, Polaroid, Pentax, Minolta, Canon
- Watches—Seiko, Bulova, Omega, Movado
- Crystal—Orrefors, Lenox, Fostoria, Baccarat

Other products include answering machines, telephones, calculators, sewing machines, luggage, tape recorders, and computers.

Deliveries can be made anywhere in the continental United States within two to three weeks.

Telecommunications access

Comp-U-Store is accessible through the CompuServe network, Tymnet, and Telenet. Both 300 and 1200 baud service is available. There is a $3 per hour surcharge on Tymnet and Telenet but none on CompuServe. There is no direct-dial facility.

Comp-U-Store can also be reached through The Source, CompuServe Information Service, and Dow Jones News/Retrieval. Online charges vary depending on the vendor.

Hardware and software requirements

The system is accessible from any dial-up terminal.

Fee structure and sign-up

All users must purchase a membership at $25 for one year or $40 for two years. Access charges are $18 per hour from 9:00 A.M. to 5:00 P.M., Monday through Friday, and $5 per hour at other times. Customers using the service via The Source, CompuServe Information Service, or Dow Jones News/Retrieval pay those vendors' standard prices.

Offline printing and remote capabilities

Not applicable.

Documentation available

Upon signing up, a Comp-U-Store member is mailed a user's manual. In addition, the Comp-U-Store system is designed with "helps and prompts" throughout.

Best Buys is a monthly newsletter sent free to Comp-U-Store members to inform them of bargains of the month.

Customer training

No training, beyond assistance from the customer-service desk, is available.

Document retrieval

Not applicable.

Other services

Members may apply for Comp-U-Store Visa cards, which carry no annual fee. Electronic mail will be added in the near future.

Comp-U-Store provides help to customers who have complaints about products purchased through its system.

Public database offerings

Comp-U-Store is the company's only public database.

*CompuServe

CompuServe, Inc., 5000 Arlington Centre Blvd., P.O. Box 20212, Columbus, Ohio 43220, 614-457-8600, 800-848-8199 (for information, except in Ohio, where the number is 614-457-0802)

Other offices

The sales offices listed below provide sales, training, and support to customers of the Business Information Service (BIS). Customers of the Executive Information Service (EIS) or Consumer Information Service (CIS) are normally assisted by retail computer stores or by CompuServe headquarters.

Sales offices: Atlanta, Boston, Chicago, Cincinnati, Columbus, Dallas, Dayton, Denver, Detroit, Houston, Indianapolis, Kansas City, Los Angeles, Louisville, Memphis, Minneapolis, Newport Beach (Calif.), New York (2 offices), Parsippany (N.J.), Philadelphia, Pittsburgh, St. Louis, San Francisco, Santa Clara (Calif.), Toledo, Tucson, Tulsa, Washington D.C., and Westport (Conn.).

Hours of operation

21 hours a day, 8:00 A.M. to 5:00 A.M. EST, seven days a week.

Customer assistance

General information about CompuServe is available at 800-848-8199 (except in Ohio, where the number is 614-457-0802).

The Customer Service Center can be reached at 800-848-8990 (except in Ohio, where the number is 614-457-8650). It is open 24 hours, and the staff size is 14.

CIS and EIS customers may also contact Customer Service via the online Feedback service. Turnaround time for responses to Feedback questions averages 48 hours.

Position in database industry

CompuServe offers a wide range of information services to its customers, who range from large corporations and government offices to individuals at home. Most of the company's customers, however, are large accounts.

CompuServe's three major services are:

♦ Business Information Service (BIS), which provides a number of computer services to large corporate and government customers.

♦ Consumer Information Service (CIS), which provides databases and other online features on a wide variety of subjects to personal and home computer users.

♦ Executive Information Service (EIS), CompuServe's newest offering, which is aimed at executives and business professionals who need easy-to-access business and general information.

CompuServe also markets Infoplex, an intracompany electronic mail communication system that is one of its fastest growing products, and CompuServe Network Service (CNS), a value-added network that gives large companies more cost-effective access to their computers.

Company background

The firm was begun in 1969 as a time-sharing service primarily for corporate and government customers. In 1979, the company decided to make its computers available at night and on weekends to members of a personal computing club in the Midwest in exchange for their evaluation of a new system aimed at computer hobbyists. This system, known as Micronet, initially offered utility programs, language processors, and a bulletin-board feature. Micronet evolved into CompuServe Information Service, offering a variety of information products aimed at a larger audience. CIS began operating in July 1980.

In October 1983, CompuServe introduced the Executive Information Service, which is aimed at the same market as Dow Jones News/Retrieval. At that time, CIS's name was changed from CompuServe Information Service to Consumer Information Service.

CompuServe, Inc., became a wholly-owned subsidiary of H & R Block, a $300-million corporation, in May 1980. CompuServe currently employs about 500 people nationwide. Its revenue in 1982 was $33 million, an increase of 20 percent over 1981.

Computer facilities

CompuServe operates two data centers in Columbus and Dublin, Ohio. Twenty-seven DEC KI-10 and KL-20 computers are used along with DEC system 2050 processors. Over 700 simultaneous users can be supported. Operation is 24 hours a day, seven days a week.

Summary of database services

Business Information Service BIS has grown in its 14 years of operation from offering only raw computer time to providing very sophisticated information-processing applications, software, databases, and other services. Numerous advanced application packages have been designed to help over 2,000 corporate and government customers solve business and technical problems. Nearly 100 software products and online services are available, including EMPIRE, an interactive modeling and forecasting system, and COMPUSTAT, a database containing financial information on publicly held companies.

The new Private Vidtex service enables customers to create a private, in-house database and to access it via a menu-driven format.

Users can access BIS anywhere in the continental United States through CompuServe's own communications network or inbound WATS lines.

Executive Information Service   EIS is designed for professional people who own a home computer and want an easy-to-use package of business and financial information, news, decision-support research, and communications options.

Subscribers to EIS can choose from databases on business and finance (such as Standard & Poor's, which provides extensive information on over 3,000 companies, and TICKER RETRIEVAL, which provides price information on a 20-minute delayed basis on over 9,000 security issues); news (the Associated Press news wire); travel (the online version of the Official Airline Guide); and decision support (SITE II and SITE POTENTIAL, for example, which offer demographic information on any area of the United States). Customers also have access to communications services, such as electronic mail, conferencing, forums, and bulletin boards; Infoplex, an electronic mail service that utilizes the U.S. Post Office's E-COM hard-copy delivery service so that users can send mail to associates who do not have online equipment; online shopping; more advanced professional and technical information services; and the versatile Consumer Information Service (see description below). EIS also offers an automatic news-clipping service on topics of the customer's choice.

EIS's menu-driven format makes it relatively easy to learn and use. No prior computer experience is necessary. This format allows the user to move through the system to the type of service he desires by choosing among clear, functional alternatives. Simple commands can be learned later to progress through the service more directly. The starter kit for EIS is available in either a standard version or an IBM PC version with special connection software.

The prime-time connect-hour charge for EIS is the least expensive of any CompuServe service ($12.50 for 300 baud, $15 for 1200 baud). Nonprime, the charge is $6 per connect hour at 300 baud. EIS (like CIS below) offers the advantage of relatively straightforward charge structures and billing options (major credit cards and Checkfree).

Consumer Information Service   CIS offers over 600 databases and online features. Compared to EIS, which has more extensive business and financial fferings, CIS's features are geared more toward hobbies, recreation, and consumers' needs. A great many CIS users are interested in communicating with their counterparts from all over the United States, and they can do so in less structured ways than on EIS. Both systems are menu-driven. CIS is very popular after working hours, as its price drops from $22.50 per hour to $5 after 6:00 P.M. on weekdays and all weekend. EIS customers can access CIS, but not vice versa. (CompuServe will offer a discount on EIS to CIS customers.)

CIS carries some business-related features, including databases of financial information (securities, commodities, company information, etc.); online travel guides and booking services; and the online text of news wires, newspapers, and magazines. Customers can send electronic mail to each other, peruse a bulletin board, and participate in Special Interest Groups

(SIGs), a unique feature on the system. SIGs allow subscribers with similar occupations or interests to get together and hold online meetings.

Hundreds of consumer products and services are also offered. Popular items include computer games; the CB Simulator, which provides 40 "channels" for carrying on "conversations" with other CIS subscribers in the United States; online shopping for athletic equipment, books, gifts, etc.; and a clearinghouse for renting vacation accommodations and vehicles around the world.

Many of CIS's subscribers are experienced computer users. For them, a personal computing section is available offering the more advanced capabilities of BIS. Users also have access to several applications software packages on a time-sharing basis, and they can purchase software to be downloaded to their own computers. Each new CIS user is given 128K personal storage space, and additional space may be purchased.

Telecommunications access

CIS and EIS can be accessed through Tymnet, Telenet and Datapac (in Canada) at 300 and 1200 baud. BIS members can use WATS lines. CompuServe also has its own packet-switching network in 400 U.S. cities. It can be used for any of these services.

Hardware and software requirements

Anyone with a microcomputer, terminal, or communicating word processor can use CompuServe.

CIS and EIS offer a communications software package, Vidtex, that features automatic log-on, printer support, color graphics, and user-defined function keys. Special communications packages for several brands of personal computers are planned.

Fee structure and sign-up

Customers of the Business Information Service contract with CompuServe's network of sales and service people. Rates and arrangements vary according to user requirements. Most accounts total at least $1,000 per month.

Customers of the Executive and Consumer Information services get started by purchasing "starter kits," available in most computer stores, Radio Shack stores, and through the Sears, Roebuck catalog. EIS kits retail at $89 for the standard version and $139 for the IBM PC version with connection software. CompuServe plans customized kits for other computers in the near future. CIS kits are available at $39.95 retail, with five hours of free search time, or in $19.95 and $29.95 versions, which contain less search time. Kits also contain an account number, password, computer storage space, a user's guide, and various literature.

EIS costs $12.50 per connect hour from 8:00 A.M. to 6:00 P.M. on weekdays and $6 per hour at all other times. (These rates are for 300 baud; 1200 baud costs $15 and $12.50 respectively.) Telecommunications charges other than for CompuServe's own network are additional. Some services on the system may require an extra charge. Billing for EIS Is through MasterCard, Visa or Checkfree Electronic Funds Transfer.

Connect-hour rates for CIS are $22.50 from 8:00 A.M. to 6:00 P.M. Monday through Friday and $5 per hour at all other times. Telecommunications charges, other than for CompuServe's own network, are additional. Some of the individual services on CIS require an extra charge. Payment is by Master-Card, Visa, or Checkfree.

For both EIS and CIS, there is no monthly minimum. Offline prints are available (see below).

Offline printing and remote capabilities

CompuServe produces offline prints at the Columbus, Ohio, facility using high-speed line printers. Charges are 12¢ per page, plus $1.50 for postage and handling. The minimum order is $4.

Documentation available

BIS customers have a number of programming and compiling manuals and software guides available to them.

EIS and CIS customers receive user manuals with their starter kits. Subscribers to CIS receive UPDATE, a newsletter, and TODAY, a glossy four-color magazine.

Customer training

BIS customers are trained through CompuServe sales offices. Onsite training for large-account customers is available.

EIS and CIS are designed to be self-taught through their user manuals and used right away; therefore, no special course is provided. CompuServe makes an effort to familiarize retail and computer store staffs with its product, however, so that they can supply some assistance to subscribers if necessary. More than 4,000 Radio Shack personnel have undergone this training, and CompuServe is expanding its efforts to other retailers.

Document retrieval

The Infotext service on CIS supplies research services and document retrieval. CIS and EIS users can also obtain documents from Information on Demand, a Berkeley, California firm with which orders can be placed online.

Other services

BIS customers have available custom applications consulting. CompuServe offers specialized system design and development services on a fee basis.

Public database offerings

BIS databases

COMPUSTAT II Produced by Standard and Poor's, financial information on over 6,000 industrial companies, 175 annual and quarterly industrial aggregates, and over 100 utilities and banks. Data on balance sheets, income statements, sources and uses of funds, and trading are provided. (Separate contract and license fee required)

Value Line Produced by Arnold Bernhard & Co., a broad-based library of financial information covering 95 percent of the dollar value of securities traded on the major exchanges. Data on 1,800 major U.S. companies are provided, including 10-K reports, income statements, sources and uses statements, stock market relationships, and calculated financial ratios. (Separate contract required.)

Merrill Lynch Equity Research Estimates of dividends, prices and earnings for over 1,100 of the largest U.S. companies. Estimates and projections are updated daily by 85 of Merrill Lynch's top analysts.

VALUE From Telestat Systems, contains current and historical trading, financial and descriptive information for thousands of security issues of all types. Fifteen custom-designed programs are available for plotting and graphing data. (Proprietary product of Capital Market Systems; separate contract required.)

CITIBASE A collection of historical national economic series, compiled and updated weekly by the CITIBASE Technical Group of Citibank. Monthly, quarterly and annual time series back to 1946 are included. (Separate contract and license fee required.)

SITE II Information from the U.S. Census Bureau on population, households, income, age, and race. It is searchable by zip code and county, among other factors.

SITE POTENTIAL Allows the user to define geographic areas of the United States and evaluate the market potential there for up to 29 retail and financial businesses.

A. M. Best Executive Data Service Two years' worth of information on 2,700 insurance companies, including premiums, market share, and loss and underwriting data.

FDIC and FHLBB Bank Call Report Data Data on FDIC call reports back to 1972 on FRS banks and other U.S. banks and FHLBB call reports back to 1974 on over 4,000 savings and loan institutions.

Institutional Brokers' Estimate Service Consensus estimates on earnings for 3,000 companies made by 65 institutional brokerage firms. Earnings per share for two years and growth rates for five years are projected.

New Issues Corporate Securities Data Base Historical data on the placement of corporate securities through investment bankers. It covers 6,000 transactions from 1976 to date on both public companies and initial offerings.

EIS databases—Business and finance

Ticker Retrieval Price information on over 9,000 security issues, including high, low, closing, volume, and net change. There are also company synopses, pricing and dividend histories, statistics on pricing, detailed issue examinations on securities, financials, estimates, and projections.

Standard & Poor's Descriptive and financial information on more than 3,000 companies.

Value Line (See under BIS databases.)

Institutional Brokers' Estimate System (See under BIS databases.)

Continuously Updated Quotes High, low, closing, volume, and net changes for over 9,000 securities on NYSE, AMEX, and OTC. Prices are updated continuously on a 20-minute delayed basis.

Historical Market Information   Daily trading statistics and descriptive information for ten years on over 40,000 stocks, bonds, mutual funds, government issues, and options.

Market Reports   Information on market trends, including the identification of the 20 most active stocks and the 20 largest gains.

Issues Examination   Standard and Poor's and Moody's ratings, shares outstanding, beta factor, latest bid, pricing and dividend activity, bond coupon rate, yield, maturity date, and open interest.

Prices and Dividends   Pricing and dividend information for any specified time range for a specified security.

Multiple Price Quotes   Price quote for a specified day for one or more securities, including ticker symbol, value, high/ask, low/bid, close/average prices, and CUSIP number.

Portfolio Summary   Current valuation report on a portfolio, using the issue, number of units, acquisition cost per unit, and current market price.

Summary Statistics   Descriptive statistics for an issue over a specified period of time, including high, low, close, high close, low close, volume, mean, and standard deviation.

Major Market and Industry Indexes   Indexes of NYSE, AMEX, Kuhn Loeb, NASDAQ, Value Line, Dow Jones, Standard & Poor's 400/500, Standard & Poor's Industry Composites, and Moody's.

Canadian Press Business Information Wire   Canadian and international business coverage. It is supplemented by information from Reuter's, Associated Press, and Agence Presse-France.

The National Business Wire   Continuous update of news and press releases on hundreds of companies.

Money Market Services   The largest supplier of online financial forecasting, with over 800 institutional clients around the world. The three services offered are The Daily Comment, dealing with daily aspects of market activity; Fedwatch, a weekly news bulletin focusing on interest rate trends; and The Monthly Report, presenting long-term economic and monetary trends.

EIS databases—Decision support

SITE II   (See under BIS databases.)

SITE POTENTIAL   (See under BIS databases.)

STATS II   An integrated statistical system. It permits users to store and manipulate data extracted from other areas of the system or from offline files.

Evans Economic databases   Four databases from Evans Economics, Inc. will be added to EIS during 1984:

- ◆ Michael Evans' Market Ticker—forecasts, analyses, and commentary on stocks, futures, and money markets.
- ◆ Evans Economics Barometer—consensus forecasts, historical statistics, and analysis of over 20 major economic indicators released by the federal government.
- ◆ Business Ballot Box—an interactive service that subscribers can use to express their views on pertinent issues in the U.S. and foreign markets. Evans will publish results of the polls online each week.
- ◆ Evans Executive Roundtable—answers by Evans' economists to selected questions from customers.

EIS databases—News

The Associated Press   Newsline updated continuously. It has automatic clipping service capability.

The Washington Post Electronic newsletter containing local and national news, sports, financial data, etc.

EIS databases—Travel

Official Airline Guide Latest information on schedules and fares for nearly all commercial airline flights in North America. OAG will go to international coverage during 1984.

Travel America An online travel service that assists users in booking their transportation and accommodations.

NOAA Weather Service Weather information for the U.S. and its territories.

EIS databases—Shopping

COMP-U-STORE Shopping service for users from their terminals or microcomputers for nationally advertised consumer goods at discount.

EIS databases—Communications

Communications Capabilities for electronic mail, conferencing, forums, and bulletin-board notices between users all over the United States.

CIS databases—Financial

Heinold Community Reports Information about trading commodities.

Market Reports (See under EIS databases—Business and Finance.)

Issues Examination (See under EIS databases—Business and Finance.)

Prices and Dividends (See under EIS databases—Business and Finance.)

MicroQuote Current and historical trading information on over 40,000 securities including stocks, bonds, and options.

Value Line (See under BIS databases.)

Standard & Poor's (See under EIS databases—Business and Finance.)

CIS databases—Shopping

Athlete's Outfitter A home-shopping service carrying athletic clothing and equipment from M. Handelsman Co. of Chicago. All items are available at a discount and are shipped within 48 hours of order.

Fifth Avenue Shopper A home shopping service: athletic clothing and equipment from H & J Price Co., Maplewood, New Jersey; FTD and Teleflora flowers and plants; Godiva chocolates; gift and rare books; and book searching.

National Public Radio Cassette Gazette At-home ordering of cassettes of NPR radio programs.

Primetime Radio Classics A home-shopping catalog of cassettes of old-time radio programs such as The Shadow, Burns and Allen, and The Lone Ranger.

COMP-U-STORE (See under EIS databases—Shopping.)

Worldwide Exchanges A clearinghouse for the exchange, rent or charter of condominiums, vacation homes, bed-and-breakfast inns, yachts, power boats, aircraft, and recreational vehicles throughout the world.

CIS databases—Travel

Travel America (See under EIS databases—Travel.)

U.S. Department of State Travel Advisories Travel advisories and hazardous situations from around the world that might affect U.S. travelers.

CIS databases—Other

Special-Interest Groups   Available on many subjects, including Family Matters, Food Buy-line, Games, Golf, Ham Radio Operators' Network, Literacy, Music, National Issues and People, NETWITS (for online users), Orchestra 90, Space, Sports, and Work at Home.

Popular Science   The electronic version of *Popular Science* magazine.

Rick Brough's Movie Reviews   A thorough guide to the most recent movie releases, complete with ratings.

Showtime Entertainment   Summaries and reviews of features on national pay-TV.

Victory Garden   Articles for the home gardener.

U.S. Government Publications   Index to the various booklets available from the government.

The Washington Post   (See under EIS databases—News.)

The Associated Press   (See under EIS databases—News.)

*Data Resources (DRI)

Data Resources, Inc., a division of McGraw-Hill, 24 Hartwell Ave., Lexington, Massachusetts 02173, 617-863-5100

Other offices

Regional offices: Atlanta, Boston, Chicago, Detroit, Houston, Los Angeles, New York City, Philadelphia, Pittsburgh, San Francisco, Stamford (Conn.), Washington D.C.

International offices: Toronto, Brussels, London, Milan, Paris, Durnstadt (West Germany).

Hours of operation

24 hours a day, seven days a week except Christmas and New Year's day and scheduled maintenance periods.

Customer assistance

All local offices have consultants who provide support to clients in the use of DRI's data and software. A consultant is available at every office during normal business hours for telephone assistance. In addition, a technical consulting team of five people offers software assistance by phone at the Lexington office during normal business hours.

Specialists at the DRI computer facility in Lexington can answer questions 24 hours a day, seven days a week (including major holidays).

Position in database industry

Data Resources, Inc., maintains one of the world's largest private collections of computer-accessible business, financial, and economic time-series data. Over 75 databases containing over 100 million time series are available.

Through DRI's proprietary software programming language, EPS, users can manipulate time-series data, do sophisticated simulation and regression analysis, write reports, and develop graphics.

DRI was traditionally a time-sharing vendor. Recently, however, the firm has developed DataKits, a new product aimed at users of personal computers. DataKits allow users to download preformatted data at fixed prices of $6 to $125.

Time-sharing subscribers pay annual subscription fees for access to specific data and models. These clients are generally from large corporations, and their monthly use cost averages around $10,000. DRI produces software that works on mini- and microcomputers, permitting users to process DRI's data and models on their own machines.

The firm's competitors have traditionally included other economic forecasting companies such as Chase Econometrics, other time-sharing companies such as ADP, and other consulting firms. One real strength is the firm's ability to provide consultants to help clients understand how to use the databases to meet individual information needs.

Company background

DRI was founded in 1968 by Otto Eckstein. In its early years, the company made econometric forecasting techniques available commercially to large government and business users. DRI became a public company in 1974 and was acquired by McGraw-Hill in 1979. Today DRI is one of the world's foremost sources of econometric models and a major supplier of U.S. national, U.S. regional, international, energy, and financial databases.

In 1982, DRI acquired Gnostic Concepts of San Mateo, California, and Systemetrics of Santa Barbara, California. Both companies provide proprietary data and consulting services—Gnostic to the electronics industry and Systemetrics to the hospital and health care industries.

Approximately 500 professionals, including product economists and software specialists, work at DRI's Lexington headquarters. Another 400 consultants and data specialists work in its 13 U.S. and 6 international offices.

Computer facilities

Data Resources has four Burroughs B7800 computers with over 60 billion characters of proprietary and public data.

Summary of database services

DRI makes historical and forecast data available to customers in a variety of ways.

Small-scale users can use VisiLink, a software package developed for microcomputers by DRI and VisiCorp. This package allows access to fixed-cost, preformatted segments of DRI information. These segments, called DataKits, are formatted in VisiCalc worksheets and allow users to do business, investment, and economic analyses with DRI data.

Larger corporate customers use a variable cost option that works as a traditional time-sharing service. Clients pay an annual access fee to subscribe to particular databases or sets of databases. Users also pay for access time, specific information, and computer use. This service allows customers to use DRI's sophisticated programming languages to create models and analyze information.

Data can also be downloaded for local processing and analysis using DRILINK, a new software package for supermicrocomputers capable of supporting four to eight users. This type of service has numerous applications for planning and strategy setting in government and large companies. Users require training and must use the system regularly to take full advantage of it.

Telecommunications access

DRI is accessible at 300 or 1200 baud via Uninet, Tymnet, or Drinet, DRI's own network, which is available in 24 cities of the United States, Canada, and Europe.

Hardware and software requirements

No special terminals are required to access DRI.

Several software packages can help users access and analyze information on microcomputers. Through EPS/PC, subscribers can use an IBM PC to sign on to DRI, to manipulate data using EPS, a proprietary language designed for econometric work, and to download the data into a VisiCalc file for further analysis. Through a similar procedure, subscribers can use EPSTODIF to bring data into a DIF, or Data Interchange Format. This is a standard format for file storage that can be used for other programs on a PC.

Nonsubscribers can use VisiLink on an Apple II or IBM PC to access selected data in VisiCalc format. VisiLink is available from retail computer dealers for about $250.

Fee structure and sign-up

Customers sign up for service by contacting DRI. Subscribers pay an annual fee of $3,000 to $20,000 for access to DRI, depending on the information to be accessed. Subscribers are then billed for time sharing based on computer resources used. The average subscriber spends $10,000 per month.

Nonsubscribers can use VisiLink to access preformatted segments of data called DataKits, for which there are no connect or transmission charges. DataKits cost from $6 to $125, with most in the $25 to $30 range. Registration takes place online. Billing is by DRI account or major credit card.

Offline printing and remote capabilities

For subscribers, DRI has a high-speed, high-quality printer for offline printing. Cost is $4.75 per 1,000 lines.

Documentation and customer training

DRI provides extensive documentation for EPS, its proprietary software language, and for other software and database packages. Fees are generally $20 to $30 per document. Users of DataKits receive complete documentation on how to use them as part of the VisiLink software package. *Database Updates* is sent bimonthly to subscribers.

DRI provides free classes to help clients learn to use its databases and software. Classes are held in the company's offices in the United States, Canada, and Europe.

Document retrieval

Not applicable.

Other services

DRI's economists and consultants are available for special project analysis. These services are negotiated through proposals and billed to clients as professional fees.

DRI also holds special seminars bringing together recognized experts. Fees range from $350 to $850 per day.

Public database offerings

U.S. national and regional

DRI/NPDC Census Summary data from the 1980 U.S. Census. These data are cross-sectional and include demographic and housing characteristics at the regional, state, and county levels.

U.S. Central Financial, economic, and demographic indicators that provide comprehensive measures of economic activity for the United States as an aggregate.

U.S. County Indicators of economic activity at the county level.

U.S. Prices A large collection of consumer, producer, and industry-sector price indexes compiled by the Bureau of Labor Statistics of the U.S. Department of Labor.

U.S. Regional Indicators of economic activity in various states, regions, and metropolitan areas.

California Extensive macroeconomic data for the state of California. The data is collected and maintained by the Security Pacific National Bank and made available on the DRI system.

The Conference Board A unique source of proprietary data, both historical and forecasted, measuring activity in various sectors of the U.S. economy. The database is produced by The Conference Board.

New York City Indicators of economic activity in New York City and surrounding areas.

International

Canada A wide range of economic, demographic, and financial statistics. It is available as two databases: Statistics Canada's CANSIM Mini Base containing micro and macro indicators updated via a computer-to-computer link; and DRI's primary source database of statistics not available through CANSIM.

Current Economic Indicators Extremely timely coverage of major financial and economic indicators for the United States, Europe, Japan, Canada, and selected developing countries.

Other countries covered include Argentina, Australia, Brazil, Japan, Mexico, Korea, South Africa, Taiwan, and Venezuela. Coverage of countries is being expanded.

European National Source Macroeconomic, microeconomic, and financial indicators for 14 European nations—Belgium, Denmark, France, Germany, Greece, Ireland, Italy, the Netherlands, Norway, Spain, Sweden, Switzerland, the United Kingdom, and Yugoslavia.

External Debt Time series detailing the external public debt and financial position of developed and developing nations. Data from the International Bank for Reconstruction and Development includes series on external public debt by creditor, type of transaction and estimated debt service payments. Data from the Bank for International Settlements includes liabilities, maturity distribution of assets, and nondisbursed credit commitments of commercial banks.

IBRD World Tables The national accounts, balance of payments, and central government finances of 120 countries in both current and constant prices.

IMF Balance of Payments Balance-of-payments series reflecting two established presentations—aggregated and detailed—that highlight the following categories: goods, services, and unrequited transfers; long-term capital; short-term capital; exceptional financing; counterpart items; reserves and related items; and allocation of SDRs. The data is for 114 IMF member nations.

IMF Direction of Trade For 130 countries, total import and export statistics by country of origin and destination with the trading partners of each, supplemented by world and area aggregates. All data is expressed in U.S. dollars for ease of comparison.

IMF International Financial Statistics A collection of economic and financial statistics for the 150-member nations of the International Monetary Fund (IMF).

IMF International Financial Statistics Restated Key series from the IMF International Financial Statistics database restated to consistent units—millions of U.S. dollars. This is designed to facilitate comparative analysis across countries of 22 concepts, such as deposits in and foreign liabilities of banks; money supply; government deficit, revenue, expenditures, borrowing, and consumption; imports, exports, and stocks; and gross domestic product. Data for 74 countries are included.

DRI International Trade Information Service Statistics from the Organization for Economic Cooperation and Development's Trade Series C and the United Nations's Trade Series D. These figures detail bilateral trade flows for 52 nations with over 190 trading partners. Commodity detail is to the five-digit Standard International Trade Classification level, totaling more than 1,100 commodities.

ITIS Monthly Monitor Timely primary source data on exports and imports for up to 11,000 specific commodities for nine major developed countries with each of their trading partners. Concepts available are (1) value of trade in national currencies and (2) quantity or volume of trade. Coverage includes Belgium, Canada, France, Germany, Italy, Japan, the Netherlands, the United Kingdom, and the United States.

Japan Economic, demographic, and financial indicators that provide a comprehensive economic profile of the Japanese economy.

Japan Prices The detailed price indexes collected by the Bank of Japan.

LDC Africa/Middle East National statistics from primary sources for the following countries: Egypt, Iraq, Israel, Ivory Coast, Jordan, Kenya, Kuwait, Nigeria, Oman, South Africa, Syria, Turkey, and Zambia.

LDC Asia/Australia Economic profiles of 11 Asian countries. Information is taken from primary sources and covers Australia, China, Hong Kong, India, Indonesia, Korea, Malaysia, the Philippines, Singapore, Taiwan, and Thailand.

LDC Latin America A variety of economic and financial variables designed to give an in-depth, current economic profile of this region. Coverage includes Argentina, Brazil, Chile, Colombia, Jamaica, Mexico, Peru, and Venezuela.

OECD Main Economic Indicators   A compilation of economic, demographic, and financial indicators for the 25 OECD member nations and regional aggregates.

OECD National Income Accounts   Annual and quarterly data for OECD member nations. The quarterly series are not adjusted by the OECD, but the annual series are standardized to allow comparison across countries. Coverage includes annual data for each OECD member nation and quarterly data for Australia, Austria, Canada, Finland, France, Germany, Greece, Italy, Japan, Sweden, the United Kingdom, and the United States.

OECD Trade Series A   A compilation of statistics covering trade by three categories: total imports and exports by OECD member and trading partner, total trade of OECD member nations by SITC category, and volume and average value indexes at the SITC sector subgroup level. Coverage includes 24 OECD member nations, over 100 trading partners, and five regional groupings.

Industrial/sectoral

Agriculture   Information on supply, demand, and prices of domestic and international commodities. Government policy variables and trade information complement the system. Coverage is of the United States at the state and national levels.

Automotive News   The status of the U.S. automobile market at a nameplate level. Available in detail are statistics on Canadian car production, U.S. light-duty truck sales, and imported car sales.

Budgetrack   Both a program and an information system detailing U.S. federal budget data on a timely basis, allowing examination of each year's federal budget from its inception as a presidential request until it becomes law. Currently, Budgetrack focuses on research and development as well as procurement for the defense and NASA portions of the budget.

A. M. Best Insurance   Statutory financial information for life, accident, health, and property and casualty insurance companies. Coverage is for the United States at the individual company level.

Chemical   Extensive coverage of economic, market, and financial conditions relevant to the chemical industry.

Cost Forecasting   Indicators for the construction and related industries. International coverage includes price and wage data. The United States at national and regional levels, Germany, France, Italy, and the United Kingdom are covered.

Defense   Time series necessary for analyzing defense spending and costs and how they affect defense-related industries. Coverage is at the U.S. national and state levels.

DMS/Online   A comprehensive and detailed collection of textual and statistical information on the defense and aerospace industries. Specific contract awards, defense programs, market analysis, and special studies are included. The three major components of the database are contract awards, market intelligence, and special services.

Dodge Construction Analysis System   Construction statistics at the individual project level and a variety of regional and conceptual aggregations of contracts. U.S. counties and individual projects are covered on a monthly basis.

Forest Products   Series on the U.S. and Canadian lumber and plywood industries; the U.S. particleboard, waferboard, OSB, and hardboard industries; and U.S. timber resources. Coverage of the United States is at national and regional levels; of Canada, it is at the national level.

Historical Interindustry   Databases providing the tools for analyzing the flow of goods to and from all sectors of the U.S. economy. Coverage is at the three- and four-digit industry level.

International Auto   An expanding collection of key indicators on the international automobile industry. Belgium, France, Germany, Italy, the Netherlands, Spain, Sweden, the United Kingdom, and 30 other countries are included. Annual data describes total production, total exports and imports, and total registrations.

International Truck Statistics of importance to the international automotive and truck community. Countries include Belgium, France, Germany, Italy, the Netherlands, Spain, Sweden, and the United Kingdom.

Metals Week Detailed price information for the international nonferrous metals industry on the New York Commodity Exchange, London Metal Exchange, and other U.S. regional and international markets.

Pulp and Paper Indicators directly related to the U.S. and international pulp and paper industry and its end markets. Coverage includes the United States, major European countries, Japan, and other world regions.

Random Lengths Prices in the United States and Canada for a variety of woods and wood products as found in the Lumber and Plywood Market Reporting Service publication.

Regional Insurance Statistical description of the U.S. insurance industry, along with data affecting it, for every state and the District of Columbia. Insurance lines covered are fire and allied, commercial and private auto, commercial multiperil, and homeowners.

Steel Time series on iron, steel, and raw materials, for the United States and its trading partners.

Timber Mart South Regional, high, low, and average price data for timber and timber by-products in the southeastern United States.

Transportation Databases with extensive information on the following transport modes: Class I and Class II rail and motor carrier, air, and waterborne (inland, coastwise, local, lakewise), and pipeline.

U.S. Insurance General economic data of interest to insurance companies as well as data specific to the industry. Lines of insurance detailed are life, property, and casualty.

Energy

Canadian Energy Sources and uses of major fuels by province and sector.

Coal Extensive coverage of the U.S. coal industry, including data on mine types, production, distribution, employment, delivery, and import/export. State, regional, and national details are given.

International Energy Databases with facts on the energy activity of member nations of the Organization for Economic Cooperation and Development (OECD) and the International Energy Agency (IEA). Information on production, consumption, stocks, imports, and exports is provided by country and by fuel type. These series are supplemented by more timely CIA (Directorate of Intelligence) data on production of crude oil by major producing country and consumption, stocks, and energy trade by major consuming country.

Japanese Energy Data by Nikkei, DRI's Japanese partner. There are 3,300 series on energy demand, supply, and prices as well as essential international and domestic variables.

Oil and Gas Drilling Historical time series that describe various activities of the oil- and gas-drilling industry. Coverage is at the state, substate regional, and international levels.

Oil Company Historical series describing various activities of major oil- and gas-drilling companies. Coverage is of U.S. domestic activity by company.

Platt's Domestic and international crude oil and petroleum product spot prices. Official and spot prices are available by foreign crude type; product prices, generally by market locations and subdivided by sulfur content. International prices include European bulk cargo rates and tanker and barge quotations.

U.S. Energy Databases that allow the user to track energy information on the United States statistically from resources and primary production, through transformation into petroleum and natural gas products, to final consumption by energy-consuming sectors in the United States. These data are supplemented by the Department of Energy's State Energy Data System

(SEDS) and the Department of Commerce's Survey of Manufactures for Consumption by Specific Industry.

Financial

Commodities   Price and trading activity information for all major commodities traded on the U.S., Canadian, and London markets: food and feed grains, livestock and meat products, fibers and wood, metals, and energy futures.

COMPUSTAT   Produced by Standard and Poor's, detailed balance sheet and income statement items for over 5,000 industrial companies, 250 utilities, 145 banking institutions, and 200 telecommunications firms. It provides financial information on the individual business divisions of over 3,000 companies. It also includes 300 Canadian companies.

DRI Bank Analysis Service   Databases with balance-sheet and income-statement time series for individual savings and loan associations, mutual savings banks, and commercial banks in the United States, Guam, and Puerto Rico. Concepts include major categories of assets and liabilities. Supplemental and memoranda items, such as whole loans and participations and IRA and Keogh account totals, are included for savings and loans. Full call report data, including separate breakdowns for foreign operations, are given for commercial banks, as are loan loss experience by sector and deposits by source. Seven categories of deposits are available by branch.

DRI's Financial and Credit Statistics   Extensive coverage of interest rates, commercial bank assets and liabilities, and thrift institution activity.

DRI-SEC   Daily pricing and current fundamental information for equity, debt, and government agency issues. Coverage goes back to January, 1968.

EXSTAT   The balance sheet and profit-and-loss account items for 2,500 international corporations. Specific concepts available are highly disaggregated and presented as reported by the individual firms. In general, concepts covered include balance sheet assets and liabilities and profit-and-loss account. Coverage is of corporations in the United Kingdom, Eire, Japan, Australia, and other selected European countries.

DRI/Nikkei Japan Financial   The financial position of approximately 1,700 Japanese companies, those that are publicly traded and others that must issue annual reports.

Standard & Poor's   Selected income account and balance sheet items and well-known stock price indexes for over 100 industries. Disaggregations of the industrial, transportation, financial, and public utilities sectors of the economy are included.

U.S. Flow of Funds   Statistical information that brings the financial activities of the U.S. economy into explicit relationship with one another and into direct relation to the data on the nonfinancial activities that generate income and production. The system records both the payment and receipt aspects of any transaction by sector.

Value Line   Financial histories and projections for over 1,600 major companies in the United States.

DataKits   Available for industry details (production and costs), stock market information, COMPUSTAT, money and credit markets, the U.S. economy (national, regional, and state), and the international economy.

*Datasolve

Datasolve Ltd., Datasolve House, 99 Staines Rd. West, Sunbury-on-Thames, Middlesex, TW16, 7AH, England

U.S. headquarters: Datasolve Ltd., c/o Thorn-EMI (USA) Inc., 1370 Avenue of the Americas, 9th Floor, New York, New York 10019, 212-977-8990

Hours of operation

2:00 A.M. to 6:00 P.M. EST, Monday through Friday.

Customer assistance

The American and British offices offer customer assistance during local business hours. The New York office is open 9:00 A.M. to 5:00 P.M. Monday through Friday. Subscribers needing assistance outside of normal business hours may call Datasolve's international "hotline." To do this, the user dials a number in area code 212 that transfers directly to Datasolve customer service in England. The caller is charged only for a call to New York City.

Position in database industry

Datasolve is a leading United Kingdom computing services company based in Sunbury-on-Thames. It provides a wide range of computing services to subscribers in the United Kingdom and Europe.

Recently, Datasolve created the World Reporter collection of databases on current affairs. The World Reporter is marketed in the United States, Canada, and Australia, as well as in the U.K. and Europe. Its subscribers are primarily businesspeople engaged in international trade, media professionals, and users of academic or special libraries.

Company background

Datasolve is a wholly owned subsidiary of Thorn-EMI. It was founded in 1965, and through intensive development and diversification has become a force in the computing services industry. The firm's objective is to deliver a level of service, expertise, and cost performance that exceeds that which any organization could reasonably provide for itself.

Datasolve's annual turnover exceeds 25 million pounds from computing and its computing training unit, Datasolve Education.

The World Reporter was developed by Datasolve Information Services, a business unit specializing in database applications.

Computer facilities

At its home base in England, Sunbury-on-Thames, Datasolve maintains an IBM 3081 and an Amdahl computer at a computer facility. The system can support 200 simultaneous users.

Summary of database services

The World Reporter service offers databases containing news and current affairs information from the British Broadcasting Company, The Associated Press, and *The Economist*. The company plans to add substantially more databases in the immediate future.

Telecommunications access

World Reporter is accessible at 300 or 1200 baud via Telenet. It will soon be accessible through Datapac.

Hardware and software requirements

Accessible from any ASCII terminal with modem.

Fee structure and sign-up

The basic connect hour charge is $100. Users pay $200 when they sign the agreement for service to cover a two-hour yearly minimum. Further hours are billed at $100 per hour. Reduced rates are available to prepaid subscribers. Telecommunications charges are extra.

Offline printing and remote capabilities

Offline prints are not available to U.S. subscribers at this time.

Documentation available

Datasolve provides a *World Reporter User Guide* free to subscribers. It describes the databases and search commands and contains sample searches.

Customer training

Training is arranged with Datasolve.

Document retrieval

Not applicable.

Public database offerings

World Reporter 90-Day News File   Information from updates within the past 90 days of all World Reporter databases. The General News File of the Associated Press was scheduled to be added late in 1983.

Economist Magazine   The full text of *The Economist*. The latest issue appears in the database one week after publication. Updating is weekly, and latest updates are stored in the 90-Day News File.

BBC Summary of World Broadcasts 1982 and 1983   An online summary of news gathered by the BBC Monitoring Service, which monitors radio broadcasts in 50 languages from 120 countries and a number of foreign news agencies. Economic, industrial, and political information helps users track key developments in the USSR, Eastern Europe, the Far East, the Middle East, Africa, and Latin America. The database is updated daily, with latest updates stored in the 90-Day News File.

BBC External Service News   World and British news as reported by the BBC World Service, updated weekly. Latest updates are stored in the 90-Day News File.

*DIALOG

DIALOG Information Services, Inc., a subsidiary of Lockheed Corp., 3460 Hillview Ave., Palo Alto, California 94304, 415-858-3785, 800-227-1927

Other offices

United States: Boston, Chicago, Houston, Los Angeles, New York, Philadelphia, Washington, D.C.

These offices are primarily training offices, although they offer some marketing support.

Foreign representatives: Australia—Insearch, Ltd/DIALOG, Haymarket, New South Wales; England—DIALOG Information Services, Oxford; Canada—Micromedia, Ltd., Toronto; Japan—Kinokuniya Company Ltd. (Information Retrieval Services Dept.), Tokyo; Maruzen Co. Ltd., Tokyo.

Hours of operation

Monday through Thursday, 12:00 A.M. to 10:00 P.M. EST; Friday, 12:00 A.M. to 8:00 P.M. EST; Saturday and Sunday, 8:00 A.M. to 8:00 P.M. EST.

Customer assistance

The customer-assistance office, located in Palo Alto, is available from 9:00 A.M. to 8:15 P.M. EST. The toll-free number is 800-227-1927. Staff can answer questions about system problems and specific databases as well as help with strategies for difficult searches.

Position in database industry

One of the largest database vendors, DIALOG Information Services currently offers over 180 databases covering virtually every field, from agriculture and business to medicine and patents. Over 50,000 customers subscribe to the service.

DIALOG's main competitors are SDC and BRS. In addition to the size and diversity of its files, DIALOG's main strengths are experience (see Company Background below); a command language that is relatively simple and easy to learn, yet has full Boolean capability and can be used to construct complex search strategies; an excellent training and support network (an average of 50 to 70 training sessions are given per month over a wide geographic area); and relatively straightforward billing.

Traditionally, the typical customer has been a corporate or academic librarian performing searches for third parties. Today, however, the majority of new DIALOG customers are end users from a variety of backgrounds. The company has made an initial foray into the personal computer market with its Knowledge Index. This off-peak, reduced-rate service is aimed at the business or professional person who owns a home computer.

Company background

DIALOG Information Services, Inc., is an outgrowth of a company-funded research and development program that began at Lockheed Missiles and Space Company, Inc., in 1963 when Lockheed's Information Sciences Laboratory was established. Lockheed in 1965 demonstrated a new interactive retrieval system and in 1968 won a contract from the National Aeronautics and Space Administration to design and implement a computerized information system to serve NASA's research centers. The resulting RECON system was successful, and it led to contracts with other government agencies to design search systems. Lockheed introduced its DIALOG system commercially in 1972.

In 1981, DIALOG Information Services was made a wholly owned subsidiary of Lockheed Corporation, an aerospace and defense company with over $5 billion in sales in 1982.

Computer facilities

The DIALOG system runs on redundant NAS 9080 computers. It has 140 gigabytes of online storage and over 100 million records online.

Summary of database services

Currently, DIALOG carries over 180 databases, and new ones are being added each month. Most are bibliographic databases containing references and abstracts from publications in the fields of science, technology, social sciences, humanities, business, and economics. DIALOG also features directory databases, such as Dun's Market Identifiers; statistical files, such as BLS's Producer Price Index; and full-text files, such as United Press International.

There is an online index to DIALOG's databases called DIALINDEX. The user enters a search statement into DIALINDEX and runs it against one or more files to find out how many postings on a topic are available in each. This helps identify which databases will be most useful, which generally means a significant saving of effort and money.

The DIALOG system is command-driven and has full Boolean capabilities. Depending on the database, users can restrict their search by a number of fields, such as author, corporate source, language, type of document, etc. An adjacency feature and right-handed truncation are available.

Output from some databases on DIALOG can be sorted, but at present there is no way to merge the output of various files and eliminate duplicates. There is no graphics capability, nor is there a way to manipulate the retrieved data.

The company offers a private file service for organizations that wish to have their private database resident on the DIALOG system. Access to a private file is limited to members of the database creator's organization.

SDIs are available on 45 of DIALOG's files. The user creates a profile of information he needs regularly and runs it against each new update of one or more chosen databases. New postings are automatically mailed to the user.

Costs for this service range from $5 to $10 per profile per update of a database. There are volume discounts. DIALOG has plans to offer online delivery of SDI updates.

Its newest innovation is Knowledge Index, which offers 20 of the firm's databases in a simplified command-driven format. Target customers are owners of personal computers. The cost is $24 per connect hour, including telecommunications and database royalties. Offline prints are not available, but online ordering of complete documents is. Knowledge Index operates during evening hours and on weekends—6:00 P.M. to 5:00 A.M., Monday through Friday; 8:00 A.M. to 12:00 A.M., Saturday; and 3:00 P.M. to 12:00 A.M., Sunday (all hours are local user time). Knowledge Index's competitor in this market is BRS After Dark. Observers of the industry are carefully watching to see whether this new type of service becomes popular.

DIALOG will introduce an electronic mail service during the first half of 1984.

Telecommunications access

DIALOG is accessible at 300 or 1200 baud via Tymnet, Telenet, and Uninet. It is also available through direct dial, and it has its own inbound WATS capability. There is no differential charge for using 1200 baud access. The company has announced plans to offer its own dedicated network, Dialnet, beginning in mid-1984.

Hardware and software requirements

No special terminal is needed for access to the system. Most dial-up terminals, personal computers, and communicating word processors can be used.

A simplified user interface package for the IBM Personal Computer has been prepared in cooperation with an independent software developer. Additionally, a personal-computer development group has been created within DIALOG to research and introduce custom search and telecommunications software, both in-house and in cooperation with independent software developers.

Fee structure and sign-up

Customers sign up for services in writing, using a standard contract form available from any DIALOG office. There are no sign-up fees or subscription costs, but there are charges for user manuals (see below). The Knowledge Index service has a $35 sign-up fee.

Costs per connect hour range from $25 to $300, depending on the database, and average $60 to $80. This connect hour charge includes basic royalty charges for the database.

Offline prints cost an average of 25¢ per citation. Customers must pay royalty charges for typing citations from some databases online. These charges run about 10¢ to 15¢ per citation, and the trend at DIALOG is toward adding more royalty charges.

Billing is monthly. Customers receive totals for each database's access and each day's activity. The typical inclusive cost for a search is $5 to $25.

There are several types of contracts:

♦ Standard contract—Users who log at least five hours of billable connect time per month receive progressive discounts that begin at $5 per connect hour.

♦ Discount contract—Additional discounts are available to customers who contract for a guaranteed minimum dollar amount of use.

♦ Knowledge Index contract—The $35 sign-up fee includes a self-instruction manual and two hours of search time. All access to Knowldege Index costs $24 per connect hour, which includes royalties and telecommunications.

Offline printing and remote capabilities

Offline prints are available, produced by a high-speed laser printer. Print legibility is very good. Prints are produced three times a day and are mailed out either the same day or by 6:00 A.M. the following day.

As part of its new electronic mail service, DIALOG plans to offer electronic delivery of prints and SDIs to customers' online mailboxes.

Documentation available

DIALOG publishes the following user aids to assist customers:

♦ *The Guide to DIALOG Searching*—This manual sells for $50 and gives all the necessary information about the system, including features, commands, databases, and document ordering.

♦ Bluesheets—These distinctively colored reference guides contain key information about each database—its producer, its contents, searchable fields, etc. A sample citation is also given, with fields highlighted. Bluesheets are furnished with *The Guide to DIALOG Searching*, and new ones are sent with DIALOG's monthly newsletter.

♦ *Chronolog*—This monthly newsletter intended to keep customers current on system changes, database changes, and new developments also has tips on search strategies.

♦ *Knowledge Index Workbook*—This training manual for Knowledge Index is furnished to new customers. Its separate purchase price is $25.

DIALOG also has for sale in-depth chapters on each database. These cost $5 apiece.

The majority of database producers write their own user aids as well. These vary in price and coverage. A search aids list is included with the basic guide or may be purchased separately for $5.

Customer training

Training is offered frequently throughout the United States by DIALOG and by representative companies in Canada, Europe, Japan, Australia, and New Zealand. Information and coordination is through DIALOG's Palo Alto office.

The System Seminar for new users requires one and one-half days and costs $135 per person. Basic features of the system and the command language are explained at this session; five to ten more hours of practice are needed by new users to gain some proficiency.

Subject Seminars for experienced searchers are offered at $45 per half-day session and $115 for a full day; at these seminars, one subject area (such as business) and the databases that cover it are examined in depth. DIALOG also holds an annual two-day Update Session, at which customers have a chance to meet database producers.

Knowledge Index is designed to be self-taught using the instruction manual. Up to two free connect hours are provided when a user signs up, which is considered sufficient time to become proficient.

Document retrieval

DIALOG's Dialorder is the most extensive system available for ordering documents online. There are approximately 50 document suppliers on the system. The user selects a supplier based on the type and subject of the document that he needs, and enters his request. Copies are then mailed directly by the supplier, who also bills directly. Fees vary according to supplier. DIALOG provides information on document suppliers in *The Guide to DIALOG Searching* and issues updates through *Chronolog*.

Public database offerings

A dagger (†) indicates a Knowledge Index database. Prices are subject to change.

Chemistry

CA Search   The basic bibliographic data, keyword phrases, and index entries for all documents covered in the journal *Chemical Abstracts*. Charge: $68 per connect hour, 12¢ per online citation, 25¢ per offline citation.

Chemical Exposure   Information about chemicals that have been identified in human tissues and body fluids and in feral and food animals. Charge: $45 per connect hour, 15¢ per offline citation.

Chemical Industry Notes   Index of 78 worldwide business-oriented publications on the chemical-processing industries. Charge: $70 per connect hour, 12¢ per online citation, 25¢ per offline citation.

Chemical Regulations and Guidelines System   Index to U.S. federal regulatory material relating to the control of chemical substances, including federal statutes, promulgated regulations, and available federal guidelines, standards, and support documents. As of late 1983, work on this database was suspended due to funding cutbacks; check with DIALOG for latest availability information. Charge: $70 per connect hour, 90¢ per offline citation.

CHEMLAW   The full text of U.S. federal chemical regulations as published in the *U.S. Code of Federal Regulations* and updated in the *Federal Register*. Charge: $150 per connect hour, $1.50 per offline citation.

CHEMNAME   File's purpose to provide substance searching and identification on the basis of nomenclature, trade names, synonyms, ring data, element count, and molecular formula. Charge: $138 per connect hour, 12¢ per online citation, 25¢ per offline citation.

CHEMSEARCH   Companion file to CHEMNAME. Substances that have been cited most recently in the CA Search file are listed. CHARGE: $138 per connect hour, 12¢ per online citation, 25¢ per offline citation.

CHEMSIS   A dictionary file of chemical substances cited only once during a collective indexing period of *Chemical Abstracts*. Charge: $138 per connect hour, 12¢ per online citation, 25¢ per offline citation.

CHEMZERO   Dictionary file of chemical substances for which there are no citations in *Chemical Abstracts*. Charge: $138 per connect hour, 12¢ per online citation, 25¢ per offline citation.

CLAIMS Compound Registry   A registry of specific compounds searchable in the CLAIMS U.S. Patent database. Charge: $95 per connect hour, 15¢ per offline citation.

PAPERCHEM   Indexes and abstracts of scientific and technical literature dealing with the raw materials, principles, processes, technology, and products of the pulp and paper industry. It corresponds to the printed *Abstract Bulletin* of the Institute of Paper Chemistry. Charge: $65 per connect hour, 15¢ per online citation, 25¢ per offline citation.

SCISEARCH   A multidisciplinary index to the literature of science and technology containing all the records published in the printed *Science Citation Index*. Charge: subscribers to print version: $65 per connect hour, 15¢ per offline citation; nonsubscribers: $165 per connect hour, 25¢ per offline citation.

TSCA Initial Inventory   A nonbibliographic dictionary of chemical substances in commercial use after June 1, 1979. This file provides CAS Registry numbers, preferred names, synonyms, and molecular formulas. Charge: $45 per connect hour, 15¢ per offline citation.

Agriculture and nutrition

†*AGRICOLA*   The cataloging and indexing database of the National Agriculture Library. The worldwide journal and monographic literature on agriculture and related subjects is comprehensively covered. Charge: $35 per connect hour, 10¢ per offline citation.

†*BIOSIS Previews*   Coverage of over 9,000 primary journals and monographs in the biosciences as well as symposia, reviews, research communications, and government reports. Charge: $65/connect hour, 15¢ per offline citation.

CAB Abstracts   Corresponds to the 26 major abstract journals published by the Commonwealth Agricultural Bureaux, located in England, one of the foremost research organizations in the world in the areas of biology and agriculture. Charge: $55 per connect hour; 35¢ per offline citation.

CRIS/USDA   A "current awareness" database covering research projects in agriculture and related sciences. These projects are sponsored or conducted by USDA research agencies, state agricultural experiment stations and forestry schools, and other cooperating state institutions. Charge: $35 per connect hour, 10¢ per offline citation.

EMBASE—Medicine and Biosciences   Produced by Excerpta Medica, abstracts and citations of articles from over 3,500 biomedical journals published throughout the world. It covers human medicine and related disciplines. Charge: $75 per connect hour, 8¢ per online citation, 25¢ per offline citation.

FOODS ADLIBRA   Information on the latest developments in food science, packaging, and marketing. Nutritional and toxicological information. Charge: $55 per connect hour, 10¢ per offline citation.

Food Science and Technology Abstracts (FSTA) Research and development literature in areas related to food science and technology. Charge: $65 per connect hour, 15¢ per offline citation.

Health Planning and Administration Produced by the National Library of Medicine, references from nonclinical literature on subjects related to the delivery of health care: planning, facilities, insurance, financial management, personnel administration, manpower planning and licensure, and accreditation. Charge: $35 per connect hour, 15¢ per offline citation.

†International Pharmaceutical Abstracts All phases of the development and use of drugs and professional pharmaceutical practice. Charge: $55 per connect hour, 20¢ per offline citation.

Life Sciences Collection Abstracts of articles in the fields of animal behavior, biochemistry, ecology, entomology, genetics, immunology, microbiology, toxicology, and virology. Charge: $45 per connect hour, 15¢ per offline citation.

†MEDLINE Produced by the National Library of Medicine, corresponding to three printed indexes: *Index Medicus, Index to Dental Literature,* and *International Nursing Literature*. MED-LINE indexes articles from over 3000 international journals published in the United States and 70 other countries. Charge: $35 per connect hour, 15¢ per offline citation.

Mental Health Abstracts Citations of worldwide information relating to the general topic of mental health. Sources include 1,200 journals, books, monographs, technical reports, and conference proceedings. Charge: $85 per connect hour, 5¢ per online citation, 15¢ per offline citation.

Pharmaceutical News Index (PNI) Online index to current news about pharmaceuticals, cosmetics, medical devices, and related fields. Charge: $95 per connect hour, 25¢ per online citation, 30¢ per offline citation.

Telegen Produced by EIC/Intelligence, citations to literature in the rapidly advancing fields of genetic engineering and biotechnology. Charge: $90 per connect hour, 15¢ per online citation, 25¢ per offline citation.

Zoological Record Worldwide coverage of zoological literature, with particular emphasis on systematic/taxonomic information. Charge: $78 per connect hour, 20¢ per offline citation.

Energy and environment

APTIC All aspects of air pollution, including its effects, prevention, and control from 1966 to 1976. Charge: $35 per connect hour, 10¢ per offline citation.

Aquaculture References on the subject of the growth of marine, brackish, and freshwater organisms. Charge: $35 per connect hour, 10¢ per online citation, 10¢ per offline citation.

AQUALINE All aspects of water, waste water, and the aquatic environment. Charge: $35 per connect hour, 25¢ per online citation, 30¢ per offline citation.

Aquatic Sciences and Fisheries Abstracts Life sciences of the seas and inland water as well as related legal, political, and social topics. Charge: $75 per connect hour, 20¢ per online citation, 30¢ per offline citation).

DOE Energy Produced by the U.S. Department of Energy Technical Information Service, references to a wide variety of literature (including government reports) on virtually every topic related to energy. Charge: $40 per connect hour, 15¢ per offline citation.

Electric Power Database References to research and development projects of interest to the electric power industry, produced by the Electric Power Research Institute. Charge: $55 per connect hour, 15¢ per offline citation.

Energyline Produced by EIC/Intelligence, machine-readable version of *Energy Information Abstracts*. Charge: $90 per connect hour, 15¢ per online citation, 25¢ per offline citation.

Energynet   Online directory of over 3,000 organizations and 8,000 people active in energy-related fields. Entries include a descriptive abstract. Charge: $90 per connect hour, 50¢ per offline citation.

Enviroline   Many types of information on the environment, such as management, technology, planning, law, and economics. Charge: $90 per connect hour, 25¢ per offline citation.

Environmental Bibliography   Coverage of general human ecology, atmosphere studies, energy, land and water resources, nutrition, and health. Charge: $60 per connect hour, 15¢ per offline citation.

Oceanic Abstracts   Index of technical literature published worldwide on marine-related subjects. Charge: $73 per connect hour, 25¢ per online citation, 30¢ per offline citation.

Pollution Abstracts   Online source of references to environmental-related literature on pollution, its sources, and its control. Charge: $73 per connect hour, 15¢ per online citation, 20¢ per offline citation.

WATERNET   Index to the publications of the American Waterworks Association and the AWWA Research Foundation. Charge: $80 per connect hour, 10¢ per online citation, 20¢ per offline citation.

Water Resources Abstracts   A wide range of water resource topics, including economics, ground and surface water hydrology, and metropolitan water resource planning and management. Charge: $45 per connect hour, 15¢ per offline citation.

Science and technology

BHRA Fluid Engineering   Indexes and abstracts of literature on every aspect of fluid engineering, including theoretical research and the latest technologies and applications. 1974 to the present. Charge: $65 per connect hour, 15¢ per offline citation.

†COMPENDEX   The machine-readable version of *Engineering Index*, which contains abstracts and references to the world's significant engineering and technological literature. Charge: $98 per connect hour, 30¢ per online citation, 30¢ per offline citation.

Ei Engineering Meetings   Index to published proceedings of engineering and technical conferences, symposia, meetings, and colloquia; 1979 to the present. Charge: $98 per connect hour, 30¢ per online citation, 40¢ per offline citation.

GeoArchive   Coverage of geophysics, geochemistry, geology, paleontology, and mathematical geology. More than 100,000 references are added each year. Charge: $70 per connect hour, 20¢ per offline citation.

GeoRef   Comprehensive access to literature concerned with geology, geochemistry, geophysics, mineralogy, paleontology, petrology, and seismology. Charge: $82 per connect hour, 10¢ per online citation, 20¢ per offline citation.

†INSPEC   Corresponds to the journals in *Physics Abstracts, Electrical and Electronics Abstracts*, and *Computer and Control Abstracts*. It is the largest English-language database in the fields of physics, electrotechnology, and computers. Charge: $85 per connect hour, 25¢ per online citation, 35¢ per offline citation.

†International Software   Lists of commercially available software for any type of mini- or microcomputer. Charge: $60 per connect hour, 15¢ per offline citation.

ISMEC   Indexes of significant articles on all aspects of mechanical engineering, production control, and engineering management. Charge: $73 per connect hour, 15¢ per online citation, 20¢ per offline citation.

MATHFILE   Coverage of worldwide mathematical research literature from 1973 to the present. Charge: $55 per connect hour, 20¢ per offline citation.

Meteorological and Geoastrophysical Abstracts   Lists of current citations in English to the important worldwide literature in meteorological and geoastrophysical research. Charge: $95 per connect hour, 15¢ per offline citation.

†*Microcomputer Index*   Online subject and abstract guide to magazine articles from 40 microcomputer journals, including *BYTE, Interface Age, Infoworld*, etc. Charge: $45 per connect hour, 15¢ per offline citation.

†*NTIS*   Directs users to government-sponsored research, development, and engineering reports and analyses prepared by federal agencies, their contractors, or their grantees. It is a major source of unclassified government reports. Charge: $45 per connect hour, 15¢ per offline citation.

SPIN   References from all journal articles and conference proceedings in English or Russian (translated into English) published by the American Institute of Physics, by its member societies, or in other relevant American journals. Charge: $35 per hour, 10¢ per offline citation.

SSIE Current Research   Summaries of research projects of the Smithsonian Science Information Exchange (SSIE) in progress or completed within the past 24 months in all areas of the physical, social, engineering, and life sciences. Project descriptions are furnished by over 1,300 organizations that fund research (approximately 90 percent are federal government agencies). Charge: $78 per connect hour, 20¢ per offline citation.

Standards & Specifications   File of government and industry standards, specifications, and related documents that specify requirements or characteristics—such as terminology, performance testing, safety, materials, or products—relevant to a particular technology or industry. Charge: $65 per connect hour, 20¢ per online citation, 30¢ per offline citation.

TRIS   Online index to research information on numerous modes of transportation, including highway, rail, and maritime transport and mass transit. Charge: $40 per connect hour, 10¢ per offline citation.

Weldasearch   The international literature on the joining of metals and plastics is covered, as well as related areas such as metals spraying and thermal cutting. Charge: $75 per connect hour, 20¢ per offline citation.

Materials sciences

METADEX   Comprehensive coverage of international literature on the science and practice of metallurgy. Major categories include materials, processes, properties, products, forms, and influencing factors. Charge: $80 per connect hour, 10¢ per online citation, 15¢ per offline citation.

Non-Ferrous Metals Abstracts   References to literature on all aspects of nonferrous metallurgy and technology. Charge: $45 per connect hour, 10¢ per online citation, 20¢ per offline citation.

Surface Coatings Abstracts   All aspects of paints and surface coatings, including pigments, dyestuffs, resins, solvents, inks, insulations, testing, pollution, industrial hazards, and marketing. Charge: $65 per connect hour, 15¢ per offline citation.

Textile Technology Digest   An online guide to the international literature on textiles and related subjects, including dyeing, mill operation, man-made and natural fibers, marketing, and statistics. Charge: $65 per connect hour, 15¢ per offline citation.

World Aluminum Abstracts   World coverage of the technical literature on aluminum, from ore processing through end uses. Charge: $50 per connect hour, 10¢ per offline citation.

World Textiles   Index on the science and technology of textiles; technical economics, production, and management in the textile industry; and consumption of and international trade in textile materials and processes. This database corresponds to the print journal *World Textile Abstracts*. Charge: $55 per connect hour, 10¢ per offline citation.

Patents and trademarks

CLAIMS/Citation, CLAIMS/CLASS, CLAIMS/U.S. Patent Abstracts, CLAIMS/U.S. Patent Abstracts Weekly, CLAIMS/UNITERM   Files containing citations to U.S. Patent Office records. All patents listed in the general, chemical, electrical, and mechanical sections of the *Official Gazette* of the U.S. Patent Office (1950 to the present) are covered. There is also information on the classification system and citations to other patents. Charge: $98 per connect hour, various fees for online citations, various fees for offline citations.

PATLAW   Records of reported judicial and administrative decisions pertaining to patents, trademarks, copyrights, and unfair competition law. Charge: $120 per connect hour, 70¢ per offline citation.

TRADEMARKSCAN   File of over 600,000 records currently covering all active applications and trademarks registered in the U.S. Patent and Trademark Office. Charge: $85 per connect hour, 20¢ per online citation, 25¢ per offline citation.

Business/economics

ABI/INFORM   A bibliographic database covering literature on many aspects of business management and administration with the emphasis on decision science information applicable to many businesses and industries. It is designed to meet the information needs of executives. Charge: $73 per connect hour, 20¢ per online citation, 30¢ per offline citation.

ADTRACK   Index of all advertisements of one-quarter page or larger appearing in 148 major consumer magazines in the United States. Charge: $95 per connect hour, 25¢ per online citation, 25¢ per offline citation.

Arthur D. Little/Online   Nonexclusive information sources of Arthur D. Little, Inc. (including its divisions and subsidiaries) referenced. Strategic planning, company assessments, and electronics are among the subjects covered. Charge: $90 per connect hour, $100 per online citation including management summary, 20¢ per offline citation.

Commerce Business Daily   The complete text of the printed publication issued every weekday to announce products and services wanted or offered by the U.S. government. Charge: $54 per connect hour, 25¢ per offline citation.

Economic Literature Index   Online index of journal articles and book reviews—260 economics journals and approximately 200 monographs covered annually. Charge: $75 per connect hour, 15¢ per offline citation.

Economics Abstracts International   Coverage of literature from worldwide sources on markets, industries, country-specific economic data, and economic research. Charge: $65 per connect hour, 20¢ offline citation.

FIND/SVP Reports and Studies Index   Index and description of industry and market research reports, studies, and surveys of over 300 U.S. and international publishers. Charge: $65 per connect hour, 25¢ per offline citation.

HARFAX Industry Data Sources   Information on bibliographic sources of financial and marketing data for 65 major industries. Charge: $75 per connect hour, 30¢ per offline citation.

Harvard Business Review Online   The full text of the *Harvard Business Review* since 1977. In the process of being added are citations and abstracts to articles from 1971 through 1976 and to 700 classic earlier articles. Charge: $75 per connect hour, $7.50 per article printed offline, 20¢ per offline citation with abstract.

Insurance Abstracts   Survey of specialized literature on life, property, and liability insurance. Charge: $55 per connect hour, 15¢ per offline citation.

Management Contents   Broad bibliographic coverage of literature from 1974 to the present on business and management, including accounting, advertising, banking, decision science, management and administration, finance, marketing, and personnel. Charge: $80 per connect hour, 20¢ per online citation, 35¢ per offline citation.

PTS Annual Reports Abstracts   Abstracts of annual reports issued by over 3,000 publicly held U.S. corporations and selected international companies. Charge: $114 per connect hour, 58¢ per online citation, 68¢ per offline citation.

PTS F&S Indexes   (F&S for Funk & Scott) Data on company, product, and industry information, both United States and international, with information on mergers, acquisitions, new products, and technological developments. Charge: $95 per connect hour, 20¢ per online citation, 25¢ per offline citation.

PTS PROMT   Abstracts of significant information appearing in thousands of newspapers, business magazines, government reports, trade journals, bank letters, and special reports. Charge: $95 per connect hour, 35¢ per online citation, 40¢ per offline citation.

†Standard & Poor's News Online and News Daily   Extensive information on over 10,000 publicly held corporations. One file is updated daily and contains the most recent five days of news; the other stores information back to 1979. Both financial and general news is included, as are abstracts. Charge: $85 per connect hour, 15¢ per offline citation.

Trade and Industry Index   Index and selective abstracts of business journals relating to trade, industry, and commerce. Charge: $85 per connect hour, 20¢ per offline citation.

Numeric files

BI/DATA Forecasts   Citations of extensive market forecast reports on business activities for 35 countries. Charge: $85 per connect hour, $55 per online citation, $55 per offline citation.

BI/DATA Time Series   Time-series records with a maximum of economic indicators for up to 131 countries. Charge: $85 per connect hour, $1.50 per online citation, $1.50 per offline citation.

BLS Consumer Price Index   Time series of consumer price indices for various U.S. geographic areas and population categories compiled by the Bureau of Labor Statistics. Charge: $45 per connect hour, 50¢ per offline citation.

BLS Employment, Hours, and Earnings   Time series organized by industry on employment, hours of work, and earnings in the United States. Charge: $45 per connect hour, 50¢ per offline citation.

BLS Labor Force   Time series on employment, unemployment, and nonparticipation in the labor force in the United States, classified by a variety of demographic, social, and economic characteristics. Charge: $45 per connect hour, 50¢ per offline citation.

BLS Producer Price Index   Time series of U.S. producer price indexes calculated by the Bureau of Labor Statistics. Charge: $45 per connect hour, 50¢ per offline citation.

Disclosure II   Extracts of reports filed at the Securities and Exchange Commission by publicly owned companies, including 10-K and 10-Q reports. Charge: $60 per connect hour, $6 per online citation, $10 per offline citation.

PTS International Forecasts   Abstracts of published forecasts with historical data for all countries of the world except the United States. Charge: $15 per connect hour, 20¢ per online citation, 25¢ per offline citation.

PTS International Time Series   The same type of information as PTS U.S. Time Series below, except for individual countries other than the U.S. Charge: $95 per connect hour, 35¢ per online citation, 40¢ per offline citation.

PTS U.S. Forecasts   Abstracts of published forecasts for the United States from trade journals and business and financial publications. Also included is information from the Census of Manufacturers. Charge: $95 per connect hour, 20¢ per online citation, 25¢ per offline citation.

PTS U.S. Time Series   Time series (some annual) of historical and projected data. The user can retrieve statistics about production, consumption, price, and usage in the United States for agriculture, mining, manufacturing, and service industries. There are also general economic, demographic, and national income series. Charge: $95 per connect hour, 35¢ per online citation, 40¢ per offline citation.

U.S. Exports   Statistics for exports, both governmental and nongovernmental, of domestic and foreign merchandise from the United States to other countries. Charge: $45 per connect hour, 25¢ per online citation, 25¢ per offline citation.

Business directories

Dun's Market Identifiers   Detailed information on more than 1 million U.S. business establishments having 10 or more employees. Charge: $100 per connect hour, $1.50 per online citation, $1.50 per offline citation.

D&B Principal International Businesses   Directory listings, sales volumes, marketing data, and references to parent companies of over 57,000 non-U.S. companies are available through this file. Charge: $100 per connect hour, $2.00 per online citation, $2.00 per offline citation.

EIS Industrial Plants   Current information on approximately 150,000 establishments operated by 67,000 firms with total annual sales of more than $500,000. Charge: $90 per connect hour, 50¢ per online citation, 50¢ per offline citation.

EIS Nonmanufacturing Establishments   Information on over one-quarter million nonmanufacturing establishments including location, headquarters name, percent of industry sales, industry classification, etc. Charge: $95 per connect hour, 50¢ per online citation, 50¢ per offline citation.

Electronic Yellow Pages   Listings of companies from almost 5,000 telephone books and special directories in the U.S. are compiled into this group of databases. Users can search by company name, business description, SIC code, location, etc. Industry files are available for construction, finance, manufacturers, professionals, retailers, services, and wholesalers. Charge: $60 per connect hour, 20¢ per online citation, 20¢ per offline citation.

Foreign Traders Index   A directory of manufacturers, service organizations, agent representatives, retailers, wholesalers, distributors, and cooperatives in 130 countries outside the United States. Charge: $45 per connect hour, 25¢ per offline citation.

Million Dollar Directory   Comprehensive business information on 121,000 U.S. companies from D&B's three-volume *Million Dollar Directory Series*. Charge: $100 per connect hour, $1.50 per online citation, $1.50 per offline citation.

Trade Opportunities; Trade Opportunities Weekly   Many leads in these two files on export opportunities for U.S. businesses. The information is reported by U.S. Foreign Service officers directly to the Department of Commerce. Charge: $45 per connect hour, 25¢ per offline citation.

Industry-specific

COFFEELINE   All aspects of the production of coffee, from growing coffee through its packaging and marketing. Charge: $65 per connect hour, 20¢ per offline citation.

Law and government

ASI (American Statistics Index)   A comprehensive index, with abstracts, of all statistical publications produced by government agencies. Charge: $90 per connect hour, 25¢ per offline citation.

CIS/Index (Congressional Information Service)   Coverage of the entire spectrum of the U.S. Congress's working papers—hearings, prints, reports, documents, and special publications. Charge: $90 per connect hour, 25¢ per offline citation.

Congressional Record Abstracts   Abstracts of every issue of the Congressional Record. Charge: $75 per connect hour, 15¢ per offline citation.

Criminal Justice Periodical Index   Cover-to-cover index of journals containing information on crime, the justice system, penology, criminal law, and drug abuse. Charge: $55 per connect hour, 15¢ per offline citation.

Federal Index   Coverage of federal actions—such as proposed rules, regulations, bill introductions, speeches, hearings, roll calls, reports, vetoes, court decisions, executive orders, and contract awards. Charge: $90 per connect hour, 20¢ per offline citation.

Federal Register Abstracts   Coverage of federal regulatory agency actions as published in the *Federal Register*. Charge: $75 per connect hour, 20¢ per offline citation.

GPO Monthly Catalog; †GPO Publications Reference File   Index files of documents produced by the executive and legislative branches of the U.S. government that are for sale by the Government Printing Office. Charge: $35 per hour, 10¢ per offline citation.

LABORLAW   Produced by the Bureau of National Affairs, indexes of U.S. federal, state, and administrative agency decisions pertaining to labor relations. Each point of law in a case is described by an attorney/editor in a summarized headnote or abstract. Major subject categories include labor-management relations, labor arbitration, fair employment practices, wages and hours, occupational safety and health, and mine safety and health. Charge: $120 per connect hour, 70¢ per offline citation.

†Legal Resource Index   Cover-to-cover indexing of more than 700 key law journals and 5 law newspapers, in addition to legal monographs and government publications. Charge: $90 per connect hour, 20¢ per offline citation.

National Criminal Justice Reference Service (NCJRS)   All aspects of law enforcement and criminal justice, including police, courts, corrections, juvenile justice, and crime prevention. Charge: $35 per connect hour, 10¢ per online citation, 15¢ per offline citation.

Current affairs

Chronolog Newsletter   The online version of the monthly publication of DIALOG Information Services. Charge: $15 per connect hour, 15¢ per offline citation.

†Magazine Index   Index of about 400 popular magazines, with extensive information on current affairs, performing arts, business, sports, consumer product evaluations, science, technology, and other areas. Charge: $80 per connect hour, 20¢ per offline citation.

†National Newspaper Index   Online index of *The Christian Science Monitor, The New York Times, The Wall Street Journal, The Los Angeles Times,* and *The Washington Post*. Charge: $80 per connect hour, 20¢ per offline citation.

†NEWSEARCH   Indexes on a daily basis of most of the contents of three major newspapers (*The Christian Science Monitor, The New York Times*, and *The Wall Street Journal*), over 370 popular American magazines, 660 law journals, and 6 law newspapers. Charge: $95 per connect hour, 20¢ per offline citation.

PAIS International   References to information in all fields of the social sciences, including political science, banking, public administration, international relations, and public policy. Charge: $60 per connect hour, 10¢ per online citation, 15¢ per offline citation.

UPI News   The full text of news stories carried on the United Press International wire in these categories: domestic general news, columns, standing features, financial news, international news, and commentaries. Charge: $85 per connect hour, 25¢ per offline citation.

World Affairs Report   A digest of worldwide news as seen by Moscow. It provides subject-by-subject and country-by-country analyses of the Soviet attitude toward world developments. Charge: $90 per connect hour, 10¢ per online citation, 20¢ per offline citation.

Directories

American Men and Women of Science   A biographical registry of eminent and active American and Canadian scientists. It corresponds to the book *American Men and Women of Science—Physical and Biological Sciences*. Charge: $95 per connect hour, 40¢ per offline citation.

Biography Master Index   A master index to biographical information found in more than 600 source publications. Charge: $55 per connect hour, 15¢ per offline citation.

Career Placement Registry/Experienced Personnel/Student   Two files with listings of college and university seniors and recent graduates and of experienced persons seeking new employment. The record data includes college, degrees, occupation preferences, geographical preferences and experience. Charge: $50 per connect hour, $1 per online citation, $1.50 per offline citation.

Encyclopedia of Associations   Detailed information on all kinds of associations, including trade, fraternal and patriotic associations, professional societies, and labor unions. Charge: $45 per connect hour, 20¢ per online citation, 25¢ per offline citation.

Marquis Who's Who   Detailed biographies of nearly 75,000 individuals corresponding to the publication *Marquis Who's Who in America*. Charge: $95 per connect hour, 40¢ per online citation, 50¢ per offline citation, $2.50 per record from special reports.

Ulrich's International Periodicals Directory   A file corresponding to the print publication of the same name. It also contains the contents of *Irregular Serials and Annuals*. Charge: $65 per connect hour, 20¢ per offline citation.

Social sciences and humanities

America: History and Life   The full range of U.S. and Canadian history, area studies, and current affairs, including ethnic studies and local and oral history. Charge: $65 per connect hour, 15¢ per offline citation.

ARTbibliographies MODERN   References to literature in books, dissertations, exhibition catalogs, and some 300 periodicals on modern art design. Charge: $60 per connect hour, 15¢ per offline citation.

Child Abuse and Neglect   References to materials on the subject of child abuse and neglect—research project descriptions, bibliographic references, service programs, legal references, and descriptions of audiovisual materials are included. Charge: $35 per connect hour, 10¢ per offline citation.

Family Resources   Coverage of psychosocial literature in the field, including material on marriage, divorce, family relationships, services to families, and education. Charge: $57 per connect hour, 25¢ per online citation, 25¢ per offline citation.

Historical Abstracts   Index of the world's periodical literature on history and related social sciences and humanities. Abstracts are provided. Charge: $65 per connect hour, 15¢ per offline citation.

Information Science Abstracts   Coverage of the literature on information science and related areas, including information storage and retrieval. Charge: $70 per connect hour, 35¢ per offline citation.

Language and Language Behavior Abstracts   Current selective access to the world's literature on language and language behavior. Each record includes an abstract, and over 1,200 journals are scanned. Charge: $55 per connect hour, 15¢ per offline citation.

LISA (Library and Information Science Abstracts)   Comprehensive coverage of all phases of librarianship and of information storage, retrieval, and related areas. Charge: $75 per connect hour, 25¢ per offline citation.

MLA Bibliography   Produced by the Modern Language Association, comprehensive coverage of current scholarship in modern languages and literature. About 3,000 journals and series as well as books and essay collections are included. Charge: $55 per connect hour, 15¢ per offline citation.

Philosopher's Index   Online index to information on philosophy, including such areas as aesthetics, epistemology, ethics, logic, and metaphysics. Charge: $55 per connect hour, 15¢ per offline citation.

Population Bibliography   Citations to information on demography, migration, family planning, fertility studies, population research, and law. Charge: $55 per connect hour, 10¢ per offline citation.

†PsycINFO   Coverage of the world's literature on psychology and related disciplines in the behavioral sciences. Charge: $55 per connect hour, 35¢ per online citation, 20¢ per offline citation.

Religion Index   To be available on DIALOG in 1984, an online index to literature on religion, including church history, biblical literature, theology and history of religions, and current events. Contact DIALOG for price and availability information.

RILM (REPERTOIRE INTERNATIONALE DE LITERATURE MUSICALE) Abstracts   An international database containing abstracts of all significant articles on music in over 300 journals. Charge: $65 per connect hour, 15¢ per offline citation.

Social SCISEARCH   A multidisciplinary database indexing significant items from over 1,000 social science journals throughout the world and from many journals in related scientific fields. Charge: subscribers to print version: $75 per connect hour, 15¢ per offline citation; non-subscribers: $110 per connect hour, 20¢ per offline citation.

Sociological Abstracts   Coverage of the world's literature in sociology and related disciplines in the social and behavioral sciences. Abstracts are provided for post-1973 records. Charge: $55 per connect hour, 15¢ per offline citation.

U.S. Political Science Documents   Indexes and abstracts of articles from the most significant U.S. political science journals in such areas as foreign policy, international relations, public administration, economics, and world politics. Charge: $65 per connect hour, 15¢ per offline citation.

Multidisciplinary

Comprehensive Dissertation Index   A subject, title, and author guide to virtually every dissertation accepted at every accredited American institution since 1861. Charge: $70 per connect hour, 20¢ per offline citation.

Conference Papers Index   Citations of scientific and technical papers presented at nearly 1,000 conferences and meetings around the world. Information on ordering is provided. Charge: $73 per connect hour, 15¢ per online citation, 20¢ per offline citation.

DIALINDEX   A special file on the contents of DIALOG databases. Users can find out the number of postings available on each search statement in a specified database. Charge: $35 per connect hour.

Education

AIM/ARM   A specialized index for locating materials on vocational and technical education. Related areas, such as manpower economics and development, job training, and vocational guidance are also covered. Charge: $25 per connect hour, 10¢ per offline citation.

†ERIC (Educational Resources Information Center)   Produced by the U.S. Department of Education's National Institute of Education, citations of journal articles and research reports in education and related areas. Charge: $25 per connect hour, 10¢ per offline citation.

Exceptional Child Education Resources   Comprehensive coverage of published and unpublished literature on the education of handicapped and gifted children. Charge: $35 per connect hour, 15¢ per offline citation.

IRIS (Instructional Resources Information System)   Abstracts of educational and instructional materials on water quality and water resources. Charge: $35 per connect hour, 10¢ per offline citation.

NICEM   Produced by the National Information Center for Educational Media, lists educational materials in nonprint media from preschool to professional/graduate school levels. Charge: $70 per connect hour, 20¢ per offline citation.

NICSEM/NIMIS   Special education materials for use with handicapped children. Charge: $35 per connect hour, 10¢ per offline citation.

Online training and practice

ONTAP   A set of ten databases that can be accessed at low cost for training and practice on the DIALOG system. Charge: $15 per connect hour.

Bibliographies of books and monographs

Book Review Index   An online guide for locating sources of published reviews of books and periodicals. Charge: $55 per connect hour, 15¢ per offline citation.

†*Books in Print*   The online version of the popular Bowker bibliography. It lists books that are forthcoming, in print, or going out of print, published or distributed in the United States. Only a few categories of books (such as government publications and Bibles) are excluded. Charge: $65 per connect hour, 20¢ per offline citation.

DIALOG Publications   A special-feature database for ordering DIALOG publications online. Charge: $15 per connect hour, 15¢ per offline citation.

LC MARC   Bibliographic records of all books cataloged by the U.S. Library of Congress since 1968. (This date represents English-language books; starting dates for other languages vary from 1973 to 1980). Charge: $45 per connect hour, 10¢ per online citation, 15¢ per offline citation.

REMARC   Records of works not included in the LC MARC database. Five files provide coverage of international scope from before 1900 to 1980. Charge: $85 per connect hour, 25¢ per online citation, 35¢ per offline citation.

Foundations and grants

Foundation Directory   A directory of over 3,500 foundations that have assets of $1 million or more or that make grants of at least $100,000 annually. Charge: $60 per connect hour, 30¢ per offline citation.

Foundation Grants Index   Information on grants awarded by more than 400 major American philanthropic foundations. Charge: $60 per connect hour, 30¢ per citation.

Grants   Information on 2,200 available grants sponsored by a variety of sources. Sponsors include federal, state, and local governments, commercial organizations, associations, and private foundations. Charge: $60 per connect hour, 30¢ per offline citation.

National Foundations   Information on more than 21,000 private foundations in the United States that award grants for charitable purposes. Charge: $60 per connect hour, 30¢ per offline citation.

*Dow Jones News/Retrieval

Dow Jones Information Services, a division of Dow Jones & Company, Inc., P.O. Box 300, Princeton, New Jersey 08540, 609-452-2000

Other offices

Sales offices: Palo Alto (Calif.), Orlando (Fla.), Dallas.
   News bureaus and offices are located throughout the United States.

Hours of operation

6:00 A.M. to 4:00 A.M. EST, seven days a week.

Customer assistance

Dow Jones News/Retrieval maintains customer support from 8:00 A.M. to 11:00 P.M. EST, Monday through Friday, and 9:00 A.M. to 5:00 P.M. on Saturdays. Over 25 customer-support representatives answer questions about database use, registration procedures, pricing, and applications. Representatives can be reached at 800-257-5114. In New Jersey, the telephone number is 609-452-1511.

Position in database industry

With over 100,000 customers in September 1983, Dow Jones News/Retrieval has more users than any other service. The firm is a rapidly growing information service, and it is predicted that it will have over a quarter-million users within two years. Competitors actively trying to overtake Dow Jones include CompuServe, I. P. Sharp, DIALOG, and Mead.

News/Retrieval offers 20 databases in four categories: business and economic news, financial and investment services, Dow Jones Quotes (including current and historical quotes), and general news and information services.

Typical users include corporate executives, financial and investment experts, information specialists, investors, and students. News/Retrieval is especially strong at providing up-to-date and historical information on companies, industries, and markets. The service draws on the experience and resources of Dow Jones and Company, Inc., publishers of *The Wall Street Journal, Barron's National Business and Financial Weekly*, and the Dow Jones News Service, or "Ticker."

Company background

Dow Jones Information Services is the wholly owned subsidiary of Dow Jones and Company, Inc., a $730-million provider of business information. Dow Jones and Company maintains a news service with bureau offices in nearly 100 cities around the world. *Barron's* maintains offices in 8 American cities, while AP-Dow Jones News Service has joint offices in 12 cities, most in Western Europe.

Dow Jones publishes *The Wall Street Journal* and *Barron's Weekly*. It uses a sophisticated satellite and communications network to publish the *Journal* at 17 printing plants throughout the United States. The company was the first private company licensed by the FCC to own and operate satellite earth stations. It used this technological expertise to begin its interactive News/Retrieval Service in 1974.

Today, News/Retrieval has 180 employees.

Computer facilities

Dow Jones News/Retrieval runs on four IBM 4341 machines with 16 megabytes online storage capacity. The system uses IBM's CICS, DOS/USE, TSO, and MVS software.

Summary of database services

There is a single level of access, with all users being able to access the same databases. The system offers menu- and command-driven formats. Boolean searching can be used with the Free-Text Search database. The rudimentary commands can be learned in a few hours.

Information in News/Retrieval is provided only in display form. There are no graphics or SDI capabilities. Users can access Comp-U-Store, an online shop-at-home service offering a wide range of consumer goods.

Telecommunications access

Dow Jones is accessible through Telenet, Tymnet, Uninet, and Datapac at 300 and 1200 baud. It also has its own packet-switched network available in Princeton called DowNet. Plans call for further expansion.

Hardware and software requirements

The service can be accessed on virtually any communicating computer, terminal, or word processor. Dow Jones offers special software packages for Apple and IBM personal computers to help analyze market information, do fundamental portfolio analysis, and assist with portfolio management. The packages will soon be available on other selected systems.

Fee structure and sign-up

New users can subscribe either by purchasing a software package at a computer store or by calling Dow Jones directly. The starter package, Dow Jones Connector, contains a directory of symbols and a user agreement. It retails for $49.95 and entitles the user to one free hour of unrestricted searching.

Standard fees for accessing databases vary according to the database and time of day. Prime time, 6:00 A.M. Eastern Standard Time to 6:00 P.M. local user time, varies from $72 per hour to $36 per hour. Most business databases are $72 per hour. Dow Jones Quotes is $54 per hour. Offpeak charges vary from $54 per hour for most non-Dow Jones business databases, to $36 per hour for Free-Text Search, to $9 per hour for Dow Jones Quotes. Rates are doubled for 1200 baud instead of 300 baud.

There are two discount plans available. Under Blue Chip membership, users pay $100 per year on top of initial fees and receive a $33\frac{1}{3}$ percent discount on nonprime services. Under the Executive membership, users pay $50 per month and receive $33\frac{1}{3}$ percent savings during both prime and nonprime hours. Under both the Blue Chip and Executive plans, subscribers receive a guaranteed minimum of six free hours of use each year on new databases. Prices for 1200-baud transmission are two times the standard rate.

Monthly invoices for usage are sent to subscribers. The invoices for Blue Chip or Executive plans offer one-half hour free time on a specified database.

Offline printing and remote capabilities

Not applicable.

Documentation available

Most databases on the News/Retrieval Service have "help" functions that provide instant information on how to access and use particular databases. Subscribers are given the *Dow Jones News/Retrieval Fact Finder* free. This provides directions on how to access the services and a list of all stock, bond, treasury note, and mutual fund symbols. Users also receive supplements free of charge.

An online newsletter, *INTRO*, is free and explains changes in the system. This includes changes in the telecommunications network and reports on new databases. *INTRO* also offers application ideas for new users, new information on Dow Jones software, and a list of dealers and their locations.

Finally, subscribers receive *Dowline*, a monthly magazine.

Customer training

Dow Jones does not offer classes. Most people find News/Retrieval easy to use and do not require formal training.

Document retrieval

Not applicable.

Other services

Dow Jones does not perform custom searches or do consulting. Online purchase of consumer goods is available through Comp-U-Store.

Public database offerings

Note: Executive plan offers one-third savings at all times. Blue Chip offers one-third savings during off-peak hours. These discounts apply to the rates given below.

Dow Jones News   Full text or summarized coverage of *The Wall Street Journal, Barron's,* and the Dow Jones News Service with stories as recent as 90 seconds to as far back as 90 days. Searchable by stock symbol or category code. Charge: $72 per hour peak, $12 per hour off-peak.

Wall Street Journal Highlights Online   Headlines and summaries of major stories from *The Wall Street Journal,* including front-page news items, front- and back-page features, market pages, editorial columns, and commentary. Highlights are online as early as 6:00 A.M. EST. Charge: $72 per hour peak, $12 per hour off-peak.

Free-Text Search   Full-text database covering *The Wall Street Journal, Barron's,* and Dow Jones News Service with records back to June 1979. This database is searchable using any combination of words, dates, or numbers. Charge: $72 per hour peak, $36 per hour off-peak.

Forbes Directory   Rankings of the largest U.S. corporations by sales, profits, assets, and market value, plus profitability and growth rankings for 46 industries. Charge: $72 per hour peak, $54 per hour off-peak.

Dow Jones Quotes—Current Quotes   Current quotes with a 15-minute delay during market hours of common and preferred stocks, bonds, mutual funds, U.S. Treasury issues, and options for major American exchanges. Charge: $54 per hour peak, $9 per hour off-peak.

Dow Jones Quotes—Historical Quotes   Daily volume, high, low, and close prices for the past year accessible by date. There are quarterly summaries back to 1978 and monthly summaries to 1979. Charge: $54 per hour peak, $9 per hour off-peak.

Dow Jones Quotes—Historical Dow Jones Averages   Historical coverage for the industrials, transportation, utilities, and 65 stock composites. Charge: $54 per hour peak, $9 per hour off-peak.

Weekly Economic Update   Reviews of the week's top economic events and a glimpse of the month ahead. Charge: $72 per hour peak, $12 per hour off-peak.

Financial Earnings Estimator   Produced by Zacks Investment Research, Inc., earnings forecasts for 3,000 of the most followed companies based on research of top analysts at more than 60 major brokerage firms. Charge: $72 per hour peak, $54 per hour off-peak.

Disclosure II   Produced by Disclosure, Inc., 10-K, 10-Q, and 8-K Securities and Exchange Commission filings, proxy statements, and registration statements on over 9,000 publicly held companies. Charge: $72 per hour peak, $54 per hour off-peak.

Media General Financial Services   Detailed corporate financial information on 3,150 companies and 170 industries. Charge: $72 per hour peak, $54 per hour off-peak.

Weekly Economic Survey   Produced by Money Market Services, Inc., forecasts of monetary and economic indicators by economic analysts at 40 to 50 leading financial institutions. Charge: $72 per hour peak, $12 per hour off-peak.

Academic American Encyclopedia   From Grolier publishers, over 30,000 carefully researched, concise articles. The database is revised and updated twice a year. Charge: $36 per hour peak, $18 per hour off-peak.

News/Retrieval World Report   Foreign and national news from the United Press International wire, updated throughout the day in an easy-to-use electronic package. The text is edited by Dow Jones to ensure a concise, readable format. Charge: $36 per hour peak, $18 per hour off-peak.

News/Retrieval Sports Report   Scores, statistics, standings, stories, and schedules for most major sports, continuously updated seven days a week. Charge: $36 per hour peak, $18 per hour off-peak.

News/Retrieval Weather Report   Two-day forecasts from UPI, updated twice daily for more than 50 major cities. There is also a monthly weather planner with 30-day forecasts. Charge: $36 per hour peak, $18 per hour off-peak.

Cineman Movie Reviews   Produced by Cineman Syndicate, concise reviews of the latest releases as well as reviews of thousands of films dating back to the 1930s. Charge: $36 per hour peak, $18 per hour off-peak.

Wall $treet Week Online   The full-text transcript of the four most recent programs from the popular PBS television series "Wall $treet Week." Charge: $36 per hour peak, $18 per hour off-peak.

Comp-U-Store   An electronic shopping service of Comp-U-Card, Inc. Users can choose from over 50,000 discounted brand-name products ranging from appliances to sporting goods. Charge: $36 per hour peak, $18 per hour off-peak.

News/Retrieval Symbols Directory   A list of more than 15,000 symbols used to access News/Retrieval, including stocks, corporate and foreign bonds, Treasury issues, mutual funds, options, category codes, and Media General industry groups. Charge: $36 per hour peak, $18 per hour off-peak.

*Info Globe

Info Globe, the Online Division of *The Globe and Mail*, 444 Front St. West, Toronto, Ontario, Canada M5V 2S9, 416-585-5250

From Area Code	Number
416	800-387-2600
613, 519, 705	800-387-2610
819, 418, 514	800-387-2620
807, 506, 902, 403, 204, 306, 709, 604	800-387-2630

Other offices

Sales offices in Canada: Calgary, Ottawa.

Hours of operation

6:00 A.M. to 4:00 A.M. EST.

Customer assistance

Customer service is available by calling the Toronto office from 9:00 A.M. to 5:00 P.M. EST. Local representatives in Calgary and Ottawa can also handle customer-service calls.

Position in database industry

Info Globe offers the full text of the Canadian national newspaper *The Globe and Mail* to over 2,000 subscribers. Its typical client is a librarian or information specialist in business or government; a growing percentage of new customers, however, are general business managers or people at home. Approximately 10 percent of its clients are based in the United States.

One of the database's strengths is the fact that the newspaper is available online, in full text and fully enhanced, by 6:00 A.M. on the date of publication.

The company also produces MARKETSCAN, a database of stock price data from three Canadian and two major U.S. exchanges.

Company background

Info Globe is a division of the Canadian paper *The Globe and Mail*, based in Toronto. A national edition is published via satellite in Vancouver, Calgary, Ottawa, and Moncton (New Brunswick).

Info Globe was founded in 1979 to market the online and microfilm edition of the newspaper. It currently employs 17 people.

Until 1983, Info Globe was marketed in the United States by The New York Times Information Service, which was marketed, in turn, by Info Globe in

Canada. Since Mead Data Central became the sole marketer of NYTIS, Info Globe has marketed its own services in the United States.

Computer facilities

Presently Info Globe is using computers at Canada Systems Group (CSG), the largest computer service bureau in Canada. CSG has a mix of Amdahl and IBM equipment. Info Globe's storage capacity is over 2 billion characters, with about 1 million characters added each day.

Summary of database services

Info Globe produces two databases, The Globe and Mail and MARKETSCAN. The Globe and Mail contains material from every story that has appeared in its parent newspaper of the same name since November 14, 1977, and in the *Report on Business* (Canada's only daily business publication) since January 1, 1978. MARKETSCAN contains stock quotations from the Toronto, Montreal, Vancouver, Alberta, New York, and American stock exchanges for the past 250 trading days.

Information is accessed in MARKETSCAN by stock symbol. The Globe and Mail database is searched using free text, although users can specify controlled vocabulary terms, type of material, and dates in order to enhance their searches. Searches are entered using Boolean logic, although clients may request menu-driven accounts that employ stored and programmable searches. These allow the client to have fixed elements in search strategy and to perform his search by being prompted to "fill in the blanks."

Telecommunications access

Access is by Datapac in Canada and Telenet or Tymnet in the United States.

Hardware and software requirements

Any ASCII terminal, personal computer, or communicating word processor can be used for access to Info Globe at 300 or 1200 baud.

Fee structure and sign-up

(All figures are in Canadian dollars.)

With MARKETSCAN, the customer pays a $50 sign-up fee and receives a manual, password, and free half-hour in the first month of use. Online time is billed at $2 per connect minute from 8:00 A.M. to 8:00 P.M. EST, and 50¢ per minute from 8:00 P.M. to 8:00 A.M. EST. There is also a charge of 1¢ per line of data (for example, to go back 35 days on a stock quotation would cost 35¢ plus online time).

There is no sign-up fee for The Globe and Mail. Online time is billed at $159 per hour at any time. The user's manual costs $30. There is an online training database available that costs $1 per minute.

There are no minimum monthly charges for either database, and all prices include telecommunications (Datapac, Telenet, or Tymnet).

Offline printing and remote capabilities

Offline prints are available from the Toronto and Calgary offices. Most printing is done in Toronto using a high-quality laser printer. Copies are dispatched to customers the next business day and are often received by Toronto customers by noon. Printing performed in Calgary is on an upper-case-only impact printer.

Documentation available

Info Globe provides user's manuals to customers upon registration for either The Globe and Mail (at a fee) or MARKETSCAN.

A bimonthly newsletter, *Info Globe News*, is mailed free of charge to all subscribers.

Customer training

Training sessions are offered across Canada and in the eastern U.S. A one-day introductory session costs $60 per person, and a half-day advanced session costs $40. A special training database is available at a reduced rate.

Document retrieval

Not applicable.

Other services

Custom searching is available from the Toronto office. In addition to charges for connect time and offline prints, there is a $90 per hour consulting fee (minimum $25).

Public database offerings

The Globe and Mail Full-text coverage of *The Globe and Mail*, Canada's leading newspaper. Coverage is from November 14, 1977, to date. The database is updated daily, and the day's edition is online by 6:00 A.M.

MARKETSCAN Daily information on stocks listed on the Montreal, Toronto, Alberta, Vancouver, New York, and American stock exchanges. Coverage includes daily volume, highs, lows, and closing prices. Coverage is available for the latest 250 days of trading and may be extended if there is sufficient demand.

InnerLine

InnerLine, joint venture of the Bank Administration Institute and the American Banker, 60 Gould Center, Rolling Meadows, Illinois 60008, 312-228-6200, 800-323-1321 (except Illinois), 800-942-8861 (Illinois only)

Other offices

Not applicable.

Hours of operation

24 hours a day, seven days a week.

Customer assistance

The customer-service office is open 9:30 A.M. to 5:45 P.M. EST, Monday through Friday, at the toll-free numbers above. The office provides general, technical, training, and billing information.

Position in database industry

InnerLine is the first computer-based management-support system designed specifically to serve professionals in the financial services industry. Eighty percent of the current users based at over 1,000 institutions hold the title of vice president or above. The system provides access to more than 40 different services, including the American Banker news service, weekly updates of money market deposit instrument rates, 62 statistical ratios on any bank in the country, and Frost & Sullivan's Political Risk Newsletter. Electronic mail and an information exchange enable subscribers to send and receive messages throughout the United States and around the world.

InnerLine's products are divided into five key product groupings: funds management, electronic consulting, electronic scanning, electronic communications, and franchised services.

InnerLine was named the 1983 Product of the Year by Associated Information Managers on the basis of "innovation and creativity, user acceptance, market penetration, and achievement of state of the art of the information business."

Company background

In 1981 the Bank Administration Institute began InnerLine as a pilot project. In February 1983, BAI and the American Banker joined forces to establish InnerLine as a partnership venture. The firm has developed into a commercial venture serving more than 1,000 financial institutions nationwide.

Computer facilities

Information not available at time of publication.

Summary of database services

InnerLine offers a wide range of services, ranging from traditional databases to enhanced electronic mail. Databases concentrate on information for the banking, financial, and accounting industry. The system is menu-driven and easy to use; new users generally require less than an hour to become proficient.

The company will perform SDIs on the American Banker and send results to the user's electronic mailbox. The charge is 20¢ per clipping order per day.

Other services include private files for customers to be used in conjunction with electronic mail; an Information Exchange, where interested users can exchange ideas electronically through electronic mail; and the ability to order Bank Administration Institute publications or register for BAI courses online.

Telecommunications access

The system is accessible on Telenet at 300 or 1200 baud.

Hardware and software requirements

InnerLine is accessible from any dial-up terminal.

Fee structure and sign-up

A subscriber signs up by calling the appropriate toll-free number or by mailing in a subscription order form. A personalized code word is then assigned and log-on instructions forwarded to the subscriber.

The cost for InnerLine is $20 per month, plus $36 per hour prime time (7:00 A.M. to 9:00 P.M. EST, Monday through Friday) or $24 per hour at all other times. These fees include telecommunications. Some databases have royalties, which are additional. There is no differential charge for 1200 baud.

Offline printing and remote capabilities

Not applicable.

Documentation available

Documentation published by InnerLine includes: *InnerLine Newsletter*, published monthly; *New Service Announcements; Information Kit*, sent to prospective subscribers; *Subscriber Start-up Kit*, giving log-on instructions and more detailed information.

Customer training

The *Subscriber Start-up Kit* instructs users on how to log on to the system. The customer-service office also provides assistance. Seminars are being planned.

Document retrieval

Not applicable.

Other services

Customized private communications networks for groups of users are available on InnerLine. Electronic mail is available at the standard costs of 60¢ per minute or 40¢ per minute off-peak, with no storage charges. Users can order Bank Administration Institute publications and register for BAI courses online.

Public database offerings

Standard charges are $36 per hour prime time and $24 per hour nonprime.

American Banker News Service   The full text, including headlines, commentary, and analyses, from the banking industry's only daily newspaper, *American Banker*. The latest six issues are stored. Service providers are American Banker, Bond Buyer, and Munifacts.

Nationwide Funds Marketplace   The first system of its kind that enables banks to electronically "shop for funds." A bank can enter its funds trading position—how much it wants to buy or sell and at what rate and maturity. Instruments include Fed Funds; Jumbo CDs (including issuer input, rate guidelines and rate ranges), provided by CDx, a service of Harvey Baskin & Co., Washington, D.C.; GNMAs (Government National Mortgage Association instruments) and FNMAs (Federal National Mortgage Association instruments), provided by Bond Buyer, New York; and expanded rate information, such as foreign exchange, money funds and commodities. Charge: $200 per month.

Money Market Monitor   Weekly updates of money market deposit instrument rates reported and analyzed nationally and by region. Service provider is Whittle Raddon Motley & Hanks. Surcharge: $7.50 per access.

Disclosure   Complete financial, historical, and analytical information on 8,500 publicly held corporations. This is considered a useful tool for developing prospects. Service provider is Disclosure. Charge: reports, $1.50 to $4.00 each; the online charge, $60 per hour.

Index of Bank Performance   62 statistical ratios on any bank in the country, a service that can help users compare their bank's performance against any individual or group of banks. Service provider is the Bank Administration Institute. Charge: $10 to $75 per report.

Prime Rate Service   Prime and broker prime lending rates. Banks involved in loan participation programs are invited to join the special network, which provides current and the past three primes (with effective dates) of all banks using the service. Service providers are the loan departments of the nation's top 200 banks.

Federal Reserve Services and Pricing   Current listing of check and noncheck services and pricing offered by the Federal Reserve System and detailed by its districts. Service provider is Littlewood Shain & Co.

REGSNOW   Up-to-the-minute news of bank regulations in ten different categories. The database enables subscribers to call up complete regulations as well as expert interpretations. Service providers are the United Bank of Denver and the Bank Administration Institute.

CITIBASE Economic Series   A series of 35 tables of macroeconomic data of special interest to bankers. Service provider is CITIBASE, a service of the Economics Department of Citibank, NA. Charge: $1.50 per table.

Frost & Sullivan's Political Risk Newsletter   Updates on financial risks to foreign businesses arising from political factors in 70 countries. Risk ratings are provided for six factors: export, regime stability, finance, manufacturing/extractive, social turmoil, and five-year forecast. Provider is Frost & Sullivan, New York.

Information Exchange A method for peers to exchange information. Exchanges in the areas of microcomputers, tax, accounting, and audit are currently in operation. Service providers are Arthur Young & Co., Bank Administration Institute, Ernst & Whinney, and Microbanker Inc.

Financial Hedge Management Service Technical analysis, monthly calendars detailing economic projections, and key financial futures trading dates, and Consultant's Market Comments (updated three times daily). The service allows portfolio managers and investors the opportunity to review hourly updates of future prices for T-bills, rates, bonds, GNMAs, CDs, and Eurodollars. Provider is Powers Research, Inc.

ITT Dialcom

ITT Dialcom, Inc., 1109 Spring St., Silver Spring, Maryland 20910, 301-588-1572

Other offices

U.S. sales offices: Commercial—Boston, Des Plaines (Ill.), Houston, Los Angeles, New York City, Silver Spring (Md.); Federal marketing—Washington, D.C.

International licensees: Amsterdam—Netherlands Standard Electric; Hong Kong—Cable and Wireless; London—British Telecom Gold; San Juan—All America Cable and Radio; Sydney (Austl.)—Overseas Telecommunications Commission; Toronto—Canadian National/Canadian Pacific; Vienna—Radio Austria.

Hours of operation

24 hours a day, seven days a week.

Customer assistance

Assistance is provided by more than 30 marketing support representatives in Dialcom's sales offices. Both telephone and onsite assistance is available. On-site assistance is on a per diem basis. The range of services includes training, technical support, troubleshooting, and programming. Normal support hours are 9:00 A.M. to 5:00 P.M. EST, Monday through Friday. Limited support is available 24 hours a day through Dialcom's operations center (301-588-1572).

Position in database industry

ITT Dialcom offers a range of online communications services and information databases for business. It is one of the largest providers of electronic mail.

Databases available contain information on travel, current news, industry/management articles, and stock market activity. Many of Dialcom's databases interface with its electronic mail, allowing the user to distribute information from the databases to other users in a timely, efficient manner.

Dialcom also provides gateways from its system to other commercial databases, such as Dow Jones News/Retrieval and DIALOG. This allows users who have subscriptions to other services to move quickly back and forth between different services to gather information.

Dialcom's largest market is in electronic mail. Typical customers include large corporations with hundreds or thousands of users. Dialcom continues to develop its interconnected "global mail" network through licensees in nine major countries in Europe and the Far East. Currently there are over 50,000 Dialcom electronic mail users.

Another large customer of Dialcom is the U.S. government. Nearly one-half of the House of Representatives uses its services.

Dialcom will continue to expand its marketing and support facilities both domestically and internationally. Additional general business- and industry-specific databases are currently being developed.

Company background

In 1970, Dialcom was founded as a private time-sharing company. In late 1982, it was acquired by ITT Corp. as part of that company's move into the "high-tech" online industry. Dialcom's electronic mail and information services form the hub of ITT's product offering to the office automation market.

The company started out as a simple time sharer, without its own products. It worked closely with The Source, which operated on Dialcom computers from its inception until 1982, when it initiated its own computer operations.

Over time, Dialcom began to develop online products that it marketed directly. In 1979, its electronic mail system went online. Currently, there are three online forms of electronic mail: bidirectional electronic mail, telex/electronic mail interface, and electronic mail via word processors. Dialcom also offers computer conferencing, electronic publishing, an executive calendar scheduler, a text editor, and several online databases.

Computer facilities

Dialcom has 5 Prime 850, 16 Prime 750, 2 Prime 550, and 3 Prime 250 computers at four sites: Silver Spring (Md.), London, Toronto, and Hong Kong. More computer facilities are planned in Whippany (N.J.), San Juan, and Singapore. The Dialcom system can handle over 2,500 simultaneous users. Total storage capacity is currently over 17,000 megabytes. The system runs on a PRIMOS operating system.

Summary of database services

Dialcom is a command-driven service. Its gateways can be used by subscribers to other services, such as DIALOG and BRS, to access those services. Information can be stored in private files on Dialcom's systems and disseminated via the company's electronic mail.

Dialcom's database offerings are in the fields of news (sources range from popular national wires to specialized news services), electronic publications, and travel. Some of the services are open only to subscribers. One database, Travelscan, allows subscribers not only to plan trips but also to make reservations online.

Telecommunications access

Access is via Telenet, Tymnet, and Uninet. There is direct dial-in service in Washington, D.C., and New York City. Service is available at 300 and 1200 baud.

Hardware and software requirements

Dialcom is accessible from any dial-up terminal.

Fee structure and sign-up

There is a $100 minimum monthly charge. Connect charges depend on the time of day and amount of use. During prime hours of 8:00 A.M. to 6:00 P.M., Monday through Friday, the charges are $16.50 per hour for the first 250 hours, $15.50 per hour for the next 250 hours, and $14.50 per hour after that. Nonprime-time hours are billed at a flat $12.50 per hour. Telecommunications is included. There is no surcharge for general 1200 baud service, although there is a surcharge for 1200 service for some databases. In addition, there are storage charges for private files and surcharges for various databases. Discounts are available for volume users of more than $15,000 per month.

Offline printing and remote capabilities

Dialcom offers letter-quality and laser printing of personalized letters and envelopes on a batch service basis for mass mailings. Offline storage of mailing lists is available. Normal processing for printing takes three days. Prices depend on volume, beginning at 15¢ per page for letter quality and 10¢ per page for laser printing.

Documentation available

Each of Dialcom's core products is documented with a separate user's manual. In some cases, both beginners' level and advanced manuals are available.

Dialcom provides each client company's system manager (client's employee who supervises the system's use internally) with a manual containing maintenance and management information.

Each product has a detailed online description that functions as a user guide. Additional assistance is usually available by typing HELP or ?.

Customer training

New customers' system managers are given a two-week training course on Dialcom products and system maintenance. These individuals, in turn, are responsible for training other users in their organization.

Customers can also phone marketing sales representatives with their questions.

Document retrieval

Not applicable.

Other services

Dialcom can furnish custom software development. High-volume users can lease or purchase hardware and Dialcom software.

Dialcom electronic mail service links with private files and databases. The firm is currently testing computer conferencing through software developed by Participation Systems, Inc.

Other services allow users to store mailing lists online and produce mass mailings. Dialcom also offers software for electronic publishing and scheduling.

Public database offerings

Dialcom offers a gateway link to any public database. A separate account is usually necessary to take advantage of this. Information from these sources can then be loaded into Dialcom's electronic mail system for further distribution.

In addition, Dialcom is planning to bring online The PAC Directory, a database that tracks contributions by political action committees to state and federal election candidates.

The surcharges noted for the databases below are in addition to connect charges.

United Press International (UPI)   Over 70 specific news wires (national, regional/state, business, sports) with current news, available at the same time as the standard UPI teletype. Data is available for up to seven days. The database is key-word searchable. Surcharge: $11 per hour.

Los Angeles Times/Washington Post   Stories prepared by the writers of the *Los Angeles Times* and *Washington Post* newspaper syndicates. This includes both "hard" news and feature stories and is key-word searchable.

Other electronic news services   OPEC (oil-related), the International Medical Tribune Syndicate, the West German Deutsche Presse Agentur, and the U.S. Department of Agriculture have electronic news databases that are available through Dialcom. Some of these databases are key-word searchable.

Official Airline Guide   Over 70,000 domestic and international airline flight schedule listings. The OAG database displays flight options to and from a particular city. Fares (domestic flights only), type of aircraft, and meal information are included. Connecting flight information is also available. Surcharge: $9 per hour prime and $6 per hour nonprime; 30¢ prime or 20¢ nonprime for schedules; 45¢ prime or 30¢ nonprime for fares and rules.

Travelscan   An interactive database containing over 10,000 pages of information on airline schedules (using OAG), hotels, rental cars, cruises, entertainment, and tours. Covering more than 150 cities, Travelscan provides full descriptions and rate data for domestic and international travelers. Direct bookings can be made through the database for any of the transportation and accommodation listings. The Compute-A-Trip feature allows the user to plan a trip instantly according to personal specifications. This database also features electronic mail to and from Travelscan and its affiliated travel agents.

Bureau of National Affairs   Access to this product only by a separate BNA account. Current publications covered include *Daily Tax Advance* and *Labor Advance*. Other BNA publications used intensively by attorneys, accountants, and business executives are scheduled to be added in the future.

Journal of Commerce

The Journal of Commerce, Trade Information Services, a division of Knight-Ridder Newspapers, Inc., 110 Wall St., New York, New York 10005, 212-425-1616

Other offices

Not applicable.

Hours of operation

24 hours a day, Monday through Friday.

Customer assistance

Users may call in for customer assistance from 8:00 A.M. to 6:00 P.M. EST, Monday through Friday at 212-425-1616. Everything from general inquiries to complex programming and execution of requests is handled by the customer-service department. On request, service representatives visit clients throughout the United States and overseas.

Position in database industry

The Journal of Commerce offers databases that focus on foreign trade. These databases are factual and contain numeric information gathered from shipping documents and other maritime records. The information they provide is generally not available on any other database.

Typical customers are large exporters, importers, shipping companies, freight forwarders, and banks. More than 200 customers currently use the company's online services, while 500 purchase offline custom reports containing information from the databases.

Annual revenues have grown from $1 million in 1980, when the service began, to $5 million. This includes revenues from the Import Bulletin, Export Bulletin, and all offline customized report services.

A database of shipping tariffs called R.A.T.E.S. (Rapid Access Tariff Expediting Service) is being developed for introduction in 1984 (export freight tariff edition) and in 1985 (import tariff edition).

Company background

The Journal of Commerce is a division of Knight-Ridder Newspapers, Inc., a $1.3 billion news and information company. Knight-Ridder owns over 30 daily newspapers, including the *Miami Herald*, the *Detroit Free Press*, the *Philadelphia Inquirer*, and the *Philadelphia Daily News*. Other operations include ten additional suburban newspapers, cable TV operations, and four television stations. Knight-Ridder is actively exploring videotex opportunities.

The Journal of Commerce is a business daily that has reported on import and export activity for almost 160 years. It is widely acknowledged as a leading source of information in the fields of trade and transportation.

The Journal of Commerce division began offering P.I.E.R.S. (Port Import/Export Reporting Service), its first online database, in July 1980. A staff of 120 field personnel collects and compiles daily the shipping records data used in the database and *The Journal of Commerce*; 40 other employees code, edit, and check the information; and 12 employees work in marketing and customer service.

Computer facilities

The Journal of Commerce databases run on Tandem Non-Stop II computers. The P.I.E.R.S. database alone contains 5 million shipping records of approximately 205 bytes each. Present configuration consists of 66 drives, each with a capacity of 360 megabytes. More than 100 users can be accommodated simultaneously.

Tandem's ENFORM and custom (Cobol-based) P.I.E.R.S. software constitute the software operations system.

Summary of database services

The Journal of Commerce produces two databases: P.I.E.R.S. (Port Import/Export Reporting Service) and R.A.T.E.S. (Rapid Access Tariff Expediting Service). P.I.E.R.S. has been online since 1980; R.A.T.E.S. will be released in 1984 (export freight tariff version) and 1985 (import tariff version).

The information in P.I.E.R.S., gathered from documents submitted by steamship companies to the U.S. Customs Service, lists shipments departing or arriving at major U.S. ports. It contains numeric values for quantities and pounds and various alphabetic and coded fields. These fields indicate product, exporter or consignee, carrier, port of origin, and port of entry.

P.I.E.R.S. is command-driven, and the company estimates that one to two weeks of use are necessary to achieve proficiency on the system. The P.I.E.R.S. user can take advantage of the system's special software to generate standard or custom reports. Clients may design their own formats for producing reports or may choose an "auto command" feature to produce reports in any of the ten most popular P.I.E.R.S. formats. Searches and formats can be stored for future use.

Customers need not be online subscribers to have access to P.I.E.R.S. information. Many customers purchase customized, printed reports based on the database information. The R.A.T.E.S. database, now in the pilot stage and being readied for release in 1984 and 1985, is menu-driven and "user-friendly." It contains the full text of ocean tariffs filed with the U.S. Federal Maritime Commission as well as up-to-date ship sailing schedules.

Telecommunications access

The firm's two databases can be accessed through Telenet or Uninet. Service is available at 300 or 1200 baud with no difference in price. There is no direct-dial access.

Hardware and software requirements

The company's databases are accessible from any dial-up terminal.

Fee structure and sign-up

Fees are either on a per record or unlimited-use basis. For unlimited use of P.I.E.R.S., there is a minimum charge of $1,000 per month and a six-month minimum subscription period. Users purchase unlimited use by segments of the database, which is broken down by commodity group, trade route, and shipper or consignee location. Segmented prices are as follows:

1. Commodities—These are divided into 10 groups, available for $550 per commodity group per month. Users may access a maximum of two commodity groups. If more information is required, customers must use one of the next two options.
2. Trade routes—These are shipping routes between the four major U.S. shipping regions and eight foreign regions. Trade is separated into 32 trade routes. Users may sign up for either the import or the export section of a trade route or for both. Costs of segments vary from $475 to $1,705 per month. Subscribers can select segments covering all shipments to or from a particular region or covering all shipments to or from all U.S. ports. The cost is $7,000 per month for either an export or import segment.
3. Shipper or consignee locations—These are divided into seven regions covering the United States. Monthly costs for a region vary from $600 a month for New England to $1,185 for the Pacific region. This covers all commodities at all ports shipped to or from all consignees or shippers in a region.

An hour of telecommunications is provided for each $28 paid in subscription fees; additional hours are billed at $15 each. Billing is monthly.

Under the per record billing service, there is a $250 monthly service charge, which includes ten hours of telecommunications. Additional telecommunications are billed at $15 per hour. Under this plan, users are billed for the number of records used in producing their reports.

Charges for records used are the first 1 to 10,000—5¢ each; next 10,000 to 30,000—3¢ each; over 30,000—2¢ each.

As an example, information on all chemical imports for 1982 totals 96,000 records. There are approximately 50 records covering copper sulfate, 100 covering iodine, and 500 covering MSG. An inquiry covering a year's MSG imports would cost a maximum of $25. But figures on imports to the Far East for one month (all cargoes) would consume 50,000 records and cost $1,500.

Reports generated by subscribers and printed by the Journal are billed at 10¢ per page including delivery by UPS. Printing is done on a good-quality dot matrix printer.

Offline printing and remote capabilities

Not applicable.

Documentation available

A complete set of user manuals, code schedules, and indexes is provided free to the customer. Update bulletins are sent biweekly.

Customer training

Training sessions lasting two days are held regularly in New York City and San Francisco. They are free of charge. Training may be conducted at the user's site with expenses billed as incurred. User manuals, code schedules, and indexes are provided free at sessions.

All customers attend at least one training session, and many return for additional sessions.

Other services

The Journal of Commerce offers a custom report service, which currently has 500 customers. Costs are based on programming and data fees and vary by type of request.

Public database offerings

P.I.E.R.S. Information directly from shipping records and other documents submitted by steamship companies to the U.S. Customs Service. It is a computational database that lists shipments departing or arriving at major U.S. ports coast to coast. Information is updated weekly, and it remains online for 16 months before being downloaded to tape storage. Approximately 100,000 shipping records are added per week.

R.A.T.E.S. Full service on this database to be offered in 1984 (for export freight tariffs) and in 1985 (for import freight tariffs). The database contains the full text of ocean tariffs filed with the U.S. Federal Maritime Commission. R.A.T.E.S. also contains updated ship sailing schedules based on extensive Journal of Commerce shipcards. It is updated daily.

Mead Data Central

Mead Data Central, a division of The Mead Corp., 9333 Springboro Pike, P.O. Box 933, Dayton, Ohio 45401, 513-865-6800, 800-227-9597

Other offices

California—Century City, Los Angeles (regional office), San Francisco (regional office); Colorado—Denver; Washington, D.C. (regional office); Florida—Miami; Georgia—Atlanta; Illinois—Chicago (regional office); Louisiana—New Orleans; Massachusetts—Boston; Michigan—Detroit; Minnesota—Minneapolis; New York—New York (regional office); Ohio—Cincinnati (regional office), Cleveland; Pennsylvania—Philadelphia, Pittsburgh; Texas—Dallas, Houston (regional office)

Hours of operation

Monday through Friday, 3:00 A.M. to 2:00 A.M. EST; Saturday and Sunday, 7:30 A.M. to 10:00 P.M. EST.

Customer assistance

Customer assistance is available 365 days per year at 800-543-6862 (in Ohio, 800-762-6626). In addition, staff at local and regional offices can help customers solve specific problems.

Position in database industry

Mead Data Central's clients include lawyers, businessmen, and librarians. Its services are divided between LEXIS, which provides legal information, and NEXIS, which contains databases of general business and news information. Each requires separate sign-up forms and passwords. Charges are separate for each service.

Mead Data Central has been a leader in bringing full-text databases to a wide range of fields. Both of its services concentrate on full-text access to written documents. LEXIS was the first database service to provide the full text of legal decisions. (West Publishing has since followed with a similar service.) LEXIS now covers many other subjects of interest to the legal profession, including patents, statutes, regulations, administrative rulings, and the like.

NEXIS was the pioneer of online services that provide the full text of general news and business publications. Today other services, such as Dow Jones News/Retrieval and NewsNet, offer more limited full-text databases to a similar market. Mead also competes for the same market as some bibliographic services. Other databases cover the same sources as Mead but lack full text.

Full-text databases tend to give many "false drops" when free-text searching; that is, they identify articles that contain a search term, but the term is peripheral to the article. Mead has tried to minimize some of these problems by allowing users to scan the words around the search term.

Mead has been a leader in providing relatively easy-to-use systems. Traditionally, it has done this by requiring users to use Mead-supplied, dedicated terminals that have special search function keys. While a dedicated terminal facilitates searching, it has its drawbacks. In recent years, as other vendors grew in prominence, Mead was criticized by users who complained that they had to acquire another terminal to search these other services.

As a short-term solution, Mead opened an electronic gateway to the Lockheed DIALOG service in 1982. This enabled Mead customers to search this other major vendor right from its dedicated terminals. Finally, in June 1983, Mead announced a dramatic two-pronged departure from its dedicated terminal strategy. It has developed a "smart" terminal that allows access to databases of other vendors. Mead has also signed agreements with IBM and TeleVideo allowing certain equipment from these manufacturers to be used for searching NEXIS and LEXIS. Negotiations with additional vendors continue. At present most personal and home computers cannot be used to access Mead Data Central.

Mead maintains a system of leased lines, which it calls MeadNet. This is a high-quality 1200 baud system that cuts down on transmission errors and delays.

Company background

In 1968, the Ohio Bar Association contracted with OBAR, a legal research service, to computerize Ohio case law records. OBAR was acquired by The Mead Corp. in 1970 and became Mead Data Central. The Mead Corporation is a Fortune 500 forest products and electronic publishing company.

In 1972, Mead Data Central introduced its first custom terminal and printer. In 1973, the LEXIS database was announced, along with a private database service for the American Institute of Certified Public Accountants. Beginning with its introduction in 1973, LEXIS has been the recipient of ongoing and considerable investments as special databases were developed to address the needs of the various legal specialties.

Mead established a private telecommunications network in 1974 and a litigation support service in 1975. Then, in 1980, the NEXIS family of databases was introduced, offering full-text information aimed at the business community. In the same year, a large new computer center was opened in Dayton, Ohio. Division headquarters moved from New York to Dayton in 1982. Three separate sales forces were combined into a single team.

Recently, Mead has developed a new UBIQ II terminal. Agreements opening Mead's information services to IBM and TeleVideo equipment have been reached. In 1983, Mead became the sole marketer of The New York Times Co. databases.

Today Mead Data Central is one of the largest online database vendors in the world. It has over 850 employees and expects sales of well over $100 million in 1984.

Computer facilities

Attached to two Amdahl 5860 computers are 220 disk drives with 58 billion characters online. By the end of 1983, Mead Data Central expected to have 68 billion characters online, an increase of 55.9 percent over the 38 billion characters online at the beginning of the year. The 220 disk drives have a storage capacity of 107 billion characters. The capacity of the computer center was increased in 1983; today the center utilizes computers capable of processing 26 million instructions per second, more than double the previous year's capacity. This upgrade has positioned the division for the high growth expected.

Mead Data Central maintains a computer-tape library of over 25,000 tapes containing more than 1 trillion characters. Duplicate tapes are located at two remote locations to ensure data security and backup. When there is a power fluctuation or loss of power, a bank of 192 batteries ensures uninterrupted service. They are typically needed for only ten seconds, until backup diesel generators start, producing approximately 2 million watts, or enough power to support many small cities.

Summary of database services

All Mead databases are relatively easy to use, with simple English instructions instituted through a special keyboard. It takes less than a half-day to become quite proficient. Both NEXIS and LEXIS are menu-driven but use Boolean searching. Both display the full text of information, in most cases.

The emphasis at Mead is on full-text services, though a few databases such as Infobank and Advertising and Marketing Intelligence are bibliographic. Full-text databases do not have controlled vocabularies, and thus they may be less effective in some cases than bibliographic databases with controlled vocabularies.

Mead databases are alphanumeric. There is no graphics capacity or SDI service. Databases must be searched separately, though search requests can be stored and reused during the same session.

Mead produces and manages both public and private databases for customers.

In a rapidly changing industry, Mead Data Central has been able to commit large sums of money to develop new services and products. It has been, and should continue to be, an innovator, stressing the marketing of information products to end users.

Telecommunications access

Mead Data Central's telecommunications network, MeadNet, contains over 100,000 miles of leased high-speed circuits. It uses 11 network processors and provides local communications service to over 70 cities. The network uses the X.25 packet-switched protocol and supports terminals operating at 1,200 bits per second. MeadNet is also used to support access by non-Mead terminals, and it has the ability to interconnect with other telecommunications networks such as Telenet.

Hardware and software requirements

The primary terminal used with Mead services is its UBIQ dedicated terminal, which includes a built-in, intelligent modem. The UBIQ was designed with function keys to make it as easy as possible for people not familiar with computers to use Mead services. A new UBIQ IIe was announced in June 1983. This machine retains function keys and modem, but it has an automatic dialer and is capable of accessing other databases.

In the fall of 1983, Mead allowed some IBM and TeleVideo 950 machines to access NEXIS and LEXIS. The IBM equipment involved is the PC, the Displaywriter, and the 3101 terminal. These machines use MeadNet and have designated function keys to allow easy access to LEXIS and NEXIS. Mead will expand the list of accepted terminals (which must operate at 1200 baud) in the future.

Fee structure and sign-up

Mead fee schedules are complex. They include charges for installation, rental of equipment, instruction, and use, as well as monthly charges. Installation charges on terminals range from $200 to $400. There is also a $100 to $250 charge to move equipment.

LEXIS and NEXIS charges are not identical. For instance, LEXIS users are charged monthly rental fees on terminals and printers, while NEXIS users pay rentals only on printers.

Use charges for both LEXIS and NEXIS for peak time (7:30 A.M. to 7:30 P.M. local time) are:

Monthly Use	Charge per Hour
First 5 hours (0-5)	$90
Next 5 hours (6-10)	75
Next 30 hours (11-40)	60
Next 60 hours (41-100)	45
Over 100 hours (101+)	30

Off-peak charges are $45 per hour or the peak connect rate, whichever is less.

LEXIS pricing also calls for a charge of $100 per professional at the first location and reduced rates at additional locations. Instruction on LEXIS costs $75 per professional, to a maximum of $2,250; instruction on NEXIS is free.

On both systems there is a search surcharge of 45¢ per search unit. This is defined as each 25,000 times a search word shows up in the database being searched. A maximum of seven search units may be charged for any single search.

Like the fee schedules, Mead's contracts are lengthy and confusing. The company's marketing representatives are knowledgeable and helpful, however.

Offline printing and remote capabilities

Mead Data Central has high-quality, offline/remote text printing. The turnaround time is immediate in-house and overnight from Dayton. Customer service can provide samples.

Offline printing is available at ½¢ to 1¢ per line depending upon volume. Online printing is available.

Documentation available

Free user guides are available. *LEXIS Brief* is a newsletter sent to all LEXIS subscribers. *NEXIS News* is a newsletter for NEXIS customers.

Customer training

Customer training for beginners on LEXIS and NEXIS is offered at Mead's regional offices. Call these offices directly for information about locations and dates. NEXIS classes are free to customers; LEXIS classes cost $75 per professional.

Document retrieval

Not applicable.

Other services

The organization's Private Libaries Service enables the customer to maintain a secure, private document retrieval system. Currently, over 2 billion characters are stored in these private libraries. Customers include "Big 8" accounting firms and Fortune 100 companies.

Public database offerings

LEXIS services

LEXIS   Produced by Mead, the basic LEXIS library of selected statutes and regulations, including full-text coverage of federal cases and case law of all 50 states, the United Kingdom, and France. Among the specialized law libraries in the LEXIS family of databases are tax, securities, trade regulation, bankruptcy, patent, trademark and copyright, communications, labor, public contracts, and Delaware corporations law.

LEXPAT   Produced by Mead, the full text of every patent issued by the U.S. Patent and Trademark Office since 1975. The LEXPAT library also contains the Master Classification File.

American Bar Association   Full-text coverage of the Code of Professional Responsibility and Judicial Conduct, formal and informal opinions of the Commission on Ethics and Professional Responsibility, and the Constitution and bylaws of the House of Delegates of the American Bar Association.

Auto-Cite   Produced by The Lawyers Co-Operative Publishing Company. It verifies the accuracy of virtually any case law citation by providing the names of parties, date, parallel citations, legal histories, and titles of ALR and L. Ed. annotations.

Shepard's Citations   Produced by Shepard's Division of McGraw-Hill, citations to all federal, state, and regional case law. Case history, parallel citations, and a statement of the subsequent history of the case are given.

Matthew Bender   The full text of Matthew Bender publications that deal with legal issues.

NEXIS services

NEXIS   Produced by Mead, the basic NEXIS library of the full text of more than 12 newspapers, 60-plus magazines and newsletters, and 9 wire services. Coverage, depending on the publication, goes as far back as January 1975.

Forensic Services Directory   Produced by The National Forensic Center, listings of forensic experts, litigation consultants, and legal support specialists.

Infobank   Produced by the New York Times Company, the full text and abstracts of *The New York Times* as well as bibliographic coverage of over 60 newspapers and magazines.

Advertising and Marketing Intelligence   Produced by the New York Times Company in conjunction with the J. Walter Thompson Company, bibliographic references to over 60 newspapers, newsletters, and magazines aimed at the advertising and public relations industry.

Deadline Data on World Affairs   Reports on economic and political conditions, including background information on current political leadership, for numerous countries, states, and provinces.

National Automated Accounting Research System   Produced by the American Institute of Certified Public Accountants (AICPA), authoritative accounting materials. These include statements of auditing standards and industry accounting guides issued by the AICPA, the Securities and Exchange Commission, and the Financial Accounting Standards Board (FASB) and selected annual reports and extracts of proxy statements of corporations listed on the New York and American Stock Exchanges.

Encyclopedia Britannica   Produced by Encyclopedia Britannica, Inc., the full text of *Britannica 3,* including the 10-volume Micropedia and 19-volume Macropedia, plus annual yearbooks. Users cannot print out the full text, only words in context or references. This service is only available to users with Mead terminals. It is not available to academic or public libraries.

*NewsNet

NewsNet, Inc., 945 Haverford Rd., Bryn Mawr, Pennsylvania 19010, 215-527-8030, 800-345-1301

Other offices

New York City, 212-505-8924.

Hours of operation

24 hours a day, 365 days a year.

Customer assistance

Customer service is available Monday through Friday from 9:00 A.M. to 8:00 P.M. EST. Between one and four staff members are on hand to answer questions concerning logging on, terminal compatibility and software, NewsNet features search strategy, and billing.

NewsNet users may also contact customer service online via electronic mail without charge.

Position in database industry

NewsNet distributes information produced by more than 80 independent publishers by providing online access to the full text of more than 165 specialized business newsletters plus PR Newswire and UPI News.

Users generally do not have to subscribe to the printed version of a newsletter to read the online edition. With a few exceptions, NewsNet has royalty arrangements with newsletter publishers that permit all NewsNet users to read the newsletters of their choice. In most cases, print subscribers get a reduced rate.

Information is often available on NewsNet before it is available in print. Most publishers use word processors to transmit their text to NewsNet at the same time they create the final copy for their print editions, and NewsNet can make the text publicly available as early as one hour after transmission by the publisher.

NewsNet's database covers nearly 35 industries, and coverage in each industry is expanding rapidly. The following are particularly well covered:

- Telecommunications
- Publishing and broadcasting
- Electronics and computers
- Taxation
- Farming and food
- Public relations
- Energy
- Investment
- Finance and accounting

Back issues are available for many newsletter titles since January 1982. The latest issues are often online days, even weeks, before they appear in print.

At present, NewsNet has no direct online competitors. Fewer than 10 percent of its products are offered by other online information services. The information in NewsNet costs about $200 per newsletter, annually, in print subscriptions.

NewsNet is designed for easy use by business professionals with no previous computer or information retrieval experience. Most accounts are paid for by the user's company. Typical customers include top executives in small companies, middle- to upper-level management in Fortune 500 corporations, and online information specialists in Fortune 500 companies.

Company background

NewsNet is a wholly owned subsidiary of Independent Publications, Inc., a privately held company. The parent company is the former owner of *The Philadelphia Bulletin* and currently publishes 20 daily and weekly suburban newspapers throughout the United States. Other IPI operating subsidiaries include the Qualified Lead System (QLS), the McLean Investment Company, Independence Communications–Muzak, and the East Valley Ranch Company.

NewsNet began commerical operation in April 1982 with 14 newsletters online. It has 15 employees, and as of October 1983, 2,000 users and 165 newsletters online. Gross revenues are not disclosed.

Computer facilities

NewsNet is currently supported by three Prime 750 super-minicomputers with 12 megabytes of main memory and 4,000 megabytes of disk storage. The operating system is PRIMOS. Newsletter delivery, storage, retrieval, and billing software are owned entirely by NewsNet, which also supplies computer time-sharing services to its sister company, the Qualified Lead System.

Summary of database services

Users of NewsNet can do more than just read or print the entire contents of a newsletter. Among the options are scanning headlines, searching one to three newsletters (or categories of newsletters) by key word, reviewing an index of services that is cross-referenced by industry, using the electronic mail feature, or requesting help at any stage of the process.

NewsNet customers either go directly to a newsletter using a simple command with the publication code, or display detailed menus. Key-word searches may include multiple terms that can be linked by the Boolean operators AND or OR. The two operators, however, may not be mixed in one search. Two levels of help are available at any time. Brief help is triggered by touching the "return" key in reply to any prompt; detailed help is triggered by typing the word **HELP** in reply to any prompt. The prompts and commands are simple to learn; most users can become proficient in less than one hour.

NewsNet does not support graphics display, except those that can be represented with standard ASCII characters. Although some NewsNet databases include numeric information (tables and charts), the information can only be displayed, not manipulated by special programs.

NewsFlash, NewsNet's electronic clipping service, is designed to update users automatically and continuously on any topic they specify. There is no extra charge (aside from connect time) for this special service. Each user can define up to ten words or phases for continuous and automatic searching. Once the profile has been established, NewsNet searches all database updates for matches. When matches are found, the headlines are stored. The user automatically sees the matching headlines at the next sign-on. Each headline is numbered, and the user may retrieve the full text of any story or stories by number.

Telecommunications access

NewsNet is accessible at either 300 or 1200 baud in the United States through Uninet, Tymnet, and Telenet. International access assistance is available upon request.

The customer may also dial directly. A toll-free number is not available for direct dial, however.

Hardware and software requirements

One can access NewsNet by any standard ASCII microcomputer, terminal, or word processor, providing that it is properly equipped to communicate through the public telephone network.

NewsNet rents terminals to users in the United States if needed. These terminals allow one-button automatic dialing and log-on but are otherwise not customized. Monthly rental costs are between $39 and $78, depending on configuration.

Custom telecommunications software for microcomputers is not offered. However, independently authored software is available and has been tested for use with NewsNet. Suggestions will be supplied upon request.

Fee structure and sign-up

To sign up for NewsNet, the user must complete a subscriber agreement. No initiation fee is charged.

NewsNet charges for connect time in one-minute increments. The basic hourly charge, which includes searching, headline scans, mail, and other basic NewsNet services, is as follows: Monday through Friday, 8:00 A.M. to 8:00 P.M. EST, $24 for 300 baud and $48 for 1200 baud. All other times, $18 for 300 baud and $36 for 1200 baud.

In addition, premium charges apply to the time spent reading the text of most newsletters. These premiums vary by title and are subject to change at any time. The rates depend on whether the user is a subscriber to the print version. Nonvalidated NewsNet users (those who don't subscribe to the print edition) pay additional charges to read text, while most validated users do not. The validation process is part of the subscriber agreement and can be updated at any time.

Offline printing and remote capabilities

Not applicable.

Documentation available

Various printed materials are given to subscribers. These include the *News-Net System Overview, ABCs of NewsFlash, Guide to News on NewsNet*, log-on procedures, sample searches, and a list of network phone numbers for the user's local telephone area.

NewsNet mails its subscribers *The NewsNet Action Letter* monthly. This features updates on newsletters and services and provides searching tips. *NewsNet's Online Bulletin*, an online bulletin service available to users, is constantly updated with notifications of new or discontinued services, price changes, and new software features and enhancements.

Customer training

NewsNet does not offer formal user training. Its system is designed for ease of use so that users can effectively train themselves. Call-in assistance is available.

If a company with ten or more NewsNet users requests on-site group training, NewsNet's customer service or sales staff can usually accommodate the request. There is no charge for such training, and it is designed to meet the specific needs of the group.

Document retrieval

Since NewsNet offers full-text retrieval, all documents are retrieved by the user while online. If documents are needed that are not online, the user may send an electronic message to request them from the appropriate publisher.

Other services

NewsNet does not offer custom off-line searching of its databases on behalf of customers.

It currently offers electronic mail as follows:

- ◆ User to publisher
- ◆ User to NewsNet
- ◆ Publisher to user
- ◆ NewsNet to user

Public database offerings

The electronic editions in the table that follows are available on NewsNet. The publications and "text-reading" premiums (above the basic rate) are given. Validated subscribers (those who subscribe to the print editions) pay the VAL premium (if any) to read text. Nonvalidated subscribers pay the NONVAL rate to read text. Premiums are hourly at 300 baud; 1200-baud premiums are double the rates below. TBD means prices are still to be determined at publication time.

Service	VAL	NONVAL
Access Reports/Freedom of Information	$ 0	$ 24
Advanced Office Concepts	12	36
Africa News	0	12
Agricultural Research Review	0	0
Agri-Markets Data Service	0	96
Air/Water Pollution Report	0	24
Altman & Weil Report to Legal Management	0	12
The American Banker	TBD	
Annex Computer Report	48	96
Bank Network News	0	48

Service	VAL	NONVAL
Banking Regulator	0	72
Behavior Today	12	24
Biotechnology Investment Opportunities	TBD	
The Business Computer	24	24
Cable Hotline	TBD	
CableNews	0	24
Campus Exchange	TBD	
CCH State Tax Review	24	96
CCH Tax Day—A Digest of Federal Taxes	24	96
Cellular Radio News	0	24
Charitable Giving	0	0
ChurchNews International	0	72
Communications & Distributed Resources Report	0	24
Communications Daily	12	36
The Computer Cookbook	TBD	
The Computer Cookbook Update	TBD	
Computer Farming Newsletter	0	0
Computer Market Observer	0	24
Confidential Kick-Off	48	48
Construction Computer Applications NL	0	12
Contacts Daily Report	TBD	
Contacts Weekly	TBD	
Corporate Acquisitions and Dispositions	24	XX
The Corporate Shareholder	0	24
Credit Union Regulator	0	72
Crittenden Bulletin	24	48
Crittenden Report	24	48
Daily Industrial Index Analyzer	24	24
Daily Metals Report	48	48
Daily Petro Futures	24	24
DataCable News	0	0
Data Channels	0	24
DBS News	0	24
Defense Industry Report	36	48
Defense R&D Update	36	48
Diack Newsletter	TBD	
Editors Only	24	72
Electric Vehicle Progress	0	24
Employee Retirement Plans	24	XX
Energies, Trends, Cycles	24	48
Energy & Minerals Resources	0	24
Entrepreneurial Manager's Newsletter	0	12
Executive Investing	TBD	
Executive Productivity	0	12
The Exporter	0	24
F&S Political Risk Letter	0	72
Farm Exports	TBD	
Farm Software Developments	0	0
The Fearless Taster	0	0
Federal Research Report	0	24
Federal Reserve Week	0	36

Service	VAL	NONVAL
Fedwatch	TBD	
Fiber/Laser News	0	24
Fiber Optics & Communications Newsletter	0	12
Fiber Optics & Communications Weekly News	0	24
Financial Management Advisor	0	12
Fintex All-Day Foreign Exchange Monitor	120	120
Fintex All-Day U.S. Money Market Monitor	TBD	
Fintex International Economic Summaries	TBD	
Ford Investment Review	0	12
Fraud and Theft Newsletter	TBD	
The Gold Sheet	0	0
The Gold Sheet Technical Report	0	0
Grants & Contracts Alert	0	XX
Grants & Contracts Weekly	0	XX
Hazardous Waste News	0	36
Health Benefit Cost Containment Newsletter	12	12
Hi Tech Patents: Data Communications	0	12
Hi Tech Patents: Fiber Optics Technology	0	12
Hi Tech Patents: Laser Technology	0	12
Hi Tech Patents: Telephony	0	12
Hollywood Hotline	0	0
Home Computer News	0	24
Howard Ruff's Financial Survival Report	TBD	
IBM Watch	TBD	
IIA Friday Memo	0	24
Insight: Monthly Economic Report	TBD	
Interactive Video Technology	0	12
International Intertrade Index	0	12
International Petroleum Finance	TBD	
International SOS Newsletter	12	24
IRS Practices & Procedures	24	96
Ken Winslow's Videoplay Report	TBD	
LAN	0	24
Land Use Planning Report	0	24
Latin American Energy Report	0	48
Legislative Intelligence Week	0	12
Link News Briefs	0	96
Low-Priced Stock Alert	12	12
Management Contents Preview	TBD	
Market Consensus Alert	12	12
Market Digest	TBD	
Marriage and Divorce Today	12	24
Media Science Reports	0	12
Medical Abstracts Newsletter	TBD	
Micro Moonlighter	12	24
Mini/Micro Bulletin	0	24
Modem Notes	TBD	
NA Hotline	0	24
NewsNet Action Newsletter	0	0
NewsNet's Online Bulletin	0	0

Service	VAL	NONVAL
Nuclear Waste News	0	36
Office Automation Update	0	12
On-Line Computer Telephone Directory	0	0
Online Database Report	0	96
PACs & Lobbies	0	24
Penny Stock Preview	12	12
Personal Computers Today	0	24
Petroleum Information International	0	36
The Photoletter	0	96
PR Newswire	0	0
Public Broadcasting Report	0	24
RadioNews	0	24
Real Estate Investing Letter	0	24
Remnant Review	TBD	
Research Monitor News	0	24
RFC News Service	0	36
RIA Executive Alert	TBD	
Robotronics Age Newsletter	24	24
Runzheimer on Automotive Alternatives	0	24
Satellite News	0	24
Satellite News Bulletin Service	0	XX
Satellite Week	0	24
Sexuality Today	12	24
The Seybold Report on Office Systems	0	12
The Seybold Report on Professional Computing	0	12
The Seybold Report on Publishing Systems	0	12
S. Klein Newsletter on Computer Graphics	0	24
Sludge Newsletter	0	36
The Small Business Tax Review	TBD	
SMR News	0	24
Solar Energy Intelligence Report	0	24
Source	0	12
The Stanger Report	TBD	
Stock Advisors' Alert	12	12
Tax Notes International	0	0
Tax Notes Today	0	12
Tax Shelter Insider	12	24
Telecommunications Counselor	0	12
Telephone Angles	0	12
Telephone Bypass News	0	0
Telephone News	0	24
Telepoints	12	24
Television Digest	0	24
Toxic Materials News	0	36
Trade Media News	TBD	
Travelwriter Marketletter	0	12
Trude Latimer's Stock Traders' Hotline	TBD	
two/sixteen Magazine	0	12
UNIQUE: Your Independent UNIX/C Advisor	0	12
United Methodist Information	0	0

Service	VAL	NONVAL
Update/The American States	24	36
UPI	12	12
U.S. Census Report	0	36
VideoNews	0	24
Video Week	0	24
Viewdata/Videotex Report	0	96
Viewtext	0	24
Wall Street Monitor: Weekly Market Digest	48	48
Washington Credit Letter	0	36
Weekly Marketeer	TBD	
The Weekly Regulatory Monitor	0	24
Wiley Book News	0	0
World Environment Report	0	12
Worldwide Videotex Update	0	12

*Pergamon-InfoLine

Pergamon International Information Corporation (a sister company of Pergamon Press Ltd.), 1340 Old Chain Bridge Rd., McLean, Virginia 22101, 703-442-0900, 800-336-7575

Other offices

British headquarters for Pergamon-InfoLine Ltd.: 12 Vandy St., London EC2A 2DE, England, 01-377-4650.

Canadian headquarters for Pergamon Press Ltd.: Pergamon Press Canada Ltd., 150 Consumers Rd., Suite 104, Willowdale, Ontario, Canada M2J 1P9, 416-497-8337.

Hours of operation

3:00 A.M. to 9:00 P.M. EST, 7 days a week.

Customer assistance

Customer assistance on database use and hardware problems is available 8:30 A.M. to 5:30 P.M. local time, Monday through Friday, at 800-336-7575. In London, the telephone number is 01-247-5917.

Position in database industry

Pergamon-InfoLine offers 17 bibliographic databases concentrating on patent, chemical, and applied technology information. Some databases—such as PATSEARCH, which covers U.S. patents—originated with Pergamon, while others have been acquired.

One unique feature of Pergamon is VIDEO PATSEARCH, which allows patent searchers to retrieve and display drawings from the front pages of patent documents through the use of a videodisk player.

Pergamon's typical customers are large corporations or librarians with a frequent need for technical information. Its major competitors are BRS, DIALOG, SDC, and Mead.

Company background

Pergamon International Information Corporation markets in the United States for Pergamon-InfoLine Ltd., a British database vendor. Pergamon-InfoLine is owned by Pergamon Press Ltd., a major international publisher of books and journals. InfoLine was established in the United States in 1983.

Pergamon is moving quickly to supply an increasing number of databases aimed at patent, chemical, and applied technology information users.

The company owns one of the largest U.S. document retrieval and information research firms, Information on Demand of Berkeley, California.

Computer facilities

Pergamon uses a VAX II-780 computer.

Summary of database services

Currently 17 bibliographic databases are offered. These are concentrated in the following areas: patents (United States and worldwide), chemistry, sciences, technologies, specific industries, and major British companies. Many have abstracts.

VIDEO PATSEARCH allows users with microcomputers and a video disk to access the PATSEARCH database of patent information and to display diagrams corresponding to the file records.

The Pergamon system is command-driven. Experienced database searchers can gain proficiency on the system through reading the documentation and practicing, while newcomers should probably attend a one-day class given by the company.

All Pergamon databases have SDI capability, which usually costs $4 per search. Private files are available to European customers.

Telecommunications access

Pergamon-InfoLine is accessible at 300 and 1200 baud via Tymnet, Telenet, and Uninet in the United States and Euronet in Europe. A dedicated line was introduced in fall of 1983 for U.S. users.

Hardware and software requirements

Most terminals can access InfoLine. In addition, most personal computers, microcomputers, and word processors with modems and appropriate software can be used.

Fee structure and sign-up

Users sign up for InfoLine by filling out an order form; there is no sign-up charge. They receive back a user name, password, and self-instruction manual. Pergamon charges a $10 minimum per month that the service is actually used.

Fees for databases are from $50 to $120 per hour. Telecommunications is billed at $10 per hour from the United States. Offline prints are additional (fees vary).

SDI service costs $6 per update on PATSEARCH and INPADOC and $4 on other databases (offline print charges are additional).

Offline printing and remote capabilities

Offline prints are available at fees ranging from 10¢ to 35¢ per citation for most databases. Prints are produced in London and take about two weeks to arrive in the United States. The company expects to begin producing prints in New York in early 1984 and to thereby shorten delivery time.

Documentation available

New users receive the *InfoLine Brief Guide* free (extra copies, $6). The *InfoLine User Guide*, which includes a System Reference chapter and chapters on each database, costs $50. The System Reference chapter is available separately for $10 and each database chapter for $8.

Pergamon distributes a monthly newsletter, *Update*, that is free to each customer.

Customer training

Pergamon recommends that new users attend a one-day InfoLine System Seminar, which costs $40. Three or four seminars per month are scheduled in the United States and Canada. Experienced searchers will probably be able to gain proficiency on a self-taught basis, using the documentation.

InfoLine Subject Seminars offer in-depth information on searching in the fields of patents, chemicals and applied technology. These half-day seminars cost $30 and are held throughout the United States and Canada. Check with Pergamon for dates and locations of all courses.

In-house training for companies can be arranged.

Document retrieval

The Pergamon Search Center provides copies of patents. U.S. patents cost $3 each for regular service and $7 for rush service (shipment within 24 hours). Foreign patents cost $10 each for regular service and $14 rush. These charges are for up to 10 pages; additional pages are 75¢ each.

Other documents can be retrieved through Information on Demand, a Pergamon company.

Other services

Pergamon's Patent Search Center performs custom patent and database searches for clients. Cost depends upon the type of information being searched.

Public database offerings

CA Search   Produced by the Chemical Abstracts Service, citations to documents on chemistry, biochemistry, chemical engineering, and related technologies. Sources consist of over 14,000 journals, patent specifications from 26 countries, books, conference proceedings, technical reports, reviews, and dissertations. Charge: $65 per connect hour, 15¢ per online display, 25¢ per offline print.

Chemical Engineering Abstracts   Produced by The Royal Society of Chemistry, bibliographic records with abstracts for theoretical and practical material on all aspects of chemical engineering. It is produced from 105 of the world's major chemical- and process-engineering journals. Charge: $70 per connect hour, 30¢ per offline print.

COMPENDEX   Produced by Engineering Information Inc., a bibliographic database with abstracts covering all areas of engineering, technology, and applied science: research, development, testing, design, systems engineering, construction, maintenance, production, sales, marketing, consulting, education, etc. Records cover 3,000 professional and trade journals, conference papers, reports, and technical papers from 50 countries. Charge: $90 per connect hour, 25¢ per online display, 35¢ per offline print.

Dun & Bradstreet's Key British Enterprises   Directory of the top 20,000 companies in Britain as determined by annual sales. Its company profiles include company address and telephone, names of directors, parent company, trade names, area of trade, annual sales, export sales, geographic markets, number of employees, and SIC codes and headings. The database is updated monthly and corresponds to a print directory of the same name. Charge: $90 per connect hour, 15¢ to $3.60 per online display depending on format of information desired.

Electronic Publishing Abstracts   Coverage of scientific, technical, and commercial literature on electronic publishing and information technology. Charge: $70 per connect hour, 15¢ per offline print.

Fine Chemicals Directory   Produced by Fraser Williams (Scientific Systems) Ltd., a catalog of commercially available research chemicals and names of suppliers. FCD covers over 50,000 compounds, including organics, inorganics, biochemicals, dyes, and stains. Charge: $70 per connect hour, $4 per compound for special tabular display showing suppliers—includes offline print.

Geomechanics Abstracts   Bibliographic database with abstracts containing references to literature on rock mechanics, soil mechanics, and engineering geology. It is owned by Pergamon Press Ltd. Charge: $70 per connect hour, 15¢ per offline prints.

INPADOC   Produced by the International Patent Documentation Center in Austria, bibliographic database of patent documents issued by 51 national and regional patent offices. Most coverage begins in 1973, with some major offices from 1968. Charge: $120 per connect hour, 25¢ per offline print, $6 for SDI.

Management and Marketing Abstracts   Produced by PIRA, bibliographic references with abstracts to articles of interest to management and marketing executives. Theoretical and practical areas are covered based on source material from over 100 internationally renowned journals. Charge: $70 per connect hour, 15¢ per offline print.

Mass Spectrometry Bulletin   Produced by The Royal Society of Chemistry, bibliographic references to documents on mass spectrometry and allied subjects. Over 400 primary journals, abstracting journals, reports, books, and conference proceedings are sources. Charge: $70 per connect hour, 15¢ per offline print.

PAKLEGIS   Information on national, international, and European Economic Community legislation affecting the packaging industry. Associated regulatory documents are also included. The United Kingdom, Ireland, and Belgium are currently covered; the United States, Austria, France, West Germany, the Netherlands, and Scandinavia are expected to be added. A subscription is required. Charge: $70 per connect hour, 15¢ per offline print.

PATCLASS   Produced by Pergamon International Information Corp., classification codes assigned to all U.S. patent documents since 1740. Charge: $80 per connect hour, 15¢ per offline print.

PATLAW   Produced by the U.S. Bureau of National Affairs, citations, headnotes, and other bibliographic material for judicial and administrative decisions involving patents, trademarks, copyrights, or unfair competition. It is based on information from the *United States Patents Quarterly*. Charge: $115 per connect hour, 15¢ per offline print.

PATSEARCH   The full text of the front pages of U.S. utility patents filed after January 1971. There is also coverage of reissues (since July 1975), defense publications (since December 1976); design patents (since January 1977); and all patent applications published by the World Intellectual Property Organization. This database is produced by Pergamon International Information Corp. Charge: $80 per connect hour, 20¢ per online display with abstract, 40¢ per offline print, $6 for SDI.

PIRA   Produced by the Research Association for the Paper and Board, Printing and Packaging Industries. It contains bibliographic references with abstracts to the scientific and technical literature on these industries. The database contains roughly 70,000 records from 1975 to date. Charge: $70 per connect hour, 15¢ per offline print.

RAPRA (Rubber and Plastics Abstracts)   Produced by the Rubber and Plastics Research Association of Great Britain, bibliographic citations with abstracts to the world's commercial and technical literature on polymer materials, processing, and products. Charge: $80 per connect hour, 15¢ per offline print.

World Textiles   Produced by Shirley Institute, bibliographic database with descriptors covering published literature on textiles and the textile industry. Areas covered include economics, production, and management; science and technology; consumption; international trade plus related materials and industries. Sources are over 500 international periodicals and U.S. and U.K. patents. Charge: $50 per connect hour, 10¢ per offline print.

Zinc, Lead, and Cadmium Abstracts   Produced by the Zinc Development Association, bibliographic database with abstracts covering all aspects of the production, properties and use of zinc, lead and cadmium. The database corresponds to the three print publications. Sources consist mainly of journal, patent, conference, and report literature. Charge: $65 per connect hour, 15¢ per offline print.

The following databases are scheduled to be added in the near future: Current Technology Index, Directory of Companies (U.K.), Laboratory Hazards Bulletin, Oceanographic Literature, and World Surface Coating Abstracts.

Questel

Questel, a division of Telesystems, 40 rue de Cherche-Midi, 75006 Paris, France, 01-544-3813

U.S. address: Questel, Inc., Suite 818, 1625 I St., N.W., Washington, D.C. 20006, 202-296-1604, 800-424-9600

Other offices

Informatech, Inc., Montreal, Canada (sales and customer support); Maruzen Co. Ltd., Tokyo, Japan (sales and customer support).

Hours of operation

24 hours a day, seven days a week.

Customer assistance

Questel, Inc., provides customer support and training for users in the United States. Technical assistance is available from 8:00 A.M. to 6:00 P.M. EST, toll-free at 800-424-9600. Help desks are also maintained at other offices.

Position in database industry

One of the largest European vendors, Questel is based in France. It has customers in the United States, Canada, Japan, Mexico, and Brazil. The system offers a broad range of information, from numerical data and chemical structure searching to bibliographic databases covering many subject areas, including patents. Nearly all of the databases are exclusive to the Questel system and give U.S. users access to European literature not otherwise readily available. Questel is particularly strong in information of French origin or about chemistry.

Company background

Telesystems was set up with government support as a profit-making subsidiary of Radio France and was given a broad mandate to serve information needs. Today it has five divisions that produce software, hardware, and networking products.

Questel/Paris, one of these divisions, was formed in 1979 to provide access to online information. Its first database went online that same year. Questel, Inc., was established in Washington, D.C., in 1981 to market the company's services and support users in the United States.

Computer facilities

The 40 Questel databases are maintained on an IBM 4341 and a Honeywell CIIT located in Valbonne, France. Storage capacity is 40 gigabytes.

Summary of database services

Questel offers a variety of numeric and bibliographic databases. Subjects include patents, financial information on companies, textile and food industries, agriculture, health administration, occupational safety, architecture, urban planning, law, electronics, and chemistry. Sources can be worldwide or exclusively French.

DARC, increasingly used in the United States, allows the user interested in chemistry to formulate a structural query by inputting alpha-numeric text or graphics. The system then retrieves all structures related to the query. (See Hardware and Software Requirements below.)

At least one and one-half days of training are generally required to become proficient on the Questel system (usually one day for DARC alone).

Questel offers SDI capability.

Telecommunications access

Access to Questel is via Telenet, Tymnet, Uninet, Transpac, and Datex-P at either 300 or 1200 baud.

Hardware and software requirements

No special terminal is required to access Questel databases, with the exception of DARC.

On DARC, structures may be entered and searched using any terminal. Graphics verification or viewing of answers, however, does require a terminal that can emulate a Tektronix 4010 (such as the IBM PC, Apple, VT640, Hewlett Packard, and Televideo).

Fee structure and sign-up

There is no subscription fee or monthly minimum charge. A service contract must be signed before an account can be opened. Individual databases are priced from $36 to $110 per connect hour. Telecommunications costs $20 per hour. Invoices are issued monthly. Discounts are given for volume use and to certain educational and research organizations. Deposit accounts are available. Additional users may be added to an account at no charge.

Offline printing and remote capabilities

Offline prints of bibliographic citations and chemical structural diagrams are available, printed in France and airmailed to users. Charges for this vary by database. A dot matrix printer is used.

Documentation available

Each new subscriber receives a complete set of instruction manuals at no charge. Manuals are in French, with English versions available for many databases. Additional manuals may be purchased separately; a complete set costs $25. Sheets describing each database's content and searchable fields are available free of charge.

Customer training

Training is not required on Questel, but it is recommended. Sessions are offered regularly in Questel, Inc.'s Washington, D.C. office. A session on the bibliographic search system and databases takes one day. The DARC system also requires one day (in addition, the regular Questel session is recommended). Cost is $100 for a two-day program or $50 for one. Fees are applied to user accounts. Private training sessions are available for companies.

Document retrieval

Available for some databases.

Other services

Questel does not perform custom searches.

The company licenses both Questel and DARC software for private use. The DARC Chemical Management System, for example, can be used by companies to maintain information on structures of chemicals, molecular formulas, raw data, spectral data, and patent information.

Public database offerings

BSI (Biblio Service Informatique)   Bibliographic database of computer science and related fields—electronics, teleinformatics, office data processing, automation, and robotics. Monthly updates. Charge: $62 per hour, 14¢ per offline or online print.

CANCERN   Basic research in cancer and medicine, biochemistry, virology, immunology, etc., plus administration of health services. Monthly updates. Charge: $60 per hour, 14¢ per offline or online print.

CECILE   Industrial design, visual communication, architecture, and space planning. The nineteenth and twentieth centuries are covered. Monthly updates. Charge: $80 per hour, 14¢ per offline or online print.

CIM   International bibliographic documentation covering hydraulic bindings, cements, limes, plasters, and related fields. Monthly updates. Charge: $76 per hour, 14¢ per offline or online print.

CISILO   Bilingual database (French and English) covering worldwide literature on occupational safety and health. Updates seven times a year. Charge: $85 per hour, 14¢ per offline print.

CNRSLAB   Current research funded by Centre National de la Recherche Scientifique. Yearly update. Charge: $58 per hour, 14¢ per offline or online print.

DEFOTEL   Financial information of companies on the official French list and some 400 companies on the unquoted list. Includes staff, balance sheets, subsidiaries, etc. Charge: $90 per hour, $2 per offline print or $1 per online print.

EDF-DOC   Coverage of mathematics, computer science, electronics, telecommunications, electrical material, energy sources, nuclear power stations and equipment, environment—waste pollution, etc. Charge: $76 per hour, 14¢ per offline or online print.

ESSOR   Directory of French companies employing more than ten people. Includes trademarks, abstracts of business, personnel. Charge: $77 per hour, 32¢ per offline or online print.

EUCAS67-82   Chemistry and related fields (metallurgy, biology, organic chemistry, polymers, macromolecular chemistry, applied chemistry, and chemical engineering). Updated twice a month. Charge: $66 per hour, 20¢ per offline print and 14¢ per online print.

EURECAS   Structural file of over 6 million chemical compounds, searchable by structure using the DARC system. POLYCAS contains structures of polymers. Charge: $60 to $100 per hour, depending on the nature of the search; 14¢ per online display, 20¢ for first 100 lines printed offline and 16¢ for each additional 100 lines.

FAIREC   Tropical and subtropical fruit cultivation. Charge: $70 per hour, 14¢ per offline or online print.

FRANCIS   Worldwide coverage of literature in the arts, humanities, and social sciences. Charge: $58 per hour, 14¢ per offline or online print.

IALINE   Worldwide coverage of scientific, technological, and economic subjects within agriculture and the food industry. Charge: $66 per hour, 14¢ per offline or online print.

IFP-TH   Bibliographic data concerning physicochemical properties and transer properties of pure compounds and mixtures. Charge: $90 per hour, 12¢ per offline print and 14¢ per online print.

INPI-1 All patents applied for and published in France since 1969. Charge: $107 per hour, 20¢ per offline or online print.

INPI-2 All European patents, published applications and EURO-PCT. Updated weekly on day of publication. Charge: $107 per hour, $20 per offline or online print.

INPI-3 References to patent families. Links between patent documents of major industrial countries issued on the same priority application. Updated once every three weeks. Charge: $107 per hour, $10 per offline or online print.

INPI-4 All of the terms and codes included in the 55,000 groups and subgroups of the International Patent Classification Codes. Charge: $107 per hour, 20¢ per offline or online print.

JURIS Jurisprudence of French law courts. About 50 percent of the material is unpublished references. Doctoral and ministerial replies included. Charge: $110 per hour, 32¢ per offline print and 50¢ per online print.

LABOR Worldwide journal and monographic literature on industrial relations, labor law, employment, working conditions, etc., as well as French national legislation in these fields, EEC directives, collective agreements, etc. Charges: $85 per hour, 14¢ per offline or online print.

LEX All French laws and decrees of application. Updated weekly. Charge: $96 per hour, 14¢ per offline or online print.

LOGOS French political, economic, and social matters. Chronology of French home and foreign affairs policies and cabinet meetings communiques. Charge: $76 per hour, 14¢ per offline or online print.

Meeting Announcements of congresses, conferences, meetings, workshops, exhibitions, and fairs organized around the world. Updated twice a month. Charge: $90 per hour, 12¢ per offline or online print.

NORIANE French technical standards; standards from the International Standard Organization (ISO); SRFCQ, DTU, UTE, etc. Updated bi-monthly. Charge: $110 per hour, 14¢ per offline or online print.

PASCAL Multidisciplinary coverage—plant biology, agricultural science, chemistry, physics, life science, engineering, information science. Updated monthly. Charge: $56 per hour, 18¢ per offline or online print.

QUESTA6/QUESTA7 Questions to the French National Assembly. Updated weekly. Charge: $55 per hour, 12¢ per offline print.

REDOSI Information systems in use with the emphasis on civil service, regional development, office data processing, etc. Charge: $66 per hour, 14¢ per offline or online print.

SYDONI Primary and secondary sources of French law, divided by fields. Charge: $100 per hour, 50¢ per offline or online print.

TELEDOC Coverage of telecommunications: electronics, electrical engineering, optics, acoustics, physics, computer science. Charge: $76 per hour, 14¢ per offline or online print.

TITUS-E Textiles, processes and machines for the production of fibrous materials, yarns, threads, woven fabrics, knitted fabrics, nonwoven fabrics. In addition, textile engineering, industrial management, and biological effects of textiles related to health protection. Updated monthly. Charge: $70 per hour, 14¢ per offline print.

TRANSIN Offers and requests for industrial techniques and new products. Charge: $110 per hour, 14¢ per offline or online print.

URBAMET Scientific, technical, economic, and legal information related to town planning, urban design, environment, and transportation. Offers online subject and geographic thesaurus. Charge: $70 per hour, 14¢ per offline or online print.

SDC Information Services

SDC Information Services, a division of Burroughs Corp., 2500 Colorado Ave., Santa Monica, California 90406, 213-453-6194, 800-421-7229 (outside California), 800-352-6689 (inside California). Telex: 65-2358. TWX: 910-343-6643

Other offices

All offices provide customer service, training, and sales.

East Coast office: 7929 Westpark Dr., McLean, Virginia 22101, 703-790-9850, 800-336-3313 (outside Virginia only).

Associate offices: Australia—SDC Search Service, 30 Alfred St., P.O. Box 439, Milson's Point, New South Wales 2061, Australia; England—Derwent-SDC Search Service, Inc., Stuart House, 47 Crown St., Reading, Berkshire, RG1 2SG, England; Japan—SDC of Japan, Ltd., Nishi-Shinjuku Showa Bldg., 1-13-12, Nishi Shinjuku, Shinjuku-ku, Tokyo 160, Japan.

Representative: Brazil—Barroslearn, Rua 24 de Maio 62 - 5.0, Caiza Postal 6182, Cep. 0 1000, Sao Paulo, SP Brazil.

Hours of operation

Monday through Thursday, 24 hours, except 9:45 to 10:15 P.M. EST; Friday, 3:00 A.M. to 8:00 P.M. EST; Saturday, 8:00 A.M. to 7:00 P.M. EST; Sunday, 7:00 P.M. to 3:00 A.M. EST.

Customer assistance

The two customer-service action desks are:

- ◆ Santa Monica
  800-421-7229 (outside California)
  800-352-6689 (inside California)
  Monday through Friday, 11:00 A.M. to 8:00 P.M. EST
- ◆ McLean
  800-336-3313 (outside Virginia)
  Monday through Friday, 8:00 A.M. to 5:00 P.M. EST

Position in database industry

SDC Information Services is one of the "big three" supermarket vendors along with DIALOG and BRS.

Its ORBIT Search Service offers full-text, numeric, and bibliographic databases of over 70 files concentrated mainly in the areas of patents, chemistry, energy, pharmaceuticals, government information, and engineering. The typical customers are librarians or other search intermediaries.

SDC has recently developed a software applications package for microcomputers called the ORBIT SearchMaster System. This system will allow storage of preformatted strategies, commands, passwords, and search results on a floppy disk for later editing and reformatting.

Company background

System Development Corp., a software company, introduced a publicly accessible online information system in 1972, SDC ORBIT Search Service, offering two databases, ERIC and MEDLINE. Today more than 70 databases are part of the system.

In 1981, SDC was bought by Burroughs Corp., a manufacturer of computer hardware with over $3 billion in sales in 1982. In early 1983, the Search Service became SDC Information Services in order to reflect an expanded business direction. It is part of SDC's Commercial Services Division.

Computer facilities

This service uses two Amdahl 470/V7 computers.

Summary of database services

The ORBIT Search Service is SDC's information retrieval service. A command-driven system with full Boolean logic capabilities, truncation, and an adjacency feature, ORBIT can be searched by subject, author, title, and a number of other fields, depending on the database. The system of 70-plus public databases has more than 55 million citations.

The Data Base Index (DBI) is an online index to all of the system's databases. When you enter a term, the system responds with a ranked list of the databases in which it occurs.

ORBIT has a number of sponsored files placed on the sytem by organizations and made available to selected users on a subscription basis. There is also a private file service that is similar except that access is restricted to authorized users within an organization. Consulting support from SDC is available for both of these services.

SDC has a current awareness service (SDI) available in which information on selected topics will be sent automatically to a user every time a file is updated.

SDC does not offer electronic mail or graphics at this time.

Another segment of SDC Information Services is the ORBIT SearchMaster System, which is discussed below.

Telecommunications access

The ORBIT Search Service is accessible at 300 or 1200 baud via Tymnet and Telenet commercial common carriers. It is also available through direct dial. There is no differential charge for 1200-baud access.

Hardware and software requirements

No special terminal is needed to access SDC.

The ORBIT SearchMaster System is a microcomputer software applications package that runs on standard personal computers. This system will provide the searcher with a prompted format for selected types of searches or requests. The format is designed to allow the searcher to answer simple questions that the system translates into appropriate search protocol for a number of systems, including ORBIT, DIALOG, BRS, National Library of Medicine, and Dow Jones. SearchMaster also provides the searcher with the following capabilities: automatic logon, preformatted search strategies, automatic execution and downloading of search results onto floppy disks, and editing or formatting output to meet personal specifications.

Fee structure and sign-up

There are no sign-up costs or monthly minimums for ORBIT. If SDC's ORBIT system or services are used, however, a $10 minimum per month is charged.

Hourly charges on ORBIT range from $35 to $160. Telecommunications cost an additional $8 per hour. A per citation charge is assessed for records printed offline; some databases charge per citation for online prints as well. Discounts are available for high-volume searchers.

Start-up packages range from $125 for the Self-Instructional Workbook Package to $450 for a Custom Training Package. Prices include the *ORBIT User Manual*, five database manuals, and a small amount of connect time for practice.

Offline printing and remote capabilities

Offline prints are available at a turnaround time of three days to one week.

Documentation available

The following training and search aids are available:

- ◆ *ORBIT User Manual* ($40)—the main system reference guide covering search features and techniques.
- ◆ *Quick Reference Guide* ($15)—a handy reference containing three sections: (1) system basics, log-in procedures, commands, etc.; (2) entry sheets for each database containing general information, key-to-fields, and search tips; (3) a list of document delivery services.
- ◆ Database manuals ($7.50 each)—in-depth coverage of individual databases.
- ◆ *SEARCHLIGHT* (free)—monthly newsletter, issued to password holders, with news of system changes, updates, and new databases.
- ◆ *Handy Guide* (50¢)—a flip-chart pamphlet with examples of all ORBIT system commands and features for quick reference.

There is a $2 handling fee for all document orders.

Customer training

SDC offers training workshops regularly in its own facilities and in major population centers throughout the United States. Schedules are available in print or online covering the following courses:

♦ ORBIT Basic Skills—one-day workshop for individuals with little or no online experience. It costs $150 per person and covers general search principles, search logic, system commands, and hands-on experience.

♦ ORBIT Basic Skills Primer—half-day workshop covering basic commands and everything a user would need to perform a simple search. Contact SDC for cost information.

♦ ORBIT Advanced Skills Seminars—one-day workshops for individuals who have had some ORBIT training and experience. Users may choose a general advanced systems seminar or special subject seminars in patents, chemistry, engineering, or energy. Cost is $100 per person.

Document retrieval

ORBDOC is SDC's online ordering service. At present, 35 suppliers are offered. Users are billed directly by vendors at varying fees. Further information is given in the *ORBIT Quick Reference Guide*.

Public database offerings

Accountants' Index Extensive coverage of English-language literature on accounting and related business/financial areas. Charge: $75 per hour, 25¢ per offline citation, 15¢ per online citation.

APILIT Produced by the American Petroleum Institute, citations to literature on the petroleum-refining and petrochemical industries. Coverage includes scientific and technical developments, engineering, and process-level work. Charge: subscribers to print product, $60 per connect hour, 25¢ per offline citation, 15¢ per online citation; nonsubscribers (access is limited), $100 per connect hour, 30¢ per offline citation, 20¢ per online citation.

APIPAT Produced by the American Petroleum Institute, patent citations relevant to the petroleum-refining and petrochemical industries from the United States, Belgium, Canada, France, Germany, Great Britain, Holland, Japan, and South Africa. Charge: see APILIT.

ASI Online version of the *American Statistics Index*. It cites statistical publications from major federal agencies: the Bureau of Census, the Bureau of Labor Statistics, the National Center for Social Statistics, and the Statistical Reporting Service of the Department of Agriculture. Charge: $90 per connect hour, 15¢ per offline citation.

BANKER Index of all articles and news items appearing in the American Banker newspaper. Charge: $75 per connect hour, 24¢ per offline citation, 15¢ per online citation.

BIOSIS Comprehensive coverage of the world's life science information in this online version of the Biological Abstracts publications. Charge: $65 per connect hour, 15¢ per offline citation.

BIOTECHNOLOGY Produced by Derwent Publications Ltd., all aspects of biotechnology from genetic manipulation and biochemical engineering to fermentation and downstream processing. Derwent subscribers only. Charge: $100 per connect hour, 13¢ per online citation, 25¢ per offline citation.

CAS82/CAS77/CAS72/CAS67 Files corresponding to the journal *Chemical Abstracts* from 1972 to date, providing worldwide coverage of chemical science literature. Charge: $65 connect hour, 22¢ per offline citation, 15¢ per online citation.

CASSI Online version of the *Chemical Abstracts Service Source Index*. This provides bibliographic data, library holdings, and information on publishers for journals, serials, monographs and conference proceedings cited in *Chemical Abstracts*. Charge: $65 per connect hour, 22¢ per offline citation, 15¢ per online citation.

CHEMDEX Based on the CA Registry Nomenclature file, a repository for names and nomenclature data associated with substances that have been registered by Chemical Abstracts Service. Charge: $132 per connect hour, 24¢ per offline citation, 15¢ per online citation.

Chemical Industry Notes References from over 80 worldwide publications covering the chemical industry. Charge: $70 per connect hour, 22¢ per offline citation, 13¢ per online citation.

CIS/Index Publications from the committees and subcommittees of the U.S. Congress. Charge: $90 per connect hour, 15¢ per offline citation.

COLD Produced by the U.S. Army Corps of Engineers Cold Regions Research & Engineering Laboratory, coverage of all disciplines relevant to frozen regions, including Antarctica, the Antarctic Ocean, and sub-Antarctic islands; snow, ice, and frozen ground; navigation on ice; civil engineering in cold regions; behavior and operation of materials and equipment in cold temperatures. Charge: $80 per connect hour, 30¢ per offline citation, 15¢ per online citation.

COMPENDEX Online version of the Engineering Index covering worldwide significant engineering literature from 3,500 sources including books, journals, technical reports, and conference proceedings. Charge: $98 per connect hour, 35¢ per offline citation, 25¢ per online citation.

CRDS (Chemical Reactions Documentation Service) Journal and patent literature on subjects of interest to the practicing chemist, such as novel organic reactions, reagents, synthetic methods. Derwent subscribers charge: $100 per connect hour, 13¢ per offline citation.

CRECORD A comprehensive index (with abstracts) to the *Congressional Record* from 1976 to date. Charge: $95 per connect hour, 35¢ per offline citation, 15¢ per online citation.

DBI (Data Base Index) SDC's master index to all ORBIT databases. Charge: $35 per connect hour, 5¢ per online citation, 10¢ per offline citation.

EI Engineering Meetings Published proceedings of engineering and technical conferences, symposia, meetings, and colloquia. Charge: $98 per connect hour, 35¢ per offline citation, 25¢ per online citation.

Electric Power Industry Abstracts Indexes and abstracts of literature on electric power plants and related facilities from 1975 to date. Charge: $86 per connect hour, 20¢ per offline citation, 10¢ per online citation.

Energy Bibliography & Index Access to all energy-related holdings (exclusive of journal articles) of the Texas A & M University Library. Charge: $80 per connect hour, 30¢ per offline citation, 15¢ per online citation.

Energy Data Base Journal and conference literature, patents, monographs, and technical reports on all aspects of energy production, utilization, and conservation. Charge: $45 per connect hour, 25¢ per offline citation, 10¢ per online citation.

Energyline Comprehensive literature coverage of approximately 20 different energy-related areas including economics, policy and planning, research and development, production, consumption, and traditional and alternate energy sources. Charge: $90 per connect hour, 25¢ per offline citation, 15¢ per online citation.

Enviroline Produced by EIC/Intelligence, Inc., coverage of a wide range of information sources on air, water, and noise pollution, environmental health, and resource management from 1971 to date. Charge: $90 per connect hour, 25¢ per offline citation, 15¢ per online citation.

ERIC   Prepared by the National Institute of Education, wide coverage of report and journal literature in education and related areas. Charge: $35 per connect hour, 10¢ per offline citation.

FEDREG   Abstracts of material in the *Federal Register*, including rules, proposed rules, public law notices, meetings, hearings and presidential proclamations. Charge: $70 per connect hour, 25¢ per offline citation, 10¢ per online citation.

Food Science and Technology Abstracts   The composition and properties of foods and other topics such as food handling, transport, engineering processing, quality control, legislation, storage, and packaging from 1969 to date. Charge: $75 per connect hour, 25¢ per offline citation, 12¢ per online citation.

Forest   Worldwide literature pertinent to the entire wood products industry, from harvesting of the standing tree through marketing of the final product. Charge: $90 per connect hour, 25¢ per offline citation, 10¢ per online citation.

GeoRef   Coverage of the geosciences: geology, geophysics, mineralogy, geochemistry, and related sciences. Charge: $82 per connect hour, 25¢ per offline citation, 15¢ per online citation.

Grants   Reference to grants offered by federal, state, and local governments, commercial organizations, associations, and private foundations. Charge: $55 per connect hour, 35¢ per offline citation, 15¢ per online citation.

INFORM   Coverage of hundreds of periodicals in the field of business management and administration. Banking, finance, data processing, labor relations, marketing, and planning are among the subject areas included. Charge: $70 per connect hour, 30¢ per offline citation, 20¢ per online citation.

INSPEC   Citations and abstracts of the literature of physics, electrical engineering, and electronics engineering. Source documents are journal articles, government reports, patents, and monographs. Charge: $85 per connect hour, 35¢ per offline citation, 27¢ per online citation.

International Labor Documentation   Worldwide journal and monographic literature on labor including economic and social development and industrial relations. Charge: $85 per connect hour, 30¢ per offline citation, 15¢ per online citation.

LC/LINE   Documents cataloged by the U.S. Library of Congress since 1968 and by the National Library of Canada since 1973. Charge: $85 per connect hour, 35¢ per offline citation, 25¢ per online citation.

Library and Information Science Abstracts (LISA)   References to journal articles and other documents in this field, with abstracts. Charge: $75 per connect hour, 25¢ per offline citation.

Management Contents   Indexes and abstracts of English-language proceedings and transactions in the areas of business and management. Charge: $70 per connect hour, 35¢ per offline citation, 20¢ per online citation.

METADEX   International technical literature on all aspects of metals and alloys. Charge: $80 per connect hour, 15¢ per offline citation, 10¢ per online citation.

Metals Data File   A numeric database covering information on ferrous and nonferrous metals and alloys. Charge: $50 per connect hour, varied prices for online and offline prints depending on format.

MONITOR   Index to regional editions of *The Christian Science Monitor* includes all articles and other selected material. Charge: $75 per connect hour, 24¢ per offline citation, 15¢ per online citation.

NDEX (Newspaper Index)   References to news from these U.S. newspapers: *Chicago Sun-Times, Chicago Tribune, Detroit News, Denver Post, Houston Post, Los Angeles Times, New Orleans Times-Picayune, San Francisco Chronicle, St. Louis Post-Dispatch*, and *Washington Post*. The database also indexes ten U.S. newspapers geared to black readers. Coverage is from 1976 to date in most cases. Charge: $75 per connect hour, 24¢ per offline citation, 15¢ per online citation.

NTIS Citations of U.S. government-sponsored research and development reports in areas of major technical interest from over 200 federal agencies, as well as federally sponsored translations and foreign-language reports. Charge: $40 per connect hour, 10¢ per offline citation.

NUC/CODES Names and addresses of over 300 libraries cited in the *Chemical Abstracts Service Source Index*. Charge: $35 per connect hour, 10¢ per offline citation, 5¢ per online citation.

Pacific Island Ecosystems A comprehensive multidisciplinary database of references to literature on the Pacific islands under U.S. jurisdiction. Charge: $50 per connect hour, 10¢ per offline citation.

PAPERCHEM Online version of the *Abstract Bulletin* of the Institute of Paper Chemistry. It covers scientific and technical literature on the pulp and paper industry. Charge: subscribers, $49 per connect hour, 18¢ per online citation, 23¢ per offline citation; nonsubscribers, $55 per connect hour, 18¢ per online citation, 23¢ per offline citation.

P/E News Articles from 14 major publications on petroleum and energy. The database also carries the full text of *Platt's Oilgram News*. Charge: subscribers, $95 per connect hour, 15¢ per online citation, 25¢ per offline citation; nonsubscribers, $95 per connect hour, 20¢ per online citation, 30¢ per offline citation.

PESTDOC/PESTDOC-II Designed to meet the requirements of manufacturers of agricultural chemicals (other than fertilizers) with such topics as biology, chemistry, toxicology, insecticides, herbicides, and fungicides. Charge: subscribers, $80 per connect hour, 13¢ per offline citation.

POWER Cataloging records of books in the Energy Library of the U.S. Department of Energy. Charge: $40 per connect hour, 10¢ per offline citation.

PsycINFO Online version of the journal *Psychological Abstracts*, providing comprehensive coverage of literature in psychology and other behavioral sciences. Charge: $45 per connect hour, 35¢ per online citation, 40¢ per offline citation.

RINGDOC Designed to meet the information requirements of pharmaceutical manufacturers, covering journal literature in the field. Charge: subscribers, $80 per connect hour, 13¢ per offline citation.

SAE Produced by the Society of Automotive Engineers, indexes of technical papers relevant to the automotive and related industries. Charge: $90 per connect hour, 10¢ per online citation, 25¢ per offline citation.

SPORT Online version of *Sport and Recreation Index* of literature on all aspects of sports, including practice, training and equipment, recreation, sports medicine, physical education, sports facilities, history, and individual sports. Charge: $85 per connect hour, 5¢ to 15¢ per online citation, 25¢ per offline citation.

Standard Drug File Information on 7,500 known drugs and commonly occurring compounds. Charge: subscribers, $80 per connect hour, 13¢ per offline citation.

TROPAG (Abstracts on Tropical Agriculture) The literature on tropical and subtropical agriculture. Charge: $70 per connect hour, 10¢ per online citation, 20¢ per offline citation.

TSCA Plus The inventory of the Toxic Substances Control Act. It includes formulas, registry numbers, names, and synonyms of chemical substances manufactured, imported, or processed for commercial purposes. Toxicity is not a criterion for inclusion. Charge: $45 per connect hour, 15¢ per offline citation.

Tulsa Online version of *Petroleum Abstracts*, citing literature and patents related to the exploration, development, and production of oil and natural gas. Charge: subscribers, $70 per connect hour; varied prices for online and offline prints depending on format.

USCLASS Index of over 4 million U.S. patents issued since 1860. It can be searched by patent numbers or by classification. Charge: $60 per connect hour, 50¢ per offline citation.

U.S. Government Contract Awards   Contract awards as announced in the *Commerce Business Daily*. Among the data available to users are project title, awardee, sponsoring organization, funding, and contract and request-for-proposal numbers. Charge: $105 per connect hour, 20¢ per offline citation.

USPA/USP77/USP70   Information on U.S. patents, including reissues, continuations, divisionals, designs, and defensive documents from 1971 to date. Charge: $100 per connect hour; varied prices for online and offline prints depending on the format.

Veterinary Literature Documentation   Worldwide coverage on substances used for veterinary purposes. Charge: subscribers, $80 per connect hour, 13¢ per offline citation.

WATERLIT   Produced by the South African Water Information Centre, literature on water and all water-related disciplines. Charge: $55 per connect hour, 15¢ per online citation, 30¢ per offline citation.

WPI/WPIL   Online index to patents issued by 27 issuing authorities representing 24 countries. Patents are from the following areas: pharmaceuticals, agriculture, veterinary, chemicals, polymers, and technologies. Charge: Derwent subscribers, $100 to $105 per connect hour; nonsubscribers, $150 to $160 per connect hour; varied prices for online and offline prints depending on format.

*I. P. Sharp Associates

I. P. Sharp Associates Limited, 2 First Canadian Place, Suite 1900, Toronto, Ontario, Canada M5X 1E3, 416-364-5361

U.S. Headquarters: I. P. Sharp Associates, Inc., 1200 First Federal Plaza, Rochester, New York 14614, 716-546-7270

Other offices

Regional headquarters: London, Singapore, Sydney.

Branches: Asia—Hong Kong; Australia—Brisbane, Canberra, Melbourne; Canada—Calgary, Edmonton, Halifax, London, Montreal, Ottawa, Saskatoon, Vancouver, Victoria, Winnipeg; Europe—Amsterdam, Brussels, Copenhagen, Dublin, Dusseldorf, Madrid, Oslo, Paris, Stockholm, Vienna, Zurich; United Kingdom—Aberdeen, Coventry, Warrington; United States—Atlanta, Boston, Chicago, Dallas, Denver, Houston, Los Angeles, Miami, New York, Newport Beach (Calif.), Palo Alto (Calif.), Philadelphia, San Francisco, Seattle, Washington, Wayne (N.J.), White Plains (N.Y.).

Representative agencies: Finland—TMT-Team Oy, Helsinki; Italy—Informatical Society Italia Srl., Milan and Rome; Japan—INTEC, Inc., Tokyo; Korea—Daewoo Corporation, Seoul; Mexico—Teleinformatica de Mexico S.A., Mexico City; Singapore—Singapore International Software Services Pte. Ltd.

Each office is fully responsible within its locale for sales, training, and customer support. Special backup assistance is available from Toronto as well as the regional headquarters locations.

Hours of operation
24 hours a day, 7 days a week.

Customer assistance
Every local office is staffed by at least two customer-support personnel who are responsible for both training and supporting customers in the use of database services. Local office hours are typically concurrent with the hours of business operation common within the locale. In Toronto, the hours are 8:00 A.M. to 6:00 P.M. EST. Via Sharp's electronic mail, all offices can draw upon the resources of the "help desk" in Toronto and the database group, centered in Toronto but with members throughout the world. There are 30 people in this group, and they are responsible for the development of database products.

For software or hardware problems, the customer can call the Central Data Center in Toronto. This center is open 24 hours a day and can be reached at 416-363-2051. Again, assistance is also available via electronic mail.

Position in database industry
I. P. Sharp maintains one of the world's largest collections of online numeric databases. Users of the company's time-sharing services have access to public data related to the following categories: aviation, economics, energy, finance, and actuarial. The data may be retrieved, analyzed, and displayed using a variety of techniques. Considerable flexibility in report generation includes the ability to plot results as multicolor graphics. Users may combine data from a variety of Sharp databases for analysis and manipulation. Users may also incorporate their own data into reports or plots. Customers spend between $50 and $10,000 a month. Typical usage is $1,000 a month.

Sharp's competitors have traditionally been other time-share-oriented organizations such as DRI and ADP. With the advent of sophisticated but menu-driven products (see Infomagic discussed under Summary of Database Services), Sharp is targeting competitors like Dow Jones. Sharp is only interested in serving the business user—not the home market.

Overall, Sharp views its competitive edge as being its multinational capability to support and service clients via its far-flung network of offices. For some clients, the Sharp telecommunications network is an important factor. Flexibility in retrieving and outputting Sharp data is also key. While most Sharp databases are available without a sign-up charge (which is a noted advantage compared to other large time sharers), Sharp does not view price as its most important competitive feature.

Company background
I. P. Sharp is a private Canadian company formed in 1964 by Ian Sharp and seven colleagues. Approximately 550 people are employed in 60 offices in

22 countries. Revenue in 1982 was $52 million. The company's growth is attributable to development of Sharp APL, a greatly enhanced version of the APL computer language. Sharp was one of the first organizations to offer substantial commercial application in that language.

Sharp started offering access to commercial databases in 1974. Users have access to over 50 million time series of information, making Sharp one of the world's largest suppliers of online numeric databases. Sharp's first database offerings were in the field of aviation.

Computer facilities

The company operates a central computer facility in Toronto and uses an IBM 3081 and, for backup, an Amdahl V/8. The system can support approximately 400 simultaneous users and operates 24 hours a day. The computer runs a Sharp custom version of APL software. Sharp has available 32 drives with 634 megabytes of memory; 40 drives with 200 megabytes of memory; and 8 drives with 1,400 megabytes of memory. At present, Sharp maintains 25 gigabytes of online database storage.

Summary of database services

I. P. Sharp offers two basic types of services for database access: MAGIC, a command language, and Infomagic, a menu-driven system.

MAGIC allows access to all public databases using a sophisticated command language. It is effectively an extension of Sharp's time-sharing business. Consequently, the pricing for access is based on more traditional time-sharing variables, namely connect time, CPU utilization, and the number of characters transmitted or received. In order to access public data effectively, the user must become initially proficient in the use of MAGIC. Basic training in MAGIC takes one day. This time investment is merited where the user wishes to access, manipulate, combine, and display data in the most sophisticated fashion.

Using SUPERPLOT software, the customer may plot search results in multicolor graphics. SUPERPLOT is compatible with Hewlett Packard, Calcomp, and many other graphic devices. Sharp allows save/searches (SDI). Users may combine data from various databases and even combine with their own data to facilitate special analysis.

As discussed below, Sharp offers a software package for the IBM PC to facilitate logon to the system and upload/download.

Sharp also has an easy-to-use service entitled Infomagic, which is a sophisticated, menu-driven system for accessing public databases. Of the 100 public databases on Sharp, less than 15 as of this writing are accessible via the user-friendly Infomagic. The following are a list of current databases available via Infomagic: Bidata, Cansim, Citibase, Dewitt, Disclosure, Energy Futures Group, Form 4l, Lundberg, Nastock, OAG2, PIW, TSE300. Sharp plans to expand this service. Virtually no training is required to use Infomagic. It is available on a flat per hour charge basis.

Sharp has recently introduced a new computerized information and trading system that permits producers, traders, and consumers of petroleum and petrochemical products around the world to buy and sell electronically on a spot basis. The service, known as Electronic Markets and Information Systems (EMIS), Inc., is operated by McGraw-Hill in a joint venture with I. P. Sharp. More than 20 companies are currently using EMIS from some 35 locations around the world. The system allows them to make bids and offers to buy and sell; respond anonymously to bids and offers made by others; then, if they wish, identify themselves and continue negotiations to the point where a deal is concluded.

Telecommunications access

I. P. Sharp is accessible at 300 or 1200 baud via the following commercial common carrier networks: Datapac (Canada), Datex-P (Germany), PSS (United Kingdom), Telenet (United States), Telepac (Switzerland), Transpac (France), Tymnet (United States).

Sharp also operates its own value-added network, which can be reached by a local phone call in 80 cities. Including access via the common carriers, Sharp can be reached by a local call from 600 cities in 47 countries.

Hardware and software requirements

No special terminal is required to access Sharp databases. However, I. P. Sharp offers a custom software package for interface with the IBM Personal Computer. The package is called Microcomm. The software features are as follows:

- Facilitates sign-on to the Sharp network
- Enables downloading of data to an IBM PC file as a sequence of numbers, a textual report, or in VisiCalc format
- Enables uploading of data into the Sharp system

Microcomm is designed to work on a PC with at least 64 kilobytes of memory and at least one diskette drive. Sharp is planning to introduce an Apple version of Microcomm in the near future and, eventually, a comprehensive "intelligent work station" software product. Microcomm is designed to function with both MAGIC and Infomagic.

Fee structure and sign-up

Customers sign up to access the Sharp system by executing a simple agreement with a local office. There is no initiation fee or monthly minimum charge for use of the system, whether via Infomagic or MAGIC. Discounts to the charges outlined below are available only on a special negotiated basis. Charges are invoiced monthly.

The charges to access the full-capability MAGIC system are based on time-sharing variables as follows:

- $1 per connect hour (regardless of time of day)
- 70¢ per 1,000 characters transmitted or received
- 45¢ per CPU used

Access to public databases via Infomagic (the menu-driven version) is a flat $60 per hour at 300 baud or $120 per hour at 1200 baud. There is no time of day differential.

Whether via MAGIC or Infomagic there are additional royalty charges and/or subscription requirements for a few particular databases as noted in the database discussion below. There are no special charges for offline prints except for materials and handling as discussed below.

If the customer wishes to establish a private file to supplement the public data available, there is a storage charge of 55¢ per 100,000 bytes per day.

An annual subscription to Electronic Markets and Information Systems (EMIS) is $20,000 to $32,000 depending on the range of services requested. Users of the service also pay normal time-sharing charges. The typical Sharp customer is invoiced $1,000 per month.

Offline printing and remote capabilities

Nongraphic offline prints may be had from the Toronto facility where they are produced on a low-quality printer. This service is provided as a customer convenience on a cost-recovery basis. The charge is 15¢ per 50 lines.

In addition, each local Sharp office can produce high quality offline multicolor plots. This service is again offered as a convenience. The charge for an offline plot is set by the local office. Some offices provide this service free of charge. The average charged by an office is $5 per plot.

Documentation available

To aid the user, Sharp publishes the following periodicals, which are available at no charge:

- *I. P. Sharp Newsletter*—published every two months
- *Financial and Economic Data Base Newsletter*—published quarterly
- *Aviation Data Base Newsletter*—sporadic publication
- *Energy Data Base Newsletter*—sporadic publication

The following reference guides are published semiannually:

- *Financial and Economic Data Bases Reference Guide*
- *Aviation Data Bases Reference Guide*
- *Energy Data Bases Reference Guide*

Sharp also publishes a useful *Public Data Bases Catalogue*, available online and continuously updated. In addition, Sharp produces various software user guides as well as guides for most of the respective databases offered. The charge for these guides ranges from free to $15.

Customer training

Each of the local Sharp offices provides databases and APL training. At present, all training is via custom seminars lasting from one to three days. Training costs average $85 per day. Training is indispensable for customers who wish to use the full-capability Sharp APL system.

Sharp is considering setting up a regular schedule of training seminars, especially for Infomagic customers. Even though menu-driven Infomagic is easy to use and understand, Sharp wants to teach the range of useful applications.

It should be noted that for some databases, notably Disclosure, training is provided on a regular basis by the database producer.

Document retrieval

Not applicable.

Other services

Database search services I. P. Sharp does not customarily search its databases on a client's behalf. Rather, it will try to teach the client how to do the search.

Consulting services Sharp's first business—in 1964—was the provision of specialized software consulting services. Consulting has continued as an important business area. With regard to databases, Sharp currently consults to clients on data applications, special report generation, integration of client data, etc. Consulting fees are charged on an hourly basis. Total charges can run to thousands of dollars, though informal limited consultation is free of charge.

Electronic mail Sharp runs an electronic mail system known as Mailbox. Costs for using the system on the Sharp APL time-sharing service are 75¢ per 1,000 characters transmitted or received and 55¢ per 100,000 file bytes per day.

Public database offerings

Note: Unless otherwise indicated, there is no surcharge or royalty for use of these databases.

Aviation

Air Charter Details on all charter flights originating or terminating in the United States. The database is no longer updated because of decreased interest in charter flights.

Aircraft Accidents Information on all jet and turboprop airliner losses for aircraft weighing 20,000 pounds or more. The database is updated as soon as data is available; sometimes before details appear in the newspaper.

Association of European Airlines Statistics describing the operations of European airlines. Members of the AEA update the database when they have compiled their statistics.

Canadian Operating Statistics Statistics on Canadian airlines. The database is updated quarterly, with a 6- to 12-month lag.

Combined T9/Service Segment Monthly domestic nonstop airport-pair data at the carrier and aircraft-type level (but not flight number). The database is updated monthly.

Commuter Online Origin-Destination   Statistics on point-to-point traffic by commuter airlines. The database is updated quarterly, with a lag of about six months.

ER586 Service Segment   Detailed monthly summaries of all traffic on each flight segment flown by certificated, U.S. route, air carriers. The database is updated monthly, with a lag of three to four months.

Form 41   The Form 41 schedules submitted to the United States Civil Aeronautics Board (CAB) by all U.S. certificated air carriers. The database is updated as follows: financial schedules—quarterly and yearly, with a lag of two to three months; traffic schedules—monthly, with a lag of six to seven weeks.

IATA North Atlantic Traffic   Statistics concerning flights between the United States or Canada and Europe. The database is no longer updated, for data is no longer available from the International Air Transport Association (IATA).

ICAO Air Traffic Statistics   Traffic statistics for more than 400 airlines and 280 airports. The database is updated annually, typically in October of the following year, after the International Civil Aviation Organization (ICAO) publishes its annual traffic report.

Official Airline Guide   The schedules of about 600 international and North American airlines. The data is updated monthly, about seven days before the first of the month.

Origin-Destination   The result of a continuous survey of the itineraries of 10 percent of all passengers traveling on U.S. certificated carriers. The database is updated quarterly, with a lag of about nine months.

U.S. International Air Travel Statistics   The number of passengers flying each month between United States and foreign ports, not including Canada. The database is updated monthly, with a lag of about five weeks.

Economics

Australian Bureau of Statistics Database   Economic and financial statistics relating to Australia. The database is updated quarterly, or more often when new information is released for popular series.

Australian Economic Statistics   Over 1,200 time series relating to Australia's economy. The database is updated irregularly.

Australian Export Statistics   Values and quantities of commodities exported to Australia's trade partners, updated monthly, as soon as new data becomes available from the Australian Bureau of Statistics.

Australian Input-Output Database   Statistics describing the interaction of Australian industries. The database is updated by the ABS as data becomes available.

Australian Sector Cash Flow   Trends in the four sectors of the economy: households, private corporations, government, and the rest of the world. The database is updated quarterly, with a lag of about three months.

Bank for International Settlements, Quarterly   Total liabilities and assets for approximately 200 countries (as well as some regions), updated quarterly.

Bank for International Settlements, Semiannual   Total liabilities, total assets, maturity distributions of assets, and undisbursed credit commitments for approximately 200 countries (as well as some regions), updated semiannually.

Business International Economic Forecasts   Fifty economic forecasts in text for 35 countries. This is not a time series database. The database is updated quarterly. Note: a surcharge of $50 per report for use of this database.

Business International Historical Data   Economic and demographic data for more than 130 countries. The database is updated quarterly, as data becomes available.

Canadian 1981 Agricultural Census   Socioeconomic data on the Canadian agricultural economy. The database is updated as data becomes available.

1981 Canadian Census   1981 Canadian data including information on such areas as cultural characteristics, demographics, family, and household structure. The figures are updated as soon as Statistics Canada releases new data.

Cansim Mini Base and Supplement   Socioeconomic data on Canada's characteristics, internal activities, and external trade. The database is updated daily.

CITIBASE   U.S. economic statistics. The database is updated daily.

CITIBASE Economic Forecast   Over 250 quarterly macroeconomic time series that predict statistics for a variety of segments of the U.S. economy. The series are updated quarterly. Note: subscription fee to access is $2,500 (U.S.) annually or $1,000 (U.S.) quarterly.

German Bundesbank, Monthly   Statistics from the Deutsche Bundesbank. The database is updated monthly, within seven to ten days of the release of the tape by the Bundesbank.

International Financial Statistics   Information concerning countries or governments as a whole. The database is updated monthly, about two weeks after month-end.

National Income Forecasting Model for the Australian Economy   Economic, financial, and demographic data used in the latest version of the National Income Forecasting (NIF) model of the Australian economy. The database is updated quarterly.

National Planning Association Demographic Data   Demographic data for the United States, analyzing the population by age, sex, and race. The database is updated yearly, with a lag of one to two years.

National Planning Association Economic Data   Internal economic data for the United States. The database is updated yearly, with a lag of one to two years.

Organization for Economic Co-operation and Development (OECD)   Statistics describing the domestic economies of member countries of the Organization for Economic Co-operation and Development (OECD) and international statistics. The database is updated monthly, when tapes arrive from the OECD.

S. J. Rundt World Risk Analysis Package   Country business risk analysis reports. The database is updated as a change occurs. Note: subscription fee (variable) payable to S. J. Rundt and Associates as a surcharge to access this data.

STATISBUND   Statistics from the West German Federal Statistical Bureau. The database is updated monthly, with a seven- to ten-day lag.

United Kingdom Central Statistical Office   Socioeconomic data on the United Kingdom. The database is updated monthly, with a major revision every October.

United Nations Commodity Trade Statistics   Details (values and quantities) of international trade for the selected reporting countries, Canada and the United Kingdom in 3075 commodities according to the Standard International Trade Classification Revision 2 (SITC). The database is updated quarterly as the data becomes available from the U.N.

U.S. Consumer Price Index   Indexes of the cost of consumer goods and categories of consumer goods. The database is updated monthly, with a lag of about five weeks.

U.S. Flow of Funds, Quarterly   Over 3,600 time series on the sources and uses of funds in the U.S. economy for over 50 major sectors. The database is updated quarterly.

U.S. Producer Price Index   Price indexes for commodities and groups of commodities. The update is monthly, with a lag of about four weeks.

World Bank Debt Tables   Tables, with 1,050 yearly time series on the external public and publicly guaranteed debt of 104 developing countries and 6 regions. The database is updated yearly, 10 to 12 months after the end of a calendar year.

Energy

Dewitt Petrochemical Newsletters and Price Forecasts Weekly analytical reports, price quotations, and forecasts for a broad range of petrochemical products. Sixteen distinct newsletters and forecasts are available with weekly or more frequent updates if circumstances require. Note: annual subscription fee for access to each newsletter or forecast, and slightly higher Infomagic rates.

Hughes Rotary Rig Report Counts of active drilling rigs in the United States and Canada. The database is updated weekly, about three days after the reporting period.

Independent Chemical Information Services Information relating to market activity for a range of chemical and petrochemical products as reported weekly by ICIS. The database is updated every weekend.

International Petroleum Annual Worldwide statistics on supply of, and demand for, crude petroleum and refined petroleum products. The database is no longer updated because the *International Petroleum Annual* is no longer published.

Liquefied Petroleum Gas Report Inventories of liquefied petroleum gases (LPG) in all U.S. Petroleum Administration for Defense (PAD) districts. The database is updated monthly, with a lag of about two months.

Lundberg Current and historical wholesale prices for gasoline and diesel as collected by Lundberg Survey Inc. Note: subscription fee (variable), payable to Lundberg Survey Inc., for use of this database.

Monthly Energy Review Several tables from the U.S. Department of Energy publication, *Monthly Energy Review*. The database is updated monthly, with a lag of two to six months.

Monthly Report of Heating Oil and Other Middle Distillate Sales by State Published by the American Petroleum Institute and updated 1½ to 2 months after the reporting period.

OECD Quarterly Oil Statistics A report of the International Energy Agency of the Organization for Economic Co-operation and Development (OECD). The database is updated quarterly, three to six months after the end of the quarter.

Petroleum Argus Daily Market Report Reports on spot prices for crude oil and petroleum products in leading European centers. The database is updated daily, between 20:00 and 21:00 London time. Note: annual subscription fee of $1,500 to use the database.

Petroleum Argus Prices Two tables with prices for refined petroleum products in Europe that are updated three to five days after *Petroleum Argus* is published. The Rhine data is updated about one week after *Europ-Oil Prices* is published. Note: subscription fee of $25 per month to use the database.

Petroleum Intelligence Weekly Three data series from *Petroleum Intelligence Weekly* (PIW): COP production figures, usually available six to seven weeks after the month's end; KCP and SPP prices, available the third or fourth week of the month. SPP revisions for Rotterdam and Italy are available the first or second week of the following month.

State Energy Data System Statistics on energy consumption in the United States. The database is updated annually, as information becomes available.

U.S. Department of Energy Information on stocks, production, and imports of crude oil and petroleum products and refinery operations in the United States. It is updated monthly, with a lag of about three months.

U.S. Petroleum Imports Information about every shipment into the United States of crude oil and residual, unfinished, and finished petroleum products. The database is updated monthly, with a lag of two to three months.

Weekly Statistical Bulletin Information on crude oil, petroleum products, and refinery operations in the United States. The database is updated weekly, usually late Wednesday afternoon (EST), by the American Petroleum Institute.

Finance

Agricultural Commodities   Short-term trends in prices, volumes, and other indexes for many agricultural products, including grains and oil seeds; cattle and beef products; hogs and pork products; broilers, eggs, and fowl; and special crops. Alberta Agriculture updates the figures weekly.

Australian Commodities   Daily trading information on prices (high, low, last trade, buy quote, and sell quote), open position, and volume traded for all months and commodities on the Sydney Futures Exchange. The database is updated daily, by 08:00 (Sydney time) the next business day by International Commodities Clearing House.

Australian Financial Database   Financial statistics and interest rates, updated monthly, with a lag of about one month.

Australian Financial Markets   Daily market-based interest rates, exchange rates, and commercial bill rates; weekly series on commonwealth government securities; and monthly series on semi-governmental securities. The database is updated daily, the morning of the next working day (Melbourne time).

Australian Funds Markets   Aggregate data on the total amount of money in the Australian economy and on the flows of money among the mail categories of lenders and borrowers. The database is updated yearly, in December, for the financial year ending in June.

Australian Graduate School of Management (AGSM) Corporate Data   Approximately 32,750 time series of financial data on more than 250 major Australian public companies. The database is updated yearly.

Bank of Canada Weekly Financial Statistics   Weekly banking and monetary statistics released by the Bank of Canada. The database is updated Friday afternoon.

Canadian Bonds   Price and yield statistics for about 1,100 Canadian bonds. The database is updated every Friday afternoon, as data is received.

Canadian Chartered Banks, Annual   Annual financial statement for each bank operating in Canada. The database is updated yearly, about $1\frac{1}{2}$ to 3 months after year-end (October 31).

Canadian Chartered Banks, Monthly   Balance sheet on Canada's chartered banks. This database is no longer updated.

Canadian Chartered Banks, Quarterly   Balance sheets, revenues, expenses, and dividend statistics from the banks' quarterly (interim) statements. This database is no longer updated.

Canadian Chartered Banks, Yearly   Statistics from the annual reports of the Canadian chartered banks. This database is no longer updated.

Canadian Department of Insurance   Financial information on 600 federally registered insurance or trust companies; fraternal benefit societies; and cooperative credit associations across Canada. It is updated yearly, about midyear, by the Department of Insurance.

Canadian Department of Insurance Property and Casualty Insurance   Financial data on property and casualty insurance companies and accident and sickness branches of life insurance companies. The database is updated annually, around July.

Canadian Stock Options   Daily trading statistics for both put and call options traded in Toronto and Montreal and issued by Trans Canada Options Inc. The database is updated each trading day, about 23:00 (Toronto time).

Chartered Banks Monthly Statement of Assets and Liabilities   Statistics on Canada's chartered banks. The database is updated monthly, about three to six weeks after month-end.

Chartered Banks Quarterly Income Statement   Statistics on Canada's chartered banks. The database is updated quarterly, six to eight weeks after quarter-end.

Commodities   Prices, volumes, and open interest for all major commodities traded on the London, New York, Chicago, Kansas City, Minneapolis, Winnipeg, and Toronto/Montreal futures markets. The database is updated daily by Eurocharts Limited.

Commonwealth Bank Bond Index   Price, income, and accumulation indexes, and current yield to maturity of Australian government bonds. The database is updated on Fridays, for the week up to close of business on Thursday (Sydney time), by the Commonwealth Bank.

Disclosure II   Current and historical corporate statistics and textual information for 8,500 publicly owned companies that have filed with the U.S. Securities and Exchange Commission. The database is updated weekly with relevant changes. Note: subscription fee (variable) for use of this database.

Federal Reserve Board Weekly   Weekly banking and monetary statistics released by the Board of Governors of the Federal Reserve System and the Federal Reserve Bank of New York. The statistics are updated weekly, one business day after data is released.

Financial Post Canadian Corporate Data   Data covering most of the companies in the Toronto Stock Exchange 300 Composite Index, and others chosen for their growth and interest to investors. The database is updated as new data becomes available by the Financial Post Investment Databank. Note: annual subscription fee of $6,000 Canadian payable to the Financial Post Investment Databank.

Financial Post Securities   Stock trading statistics for securities traded on the Canadian exchanges, the New York Stock Exchange, and the American Stock Exchange, updated daily from tapes containing the previous day's data.

Financial Times Actuaries Share Indices   Index values and associated information for each of the 42 Financial Times Institute of Actuaries Indices published in the *Financial Times*. The database is updated daily. Note: royalty fee of 1¢ per time series item accessed.

Financial Times Share Information   Comprehensive information on securities listed on the London Stock Exchange. The database is updated daily. Note: royalty fee of 1¢ per time series fact.

Fund Monitor Unit Trusts and Insurance Bonds   Current and historical offer (asking) prices for units of two classes of U.K. investment funds. The database is updated weekly.

Hong Kong Stock Exchange   Daily volume and high, low, and close prices, updated daily, for 113 securities listed on the Hong Kong exchange.

Money Market Rates   246 daily and weekly money market rates for several countries. The database is updated daily, as information is published.

North American Stock Market   Current and historical prices and volumes for securities on North American exchanges. The database is updated daily, on the next business day at about 11:00 Toronto time.

Singapore Corporate Statistics   Annual corporate financial statistics for over 250 companies in Singapore and Malaysia, amounting to about 53,000 time series. The database is updated monthly, as annual reports are received and compiled. Note: surcharge of $500 (U.S.) to start and $500 (U.S.) a year for using this database.

Singapore Stock Exchange   Daily trading statistics for the stocks traded on the exchange, updated daily.

Sydney Stock Exchange Share Prices   Trading statistics for more than 600 stocks on the Sydney exchange. The database is updated daily, on the next business day.

Sydney Stock Exchange Statex Service   Yearly balance sheet information on more than 430 companies traded on the Sydney exchange. The database is updated quarterly, with a lag of about six months.

Toronto Stock Exchange 300 Index   Trading statistics for the 300 stocks and 62 major and minor indexes that form the Toronto Stock Exchange 300 Composite Index. The database is updated daily each trading day, at approximately 23:00 Toronto time. There are summaries of weekly and monthly data at the end of the period from the daily file.

U.S. Banks   Balance sheet and income statement data for over 15,000 banks in the United States. Preliminary data is available 90 to 120 days after quarter-end; final data, four to six months after quarter-end.

U.S. Quarterly Financial Report   A subset of the information appearing in the *Quarterly Financial Report* published each calendar quarter by the U.S. Federal Trade Commission. It is updated quarterly.

U.S. Stock Market Database   Current and historical prices and volumes for securities on North American exchanges. The database is updated daily, on the next business day at about 02:00 Toronto time.

U.S. Stock Options   Daily trading statistics for all put and call options traded on the major stock exchanges in the United States. The database is updated each trading day, at about 01:00 Toronto time.

Actuarial

Actuarial Database   Over 200 tables, including tables of mortality on assured lives, annuitants, and general populations. Due to the nature and sources of the data, updates occur when newly published tables become available.

Other

APL Bibliography   A Mabra database consisting of bibliographic information on the APL programming language. The database is updated as needed.

National Emergency Equipment Locator System   Information on the nearest suitable equipment and material in Canada for combatting spills of oil or hazardous material. The database is updated interactively by users.

*The Source

Source Telecomputing Corporation, 1616 Anderson Rd., McLean, Virginia 22101, 703-734-7500

Other offices

Regional offices and field representatives: Boston, Chicago, Dallas-Fort Worth, Fort Lauderdale (Fla.), Los Angeles, San Francisco, Washington, D.C.

Hours of operation

6:00 A.M. to 5:00 A.M. EST daily.

Customer assistance

Customer service is available from 8:00 A.M. to 1:00 A.M. EST, Monday through Friday, and 9:00 A.M. to 1:00 A.M. EST, Saturday and Sunday. Users can call 800-336-3330, except in Virginia and outside the United States, where the number is 703-734-7540. Fifteen people provide answers to a variety of questions ranging from the services themselves to the use of specific equipment or software.

Position in database industry

The Source was one of the first computerized information services to go after the home computer market. It offers a variety of electronic information and communications services along with games aimed at personal rather than business use. More recently the company has begun to emphasize sales to the business community. Typical customers have high incomes, are well educated, and fit a professional/executive profile. Thirty-five percent of the accounts are corporate; the rest are individuals. Membership is reported growing at 1,500 per month with 40,000 subscribers as of September 1983.

The Source competes with information utilities such as CompuServe Information Service. It also competes with companies that stress electronic communication, such as ITT-Dialcom.

In the future, the system will probably add more business databases in an attempt to appeal more to corporate users. Initially, service was provided on time-shared computers rented from Dialcom. In 1982, it opened its own computing center to meet growing demand. This is being expanded to overcome complaints of slow response time, which can occur at peak times, such as late afternoon and early evening.

Company background

Source Telecomputing Corporation (STC) was founded in June 1979. It was purchased in October 1980 by Reader's Digest Association, Inc., which made a major commitment at a time when The Source was reportedly losing as much as $1 million per month. In April 1983, Control Data Corporation also made a major investment in the company.

STC provides three mail services: (1) Update, an information service for ITT Telex users overseas; (2) Sourcecable, an entertainment and news cable service being tested in a small number of U.S. cities; and (3) The Source, an online provider of information, games, and communication services for personal computer owners. Services are divided into business/financial, news and sports, travel services, consumer services, games, and communications.

The Source has pioneered many new services, such as computer conferencing and computer barter networks. It provides special electronic mail services for companies and groups as part of its move to attract corporate clients.

Computer facilities

STC has 14 Prime 750 computers running the PRIMOS operating system.

Summary of database services

The Source offers a number of different online services. They are broken down into six categories: business/financial, news and sports, travel services, consumer services, games, and communications. The services are accessible through a menu-driven program using simple English commands. Some programs have had bugs in the past, many due to their inherently experimental nature. New users can begin to use The Source by reading the manual and spending one or two hours online.

Graphics are currently available for the IBM PC using Sourcelink, Source Telecomputing Corp.'s telecommunication software. The Source is also reported to be working on true videotex services that will allow users access to full-color graphics using simple commands.

Telecommunications access

One can access The Source through Telenet, Tymnet, Uninet, Datapac, and Sourcenet, which is STC's own network. Incoming WATS telephone service is available at a 25¢ per minute surcharge for members calling from remote areas. STC supports both 300- and 1200-baud rates. There is a $5 per hour surcharge for 1200 baud between 7:00 A.M. and 6:00 P.M. local time, weekdays, and a $3 per hour surcharge at other times.

Hardware and software requirements

The Source supports most portable terminals and microcomputers with modems. Special Sourcelink software ($49.95) is available for use with IBM PCs, and a second version is being developed for Apple computers. Sourcelink allows users to sign on to The Source automatically, easily transfer files to and from their computers, and save each session for later review.

Fee structure and sign-up

Users can sign up directly with STC or through any of 2,000 computer stores nationwide that are authorized to sell The Source. There is a $100 registration fee. Discounts are available for groups. Some "bundling" programs provide membership without the registration fee with purchase of certain personal computing equipment.

There is a $10 monthly minimum charge; $9 is applied to use. For most services, members are charged a flat $20.75 per hour between 7:00 A.M. and 6:00 P.M. local time, weekdays. The charge drops to $7.75 per hour at all other times. The rates for 1200 baud are $25.75 per hour prime time and $10.75 per hour nonprime time. These rates include telecommunications charges. Users can check rates online through the "help rates" command.

Five database services on The Source are charged at higher rates. These "Source-Plus" services contain business/financial information, including Commodity News Service and Media General Financial Service. They are billed at $39.75 per hour 7:00 A.M. to 6:00 P.M. weekdays and $34.75 per hour at all other times.

The Source charges a fee for storing files. This does not apply to mail stored in STC's electronic mailboxes, but it does apply to computer conferences and regular private files.

Offline printing and remote capabilities

Not applicable.

Documentation available

New users receive an illustrated user's manual free with their subscriptions. The manual sells for $19.95 to others, including those who join through bundling programs.

The Source publishes a monthly newsletter, *Sourceworld. Update*, a monthly flyer, discusses new or changed services. Both of these publications are sent free to subscribers.

Prospective members receive a kit that details The Source's services.

Customer training

Free demonstrations of The Source are available in any store where it is sold. Periodic Source Days are held in dealer stores across the country. For corporate members and sponsors of private networks on The Source, STC field representatives conduct on-premises training sessions.

For most members, the manual is sufficient for training.

Document retrieval

The Source does not have a retrieval service, but users may contact document retrieval and delivery firms through electronic mail. For example, Management Contents provides articles from business publications, and Professional Book Center can provide most books in print. Other information providers may be contacted online, such as Information on Demand, a Berkeley, California, service that will carry out many kinds of research projects.

Other services

Many services are offered besides databases. These fall into the categories of games (over 80 are available), communications, and software packages.

Under communications services, The Source provides the following:

- Sourcemail—a multifeature electronic mail service
- Post—over 80 electronic bulletin boards, each with a special topic, including one for most popular personal computers
- PARTI—by Participation Systems, Inc., an advanced computer conferencing system that allows both public and private conferences
- CHAT—synchronous (same-time) communications between two Source users

The Source also contains software packages for programmed learning, statistics, and text editing.

Public database offerings

These are The Source's major news or information databases. The Source also carries a large number of entertainment or educational offerings—from I Ching to movie reviews. Though most of these are technically databases, we have omitted them from this list.

Regular databases

Bylines   Produced by United Media Features Syndicate, full-text coverage of nearly 50 regular columns and features syndicated in newspapers and magazines. Subjects include personal viewpoints, the arts, sports, and general household information. Most bylines are updated weekly, though some are updated more frequently.

Commodity News Service   The news wire and price wire of the Commodity News Service. CNS tracks news and price activity on America's major commodity markets, including the Chicago Board of Trade, the Kansas City Board of Trade, the Minneapolis Grain Exchange, the New Orleans Commodity Exchange, and the New York Futures and Commodity exchanges. The news wire covers news about commodities and financial instruments as well as political, agricultural, economic, and weather news. It is billed at the standard Source rate. The CNS price wire is a Source-Plus component updated every 20 minutes while exchanges are open.

Currency   A database providing reports on currency trading activity of 27 currencies on the New York Foreign Exchange. The file is updated twice daily with information provided by Multinational Computer Models, Inc.

Employ   A service of Computer Search International Corporation. Resumes of job seekers categorized into more than 40 professions. It also lists available positions broken down by profession, location, and salary level.

Management Contents   Produced by Management Contents, bibliographic references, including abstracts, for 27 leading business and financial publications. This is a subsection of the Management Contents files found on other vendors.

BIZDATE   A compendium of business news updated 80 times throughout the day. Much of the information is gathered from other Source databases.

Stockvue   Produced by Media General Financial Services, comprehensive analyses of the performance of more than 3,100 common stocks traded on the New York, American, and OTC exchanges.

UNISTOX   A service of United Press International, trading activitity for stocks, bonds, money markets, mutual funds, metals, and commodities from the New York, American, and OTC exchanges.

UPI   Up-to-the-minute coverage of the UPI news wires, including business, sports, state news, and weather. News stories are retained online for seven days.

U.S. News Washington Newsletter   Online version of the *Washington Newsletter*, a weekly publication of U.S. News & World Report. It assesses the latest news and trends, particularly as they relate to American business and the economy. The file is updated weekly and information is kept online for four weeks.

Wine   Detailed listings of wines, including where they come from, when to buy them, and what to serve them with.

Online ordering services

Barter   A service of Barter Worldwide, Inc., an online posting and trading service for businesses wishing to barter goods and services. Fees are based on the value of the exchange.

Books   By the Professional Book Center, allows online ordering of in-print books published or distributed in the United States. Prices charged are suggested retail.

Comp-U-Store   Produced by Comp-U-Card of America, online shopping and price information service. Over 50,000 brand-name products are offered at up to 40 percent off list prices.

Other Source databases allow online ordering of books, records and tapes, and classic radio programs.

Travel services

AIRSCHED; CITYCON   Produced by Dittler Brothers, domestic and international flight information.

Travel Club   Produced by Firstworld Travel Corp., allows users to make travel, accommodation, and car rental reservations online.

U.S. REST   Online version of the *Mobil Restaurant Guide* for the United States and Canada.

U.S. ROOMS   The *Mobil Travel Guide* for the same areas as the U.S. REST database.

NY Guide   A catalog of shopping, entertainment, and sightseeing in New York.

Other databases offer information on and reviews of restaurants in New York and Washington, D.C.

25 Other Vendors— In Brief

Chase Econometrics/Interactive Data

Chase Econometrics/Interactive Data Corporation, a subsidiary of the Chase Manhattan Bank, N.A., 486 Totten Pond Rd., Waltham, Massachusetts 02154, 617-890-1234

Other offices: In 18 North American cities, 4 European cities, and Tokyo.

Interactive Data Corporation was formed as an independent company in 1968 as the result of a merger between the Interactive Data Services Division of White, Weld & Co. and the Computer Communications Center. IDC developed its services around two major facilities: large online databases and proprietary software to access and work with that data.

In 1974, Interactive Data was acquired by the Chase Manhattan Bank, N.A. In 1978, Chase merged Interactive Data with Chase Econometrics to become Chase Econometrics/Interactive Data Corporation (CE/IDC).

CE/IDC is organized to deliver applications expertise to customers via specialized product divisions:

- *Chase Econometrics* serves the needs of economists, corporate planners, and market researchers in public and private organizations. Key products include econometric models, economic forecasting, and economic data.
- *Decisions Systems* serves the needs of controllers, financial planners, and bankers within corporations and financial institutions. Key products include integrated applications solutions for budget and control, asset/liability management, merger and acquisition, loan and credit analysis, and bank trust and custody products.
- *Securities Products* serves the needs of directors of research, portfolio managers, and corporate finance managers who deal with securities and investments in all organizations. Key products include a compre-

hensive set of securities databases containing prices and fundamental financial data, investment research tools, and portfolio management systems.

♦ *Treasury Management Services* serves the needs of treasurers and cash managers in banks and corporations as well as banks that offer services to their customers. Key products include tools for balance reporting, cash analysis, cash movement, investment planning, and capital planning.

Clients include 300 of the Fortune 500 companies, and revenues exceed $100 million.

CE/IDS provides decision support systems, processing, training, and consulting services in addition to financial and economic databases. Extensive mainframe computing capabilities and software that integrates microcomputer technology into the process are available, maintained on a 24-hour international communications network.

Public database offerings

CE/IDC provides business decision makers one of the largest, most comprehensive collections of economic and financial databases containing U.S. and international information. Economic historical databases cover agriculture, automotive, energy, finance, general industry, insurance, macroeconomic multicountry, macroeconomic single country, metals trade, U.S. regional, and U.S. national information. Forecast databases cover Canada, Europe, the Far East, Latin America, regional, state, and U.S. national information. Other forecast databases cover agriculture, fertilizers, insurance, inflation, steel, energy, and passenger cars and light trucks.

Financial database information includes fundamental and securities data, commodities and financial futures, foreign exchange rates, and forecast and estimate data available through time sharing or in the convenience of the microcomputer environment.

Control Data—Business Information Services

Control Data Corporation—Business Information Services, P.O. Box O, 8100 34th Ave. South, Minneapolis, Minnesota 55440, 612-853-8100

Business Information Services (BIS) provides applications software and databases to meet the needs of business people for specific kinds of information. We list 25 of its databases below.

NOTE: Business Information Services operates independently of Control Data's Cybernet Services.

Public database offerings

In the area of economics there are the two Evans Economic, Inc., databases, including the EEI Capsule. In the area of finance, offerings include Bank

Analysis System; COMPUSTAT; COMPUSTAT II; Corporate COMPUSTAT; EARLYOPT; EURABANK; EURARATE; EXSTAT; FDIC/FSLIC/NCUA; FEDWIR; Insurance Industry Data Base; and X/Disclosure. In the area of investment are MISTI II; MUNIPRICE; and VALPORT. Marketing databases include American Profile; Doane Farm Media Measurement Study; SITE II; SITE-POTENTIAL; X/Market; and X/Profile. In addition, BIS offers Orr System, which estimates construction costs, and FAPRS2, which contains information on federal domestic assistance loans, grants, and programs.

Control Data—Cybernet Technology Management Services

Control Data Corporation—Cybernet Technology Management Services, P.O. Box O, 8100 34th Ave. South, Minneapolis, Minnesota 55440, 612-853-8100, 800-328-1870

Cybernet is a time-sharing service of Control Data Corporation. It offers applications software programs in both broad and technical fields such as management science, consumer products, financial analysis, electrical engineering, and microwave circuits. Cybernet also supplies four online databases.

NOTE: Cybernet Technology Management Services operates independently of Control Data's Business Information Services.

Public database offerings

TECHNOTEC   Produced by Control Data, a database for licensing technology listing parties who seek to sell licenses or consulting services as well as those seeking to buy.

Trade Opportunities   Produced by the U.S. Department of Commerce International Trade Administration, trade leads and proposal requests gathered by economic and commercial officers at U.S. foreign embassies.

Develop   A resource for business people, government officials, and members of the scientific community who are interested in knowing about products, services, and experts in their particular areas of research and development. Among the purposes for which this database is used are development of new technologies, selection of foreign enterprises for technology transfer, and location of new research methods. Agriculture, business, energy, education, medicine, and natural resources are some of the fields covered. Users can communicate with each other by electronic mail.

Renewable Energy   Used by contractors, architects, manufacturers, and researchers of solar and related technologies to identify applications that meet their needs. Among the technologies covered by over 6,000 entries are solar heating and cooling (active and passive), solar-photovoltaic cells, biomass, small-scale hydro power, wind power, ocean thermal and tidal energy, small-scale geothermal energy, and energy conservation.

Defense Technical Information Center (DTIC)

Defense Technical Information Center, Building 5, Cameron Station, Alexandria, Virginia 22314, 202-274-7633

Field offices: Bedford (Mass.), Los Angeles.

The Defense Technical Information Center (DTIC) is a component of the Department of Defense Scientific and Technical Information Program. DTIC contributes to the management and conduct of defense research and development by providing access to and transfer of scientific and technical information for DOD personnel, DOD contractors, and other U.S. government agency personnel and their contractors. The four DTIC databases provide access to planned, ongoing, and completed research activities of the DOD and DOD contractors.

DTIC is available to registered Department of Defense contractors and potential contractors and can be searched by one of three methods:

◆ Dedicated, hard-wired access to DTIC's DROLs computers using UNIVAC terminals. The costs are for the hardware and the communications lines, searching is free.

◆ Dial access to the system using Tymnet, available at either 300 or 1200 baud. This carries a charge of $20 per connect hour.

◆ Customized online searches are performed free of charge at any one of the three DTIC locations for registered users.

DTIC's collection contains information on aeronautics, missile technology, space technology, navigation, and nuclear science. Also covered are such areas as biology, human factors, engineering, and environmental sciences.

Public database offerings

Technical Reports   Contractor's reports on completed research efforts.

Research and Development Work Unit Information Summary   Information on research projects at the work unit level currently being performed by DOD or under contract.

Research and Development Program Planning   Projects that forecast and propose future research efforts.

Independent Research and Development   A collection of contractors' independent R&D efforts shared with DOD.

*ESA-IRS

European Space Agency Information Retrieval Service (ESA-IRS), ESRIN, Via Galileo Galilei C.P. 64, 00044 Frascati, Italy, 010-396-94011

Other offices: Contacts in eight Western European member countries and Australia. U.S. contact planned for 1984.

The European Space Agency was established in 1966 to promote cooperation among European countries in space research and technology for exclusively peaceful purposes. ESA-IRS is the agency's online service.

ESA-IRS maintains over 50 databases, most in the areas of science, technology, and social science. Both specialized and multidisciplinary databases are offered. In our Public Database Offerings list below we note 34 of them.

U.S. customers can gain access to ESA-IRS services through Telenet or Tymnet. Computer service is 20 hours per day, Monday through Friday, with shutdown from 6:30 P.M. to 10:30 P.M. local Italian time. Connect hour charges range from $40 to $100. There are no subscription fees or required minimum amounts. Rebates may apply to users of at least five hours per month.

Sign-up for the service is accomplished by contacting ESA-IRS and filling out a contract. The new user receives a password and two free connect hours for the first month of use. About one-half dozen training databases are available. Documentation includes a user manual and a bimonthly newsletter.

Training seminars are not offered in the United States at this time.

Other ESA-IRS services include electronic mail; online ordering of documents, delivered in hard copy or microfiche; private files; stored automatic searches; online tutorials; online entry and editing of documents; online statistical analysis; custom searching on the system's databases; and consulting.

Public database offerings

ABI/INFORM   Management information.

ACOMPLINE   Urban environment.

AGRIS   Agriculture.

ALUMINUM   Aluminum.

AQUALINE   All aspects of water.

BIOSIS   Biosciences.

CAB   Agriculture.

CHEMABS   Chemistry.

COMPENDEX   Engineering.

COSMIC   Computer programs for aerospace and high-technology industries.

CPI   International conference papers.

EDF-DOC   Energy.

Ei Engineering Meetings   Engineering meetings and conferences.

Energyline   Energy.

Enviroline   Environment.

ETIM   Mechanical engineering.

EUDISED   Documentation and information on education.

FLUIDEX   Fluid engineering.

FSTA   Food industry.

HSELINE   Health and safety.

INIS   Peaceful applications of nuclear energy.

INSPEC   Electronics, computer and control, physics.

IRRD   Road research.

MERLIN-TE   Electrical and electronic engineering.

METADEX Metallurgy.

NASA Aerospace and related sciences, restricted access.

OCEANIC Marine environment.

PASCAL Multidisciplinary science and technology.

Pollution Pollution.

PRICEDATA A manipulative database on worldwide raw materials prices and currency rates.

SPACECOMPS Spacecraft components.

Standards & Specifications Industry and government standards and specifications.

Telegen Worldwide genetics engineering.

WTI (World Transindex) Directory of translations to/from Western European languages.

Finsbury Data Services

Finsbury Data Services Limited, 68-74 Carter Lane, London EC4V 5EA England, 01-236-9771

In 1979, three leading U.K. financial institutions—Scottish Northern Investment Trust, Scottish Amicable Life Assurance Society, and British and Commonwealth Shipping—formed Finsbury Data Services Limited to initiate and develop online business text retrieval.

Public database offerings

Finsbury produces the Textline and Newsline databases (see also Chapter 14).

Textline Bibliographic coverage with abstracts for national and international newspapers, business journals, press releases, news tapes, corporate financial reports, newsletters and broker surveys. Sources are originally published in English, French, German, Italian, Japanese, and Spanish. All are translated into English. Coverage of the U.K. and Western Europe is particularly strong, with emphasis upon information about companies, industries, markets, and products. Current economic data, attitudes, trends, and forecasts are also available, along with political and general coverage.

Newsline Concise summaries of one day's news and commentary from about 40 British and European newspapers. Most of the information is online by 9:00 A.M. London time on the day of publication (this is five to seven days ahead of Textline). Dailies covered include *The Times, The Financial Times, Glasgow Herald, The Guardian, International Herald Tribune, Die Welt, Frankfurter Allgemeine Zeitung,* and *Le Monde*. Weeklies include *The Sunday Times, The Observer, The Economist,* and *The Financial Weekly*. Unlike Textline, Newsline contains no back files.

GEISCO

General Electric Information Services Company, a subsidiary of General Electric Co., 401 N. Washington St., Rockville, Maryland 20850, 301-340-4000

Regional offices or representatives: Atlanta, New York, Oak Brook (Ill.), San Francisco, and 23 foreign countries.

General Electric Information Services Company (GEISCO) is one of the largest time-sharing companies, with revenues of over $600 million and over 6,000 customers. Clients access GEISCO computers via the world's largest commercially available teleprocessing network.

The company's services include interactive time sharing, online computer-to-computer processing, batch processing, custom software design, distributed data processing, and terminal devices. G.E. Information Services is a leading vendor of electronic mail.

In addition, customers can access databases on economics, finance, industries, companies, demographics, science, engineering, petroleum, and pharmaceuticals.

Public database offerings

Economic databases   ABC Financial Planning, Analysis and Reporting System; A. Gary Shilling and Co. Economic Forecasting Services; CITIBASE; IFS Data; Lochrie & Associates, Inc.; Quick Model System; Business International Corporation BI/DATA; FUTURSCAN; WRI/E JAPAN Economic & Business Data Bank; Producer Price Index (PPI); Sibyl/Runner; State Space Systems, Inc.

Financial databases   Caploan Euroloan Information System; Currency Exchange Data Base; Federal Trade Commission and Security Exchange Commission Data Banks; Commodity Futures Data Base.

Industry databases   American Home Appliance Manufacturer's Data Base; National Electrical Manufacturers Association Data Base (NEMA); SIC; SIC72.

Company databases   Value Line II; Securities Data Base System; Industrial Bank of Japan Data Base.

Petroleum databases   Dwight's Energydata Oil and Gas Production History; Petroleum Product Data Clearinghouse; Petroleum Data System; Drilling Activity Analysis System.

Demographic, science, and engineering databases   Demographic Retrieval System (SITE II); Marine Industry Data Bases; World Fertilizer Market Information Service; Physical Property Data Service; SITE POTENTIAL.

Pharmaceutical and medical databases   Pharmaceutical Futures Data Base.

*General Videotex

General Videotex Corp., 3 Blackstone St., Cambridge, Massachusetts 02139, 617-491-3393, 800-544-4005

General Videotex produces Delphi, a new electronic information, communications and entertainment system intended for consumers. Delphi offers electronic mail and bulletin boards, and users can send mail to subscribers of The Source and CompuServe. There is a gateway to DIALOG allowing users to search Dialog databases. With Delphi's travel service, users can review airline schedules and prices and then make reservations. The banking service allows users to pay bills and transfer money through electronic funds transfers.

ISI

Institute for Scientific Information (ISI), 3501 Market St., Philadelphia, Pennsylvania 19104, 215-386-0100, 800-523-1850

Other offices: In 10 countries.

ISI is an international corporation that provides bibliographic information services to help research personnel, librarians, educators, managers, and others locate and obtain relevant information published worldwide. Scholarly, scientific, and technical journals, books, and proceedings are covered.

Public database offerings

Much of the information in the ISI databases is derived from the company's print product, the *Science Citation Index*. Their offerings include ISI/ BIOMED; ISI/CompuMath; ISI/GeoSciTech; ISI/Index to Scientific & Technical Proceedings & Books (see Chapter 21); SCISEARCH; and Social SCISEARCH.

*ITM

ITM, 2835 Mitchell Dr., Walnut Creek, California 94598, 415-947-0850, 800-334-3404

ITM is producer and vendor of the ONE POINT Electronic Catalog, a database listing over 30,000 IBM PC-compatible software products. The database is menu-driven and requires no special training or instructions to use. There is a $100 initial sign-up fee and additional charges based on the amount of information accessed during a search.

ITM also sells, through the online service or by telephone, virtually all IBM PC compatible software products.

Legi-Slate

Legi-Slate, a subsidiary of the Washington Post Co., 444 N. Capitol St. N.W., Washington, D.C. 20001, 202-737-1888

Public database offerings

Legi-Slate provides two databases dealing with the U.S. federal government.

Legi-Slate A database covering all bills and resolutions filed in the U.S. Congress beginning with the 96th session to the present. Information contained includes bills' sponsors and co-sponsors, subject references, citations of other laws, committee or floor actions, and votes. Legi-Slate also covers the Texas State Legislature. Users can check on bills or investigate how legislators vote.

Reg-Ulate   Information on all announcements contained in the *U.S. Federal Register* since 1981. This bibliographic database with descriptors allows users to search for regulations affecting their interests and identify the agencies issuing the regulations.

MCI Mail

MCI Mail, 200 M St. N.W., Washington, D.C. 20036, 202-293-4255, 800-MCI-2255 (customer service)

MCI Mail provides an electronic mail service that offers a number of unique options for sending mail to recipients without MCI Mail addresses. The four-hour letter service guarantees hand delivery of correspondence within four hours in many major U.S. cities; the overnight letter service provides hand delivery by noon the next day by Purolator Courier; and MCI Letter provides electronic transmission to a post office in the recipient's region, where the correspondence is printed and delivered by the U.S. Postal Service.

MCI Mail is accessible via a local call in 35 cities and via a toll-free 800 number elsewhere. The system will be connected to Telex, allowing messages to be sent and received virtually anywhere in the world.

There are no sign-up charges. The sender pays all the costs; recipients can read electronic mail without charge. There are no connect-time charges. Costs of totally electronic mail are $1 per message. MCI Letters cost $2, overnight letters are $6, and four-hour letters cost $25.

MCI Mail users receive a free subscription to Dow Jones News/Retrieval; a gateway allows users to access News/Retrieval through MCI Mail. Dow Jones services are billed at the standard News/Retrieval hourly rates.

MEDLARS

MEDLARS Management Section, Bibliographic Service Department, National Library of Medicine, 8600 Rockville Pike, Bethesda, Maryland 20209, 301-496-6193

MEDLARS is an online information system produced by the National Library of Medicine (NLM). It contains over a dozen databases, some of them very large and extensive, of information on the following areas: chemistry, toxicology, medicine, cancer research, bioethics, health planning and administration, and population planning.

MEDLINE, a well-known database of worldwide biomedical literature, is available on DIALOG and BRS. It and the other MEDLARS databases listed below are also available through NLM directly. Users accomplish this by becoming designated MEDLARS Centers. There are over 2,000 such centers in the U.S., primarily hospitals, universities, and corporations. Seven regional

MEDLARS centers make available custom searching on the system and document retrieval through the National Library of Medicine.

The MEDLARS system is complex, and three days of basic training is required for issuance of an access code. Representatives of institutions interested in becoming a MEDLARS Center should contact the Management Section at the above address.

Public database offerings

AVLINE   The NLM catalog of audiovisual materials.

BIOETHICSLINE   Produced by the Kennedy Institutes of Ethics at Georgetown University, citations to the literature on issues in this field.

CANCERLIT   Summary of the literature on cancer found in the International Cancer Research Data Bank (ICRDB).

CATLINE   The National Library of Medicine's catalog online.

CHEMLINE   An online chemical dictionary.

CLINPROT   File of the Clinical Protocols from ICRDB.

HISTLINE   Cites a variety of literature on the history of medicine.

MEDLEARN   A self-tutorial for the MEDLARS system.

MEDLARS   Coverage of international biomedical literature.

MEDLINE   A database of citations to the world's biomedical journal information.

PDQ   Lists of cancer therapy research programs that are currently in progress.

POPLINE   Citations to worldwide literature on family planning and fertility control.

RTECS   The online Registry of Toxic Effects of Chemical Substances.

SERLINE   The NLM catalog of its serials.

TDB   Information on the reported toxic effects of various compounds.

TOXLINE   Coverage of the Toxicity Bibliography and toxicology information from the journals *Chemical Abstracts* and *Biological Abstracts*.

NASA/RECON

National Aeronautics and Space Administration, Scientific and Technical Information Branch, Washington, D.C. 20546, 202-621-0100

NASA/RECON is available to NASA contractors, other federal agency contractors, and universities assisting in aerospace research.

Public database offerings

The NASA/RECON system contains the following components: technical reports and series including those listed in the printed *NASA STAR* (Scientific and Technical Aerospace Reports); International Aerospace Abstracts; Research and Development Contract Search File; Research and Technology

Operating Plan; NASA Technical Briefs; NASA Library Network Books; NASA Library Network Periodicals File.

National Data Corp.

National Data Corporation, Rapidata Division, 20 New Dutch Lane, Fairfield, New Jersey 07006, 201-227-0035

National Data Corporation (NDC) is a large independent computer services company. Products and services include cash and credit management, information services, telemarketing networking services, and health-care data management. Competitors include ADP and Comshare.

The Rapidata Division specializes in microcomputer applications software and interactive computing services. It provides information to support finance, sales, and marketing functions for business.

Public database offerings

Demographic Database   Produced by Demographic Research Co., demographic information based on the 1970 and 1980 census data, including zip code, census tract, population, income, DMA, county, and state. It can be used for market analysis and site selection.

Global Finance Database   Produced by Global Finance, international economic indicators, analyses, and money market rates.

International Financial Statistics   Time series covering various types of international financial information.

Conference Board Data Base   Produced by The Conference Board, economic time series on the U.S. economy.

New York Regional Economic Database   Produced by Professor Mathew Drennen, historical statistics and forecasts for New York City and its environs. The database contains 12,500 time series on employment and income in 53 industries.

CITIBASE   Produced by the Economics Department at Citibank, over 4,000 time series on the U.S. economy, which are of value in analyzing U.S. economic activity.

Telerate Historical Domestic   Information on U.S. money markets.

Rapidquote II Securities   Information for $12\frac{1}{2}$ years of data on 40,000 securities traded on major exchanges. There are time series on 200 key market indicators. The file is updated daily.

NIH/EPA Chemical Information System

NIH/EPA Chemical Information System (CIS), Computer Sciences Corporation, P.O. Box 2227, Falls Church, Virginia 22042, 800-368-3432, 703-237-1333

The NIH/EPA Chemical Information System contains scientific and regulatory databases and computer programs to perform data analysis. There are numeric, textual, and bibliographic databases in the areas of toxicology, environment, regulations, spectroscopy, chemical and physical properties, and nucleotide sequencing. CIS also has electronic mail for communication between users.

Public database offerings

Analysis and modeling

Chemical Modeling Laboratory (CHEMLAB) Capabilities for three-dimensional conformational analysis, molecular orbital calculations, and estimation of many properties of a chemical such as partition coefficient and molecular connectivity.

Biology

Nucleotide Sequencing Search System (NUCSEQ) Nucleotide sequence information searchable by author, journal, year, material, specific sequence, or reverse complement.

Chemical and physical properties

NBS Single Crystal Data Identification File (XTAL) An automated search system derived from the Crystal Data Determinative Tables published by the National Bureau of Standards. Space group, density, unit cells, and chemical types are searchable. The system currently contains over 57,000 compounds.

Thermodynamics (THERMO) Evaluated data on over 15,000 substances at STP, including enthalpy of formation, Gibbs free energy, entropy, enthalpy, and heat capacity, as well as evaluated data at 0 °K on enthalpy of formation, physical state, and crystal structure.

X-ray Crystallographic Search System (CRYST) The bibliographic and structural files of the Crystallographic Data Centre (Cambridge, England). Over 28,000 compounds have space groups assigned that may be used as a search element. Approximately 22,500 compounds have atomic coordinates and cell parameters.

Chemical structure name searching

Structure and Nomenclature Search System (SANSS) Information from 72 different sources on over 800,000 chemical names representing 250,000 unique substances, including CAS registry numbers, structural diagrams, molecular formulas, systematic names, and synonyms. The database has structure, substructure, and full or partial name search capabilities.

Environment

Oil and Hazardous Materials Technical Assistance Data System (OHM-TADS) Up to 126 different fields of information for some 1,200 materials, including physical, chemical, biological, toxicological, and commercial data on these materials, with emphasis placed on their harmful effects to water quality.

TSCA Plant and Production Data (TSCAPP) Information (including 127,000 production citations) for about 55,000 chemicals on the Toxic Substances Control Act Inventory. Manufacturer, plant location, and volume category are included.

Regulations

Federal Register Search System (FRSS) A cross-reference to all citations to a chemical or class of chemicals cited in the *Federal Register* since January 1, 1977. The listing contains the title, part, subpart, and a short description of the notice of the chemical of interest for over 150,000 citations.

Spectroscopy

Carbon-13 Nuclear Magnetic Resonance Spectral Search System (CNMR) Over 6,500 CNMR spectra of more than 5,500 compounds. Searches by chemical shift requirements are permitted; analysis and display are available.

Infrared Search System (IRSS) A parallel of MSSS for retrieval of known spectra and analysis of unknowns, consisting of approximately 4,100 spectra taken from the EPA collection and contributions from the Boris Kidric Institute in Yugoslavia. An extensive graphics package allows for display of actual spectra on graphics-compatible terminals.

Mass Spectral Search System (MSSS) Mass spectra of over 41,000 compounds that can be searched on the basis of peak and intensity requirements, as well as by Biemann and probability based-matched (PBM) techniques.

Toxicology

Chemical Carcinogenesis Research Information System (CCRIS) Results of carcinogenicity, mutagenicity, and tumor promotion and cocarcinogenicity tests in chemicals compiled, but not independently reviewed, by the National Cancer Institute (NCI). CCRIS contains test data for over 2,800 animal bioassay, in vitro mutagenicity, and epidemiological results covering over 900 chemicals.

Chemical Evaluation Search & Retrieval System (CESARS) Detailed, evaluated chemical profiles taken from primary literature for over 170 compounds, including toxicity data and environmental fate. It is sponsored by EPA Great Lakes Program and Michigan State Department of Natural Resources.

Clinical Toxicology of Commercial Products (CTCP) Toxicity data for approximately 20,000 common commercial products derived from some 3,000 chemicals. Symptom and treatment data are expected soon. It is based upon the fifth edition publication of the same name by Gleason, Hodge, Gosselin, and Smith.

Registry of Toxic Effects of Chemical Substances (RTECS) Toxicity information on over 50,000 substances, including some 70,000 toxicological measurements. Provided by the National Institute of Occupational Safety and Health.

Scientific Parameters for Health and the Environment, Retrieval and Estimation (SPHERE) Consisting of two databases, a Dermal Absorption database and an Aquatic Information Retrieval database (AQUIRE), both developed by the Environmental Protection Agency's Office of Toxic Substances. The information is individual assay data extracted from international literature published between 1970 and 1981.

*Official Airline Guides

Official Airline Guides, a subsidiary of Dun & Bradstreet Corporation, 2000 Clearwater Drive, Oak Brook, Illinois 60521, 312-654-6000

Customer service: 800-323-4000, 800-942-3011 (in Illinois)

Official Airline Guides produces OAG-EE (Official Airline Guide Electronic Edition), which is the electronic equivalent of the *Official Airline Guide* (North American Edition and Worldwide Edition). The printed versions of the Official Airline Guides have provided airlines, travel agents, and travelers with schedule, fare, and rules information about air travel for over 50 years. The OAG-EE began online in May 1983. It provides most schedules, fares, and rules maintained for over 640 worldwide airlines.

Data coverage is from the current day to 364 days in the future. Fares and rules are updated daily; schedules are updated weekly. OAG-EE is available to subscribers of Dow Jones News/Retrieval, CompuServe, Dialcom, iNet (Bell Canada), and Delphi. Rates vary depending on the vendor.

Users can also subscribe directly through Official Airline Guides, accessible through Telenet and Tymnet. There is a $50 one-time subscription fee for direct subscribers. Users are billed 10¢ a unit, with one unit charged for each connect minute, two units for schedule information, and three units for fare or rules information. The average session costs about $3.50.

*PAC Researchers

PAC Researchers Ltd., 1925 North Lynn St., Suite 903, Arlington, Virginia 22209, 703-247-3930

A subsidiary of MIW Associates, Inc., PAC Researchers is preparing to launch a system of databases known as Politics Online (POL). POL is what is known in the industry as a "boutique" of databases. It comprises a collection of data files designed to serve the diverse needs of one main audience— the political community. The various databases that comprise POL are integrated via a menu-driven search system. This enables the user to search across the respective POL databases concurrently. The core POL database is the Federal PAC Directory. This large database tracks, dollar for dollar, all contributions from political action committees to candidates for federal office since 1977. A complementary database, the State PAC Directory, tracks contributions to selected local candidates from various organizational sources (including nonfederal PACs).

In addition, POL will contain a database profiling congressional incumbents and will give over 40 interest-group ratings of those incumbents. Additional databases are scheduled to be added to POL in 1984.

Selected data from POL is published by Ballinger Publishing Co., a division of Harper & Row, in a series known as *The PAC Directories*. The updated two-volume set of these directories is planned to be on sale in hardcover in Spring 1984, at a cost of $200.

Public Affairs Information

Public Affairs Information, 1024 10th St., Suite 300, Sacramento, California 95814, 916-444-0840

Public Affairs Information (PAI) provides a series of databases containing information on all bills introduced in Congress and in the fifty states. Bills can be screened, tracked, and monitored by subject, state, house of origin, date of introduction, sponsor, title, and committee reference. Each bill has a summary that is updated as bills are amended.

In combination with Capitol Services Inc. (CSI), PAI provides a daily online version of CSI's Congressional Record and Federal Regulatory Information.

PAI also covers all state and federal regulations. Information includes agency, topic, summary, agency contact, citation, source, proposal date, comment deadline, and hearing date.

In early 1984, PAI will make available a database on environmental compliance, including existing federal laws, laws of 35 states, and related rules and regulations.

During the second quarter of 1984, PAI will provide a federal and ten-state political database covering campaign contributions for state and federal offices, district profiles for state and federal offices, and district demographic data.

Annual subscriptions begin at $2,000 and include connect charges.

*QL Systems

QL Systems Limited, 797 Princess St., Kingston, Ontario, Canada K7L IGI, 613-549-4611

Sales offices: Kingston, Ottawa, Toronto.

QL Systems grew out of a joint project between Queens University and IBM to develop QUIC/LAW, an information retrieval system. Today the company supplies over 80 databases, in addition to text-editing and electronic mail services.

Most of the information in QL's databases concerns Canada. There are 30 legal databases on Canadian federal and provincial statutes, case summaries, and decisions; 7 databases on Canadian energy and environmental issues; and 10 concerned with science and engineering. Others contain information on Canadian business, government, and research.

QL Systems is accessible at baud speeds of up to 9600, making it one of the first vendors to operate such high-speed lines.

Quotron Systems

Quotron Systems, Inc., 5454 Beethoven St., Los Angeles, California 90066, 213-827-4600

Sales offices: 9 U.S. cities, London, Hong Kong, Singapore.

Established in 1957 to supply online financial information services to brokerage houses, banks, insurance companies, and other financial institutions, Quotron Systems by 1984 had grown to be a $100 million company. Its customers have access to complete transactions information on all stocks, bonds, options, mutual funds, and commodities quoted on major American, Canadian, European, and Far Eastern exchanges. The system serves more than 4,800 brokerage offices in over 1,100 cities. Typical users are financial brokers or experts who need a constant source of current market information.

Clients use dedicated Quotron terminals connected via Quotron's own network to central computers. Representative databases offered by the system are listed below. A new service called Quotdial makes some of this data available to microcomputer users (see Chapter 19).

Public database offerings

Databases available on Quotron include ARGUS Research; Citicorp Economic Report; Dow Jones 90-Day News Retrieval; Innovest; Market Advisory; Quotron Financial; Vickers; Wall Street Estimates; and Wright Investor's Service.

Samsom Data Systemen

Samsom Data Systemen B.V./Data Base Services, a division of Wolters Samsom Groep, Wilhelminalaan 1, Postbus 180, 2400 AD Alphen aan den Rijn, The Netherlands, 01720-62195 (in the Netherlands), 31-1720-62195 (outside)

Temporary U.S. information desk: Aspen Systems Corporation, Rockville, Maryland, 301-251-5360 or 301-251-5363.

Samsom is a division of the Wolters Samsom Groep, an international corporation made up of 20 companies involved in publishing, printing, databases, correspondence courses, and efficiency systems. 800 of the company's 2500 employees work in subsidiaries outside the Netherlands.

Through its Datanet system, Samsom provides a series of databases containing bibliographic information on the shipping, hydraulics, and offshore industries, telecommunications, library and information sciences, and tropical agriculture. Databases concentrate on source material from acknowledged experts and world-famous scientific authors.

Samsom's first databases, concentrating on the maritime and hydraulics fields, were introduced in 1980. In 1983 Samsom decided to expand the focus of its offerings. Many databases were added and more will be added in the future. The hourly charge is about $60 to $80.

The Telecom database, produced by a leading Dutch telecommunications company, contains over 100,000 bibliographic references (30 percent with abstracts) to information about telecommunication and its applications.

Samsom Datanet is accessible via Tymnet, Telenet, Datapac, Teleglobe, and Euronet.

TRW Information Services

TRW Information Services Division, TRW Inc., 505 City Parkway West, Orange, California 92668, 714-937-2000

TRW Information Services operates and markets two nationwide computerized credit-reporting services: TRW Credit Data, one of the largest available files on consumer credit, and TRW Business Credit Profile, a business credit-reporting service.

TRW Credit Data contains credit information on more than 90 million consumers and serves 24,000 subscribers at 35,000 locations. The company collects and stores factual credit information on consumers and provides it to credit grantors that subscribe to the service. This updated credit profile (see Chapter 16) contains credit account information provided by subscribers, including positive and negative information about retail credit card accounts, bank charge card accounts, lines of credit, secured loans, and finance company accounts. The profile also includes selected public record information limited to tax liens, judgments, and bankruptcies.

TRW provides the information to bona fide credit grantors who have a legitimate business need for it, as in considering applications for credit. Typical customers are banks, retailers, and finance companies. Individual consumers may also obtain copies of their own profiles.

TRW Business Credit Profile (see Chapter 18) provides credit executives with trade payment information on nearly 8 million business locations representing all major industries, with key business facts on over 400,000 companies and with comprehensive business and financial data supplied by Standard & Poor's Corp.

The reports in TRW Business Credit Profile can be obtained in minutes from teleprinter terminals linked via high-speed data communications lines to the central file in Anaheim, California. Nearly 7,000 companies contribute their automated and manual accounts-receivable information to the file every 90 days. The file currently contains over 20 million lines of payment experiences.

Tymshare

Tymshare, Inc., 20705 Valley Green Dr., Cupertino, California 95014, 408-446-6000

Tymshare is a large computer services company with nearly $300 million in annual revenues. Its "Ontyme" product is a major electronic mail service. Other online services include numerous applications programs aimed at particular industries or functions. Tymshare owns Tymnet, a major value-added network serving as a common carrier for data communications in 400 U.S. metropolitan areas and 40 countries.

Public database offerings

Tymshare public databases include CITIBASE; DORIS; SITE II; SITE POTENTIAL; Solo; TYMQUOTE Securities; and Value Line.

VU/TEXT

VU/TEXT, P.O. Box 8558, Philadelphia, Pennsylvania 19101, 215-854-8297

VU/TEXT started as a private database to automate the editorial libraries of The Philadelphia Inquirer and The Philadelphia Daily News. Today VU/TEXT provides online access to databases primarily containing information from and about the Mid-Atlantic section of the United States. VU/TEXT is accessible via Telenet.

Public database offerings

VU/TEXT provides full-text coverage of *The Philadelphia Inquirer, The Philadelphia Daily News, Lexington Herald-Leader*, and *The Washington Post*. Other VU/TEXT databases include Academic American Encyclopedia; Mediawire, a public relations service carrying news releases from Pennsylvania, Maryland, Delaware, and West Virginia; and Pennsylvania Legislative Database.

Westlaw

Westlaw, a division of West Publishing Company, 50 West Kellogg Blvd., P.O. Box 3526, St. Paul, Minnesota 55165, 612-228-2500, 800-328-9833

West Publishing Company is a major publisher of federal and state legal decisions. Westlaw is the company's computer-assisted legal research service. It began online in 1975. Since 1978 Westlaw has been offering full-text files of legal decisions. It has case records from all U.S. Federal District and Appeals Courts and the U.S. Supreme Court. Other Westlaw libraries include federal statutory and administrative law, federal tax law, and many federal special-interest libraries, such as securities, patents, trademarks, copyrights, antitrust and business regulations, communications, and bankruptcy. There are 50 state case law libraries, including attorney general opinions, insurance, and family law for some states.

In addition to its vast libraries, Westlaw has also added other vital research capabilities: Shepard's Citations; Insta-Cite (West's online case history service); Black's Law Dictionary; Forensic Services Directory; and Eurolex, the full-text computer-assisted legal research service offered by The European Law Centre, Ltd., London. Eurolex offers the important libraries covering Common Market, European, and United Kingdom law.

Westlaw is compatible with over 200 different models of computer terminals, word processors and microcomputers.

Wharton Econometric Forecasting Associates

Wharton Econometric Forecasting Associates, Inc., 3624 Science Center, Philadelphia, Pennsylvania 19104, 215-386-9000

Wharton Econometrics is an internationally known econometric forecasting group. It has close ties to the Wharton School at the University of Pennsylvania. Today it is a subsidiary of Compagnie International de Services en Informatique (CISI), a French-based company. CISI has one of the largest commercial data networks in Europe. Wharton produces models for study and analysis of the U.S. and world economies for a customer base consisting primarily of major corporations and government agencies. The company also designs models to track and forecast data according to customers' specific needs.

Public database offerings

A number of the Wharton Econometric online databases contain historical time series and forecasts for the U.S. economy by year, quarter, and month. Other databases cover the Producer and Consumer Price indexes, gross product originating series for many industries, the flow of funds in the U.S. economy, the automobile industry, and various data on the New York and Philadelphia metropolitan areas. International databases offer global econometric coverage with special detailed series for Mexico, Brazil, the Middle East, the U.S.S.R, China, and other centrally planned economies. A World Economic Model is also available.

PART FOUR

MAKING THE CONNECTION

*T*his section deals with the technical side of searching databases—the hardware and software you'll need. We start with a discussion of old-fashioned "dumb" terminals, which people used for database searching in the decade before microcomputers. Then, in Chapter 27, we come more up to date with an examination of microcomputers for online communications. Chapter 28 explains the other side of the equation—the telecommunications networks that transmit messages to and from your terminal. Finally, Chapter 29 describes how to select a software package and modem for on-line searching.

Old-Fashioned
26 (and Modern) Terminals

There's an old-fashioned way to go online and a modern way. The old fashioned way uses a "dumb" communicating terminal. The modern way uses a microcomputer. (Some terminals are now "smart" or "intelligent," but not very, when compared to microcomputers.)

Let's define our terms. A terminal isn't a computer. Or more precisely, it is a "dedicated" computer, programmed for just one application. It cannot run other kinds of software; it usually has little or no memory; and it usually cannot be connected to an external memory device. A terminal is simply *a device for sending messages to, or receiving them from, an actual computer*. If you plug a terminal into the electricity and turn it on, it will just sit there humming. There's nothing it can do for you without being connected to a computer.

Terminals can be linked with computers in one of two ways. One is by being "hard wired," connected directly to the computer by a cable. This is how an organization with a large computer might connect work stations throughout a building. This method of connection will not concern us here.

The other method of connecting to a computer, which does concern us, is by telephone. This requires a modem, which, as we've said before, turns data bits into tones that can travel over phone lines (modulation) or turns tones back into electronic pulses when they arrive at their destination (demodulation). Many terminals have modems built in (these are called *communicating* terminals, though often referred to as just terminals); for those that don't, you must hook one up. If you need to buy a separate modem, take a look at Chapter 30 and Appendix E, which are all about modems for your terminal or microcomputer.

Communicating terminals were invented in the late 1960s, about the same time that computer time sharing was coming into existence. It was a natural development. Time sharing meant that many people could use a single large computer at the same time. That being possible, it made sense to

428 / Making the Connection

allow individual users to be in widely dispersed locations. Thus communicating terminals have been with us for more than a decade.

Why are we telling you about terminals, if they're so old-fashioned? If you already have a microcomputer, this chapter might be irrelevant for you. Then again, it might not. Your business might well already own dumb terminals that you could use for searching databases. Or your company might own a portable terminal convenient for taking along on trips.

Even if your company doesn't have a communicating terminal, it might want to buy a new one. Even though they're old-fashioned, spiffy new models are being manufactured, and in general they are cheaper than microcomputers (though you'll find plenty of exceptions to that rule). Also, terminals in general are simpler machines to use.

A computer, of course, is a far more versatile machine. A terminal, however, might be right for you (or your company), at the right price, particularly if you want to use online databases or electronic mail exclusively.

A communicating terminal usually looks like a typewriter, with a keyboard and built-in printer. Some terminals use a video display rather than printer, but for database searching the printing kind (also known as "teleprinters") are more widely used. Why? Because you need some way to preserve the information that arrives at the terminal! Remember, terminals have little or no memory; so with a "dumb" video terminal, information that rolls off the screen is lost. You can attach a printer to a video terminal; however, that tends to be a more cumbersome or more expensive arrangement.

Like typewriters, teleprinters come in portable and nonportable models. Portables are usually cheapest; on the other hand, they generally use thermal printing, which offers the poorest quality and takes relatively expensive, special paper. Larger models may use impact printing—either dot-matrix (medium quality) printing or full-character printing (best quality, like a typewriter).

A portable terminal with built-in printer can now be had for $395 (the Lexicon LEX-21), and a communicating video display terminal (no printer or memory) goes for as little as $250 (the Quazon QUIK-LINK 300) or possibly even less by the time you read this. But in acquiring one of the less expensive terminals, check to see whether it can transmit all 128 ASCII characters. Some may lack a control key, break key, or other crucial button. (All the ones we list in Appendix C have full ASCII character sets.)

In Appendix C, we describe a number of terminals on the market. We have not prepared a comprehensive list nor are these models necessarily the best or least expensive. We don't mean to recommend them over others you might find. Rather, our goal is to illustrate the range of products available. For each one listed, we have tried to provide most of the data you might need for evaluating it and comparing it to others on the market.

Microcomputers
27 for Communicating
Online

If you begin doing a great deal of searching on a communicating terminal, you're bound to notice something: it isn't very efficient.

There you are, online with DIALOG. The clock is running at around $95 an hour. You are entering a search command: SEARCH JAPAN AND (IMPORT OR TRADE) AND (QUOTA? or RESTRICTION?). You get the line almost done, then notice that you misspelled IMPORT. You backspace, fix the error, then retype the rest, leaving off the closing parentheses after TRADE. You go back and fix that. After a minute of this, you get it right, hit the return key, then remember that you should have put a question mark after JAPAN, which makes the system search for the term "JAPANESE" as well. It may end up costing you $3 or $4 just to get a single search statement executed correctly, and you still haven't received any information.

Then you hit a TYPE command to print out the titles of the "hits" that you uncovered, pick a dozen or so that look promising, print the full records on your terminal, and log off. Now you have a roll of poor-quality thermal paper with the results of your search on it. That's unfortunate because what you really need is some neat material for a report that must be presented at a board meeting. So you mark up the printout and hand it to your secretary, who spends part of the afternoon retyping it in a more readable and condensed form. The whole affair costs you about $10 in online time and perhaps four times that in personnel cost.

With all this high technology, isn't there a better way? Yes. Using a microcomputer instead of an old-fashioned dumb terminal can save lots of time and money. Consider the following record from the ABI/INFORM database.

83816725
Productivity and QWL Success Without Ideal Conditions
  Ashkenas, Ronald N.; Jick, Todd D.
  National Productivity Review   vin4   PP: 381-388   Autumn 1982   ISSN:
8277-8556   HRNL   CODE: NLP

DOC TYPE: Journal Paper   LANGUAGE: English   LENGTH: 8 Pages
AVAILABILITY: ABI/INFORM

Severe competitive pressure and some well-publicized cases have sparked management interest in greater employee involvement in improving productivity and the quality of work life (QWL). Experiences of the past few years suggest that long-lived successes occur most often in organizations that meet a number of preconditions, including: 1. strong managerial commitment, 2. adequate resources for change, 3. planning for change, 4. long lead time, 5. well-managed firms, and 6. a stable leadership environment. Few organizations meet these preconditions. This analysis offers examples of the risks that are present when well-meaning, committed managers attempt to initiate employee involvement programs. It is possible, however, to be successful in such programs without meeting the preconditions for success. The key is to build an employee involvement effort around existing organizational imperfections, rather than the reverse. By beginning with bottom-line results and accomplishing some early small successes with those managers and supervisors who are most ready to involve their staff more fully, an expanding pattern of involvement can be created. Charts. References.

DESCRIPTORS: Quality of work; Productivity; Improvements; Planning; Programs; Quality circles

CLASSIFICATION CODES: 2500 (CN = Organizational behavior); 5318 (CN = Production planning & control)

This record was obtained as a result of a search for the term "quality circles" and "productivity." The article is exactly what was sought, but if included in a report in its present form, it might cause the reader's eyes to glaze over.

It was saved on disk, however, which made it easy to manipulate with a word processing program. About five minutes' work turned it into this:

Productivity and QWL Success Without Ideal Conditions

by Ronald N. Ashkenas & Todd D. Jick
National Productivity Review
Autumn 1982, page 381-388

Severe competitive pressures and some well-publicized cases have sparked management interest in greater employee involvement in improving productivity and the quality of work life (QWL). Experiences of the past few years suggest that long-lived successes occur most often in organizations that meet a number of preconditions, including:

1. strong managerial commitment
2. adequate resources for change
3. planning for change
4. long lead time
5. well-managed firms
6. a stable leadership environment

Few organizations meet these preconditions. This analysis offers examples of the risks that are present when well-meaning, committed managers attempt to initiate employee-involvement programs. It is possible, however, to be successful in such programs without meeting the preconditions for success. The key is to build an employee-involvement effort around existing organizational imperfections, rather than the reverse. By beginning with bottom-line results and accomplishing some early small successes with those managers and supervisors who are most ready to involve their staff more fully, an expanding pattern of involvement can be created.

The format here is cleaner, easier to read, and free of such details as accession numbers, CODENs, journal codes, descriptors, and so on. Such enhanced records can be integrated smoothly into reports and proposals without breaking the flow of the surrounding text.

This can involve more than mere cosmetics. The typical online printout is littered with search commands, typographical errors, wild goose chases, and cost statements. Some databases, such as Disclosure II, are full of spelling errors as well, which can be embarrassing if you are striving for a professional appearance in your report.

A microcomputer affords many other potential advantages:

♦ The cost of "hunting and pecking" goes down considerably when you can edit your search statements offline and then transmit them smoothly and accurately at 30 or 120 characters per second.

♦ Much of the detail of online searching can be eliminated if the microcomputer takes care of dialing the phone, signing on, remembering your password, etc.

♦ With some databases, you can save quite a bit of money (while sacrificing some flexibility) by letting the microcomputer automatically sign on late at night and perform a predefined search. With few users online, the response time at night usually is brisk, resulting in lower connect charges.

♦ With some microcomputer software, such as the Institute for Scientific Information's Sci-Mate, the results of your search can be integrated into an "electronic library" of your own. While open to copyright questions, this technique can be of considerable value in managing the files for a specific project or specialty.

♦ Equipped with other software, the microcomputer can serve as a low-cost training aid, allowing new users to practice on simulated databases without accumulating heavy online charges.

To communicate with online vendors by microcomputer, you need a modem and a communications software package. Selecting these can get a bit complicated. To help you, we discuss each in more detail in the following chapters.

28 How Computers Communicate

Thus far all that we have told you about connecting your terminal or computer to a database vendor is that it takes a simple telephone call. There are a few more facts you ought to know about the process.

First, as we mentioned earlier, the telephone call doesn't cost much. Computers have their own long-distance telephone networks, which are considerably cheaper to use than your telephone company's. Within the continental United States, the price averages $2 to $8 an hour, regardless of distance.

What makes the call cheaper than a voice telephone call? As you may know, computers "communicate" (or humans communicate by computer) in a manner not much different from the nineteenth-century telegraph: they transform numbers and letters of the alphabet into a kind of Morse Code of dots and dashes. Rather than Morse Code, of course, they usually use the American Standard Code for Information Interchange (ASCII) or one of a few others modern codes.

Human communication, whether by voice, Morse Code, or ASCII, is fundamentally "asynchronous" (sporadic). Humans stop to think about what to say next. They emit quick bursts of conversation. At one moment a lot of data may be traveling across the phone line; at another, there's little or no flow at all.

Whether a person communicates with another human or with a computer, the same holds. When you're online communicating with a database system through a modern computer telephone network, you naturally type slowly, pausing to think about what command to give next.

If you tied up a long-distance telephone line to accomplish that, you could run up a large bill quickly. But in the 1960s, the computer industry found a way to conserve valuable long-distance capacity when sending asynchronous computer signals. The solution, in essence, is that at each pause, the telephone network jumps in and transmits a portion of somebody else's message over the path yours was traveling on. In effect, many computer conversations travel over a path that could carry only one voice conversation. During a voice call, you must monopolize a path; no other data can travel over it.

The technique is called "packet switching," after the way the characters you type are bundled together and switched in and out among other packets. In this way the cost is held considerably below the long-distance charges for voice calls. Packet switching also makes distance largely irrelevant, as each packet of information may travel paths of very different length. That's why computer telephone network charges don't vary with distance (except when going overseas).

How do you take advantage of a packet-switching network? It's very similar to using one of the alternative long-distance phone companies, such as MCI or Sprint. You dial a local "access node," then punch in another number that tells the network where you want to be connected.

There are three major "common-carrier" packet-switching networks (also referred to as "value-added networks" or VANs). Tymshare Inc.'s Tymnet helped bring about the online industry when it became the first public packet-switched network in 1972. GTE's Telenet joined the business in 1975, and the newest, United Telecom's Uninet, began operation in 1983. All three are expanding rapidly, and you can expect to see other competitors in the future, possibly including AT&T or IBM. Most database vendors can be reached through at least one of these three networks.

In addition to the three common carriers, a number of time-sharing computer companies and database vendors operate their own packet-switching networks primarily for users of their own services. These include ADP, Control Data, CompuServe, National Data, The Source, DIALOG, Dow Jones, General Electric Information Service, and Data Resources. (Their networks aren't necessarily available in all cities.)

There are just a few easy steps to do to be able to use the packet-switching networks—but more than a few things could go wrong. Here are some tips that may help you when you go online:

♦ *For each of the three common carriers, get an instruction booklet and keep it handy.* You can request one by calling Tymnet at 800-336-0149 or Telenet at 800-336-0437. (At press time, Uninet did not have a toll-free number.)

♦ *Figure out how your terminal or computer and modem work.* There are hundreds of terminals and modems on the market—and equally many varieties no longer manufactured but still in wide use. Each one operates slightly differently. Some, for example, have a light that goes on when you've established a connection; some don't. Some may require you to push an arbitrary button to get communication flowing. The sequence of steps required to make it work probably isn't obvious. The best way to learn to use a terminal is to have someone show you how. If someone else in your company uses the machine, ask for a demonstration. Then have that person stick around while you attempt your first log on. If you're buying a new machine, by all means, insist that the salesman help you through a "live" demonstration, calling the actual service you plan to use later.

♦ *Make sure you have the correct telephone numbers*. Even though database vendors will send you a list of phone numbers when you sign up, the packet-switching networks change numbers often. They are so busy building new facilities that access numbers in a city may be changed every few months. To get the latest phone numbers for your area, call the networks toll-free at the numbers given above.

♦ *Make sure you get a list of* all *the local access numbers for each network*. In major cities, each network may have several numbers that you can use. One may be more reliable than another. Also note other numbers in the suburbs or nearby cities that are a local call from your location. These may be easier to get through to.

♦ *If a local node doesn't answer your call after a couple of rings, don't wait; hang up and try a different one*. An endlessly ringing number signifies that the node is busy handling its maximum number of callers, or that it is out of order.

♦ *Get used to using all three networks*. When one doesn't function, another will.

♦ *Be sure to note which of the local numbers are compatible with your modem*. There are basically three kinds of modems that you have to be aware of—the Vadic 3400, the Bell 103, and the Bell 212A. Your modem is of one of these three types. Some network phone numbers work for all three, but others may be compatible with only one or two. (More on modems in Chapter 30.)

♦ *Is the phone number compatible with transmission at 30 characters per second, 120 characters per second, or both?* If your connection generates gibberish, it may be because you're calling a 30-cps node with a 120-cps modem.

♦ *If you have problems receiving "garbage characters," try another telephone line* (if you're in a location with more than one) *or, if possible, another location in your facility*. You may be picking up electrical interference. The longer the wire between your telephone and the lines outside, the more likely you are to pick up interference.

♦ *Be aware of your "terminal identifier."* Each time you connect with Telenet or Tymnet, you'll first get a message asking for your identifier. Often, the connection will work just fine if you respond with one of these all-purpose answers: "A" for Tymnet or the "Return" button for Telenet. If you have trouble receiving information, though, you may have to find out your terminal's correct identifier. To do so, do any one or all of the following: (1) consult the documentation from the database vendor your're trying to reach; (2) call the vendor; (3) consult the network brochures mentioned; or (4) call the network at the numbers we have listed.

♦ When "uploading" stored information from your microcomputer, your computer actually sends data in a steady stream. If the packet-switching network is expecting your usual start-and-stop communication, then it will probably lose words and characters. The solution— *warn the packet-switching network in advance that a steady stream is going to arrive*. You do that by giving the network a special command. On Telenet, you type @ to get the network's attention and then say DTAPE; on Tymnet you type Control X after the terminal identifier. In either case, you will be switched to half duplex (the meaning of this is discussed just below) and must adjust your terminal accordingly.

♦ *Pay attention to the half-duplex/full-duplex switch or setting.* When operating in full duplex, your signal travels to the vendor computer and then is "echoed" back to your computer screen or printer. This provides a convenient check on whether your signal is getting through properly. If a character you type doesn't appear on the screen, then it hasn't yet been received by the vendor. In half duplex, on the other hand, your signal takes only a one-way trip. In order to display the character sent, your own computer simultaneously sends a duplicate to your screen. The majority of vendors ordinarily operate at full duplex, though they may also work at half duplex.

If, when you begin an online session, every character you type appears double, then you're set at half duplex when you should be in full (you're getting one display character from your own computer and an echo from the vendor). If your characters don't appear on your screen at all, but you still receive proper responses from the vendor, then you have the opposite problem: You're set at full but communicating at half (your terminal is expecting an echo that never comes).

♦ *Find out the communications protocol for each database vendor that you use.* Often you will not learn this information in the vendor's literature; you may have to call and ask or experiment with one or two protocols to find what works.

The ASCII characters you send out from your computer should be made up of ten bits. At the beginning and end will be a "start" and "stop" bit. These simply help the host computer ascertain that there is an eight-bit character code in-between. Of the eight remaining bits available to specify a letter, number, or other symbol, most host computers use only seven. That's because seven bits are enough to create the 128 (2 to the 7th power) unique characters that make up the standard ASCII set as defined by the American National Standards Institute. Some communications software use all eight bits, allowing double that many characters (2 to the 8th power equals 256). But these additional "high" ASCII codes aren't standardized; they mean different things to different computers.

In place of the eighth bit, the vendor's computer may require an odd or even (usually even) parity bit. This is simply a 0 or 1 added to the other seven digits, which makes their sum odd or even. A parity bit helps the host spot garbled transmissions: if a computer using even parity encounters an eight-bit code whose sum is odd, it knows there has been some interference and can warn the user.

Even if the vendor doesn't use parity, you generally still must fill that eighth bit's place with something. Thus the vendor's protocol might require two stop bits; or it might specify use of eight-bit characters even though the eighth bit will be ignored; or it might ask for a parity bit that will be ignored. All of these options accomplish essentially the same thing.

♦ *Check the vendor's Xon/Xoff or "flow-control" specification.* If it uses this feature, you should set your communications software accordingly. You may also have to enable this option at the network level (CON-TROL-R after the terminal identifier on Tymnet; or ENAB TFLO after Telenet's @ sign). With this feature enabled, your computer can automatically send a temporary halt (Xoff) command when its buffer fills up. When it is ready to start receiving data again, it sends the vendor a start command (Xon). You can also send the commands manually: CONTROL-S sends an Xoff and CONTROL-Q sends an Xon.

Don't, however, try to use Xoff/Xon unless the vendor allows it. On some vendor systems such as DIALOG, the telecommunications network will intercept the Xon and not pass it through to the vendor. The transmission will appear to pause on your end, but the vendor will continue sending data into the network's buffers; in a short time the buffers will overflow, and you'll lose information.

There are other minor specifications that you might have occasion to adjust. These include the auto-linefeed, dial pulse rate, length of the break signal, and other obscure settings. Most of these will be correct in their "default" status—the way they come out of the box. But if you find that something just doesn't function the way it is supposed to, you may have to try reading some of the fine print in your user manual.

All About
29 Communications Software[1]

Most microcomputers were not designed with communications as a principal function; they were originally envisioned only as stand-alone processors. Consequently, many microcomputers require a number of hardware "add-ons" before they will operate as terminals. These add-ons might include clocks, serial interfaces, printer controllers, upper/lower-case or 80-column displays, and so on. (Some microcomputers, the Apple II in particular, require more add-ons than others.) The complete purchase price may increase substantially before the microcomputer is ready to talk to the outside world.

In addition to hardware modifications, a microcomputer also needs appropriate software to allow it to appear as a terminal to the remote vendor. A few have this capability as part of their operating systems, but most of these allow for strictly "dumb" operations only—that is, they will send the proper signals back and forth, but not much else. This is not a very effective way to use a microcomputer. What is needed is a "smart-terminal" software package.

There are a great number of these packages available now (easily over 200), and more are being released all the time. You don't, however, need to evaluate dozens of packages before selecting one to purchase. Virtually all communications software packages are quite hardware dependent: each will operate on only selected hardware configurations, including any add-on boards or peripherals. Thus, if the hardware has already been acquired, the software selection is greatly narrowed. If the hardware has not been purchased or selected, the software should be examined as part of the evaluation and selection process. Some software is even "bundled" with other

[1]This chapter is reprinted, with changes, from *Communication Software for Microcomputers* by Janet L. Bruman (Cooperative Library Agency for Systems and Services, San Jose, CA., January 1983), by permission of the author and CLASS.

software packages such as spreadsheet analysis (the Context MBA, listed in Appendix D, is an example).

Terminal software packages range from top-of-the-line, do-everything wonders, down to bare basics. They range in price from $35 to $900 or more. The functions of this software include communications protocols, display characteristics, command operations and data transfers. When considering the purchase of such programs, examine how thoroughly and easily they perform each of the following operations.

Communications protocol

Configuring the communications protocols means determining the word length (number of data bits per character), the number of start/stop bits, and the number and type of parity bits. The same process will usually also encompass setting the baud rate, the duplex (half or full) generation of line-feed characters, and various other CONTROL functions. Whatever software package is acquired, it will have default settings, but since the requirements of the various vendors differ, it is important that the user be able to alter these. The program should then store the changes, so the user need not go through the process every time the software is used. Because online vendors do have very different requirements, a program should be able to store a number of configurations.

Keyboard redefinition

Another capability that the software should have is character redefinition, which is sometimes referred to as "keyboard mapping." Many microcomputers lack full character sets and cannot generate all of the ASCII characters or all of the control codes needed to converse properly with the vendor. (Sometimes the missing codes are quite essential ones, like BREAK.) Other microcomputers may define the function of certain CONTROL or ESCAPE sequences differently than what the vendor expects or requires. The software should allow the user to alter the code or character that is generated by particular keys or key combinations. These redefinitions should also be stored, so that this step need not be repeated with each use. The better packages allow the user to have it both ways—the user can retain the original function of the key and add desired functions through ESCAPE or CONTROL combinations. While this may require that more than one keystroke be used to generate the appropriate signal, at least no functions are lost.

Screen display

It is only quite recently that microcomputers have had 80-column displays or upper- and lower-case character sets as standard features. The smart terminal software can be used to substitute or compensate for these lacks, although more generally the solution is a hardware modification.

When the software is used to generate both upper and lower case, the screen may display it by using reverse video. The software will recognize the differences and will send the right signals to the vendor. This is particularly useful for electronic mail applications, where the use of upper and lower case is more important than for database searching.

A related function is changing the screen format. The output from the vendors is typically in lines of up to 75 characters; without a full-size 80-column display, the vendors' output must be wrapped around to the next line. Smart terminal software can make the display easier to read by breaking the lines at the end of the words rather than arbitrarily in mid-word. The full-length line should still be passed unbroken to the printer, however.

RAM buffer operation

Perhaps the most important feature to be gained from a microcomputer with communications package is the buffer. This is a section of RAM (random-access memory) used for temporary storage of data transmitted between the user and the vendor. The buffer's contents can then be viewed, edited, saved to disk, dumped to the printer, etc. (The RAM buffer should not be confused with the print buffer that many packages provide. The print buffer is a separate area located within the memory.)

The RAM buffer size will vary widely, depending both on the hardware being used and on the terminal software itself. For most purposes, the larger the buffer, the better. The software packages can provide as little as 4K of space or as much as an entire disk. The buffer needs to be large enough to accommodate both the data to be captured from the vendor (downloaded) and the data to be sent to the vendor (uploaded). The program should permit the user to toggle the buffer open and closed without exiting from the terminal program or interrupting the vendor in any way. This allows the user to be selective about what is captured. The software should also inform the user if the buffer is open or closed and how much space it has left.

Most software programs will not allow simultaneous receipt of data and saving to disk. This means that to prevent data loss, the *save* must be done while the vendor is "on hold," which wastes connect time. The best situation is to have a buffer large enough to capture the entire online session, so that the *write* to disk can be done while offline. The Dtrans program (Automata Design Associates, 1570 Arran Way, Dresler, Pennsylvania 19025) permits five open buffer files to place data in, simultaneously. Another package, Crosstalk (Microstuf Co.; see listing in Appendix D), allows the user to capture directly onto disk rather than into buffer, but the function depends on using the Xon/Xoff flow-control protocols, which are not available on DIALOG, BRS, or some other vendors.

Be wary of how the buffer operates. On some packages, reopening the buffer erases its current contents. As a consequence, if the user has forgotten to *write* the contents to disk after the last close of the buffer, whatever was in it will be lost. Another problem area is the *buffer full* message, which some packages will not give until already out of space. Most will simultaneously send the vendor an Xoff to handle the data flow, but since many vendors unfortunately will ignore this signal, some of the data will be lost. The Transend package (Transend Corp., 2190 Paragon Dr., San Jose, California 95131) sounds a warning "bell" when the space remaining in the buffer goes below 3K.

Uploads, downloads, and editing

Capturing data from the vendor (downloading) and sending preconstructed text back (uploading) are among the major justifications for using a microcomputer for communications. In order to perform these transfers, the user must be able to create and manipulate text. This means an editor is needed. Some terminal packages include an editor; others provide compatibility with standard word-processing packages for the same hardware, so that files can be used and manipulated within both programs. Commwhiz (Volks Micro Computer Systems, Inc., 202 Packets Ct., Williamsburg, Virginia 23185) does this for Scripsit and Electric Pencil, for instance. Still other packages both create short text files within the terminal program and utilize other files created by the word-processing package or operating system. You should beware of terminal programs that can do neither, as with the TRS-80 Model II "Terminal" function. They will leave the user with downloaded blocks of unalterable text; uploads are not possible at all.

Whatever editor is being used, be certain that the transfer process allows for imbedding CONTROL characters. This allows instructions to the vendor to be included in uploaded text, without them being acted on by the microcomputer. It is also important to be able to instruct the microcomputer to ignore certain characters or CONTROL sequences transmitted by the vendor—top of form, clear screen, change screen characteristics, etc.—that could cause unwanted reactions.

The better smart terminal programs allow the user a variety of ways to perform uploads. Almost all will allow dumping of a block of text (or the contents of the buffer) to the vendor, but not all vendors can accept large uninterrupted streams of data. The software should allow the user to choose between transmitting a block or a line at a time. If transmitting a block, which is really a stream of characters in asynchronous transmission, the user should be able to insert delays between characters. This does not alter the baud rate. Zterm (Southwestern Data Systems, P.O. Box 582, Santee, California 92071) provides six stepped delays in addition to a carriage return delay; Commwhiz has nine stepped delays.

When transmitting line by line, even more control of the data flow is needed. The microcomputer must recognize when it has reached the end of the a line to be uploaded (usually by a CR/LF). It must also recognize, as part of the configurations for that vendor, the prompt character(s) to wait for before sending the next line (i.e., whether the vendor uses a question mark, underscore/colon, greater than, or other characters). Alternatively, there are other mechanisms for controlling the data flow. Some packages use a WAIT (defined as a number of seconds) or else define the number of characters to be received from the vendor sending the next line.

Printer controls

There is wide variation in the way software packages control printer output. Some allow printing directly from the incoming modem line; some will print directly from the RAM buffer while data is incoming; others allow printing only when the communications line is "quiet." The user should consider very carefully whether it is important to print while in TERMINAL mode and in what volume. Since it is unusual to want to print everything coming over the line (and into the RAM buffer), the program should have a simple way of toggling the printer on and off without interrupting other functions unduly.

In addition to simply turning the printer on and off, the software should provide some interface or controls over the print speed. Printers that can keep up with high-speed output are costly compared to the slower models, and the typical printer sold with a microcomputer system may be even slower (particularly in performing carriage returns) than teleprinters. Unless the software provides some controls, the printer will fall behind the data stream and lose characters.

These speed controls can be in the form of a separate print buffer or spooler. This is an area of the RAM that is allocated to compensate for the difference between the speed of data reception and the speed of printing. The print buffer receives data at the same rate as the modem but releases it at the speed of the local printer. The size of the print buffer can be small (Zterm allows 255 characters) or large (Transend sets no limit). Other programs rely on Xon/Xoff controls or other techniques. How well the controls work may depend in part on what type of printer is used, as they must interact properly.

Automatic log on

Automatic log on is one of the features that every searcher of online database systems associates with the joys of owning a micocomputer: no more remembering passwords, terminal identifiers, etc. Users should be aware, however, that there is considerable variation in the provisions that the terminal software packages make for these functions. Storing and automatically transmitting strings of characters are referred to as Keyboard Macros. Some terminal packages have very limited parameters for macros (i.e., only so many strings, of so many characters). Some tie each string to a particular key; others allow the user to program one or more groups or sets of such strings. The Crosstalk package allows four strings of 50 characters each.

Some packages allow as many as can be stored in a certain space. Zterm provides a maximum of 2K; Datalink allows 1K.

Be careful about whether, and how, these macros incorporate control codes, as some log-on sequences need to use them. One program, Terminal Program (Telephone Software Connections; see listing in Appendix D) has taken a very clever approach to creating log-on macros. It simply captures the entire sign-on process during the initial (manual) session. At later sessions, the software repeats the user's input to the vendor's prompts. If the vendor changes the procedures, the package can just capture it again. Other packages come preprogrammed to log on to major vendors—you need only supply your confidential ID (for example, see the LINK Systems package listed in Appendix D).

Command execution

Virtually every software package will have at least two operating modes—one for COMMAND level or local interaction between the user and the microcomputer and another TERMINAL mode for conversing with the vendor mainframe. The program can only be in one mode at a time, so a mechanism must be provided for switching back and forth. Most packages do allow the user to perform COMMAND functions without disconnecting the communications line, but not all will allow this to happen without losing whatever the vendor has transmitted while the user was "away." Similarly, some may continue to capture the vendor's transmissions into the memory but will not restore it on the screen display when returning to TERMINAL mode. (Comwhiz is one that does restore the screen display.)

The mechanism that allows the user to change modes is usually a CONTROL or ESCAPE sequence. Sometimes this is a single keystroke, sometimes more. The return (from COMMAND to TERMINAL mode) may be accomplished automatically after completion of each COMMAND function, or may require an additional keystroke or menu selection. Obviously, the fewer keystrokes that are required, the faster the user will be able to perform the desired operation. A few of the better packages allow the performance of certain functions (open/close buffer, printer on/off) without leaving TERMINAL mode at all.

Status line

Another very useful feature to have, which will contribute to smooth operation, is a "status line." This is simply a line on the screen, usually at the very top or very bottom, that tells the user what the current settings are. This can include communications protocols that have been selected (helpful in identifying transmission problems), whether the RAM buffer is opened or closed and how much space is left in it, whether the printer is on or off, whether auto-linefeed is enabled, and so on. Being able to check on any of these conditions without exiting from the online conversation is quite helpful. A few packages enlarge on the status line by including in it a list of the key commands.

Menu operation

It is generally accepted that the best way to structure communications software is to make it menu-driven. This means that for any function, the user is prompted to select from a menu of options. Certainly it is less strain on the human memory to select from a list of choices than it is to remember what all the possible alternatives are. But the very experienced user may also get quite annoyed at being forced to look at a menu for every single operation (or even more than one menu, such as Transend uses). The user must judge what his tolerance is for menus and submenus (sometimes called "tree" structures), or for a system that asks him to verify (Are you sure? Y/N) even routine selections. A few packages allow the experienced user to bypass the menu displays by "typing ahead" or using a different CONTROL sequence.

Documentation

The user manual itself is a critical factor in the success of the software package. Unfortunately, the failings may not reveal themselves until the user is tangled in error messages. Look for indexes, logical organization, reference cards or command summaries, and training exercises or sample sessions. The manual for Visiterm (VisiCorp; see listing in Appendix D) includes a "Primer on Data Communications" and "Introduction to Communication Cards"; Micro/Terminal (MICROCOM, 1400A Providence Hwy, Norwood, Massachusetts 02062) gives a telecommunications oveview and ASCII character code chart. All are very useful items. Although good documentation does not guarantee a good program, poor documentation can ruin the usefulness of excellent ones.

Hardware compatibility

Communication speed is a variable that depends on both hardware and software. Unfortunately, many of the current software packages were written before the recent drop in 1200-baud modem prices; consequently, they did not anticipate the demand for 1200-baud compatibility. Many packages are being revised for 1200 baud, as the 300-baud modems have really lost their low-price advantage.

Some terminal software packages will support a wide range of modems and interface boards, while others are quite limited. The compatible modems are generally clearly stated in the software specifications. The most widely used are those from Hayes Microcomputer Products and Novation, in part because those companies have actively sought the microcomputer market. There are now also a number of firms selling both the modems and smart-terminal software sometimes as a "package deal."

Auto dial

The most commonly found enhancement is automatic telephone dialing from a directory of stored numbers. The software provides the proper instructions to the modem to make the connection. The function is often linked to the vendor log-on macro (see Automatic Log On, page 443). Automatic dialing cannot be accomplished by the software alone; it will only work in conjunction with the appropriate hardware.

Automatic dialing can be a great saver of time and frustration for the user, especially if more than one telephone number is accessed often. Packages that support automatic dialing will usually support re-dialing also, so busy ports are no longer such an annoyance. Some packages will "link" numbers, so that a busy signal or no answer will result in the software trying an alternate number for the same vendor. One new package, Perfect Software's Perfect Link, comes programmed with local-access telephone numbers.

File transfer protocols

So far, the emphasis has been on communications where the microcomputer and software function with a commercial database vendor. There are a number of other applications that are available when the system is operating in pairs—i.e., where there is a microcomputer on the other end of the line, running the same software package. The most common use for such connections is to transfer programs, as opposed to text.

When transferring nontext files, it is highly desirable to use some form of error checking. Several software packages incorporate this feature, using a variety of techniques such as check-sum verification to detect and correct errors.

Some packages will translate certain error-prone characters prior to transferring files, such as changing tab characters to eight spaces. This enables the files to be used by communicating word-processing systems, an application that more and more organizations are finding useful. Other packages will translate entire files from ASCII to binary, from BASIC to CP/M-based operating systems, or from "compressed" to "uncompressed" formats. All of these abilities are useful if the user expects to be involved in transferring program files.

If the hardware and software are appropriate and compatible, such operations can be conducted unattended. Several packages are available that allow for automatic origination and answering of telephone calls without any human intervention. Some communications packages that specifically address these applications are Micro Courier, Online (Southwestern Data Systems), Transend, and CommuniTree (CommuniTree Group, San Francisco). This application does result, however, in the microcomputer being "dedicated" to this function alone.

Database creation

All of the communications software packages will allow the user, to one extent or another, to download information—i.e., capture data from the vendor into local memory. However, the captured text usually can be used only for word processing. There is no easy way to transfer the file into a database management system, where it would be possible to merge, search, sort, or otherwise manipulate the data as if it were a locally created database. The only way this can be done is for the user to create the necessary programming locally.

Significant progress is being made in the direction of generalized data-capture-and-file-creation packages. Several products that provide the ability to download from vendor systems into a local database format have been released by online vendors and database publishers. ISI's PRIMATE, BIO-SIS's BITS, and Disclosure's Micro-DISCLOSURE programs are all specific to their own databases. BRS's Search and Cuadra Associates' STAR are more sophisticated (and more costly, both for software and hardware) and will perform downloading from many vendors as long as the data is formatted with recognizable tags.

Nonbibliographic databases and vendors are also progressing in this direction. Data Resources will now provide for downloading into a VisiCalc spreadsheet. Dow Jones is now selling software that allows for the collection and analysis of stock data from the Dow Jones News/Retrieval Service.

Serial interfaces

If the microcomputer has not been designed with a serial port, the first add-on that will be needed is a serial interface board and a clock that will enable the microcomputer to generate the proper signals for the modem and thus the vendor. Most of the newer machines will not require any modifications or enhancements in this area, as communications is now regarded as an important user priority.

Display monitors

The microcomputer display should be able to generate both upper- and lower-case characters in an 80-column format. It should also be able to scroll at least fast enough to keep pace with 1200-baud transmissions from the vendor. Because these features were not provided on some "personal" computers, most notably Apple, numerous other manufacturers have introduced plug-in boards with these features. The communications packages may be written for one specific manufacturer's boards; as with the modems, this should be checked against the software's specifications.

30 All About Modems[1]

The word "modem" is a contraction of the words *mod*ulate and *dem*odulate. Modems are solid-state devices that change (modulate) the digital signals from computers and computer equipment into tones that are suitable for transmission over phone lines, and then change (demodulate) them back.

Our discussion outlines the major features offered in modems targeted at personal computer users. (Appendix E lists some of the major modems available.) This includes modems that connect directly to the network through modular jacks and acoustic couplers with rubber cups that cradle a telephone handset.

In general, direct-connect modems are less error prone and more reliable than acoustic couplers. But in situations where direct connection is impossible or impractical—for example, when using a portable terminal or computer or in an office with a hard-wired PBX (in-house telephone switch)—an acoustic coupler is indispensable. Some modem models support both direct connection and acoustic coupling, providing the user with a choice of options.

Personal computer modems range in price from about $65 to $1,800, depending on their features. The major cost factor is the data rate—or speed—of the modem, measured in bits per second (baud). Ten baud equals one character transmitted per second.

Popular rates are 0 to 300 baud (30 characters per second), 1200 baud, and 2400 baud, with correspondingly higher prices for the higher-speed units. The 300-baud modems at the low end, called Bell 103—compatible with AT&T's standard model—have been popular for a number of years.

---

[1]The basic material in this chapter and Appendix E, A Smorgasbord of Modems, was provided by Data Decisions, a research and consulting firm that publishes information services on computer systems, software, and communications. Additional information on the company's services is available from Data Decisions, 20 Brace Road, Cherry Hill, New Jersey 08034; telephone, 609-429-7100.

They will continue to attract the home computer and casual business user because of their low price and ubiquity.

The 1200-baud modems, the majority of which are compatible with the Bell 212A model, are becoming increasingly popular and reportedly represent 85 percent of current personal computer modem sales. At four times the speed of Bell 103-compatible modems, the 212A lessens the lengthy wait (and associated costs) that comes with retrieving entries from online database services. In addition, the 212A is compatible with the Bell 103 standard. It is actually two modems in one, so it can communicate with the widely established base of Bell 103 users at 300 baud as well as with other 212A users.

It should be noted, however, that not all 1200-baud modems are compatible with the 212A. A sizable number of modems compatible with the Racal-Vadic VA3400 standard are also in use, and the two cannot communicate. Therefore, modem purchasers might also want to consider a triple modem, a device made by Racal-Vadic and Anderson Jacobson that communicates with modems using both the Bell 212A and Racal-Vadic standards.

Until recently, 1200 baud was the fastest speed at which modems could communicate over the telephone network in full duplex, or two-way simultaneous, transmission mode. Almost all personal computers are designed to communicate in full-duplex mode only; they cannot operate with half-duplex modems. Today several modem vendors provide 2400-baud full-duplex modems, which, because of the twofold speed increase over the 212A standard, are attractive to corporate personal computer users who can afford high-volume transactions. The 2400-baud modems are or will be available from vendors such as Concord Data, Rixon, Racal-Vadic, and Codex. Users should be aware, however, that 2400-baud modem communication is sanctioned only for international use by the CCITT (International Telegraph and Telephone Consultative Committee); U.S. versions of these modems from different vendors may not be able to communicate with each other. Prospective users may wish to wait until AT&T or another U.S. organization develops a standard for 2400-baud communication, a standard that may not be long in coming.

Because of the growing number of personal computers in the corporate environment, potential users should consider one important factor before placing large orders for personal computer modems: the level of service and support provided by the vendor. Many high-speed modem vendors that traditionally service and support large computer installations tend to view personal computer modems as a low-margin, consumer-oriented enterprise, and they are not entering the low-speed marketplace. Therefore, corporate users who want to install large numbers of low-cost 212A-type modems may have to go with a "non-traditional" supplier.

Other pitfalls await the unwary buyer of personal computer modems. For example, just because a modem is advertised for personal computers, this does not mean it will work with all personal computers. A computer needs more than a modem to communicate over telephone lines. Modems send data in serial fashion one data bit at a time over the telephone wires, while computers transmit data in parallel fashion, one whole byte or word of data (several bits) at a time. Therefore, special hardware and software are required to convert the parallel format into the serial format. A special code protocol for communicating data over the telephone lines is also required, and a hardware serial interface (usually RS-232C cable) or other computer-specific interface adapter is needed because of the vagaries of many personal computers.

Some independent vendors are now packaging a modem and input/output converter onto a single plug-in card that fits into a personal computer card slot, with communications software (usually supplied on cassette or diskette) thrown in as part of the deal. These packages simplify the chore of choosing a PC communications "system," taking the guesswork out of the buying decision. Hence, they are ideal for the novice, who need purchase only one item instead of two or three separate devices. Personal computer manufacturers are beginning to realize the advantages of a packaged communication system. You can expect to see most personal computers sold with built-in modems in the next few years.

The capabilities of the plug-in modems vary greatly, however, and sophisticated users may require communications features not supported by plug-in modem combos. These users will still need to purchase an external modem, preferably one that is compatible with and matches the capabilities of the desired communications software.

Unfortunately, stand-alone modems can become a Pandora's box to an unsuspecting user. For example, most of the Bell 103- and 212A-type modems now on the market were designed for communicating terminals; they will not work with a personal computer that is coupled with one of the new communications software packages unless interface signal assignments are adjusted. Briefly, a display terminal requires that pin number 8 (carrier detect) on the RS-232C interface cable be "high," or on, all of the time. Most communications software designed for personal computers requires that pin 8 be high only when the modem carrier signal is present. Modems originally designed for the personal computer marketplace, such as the popular Hayes Smartmodem, are already adjusted for this difference; some other modems go one step further, providing switch selection between communicating terminal or personal computer operation (Bytcom's 212AD has this capability). However, most stand-alone modems designed prior to 1983 will probably not work when attached to personal computers without custom cable modifications.

Some personal computers must have Data Terminal Ready (DTS, pin 6) fixed permanently in the high, or on, position. Thus the modem always sees the personal computer in an operational condition (when, in fact, it may be idle or off) and will keep the telephone connection open until physically disconnected by the user. This condition has caused phone lines inadvertently to remain connected overnight or over a weekend unnoticed by the users, resulting in exorbitant phone bills. An open line is also an invitation for unscrupulous third parties to breach an otherwise secure system. If users wth secure applications need to communicate over the telephone network, they should ensure that their personal computers do not require DTR high.

Interface problems in general are common when attaching modems to personal computers. Sometimes, personal computers are configured to look like a data circuit equipment (DCE) such as a modem in order to attach directly to a host computer. This, in turn, makes communication with a modem impossible because the send and receive signals from the modem and personal computer are configured exactly alike. Because of this, a crossover cable must be installed to reverse the signals and ensure communication.

Other odd interface problems can and do crop up; so, when buying a stand-alone modem, prospective users should determine beforehand that it will work with their personal computers. Users should ask their computer or software dealer for a list of compatible stand-alone modems and be prepared to make adjustments themselves if they buy an unsanctioned modem. Most modem vendors will not invest the time or expense required to adjust their product to a single personal computer, and most computer stores do not have the requisite communications expertise.

There are many other functions—and associated pitfalls—that a user should consider before buying a modem. For instance, many modem models include an integral—or optional integral—automatic number dialer. An autodialer permits user to store frequently called telephone numbers and dial them at the press of a button—a useful (but often expensive) feature. A related convenience feature allows autodialer functions, and often modem communication parameters, to be selected directly from the personal computer keyboard for loading into the modem. The thing to look for here is nonvolatile storage of autodialer and modem parameters, since a temporary power shortage or brownout will erase the modem's prestored program and require a lengthy resetting of parameters. Users shopping for sophisticated modems should determine that battery backup is available or that a desired model uses nonvolatile RAM.

Bell 212A-type modem buyers should look out for another potential drawback. Although the Bell 212A standard specifies 1200-baud communication in either asynchronous (start/stop) or synchronous modes, some 212A manufacturers provide 1200 baud in asynchronous mode only. Most personal computer users will be interested only in the asynchronous data rate, for reasons of simplicity and because popular communications are themselves asynchronous in nature. However, for those who require synchronous transmission, such as IBM mainframe communications using BSC or SNA protocols, the stripped-down 212A's will not be acceptable.

When purchasing a personal computer modem, the final consideration is where one is purchased. Most personal computer stores and outlets carry one or more modem lines, but in almost all cases the selection will be small. Perhaps the best thing to do is to call the prospective modem vendor and obtain a list of distributors or retail outlets in one's immediate area. Upon contacting the retailer, be sure to ascertain the level of support provided or whether telephone consultation is available, and check out the warranty and repair procedures. These measures could save a lot of grief if problems develop later on.

PART FIVE

ONLINE INFORMATION IN THE FUTURE

"I never use my crystal ball anymore."

*T*his section, by Steven K. Sieck, takes a look at the future of the online information industry. Sieck touches briefly on the innovations you're likely to see in the next year or two, as well as those that may be five or ten years away.

Steven K. Sieck is director of research at LINK Resources Corp. of New York, a market research and consulting firm specializing in new communications media. He also serves as director of LINK's Electronic Information Program, a multiclient research service for database producers, vendors, and others in the information industry; and as editor of *Online Database Report*, a monthly industry newsletter.

31 What's Coming

All of the basic technologies involved in delivering electronic information—data communications, microcomputers, storage technologies, software—are in a virtual state of perpetual revolution. One information technology firm has, attached to the door of its main research offices, a clipping that reads: "If you understand it, it's probably obsolete"—to which has been added, "It's a safe assumption that it's obsolete even if you don't understand it."

Difficult as it is to forecast and control, it's possible to divine the outlines of the sweeping changes that are in store for tomorrow's legions of online information users. For legions they WILL become. From about 50,000 online users in 1975—mainly stockbrokers and librarians—the number has grown to over 400,000 in 1983, representing well over 600,000 different passwords on commercial, public database services. And the numbers of new users of online information will continue to mushroom in parallel with the personal computer phenomenon.

Analysts at LINK Resources Corporation and International Data Corporation estimate a worldwide personal computer population at the end of 1983 of 13 million (10 million in the United States). The total is expected to reach 82 million by 1987. LINK forecasts that more than half of the low-end or "home" computers in the United States will be communications-ready by 1987, and there will be a somewhat lower percentage internationally. Nearly all of the 17 million "general-purpose" personal computers, used primarily in business, will have communications capability by that time. Overall, a reasonable expectation is for 35 million potential online terminals to be in place by 1987, or roughly the total 1982 circulation of morning newspapers in the United States.

A new industry is rising to meet the challenge of this prospective mass market. Billions of dollars will be invested to make information easier to obtain, more economical, and more readily applicable to both real-world tasks and esoteric research pursuits. You just may be tempted, after reading the wonders envisioned in the following pages, to sit back and wait for the

Information Age to come to you. But can you afford to wait? Your competitors are already strengthening themselves by tapping into databases.

What's more, being a pioneer in a developing field, while not always easy, often lends an understanding, a "feel" for how things work that just can't be earned once a new territory has been tamed. So let's embark on a tour of what online information services may be like in the future. As a navigational aid, this chapter is divided (with a bow to the late Marshall McLuhan) into two aspects: medium and message.

The medium

Format

Until recently, electronic information delivery implied a stream of ASCII characters, usually broken into lines of 40 or 80 characters and perhaps pages of about 24 lines. ASCII stands for American Standard Code For Information Interchange, and consists of a set of 128 characters. ASCII format still represents the overwhelming bulk of electronic information delivery, but other formats are arriving, "teletext" and "videotex" (the last "t" in videotext is commonly dropped) graphics being the most important.

Videotex is a more elaborate code than ASCII—actually, it is an overlay on the original ASCII—which transmits graphics such as lines, circles, and polygons as well as character fonts. Teletext is a one-way version of videotex (as opposed to two-way interactive) and usually travels via television signals, not telephone wires.

Videotex in the broadest sense is in many minds almost synonymous with the future of information retrieval. Some people in the industry even refer to simple ASCII transmissions as a variety of videotex, ignoring the distinction between "plain vanilla" ASCII characters and more sophisticated graphics.

The original intention behind videotex was to use graphics to improve the readability of digital text delivered over home television screens. The United States and Canada adopted a "North American standard" for videotex signals more ambitious than its European counterparts because it was felt that the success of the new, color format videotex and teletext media in the United States would ultimately depend on advertising. It was conceived as a consumer service.

As a result, business information applications have been little explored. The few applications of videotex graphics to business information to date have been pursued by entrepreneurs such as Faxtel, a small firm in Toronto. Faxtel has two databases, Marketfax and Telichart. Marketfax can display information on 5,000 stocks in three types of color presentations: simple price and volume listings, point and figure charts, and price and volume charts. Any of seven technical indicator curves can be overlaid, each in a distinctive color. Telichart sends Canadian socioeconomic statistics coded for presentation as colored curves or bar charts.

In the final analysis, though, it's difficult to believe that videotex graphics (except for specialized display purposes such as point-of-sale applications) will become the standard for business information delivery. Videotex was invented before the microcomputer boom. Charts, plots, and even greeting cards can be handled at least as well, and arguably more flexibly and efficiently, with a variety of microcomputer software packages linked to plain ASCII database services.

That is the approach that Dow Jones has exemplified. Having participated in many experiments with graphically enhanced videotex systems, Dow Jones has chosen instead to develop the market with personal computer software capable of turning plain ASCII data from the Dow Jones News/Retrieval Service into pictures.

But it's likely that a variety of competing formats will survive. Traditional printed information entails a fixed format, whereas electronic information is essentially a neutral collection of impulses that can be clothed or interpreted in manifold ways. Beyond the videotex options, other electronic options include so-called "audiotex," an interactive form of telephone "dial-it" services, which will be used to deliver stock quotes, account balances, credit reports, and other information selected by tone-keyed commands that are requested by voice prompts. "Digital voice mail," an advanced version of the telephone answering machine, will spread once current storage limitations are significantly improved. And chips are already in widespread use to translate ASCII characters into speech (discussed further below). Even pictures and motion will be available in an online, on-demand mode (the way data is today), but not until the 1990s.

Transmission/distribution media

There are three basic kinds of communications carriers that can deliver information. Systems ranging from walkie-talkies to communications satellites are called spectrum-utilizing media because they use radio frequencies or other parts of the electromagnetic spectrum. Systems that use cables or wires are often called "bound media" since the wires or cables prevent the signals from radiating into space. Finally, systems using magnetic tapes, disks, or other goods as the communications medium are called "physical media."

All three types of distribution media are exploding in a plethora of competing and complementary forms. The trade-offs in cost and performance between conventional twisted copper wire, coaxialcable, microwave systems, direct satellite transmissions, etc., will likely keep users, service providers, and regulators guessing for the next decade or so—until the construction of a universal, fiber-optic network is realized. AT&T and many smaller competitors all expect the country one day to arrive at an integrated fiber-optic network. Fiber-optic cable has a wide range of advantages—it's cheap, can carry a large number of signals, is electrically impossible to tap, and can combine video, audio, and data transmissions.

In the meantime, other delivery channels will compete to provide the best means of delivering information, especially in their ability to download data to local storage very rapidly and efficiently. Today, for example, cable is being used for high-speed data transmission between banks in New York City, while a satellite company called Equatorial Communications is providing $2,500 two-foot diameter earth stations capable of receiving 9600-baud satellite transmissions.

And the use of the FM sideband as a delivery channel for database services has started a flurry of activity since the April 1983 FCC authorization of the use of the sideband for data transmission; Dataspeed Inc., a California start-up, has developed a pocket radio/terminal that can receive and display ticker quotes for up to 40 stocks transmitted over sideband by National Public Radio affiliates. National Information Utilities, run by Jack Taub, the original moneyman behind The Source, also intends to deliver financial data as well as computer software and data services over NPR sidebands. And many other radio stations, as well as cable operations, are expected to follow the example of KMPS in Seattle, which has been downloading computer software by radio since March 1983.

Networking and gateway services

New conduits will bring enormous improvements in the speed and efficiency with which information can be delivered to the user. Even more important changes, however, will come in how information is located, selected, and retrieved.

The development of network or "gateway" services will smooth the interaction between user and information. It will make possible automatic connections between database systems, intelligent selection and use of different databases, a variety of centralized administrative services (billing, subscription, and password assignment services, etc.), and an "umbrella" of marketing and customer support for all database services.

As such "supernetworks" are implemented, database users will tend to see the world of online information as a single database, contributed to by many sources but accessible via one set of commands and billed for and supported by one of a few dominant suppliers. These will include services aimed at business users, consumers, and "boutique" vendors who serve customers in special fields. Each will offer electronic mail to facilitate dialogue among customers with complementary interests.

In contrast to today's "supermarket" database vendors, with hundreds of databases brought together on a single computer system (and often duplicated on other computer systems as well), databases will reside on many dispersed computers, often on the facility of the actual producer of information. Such a "distributed database" arrangement will make it possible for many relatively small databases (which might never justify electronic access on their own) be kept available online. The gateway will distribute database storage costs among many distributors, resulting in lower costs for the user.

Eventually, gateways will incorporate much of the technique and experience of information specialists who know the strengths, weaknesses, indexing schemes, and other particulars of various databases. An existing example, the Chemical Substance Information Network (CSIN) was developed by the U.S. government to coordinate retrieval of scientific data relating to toxic substances. CSIN links many autonomous database vendors oriented to chemical substances. And because CSIN maintains a "knowledge base" of the procedures, protocols, communication interactions, and functions of its component systems, a user can tap several systems while using a single interactive language and menu display.

At its simplest levels, CSIN can automatically dial up and log on to a given system, translate high-level commands, and "capture" files in network storage. A user may, for example, opt to use a set of search terms learned through one system, allow CSIN to translate them into the format acceptable to another system, and transmit them to that system. In its most sophisticated mode of operation (likely to be a model for similar specialized gateway systems of the future), CSIN uses menus that allow the user to tailor the search logic and query terms to fit his immediate need and to select the appropriate databases.

As a modest interim step toward full-scale gateways, "facilitating" services will develop that are designed to ease the dial-up and log-on process. One prototype for this kind of service was introduced two years ago by iXO Corp. in the form of a hand-held computer terminal (described in the terminals listing in Appendix C). Users could connect it to the iXO support computer and tell it what services they use, and the computer would automatically program the terminal with the entire log-on sequence. After that, the user would have true one-button access. This kind of service will become essential as online vendors and telecommunications networks proliferate.

Terminals

Terminals have already come a long way from the days when standard equipment consisted of large, "dumb" computer terminals or teleprinters like the once ubiquitous Texas Instruments Silent 700. Besides becoming smaller, cheaper, and more powerful, personal computers used for database access are coming to seem less like computers that can communicate and more like telephones that can compute. The terminals everyone will be using in a few years, whether desktop workstations or portable receivers, will be able to dial telephone numbers and perform other telephone management functions for voice and data, perform preprogrammed searches, and upload and download files from a variety of different network types. Portables will be small enough to carry in your pocket; communications terminals will be diverse enough to include graphics generators and CAD/CAM systems, energy management devices, and multimedia kiosks.

Now that modems are being designed on chip sets, their prices will quickly come down as capabilities increase. Texas Instruments, Racal-Vadic, and Motorola are rolling out single-chip modems already. Modems that operate at 2400 baud should be in widespread use by mid-decade; 4800 baud by 1990.

Many kinds of different devices will be used to access databases, depending on the situation—office, home, or travel—and on primary applications—quick look-ups, exhaustive searches, or tailored analyses. Costs? Fifty 1983 dollars will get you one heck of a terminal in 1990, including modem. Terminals, like razors, will practically be given away in order to sell the information "blade."

Storage

Today there is an obvious trend, driven by the personal computer, toward the storage of more and more data on the user's desktop. This trend, however, ultimately runs into a barrier. Even though magnetic storage media such as floppy diskettes and hard disks are constantly increasing in capacity, large-scale, full-text databases require another degree of magnitude of storage, an inexpensive medium that can store billions of searchable characters on a single surface. The breakthroughs required will come in the form of optical disk technology—storage media on which information is read by a laser beam.

Optical disk technology takes several forms. The most exciting, for users of online information, employs standard optical videodisks or digital audiodisks, usually referred to as compact disks. (The videodisks must be "laser disks" rather than the CED variety produced by RCA. The latter use a stylus and are therefore basically unsuited for interactive uses; the stylus is slow and eventually destroys the disk.)

Although the current generation of optical disks is "read only"—new information cannot be added once they have been published—they will offer the ability to search gigantic databases without recourse to telecommunications or online charges. A number of companies, including several start-ups (LaserData, Reference Technologies) as well as major companies (IBM, Digital Equipment Corp.) have demonstrated the capacity to store a million pages or more, searchable to the word, on durable, inexpensive, mass produced videodisks. And erasable "read-write" disks are not far off commercially.

Although it has less sheer capacity than the full-size videodisk, the compact disk, nevertheless, can store about 600,000 to 700,000 megabytes (million characters) and has several advantages over videodisks for electronic publishing purposes. For one thing, being much smaller, they can use a smaller, cheaper player, and the disks themselves are capable of being replicated for less than a dollar.

Videodisks, of whatever size, are highly versatile. They can store, on the same disk, large textual databases, diagrams, moving-picture sequences, and even parallel sound tracks in different languages. Online remote systems will not disappear as a result of the optical revolution; rather, they will concentrate on fast-changing information and make available information from peripheral and disparate sources not available in disk form.

Language recognition

Artificial intelligence advances will transform the information world more profoundly than any other technology. It figures importantly in the following four aspects of the future of online information retrieval: natural language querying, sound recognition, intelligent screens, and intelligent report generation.

"Natural language querying," or the ability to converse with database retrieval systems in everyday parlance, is fairly close at hand and probably is critical to the mass acceptance of computing.

The best-known natural language query system at this writing is Intellect, a product of Artificial Intelligence Corp. (Intellect was recently licensed by IBM for use in its "information centers." These, as IBM currently defines the concept, are places where data-processing pros train novices to meet some of their own information needs.) Intellect relies on "syntactical analysis" to enable users to retrieve information from large, structured databases with queries framed in more or less random, everyday English. For example, a user today can type "Who works in the sales and accounting departments?" rather than the clumsy formalism of IBM's "user-friendly" query language Sequel: "Select name from emp.dept where (dept.dname = 'sales' or dept.d-name = 'accounting') and emp.dept# = dept.dept#)."

Intellect, a large program, currently requires a minicomputer to operate, but a simplified personal computer version is under development. While Intellect does make it easier to pull information out of structured databases that store information according to rigidly defined rules, future AI systems will bring these capabilities to free-form, unstructured text.

Another approach to interaction with databases on your terms rather than the computer's comes from a tiny Albuquerque start-up, Excalibur Technologies Corporation. Excalibur has developed a natural language processor called Savvy, implemented to date on plug-in cards for Apple and Microdata computers. Similar to Intellect, Savvy interprets the meaning of simple requests phrased any number of different ways—even misspelled or in different languages—using a technology it calls "adaptive pattern recognition processing."

Savvy has to be "trained" on an ongoing basis by its users. If it fails to understand the meaning of a particular phrase, it can be taught the new phrase's meaning. Because it deals with abstract patterns rather than specific meanings, Savvy occasionally provides a wrong answer, or one that shows only an approximate understanding of the question. That may be because of the limited processing power that can be applied on small systems; on the more powerful machines of the future, it, or something like it, may finally bring computers the ability to adjust to the idiosyncracies of their users rather than vice versa.

Speech synthesis and speech recognition

Two increasingly prominent features of information terminals that will occur in the future will be speech synthesis and speech recognition. Although managers with no typing skills—and no intention of learning any—have been put on the defensive by the computer revolution, their eventual deliverance is in sight, thanks to developments in voice recognition technology.

It will not be an overnight rescue, however. While text-to-speech processors are becoming commonplace, the task of recognizing speech (converting it to text or to a command) is proving much more difficult to perfect. In fact, the ultimate goal of speech recognition research—to develop perfectly accurate, speaker-independent systems that recognize connected words—will be the subject of ongoing research and development, probably through the end of the century.

The first systems require that users speak with distinct pauses between words, limiting applications to narrow market segments where acceptable vocabularies can be small. Systems that need to understand large vocabularies will be restricted to use by a single individual, whose unique pronunciations the terminal will have been "trained" to recognize. Texas Instruments has made widely publicized (albeit technically limited) advances in this area as represented by the Natural Language Interface program now available for their Professional computer. The company also recently introduced a language recognition program called NaturalLink, which is designed to facilitate online use of Dow Jones News/Retrieval.

In 1983, Nippon Electric developed a speaker-dependent word processor that could recognize an unlimited Japanese vocabulary. By contrast, its speaker-independent models came with a maximum vocabulary of 128 words. Meanwhile, IBM was working toward a mainframe-based system using large speaker-independent vocabularies of over 5,000 words.

Voice simulators are much easier to implement, but they are likely to keep their mechanical-sounding character. Natural speech is extremely hard to simulate: The sound source of human speech—the larynx and vocal cords—is highly dynamic and subject to biological variation, and the open end—the mouth and lips—can adopt varying sizes and shapes. Digital Equipment Corp. and the Kurzweil Computer Products Division of Xerox Corp. are leading the work in this area.

Most of the speech technologies being developed in the early 1980s were intended for use in telephony and take advantage of the fact that recognizable speech can be based on the lower-frequency part of a signal. But this prevents simulated speech from ever sounding really natural. Telephones can only handle a bandwidth of 3 kilohertz; this leaves off about two-fifths of the resonant frequencies.

Intelligent screens

Intelligent screens are probably the first application of artificial intelligence that you will actually employ in retrieving information from a database. An "intelligent screen" is a software-based "filter" that can evaluate whether or not a given fact or document is really the one you are looking for. This goes beyond the usual free-text search, "does it contain this word in the same paragraph as that word," to take into consideration the semantics surrounding the word in the database.

By the late 1980s this application will have become an essential, though controversial, armament in the battle against "information overload." The precursors are existing capabilities such as SDI (selective dissemination of information) profiles, which are searches run against updates on bibliographic databases, or the fixed "pages" that users can set up on a quotation terminal, for example, to be constantly updated as the component data items (such as stock prices) change.

The use of artificial intelligence techniques for maximizing the retrieval of relevant items and minimizing the irrelevant "outtakes" has been the focus of a great deal of research in the defense/intelligence community and the academic research centers that it funds. One early (perhaps too early, as it turns out) application of such an approach was in a hugely ambitious international private intelligence service called IRIS (International Reporting and Information Services). IRIS was set up to take field reports and published data from around the world to be analyzed, routed, reanalyzed, and rerouted until they reached customers in banks, governments, and major corporations with exactly the information they needed.

After a period of ludicrous mismanagement, IRIS collapsed in 1983 before having signed up a single customer. But the technology, which uses "syntactical algorithms" to determine relevance, had become operational and will sooner or later find its way into more successful commercial services—probably in the form of a "black box" added to a personal computer that scans streams of data broadcast on the FM sideband. Eventually, you'll be able to program and store your topics of interest so that a wide variety of information sources can contribute to a "personal" briefing—the kind previously available only to executives who could marshall a staff of readers, clippers, and analysts.

Users who store their interests on interactive systems may also have automatically identified themselves to advertisers. Indeed, many will desire this so that advertisers can inform them of new products. Such information stored on large databases may also facilitate the formation of networks of individuals with shared interests.

Intelligent report generation

Another important application of artificial intelligence to online information is that of intelligent report generation. Imagine a computer that can provide custom-tailored reports on whatever information you want. A glimpse of such a product of the future can be seen in an automatic stock report generator being developed at Bell Laboratories.

The system, called Ana, is fed numeric data from a database of securities prices. It then produces natural-language stock market reports similar to those found on the financial pages of daily newspapers. It "knows," for example, that "if the degree of change of the Dow Jones average of 30 industrials at the close of the day was greater than 10 points, then the degree of change was great."

Ana takes input data and computes facts, such as the hourly changes in the Dow Jones indexes. The facts are then sent to a "message generator," which looks, using the inference rules of the program, for specific patterns. Using historical knowledge, such as records of previous highs, lows, or interesting events in the market, Ana can "infer" messages and can update its records when new patterns are set. The messages are then sent to a module that performs the most complicated processing: changing conceptual messages into rough phrases.

For example, Ana might map the closing market status message into the phrase "was/were swept into a broad and steep decline" and the volume of trading message into the phrase "in heavy trading." A final module takes these phrases and converts them to polished text by choosing appropriate nouns or pronouns for subjects and selecting the singular or plural form of the verb as appropriate.

A "knowledge-based" report generator such as Ana cannot generate anything for which it does not have explicit knowledge. For example, after the great surge in trading volume that occurred in August 1982, Ana's rules for evaluating volume of trading had to be adjusted. But a knowledge-based report generator can be initially designed to incorporate some general knowledge of a particular area and later be augmented with more specific knowledge so as to draw finer distinctions and make subtler points.

The message

The amount of and demand for information is increasing exponentially in nearly every field. It's confusing enough to end users; likewise, the producers of information—authors and compilers, reporters and publishers, statisticians and forecasters, programmers and software designers—find themselves in the middle of the greatest upheaval since the invention of the printing press.

The press extended information to a mass readership, based on the scale economies of selling many copies of the same book. The resulting regimentation of information production is in the process of being dissipated by electronic technology. One electronic version can almost instantly serve to produce an unlimited number of copies, distributed on demand in various forms around the world.

As the percentage of the world's knowledge that's available electronically increases, so will the premium placed on fresh and original information. A natural consequence of breaking the chains of industrial mass production and physical distribution will be intensified demand for instantly changing information, supplied by hosts of small information entrepreneurs. Established repositories of information will continue to be maintained by the large publishers, though. With their sheer organizational inertia and masses of computers and information workers, large publishing enterprises will provide the "glue" that holds information together. Entrepreneurs will be best suited to meet the customized demands that the information age makes possible.

The information you have available in the future should therefore be more timely, more complete, and, most importantly, tailored to your specific needs. You'll have the benefit of more opinions, and more facts if you need them (and you probably will). Let's take a look at the new varieties of information that will be at your disposal.

New kinds of online services

Today, a significant percentage of the world's knowledge is already online. The bulk of the most important statistics and other public records produced by public and private sources are widely available. More than 50 million journal articles are cited in bibliographic databases, most of which currently go back five to ten years. Gradually, the most important magazines, newsletters, and newspapers, both specialized and of general interest, are becoming available in full text. These sources will be joined by other kinds of information, especially directories of individuals, products, and services available in different subject areas and locations.

We will see more and more electronic "bridges" between, on the one hand, organizations and individuals with products, services, or simply identities to make known to the world, and, on the other hand, those of us who might want to learn of their existence. Such bridges not only will supply information, but in many cases will enable us to take the next step, be it a purchase, agreement, or conversation, through the same online connection. "Sponsored" databases increasingly will be used to make potential buyers of products and services aware about what is available. These databases, a mixture of information and advertising, will be offered in such a way that the cost is borne by the sponsor in proportion to the amount of use by target readers.

The more distant future will also bring online visual and aural information. Tied closely to falling storage, communications, and display costs will be online scientific drawings, photographs, medical imagery, recorded voice messages, and even music. (Home Music Store, a venture to deliver albums in digital form via satellite and cable television systems, recently demonstrated the technical viability of such an approach, though it failed to win the support of the major record companies.)

As the medium is enhanced by voice recognition, automatic access routines, high-speed transmission, etc., electronic mail and computer conferencing will become as simple as the telephone to use—and a crucial component of the business environment. The ability to gather knowledge directly from experts and experienced everymen without playing telephone tag or relying on the mails, and the ability to form impromptu discussion groups and task forces that impose no time/space constraints on the participants, are powerful communications benefits now enjoyed by the pioneers of the "network nation." Imagine how much more powerful these techniques will be when most professionals, writers, experts, teachers, etc., are sharing the same network(s)!

The full-text gap

Today's most noticeable gap between what's online and what isn't is between the number of sources covered by abstracts or citations, and the online availability of the information to which they refer. Currently, once a bibliographic database search has helped you identify a number of relevant documents, you still must order them delivered by mail, or else go to the library—something that you were hoping to avoid by using an online search in the first place.

Recognizing the demand for instant accessibility of documents, the database industry has been rushing to mount more and more full-text documents, beginning with the ones perceived as most important and most marketable. Although this trend will continue and even accelerate in the near future, there are three powerful constraints on the availability of full-text documents: the cost of online storage, the cost of computer muscle-power to search more data faster, and the cost of converting existing printed text to electronic form.

All three of these costs are steadily declining, and it's reasonable to assume that—eventually—they will drop low enough to remove most of the economic constraints. In the meantime, full text is likely to become available where the costs of data entry can be avoided, for example, in the output of publishers who have created computer tapes for phototypesetting. There are a few areas where a large, focused market will justify the costs of creating full-text databases from hard copy, for example, the full text of court decisions on LEXIS and Westlaw.

With the costs of data entry and online computer storage continuing to drop, economic constraints will eventually almost cease to be a factor in what is available. But this will by no means be a panacea to users; in many respects, it will simply transfer the information explosion from paper to electronic form. A manifold increase in the amount of text online in no way indicates a parallel increase in the amount of information that's accessible, for much of the text will be redundant, overlapping, inaccurate, and disorganized.

To sort it all out will require the development of more and more secondary (or indexing) tools, compilation schemes, and evaluative services that can help users find the most valuable of a multitude of possible sources. At higher and higher price tiers, collections of obscure and abstruse information, of interest to very few people but extraordinarily valuable to some, will become available. But online combinations of databases with networks of people interested in common topics will also enable many to dig up facts and opinions.

Knowledge bases

Well within the foreseeable future, millions of information sources will enter the electronic realm. Just in time, a new generation of software, based on artificial intelligence, will provide a quantum leap in the ability of mankind to assimilate the information. Increasingly, we will use not databases but something called knowledge bases, as in "knowledge-based systems" (or "expert systems") and "knowledge-based report generators." What is a knowledge base, and what makes it different from a database?

Unlike a database, which is normally stored in a uniform, structured way, a knowledge base consists of an unstructured set of facts, along with rules of inference for determining new facts. For example, when a full-text database is loaded into a search system, the search software creates a dictionary of all the individual words it contains, with pointers to the articles they come from. Similarly, in systems for handling tabular and hierarchical information, such as in relational and network databases, the relationships between facts are designed into the database in advance.

In a knowledge base, the paths by which facts are related are determined "on-the-fly," and most of the information is inferred from a few basic facts. For example, UPI has been working with artificial intelligence researchers at Yale and other academic centers for several years on the application of knowledge bases to news copy. During the Carter administration, a program called Cyrus kept tabs on the doings of Secretary of State Cyrus Vance as reported on the UPI wire. It could, for example, make a stab at answering such questions as whether Vance's wife had ever met the wife of Israeli Prime Minister Menachem Begin. Even though the database had never found that specific piece of information on the wire, it had learned that the two statesmen had attended state banquets together. Knowing also that wives were often present on such occasions, it surmised that the two had probably met. (They had.)

Knowledge bases introduce the possibility of whole new kinds of services, including "expert systems" such as those for diagnosing illnesses, finding oil, determining personal tax and investment strategies, and so on. They also add tremendously to the practical value of existing databases. For one thing, expert systems that incorporate the knowledge of trained search specialists will bring a whole new dimension of thoroughness and efficiency to database retrieval by nonprofessional searchers. The difference is between putting the *Encyclopedia Britannica* online for keyword searching and having a computer read and understand the material to the point where it can make inferences and answer questions about information not explicitly present in the text.

Expert systems are certain to be an exciting and controversial development. They will bring the threat of "being replaced by a computer" to professionals for the first time. However, it is unlikely that machines will ever "replace" the faculties of human judgment; rather, the "experts-on-a-chip" will be used as highly intelligent assistants. And while some people may see a sinister element to diagnosis by machine, it must be remembered that in many fields, human expertise is in short supply. In many developing countries, for example, a machine diagnosis which is only 80 percent accurate will still save many lives that otherwise would be lost for lack of a real doctor.

Conclusion

Where does it all lead? Management of the information explosion is the goal, and if information technology fulfills its vast promise, an attainable one. The costs of information access and assimilation will diminish astonishingly as information technology diffuses throughout society.

While our ability, aided by the computer, to produce ever multiplying amounts of information seems to know almost no limits, the ability of people to absorb informaion is crunchingly finite, and unlikely to increase much beyond the present capacities of literate society (though it is possible that the deluge of data will produce new learning skills).

That's why the challenge to the information industry is to provide not just information, but answers; and why the challenge to all of us is to make sure that along with the capacity to generate answers comes a method by which the answers can be tested and evaluated.

The "personal information revolution" should have a salutary effect on democracy. Individuals, by harnessing the power of information, will be capable of feats previously reserved for corporate and governmental monoliths. Although the enhancement of individual access to information may be tempered by the government's use of the same technologies, the individual and the state will, at least potentially, be on a more equal information footing than has existed since Thomas Jefferson's time.

Perhaps we can be guided, in our quest to synthesize and advance mankind's knowledge, by a vision expressed almost 50 years ago. In his paper delivered at the weekly evening meeting of the Royal Institute of Great Britain on November 20, 1936, H. G. Wells spoke first of the collective wisdom and knowledge of mankind and our need to synthesize it. Wells called his concept a "world encyclopedia."

"This world encyclopedia," he said, "would be the mental background of every intelligent man in the world. It would be alive and growing and changing, continually under revision, extension, and replacement from the original thinkers in the world everywhere. Every university and research institution should be feeding it. Every fresh mind should be brought into contact with its standing editorial organization. And on the other hand, its contents would be the standard source of material for the instructional side of school and college work and for the verification of facts and testing of statements everywhere in the world. Journalists would deign to use it. Even newspaper proprietors might be made to respect it. Such an encyclopedia would play the role of an undogmatic bible to a world culture. It would do just what our scattered and disoriented intellectual organizations of today fall short of doing. It would hold the world together mentally . . . to hold men's minds together in something like a common interpretation of reality."

APPENDIXES

Selected Books,
A Periodicals, and Directories

DIRECTORY OF ONLINE DATABASES. Cuadra Associates, Inc., 2001 Wilshire Blvd., Suite 305, Santa Monica, CA 90403. Published quarterly (complete directory in spring and fall; supplements in summer and winter). $75 per year.
A well-organized, thorough listing of online databases. The fall 1983 edition listed about 1,730 databases, 900 producers, and 260 vendors. This is the primary reference source of its kind for people in the database industry.

COMPUTER-READABLE DATABASES: A DIRECTORY AND DATA SOURCEBOOK. By Martha E. Williams. 1982. Published for the American Society for Information Science by Knowledge Industry Publications Inc., 701 Westchester Ave., White Plains, NY 10604, 800-431-1880. 1,472 pages. $120.
Another industry standard. The 1982 edition of this is considerably out-of-date compared to Cuadra's quarterly Directory, *but this book has more thorough coverage of non-U.S. databases. A new edition is planned in 1984.*

INFORMATION SOURCES: THE ANNUAL DIRECTORY OF THE INFORMATION INDUSTRY ASSOCIATION. 1984 Edition. $49.50. Information Industry Association, 316 Pennsylvania Ave., S.E., Suite 400, Washington, DC 20004.
Published by the major trade association for database producers and vendors. It also counts among its members telecommunications, publishing, and computer time-sharing organizations. Leading information brokers also participate. Each member supplies a one- or two-page description of itself for the directory. (The book doesn't list individual databases.) Companies are indexed according to their main activities.

DATABASES FOR BUSINESS: PROFILES AND APPLICATIONS. By Van Mayros and D. Michael Werner. 1982. Chilton Book Co., Radnor, PA 19089. 178 pages. $19.95.
The only book on the list that attempts to address business databases as a distinct field. It's useful, but it doesn't substitute for a more complete database directory: what's business to one person may be technology or government or economics or psychology to another.

INFORMATION INDUSTRY MARKETPLACE: AN INTERNATIONAL DIRECTORY OF INFORMATION PRODUCTS AND SERVICES. R. R. Bowker Co., New York, NY. Order Department: P.O. Box 1807, Ann Arbor, MI 48106, 800-521-8110. Annual. Fourth Edition, $39.95. Fifth Edition due April 1984.
A useful but somewhat spotty guide to databases, producers, and vendors. It also lists information brokers, associations, and various other useful research services.

ENCYCLOPEDIA OF INFORMATION SYSTEMS AND SERVICES. Edited by John Schmittroth Jr., Gale Research Co., Book Tower, Detroit, MI 48226, 800-521-0707. Fifth Edition, 1983. 1,242 pages. $250. Two periodical supplements scheduled before publication of Sixth Edition, $180 for both.

A very useful and comprehensive guide to the database industry. It differs from other database directories in that its emphasis is on describing organizations that produce databases rather than individual databases. Included among the 2,500 organizations listed are research firms, videotex operators, information brokers, specialized libraries, and a variety of other organizations that supply information.

DATAPRO DIRECTORY OF ON-LINE SERVICES. Datapro Research Corp., 1805 Underwood Blvd., Delran, NJ 08075, 800-257-9406. Two looseleaf volumes with monthly updates and monthly newsletters. $415 per year. Newsletter subscription individually, $95 per year.

Coverage of not only online databases, but also computer time-sharing services. The database listings are less complete than Cuadra's Directory of Online Databases, *but Datapro's information on database vendors is much more comprehensive. A subscription includes free access to Datapro's research staff, who answer questions by telephone. The newsletter separately is of modest value.*

THE COMPLETE HANDBOOK OF PERSONAL COMPUTER COMMUNICATIONS: EVERYTHING YOU NEED TO GO ONLINE WITH THE WORLD. By Alfred Glossbrenner. 1983. St. Martin's Press, 175 Fifth Ave., New York, NY 10010. 325 pages. $14.95.

Not by any means "complete" as the title implies; however, a very good book. It introduces a wide range of online services, both business- and consumer-oriented. It also gives good nontechnical explanations of a number of technical topics related to computer communications.

OMNI ONLINE DATABASE DIRECTORY. By Mike Edelhart and Owen Davies. 1983. Collier Books/Macmillan Publishing Co., 866 Third Ave., New York, NY 10022. 292 pages. $10.95 (paperback), $19.95 (hardcover).

A useful listing of more than 1,000 major databases available in 1983, grouped by subject with brief descriptions. Sketchy information on database vendors.

ONLINE BIBLIOGRAPHIC SEARCHING: A LEARNING MANUAL. By Ching-chih Chen and Susanna Schweizer. 1981. Neal-Schuman Publishers Inc., 23 Cornelia St., New York, NY 10014. 227 pages. $22.95.

A textbook that has become popular in library schools. It deals only with the three major "supermarket" database vendors: DIALOG, SDC, and BRS, with illustrations and examples primarily from DIALOG. We recommend it for professional researchers who seek a thorough introduction to these vendors.

ONLINE SEARCH STRATEGIES. Edited by Ryan E. Hoover. 1982. Knowledge Industry Publications Inc., 701 Westchester Ave., White Plains, NY 10604, 800-431-1880. 345 pages. $34.50.

An excellent book that assumes you already know the basics about online databases. It concentrates on tips to help you get better search results. The book is divided into ten chapters that compare databases within a particular field: government information; chemical information; bioscience; energy and environment; social-behavioral sciences; patents; legal research; health sciences; news databases; business and economics. It contains many helpful printouts from actual searches.

IDP REPORT (INFORMATION AND DATABASE PUBLISHING REPORT). Knowledge Industries Publications Inc., 701 Westchester Ave., White Plains, NY 10604, 800-431-1880. Biweekly. $225 per year.

A newsletter billed as being "for informational, professional, sci-tech, and business publishers." It reports on news affecting companies in the online industry and on how online business ventures are faring.

ONLINE DATABASE REPORT. LINK Resources Corp., 215 Park Ave. South, New York, NY 10003. Monthly. $295 per year.
Billed as "the monthly newsletter for executives concerned with the online database industry." It goes into more depth than IDP Report, offering analysis rather than just news. LINK Resources also offers a service called the Electronic Information Program, at $16,800 a year, which provides research reports and consulting services related to the online database industry. Many major information companies subscribe to the service.

DATABASE ALERT. Knowledge Industries Publications Inc., 701 Westchester Ave., White Plains, NY 10604, 800-431-1880. Monthly. $48 per year.
For the experienced or frequent database user, a monthly bulletin on new products and services.

DATABASE UPDATE. Newsletter Management Corp., 10076 Boca Entrada Blvd., Boca Raton, FL 33433, 800-345-8112. Monthly. $97 per year.
For the experienced or frequent database user, a monthly bulletin on new products and services. Somewhat more selective than Database Alert, it gives more space to important announcements.

ONLINE: THE MAGAZINE OF ONLINE INFORMATION SYSTEMS. Online Inc., 11 Tannery Lane, Westport, CT 06880. Six issues a year. $78.
Reviews of new and existing databases; also user hints, news on new products and price changes, etc. It is intended for frequent database users, professional researchers, and librarians. Some of the "reviews" are written by a representative of the company whose product is under review.

ONLINE REVIEW. Learned Information Inc., 143 Old Marlton Pike, Medford, NJ 08055. Six issues a year. $70.
Articles comparing and evaluating databases in many fields, articles about the impact of new information technologies on society, user's tips, new product news, etc., intended for professional researchers. It is more scholarly than Online and the other periodicals listed here.

LINK-UP: COMMUNICATIONS AND THE SMALL COMPUTER. On-Line Communications Inc., 6531 Cambridge St., Minneapolis, MN 55426. Monthly. $19.83 per year.
A glossy magazine with emphasis on hardware and software for microcomputer communications. It also carries features and columns about online services.

ONLINE DATABASE SEARCH SERVICES DIRECTORY. John Schmittroth, Jr., Editor. Gale Research Co., Book Tower, Detroit, MI 48226, 800-521-0707. First edition, in two volumes; Vol. 1 due out January 1984, Vol. 2 due August 1984. $75 for both volumes.
Not published as we go to press; we have seen only an announcement. It promises to provide "detailed descriptions" of more than 1,000 information brokers who offer to search online databases for a fee.

B Major Information Brokers

Access Innovations

Address: P.O. Box 40130
Albuquerque, NM 87196
Telephone: 505-265-3591
Electronic mail addresses: None specified.

Overview

Typical clients include small R&D companies of 50 or fewer employees as well as scientific and technical companies (including some of the largest corporations, laboratories, and government agencies). Databases are created for large corporation libraries or information centers. Experience in creating databases is helpful in searching databases for clients for it enables the firm to search with greater accuracy. The largest fee charged to date was $300,000 to create a large database. *Subject Specialties:* Science, engineering, and energy-related technology. *Other Specialties:* Translations, verifications, searching European databases, technical writing and editing, abstracting, and indexing. *Date Founded:* 1978. *Employees:* 25, including librarians, abstractors, indexers, and data entry group. Two owners: Marjorie Hlava, President, and Jay Ven Eman, CEO. Robert Spiegal, Projects Coordinator. Two employees worked for NASA and are experienced online searchers. *Facilities:* Small corporate library. Searches are done at both 300 and 1200 baud on CDC 751, Wang 2200, and Apples.

Services

Database Services: Clients may receive a copy of the actual search or a report based on the search depending on the project. The search is often but one source of information for a report prepared for the client. Search results are downloaded or reformatted only at a client's request and after the copyright is cleared. A client is permitted to be present when a search is done. *Vendors/Databases Searched:* DIALOG, ESA-IRS, SDC, MEDLINE, BRS, TEXTLINE, Finsbury, Samsom, Sligos, Questel, Echo, Inka, Dimidi, and others. DIALOG and ESA-IRS are the most frequently accessed vendors. *Document Delivery:* Contact Michelle Lohr. There is no subject specialization. Materials are ordered by either phone or mail. The average turnaround time is two weeks. Document copies are retrieved from the University of New Mexico and other libraries in the area. Photocopies are provided. Copyright compliance is through the Copyright Clearance Center. *Consulting Services:* Provided in the fields of database creation and information center management. *Other Services:* Interviews and occasional surveys are used to complete some research projects. There are no geographic limitations attached to these surveys. *Service Restrictions:* None specified.

Charges

Database Charges: $25 per hour and all direct costs. The minimum charge is $25 with $\frac{1}{4}$-hour breakdowns billed after the first hour. The average charge for a search is $50. Searches are done at 300 and 1200 baud. *Document Retrieval Charges:* The minimum charge is $6.50 per article and 15¢ per page. Postage, special verification fees, and special phone charges are added. Prepayment or a deposit is not required. A retainer account can be established by forwarding a deposit. There is no minimum. *Charges—Other Services:* Billed at $35 to $50 per hour. There is a one-day minimum for consulting. Charges for abstracting and indexing, data entry and data conversion are usually quoted at a per 1,000-character rate, based on the complexity of the materials. *Credit Cards:* None specified. *Guarantee:* All data entry guaranteed for errors.

Katherine Ackerman and Associates

Address: P.O. Box 408472
  Chicago, IL 60640
Telephone: 312-764-7407
Electronic mail addresses: None specified.

Overview

Katherine Ackerman and Associates serves companies of all sizes, many of which do not have their own libraries. The company takes on large projects and furnishes a complete research package, including the search and all supporting documents. *Subject Specialties:* All subjects are researched, and document retrieval is performed without restriction. *Other Specialties:* Information services for personal computer users. *Date Founded:* 1983. *Employees:* 1 information specialist, 3 newsletter support staff, 1 clerical. Katherine Ackerman, Director (M.L.S.). *Facilities:* IBM equipment. Searches are done at 1200 baud.

Services

Database Services: Clients receive a computer printout of the search as well as a report based on the search results. The degree to which results are analyzed varies with the client. There is an average turnaround time of two to five days. Search results may be downloaded and reformatted at the client's request, depending upon the database producer. Clients need not be present when the search is done. Follow-up services available include consulting, document delivery, and SDI/update searches. *Vendors/Databases Searched:* DIALOG, SDC, BRS, Dow Jones, and other vendors. *Document Delivery:* Document delivery is usually provided in conjunction with larger projects; there are no special subject areas. The average turnaround time is five days. Both rush and watch services are available. Orders are taken by phone and mail. Materials are regularly retrieved from the Chicago Public Library and all major Chicago collections. Materials are also electronically retrieved from collections worldwide. Actual documents or photocopies are delivered and copyright compliance policies are followed. *Consulting Services:* Provided in the field of information services for personal computer users. *Other Services:* Manual research, expert interviews, and surveys can be performed. The company gives seminars to computer dealers called Online Information Services for Personal Computer Users. It also publishes *Modem Notes*, a monthly publication that teaches end users about online databases and their applications as well as other online information services. *Service Restrictions:* None specified.

Charges

Database Charges: $35 per hour, plus any incurred costs. There is no markup on direct database charges. The minimum charge is $35, and the average charge for a search is $100. Searches are done at 1200 baud. Clients may set up a retainer account by sending a minimum of $75 as a deposit. *Document Retrieval Charges:* $12 per document up to 10 pages, plus 20¢ per page for each additional page. Delivery charges are added to these costs. No discounts are provided for volume accounts, and a prepayment or deposit is required for first-time users. *Credit Cards:* None specified. *Guarantee:* "If we make a mistake, we will redo the work at no cost." *Notes:* "We provide personal service."

American National Standards Institute Inc. (ANSI)

Address: 1430 Broadway
New York, NY 10018
Telephone: 212-354-3300
Electronic mail addresses: Telex: 42 42 96 ANSI UI

Overview

ANSI serves industry, government, organizations that develop standards, and the public by co-ordinating private-sector domestic standards activities, approving American National (consensus) Standards, managing and coordinating U.S. participation in international standardization, and serving as a clearinghouse and information center on national and international standards. *Subject Specialties:* Standards. *Date Founded:* 1918. *Employees:* 100 professional and support personnel in its New York headquarters. Staff is managed by a president and staff directors for its principal functions. A Washington office is maintained for government liaison and technical affairs services to the Washington community. *Facilities:* An in-house library that consists of standards only.

Services

Database Services: A database developed by ANSI and Information Handling Services in Englewood, Colorado, provides online access to information on voluntary national, international, and regional standards, on drafts being considered for approval, and on proposed standards-related foreign government regulations. This Voluntary Standards Information Network Service (VSIN) is available through IHS and its subsidiary, BRS. *Vendors/Databases Searched:* VSIN. *Document Delivery:* ANSI is the sole source of ALL approved American National Standards. It is also the U.S. source for international standards and drafts of the International Organization for Standardization (ISO), the International Electrotechnical Commission (IEC), and 89 national standards organizations in other countries that belong to ISO. ANSI standards are available in microform from Information Handling Services (IHS), Englewood, Colorado, and from Information Marketing, Inc., Oak Park, Michigan. Also available from IHS in microform are ISO and IEC standards. A biweekly periodical, *Standards Action*, an annual catalog with supplements, and specialized listings keep the public aware of available standards. *Standards Action* also provides an opportunity to comment on proposed American National Standards and of ISO, IEC, the European Committee for Standardization (CEN), the European Committee for Electrotechnical Standardization (CENELEC), the International Organization of Legal Metrology (OIML), and proposed foreign government regulations. *Standards Action* is available on line through IHS and BRS. *Consulting Services:* None specified. *Other Services:* A watch service is available. Clients may call the standard developers to comment on standards that are pending. *Service Restrictions:* None specified.

Charges

Document Retrieval Charges: The minimum charge for a published document is $7. Discounts are available to members and on quantity orders for standards published by ANSI. Nonmembers must prepay orders. Coupon books and deposit accounts are available. Sales policies may be requested from the Institute's sales department. *Credit Cards:* None specified. *Guarantee:* None specified.

Bureau of National Affairs (BNA)

Address: 1231 25th St. N.W., Suite 260
Washington, DC 20037
Telephone: 202-452-4323
Electronic mail addresses: Telex: 892 692
Dialorder: Order RSPD
SDC: Order RSPD

Overview

Typical clients are law firms, government agencies, and corporations. Corporate requests come from all departments, not just the legal offices. The search division has considerable resources at its disposal, including an editorial division of 600 employees and extensive contacts (public and private) in Washington, D.C. A client interested in periodic updates on a particular subject may be sent a special newsletter available from the editorial department. Some services, such as quick reference questions, are free to BNA subscribers. *Subject Specialties:* Legal and other current information concerning labor and human relations, business and economics, environment and safety. *Date Founded:* 1950. *Employees:* 5 searchers, 18 information specialists; these employees have an M.L.S., J.D., or M.B.A. Harriet G. Berlin, Director of Research and Special Projects Division. *Facilities:* The BNA Library has a complete current and historical collection of BNA services and books, comprehensive coverage of all state administrative codes and registers, and a strong legal, labor, congressional, and business reference collection. Many types of computers are used for search purposes.

Services

Database Services: A cover letter explains a printout of the search, which may be reformatted. The amount of analysis devoted to the search product depends on the project. Search results are not downloaded unless they need to be reformatted to make sense to the client. Follow-up services include SDI/update and document delivery. Turnaround time for search services varies, but clients are always informed beforehand as to how long a search will take. Average turnaround time is 24 hours. Database search request may be made by telephone. *Vendors/ Databases Searched:* Every major vendor is accessed. On a frequent basis, the bureau searches its own databases, ABI/INFORM, Management Contents, and Disclosure. Thousands of searches are done annually. *Document Delivery:* The bureau specializes in retrieving all kinds of documents (including legal) and published and unpublished materials concerning business, economics, safety, environment, and labor and human relations. In-house and U.S. documents are retrieved very quickly, but documents from other countries require some time for delivery. Orders are taken by phone, mail, or electronic mail. Documents are retrieved throughout the world. A watch service is available. The bureau pays Copyright Clearing House Center fees and is a Dialorder supplier. Contact Harriet G. Berlin for document delivery services. *Consulting Services:* None specified. *Other Services:* Multiclient studies, manual research, specialized bibliographies, fact finding. Any library in the world can be searched; watch services are available covering federal and state legislative and regulatory activities. Customized surveys are also available. *Service Restrictions:* None specified.

Charges

Database Charges: Fees for commercial vendor searches include the online charges, a $5 "origination" fee, plus the database researcher's time of $40 per hour. Minimum research time is 30 minutes. The average cost of a search is $60 to $70. Searches are done at both 300 and 1200 baud. A prepayment or deposit is not required. BNA subscribers receive a 50 percent discount for searches on BNA's exclusive in-house database. *Document Retrieval Charges:* The minimum charge per document is $15. Photocopy charges are 50¢ per page, plus copyright fees. Only costs such as Federal Express, etc., are added on. BNA subscribers receive discounts that bring down costs to about half of what other customers pay for retrieval services. A prepayment or deposit is not required. *Charges—Other Services:* Costs depend on the project. A watch service is available for a monthly charge that depends on the scope of the service. The standard research charge of $50 per hour is doubled for nonsubscribers. *Credit Cards:* None specified. *Guarantee:* "It's rare that a customer is dissatisfied. We know that our reputation depends on the quality of our work."

Disclosure

Address: 5161 River Rd.
 Bethesda, MD 20816
Telephone: 301-951-1350 (Maryland)
 212-732-5955 (New York City)
 213-934-8313 (Los Angeles)
Toll-free telephone: 800-638-8241
Electronic mail addresses: Telex: 898 452

Overview

Disclosure is the only contractor of the SEC charged with retrieving filings for the public. Many information brokers who obtain SEC filings for clients actually get them from Disclosure. Disclosure has the only historical collection of SEC filings available, which is complete back to 1966. Disclosure picks up documents twice a day from the SEC and releases them almost immediately. Clients are notified of new services by direct mail, brochures, sales staff, etc. *Subject Specialties:* None specified. *Other Specialties:* Disclosure deals exclusively in retrieving SEC filings. *Date Founded:* 1968. *Employees:* 190 employees. Philip Hixon, President. *Facilities:* Disclosure has no library but does have a substantial collection of SEC filings on microfiche, which forms the basis of the delivery service. The collection consists of every SEC filing since 1966.

Services

Database Services: The Disclosure database, with extracts of SEC filings, is described in Chapter 18. *Vendors/Databases Searched:* None specified. *Document Delivery:* Disclosure provides copies of all types of filings with the Securities and Exchange Commission (SEC). Turnaround time in New York City is 2 hours, elsewhere 24 hours. Copies of filings can be ordered by phone or mail. Documents are retrieved only from the SEC and Disclosure's archive. Clients may request either. Files include documents back to 1966. *Consulting Services:* None specified. *Other Services:* A watch service is available at no charge. The client pays only when the document becomes available. *Service Restrictions:* None specified.

Charges

Document Retrieval Charges: If a document has been archived on microfiche, there is a $5 minimum charge. If it has just been filed with the SEC and is not yet on microfiche, the minimum charge is $25. Photocopy charges range from 37¢ to $50 per page. A prepayment or deposit is not required. A retainer account can be opened with a deposit of $250; account customers receive a 5 percent discount. *Credit Cards:* None specified. *Guarantee:* Money-back guarantee if the work product is unsatisfactory. *Notes:* Disclosure originates the popular online database by the same name, which is available via DIALOG, Dow Jones, I. P. Sharp, and other vendors.

Engineering Societies Library

Address: 345 East 47th St.
 New York, NY 10017
Telephone: 212-705-7611
Electronic mail addresses: Dialorder: ESL

Overview

Clients are generally individual engineers, engineering firms, and consultants. The most charged for a single project has been $1,129. The Engineering Societies Library is an important resource in that its collection includes publications not available elsewhere. *Subject Specialties:* Engineering. *Date Founded:* 1913. *Employees:* 13 professional librarians. Ms. Barbara Dege, Search Librarian, the contact for document retrieval (M.L.S. and DIALOG training). *Facilities:* Largest engineering library in the country. Radio Shack TRS-80 III (1200 baud) and dumb terminal (300 baud).

Services

Database Services: Clients receive either a photocopy of the computer printout or an offline print. No analysis of the database search is provided, and searches are not downloaded or reformatted. Average turnaround for a search assignment is approximately one week. Document delivery is provided as a follow-up service, and SDI is available. Approximately 250 searches are done annually. *Vendors/Databases Searched:* DIALOG, INSPEC, and COMPENDEX. *Document Delivery:* The library specializes in delivering engineering-related documents. Turnaround time is one week through Dialorder. Otherwise delivery time averages one to two weeks. It is preferred that orders be made by mail or through Dialorder. Phone orders are assessed a $10 surcharge. The Engineering Society Library is the only location from which materials are retrieved. Only photocopies of requested materials are provided. A watch service is available on request. Clients pay copyright fees unless the order is placed through Dialorder. Contact Barbara Dege concerning document delivery services. *Consulting Services:* None specified. *Other Services:* Manual searches and watch services are available. *Service Restrictions:* Documents are retrieved only from the Engineering Societies Library.

Charges

Database Charges: Connect-time charges are rounded off to the nearest $5, e.g., a $33 search becomes $35; $35 per hour is charged for the professional searcher's time. There is no minimum charge for a search. Searches are done at both 300 and 1200 baud. A prepayment or deposit is not required. Discounts are not granted to regular users, but members of the five engineering societies that support the library receive a 20 percent discount. Retainer accounts may be set up by sending a deposit of at least $50. *Document Retrieval Charges:* The minimum charge for single documents is $4.40. Photocopy charges are 40¢ per page, and there is a $4 handling charge. The billing charge is $1. Discounts are not given for volume accounts. Retainer accounts may be set up by sending a deposit of at least $50. A prepayment or deposit is not required for document retrieval services. *Credit Cards:* None specified. *Guarantee:* No formal guarantees.

FIND/SVP

Address: 500 5th Ave.
New York, NY 10110
Telephone: 212-354-2424
Electronic mail addresses: Telex: 148358
The Source: TI3676

Overview

FIND/SVP, one of the largest firms in the information brokerage field, serves all types of clients. A newsletter and announcements at conferences inform clients of new services. *Subject Specialties*: Health care, technical and industrial topics, computers, finance, banking, and consumer information are areas frequently investigated, but FIND/SVP researches all subjects. *Date Founded:* 1970. *Employees:* Approximately 100 employees, including 40 subject specialists. Andrew Garvin, President; Kathleen Bingham, Vice-President; Anne Dennis, Director of Information Resources. *Facilities:* The in-house library has 900 journals and 15,000 subject files; TI, DECwriter, and NEXIS equipment.

Services

Database Services: The averge turnaround time for search results is 24 to 48 hours; sometimes results can be obtained in less than a day. Search results are not downloaded and reformatted. Clients need not be present when a search is done. *Vendors/Databases Searched:* DIALOG, SDC, NEXIS, Dow Jones, BRS, Predicasts, MEDLARS, NewsNet, Comp-Mark, CompuServe, The Source, and others. *Document Delivery:* Available. *Consulting Services:* None specified. *Other Services:* A Quick Information Service is available on a retainer basis. It provides direct telephone access to a comprehensive information center for quick answers to a wide variety of business quotations. The Research Projects Service is a special service designed to handle more extensive research including custom market and industry studies available on an industrial project basis. *Service Restrictions:* None specified.

Charges

Database Charges: FIND/SVP prefers to deal with clients on a retainer basis (database searching comes under this retainer). Initially, most clients pay from $300 to $400 a month as a retainer. Searches are done at 300 or 1200 baud. *Credit Cards:* None specified. *Guarantee:* Informal.

FOI Service, Inc.

Address: 12315 Wilkins Ave.
         Rockville, MD 20852
Telephone: 301-881-0410
Electronic mail addresses: CompuServe 76703, 274

Overview

FOI is the only document delivery service concerned exclusively with retrieving materials from the FDA. The firm considerably shortens delivery time for documents that would otherwise have to be ordered from the FDA. All requests for documents are kept confidential. *Subject Specialties:* None specified. *Date Founded:* 1975. *Employees:* 10 employees. John Carey, General Manager. *Facilities:* FOI library with 35,000 documents is the largest food and drug library outside the FDA.

Services

Database Services: FOI searches only its own database, DocuSearch. Presently, the database can be accessed only by FOI, but it will be available to users in 1984 with FOI as the probable vendor. *Vendors/Databases Searched:* DocuSearch exclusively. *Document Delivery:* FOI specializes in retrieving documents concerning foods and drugs from Food and Drug Administration (FDA) sources. There is a 24-hour processing time for orders. The actual time to retrieve documents varies with the source. Orders are taken by phone, mail, or electronic mail. Documents are retrieved primarily from the FDA and its own library. A watch service is provided for FDA documents only. Nothing retrieved is copyrighted. *Consulting Services:* None specified. *Other Services:* None specified. *Service Restrictions:* None specified.

Charges

Document Retrieval Charges: The minimum charge per document is $25, but less is charged for advertised items. The photocopying charge is 20¢ per page. Shipping costs and costs such as computer time charged by the government are added to basic charges. Clients who subscribe to printed publications receive a discount. Prepayment is required, except for rated companies. A retainer account can be opened by forwarding a deposit. *Credit Cards:* VISA, MasterCard, American Express. *Guarantee:* No formal policy.

IFI/Plenum Data Co.

Address: 302 Swann Ave.
Alexandria, VA 22301
Telephone: 703-683-1085
Toll-free telephone: 800-368-3093
Electronic mail addresses: Dialorder: IFIPATS

Overview

Typical clients include industrial research companies, patent lawyers, and information scientists in need of patent information. An average of 250 assignments are completed each year. IFI/Plenum has the world's largest U.S. patents database with patents retrospective to 1950. The firm has a systematic method of indexing chemical patents that is accepted by companies worldwide. *Subject Specialties:* Patents; intelligence information and competitive aspects of patents. *Date Founded:* 1955. *Employees:* 14 scientists, 3 programmers, 4 management employees, and 6 clerical employees. Mary Last, Management Consultant (B.A. chemistry, M.B.A.); Rick Myrick, Manager of Technical Services (B.A. chemistry); Harry Allcock (marketing and production development background); Susan Goldberg, Document Retrieval. *Facilities:* Patent library and in-house database.

Services

Database Services: Clients receive an actual computer printout of the search. A cover letter is included explaining how the search was done and which files were used. The average turnaround time for an assignment is about five days. A client need not be present when a search is done. Follow-up services available include consulting, document delivery, and update searches. Searches are downloaded and reformatted on an IBM mainframe owned by the firm. Approximately 150 searches are done each year. *Vendors/Databases Searched:* Only DIALOG. *Document Delivery:* IFI/Plenum specializes in the delivery of patent related documents. The average turnaround time is five days but a one-day rush service is available. Orders are taken by phone or mail. A patent number is required as is the publication date for foreign patents. The U.S. Patent Office is the primary source of material retrieved. Clients normally receive photocopies of requested material. A watch service is available. IFI/Plenum is a Dialorder supplier. Contact Susan Goldberg to request documents. *Consulting Services:* Provided in the patent field. *Other Services:* IFI/Plenum has an in-house database that is applicable to some patent-related information requests. Multiclient studies will be done on request. A watch service is also available. *Service Restrictions:* None specified.

Charges

Database Charges: $75 per search, plus 50¢ per record printed for full abstract or claim. If technical research is required beyond one hour, it is billed at the rate of $30 per hour. Searches are done at 300 and 1200 baud. *Document Retrieval Charges:* $4, plus 30¢ per page for U.S. patents; $4, plus 75¢ per page for foreign patents. Actual delivery charges are added to these costs, and $10 is added when the publication date is not included with an order. Rush service is available for $10. A prepayment or deposit is not required. Discounts are not provided for volume accounts and retainer accounts are not available. *Charges—Other Services:* $30 per hour. *Credit Cards:* None specified. *Guarantee:* Yes.

ILR:ACCESS

Address: Martin P. Catherwood Library
New York State School of Industrial and Labor Relations
Cornell University
Ithaca, NY 14853
Telephone: 607-256-2277
Electronic mail addresses: BRS: T 938

Overview

Typical clients are industrial corporations and law firms. Approximately 2,300 searches are performed each year for Cornell affiliates, and 200 searches for ILR:ACCESS. To date, $2,700 has been the greatest amount charged for a search that included manual and online searching. *Subject Specialties:* Industrial relations, labor relations, and personnel. *Date Founded:* 1977. *Employees:* 2 full-time librarian/searchers—Constance Finlay (M.L.S.; vendor training and experience on DIALOG, BRS, SDC, NEXIS, Dow Jones, Westlaw, and others); Carla Weiss (M.L.S., vendor training and experience). *Facilities:* Largest collection of industrial relations materials in an academic library, approximately 150,000 books. IBM PC, TI Portable, and TI 800 standard searches at 1200 baud.

Services

Database Services: Clients receive the actual printout or a photocopy of the search. The searcher will discuss the results by phone and will annotate the printout if necessary. Search results currently are not downloaded and reformatted, but there are plans to do so in the future. It is advisable that clients be present when a search is done, but this is often not possible. Turnaround time depends on client needs. Every effort is made to deliver results within the time requested by the client. The major follow-up service is document delivery. All database searches are confidential. Approximately 2,500 searches are performed each year, about 200 of which are done for ILR:ACCESS. The remainder are done for Cornell faculty and students. *Vendors/Databases Searched:* Vendors include DIALOG, BRS, TEXTLINE, Questel, SDC, Dow Jones, Westlaw, The Source, and Labor Relations Press. Databases include Management Contents, ABI/INFORM, ERIC, NTIS, and LABORLAW. *Document Delivery:* ILR:ACCESS specializes in materials concerning industrial relations, labor relations, and personnel. Turnaround is usually only one day. Orders are taken by phone, mail, or electronic mail. Most items are retrieved from Cornell collections but when necessary from other sources as well without restriction. Photocopies of requested documents are normally provided. Contact Constance Finlay for document delivery services. *Consulting Services:* None specified. *Other Services:* Manual research is done in Cornell libraries exclusively. A watch service is also available. *Service Restrictions:* None specified.

Charges

Database Charges: $90 per hour for professional time, plus database costs. The minimum charge for professional time is $22.50 ($\frac{1}{4}$ hour of time). The average charge for a search is $150 to $225. Prepayment or a deposit is not required. Discounts are not provided to regular users, and retainer accounts are not available. *Document Retrieval Charges:* A $5.50 handling fee is charged, plus 20¢ per page. If verification of bibliographic details is needed, the professional fee of $90 per hour is charged for time spent. Discounts are not given for volume accounts. A prepayment or deposit is not required. Retainer accounts are not available. *Credit Cards:* None specified. *Guarantee:* No formal guarantees, but if the client has a problem, e.g., bad photocopies, replacements will be made.

InfoQuest

Address: 1301 Rockville Pike
        Kensington, MD 20895
Telephone: 301-881-9400
Electronic mail addresses: Telex: 904059 WSH
                Dialorder: QUEST
                SDC: Order INFOQUEST

Overview

Typical clients include R&D companies, Fortune 500 companies, lawyers, and chemical companies. *Subject Specialties:* InfoQuest provides information on all subjects. Data on the government, environment, and patents exemplify the subject areas of interest to many clients. *Other Specialties:* Chemical and medical topics are a specialty in nondatabase research. *Date Founded:* 1969. *Employees:* 3 professional and 2 clerical employees. Paula Eiblum, Project Director (four years experience as information specialist). *Facilities:* Hazeltine computer. Searches are done at 1200 baud.

Services

Database Services: Analysts usually devote about an hour of time to design a search. A written order from the customer is requested. Follow-up services available include translation, document delivery, and update searches. Turnaround is usually "same day" if results are retrieved online. Turnaround time for offline results depends on the vendor involved. Search results are not downloaded or reformatted. Clients generally receive offline prints of the search results, but online prints can be requested for rush service. *Vendors/Databases Searched:* SDC, BRS, DIALOG, and MEDLINE. *Document Delivery:* All kinds of materials are retrieved. The average turnaround time is two working days. Orders are taken by phone, mail, or electronic mail. Libraries regularly used for document retrieval include the Library of Congress, National Library of Medicine, National Agricultural Library, University of Maryland, and other Washington area libraries. Customers usually receive a photocopy of the requested material. Copyright compliance policies are followed. InfoQuest supplies documents ordered through Dialorder and SDC Orbdoc. Contact Paula Eiblum to request documents or other materials. About 5,000 document requests are handled each year. *Consulting Services:* None specified. *Other Services:* Manual research services are provided. *Service Restrictions:* None specified.

Charges

Database Charges: $35 per hour analyst time, plus online charges; there is a one-hour minimum for analyst time. The average charge for a search is $100. Searches are done at 1200 baud. Prepayment is generally required, depending on the scope of the search. There are no retainer accounts and no discounts to regular users. *Document Retrieval Charges:* $10, plus 25¢ per page for each document; rush service is provided for $20, plus 25¢ page. Actual delivery charges and copyright fees are added to these costs when applicable. A 10 percent discount on handling charges is provided for volume accounts. A prepayment or deposit is not required except for non-U.S. clients; clients may set up a retainer account by depositing $50. Clients are invoiced once a month. *Charges—Other Services:* Manual research is billed at the rate of $35 per hour with a one-hour minimum charged. *Credit Cards:* VISA, MasterCard. *Guarantee:* Yes. *Notes:* "There are no 'hidden fees' tacked onto our service charges."

Information Intelligence, Inc. (III)

Address: P.O. Box 31098
          Phoenix, AZ 85046
Telephone: 602-996-2283
Electronic mail addresses: Telex: 704787
          III Online System (Information Intelligence's own system, can be reached at 602-996-2573)
          SDC: Order INFOINT
          DIALOG: IIIA2. (Note that DIALOG and SDC access may be discontinued in 1984)

Overview

Documents are often delivered to firms in energy-related fields and to law firms. Consulting is usually provided to major public and private agencies concerned with establishing information services. A charge of $5,000 to $10,000 is typical for consulting projects. Information Intelligence is a publisher and considers itself a leading source for information on the online industry. III maintains its own online database services and hard copy publications. *Databases:* Online Hotline and Online Careers. *Publications: Information Intelligence Online Hotline, In-*

485 / *Major Information Brokers*

formation Intelligence Online Newsletter, Information Intelligence Online Libraries and Micro-computers. III publications go to subscribers in over 45 countries. New services are announced by direct mail and through press announcements. *Subject Specialties:* Documents and materials concerning all subjects are retrieved. *Date Founded:* 1979. *Employees:* Richard Holeatt, President; George S. Machovec, Managing Editor. Mr. Holeatt has worked in the information field for over 25 years. III maintains a "network" of 25 people. *Facilities:* III has its own online systems for free 24-hour online ordering and also produces and maintains its own online systems for the Online Hotline and Online Careers databases.

Services

Database Services: None specified. *Vendors/Databases Searched:* None specified. *Document Delivery:* Documents and materials concerning all subjects are retrieved. Average turnaround time is less than two working days. Orders are taken by phone, mail, and electronic mail. Libraries from which materials are regularly retrieved include the Library of Congress, National Library of Medicine, National Agriculture Library, University of Arizona, and University of California. Materials can be retrieved from other locations. Original documents or photocopies are delivered. Copyright compliance regulations are adhered to and Information Intelligence is a supplier to Dialorder and SDC. There is no watch service. *Consulting Services:* Provided in the field of information services, particularly information storage and retrieval. *Other Services:* Multiclient studies are done on an individual basis. Manual research is also available. Information Intelligence is primarily a publisher and database producer. *Service Restrictions:* None specified.

Charges

Database Charges: None specified. *Document Retrieval Charges:* $10, plus 25¢ per page plus costs. For rush service, add $5; for special documents, $15, plus costs. Additional costs include postage and copyright charges. There is a discount of 5 percent to 50 percent on deposit accounts depending on volume. Call to establish an account, and a statement will be forwarded. Prepayment or deposit is required on all orders. There is no minimum charge on credit card or deposit accounts. *Charges—Other Services:* Average rate is $500 per day, plus expenses. *Credit Cards:* VISA, MasterCard. *Guarantee:* Yes.

Information on Demand

Address: P.O. Box 9550
Berkeley, CA 94704
Telephone: 415-841-1145
Toll-free telephone: 800-227-0750
Electronic mail addresses: Telex number: 137328 answerback Pergamon EMSD
Dialorder: Order INFO
The Source: DATAIOD or TCB352
BRS: TJ52
CompuServe: 76703, 316
ONTYME: :SENDIOD
ScienceNet: INFO.ON.DEMAND
SDC: Order IOD

Overview

Research service clients are generally marketing and management people in firms of all sizes, from Fortune 500 companies to local entrepreneurs. Document delivery clients are usually corporate and government librarians. Information on Demand (IOD) was founded in 1978 following the break up of Information Unlimited, which was formed in 1971. The firm, which has worldwide resources and an electronically connected field network, is considered one of the industry leaders and a model for fledgling firms. It is owned by Pergamon International and Pergamon

Press. *Subject Specialties:* All subjects are researched. *Other Specialties:* Secondary market research. *Employees:* 32 professional and 20 clerical employees. Sue Rugge, President (ran three corporate libraries, 12 years prior experience); Barbara Newlin, Director of Research (M.L.S.; 13 years experience, 5 years online experience); Emily Rosenberg, Marketing Manager. *Facilities:* TI 820 Terminals with 1200-baud search capability. Micromation and Datapoint in-house computers.

Services

Database Services: Online or offline prints from systems are provided to client. All types of follow-up services are available. The average turnaround time for an assignment is approximately one week. Search results are not downloaded and reformatted but can be sent by electronic mail. Each year 1,500 online searches are performed. About 75 percent of the research projects undertaken involve some online searching. The Current Awareness Service provides for periodic online searches of all applicable databases to monitor current developments in any field. *Vendors/Databases Searched:* InfoLine, DIALOG, BRS, SDC, MEDLARS, ORBIT, NEXIS, Dow Jones, LEXIS, CompuServe, The Source, VuText, Info Globe, I. P. Sharp, Standard & Poor's, Dun & Bradstreet, TEXTLINE, ESA-IRS, and Samsom. The final three systems are European. *Document Delivery:* IOD locates, photocopies, or acquires published information in any form, from any country, including annual reports, census data, catalogs, conference papers, competitors' brochures, government documents, journal articles, patents, specifications/technical reports, 10-Ks, and theses. The IOD staff has daily access to the following "IOD Source Libraries": University of California at Berkeley, at Davis, at Los Angeles; Stanford University; San Francisco Public Library; Linda Hall Library (Kansas City, MO); John Crerar Library (Chicago); Cornell University Libraries; Harvard University; Massachusetts Institute of Technology; Engineering Societies Library (New York, NY); U.S. Patent Office; National Technical Information Service (Springfield, VA); National Library of Medicine; National Agricultural Library; Library of Congress; University of Texas; University of Michigan. Materials concerning all subjects are retrieved, and the average turnaround time is three to five days. Orders are taken by phone, mail, or electronic mail. Fascimile receipt and delivery (any group 2 or 3 machine: 415-841-6311) is also available. Contact person is Sue Rugge. Copyright royalties are paid to the Copyright Clearance Center and directly to publishers. *Consulting Services:* Provided in the field of information services. *Other Services:* A translation service is available. Materials are translated into the target language by translators with advanced degrees in engineering and the sciences. IOD specializes in foreign patent translations. It also does small-scale, informal interviewing of industry experts and top-level management. Telephone interviews are used to enhance other research techniques. Manual and secondary market research services are also available. There are no geographic limitations restricting these services. Multiclient studies are not available at present. The Current Awareness Service monitors developments in any field. *Service Restrictions:* None specified.

Charges

Database Charges: $60 per hour labor, plus all other direct costs. There is a markup on direct database charges, and the minimum labor charge is $120 for two hours. The average charge for a search is $200 to $300. A $1,500 deposit earns a discount of $15 per hour labor and lowers the minimum labor charge to one hour. A prepayment or deposit is required of first-time users only. Searches are done at 1200 baud. *Document Retrieval Charges:* The basic document delivery charge is $14. The first 20 pages are free, and 25¢ is charged for each additional page. There are usually no charges added to the basic document delivery unless copyright charges exceed $4. Volume account discounts: 25+ items per month receive a $2 per document discount; 100+ items per month receive a $3 per document discount. No prepayment is required for document delivery. Contact the company to set up a deposit account. This is not required, but there is an additional 5 percent discount for deposit account holders. There is a $6 per item charge for rush service. Delivery of documents cited in research reports is $11 per item if available from the IOD source libraries noted above. *Charges—Other Services:* Price quotations upon request. *Credit Cards:* VISA, MasterCard, American Express, Diner's Club. *Guarantee:* None specified. *Notes:* "We are a full-service information-gathering company, not just a computer search company. You do not need to know anything about computers or databases to use our services."

Information Store, Inc.

Address: 140 Second St., 5th Floor
San Francisco, CA 94105
Telephone: 415-543-4636 (San Francisco)
213-624-3865 (Los Angeles)
619-239-4649 (San Diego)
415-543-9147 (facsimile)
Electronic mail addresses: Dialorder: INFOSTOR or LAWINFO
OnTyme: INFOSTORE
BRS: T191
CompuServe: 74105, 1661
Cable: INFOSTORE
ORBDOC: INFOSTORE
The Source: TCC 598

Overview

Research services are generally provided to executives, and document delivery is usually requested by major corporations. Thousands of assignments are completed each year. The highest charges for assignments are in the $15,000 to $20,000 range. The Information Store was founded in 1978 followng the break up of Information Unlimited, which was formed in 1971. Notification of new services is provided by a news bulletin called *Infogram*. The company also updates its corporate brochure periodically and sends out direct mail pieces from time to time. *Subject Specialties:* Business, marketing, market research, law. Materials concerning all subjects are available through the document retrieval service. *Other Specialties:* Executive interviewing, competitive research. *Employees:* 35 employees. Georgia L. Finnigan, President, CEO (M.B.A., M.S.L.S., training in major bibliographic databases). *Facilities:* The Information Store maintains a library of directories, database manuals, union lists, and other verifying and source tools. The firm has various terminals and computers, all high speed. Searching is done at 1200 + baud.

Services

Database Services: Searches are done at 1200 + baud and are delivered in a variety of formats, depending on the requirements of the client. The degree to which search results are analyzed also depends on client requirements. All types of follow-up services are provided. Turnaround time is per client request whenever possible. Some downloading of searches can be done if desired. *Vendors/Databases Searched:* All available bibliographic and some numeric databases are searched. Business databases are searched most frequently. Hundreds of searches are performed each year. *Document Delivery:* All types of materials are retrieved worldwide. Delivery usually takes two to five days. Orders can be taken by phone, mail, electronic mail, or office visit. Sources from which documents are regularly retrieved include University of California libraries, the Library of Congress, the National Library of Medicine, and others. Photocopies of requested materials are generally delivered. Clients may request materials in any format they desire. A watch service called Special-Interest Monitoring is available. The Information Store belongs to and pays into the Copyright Clearance Center. *Consulting Services:* Advice is provided on sources of information. *Other Services:* Executive interviewing, multiclient studies, and manual research services are available. The Information Store also has a watch service called Special-Interest Monitoring. *Service Restrictions:* The firm does not do chemical searching.

Charges

Database Charges: The average charge is $500 to $1,000. Time and shipping charges are added to online costs, but charges added to online costs depend on the hourly rate charged for an assignment and the type of account the client has with the company. Minimum charges vary with assignment type. Prepayment or retainer accounts are preferred, depending on the client. Clients may open an account with an agreed-upon deposit depending on anticipated use. A discount of up to 25 percent is available to regular users. *Document Retrieval Charges:* The basic charge for document retrieval is $8 per item. The first ten pages are free; thereafter, 30¢ per page. Copyright, copyright checking, direct charges, and phone calls are added to basic charges when applicable. Prepayment is not normally required, but a deposit is encouraged. Contact the company about setting up a retainer account. *Charges—Other Services:* Depends on project. *Credit Cards:* VISA, MasterCard, American Express. *Guarantee:* "We guarantee that we have done what we say we have done. We cannot guarantee the quality of information created by others."

Library of Congress

Address: Library of Congress
            Photoduplication Service
            Washington, D.C. 20540
Telephone: 202-287-5640
Electronic mail addresses: Telex: 710-822-0815

Overview

The Photoduplication Service was organized in 1938 as a result of a grant by the Rockefeller Foundation establishing a revolving fund. The service maintains a searching staff to investigate the availability of requested material, prepare cost estimates, and secure materials from the collections. It also acts as custodian for and supplies photoduplicates of over 100,000 scientific and technical reports released through the Publication Board of the Department of Commerce, Office of Technical Services, prior to June 1, 1961. These reports were either never printed in quantity or are now out-of-print. In addition, the Photoduplication Service is the custodian of the library's Master Negative Microform Collection, totaling more than 282,000 reels of microfilm and 58,000 of microfiche. Of particular interest are the microfilms of the Presidential Papers, the manuscript collections in the libraries at Mt. Sinai, and the Greek and Armenian Patriarchiates in Jerusalem, Early State Records of the United States, Official Papers in the Japanese Ministry of Foreign Affairs, and both current and retrospective files of more than 1,000 domestic and foreign newspapers and other serials. Detailed information about the material in these and other special collections is available from the Photoduplication Service or may be found in the the *Guide to Microforms in Print, Newspapers in Microform*, and the *National Register of Microform Masters*. A circular series announcing outstanding research collections is sent to selected institutions, primarily large research libraries. The largest customer is the Library of Congress and secondarily U.S. and foreign research libraries. In fiscal 1982, 51,762 searches were conducted for 107,175 items. It is not uncommon for the service to receive orders in the amount of $20,000 to $30,000. Given the large size of the Library of Congress, the service sometimes experiences considerable difficulty in finding items that should be in the collections. *Subject Specialties:* The Library of Congress has excellent holdings in Slavic materials and American history, as well as strong holdings in almost all subjects from all over the world. *Employees:* 160 employees. Approximately 95 employees are involved in the production of micrographic copies, 7 in electrostatic print copy work, 13 in photographic work, 22 in reference and searching activities, and 23 persons in administration. *Facilities:* The Library of Congress collection includes 20 million volumes and pamphlets, 1.25 million technical reports, 3.5 million maps, 34 million manuscripts, and 8.5 million photographic negatives, prints, and slides.

Services

Database Services: All readily available Library of Congress databases are searched. *Vendors/Databases Searched:* Library of Congress databases. *Document Delivery:* The Photoduplication Service of the Library of Congress supplies photoreproductions of materials in the library's collections to Congress, other government agencies, individuals, and institutions. Turnaround time depends upon the format desired and the size of the order. Generally, turnaround time is two to three weeks. Ordering procedure is primarily by mail, but phone orders are taken for patrons having deposit accounts. Orders may also be placed in person at the Public Services Section of the Library of Congress, which is located on the ground floor of the John Adams Building (Room Gl009). The service relies almost solely on the resources of the Library of Congress to fill order requests. Clients receive requested materials in the format best suited to their needs. The Photoduplication Laboratory produces photodirect prints, electrostatic prints, photographs, microfilm, microfiche, enlargement prints, color transparencies, slides (black and white or color), blueprints, ozalid prints, etc. The Photoduplication Service is a member of the Coypright Clearance Center and complies with all the copyright regulations. *Consulting Services:* The Photoduplication Service serves as a reference source on micrographic technology. *Other Services:* Primary searching is available. Searches are done either manually or by utilizing the Library of Congress databases. Primary searching is done exclusively with the Library of Congress collection. A watch service is provided in that orders are taken for subscriptions of materials that are being filmed on a continuing basis—primarily foreign newspapers and periodicals. Manual searching in the Library of Congress Card Catalogs is available. *Service Restrictions:* Most services are provided using only Library of Congress collections and available databases.

Charges

Document Retrieval Charges: For most routine items the minimum charge is $7. Complete price lists and order forms are available on request. Customers pay postage costs and copyright fees, if required. Special rules are occasionally given for very large ongoing projects. A prepayment or deposit is required. Deposit accounts are available. *Credit Cards:* None specified. *Guarantee:* Yes.

Michigan Information Transfer Source (MITS)

Address: 205 Harlan Hatcher Graduate Library
University of Michigan
Ann Arbor, MI 48109
Telephone: 313-763-5060
Electronic mail addresses: Telex: 8102236016 (requests made over Telex should start with "Attention MITS")

Overview

MITS is a division of the University of Michigan Library. Typical clients include small companies and Fortune 500 firms. About 40 percent of the clients are from outside Michigan. MITS has the advantages of having easy access to both the University of Michigan Library and the skills of specialists employed at the library for reference requests. *Subject Specialties:* All subjects are researched. *Other Specialties:* Training is provided for library research. MITS can identify University of Michigan faculty doing research in specific areas. *Date Founded:* 1980. *Employees:* 9 employees, including a librarian, a marketing consultant, and researchers. Anne Beaubien, MITS director and creator (ten years experience as reference librarian; author of *Learning the Library: Concepts and Methods for Effective Bibliographic Instruction*). *Facilities:* University of Michigan Library; TI 785 terminal.

Services

Database Services: Clients receive an actual computer printout or offline prints of a search. No analysis of the search product is provided but some follow-up services, such as document retrieval, are available. The average turnaround time for an assignment is one day unless offline prints are obtained. Search results are not downloaded or reformatted. *Vendors/Databases Searched:* The following databases or vendors are used regularly: ABI/INFORM, Predicasts, Psych Abstracts, NTIS, INSPEC, MEDLINE, COMPENDEX, U.S. Patents, DIALOG, SDC, and BRS. ABI/INFORM and Predicasts are the most frequently used databases. *Document Delivery:* All types of documents are retrieved, and the average turnaround time is two days. Clients may order by phone, mail, Dialorder, or Telex. The University of Michigan Library, RLIN (Research Libraries Information Network), and Center for Research Libraries are the most frequently used sources for documents. Documents can be retrieved from all geographic locations and may be delivered in original form or as a photocopy or film. Copyright compliance procedures are followed. *Consulting Services:* None specified. *Other Services:* Manual research will be done but is generally limited to the University of Michigan collection. *Service Restrictions:* None specified.

Charges

Database Charges: $35 per hour or portion of hour necessary to prepare and run search; offline prints and online time are charged at cost; minimum charge for search is $10; average charge for a typical search is $50 to $100; searches are done at 1200 baud. A prepayment or deposit is not required. A retainer account may be set up by filling out a form. *Document Retrieval Charges:* Photocopying charges are billed according to a unit pricing policy; $10.50 is charged for one article up to 30 pages; the minimum overall charge is $10. Charges that may be added include the UPS cost for book delivery, copyright clearance center charges, and costs incurred in obtaining a needed document from another institution; verification charges may also be billed. Completion of a form is necessary to initiate a retainer account. *Charges—Other Services:* Other services are billed at a rate of $15 to $30 per hour, plus direct cost for other expenses incurred, such as long-distance calls and photocopying. *Credit Cards:* None specified. *Guarantee:* "If we make a mistake, we will redo the work without additional cost to the client."

Micromedia Ltd.

Address: 144 Front St. West, 5th Floor
Toronto, Ontario
Canada M5J 2L7
Telephone: 416-593-5211
Electronic mail addresses: Telex: 06524668
ENVOY: MICROMEDIA
Dialorder: CANDOCS

Overview

Typical clients are industrial or business firms having 100 to 200 employees. Micromedia provides quick service for routine assignments but does not have specialists who provide higher-priced consulting services. *Subject Specialties:* Micromedia's major area of interest is business, particularly Canadian business. The document retrieval service specializes in the following materials: Canadian documents, especially corporate reports, government documents, patents, and standards. *Date Founded:* 1972. *Employees:* 35 employees. Robert Gibson, President; other key personnel: Frank Gagne, Victor Brunke, Ulla DeStricker, Louise Fast, Tony Olshen. *Facilities:* TI Silent 700; searches are done at 300 baud.

Services

Database Services: Depending on the request of the client, search results may consist of the actual computer printout, a photocopy of the printout, and/or a report based on the search. An analysis of the search results may be included, depending on the wishes of the client. Some follow-up services are available. The average turnaround time for a search assignment is two days. Searches are not downloaded or reformatted. *Vendors/Databases Searched:* DIALOG, Info Globe, CAN/OLE, I. P. Sharp, and Dow Jones. DIALOG is searched most frequently, and Info Globe is second. *Document Delivery:* Materials most frequently provided consist of Canadian documents, especially corporate reports, government documents, patents, and standards. Average turnaround time is seven days with the exception of corporate reports, which can be provided in 24 hours. A 24-hour turnaround time is available for rush orders on all documents. Libraries from which materials are most frequently retrieved include the University of Toronto Library, Metropolitan Toronto Central Library, and National Library of Canada. Micromedia usually limits searches for documents to Canandian sources. Documents are usually delivered in either a photocopy or fiche format. Micromedia is a member of the Copyright Clearance Center and is a Dialorder supplier. *Consulting Services:* None specified. *Other Services:* Manual research, expert interviews, and surveys will be done within Canada. *Service Restrictions:* Research and document retrieval are done only in Canada.

Charges

Database Charges: There is a $50 minimum for online searches; a typical search costs $100. Searches are done at 300 baud. Discounts are not provided to regular users. A prepayment or deposit is required. A retainer account can be established by forwarding a $200 deposit or by paying a $85 per year membership, which gives a client access to research services on a "pay as you go" basis. *Document Retrieval Charges:* Minimum charge is $15; photocopying charges are 17¢ to 60¢ per page, $3 per page for patents. There are no additional charges beyond these costs. Discounts are provided for volume accounts. A prepayment or deposit is required of new clients. A retainer account can be established by depositing a minimum of $200 in the account. *Credit Cards:* VISA. *Guarantee:* None specified.

MIW Associates, Inc.

Address: 9 Carleton Rd.
Belmont, MA 02178

1925 N. Lynn St.
Suite 903
Arlington, VA 22209
Telephone: 617-484-2361
703-247-3930 (Washington D.C. office)
Electronic mail addresses: Telex: 955-318 INTL DIV ATTN: MIW
ITT/Dialcom: 98:PAC004
The Source: BBW959
CompuServe: 72446, 3140
MCI Mail: 151-6146 (Databasics)

Overview

MIW Associates is the copublisher of the present book. The company uses a variety of methods to gather information. The repertoire includes database searching, manual research (in libraries and archives), interviews with experts, and direct opinion surveys. MIW draws upon a proprietary network of research contractors to aid in data gathering. The firm typically accepts only large, sophisticated assignments requiring substantial data synthesis and analysis. Fees range from $1,000 to $50,000 per assignment. MIW is actively involved within the online industry and is a corporate member of the Information Industry Association. Heavy emphasis is placed on consulting regarding the development and marketing of database services. There is also much emphasis on developing foreign trade opportunities for clients in the United States and in the Asia-Pacific region. *Subject Specialties:* Multidisciplinary; assignment topics have ranged from hotel development in Singapore, to Japanese robotics software, to U.S. office automation. Extensive research has been completed in the fields of artificial intelligence, biotechnology, database systems, political finance, electronic conferencing, and consumer electronics. *Date Founded:* 1977. *Employees:* 12 in-house staff, plus a large network of independent research contractors throughout the United States and in various other countries. Marvin I. Weinberger, President (J.D. and Chairman of the Artificial Intelligence Task Force for the Information Industry Association); Israel J. Melman, Chairman; David U. Greevy, Director of Washington office. *Facilities:* Exhaustive library regarding database services of virtually every vendor; proprietary files on over 750 international information/research organizations; proprietary database of federal/state political finance. Online searching is done on a variety of terminals and microcomputers, at both 300 and 1200 baud. Offices are maintained in both Belmont, Massachusetts and Washington, D.C.

Services

Database Services: Database research is only performed as part of a comprehensive data-gathering program executed on the client's behalf. The printout is reformatted and published in a bound information package which includes a narrative summary and analysis along with the text of other supporting documentation. *Vendors/Databases Searched:* MIW Associates has access to virtually all significant vendors, both domestic and international. These include DIALOG, SDC, BRS, Control Data, ESA-IRS, Finsbury, Dow Jones, Datasolve, CompuServe, Dialcom, Samsom, QL Systems, Info Globe, NewsNet, Pergamon, Questel, and I. P. Sharp. MIW Associates also searches the proprietary political databases of its subsidiary—PAC Researchers, Ltd. *Document Delivery:* Comprehensive document retrieval is available but only as part of the overall information service provided. *Consulting Services:* MIW Associates provides consulting assistance to a number of leading information-industry companies regarding database development and marketing. The firm also serves as consultant to large organizations in implementing electronic conferencing networks. Additionally, MIW Associates renders merger and acquisition analysis. *Other Services:* MIW Associates writes and copublishes books/directories in selected fields. The present book is copublished with Garland Publishing and The Goldhirsh Group. *The PAC Directory* is copublished with Ballinger Publishing Inc. MIW Associates also copublishes *The Telegen Directory of Japanese Biotechnology* with EIC/Intelligence. *Service Restrictions:* Bounded by strict ethical guidelines regarding provision of advisory services to competitors within an industry.

Charges

Database Charges: The cost of database research is a function of the time spent by the information specialist (at $75 per hour) plus direct expenses. *Document Retrieval Charges:* Document retrieval expenses are passed along at direct cost plus time spent by the information specialist involved. *Charges—Other Services:* The comprehensive information service provided by MIW Associates includes database and manual research, document retrieval, interviews with experts, direct surveys, and consulting. The charges for personnel (other than clerical) range from $75 to $200 per hour. Expenses are passed along at cost. The minimum fee for any type of assignment is $900. Some assignments are contracted on a flat fee basis (irrespective of hours expended). Prepayment in full is typically required for all but very large assignments. Many clients retain MIW Associates' services on a monthly fee basis. *Credit Cards:* None specified. *Guarantee:* "Every reasonable effort is made to satisfy the client. We guarantee our best efforts; mistakes are corrected at our cost." *Notes:* "We are the information specialists to call upon for substantial and complex assignments. All client confidences are strictly maintained."

NASA/Florida/STAC

Address: 307 Weil Hall
University of Florida
Gainesville, FL 32611
Telephone: 904-392-0853
Electronic mail addresses: BRS: TBS5

Overview

NASA/Florida/STAC (State Technology Application Center) is funded by NASA and the university system of Florida. Clients include individuals, businesses, and some government agencies. Between 600 and 700 assignments are handled each year. The service has access to European databases and will search worldwide. A quarterly newsletter provides clients with information on new services. *Subject Specialties:* All subjects can be researched. There is no single specialty. *Date Founded:* 1977. *Employees:* The service draws on the skills of personnel employed at the University of Florida. There are five area directors with diverse interests and backgrounds at five sites in Florida. Lynne Heer is Library Center Director (M.L.S.; BRS, DOE, and DIALOG vendor training). *Facilities:* University of Florida Library is available for document retrieval. Microcomputers are not yet utilized for searching.

Services

Database Services: Clients receive the actual printout of a search, which will be explained on request. Referrals are made to experts or consultants if appropriate. SDI is provided on a regular basis if a client wants this. Searches are not downloaded and reformatted, although there are plans to provide this in the future to speed up the search service. Clients need not be present when a search is done. Turnaround time is generally four to five working days, although same-day service is available as workload permits. *Vendors/Databases Searched:* DOE Recon, Darc/Questel, ESA-IRS, NASA/Recon, BRS, DIALOG, SDC, NEXIS, Occupational Health Services, several demographic databases for site selection and analyses, and several European and British business databases. *Document Delivery:* Materials concerning all subjects can be delivered. Document delivery is provided as part of a search or can be requested as a separate service. Turnaround time currently averages ten days to three weeks, but downloading and electronic mail are expected to cut this time in the near future. Orders for document retrieval and searching are taken by phone, mail, or electronic mail. The University of Florida and the Engineering Societies Library are the most frequently used sources for documents. Materials can be retrieved from other locations without geographic limitation. Photocopies of unclassified NASA documents can be provided. Copyright fees are paid. *Consulting Services:* Such services are not directly provided, but referrals to specialists will be made on request or as appropriate. *Other Services:* Manual research is available and searching will be done worldwide if requested. Preliminary patent infringement searching is also available. *Service Restrictions:* None specified.

Charges

Database Charges: The price varies depending on the database(s) searched. Generally the fee amounts to no more than direct database charges plus a 15 percent surcharge. Pricing is negotiated with the client prior to the search. Searches are done at 1200 baud. A prepayment or deposit is not required. Subscription services are available to clients on an individual basis. Contracts are tailored to meet the specific needs of each client. *Document Retrieval Charges:* Photocopying charges consist of the fee charged by the library retrieving the document plus a 15 percent handling cost. A prepayment or deposit is not required. Discounts are provided for volume accounts. *Charges—Other Services:* Charges are made on an individual basis depending on costs. *Credit Cards:* None specified. *Guarantee:* No formal guarantee, but if there is a problem with a document or search, an informal agreement will be worked out.

Notes: NASA/Florida/STAC is one of two NASA-sponsored State Technology Application Centers. The other is:

NASA/University of Kentucky/STAC
109 Kinkead Hall
University of Kentucky
Lexington, KY 40506
William R. Strong, Manager
606-258-4632

These centers are integrated into existing state technical assistance programs and are intended primarily to service government and private industry in the host states. NASA also sponsors eight IACs (Industrial Applications Centers). These centers are intended to serve regional and national needs and, like the STACs, charge only modest fees for a broad range of information services. The IACs are as follows:

Aerospace Research Applications Center
1201 East 38th Street
Indianapolis, IN 46205
John M. Ulrich, Director
317-264-4644

Computer Software Management and Information Center (COSMIC)
Suite 112, Barrow Hall
University of Georgia
Athens, GA 30602
John A. Gibson, Director
404-542-3265

Kerr Industrial Applications Center
Southeastern Oklahoma State University
Durant, OK 74701
James Harmon, Director
405-924-0121, Ext. 413

NASA Industrial Applications Center
701 LIS Building
University of Pittsburgh
Pittsburgh, PA 15260
Paul A. McWilliams, Executive Director
412-624-5211

New England Research Applications Center
Mansfield Professional Park
Storrs, CT 06268
Daniel Wilde, Director
203-486-4533

North Carolina Science and Technology Research Center
P.O. Box 12235
Research Triangle Park, NC 27709
James E. Vann, Director
919-549-0671

Technology Applications Center
University of New Mexico
Albuquerque, NM 87131
Stanley Morain, Director
505-277-3622

NASA Industrial Applications Center
University of Southern California
Denny Research Building
University Park
Los Angeles, CA 90007
Robert Mixer, Acting Director
213-743-6132

National Technical Information Service

Address: U.S. Department of Commerce
           Springfield, VA 22161
Telephone: 703-487-4600
Toll-free telephone: 800-336-4700 (rush handling orders only)
Electronic mail addresses: Telex: 89-9405

Overview

Approximately 45 percent of customers are from business and industry. The remainder include government agencies, academia, individuals, and nonprofit agencies. Clients are notified of new services by newsletter, direct mail, and through a periodically updated brochure. *Subject Specialties:* Multidisciplinary. *Other Specialties:* Government-funded research reports on all subjects are provided by the document retrieval service. *Date Founded:* 1970 (predecessor agencies 1946). *Employees:* 380 civil service employees, including management, professional, clerical, and blue-collar workers. *Facilities:* None specified.

Services

Database Services: Clients receive an actual computer printout of search results with no additional analysis. The average turnaround time is seven to ten days. Search results are not downloaded or reformatted. *Vendors/Databases Searched:* DIALOG, SDC, and BRS. NTIS on DIALOG is the database most frequently searched. Approximately 350 searches are done each year. *Document Delivery:* The service specializes in providing copies of government-funded research reports on all subjects. The average turnaround time is five working days. Orders are taken by phone, mail, online ordering, or Telex. Documents are provided in either paper copy or microform. There is no watch service. The service is a Dialorder supplier. *Consulting Services:* None specified. *Service Restrictions:* None specified.

Charges

Database Charges: The minimum and average charge for a search is $125, which includes all operating costs. A prepayment or deposit is required and clients may set up a retainer account. *Document Retrieval Charges:* Cost depends on document(s) selected. There is no minimum charge, and a discount of 15 percent is provided if more than 20 but less than 100 copies of the same title are ordered. When at least 100 copies of one title are order, the total price is reduced by 25 percent. Clients may set up a retainer account, although prepayment is not required. There is an extra charge for the "ship & bill" service. Extra charges are also made for priority mail and rush handling. *Credit Cards:* VISA, MasterCard, American Express. *Guarantee:* None specified.

National Translations Center

Address: John Crerar Library
         35 W. 33rd St.
         Chicago, IL 60616
Telephone: 312-225-2526
Electronic mail addresses: Telex: 910-221-5131

Overview

The National Translations Center is an international clearinghouse for translations. Typical clients include large research corporations and government agencies, particularly the EPA. The center provides English translations of documents and is the only such comprehensive service in the United States and abroad. It receives from 12,000 to 15,000 inquiries and orders per year. A monthly translation accession list, the *Translations Register-Index*, is provided to clients at a subscription cost of $95 per year with 1,200 to 1,500 new translations listed. *Subject Specialties:* Overall subject specialties include translations in all fields of theoretical and applied sciences, including medicine. *Date Founded:* 1953. *Employees:* 2 librarians, 2 nonprofessionals. Ildiko Nowak, Chief (M.A. chemistry, M.S. library science, both degrees from Czechoslovakia); Donald D. Hinton, Bulletin Production Manager. *Facilities:* Crerar Library, which has more than 1.2 million books and bound periodicals and subscribes to 11,000 periodicals.

Services

Database Services: None specified. *Vendors/Databases Searched:* None specified. *Document Delivery:* Translations of documents are the major type of material provided. The average turnaround time is three to four days but a 24-hour rush service is available for an additional $1. Orders can be taken by phone, mail, electronic mail, TWX, or in person. Documents are retrieved from Crerar Library; when not available there, customers are referred to other sources. The center has plans to retrieve documents from additional sources in the near future. Customers receive a photocopy, microfilm, or occasionally the actual document of the material requested. A watch service is available on request. Copyright compliance is the responsibility of the customer. *Consulting Services:* None specified. *Other Services:* Manual searching is provided as part of the translations service. *Service Restrictions:* None specified.

Charges

Document Retrieval Charges: Minimum charges: one search, $5; photocopying charge, $15 up to ten pages, $3 for each additional ten pages; 24-hour rush service, $1. These prices include delivery charges and all other fees. Clients may open a retainer account with Crerar Library that can be used for the center's services. Discounts are not provided for volume accounts. A prepayment or deposit is not required. *Credit Cards:* None specified. *Guarantee:* Guarantee offered, but not on quality of translation.

Nichols Applied Management

Address: Bentall Building
10180 102nd St.
Edmonton, Alberta
Canada T5J OW5
Telephone: 403-424-0091
403-263-9166 (Calgary office)
Electronic mail addresses: None specified.

Overview

Clients are generally medium to large firms and government agencies. Approximately 250 assignments are completed each year. The most ever charged for a single assignment was $150,000. *Subject Specialties:* Information management, finance, economics. *Other Specialties:* Market research. *Date Founded:* 1973. *Employees:* 7 professional and 2 nonprofessional employees. Bruce Butler, Partner (B.S. in computer science, M.S.E. in management science); Jean Andruski, Certified Records Manager (M.L.S.). *Facilities:* In-house library. IBM PC and Apple III. Searching is done at 300 baud.

Services

Database Services: Clients receive an analytical report based on results of a search. Search results are not downloaded and reformatted. *Vendors/Databases Searched:* DIALOG. *Document Delivery:* None specified. *Consulting Services:* Provided in the fields of finance, economics, market research, and records management/library services. *Other Services:* Manual research, expert interviews, surveys, and multiclient studies. There are no geographic limitations for such services. *Service Restrictions:* None specified.

Charges

Database Charges: Prepayment or a deposit is not usually required. Searches are done at 300 baud. *Credit Cards:* None specified. *Guarantee:* None specified.

Regional Information & Communication Exchange

Address: Fondren Library
Rice University
P.O. Box 1892
Houston, TX 77251-1892
Telephone: 713-528-3553
Electronic mail addresses: Telex: 910-881-3766
Part of the OCLC network

Overview

The exchange is part of Rice University Library. All types of clients are served, including individuals and major corporations. About 25,000 to 30,000 assignments are completed each year. Affiliation with Rice, reasonable prices, and fast personal service are considered to be the most important features of the exchange. Clients are notified of new services as they become available. *Subject Specialties:* All subjects are covered. *Other Specialties:* Consulting is provided in information science. *Date Founded:* 1969. *Employees:* 11 total—1 director, 3 information specialists, 7 support staff. Elizabeth Lunden (M.L.S.), Director. Marsha Fulton, Assistant Director. Paula Garrett (M.L.S.) and Laura Wilder (M.L.S.), Information Specialists. *Facilities:* Rice University libraries. Searches are done on a TI Omni 800 at 1200 baud.

Services

Database Services: Clients receive the actual computer printout. No analysis of the printout is provided. Rush orders can be completed in one day. A watch service is provided for online searching, as are SDI-update searches. *Vendors/Databases Searched:* DIALOG and SDC mainly. Over 500 searches are done annually. *Document Delivery:* Materials concerning all subjects are retrieved. Average turnaround time is three days. Rush orders can be filled in 24 hours. Orders are taken by phone, by mail, and through OCLC. Materials are retrieved directly from Rice University and major Texas libraries as well as other libraries and sources in the United States and abroad. Actual documents or photocopies are provided. The service provides documents to OCLC. Copyright compliance policies are available upon request. *Consulting Services:* Some services are available in information science. *Other Services:* Manual research is available for clients in the Texas region. *Service Restrictions:* None specified.

Charges

Database Charges: Online charges include all incurred costs, plus $25 per hour. The minimum charge is $25, plus costs. Prepayment is required for clients without accounts. A retainer account can be opened by completing an application and depositing a minimum of $100 with the exchange. No discounts are given to regular clients. *Document Retrieval Charges:* Charges are $5 handling and 15¢ per page from Fondren Library. Materials obtained from institutions and sources other than Rice University cost $7.50 handling plus incurred costs. Rush service is available at additional cost. Prices are subject to change; a complete price list is available upon request. Delivery charges are billed to the client. Payment of copyright royalties is done on client request, and an additional service charge of $1.50 is added to the fee. Deposit accounts are not required but are preferred for out-of-state clients. Accounts can be set up by filling out account credit applications and library loan agreements. No discount arrangements are available at present. *Charges—Other Services:* Charges are per diem plus expenses or fixed bid. *Credit Cards:* None specified. *Guarantee:* None specified.

Research Counsel of Washington

Address: 226 4th St., N.E.
Washington, DC 20002
Telephone: 202-544-2700
Electronic mail addresses: Telex: IMD1248698

Overview

The Research Counsel is primarily a custom research company providing expertise in the fields of government procurement and banking. Law firms generally ask for small searches, and Fortune 500 companies request large studies. Approximately 250 market studies are done each year. The highest fee charged to date was $75,000 for a custom research project. Clients are notified of new services by phone and direct mail. *Subject Specialties:* Government procurement and banking (but database research is not limited to these areas). *Other Specialties:* Telephone interviewing. *Date Founded:* 1979. *Employees:* 5-member banking group consists of 4 banking researchers and 1 vice-president who heads group; there are other researchers and clerical workers. David Bradley, President; Derek Van Bever, Executive Vice-President; Matthew Olson, Head of Banking Group; Karen Ericksen, Research Manager. *Facilities:* NEXIS terminal.

Services

Database Services: Database searching is done as part of a research project requested by a client. Normally the computer printout is not provided; documents retrieved from the printout are provided instead. The average turnaround time for an assignment is 24 hours. Search results are not downloaded or reformatted. Technical write-up and analysis of findings are available as complementary services. Searches are done at 1200 baud. *Vendors/Databases Searched:* LEXIS, Dun & Bradstreet, and NEXIS. *Document Delivery:* The Research Counsel specializes in providing materials on government procurement and banking. Average turnaround time is 24 hours. Orders are taken by phone or mail. Materials are retrieved from any federal source. The organization will also arrange to retrieve materials from other locations throughout the world. Retrieval of government documents is occasionally handicapped by publication delays. *Consulting Services:* Provided to "selected clients only." *Other Services:* Manual research, expert interviews, telephone surveys, multiclient studies. A watch service is also available.

Charges

Database Charges: In addition to online charges, a client may be billed for researcher's time and writer's time if necessary. The minimum charge per hour for researcher's time is $50. All other charges for service vary with the type of project. The average charge for a search and report is $300. A prepayment or deposit is required of individuals but not companies. *Document Retrieval Charges:* The cost for documents requested depends on the amount charged by the source. This amount is billed back to the client. There is a minimum charge of $50 per hour for services related to document retrieval. Individuals must prepay for services, but this is not required of companies. There is no discount for large-volume requests as these are not normally encountered. *Charges—Other Services:* $75 per hour for short-answer research; $2,000 per week for research; large project fees are negotiated. *Credit Cards:* None specified. *Guarantee:* Informal guarantee.

SEARCHLINE

Address: 8 Griggs Terrace
          Brookline, MA 02146
Telephone: 617-277-2991
Electronic mail addresses: None specified.

Overview

Clients are usually repeat customers requiring research and document delivery on an ongoing basis. Research may consist of both database and manual searching. Turnaround time is short for most projects. *Subject Specialties:* Business, science/technology, patents, marketing, medicine, medical instrumentation. *Other Specialties:* Manual research, compilation of government data, and marketing/mailing lists development. Documents often retrieved include government reports and market studies in business and high technology. *Date Founded:* 1981. *Employees:* 1 full-time, plus subcontractors. Judith Sovner (M.L.S.; training on DIALOG, BRS, SDC, and NYTIB; 15 years experience in research). *Facilities:* The in-house library includes an index to indexes in business and high-technology and online thesauri. DEC and TI terminals and an Apple II +.

Services

Database Services: A computer printout of search results along with supporting documents and statistical research are compiled into a notebook for one client. Supporting materials are intended to answer a specific business problem. Search results are not downloaded and reformatted. It is recommended that clients be present when searches are done, but this is not required. Follow-up services that are available include SDI/updates, document delivery, and watch services. *Vendors/Databases Searched:* BRS, SDC, DIALOG, Pergamon, NewsNet, Dow Jones News/Retrieval. DIALOG and BRS are most frequently used. *Document Delivery:* Materials regularly retrieved include articles, government reports, and market studies in business and high technology. The average turnaround time is 48 hours depending upon the request. Orders are taken by phone or mail. Materials are retrieved from sources located primarily within the United States. Clients receive photocopies of requested materials. A watch service is available. Document delivery services are only provided in conjunction with research. *Consulting Services:* Consulting is done for firms interested in establishing online research facilities in a corporate environment. Services are also provided to database publishers in defining the market for, or parameters of, a new database. *Other Services:* Manual research, telephone research, interviews, surveys, compilation of government data, multisystem search training, and single- or multiple-database training. *Service Restrictions:* None.

Charges

Database Charges: The minimum charge for a search is $100. The basis for search charges is $40 per hour and online costs (plus 20 percent). The average charge for a search is $500. Searches are done at 1200 baud. A prepayment or deposit is required. Discounts are provided to retainer account customers. A retainer account may be opened by forwarding a deposit. *Document Retrieval Charges:* The basic charge for photocopied documents is $8.50 per document, plus 10¢ per page. Prepayment or deposit is preferred but not required. *Charges— Other Services:* Consulting fees are negotiated on an individual basis. *Credit Cards:* None specified. *Guarantee:* None specified.

Warner-Eddison Associates, Inc.

Address: 186 Alewife Brook Parkway
            Cambridge, MA 02138
Telephone: 617-661-8124
Electronic mail addresses: Telex: 710-320-0094

Overview

Typical clients are Fortune 1000 clients having needs in the field of information management. Warner-Eddison is an experienced firm and offers services not provided by other information brokers. It has a software division that handles INMAGIC, the firm's primary software product. Notification of new services is made through the INMAGIC Newsletter articles, conferences, and exhibits. *Subject Specialties:* Business and management, law, engineering, and automation. *Other Specialties:* Constructing thesauri in all fields of knowledge. (Warner-Eddison Associates created a thesaurus for ABI/INFORM.) *Date Founded:* 1973. *Employees:* 8 professionals, 2 business managers, 4 support staff; Elizabeth G. Eddison, Founder and President (M.L.S., Board of Directors of Information Industry Association); Madeline Miele, Vice-President of Marketing and Sales (employed at R.R. Bowker in market research and book editing; chairperson of their publication committee); Karen Brothers, Vice-President of Software Development (12 years software experience). *Facilities:* In-house library and various computers.

Services

Database Services: Not currently emphasizing this service, though very active previously. *Vendors/Databases Searched:* None specified. *Document Delivery:* Not currently emphasizing this service. *Consulting Services:* Consulting is provided in the field of information management. The firm assists in the development of corporate information centers and libraries. Database design and development, custom card-file production, and indexing services are supplied for many corporations. *Other Services:* None specified. *Service Restrictions:* None specified.

Charges

Charges and Payments: Charges may be by hour, day, or project. Hourly rates are usually $40 to $60. Software charges are by the program, with different prices for micro- vs. minicomputer packages. *Credit Cards:* MasterCard, VISA. *Guarantee:* Yes. *Notes:* "Most of corporate America is ill served in terms of information. The challenge is to bring information services to corporate headquarters."

C A Smorgasbord of Terminals

Many teleprinter terminals aren't sold in a retail store. They're usually distributed directly by the manufacturer or else by computer "systems houses" or computer equipment dealers. (You'll find these listed in the yellow pages.) Like other computer equipment, it's often possible to rent or lease teleprinters; a typical rental price is $100 to $175 a month.

In this listing, we have also included several machines that are full-fledged computers rather than just terminals: the Radio Shack TRS-80 Model 100, the Convergent Technologies WorkSlate, and the Grid Systems Compass "lap" computers. Though they have programming capabilities, many buyers have been acquiring these—especially the Radio Shacks—for their convenience and built-in telecommunications abilities (which include the uploading and downloading functions discussed in the following chapter).

For each machine that we list, we first give basic data about the manufacturer, then the terminal, size, style, communication speed, information on where to purchase it, and any warranties offered. A considerable amount of more technical data follows this.

The keyboard style is an important consideration. If you're a touch typist, you probably wouldn't be happy with anything other than a keyboard of the same size and alignment as the industry standard, the IBM Selectric. Hunt-and-peck typists might be satisfied with smaller keys or a nonstandard alignment. In general, the more keys, the better; a numeric key pad or detachable keyboard are options that some people desire.

Teleprinters, as discussed in Chapter 26, come with a built-in printer, and most display terminals have optional printers. We indicate whether the printer is thermal or impact and how fast it can go. Display terminals may have displays ranging from one line of 20 characters to 24 lines of 80 characters. In general, more is better. And a terminal may or may not display lower-case letters (if not, it may still be able to distinguish between upper and lower case in transmissions).

Aside from a printer, it may be possible to connect any number of accessories, such as a memory device, to a terminal. Our listing gives details of some of these options.

A number of other advanced features are appearing on terminals. RAM (random-access memory) indicates the ability to program in phone numbers, text for uploading, etc. In general, the more, the better. The amount of RAM specifically set aside for text storage is also indicated; a terminal that allows text storage generally also has text editing capabilities (particularly important in electronic mail applications), ability to perform automatic dialing, log on, redialing, or answering are also indicated.

Finally, we list the basic and option prices, and note any published reviews that have come to our attention.

The information below was supplied or checked by the manufacturer; we have tried out some of the machines, but not all of them.

A title marked with an asterisk (*) indicates a company that offers a discount described in the coupon section at the back of the book.

Business Communications Products Division/3M

Address: 3M Center
St. Paul, MN 55144
Telephone: 612-736-0865

Company information

Employees: Information not available at time of publication.   *Date Founded:* Information not available at time of publication.   *Annual Sales (Last FY):* Information not available at time of publication.

3M Whisper Writer

Terminal specifications

Name and Model: 3M Whisper Writer, model 1980 Teleprinter, model 1945 Intelligent Keyboard. *Release Date:* 1981. *Dimensions:* Teleprinter: 3 in. × 12$\frac{1}{4}$ in. × 10$\frac{1}{2}$ in. *Keyboard:* 2$\frac{1}{2}$ in. × 11$\frac{1}{2}$ in. × 6 in. *Weight:* Teleprinter: 8$\frac{3}{4}$ lbs. *Keyboard:* 2$\frac{1}{2}$ lbs. *Portability Characteristics:* Full briefcase. *Case:* Available at extra charge of $99. *Modem Speed:* 110/300 baud. *Modem Style:* Direct connect or acoustic coupler with optional attachment.

Keyboard

Size Compared to IBM Selectric: Somewhat smaller. *Key Alignment Same as IBM Selectric:* Yes. *Number of Keys:* 60. *Numeric Key Pad:* No. *Number of Programmable Function Keys:* 4. *Keyboard Detachable:* Yes.

Printer

Integral Printer: Yes. *External Printer Available:* No. *Printer Type:* Thermal, 80 characters per line. *Characters per Second:* 35.

Display

Not applicable.

Interfaces

Number of RS-232: 1 (only on Model 1482, which doesn't have built-in modem). *Other Input-Output Ports:* RJ11 phone hookup; port for optional acoustic adapter. *Peripherals Available:* Automatic line selector; acoustic coupler.

"Smart" features

Total RAM: 8K. *RAM Available for Text Storage:* 8K. *Can Attach External Memory Device:* No. *Text Editing:* Yes. *Auto Dial:* Yes, 4 numbers. *Auto Log On:* Yes, 4 log ons. *Auto Redial:* Yes. *Auto Answer:* Yes. *Other:* 8K message memory; answer-back programmable; number of rings for auto-answer programmable; auto repeat on all keys; built-in Telex/TWX interface; Xon/Xoff protocol; status indicator.

Sales information

Availability: Through distributors or 3M's own sales force. *Warranty:* 90 days. *Type of Service:* On site (any location), dealer, depot, factory. *Service Contract:* Yes.

Prices

Basic Price: Teleprinters: with 80-column printer and modem, $750; with 40-column printer, internal modem, $700; with 40-column printer, RS-232 interface, no built-in modem, $600; with 80-column printer, RS-232 version, no built-in modem, $650; with Telex 1 keyboard and 4K memory, $1,300; intelligent keyboard with 8K memory, $395. *Pricing Date:* Information not available at time of publication. *Prices for Options:* Acoustic adapter, $75; carrying case, $99.

Computer Devices, Inc.

Address: 25 North Ave.
Burlington, MA 01803
Telephone: 617-273-1550
800-225-1387

Company information

Employees: 300. *Date Founded:* 1969. *Annual Sales (Last FY):* $17 million.

Terminal specifications

Name and Model: Series 2000. *Release Date:* May 1981. *Dimensions:* l5 in. × l7 in. × 5 in. *Weight:* 15½ lbs. without case. *Portability Characteristics:* Desktop. *Case:* Furnished with unit. *Modem Speed:* 300/1200 baud. *Modem Style:* Direct connect and built-in acoustic coupler.

Keyboard

Size Compared to IBM Selectric: Approximately the same. *Key Alignment Same as IBM Selectric:* Yes. *Number of Keys:* 66. *Numeric Key Pad:* No. *Number of Programmable Function Keys:* 6. *Keyboard Detachable:* No.

Printer

Integral Printer: Yes. *External Printer Available:* No. *Printer Type:* Thermal, 80 or 132 columns. *Characters per Second:* 160.

Display

Not applicable.

Interfaces

Number of RS-232: 1. *Other Input-Output Ports:* Telephone jack. *Peripherals Available:* None specified.

Computer Devices Series 2000

"Smart" features

Total RAM: 1K (additional 2K optional). *RAM Available for Text Storage:* None. *Can Attach External Memory Device:* No. *Text Editing:* Not available. *Auto Dial:* Yes, up to 6 numbers. *Auto Log On:* Yes, up to 6 log ons. *Auto Redial:* No. *Auto Answer:* Yes. *Other:* Graphics, answer-back memory, diagnostic self-testing.

Sales information

Availability: From manufacturer or through distributors. *Warranty:* 90 days. *Type of Service:* On site in selected areas. *Service Contract:* $288 per year and up.

Prices

Basic Price: $1,695 (300 baud); $2,195 (300/1200 baud). *Pricing Date:* Late 1982. *Prices for Options:* International power supply, $150; graphics, $180; additional 2K memory, $100; answer-back memory, $75.

Computer Transceiver Systems, Inc.

Address: P.O. Box 15
East 66 Midland Ave.
Paramus, NJ 07652
Telephone: 201-261-6800
800-526-9068

Company information

Employees: 100. *Date Founded:* 1968. *Annual Sales (Last FY):* Information not available at time of publication.

Terminal specifications

Name and Model: Execuport 4120. *Release Date:* 1981. *Dimensions:* 18 in. × 16 in. × 6 in. *Weight:* 19 lbs. *Portability Characteristics:* Full briefcase. *Case:* Furnished with unit. *Modem Speed:* 300/1200 baud, Vadic and Bell compatible. *Modem Style:* Direct connect; built-in acoustic coupler.

Keyboard

Size Compared to IBM Selectric: Somewhat smaller. *Key Alignment Same as IBM Selectric:* Yes. *Number of Keys:* 69. *Numeric Key Pad:* Embedded. *Number of Programmable Function Keys:* 2. *Keyboard Detachable:* No.

Printer

Integral Printer: Yes. *External Printer Available:* No. *Printer Type:* Thermal. *Characters per Second:* 120.

Display

Not applicable.

Interfaces

Number of RS-232: 2. *Other Input-Output Ports:* None specified. *Peripherals Available:* None specified.

Computer Transceiver Systems Execuport 4120

"Smart" features

Total RAM: 43K, available as option. *RAM Available for Text Storage:* Up to 43K. *Can Attach External Memory Device:* No. *Text Editing:* Yes. *Auto Dial:* Yes. *Auto Log On:* No. *Auto Redial:* Yes. *Auto Answer:* Yes. *Other:* Answer-back storage, self-testing, fully formed descenders, double-width print, compressed print (up to 233 characters), print intensity selector.

Sales information

Availability: Directly from manufacturer or through manufacturers' representatives. *Warranty:* 90 days or varies with rental or lease-purchase plan. *Type of Service:* On site (selected areas), depot, factory. *Service Contract:* Yes, $300 per year.

Prices

Basic Price: $3,495 for standard unit. *Pricing Date:* 1983. *Prices for Options:* Execuport 4120 BSR, with text editing and 43K memory, $3,995.

Convergent Technologies, Inc.

Address: Great American Technology Center
2441 Mission College Blvd.
Santa Clara, CA 95050
Telephone: 408-980-9222

Company information

Employees: 900. *Date Founded:* 1979. *Annual Sales (Last FY):* $96.5 million (calendar 1982).

Terminal specifications

Name and Model: WorkSlate (a machine designed specifically to be a portable electronic work-sheet with built-in communications capability). *Release Date:* November 1983. *Dimensions:* 8½ in. × 11 in. × 1 in. *Weight:* 3 lbs. *Portability Characteristics:* Half briefcase. *Case:* Furnished with unit. *Modem Speed:* 300 baud. *Modem Style:* Direct connect.

Keyboard

Size Compared to IBM Selectric: Somewhat smaller. *Key Alignment Same as IBM Selectric:* No. *Number of Keys:* 60. *Numeric Key Pad:* Yes. *Number of Programmable Function Keys:* 5. *Keyboard Detachable:* No.

Printer

Integral Printer: No. *External Printer Available:* Yes. *Printer Type:* Impact (multicolor—automatically shows negative numbers in red; prints 40/80 columns horizontal or vertical and is battery powered). *Characters per Second:* 30.

Display

Type: LCD. *Size:* 6½ in. *Characters and Lines:* 16 lines × 46 characters. *Lower Case Displayed:* Yes.

Interfaces

Number of RS-232: 1 in optional communications box. *Other Input-Output Ports:* 2 RJ11 (telephone) jacks so phone line can be connected to machine and to desk phone handset at same time. 1 Centronics-compatible printer port in communications box. *Peripherals Available:* Communications box; printer.

"Smart" features

Total RAM: 16K. *RAM Available for Text Storage:* 16K (operating system, etc., one in 64K of read-only memory). *Can Attach External Memory Device:* No. *Text Editing:* Limited. *Auto Dial:* Yes, 1,000 numbers. *Auto Log On:* Yes, as many as RAM will hold. *Auto Redial:* No. *Auto Answer:* Yes. *Other:* Can be programmed for automatic operation such as calling

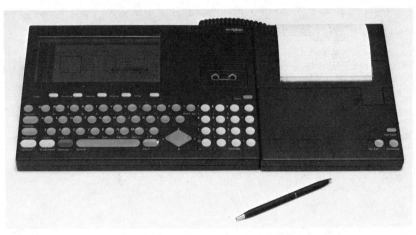

Convergent Technologies WorkSlate

Dow Jones at the stock market close and recalculating value of a portfolio. Built-in worksheet for numeric calculations and financial formulas for building spreadsheet models. Battery operated. Records data as well as voice on a built-in microcassette drive. Built-in speaker phone—machine can be shifted from voice to data transmission without disconnection. Will automatically answer phone and play a voice message (but does not record caller's answer). Alarm will retain multiple alarms for specific dates and times.

Sales information

Availability: Directly from manufacturer, through distributors, and through retail stores. *Warranty:* 90 days. *Type of Service:* Dealer or factory. *Service Contract:* Yes.

Prices

Basic Price: Basic machine, including built-in software, modem, built-in tape drive, $895. *Pricing Date:* 1983. *Prices for Options:* Communications box, $200; printer, $250; taskware (specialized software), $19.95 to $49.95. *Major Published Reviews: Smith Barney Dataquest; InfoCorp; Computers & Electronics* (October 1983), *Personal Computing* (October 1983), *Byte* (November 1983).

Grid Systems Corp.

Address: 2535 Garcia Ave.
　　　　　Mountain View, CA 94043
Telephone: 415-961-4800
　　　　　800-222-4743

Company information

Employees: 225. *Date Founded:* 1980. *Annual Sales (Last FY):* Information not available at time of publication.

Terminal specifications

Name and Model: Grid Compass Computer. *Release Date:* 1982. *Dimensions:* 11 in. × 15 in. × 2 in. *Weight:* 10 lbs., 12.5 oz. *Portability Characteristics:* Full briefcase. *Case:* Available at extra charge of $60 or $120. *Modem Speed:* 1200 baud. *Modem Style:* Direct connect.

Keyboard

Size Compared to IBM Selectric: Approximately same size. *Key Alignment Same as IBM Selectric:* Yes. *Number of Keys:* 57. *Numeric Key Pad:* Yes. *Number of Programmable Function Keys:* Zero. *Keyboard Detachable:* No.

Printer

Integral Printer: No. *External Printer Available:* Yes. *Printer Type:* Impact, 3 available. *Characters per Second:* Information not available at time of publication.

Display

Type: Advanced electroluminescense. *Size:* 6 in. *Characters and Lines:* 52 columns × 24 lines. *Lower Case Displayed:* Yes.

Interfaces

Number of RS-232: 1. *Other Input-Output Ports:* IEEE-488, a general-purpose interface bus that is not widely used in personal computers. *Peripherals Available:* Disk system with both hard and floppy disks; portable diskette drive; various software packages.

Grid Compass Computer

"Smart" features

Total RAM: 256K. Also 384K of bubble memory that can receive information online, then emulate a disk drive. *RAM Available for Text Storage:* 256K. *Can Attach External Memory Device:* Yes. *Text Editing:* Depends on software purchased. *Auto Dial:* Depends on software purchased. *Auto Log On:* Depends on software purchased. *Auto Redial:* Depends on software purchased. *Auto Answer:* Depends on software purchased. *Other:* Built-in voice telephone, optional.

Sales information

Availability: Directly from manufacturer, through retail stores. *Warranty:* 90 days. *Type of Service:* Factory. *Service Contract:* Yes.

Prices

Basic Price: Basic computer with display, $8,150. *Pricing Date:* 1983. *Prices for Options:* Portable diskette drive, $1,195; communications software, $200 and up; phone accessory kit, $25.

iXO, Inc.

Address: 5757 Uplander Way
Culver City, CA 90230
Telephone: 213-417-8080
800-421-3911
800-242-1100 (in California)

Company information

Employees: Approximately 25. *Date Founded:* 1981. *Annual Sales (Last FY):* Information not available at time of publication.

Terminal specifications

Name and Model: iXO Telecomputing System, TC-101. *Release Date:* March 1982. *Dimensions:* 4 in. × 7 in. × 1 in. *Weight:* 13 oz. *Portability Characteristics:* Hand-held. *Case:* Furnished with unit. *Modem Speed:* 300 baud. *Modem Style:* Direct connect; acoustic coupler with optional attachment.

Keyboard

Size Compared to IBM Selectric: Much smaller. *Key Alignment Same as IBM Selectric:* Yes. *Number of Keys:* 63. *Numeric Key Pad:* No. *Number of Programmable Function Keys:* 16. *Keyboard Detachable:* No.

Printer

Integral Printer: No. *External Printer Available:* Yes. *Printer Type:* Thermal in 20-, 40/80-, or 80-column format. *Characters per Second:* 32.

Display

Type: Liquid crystal display. *Size:* Single-line display. *Characters and Lines:* 16. *Lower Case Displayed:* No (keyboard transmits both upper and lower case).

Interfaces

Number of RS-232: 1 available as option. *Other Input-Output Ports:* Peripheral port. *Peripherals Available:* Acoustic interface, RS-232 interface, video interface, printers, video monitors, software.

iXO Telecomputing System

"Smart" features

Total RAM: 4K. *RAM Available for Text Storage:* 4K. *Can Attach External Memory Device:* No. *Text Editing:* Yes, on another model, the TC-200 (see below). *Auto Dial:* Yes, 16 numbers. *Auto Log On:* Yes, 16 log ons. *Auto Redial:* Yes. *Auto Answer:* No. *Other:* Special standard English command keys (e.g., "yes," "no," "don't know"), security protection system (3 separate mechanisms), battery backup on memory, built-in interface for 13 commercial database vendors.

Sales information

Availability: Directly from manufacturer, through distributors, through manufacturers' representatives. *Warranty:* 90 days. *Type of Service:* Factory. *Service Contract:* Yes; after warranty expires, company will replace with new unit for $45.

Prices

Basic Price: TC 101, $300; includes terminal, modular cable, and carrying case. *Pricing Date:* April 1983. *Prices for Options:* Video monitors, $235 and $325; video interface, $175; 20-column printer, $199; 40/80-column printer, $250; 80-column printer, $199; answer modem to printer, $149; serial/parallel interface, $119; acoustic coupler, $95; TC-102, for full/half duplex and larger buffer, $325; TC-200, data input device specifically designed for offline preparation of and automatic transmission of alphanumeric data, $395; TC-103, RS-232 direct connect model, $400. *Major Published Reviews: Byte*, April 1982.

Lear Siegler, Inc.

Address: Data Products Division
714 North Brookhurst St.
Anaheim, CA 92803
Telephone: 714-774-1010
800-532-7373

Company information

Employees: 25,000 (for Lear Siegler as a whole). *Date Founded:* 1954. *Annual Sales (Last FY):* $1.5 billion.

Terminal specifications

Name and Model: ADM 24E. *Release Date:* May 1983. *Dimensions:* 14 in. × 13 in. × 14½ in. *Weight:* 2 lbs. *Portability Characteristics:* Desktop. *Case:* None. *Modem Speed:* 300 baud, optional 1200 baud. *Modem Style:* Direct connect.

Keyboard

Size Compared to IBM Selectric: Much smaller. *Key Alignment Same as IBM Selectric:* Yes. *Number of Keys:* 104. *Numeric Key Pad:* Yes. *Number of Programmable Function Keys:* 16, shiftable to 32. *Keyboard Detachable:* Yes.

Printer

Integral Printer: No. *External Printer Available:* Yes. *Printer Type:* Impact, Lear Siegler Model 500. *Characters per Second:* 180.

Display

Type: CRT. *Size:* 12 in. diagonal or optional 14 in. *Characters and Lines:* 80 × 25. *Lower Case Displayed:* Yes.

Lear Sigler ADM 24E

Interfaces

Number of RS-232: 2. *Other Input-Output Ports:* An RS-232 extension port is also available as an option for adding on additional peripherals such as a bar code reader. *Peripherals Available:* None specified.

"Smart" features

Total RAM: 4K, with option for 8K (up to 22K achievable through OEM). *RAM Available for Text Storage:* Up to 22K of RAM can be installed for downloading user's own programs. *Can Attach External Memory Device:* No. *Text Editing:* Yes. *Auto Dial:* Yes, up to three 30-digit numbers (optional). *Auto Log On:* No. *Auto Redial:* Yes. *Auto Answer:* Yes. *Other:* 7 selectable international character sets; jump or smooth scrolling; horizontal split screen; business graphics; answer-back programmable; "highlight" background selectable, Xon/Xoff protocol.

Sales information

Availability: Through distributors. *Warranty:* 90 days. *Type of Service:* On site (selected areas), depot, factory. *Service Contract:* Yes, for maintenance and extended warranty; $360 per year for on-site maintenance.

Prices

Basic Price: $1,250 for ADM-24E basic unit (300 baud). *Pricing Date:* Information not available at time of publication. *Prices for Options:* $50 for extra display memory, $40 for 10-foot output cable, $1,695 optional Model 500 printer, $30 for 2K print buffer, $50 for 4K print buffer, $25 for extension port, $70 for current loop interface, $60 for RS-422 interface, $90 for key-cap sets installed in field (no additional charges when ordered with unit), $170 for 14-in. screen.

Lexicon Corporation

Address: 1541 N.W. 65th Ave.
Fort Lauderdale, FL 33313
Telephone: 305-792-4400
800-327-8913

Company information

Employees: 37. *Date Founded:* 1976. *Annual Sales (Last FY):* $2.5 million.

Terminal specifications

Name and Model: Lexicon 21 (LEX-21). *Release Date:* March 1981. *Dimensions:* 8½ in. × 11 in. × 2¾ in. *Weight:* 5 lbs. *Portability Characteristics:* Half briefcase. *Case:* Available at extra charge of $20. *Modem Speed:* 0/300 baud. *Modem Style:* Direct connect—through modular-equipped handset (not wall jack) or acoustic coupler, with optional attachment.

Keyboard

Size Compared to IBM Selectric: Much smaller. *Key Alignment Same as IBM Selectric:* Yes. *Number of Keys:* 59. *Numeric Key Pad:* Yes; optional at extra cost. *Number of Programmable Function Keys:* 1 on model 21DJ for Dow Jones News/Retrieval. *Keyboard Detachable:* No.

Printer

Integral Printer: Yes. *External Printer Available:* No. *Printer Type:* Thermal, 40 columns wide. *Characters per Second:* 30.

Lexicon 21 (LEX-21)

Display

Not applicable.

Interfaces

Number of RS-232: None. *Other Input-Output Ports:* Port for connecting optional acoustic coupler; port for connecting optional numeric key pad. *Peripherals Available:* Numeric key pad, acoustic coupler, access connector for direct phone line connect.

"Smart" features

Total RAM: 2K. *RAM Available for Text Storage:* IK. *Can Attach External Memory Device:* No. *Text Editing:* Yes. *Auto Dial:* No. *Auto Log On:* No. *Auto Redial:* No. *Auto Answer:* No. *Other:* Terminal connects to telephone handset rather than the wall line; battery backup on user memory and control settings.

Sales information

Availability: Directly from manufacturer, through mail-order sales, or independent manufacturers' representatives. *Warranty:* 90 days. *Type of Service:* Factory. *Service Contract:* Yes; $30 to $90 per year.

Prices

Basic Price: Terminal, $395. *Pricing Date:* September 1983. *Prices for Options:* Case, $20; acoustic cups, $38; numeric key pad, $180; box of 24 paper rolls, $36; LEX-21RS, $395, has no modem, but instead RS-232 connector. *Major Published Reviews: Datapro,* May 1982.

Northern Telecom, Inc.

Address: Integrated Office Systems
P.O. Box 1222
Minneapolis, MN 55440
Telephone: 612-932-8000
800-328-6760, Displayphone Marketing Group

Company information

Employees: 37,000. *Date Founded:* 1895. *Division of:* Northern Telecom Ltd. *Annual Sales (Last FY):* $3 billion.

Terminal specifications

Name and Model: Displayphone 1000. *Release Date:* 1982. *Dimensions:* 11½ in. × 14½ in. × 8½ in. *Weight:* 13½ lbs. *Portability Characteristics:* Desktop. *Case:* None. *Modem Speed:* 300/1200 baud. *Modem Style:* Direct connect.

Keyboard

Size Compared to IBM Selectric: Much smaller. *Key Alignment Same as IBM Selectric:* Yes. *Number of Keys:* 55. *Numeric Key Pad:* No. *Number of Programmable Function Keys:* 32 maximum (5 at any given time). *Keyboard Detachable:* No.

Printer

Integral Printer: No. *External Printer Available:* Yes (made by Okidata). *Printer Type:* Impact. *Characters per Second:* 80.

Northern Telecom Displayphone 1000

Display

Type: CRT. *Size:* 7 in. diagonal. *Characters and Lines:* 40 or 80 columns × 25 lines. *Lower Case Displayed:* Yes.

Interfaces

Number of RS-232: 1. *Other Input-Output Ports:* None specified. *Peripherals Available:* 1200-baud modem, coaxial adapter.

"Smart" features

Total RAM: 6K. *RAM Available for Text Storage:* None. *Can Attach External Memory Device:* No. *Text Editing:* No. *Auto Dial:* Yes, 81 numbers. *Auto Log On:* Yes, number depends on length of auto log-on sequences. *Auto Redial:* Yes. *Auto Answer:* No. *Other:* 40K ROM, clock with time/date, telephone call timer, reminder feature, built-in voice phone, hands-free operation, built-in 2-line operation.

Sales information

Availability: Directly from manufacturer, through distributors, through retail stores. *Warranty:* 90 days. *Type of Service:* Depot. *Service Contract:* No.

Prices

Basic Price: $1,295 for Displayphone, power unit, cables. *Pricing Date:* June 1983. *Prices for Options:* $695 for printer; $495 for 1200-baud modem; $925 for coaxial adapter. International version available.

Quazon Corporation

Address: 3330 Keller Springs Rd.
  Suite 200
  Carrollton, TX 75006
Telephone: 214-385-9200
  800-527-4045
  800-442-4764 (in Texas)

Company information

Employees: 70.   *Date Founded:* Mid-1982.   *Annual Sales (Last FY):* Start-up company.

Terminal specifications

Name and Model: Quik-Link 300.   *Release Date:* September 1983.   *Dimensions:* 15 in. × 5½ in. × 2½ in.   *Weight:* 3 lbs.   *Portability Characteristics:* Size is compact, but unit is not expressly designed to be portable.   *Case:* None.   *Modem Speed:* 300 baud, originate only. 1200-baud option is under development.   *Modem Style:* Direct connect.

Keyboard

Size Compared to IBM Selectric: Approximately same size (membrane keyboard).   *Key Alignment Same as IBM Selectric:* Yes.   *Number of Keys:* 61.   *Numeric Key Pad:* No.   *Number of Programmable Function Keys:* 4.   *Keyboard Detachable:* No.

Printer

Integral Printer: No.   *External Printer Available:* Terminal will interface with almost any serial printer.   *Printer Type:* Not applicable.   *Characters per Second:* Not applicable.

Display

Type: CRT (TV or composite monitor).   *Size:* Not applicable.   *Characters and Lines:* 40 columns with TV screen, 80 with monitor interface; 24 lines.   *Lower Case Displayed:* Yes.

Interfaces

Number of RS-232: None.   *Other Input-Output Ports:* Port that is electrically compatible to RS-232; video composite port; modular telephone jacks.   *Peripherals Available:* Video monitor interface.

Quazon Quik-Link 300

"Smart" features

Total RAM: Information not available at time of publication. *RAM Available for Text Storage:* None. *Can Attach External Memory Device:* No. *Text Editing:* No. *Auto Dial:* Yes. *Auto Log On:* Yes. *Auto Redial:* No. *Auto Answer:* No. *Other:* Audio feedback through TV; package comes with introductory offers for various databases valued at over $250; single-button access.

Sales information

Availability: Directly from manufacturer, through retail dealers, or through mail-order sales. *Warranty:* 90 days. *Type of Service:* Factory. *Service Contract:* No.

Prices

Basic Price: $249.95. *Pricing Date:* September 1983. *Prices for Options:* Cable for using printer, extra.

*Radio Shack

Address: 1500 One Tandy Center
Fort Worth, TX 76102
Telephone: 817-390-3011

Company information

Employees: Approximately 32,000. *Date Founded:* 1921. *Division of:* Tandy Corporation. *Annual Sales (Last FY):* $2.5 billion.

Terminal specifications

Name and Model: Radio Shack PT-210. *Release Date:* September 1982. *Dimensions:* 5 in. × 15½ in. × 14½ in. *Weight:* 15 lbs. *Portability Characteristics:* Full briefcase. *Case:* Furnished with unit. *Modem Speed:* 110/300 baud. *Modem Style:* Built-in acoustic coupler.

Keyboard

Size Compared to IBM Selectric: Approximately same size. *Key Alignment Same as IBM Selectric:* Yes. *Number of Keys:* 54. *Numeric Key Pad:* Yes. *Number of Programmable Function Keys:* None. *Keyboard Detachable:* No.

Printer

Integral Printer: Yes. *External Printer Available:* No. *Printer Type:* Thermal. *Characters per Second:* 50.

Display

Not applicable.

Interfaces

Number of RS-232: 1. *Other Input-Output Ports:* None specified. *Peripherals Available:* RS-232 interface module.

"Smart" features

Total RAM: None. *RAM Available for Text Storage:* None. *Can Attach External Memory Device:* No. *Text Editing:* No. *Auto Dial:* No. *Auto Log On:* No. *Auto Redial:* No. *Auto Answer:* No. *Other:* 48-character buffer.

Radio Shack PT-210

Sales information

Availability: At any Radio Shack Computer Department, Radio Shack Computer Store, and at selected dealers. *Warranty:* 90 days. *Type of Service:* Dealer. *Service Contract:* No.

Prices

Basic Price: $795, includes terminal and case. *Pricing Date:* July 1983. *Prices for Options:* $69.95 for RS-232 interface module; $24.95 for deluxe padded cover.

*Radio Shack

Address: 1500 One Tandy Center
  Fort Worth, TX 76102
Telephone: 817-390-3011

Company information

Employees: Approximately 32,000. *Date Founded:* 1921. *Division of:* Tandy Corporation. *Annual Sales (Last FY):* $2.5 billion.

Terminal specifications

Name and Model: Radio Shack TRS-80, Model 100. *Release Date:* March 29, 1983. *Dimensions:* 11⅘ in. × 8⅖ in. × 2 in. *Weight:* 3 lbs., 13.5 oz. *Portability Characteristics:* Half briefcase. *Case:* Furnished with unit. *Modem Speed:* 300 baud. *Modem Style:* Direct connect; optional acoustic interface.

Keyboard

Size Compared to IBM Selectric: Same size. *Key Alignment Same as IBM Selectric:* Yes. *Number of Keys:* 72. *Numeric Key Pad:* Yes. *Number of Programmable Function Keys:* 8. *Keyboard Detachable:* No.

Printer

Integral Printer: No. *External Printer Available:* Yes, 9 printers available. *Printer Type:* Not applicable. *Characters per Second:* Not applicable.

Display

Type: LCD. *Size:* 2 in. × 8 in. *Characters and Lines:* 40 columns by 8 lines. *Lower Case Displayed:* Yes.

Interfaces

Number of RS-232: 1. *Other Input-Output Ports:* Centronics compatible parallel port; cassette plug; bar code reader plug. *Peripherals Available:* Cassette tape recorder; bar code wand; acoustic modem cups.

"Smart" features

Total RAM: 8K, expandable to 32K. *RAM Available for Text Storage:* 8K, expandable to 32K. *Can Attach External Memory Device:* Yes, cassette tape recorder. *Text Editing:* Yes. *Auto Dial:* Yes, limited to amount of RAM available. *Auto Log On:* Yes, limited to amount of RAM available. *Auto Redial:* No. *Auto Answer:* No. *Other:* Basic programming; scheduling program.

Radio Shack TRS-80, Model 100

Sales information

Availability: Through Radio Shack Computer departments or stores.   *Warranty:* 90 days. *Type of Service:* Dealer.   *Service Contract:* No.

Prices

Basic Price: Computer with display, internal memory, 5 built-in programs, modem, $799 with 8K memory, $999 with 24K memory.   *Pricing Date:* March 1983.   *Prices for Options:* Basic package with 24K memory, AC adapter, modem cable, and cassette recorder, $1,085.   *Major Published Reviews: PC Magazine,* June 1983; *Creative Computing,* August 1983; *High Technology,* September 1983; *Computers & Electronics,* May 1983; *Popular Computing,* May 1983; *BYTE,* May 1983; *BYTE,* July 1983.

RCA Microcomputer Products

Address: New Products Division
          New Holland Ave.
          Lancaster, PA 17604
Telephone: 717-397-7661
          800-233-0187 (Marketing)
          800-233-0094 (Customer Service)

Company information

Employees: 100 in area.   *Date Founded:* Information not available at time of publication.   *Annual Sales (Last FY):* Information not available at time of publication.

Terminal specifications

Name and Model: APT (All-Purpose Terminal).   *Release Date:* May 1983.   *Dimensions:* 17 in. × 7 in. × 2 in. (terminal only, no display); $12\frac{1}{2}$ in. × $10\frac{3}{4}$ in. × $12\frac{3}{4}$ in. (display).   *Weight:* 4 lbs. (terminal only, no display); display, 20 lbs.   *Portability Characteristics:* Full briefcase.   *Case:* Case will be available in mid-1984.   *Modem Speed:* 0-300 baud.   *Modem Style:* Direct connect or acoustic coupler with optional attachment.

Keyboard

Size Compared to IBM Selectric: Much smaller.   *Key Alignment Same as IBM Selectric:* Yes. *Number of Keys:* 76.   *Numeric Key Pad:* Yes.   *Number of Programmable Function Keys:* 8.   *Keyboard Detachable:* No.

Printer

Integral Printer: No.   *External Printer Available:* No (port for optional Centronics-type parallel printer).   *Printer Type:* Not applicable.   *Characters per Second:* Not applicable.

Display

Type: CRT.   *Size:* 12 in. diagonal.   *Characters and Lines:* 40 or 80 columns × 24 lines.   *Lower Case Displayed:* Yes.

Interfaces

Number of RS-232: 1.   *Other Input-Output Ports:* Video output; VHF output for 40-character television display; acoustic coupler for nondirect connect application; Centronics-type parallel printer port.   *Peripherals Available:* Data display monitor, acoustic coupler, printer cable.

RCA   VP4801TD   (APT)
Full Keystroke Terminal and Display

RCA   VP3801TD   (APT)
Membrane Keyboard Terminal and Display

RCA APT

"Smart" features

Total RAM: 2K. *RAM Available for Text Storage:* 1 page of 80 or 40 characters × 24 lines. (New models will have 16K electronic mail work space.) *Can Attach External Memory Device:* Yes. *Text Editing:* No (but new models will have). *Auto Dial:* Yes, 26. *Auto Log On:* Yes, 26. *Auto Redial:* Yes. *Auto Answer:* Yes. *Other:* Password protection; ability to be configured to the "escape" and "control" specifications of multiple terminals or vendor computer systems; membrane keyboard option; speaker; user can monitor phone lines, hear aural feedback from keyboard; 48-hour power backup; status line menu (selectable); connectable to any standard TV.

Sales information

Availability: Directly from manufacturer, through distributors, through retail stores, through manufacturers' representatives. *Warranty:* 6 months. *Type of Service:* Factory for flat fee. *Service Contract:* Yes.

Prices

Basic Price: Regular or membrane keyboard with 12-in. display monitor, $598. *Pricing Date:* Information not available at time of publication. *Prices for Options:* Display monitor alone, $229; printer cable, $32; acoustic coupler, $59.

*Teleram Communications Corp.

Address: 2 Corporate Park Drive
White Plains, NY 10604
Telephone: 914-694-9270

Company information

Employees: Approximately 100. *Date Founded:* 1973. *Annual Sales (Last FY):* Information not available at time of publication.

Terminal specifications

Name and Model: Portabubble/81. *Release Date:* 1979. *Dimensions:* 16 in. × 16 in. × 7 in., including cover. *Weight:* 15 lbs. *Portability Characteristics:* Desktop, transportable. *Case:* Furnished with unit. *Modem Speed:* 300 baud. *Modem Style:* Built-in acoustic coupler.

Keyboard

Size Compared to IBM Selectric: Approximately same size. *Key Alignment Same as IBM Selectric:* Yes. *Number of Keys:* 70. *Numeric Key Pad:* No. *Number of Programmable Function Keys:* Zero. *Keyboard Detachable:* No.

Printer

Integral Printer: No. *External Printer Available:* Yes. *Printer Type:* Impact, 32 column. *Characters per Second:* 80.

Display

Type: CRT. *Size:* 5 in. diagonal. *Characters and Lines:* 34 or 51 columns by 17 lines. *Lower Case Displayed:* Yes.

Interfaces

Number of RS-232: 1. *Other Input-Output Ports:* None specified. *Peripherals Available:* Miniprinter kit (includes printer, case, cable, paper); RS-170 monitor (for video screen).

Teleram Portabubble/81

"Smart" features

Total RAM: 62K (up to 256K as option). *RAM Available for Text Storage:* 62K (up to 256K as option). *Can Attach External Memory Device:* No. *Text Editing:* Yes. *Auto Dial:* No. *Auto Log On:* No. *Auto Redial:* No. *Auto Answer:* No. *Other:* Nonvolatile memory; two-way communications capability as option; up to 52 stored formats or headers; accepts up to 9 revisions of copy.

Sales information

Availability: Teleram's own sales force. *Warranty:* 90 days. *Type of Service:* Depot. *Service Contract:* Yes.

Prices

Basic Price: Basic terminal with 62K bubble memory, including automatic copy retention, $3,995; with 94K memory, $4,195; with 125K memory, $4,395; with 256K memory, $5,195. *Pricing Date:* 1983. *Prices for Options:* Miniprinter kit, $930; shipping case for checking unit as regular baggage, $95; 6 software options, $150 to $795. *Major Published Reviews: Intel Solutions*, November/December 1981.

Televideo Systems, Inc.

Address: 170 Morse Ave.
Sunnyvale, CA 94086
Telephone: 408-745-7760

Televideo Personal Terminal

Company information

Employees: About 850. *Date Founded:* 1977. *Annual Sales (Last FY):* About $170 million.

Terminal specifications

Name and Model: Personal Terminal (PT). *Release Date:* January 1984. *Dimensions:* 9.6 in. × 12.5 in. × 15.1 in. *Weight:* 14 lbs. *Portability Characteristics:* Transportable. *Case:* Available for $60 extra. *Modem Speed:* 300 or 300/1200 baud. *Modem Style:* Direct connect.

Keyboard

Size Compared to IBM Selectric: Somewhat smaller. *Key Alignment Same as IBM Selectric:* Yes. *Number of Keys:* 74. *Numeric Key Pad:* No. *Number of Programmable Function Keys:* 14. *Keyboard is Detachable:* No.

Printer

Integral Printer: No. *External Printer Available:* Yes, compatible with many types. *Printer Type:* Not applicable. *Characters per Second:* Not applicable.

Display

Type: CRT. *Size:* 9 in. diagonal. *Characters and Lines:* 25 lines × 80 columns. *Lower Case Displayed:* Yes.

Interfaces

Number of RS-232: 2. *Other Input-Output Ports:* 2 ports for phone line and telephone; 2 additional phone ports optional. *Peripherals Available:* None specified.

"Smart" features

Total RAM: 2K. *RAM Available for Text Storage:* 2K. *Can Attach External Memory Device:* Yes. *Text Editing:* Yes. *Auto Dial:* Yes (28 phone numbers). *Auto Log On:* Yes (14 log-on strings can be stored). *Auto Redial:* Yes. *Auto Answer:* Yes. *Other:* None specified.

Sales information

Availability: Distributor, retail stores, mail order. *Warranty:* 90 days. *Type of Service:* Factory. *Service Contract:* Yes.

Prices

Basic Price: $499 without modem. *Pricing Date:* January 1, 1984. *Prices for Options:* 300-baud modem, $150; 1200-baud modem, $549; telephone handset and cradle, $79; carrying case, $60.

Texas Instruments Inc.

Address: P.O. Box 402430
Dallas, TX 75240
Telephone: 800-527-3500

Company information

Employees: 80,000. *Date Founded:* 1930. *Annual Sales (Last FY):* $4.2 billion.

Terminal specifications

Name and Model: TI Silent 700. *Release Date:* April 1983. *Dimensions:* $11\frac{3}{4}$ in. × $8\frac{1}{2}$ in. × $2\frac{3}{4}$ in. *Weight:* 4.5 lbs. (terminal alone); 6 lbs. (terminal and transformer). *Portability Characteristics:* Half briefcase. *Case:* Available at extra charge of $75. *Modem Speed:* 300 baud. *Modem Style:* Direct connect or acoustic coupler with optional attachment.

Keyboard

Size Compared to IBM Selectric: Approximately same size. *Key Alignment Same as IBM Selectric:* Yes. *Number of Keys:* 52. *Numeric Key Pad:* No. *Number of Programmable Function Keys:* Zero. *Keyboard Detachable:* No.

Texas Instruments Silent 700

Printer

Integral Printer: Yes. *External Printer Available:* No. *Printer Type:* Thermal, 80 or 132 columns. *Characters per Second:* 45.

Display

Not applicable.

Interfaces

Number of RS-232: None. *Other Input-Output Ports:* None specified. *Peripherals Available:* Auto-access cartridge for auto dial and auto log on; battery pack; acoustic coupler; carrying case.

"Smart" features

Total RAM: 4K. *RAM Available for Text Storage:* None; 4K nonvolatile RAM. *Can Attach External Memory Device:* No. *Text Editing:* No. *Auto Dial:* Yes, up to 1.2K. *Auto Log On:* Yes, up to 1.2K, shared with phone numbers. *Auto Redial:* No. *Auto Answer:* Yes. *Other:* 1K receive buffer; series of solid-state software cartridges in preparation, 2 available as of first quarter 1984; true underliners and descenders; optional international character set; programmable answer back; optional battery pack (for 1 to 2 hours continuous printing).

Sales information

Availability: Directly from manufacturer and through distributors. *Warranty:* 90 days. *Type of Service:* On site, any location, depot, or factory. *Service Contract:* Yes.

Prices

Basic Price: Terminal only, $695. *Pricing Date:* April 1983. *Prices for Options:* Auto-access cartridge, $100; battery pack, $95; acoustic coupler, $100; carrying case, $75.

Tymshare, Inc.

Address: 20705 Valley Green Drive
Cupertino, CA 95014
Telephone: 408-446-6111·
800-622-2260

Company information

Employees: 3,500. *Date Founded:* 1966. *Annual Sales (Last FY):* Information not available at time of publication.

Terminal specifications

Name and Model: Scanset XL. *Release Date:* December 1982. *Dimensions:* 10 in. × 14 in. × 14 in. *Weight:* 14 lbs. *Portability Characteristics:* Desktop. *Case:* None. *Modem Speed:* 300/1200 baud. *Modem Style:* Direct connect.

Keyboard

Size Compared to IBM Selectric: Much smaller. *Key Alignment Same as IBM Selectric:* No. *Number of Keys:* 68. *Numeric Key Pad:* No. *Number of Programmable Function Keys:* 6. *Keyboard Detachable:* No.

Printer

Integral Printer: No. *External Printer Available:* Yes. *Printer Type:* Impact, Scanset 725 miniprinter. *Characters per Second:* 120.

Tymshare Scanset XL

Display

Type: CRT. *Size:* 9 in. diagonal. *Characters and Lines:* 40 or 80 columns × 25 lines. *Lower Case Displayed:* Yes.

Interfaces

Number of RS-232: 1. *Other Input-Output Ports:* Centronics-type printer port. *Peripherals Available:* Accessories for use with the telephone.

"Smart" features

Total RAM: 3K. *RAM Available for Text Storage:* None. *Can Attach External Memory Device:* No. *Text Editing:* No. *Auto Dial:* Yes, 36. *Auto Log On:* Yes, up to 4. *Auto Redial:* No. *Auto Answer:* No. *Other:* Battery backup of memory; one-button auto dial with auto log on; hands-free dialing; speaker; 2-line capability; emergency phone (during power outage); tone, pulse, or manual dialing.

Sales information

Availability: Directly from manufacturer or through mail-order sales. *Warranty:* 90 days on printer, 1 year on terminal. *Type of Service:* Depot. *Service Contract:* Yes.

Prices

Basic Price: Scanset XL, ivory case (300 baud), $895; wood-grain case (300 baud), $995. Scanset XL/HS, ivory or wood-grain case (300/1200 baud), $1,495. Scanset XL/DC, ivory or wood-grain case (RS232C for direct connect), $895. *Pricing Date:* December 15, 1983. *Prices for Options:* Printer, $695.

A Smorgasbord
D of Communications
Software

To help you sort out the software market, this appendix describes in considerable detail programs by 26 companies. We have picked a representative sample, not necessarily the most popular packages. We checked this data with the software publishers, but we haven't necessarily tried out the products ourselves. Therefore, these listings carry no recommendations. We offer the information for comparative purposes only.

First, a few comments on some of the information in the listings. We have given certain basic data about each software publisher, such as when the company was founded, number of employees, estimated sales, primary market, etc., in order to help you understand the company you're dealing with. If you're more comfortable dealing with a larger company that can offer some support or an assurance that it's going to be around for some time to come, then buy accordingly. On the other hand, if you don't mind buying from a small, young company, you may get a more sophisticated product or a better price. After all, that's what new companies must offer to break into the market. Likewise, the release date, number of packages sold, and other products offered by this firm may also influence your choice.

Generally, software vendors make no guarantee on their product except to assure you that it will load in your computer. We have indicated any guarantee, if offered.

If you know how to program computers, you might consider buying a package whose source code is available. That allows you to make possible modifications to the program. You could also, of course, hire a programmer to make changes for you. In general, source codes are not available.

Sometimes publishers commit themselves to give updated programs to buyers, either free or for a fee. Updates can correct any "bugs" uncovered after the program is on the market, or just add more sophisticated capabilities. The more a program costs, the more you'll want to take the availability of updates into consideration.

We have indicated the length of the user manual in pages. The length, however, has no bearing on how easy the manual is to use; but other things being equal, more information about your product is better than less.

As noted already, many software packages are tailored to a specific machine; if so, it is indicated. In addition, in buying any software package, you must match it to your computer's operating system and RAM. Sometimes a publisher specifies a computer or microprocessor (CPU) rather than an operating system. In that case, it's taken for granted you're using the particular operating system that usually accompanies that hardware.

Some communications packages are tailored to facilitate access to particular database services; if so, we have indicated which ones.

Some software packages offer baud rates up to 9600. In general, 300 and 1200 baud are the only ones available on public telecommunications networks. (In a couple of years, 2400-baud communications channels are expected to come into common use; so if you're a forward thinker, you might want to have that option.) Higher rates are for special "dedicated" phone lines between your computer and another.

Variable protocols, as mentioned in Chapter 29, are offered by most database packages. Automatic dial up and log on can be a great convenience; if offered, you should also ask how many phone numbers or log-on sequences the program can store, as well as how long the sequences can be.

Uploading and downloading are capabilities of most software packages. We have also indicated whether the package has a built-in text editor to facilitate preparation of text for uploading.

As indicated in Chapter 29, the software's RAM buffer is a crucial item; we have listed the figure supplied by the publisher and have noted if it automatically writes to disk.

A number of related points discussed in Chapter 29 include toggling the buffer on and off without interrupting communication, presence of a buffer status indicator and buffer memory alert, ability to redefine characters, and variable printer controls.

The screen display line length, generally 40 or 80 columns, is given, and if 40, we indicate whether the rest of an 80-column line is "wrapped around" (rather than a word being cut in half).

Finally, we indicate whether the package is menu-driven and has convenient help commands, and we list any further notable features or requirements.

A title marked with an asterisk (*) indicates a company that offers a discount described in the coupon section at the back of the book.

Abt Microcomputer Software

Address: 55 Wheeler St.
Cambridge, MA 02138
Telephone: 617-492-7100

Publisher background

Division of: Abt Associates, Inc. *Date Founded:* 1965. *Number of Employees:* 300. *Annual Sales (Last FY):* $18 million. *President:* Clark C. Abt. *Applications Emphasis:* Data communications, education, mathematics, and statistics. *Intended Users:* Statisticians, general microcomputer users, and small businesses.

Package specifications

Package Name: DATA*TRANS. *Release Date:* April 1982. *Number Sold to Date:* Under 200. *How Sold:* By mail direct from the publisher. *Published Reviews/Listings:* International Software Database; *Datapro Directory of Microcomputer Software.* *Warranties:* Yes. Guaranteed to load. *Source Code Available:* No. *Program Updates Available:* No. *Special Modem Required:* No. *Size of User Manual:* 60 pages.

Systems available

Machines: Apple II +, IIE. *Operating Systems:* DOS 3.3. *Distribution Medium:* $5\frac{1}{4}$-inch disk. *Minimum RAM Required:* 48K. *Other Special Requirements:* None specified. *Price:* $100.

Communications features

Communications to Public Databases: Yes. *Dedicated to a Particular Database Service:* No. *Communications to Other Microcomputers:* Yes. *Baud Rates for Communication:* 300, 1200. *Variable Protocols for Communications:* Yes. *Auto Dial-up:* Yes. *Auto Log On:* Yes. *Uploading of Data:* Yes. *Downloading of Data:* Yes. *Alteration of Data Through Built-in Text Editor:* Yes. *RAM Buffer:* Yes. *Size of RAM Buffer:* 19K. *Automatically Writes to Disk When Buffer Full:* Yes. *On/Off Buffer Toggle Without Interrupting or Exiting the Program:* Yes. *Buffer On/Off Status Alert:* Yes. *Remaining Buffer Memory Status Alert:* Yes. *Character Redefinition:* No. *Printer Controls:* Yes. *Number of Columns in Screen Display:* 40/80. There is line wrapping on 40-column display. *Package Menu-driven:* Yes. *Break or Help Command Without Interrupting or Exiting the Program:* Yes.

Other features and comments

Converts data input to VisiCalc, VisiTrend/VisiPlot, or programs that read the DIF format.

Other communications packages by publisher

None.

American Teledata Corporation

Address: 2851 South Parker Rd.
Suite 1080
Aurora, CO 80014
Telephone: 303-671-7000

Publisher background

Date Founded: 1971. *Number of Employees:* 100. *Annual Sales (Last FY):* $6 million. *President:* Robert Goard. *Applications Emphasis:* Data communications, text editing. *Intended Users:* Credit bureaus, banks, and other Fortune 500 clients.

Package specifications

Package Name: SCOTTY. *Release Date:* January 1982. *Number Sold to Date:* 100. *How Sold:* By mail direct from the publisher and through distributors. *Published Reviews/Listings:* International Software Database; *Datapro Directory of Microcomputer Software.* *Warranties:* Yes. *Source Code Available:* No. *Program Updates Available:* Yes, free. *Special Modem Required:* No. *Size of User Manual:* 28 pages.

Systems available

Machines: IBM PC. *Operating Systems:* CP/M86, MS DOS. *Distribution Medium:* $5\frac{1}{4}$-inch disk. *Minimum RAM Required:* 64K. *Other Special Requirements:* None specified. *Price:* $495.

Communications features

Communications to Public Databases: Yes. *Dedicated to a Particular Database Service:* No. *Communications to Other Microcomputers:* Yes. *Baud Rates for Communication:* 50 to 9600. *Variable Protocols for Communications:* Yes. *Auto Dial-up:* No. *Auto Log On:* No. *Uploading of Data:* Yes. *Downloading of Data:* Yes. *Alteration of Data Through Built-

in Text Editor: Yes. *RAM Buffer:* Yes. *Size of RAM Buffer:* 56K. *Automatically Writes to Disk When Buffer Full:* Yes. *On/Off Buffer Toggle Without Interrupting or Exiting the Program:* Yes. *Buffer On/Off Status Alert:* Yes. *Remaining Buffer Memory Status Alert:* No. *Character Redefinition:* No. *Printer Controls:* Yes. *Number of Columns in Screen Display:* 80. *Package Menu-driven:* Yes. *Break or Help Command Without Interrupting or Exiting the Program:* Yes.

Other features and comments

Xon/Xoff protocol supported; global find and replace and other sophisticated text-editing features.

Other communications packages by publisher

None.

Apple Computer, Inc.

Address: 20525 Mariani Ave.
　　　　　Cupertino, CA 95014
Telephone: 408-996-1010

Publisher background

Date Founded: 1977. *Number of Employees:* 5,000. *Annual Sales (Last FY):* $50 million or more. *President:* John Sculley. *Applications Emphasis:* Diverse packages for company's personal computers. *Intended Users:* Manufactures personal computers for use in education, business, home, and scientific markets.

Package specifications

Package Name: Apple Access III. *Release Date:* 1981. *Number Sold to Date:* Information not available. *How Sold:* Through retail stores. *Published Reviews/Listings:* International Software Database; *List Magazine*, Summer 1983. *Warranties:* No. *Source Code Available:* No. *Program Updates Available:* No. *Special Modem Required:* No. *Size of User Manual:* 120 pages.

Systems available

Machines: Apple III. *Operating Systems:* SOS. *Distribution Medium:* 5¼-inch disk. *Minimum RAM Required:* 128K. *Other Special Requirements:* Monitor III. *Price:* $150.

Communications features

Communications to Public Databases: Yes. *Dedicated to a Particular Database Service:* No. *Communications to Other Microcomputers:* Yes. *Baud Rates for Communication:* 300, 1200 to 9600. *Variable Protocols for Communications:* Yes. *Auto Dial-up:* Yes. *Auto Log On:* Yes. *Uploading of Data:* Yes. *Downloading of Data:* Yes. *Alteration of Data Through Built-in Text Editor:* Yes. *RAM Buffer:* Yes. *Size of RAM Buffer:* 32K. *Automatically Writes to Disk When Buffer Full:* Yes. *On/Off Buffer Toggle Without Interrupting or Exiting the Program:* Yes. *Buffer On/Off Status Alert:* Yes. *Remaining Buffer Memory Status Alert:* Yes. *Character Redefinition:* Yes. *Printer Controls:* Yes. *Number of Columns in Screen Display:* 80. *Package Menu-driven:* Yes. *Break or Help Command Without Interrupting or Exiting the Program:* Yes.

Other features and comments

Allows computer to emulate DEC VT-100 and VT-52 terminals.

Other communications packages by publisher

Information not available at time of publication.

Cawthon Scientific Group

Address: 24224 Michigan Ave.
Dearborn, MI 48124
Telephone: 313-565-4000

Publisher background

Date Founded: 1978. *Number of Employees:* 12. *Annual Sales (Last FY):* Information not available. *President:* William L. Cawthon. *Applications Emphasis:* Data communications, engineering, and scientific. *Intended Users:* General business and engineering professionals.

Package specifications

Package Name: Computer Phone Link (CPL). *Release Date:* 1982. *Number Sold to Date:* 300 +. *How Sold:* By mail direct from the publisher and through retail stores. *Published Reviews/Listings:* International Software Database. *Warranties:* Yes. Guaranteed to load. Will perform to user-guide specifications or money back. *Source Code Available:* No. *Program Updates Available:* Yes; cost, $75. *Special Modem Required:* No. *Size of User Manual:* 50 pages.

Systems available

Machines: Various microcomputers that function under the specified operating systems. *Operating Systems:* CP/M, CP/M80, CP/M86, MP/M86, MP/MII, MS DOS, PC DOS. *Distribution Medium:* 5¼-inch disk and 8-inch disk. *Minimum RAM Required:* 64K. *Other Special Requirements:* None specified. *Price:* $165.

Communications features

Communications to Public Databases: Yes. *Dedicated to a Particular Database Service:* No. *Communications to Other Microcomputers:* Yes. *Baud Rates for Communication:* 110 to 2400. *Variable Protocols for Communications:* Yes. *Auto Dial-up:* Yes. *Auto Log On:* Yes. *Uploading of Data:* Yes. *Downloading of Data:* Yes. *Alteration of Data Through Built-in Text Editor:* No. *RAM Buffer:* Yes. *Size of RAM Buffer:* 1K. *Automatically Writes to Disk When Buffer Full:* Yes. *On/Off Buffer Toggle Without Interrupting or Exiting the Program:* Yes. *Buffer On/Off Status Alert:* Yes. *Remaining Buffer Memory Status Alert:* No. *Character Redefinition:* No. *Printer Controls:* Yes. *Number of Columns in Screen Display:* 80. *Package Menu-driven:* Yes. *Break or Help Command Without Interrupting or Exiting the Program:* Yes.

Other features and comments

Compatible with word processor.

Other communications packages by publisher

TXL Telex Link ($350); CTL Computer Telex Link ($165); WSL Wall Street Link ($165). All of these packages are available for the same machines as Computer Phone Link.

Compuview Products, Inc.

Address: 1955 Pauline
Suite 200
Ann Arbor, MI 48103
Telephone: 313-996-1299

Publisher background

Date Founded: 1979. *Number of Employees:* 20. *Annual Sales (Last FY):* $1 million. *President:* Theodore J. Green. *Applications Emphasis:* Programming aids, word processing, and text editing. *Intended Users:* Computer professionals.

Package specifications

Package Name: Modem-86. *Release Date:* September 1, 1982. *Number Sold to Date:* 1,400. *How Sold:* By mail direct from the publisher and through OEMs. *Published Reviews/Listings:* International Software Database. *Warranties:* Yes. Guaranteed to load. *Source Code Available:* No. *Program Updates Available:* Yes; cost, $25. *Special Modem Required:* No. *Size of User Manual:* 30 pages.

Systems available

Machines: DEC Rainbow, IBM PC, IBM XT, NEC APC, TI Professional, IBM Displaywriter, Zenith Z-100, Victor 9000, Seattle Computer Products, CompuPro 8086. *Operating Systems:* CP/M86, MS DOS. *Distribution Medium:* 5¼-inch and 8-inch disks. *Minimum RAM Required:* 64K. *Other Special Requirements:* None specified. *Price:* $89.

Communications features

Communications to Public Databases: Yes. *Dedicated to a Particular Database Service:* No. *Communications to Other Microcomputers:* Yes. *Baud Rates for Communication:* 300 to 19,200. *Variable Protocols for Communications:* Yes. *Auto Dial-up:* Yes. *Auto Log On:* Yes. *Uploading of Data:* Yes. *Downloading of Data:* Yes. *Alteration of Data Through Built-in Text Editor:* No. *RAM Buffer:* Yes. *Size of RAM Buffer:* Uses balance of available RAM. *Automatically Writes to Disk When Buffer Full:* Yes. *On/Off Buffer Toggle Without Interrupting or Exiting the Program:* Yes. *Buffer On/Off Status Alert:* No. *Remaining Buffer Memory Status Alert:* No. *Character Redefinition:* Yes. *Printer Controls:* No. *Number of Columns in Screen Display:* 80. *Package Menu-driven:* Yes. *Break or Help Command Without Interrupting or Exiting the Program:* Yes.

Other features and comments

Compatible with separately sold text editor.

Other communications packages by publisher

None.

*Context Management Systems

Address: 23868 Hawthorne Blvd.
     Torrance, CA 90505
Telephone: 213-378-8277

Publisher background

Date Founded: 1980. *Number of Employees:* 50. *Annual Sales (Last FY):* Over $4 million. *President:* David M. Saykally. *Applications Emphasis:* Decision-support software for managers and professionals, including spreadsheet modeling, database management, telecommunications, business graphics, word processing, and custom forms. *Intended Users:* Professional managers in large and medium-sized companies and MIS department managers.

Package specifications

Package Name: Context MBA. *Release Date:* June 1982. *Number Sold to Date:* 10,000 +. *How Sold:* By mail direct from the publisher, through retail stores, and through VARs and OEMs (including IBM, DEC, and Hewlett Packard). *Published Reviews/Listings:* International Software Database; *Datapro Directory of Microcomputer Software; List Magazine*, Summer 1983; *Computerworld*, July 1982; *Wall Street Journal*, September 1982. *Warranties:* Yes. Guaranteed to load. Extended services available for future releases. *Source Code Available:* No. *Program Updates Available:* Yes; cost, $150 a year for all updated versions. *Special Modem Required:* No. *Size of User Manual:* 200 tutorial, 200 reference pages.

Systems available

Machines: HP 200 series, HP 9816, HP 150, HP 9836, HP 9836C, NEC APC, DEC Rainbow, IBM XT, IBM PC, Victor 9000. *Operating Systems:* OS-200, MS DOS. *Distribution Medium:* 3½-inch disk (HP 150); 3½-inch or 5¼-inch disk (HP 200 series, HP 9816); 5¼-inch disk (HP 9836, IBM PC, DEC Rainbow, IBM XT, Victor 9000, HP 9836C); 8-inch disk (NEC APC). *Minimum RAM Required:* 256K (IBM PC, IBM XT), 512K (HP 9816), 576K (HP Models 9836 and 9836C). *Other Special Requirements:* Color graphics board required for IBM PC, IBM XT, and DEC Rainbow; two disk drives required for IBM PC and IBM XT. *Price:* $595 (Victor 9000); $695 (IBM PC, IBM XT, NEC APC, DEC Rainbow); $795 (all HP models).

Communications features

Communications to Public Databases: Yes. *Dedicated to a Particular Database Service:* No. *Communications to Other Microcomputers:* Yes. *Baud Rates for Communication:* 300 to 1200. *Variable Protocols for Communications:* Yes. *Auto Dial-up:* Yes. *Auto Log On:* Yes. *Uploading of Data:* Yes. *Downloading of Data:* Yes. *Alteration of Data Through Built-in Text Editor:* Yes. *RAM Buffer:* Yes. *Size of RAM Buffer:* Machine size less 160K. *Automatically Writes to Disk When Buffer Full:* Yes. *On/Off Buffer Toggle Without Interrupting or Exiting the Program:* Yes. *Buffer On/Off Status Alert:* Yes. *Remaining Buffer Memory Status Alert:* Yes. *Character Redefinition:* No. *Printer Controls:* Yes. *Number of Columns in Screen Display:* 80. *Package Menu-driven:* Yes. *Break or Help Command Without Interrupting or Exiting the Program:* Yes.

Other features and comments

Converts VisiCalc modems (including formulas); creates a phone directory; imports and exports plain text and DIF files; supports ETX/STX and Xon/Xoff protocols; 327x emulation available on IBM versions. Context MBA is an integrated package that contains many other capabilities, including graphics, word processing, and a spreadsheet.

Other communications packages by publisher

None.

Dynamic Microprocessor Associates

Address: 545 5th Ave.
New York, NY 10017
Telephone: 212-687-7115

Publisher background

Division of: Cosyde Corp. *Date Founded:* 1979. *Number of Employees:* 20. *Annual Sales (Last FY):* Information not available. *President:* Howard Radin. *Applications Emphasis:* Communications, database management, utility programs, application creation, and programming aids. *Intended Users:* Business community.

Package specifications

Package Name: Asynchronous Communication Control Program (ASCOM). *Release Date:* March 1979. *Number Sold to Date:* 20,000+ (includes OEM installations). *How Sold:* By mail direct from the publisher, through dealers, and through OEMs (including Xerox, NCR, and Monroe). *Published Reviews/Listings:* International Software Database; *Datapro Directory of*

Microcomputer Software; InfoWorld, June 28, 1982; *PC Magazine*, January 1983. *Warranties:* Yes. Guaranteed to load. Free from errors. *Source Code Available:* No. *Program Updates Available:* Yes; cost, $50. *Special Modem Required:* No. *Size of User Manual:* 190 pages.

Systems available

Machines: Various microcomputers that function under the specified operating systems. *Operating Systems:* CP/M, CP/M86, PC DOS, MS DOS, Turbo DOS, MP/M. *Distribution Medium:* 5¼-inch and 8-inch disks. *Minimum RAM Required:* 24K. *Other Special Requirements:* None specified. *Price:* $175.

Communications features

Communications to Public Databases: Yes. *Dedicated to a Particular Database Service:* No. *Communications to Other Microcomputers:* Yes. *Baud Rates for Communication:* 50 to 38,400. *Variable Protocols for Communications:* Yes. *Auto Dial-up:* Yes. *Auto Log On:* Yes. *Uploading of Data:* Yes. *Downloading of Data:* Yes. *Alteration of Data Through Built-in Text Editor:* No. *RAM Buffer:* Yes. *Size of RAM Buffer:* Uses balance of available RAM. *Automatically Writes to Disk When Buffer Full:* Yes. *On/Off Buffer Toggle Without Interrupting or Exiting the Program:* Yes. *Buffer On/Off Status Alert:* No. *Remaining Buffer Memory Status Alert:* No. *Character Redefinition:* Yes. *Printer Controls:* Yes. *Number of Columns in Screen Display:* 40/80. There is line wrapping on 40-column display. *Package Menu-driven:* Yes. *Break or Help Command Without Interrupting or Exiting the Program:* Yes.

Other features and comments

Compatible with word-processing package; unattended operations; remote mode; Xon/Xoff protocol supported; batch file processing for such functions as dialing directories.

Other communications packages by publisher

SYNC/COM ($395); TERMCOM ($145). These packages operate on the same machines as ASCOM.

Hawkeye Grafix

Address: 23914 Mobile St.
           Canoga Park, CA 91307
Telephone: 213-348-7909

Publisher background

Date Founded: 1976. *Number of Employees:* 4. *Annual Sales (Last FY):* Under 200,000. *President:* William B. Pierce. *Applications Emphasis:* Data communications, data and database management, management sciences, programming language processors, system programs, and utility programs. *Intended Users:* All microcomputer users.

Package specifications

Package Name: Communications Exchange (COMMX). *Release Date:* January 1980. *Number Sold to Date:* 5,000 + . *How Sold:* By mail direct from the publisher, through retail stores, and through OEMs. *Published Reviews/Listings:* International Software Database; *Datapro Directory of Microcomputer Software; List Magazine*, Summer 1983; *DATAC* #4, p. 51; *Infoworld*, December 1981. *Warranties:* Yes. Guaranteed to load. *Source Code Available:* Yes. *Program Updates Available:* Yes; cost, $45. *Special Modem Required:* Yes. Any Hayes, DMMI, U.S. Robotics, or others that have auto dial/answer. *Size of User Manual:* 120 pages.

Systems available

Machines: Various microcomputers that function under the specified operating systems. *Operating Systems:* C DOS, CP/M, CP/M 2.2, CP/M 80, CP/M 86, MS DOS, Turbo DOS. *Distribution Medium:* 5¼-inch disk (also available in 8-inch disk for CP/M 2.2). *Minimum RAM Required:* 16K. *Other Special Requirements:* None specified. *Price:* $150.

Communications features

Communications to Public Databases: Yes. *Dedicated to a Particular Database Service:* No. *Communications to Other Microcomputers:* Yes. *Baud Rates for Communication:* 300 to 56,000. *Variable Protocols for Communications:* Yes. *Auto Dial-up:* Yes. *Auto Log On:* Yes. *Uploading of Data:* Yes. *Downloading of Data:* Yes. *Alteration of Data Through Built-in Text Editor:* No. *RAM Buffer:* Yes. *Size of RAM Buffer:* Uses balance of available RAM. *Automatically Writes to Disk When Buffer Full:* Yes. *On/Off Buffer Toggle Without Interrupting or Exiting the Program:* Yes. *Buffer On/Off Status Alert:* Yes. *Remaining Buffer Memory Status Alert:* Yes. *Character Redefinition:* Yes. *Printer Controls:* Yes. *Number of Columns in Screen Display:* 80. *Package Menu-driven:* Yes. *Break or Help Command Without Interrupting or Exiting the Program:* Yes.

Other features and comments

Includes a complete electronic mail subsystem. Also supports Western Union Telex and TWX. Supports Xon/Xoff protocol.

Other communications packages by publisher

EMM Electronic Mail Manager written in dBASE II ($400, for two-branch system).

Hayes Microcomputer Products, Inc.

Address: 5923 Peachtree Industrial Blvd.
Norcross, GA 30092
Telephone: 404-449-8791

Publisher background

Date Founded: 1978. *Number of Employees:* 200. *Annual Sales (Last FY):* Information not available. *President:* Dennis Hayes. *Applications Emphasis:* Communications. *Intended Users:* Business and home users of Hayes modem products.

Package specifications

Package Name: Smartcom II. *Release Date:* March 1983. *Number Sold to Date:* 10,000+. *How Sold:* Through retail stores. *Published Reviews/Listings:* International Software Database; *Datapro Directory of Microcomputer Software*; *List Magazine*, Summer 1983; *PC Magazine*; *PC World*, Vol. 1, #5, 1983. *Warranties:* Yes. Guaranteed to load. One-year warranty that it will perform as specified or be replaced. *Source Code Available:* No. *Program Updates Available:* Yes; cost, none. *Special Modem Required:* Yes. Hayes Smartmodem 300, 1200, or 1200B. *Size of User Manual:* 100 pages.

Systems available

Machines: IBM PC (including Compaq and other compatibles), DEC Rainbow 100, Xerox 820-II, KayPro, Wang Professional, HP150, TI Professional. *Operating Systems:* CP/M86, CP/M80, MS DOS versions 1.0, 1.1, 2.0. *Distribution Medium:* 3 1/2-inch disk (HP-150), 8-inch disk (Xerox 820-II), 5¼-inch disk (all others). *Minimum RAM Required:* 96K. *Other Special Requirements:* None specified. *Price:* $149.

Communications features

Communications to Public Databases: Yes. *Dedicated to a Particular Database Service:* No. *Communications to Other Microcomputers:* Yes. *Baud Rates for Communication:* 110, 300, 1200. *Variable Protocols for Communication:* Yes. *Auto Dial-up:* Yes. *Auto Log On:* Yes. *Uploading of Data:* Yes. *Downloading of Data:* Yes. *Alteration of Data Through Built-in Text Editor:* Yes (limited). *RAM Buffer:* Yes. *Size of RAM Buffer:* Up to 128K depending upon available memory. *Automatically Writes to Disk When Buffer Full:* Yes. *On/Off Buffer Toggle Without Interrupting or Exiting the Program:* Yes. *Buffer On/Off Status Alert:* Yes. *Remaining Buffer Memory Status Alert:* Yes. *Character Redefinition:* No. *Printer Controls:* Yes. *Number of Columns in Screen Display:* 80. *Package Menu-driven:* Yes. *Break or Help Command Without Interrupting or Exiting the Program:* Yes.

Other features and comments

Comes preprogrammed for access to OAG, Western Union EasyLink, CompuServe, The Source, Dow Jones, and Knowledge Index; compatible with word-processing package (Wordstar recommended); multiple simultaneous tasking; supports Xon/Xoff protocol and other important protocols; program allows incompatible microcomputers to communicate with each other; page-up, page-down buffer (allows for freezing of display and reviewing of up to 40 screens of prior information without interrupting data receipt).

Other communications packages by publisher

Hayes Terminal Program for Apple II, II +, IIE ($99); Smartcom I for Apple II, II +, IIE, III ($119).

Infosoft Systems, Inc.

Address: P.O. Box 640
         Norwalk, CT 06856
Telephone: 203-866-8833

Publisher background

Date Founded: 1976. *Number of Employees:* 13. *Annual Sales (Last FY):* Over $1 million. *President:* Jerry Koret. *Applications Emphasis:* Computer management aids, data communications, data and database management, word processing and text editing, and operating systems development. *Intended Users:* Business users, particularly Fortune 1000 companies, and home users.

Package specifications

Package Name: Intelligent Terminal (I/TERM). *Release Date:* August 1976. *Number Sold to Date:* 25,000 + (includes OEM sales). *How Sold:* Through computer manufacturers and other OEM's (including Sony). *Published Reviews/Listings:* International Software Database; *Datapro Directory of Microcomputer Software*. *Warranties:* Yes. Guaranteed to load. Will function according to specifications. *Source Code Available:* Yes. *Program Updates Available:* Yes; cost, depends on OEM contract. *Special Modem Required:* No. *Size of User Manual:* 10 pages (help menus and tutorials are integral to the package).

Systems available

Machines: Sony offers for SMC-70 machine. Other OEMs also offer. Written in "C" to be transportable to any CPU with a C compiler. *Operating Systems:* Written in "C." *Distribution Medium:* Varies according to OEM from $3\frac{1}{4}$-inch disk to $5\frac{1}{4}$-inch disk and 8-inch disk. Also supplied as ROM on some units. *Minimum RAM Required:* 8K to 10K. *Other Special Requirements:* None specified. *Price:* $95 to $450 depending on OEM. There are some differences in features offered by the respective OEMs.

Communications features

Communications to Public Databases: Yes. *Dedicated to a Particular Database Service:* No. *Communications to Other Microcomputers:* Yes. *Baud Rates for Communication:* 110 to 56,000. *Variable Protocols for Communications:* Yes. *Auto Dial-up:* Yes. *Auto Log On:* Yes. *Uploading of Data:* Yes. *Downloading of Data:* Yes. *Alteration of Data Through Built-in Text Editor:* Yes. *RAM Buffer:* Yes. *Size of RAM Buffer:* Uses balance of available RAM. *Automatically Writes to Disk When Buffer Full:* Yes. *On/Off Buffer Toggle Without Interrupting or Exiting the Program:* Yes. *Buffer On/Off Status Alert:* Yes. *Remaining Buffer Memory Status Alert:* Yes. *Character Redefinition:* Yes. *Printer Controls:* Yes. *Number of Columns in Screen Display:* 40/80 (depends on machine). There is line wrapping on 40-column display (can break or wrap). *Package Menu-driven:* Yes. *Break or Help Command Without Interrupting or Exiting the Program:* Yes.

Other features and comments

Used by U.S. Army and other government agencies; Xon/Xoff protocol and other protocols are supported.

Other communications packages by publisher

Package is available in various versions through different OEMs. Sony sells ITERM as an after-market package under the name TWX DBA. C3, Inc., sells DCOMM to defense and other government contractors.

Institute for Scientific Information

Address: 3501 Market St.
University City Science Center
Philadelphia, PA 19104
Telephone: 215-386-0100

Publisher background

Date Founded: 1958. *Number of Employees:* 600+. *Annual Sales (Last FY):* $25 million. *President:* Eugene Garfield, Ph.D. *Applications Emphasis:* Communications and database management. *Intended Users:* End users in scientific, business, health, professional, and education markets.

Package specifications

Package Name: Sci-Mate. *Release Date:* July 1983. *Number Sold to Date:* Information not available. *How Sold:* By mail direct from the publisher and through retail stores (if the store is a dealer). *Published Reviews/Listings:* International Software Database; *Datapro Directory of Microcomputer Software; Microsoftware Report; Online Microsoftware Guide and Directory.* *Warranties:* Yes. Guaranteed to load. *Source Code Available:* No. *Program Updates Available:* Yes. *Special Modem Required:* No. Does not accommodate Hayes Micromodem. Accommodates all others. *Size of User Manual:* 288 pages.

Systems available

Machines: Apple IIE and II+, IBP PC, IBM XT TRS-80 II, Vector 3 and 4, KayPro, and other CP/M 80 machines. *Operating Systems:* CP/M 80, PC DOS. *Distribution Medium:* 5¼-inch and 8-inch disks. *Minimum RAM Required:* 56K (Apple IIE, II+), 128K (IBM PC and IBM XT), 54K (all others). *Other Special Requirements:* Z-80 board and 80-column board for Apple IIE and II+. *Price:* $880.

Communications features

Communications to Public Databases: Yes. Dedicated to a Particular Database Service: No (but designed to facilitate access to DIALOG, BRS, NLM, SDC, and ISI). *Communications to Other Microcomputers:* Yes. *Baud Rates for Communication:* 300, 1200. *Variable Protocols for Communications:* Yes. *Auto Dial-up:* Yes. *Auto Log On:* Yes. *Uploading of Data:* Yes. *Downloading of Data:* Yes. *Alteration of Data Through Built-in Text Editor:* Yes. *RAM Buffer:* Yes. *Size of RAM Buffer:* 4K. *Automatically Writes to Disk When Buffer Full:* Yes. *On/Off Buffer Toggle Without Interrupting or Exiting the Program:* Yes. *Buffer On/Off Status Alert:* Yes. *Remaining Buffer Memory Status Alert:* Yes. *Character Redefinition:* Yes. *Printer Controls:* Yes. *Number of Columns in Screen Display:* 80. *Package Menu-driven:* Yes. *Break or Help Command Without Interrupting or Exiting the Program:* Yes.

Other features and comments

Designed for text-processing applications and for searching databases' native language via a front-end menu. DIALOG, BRS, SDC, NLM, ISI hosts (offering access to approximately 450 databases) are all translated through a standard menu. Other files (Dow Jones, The Source, CompuServe) can be accessed in their own language. Sci-Mate can also be purchased as two separate software packages: the Universal Online Searcher, which provides the data-com link and universal search language, and the Personal Data Manager, which is a text-management system.

Other communications packages by publisher

None.

*Link Systems

Address: 1640 19th St.
Santa Monica, CA 90404
Telephone: 213-453-8921

Publisher background

Date Founded: 1980. Number of Employees: 15. Annual Sales (Last FY): Information not available. President: Hindy Kellerman Tolwin. Applications Emphasis: Data communications, education, and utility programs. Intended Users: Business and home markets.

Package specifications

Package Name: Datalink. Release Date: 1981. Number Sold to Date: Over 1,000. How Sold: By mail direct from the publisher, through retail stores, and through dealers and distributors. Published Reviews/Listings: International Software Database; Datapro Directory of Microcomputer Software; List Magazine, Summer 1983; Infoworld, May 10, 1982; Softalk Magazine, August 1982; The Book of Apple Software, 1983 Edition, p. 234. Warranties: Yes. Guaranteed to load. Source Code Available: No. Program Updates Available: Yes. Special Modem Required: Yes. Hayes Micromodem II or IIE (for Apple Package), Hayes SmartModem (for IBM Package). Size of User Manual: 70 pages.

Systems available

Machines: Apple II, Apple IIE, and IBM PC. Operating Systems: P system. Distribution Medium: $5\frac{1}{4}$-inch disk. Minimum RAM Required: 64K for Apples and 128K for IBM PC. Other Special Requirements: None specified. Price: $99.95.

Communications features

Communications to Public Databases: Yes. Dedicated to a Particular Database Service: No (but designed to facilitate access to The Source, Westlaw, DIALOG, MEDLINE, CompuServe, and Dow Jones). Communications to Other Microcomputers: Yes. Baud Rates for Commu-

nication: 110 to 9600 (for IBM), 300 (on the Apple). *Variable Protocols for Communications:* Yes. *Auto Dial-up:* Yes. *Auto Log On:* Yes. *Uploading of Data:* Yes. *Downloading of Data:* Yes. *Alteration of Data Through Built-in Text Editor:* No. *RAM Buffer:* Yes. *Size of RAM Buffer:* 4K. *Automatically Writes to Disk When Buffer Full:* Yes. *On/Off Buffer Toggle Without Interrupting or Exiting the Program:* Yes. *Buffer On/Off Status Alert:* Yes. *Remaining Buffer Memory Status Alert:* No. *Character Redefinition:* Yes. *Printer Controls:* Yes. *Number of Columns in Screen Display:* 40/80. *Package Menu-driven:* Yes. *Break or Help Command Without Interrupting or Exiting the Program:* Yes.

Other features and comments

Compatible with word-processing package; Xon/Xoff protocol supported; emulates various terminals including Televideo, Zenith, Soroc, Hewlett Packard, Ampex, Freedom, and DEC VT 100; unattended operation capability.

Other communications packages by publisher

Datalink for the IBM PC ($199).

Mark of the Unicorn, Inc.

Address: 222 Third St.
Cambridge, MA 02142
Telephone: 617-576-2760

Publisher background

Date Founded: 1980. *Number of Employees:* 20. *Annual Sales (Last FY):* $1 million. *President:* Jason T. Linhart. *Applications Emphasis:* Word-processing, text-editing, and communications packages. *Intended Users:* Secretaries, writers, technical writers, and general business users.

Package specifications

Package Name: PC/Intercomm. *Release Date:* November 1982. *Number Sold to Date:* Information not available. *How Sold:* By mail direct from the publisher, through retail stores, and from Software Wholesalers, Inc. (a distributor). *Published Reviews/Listings:* International Software Database; *Datapro Directory of Microcomputer Software.* *Warranties:* No. *Source Code Available:* No. *Program Updates Available:* Yes; no cost has been set for future updates—current updates have been free. *Special Modem Required:* No. *Size of User Manual:* 70 pages.

Systems available

Machines: IBM PC and IBM XT. *Operating Systems:* PC DOS. *Distribution Medium:* 5 $\frac{1}{4}$-inch disk. *Minimum RAM Required:* 64K. *Other Special Requirements:* None specified. *Price:* $99.

Communications features

Communications to Public Databases: Yes. *Dedicated to a Particular Database Service:* No. *Communications to Other Microcomputers:* Yes. *Baud Rates for Communication:* 50 to 19,200. *Variable Protocols for Communications:* Yes. *Auto Dial-up:* Yes. *Auto Log On:* Yes. *Uploading of Data:* Yes. *Downloading of Data:* Yes. *Alteration of Data Through Built-in Text Editor:* No. *RAM Buffer:* Yes. *Size of RAM Buffer:* Uses balance of available RAM up to 64K. *Automatically Writes to Disk When Buffer Full:* Yes. *On/Off Buffer Toggle Without Interrupting or Exiting the Program:* Yes. *Buffer On/Off Status Alert:* No. *Remaining Buffer Memory Status Alert:* Yes. *Character Redefinition:* No. *Printer Controls:* Yes. *Number of Columns in Screen Display:* 80. *Package Menu-driven:* Yes. *Break or Help Command Without Interrupting or Exiting the Program:* Yes.

Other features and comments

VT 100 terminal emulation.

Other communications packages by publisher

None.

The Microstuf Company, Inc.

Address: 1845 The Exchange
Suite 140
Atlanta, GA 30339
Telephone: 404-952-0267

Publisher background

Date Founded: 1978. *Number of Employees:* 18. *Annual Sales (Last FY):* Over $3 million. *President:* Les Freed. *Applications Emphasis:* Data communications. *Intended Users:* All microcomputer users.

Package specifications

Package Name: Crosstalk XVI. *Release Date:* March 1983. *Number Sold to Date:* Information not available. *How Sold:* By mail direct from the publisher, through retail stores, and through dealers. *Published Reviews/Listings:* International Software Database; *Datapro Directory of Microcomputer Software; List Magazine*, Summer 1983. *Warranties:* Yes. Guaranteed to load. *Source Code Available:* No. *Program Updates Available:* Yes; cost, $30 for major updates, otherwise free. *Special Modem Required:* No. *Size of User Manual:* 150 pages.

Systems available

Machines: IBM PC and IBM XT and compatibles; most machines with Z/80 8088 CPUs. *Operating Systems:* CP/M, CP/M 86, PC DOS, MS DOS. *Distribution Medium:* 5¼-inch and 8-inch disks. *Minimum RAM Required:* 32K (on Z/80 machines), otherwise 96K. *Other Special Requirements:* None. *Price:* $195.

Communications features

Communications to Public Databases: Yes. *Dedicated to a Particular Database Service:* No. *Communications to Other Microcomputers:* Yes. *Baud Rates for Communication:* 110 to 9600. *Variable Protocols for Communications:* No. *Auto Dial-up:* Yes. *Auto Log On:* Yes. *Uploading of Data:* Yes. *Downloading of Data:* Yes. *Alteration of Data Through Built-in Text Editor:* No. *RAM Buffer:* Yes. *Size of RAM Buffer:* Uses balance of available RAM. *Automatically Writes to Disk When Buffer Full:* No. *On/Off Buffer Toggle Without Interrupting or Exiting the Program:* Yes. *Buffer On/Off Status Alert:* Yes. *Remaining Buffer Memory Status Alert:* Yes. *Character Redefinition:* Yes. *Printer Controls:* Yes. *Number of Columns in Screen Display:* 80. *Package Menu-driven:* Yes. *Break or Help Command Without Interrupting or Exiting the Program:* No.

Other features and comments

Compatible with word processor. Program can emulate various terminal formats, including IBM 3101, DEC VT 100, ADDS Viewpoint, and the Televideo 910 and 920 series.

Other communications packages by publisher

Remote for CP/M or MS DOS operating systems ($150); Transporter for IBM PC DOS operating system ($295); Crosstalk for CP/M, MP/M, and CP/M 86 ($195).

Mycroft Labs

Address: P.O. Box 6045
Tallahassee, FL 32314
Telephone: 904-385-1141

Publisher background

Date Founded: 1980. *Number of Employees:* 10. *Annual Sales (Last FY):* $500,000 +. *President:* Howard C. Huff. *Applications Emphasis:* Data communications, graphics, and systems software. *Intended Users:* Business professionals who require access to their corporate data center or online information services; also programmers and systems developers.

Package specifications

Package Name: MITE 2.5. *Release Date:* September 1982. *Number Sold to Date:* 1,400. *How Sold:* By mail direct from the publisher and through retail stores. *Published Reviews/Listings:* International Software Database; *Datapro Directory of Microcomputer Software; List Magazine*, Summer 1983. *Warranties:* Yes. Guaranteed to load. *Source Code Available:* No. *Program Updates Available:* Yes; cost, $25 per update. *Special Modem Required:* No. *Size of User Manual:* 120 pages.

Systems available

Machines: Various microcomputers that function under the specified operating systems. *Operating Systems:* CP/M 2.2, CP/M 86. *Distribution Medium:* 5¼-inch and 8-inch disks. *Minimum RAM Required:* 16K. *Other Special Requirements:* None specified. *Price:* $150 (for CP/M 2.2), $195 (for CP/M 86).

Communications features

Communications to Public Databases: Yes. *Dedicated to a Particular Database Service:* No. *Communications to Other Microcomputers:* Yes. *Baud Rates for Communication:* 300, 1200 to 19,200. *Variable Protocols for Communications:* Yes. *Auto Dial-up:* Yes. *Auto Log On:* Yes. *Uploading of Data:* Yes. *Downloading of Data:* Yes. *Alteration of Data Through Built-in Text Editor:* No. *RAM Buffer:* Yes. *Size of RAM Buffer:* 13K to 19K. *Automatically Writes to Disk When Buffer Full:* No. *On/Off Buffer Toggle Without Interrupting or Exiting the Program:* Yes. *Buffer On/Off Status Alert:* Yes. *Remaining Buffer Memory Status Alert:* No. *Character Redefinition:* No. *Printer Controls:* Yes. *Number of Columns in Screen Display:* 80. *Package Menu-driven:* Yes. *Break or Help Command Without Interrupting or Exiting the Program:* Yes.

Other features and comments

Access to TWX; compatible with text editor; user manual includes a data communications tutorial; package engineered to allow user to recover from most errors.

Other communications packages by publisher

Clink/A for Apple II, Apple II+ ($145); Clink/H for CP/M operating system ($75); Mite/86 for CP/M 86 operating system ($195).

*Peachtree Software, Inc.

Address: 3445 Peachtree Rd., N.E.
8th Floor
Atlanta, GA 30326
Telephone: 404-239-3000

Publisher background

Subsidiary of: Management Science America (MSA). *Date Founded:* 1976. *Number of Employees:* 140 to 150. *Annual Sales (Last FY):* $9.4 million. *General Manager, Vice-President:* John Hale. *Applications Emphasis:* Office automation (word processing and text editing, graphics, file convertors, general accounting, database management, mailing lists, telecommunications, scheduling, payroll inventory); educational programs (math, reading, spelling, physics, calculus—many levels and subjects). *Intended Users:* Business (general) and educational market.

Package specifications

Package Name: Telecommunications. *Release Date:* 1981. *Number Sold to Date:* Information not available. *How Sold:* Through retail stores, distributors, OEMs, and major manufacturers. *Published Reviews/Listings:* International Software Database; *Datapro Directory of Microcomputer Software; List Magazine*, Summer 1983; *Data Source; The Microcomputer Software Directory; The Evaluator; Microsoftware for Business; Desktop*. *Warranties:* Yes. Guaranteed to be free from disk defects. *Source Code Available:* No. *Program Updates Available:* Yes; cost, $25. *Special Modem Required:* Yes. For auto-dial and redial functions, a Hayes Smartmodem, Smartmodem 1200, or equivalent. *Size of User Manual:* 100 pages.

Systems available

Machines: IBM PC, Compaq, Zenith Z-100, and others. *Operating Systems:* CP/M (version 2.0 or later), PC DOS 1.1, MS DOS (version 1.0 or later). *Distribution Medium:* $5\frac{1}{4}$-inch disk (also available on 8-inch disk for CP/M). *Minimum RAM Required:* 64K (for PC DOS 1.1 + MS DOS), 48K (for CP/M). *Other Special Requirements:* None specified. *Price:* $150.

Communications features

Communications to Public Databases: Yes. *Dedicated to a Particular Database Service:* No. *Communications to Other Microcomputers:* Yes. *Baud Rates for Communication:* Up to 9600. *Variable Protocols for Communications:* Yes. *Auto Dial-up:* Yes. *Auto Log On:* No. *Uploading of Data:* Yes. *Downloading of Data:* Yes. *Alteration of Data Through Built-in Text Editor:* No. *RAM Buffer:* Yes. *Size of RAM Buffer:* Uses balance of available RAM. *Automatically Writes to Disk When Buffer Full:* Yes. *On/Off Buffer Toggle Without Interrupting or Exiting the Program:* No. *Buffer On/Off Status Alert:* Yes. *Remaining Buffer Memory Status Alert:* Yes. *Character Redefinition:* Yes. *Printer Controls:* Yes. *Number of Columns in Screen Display:* 80. *Package Menu-driven:* Yes. *Break or Help Command Without Interrupting or Exiting the Program:* Yes.

Other features and comments

Can communicate with TWX. Compatible with PeachText word processor.

Other communications packages by publisher

None.

*Perfect Software, Inc.

Address: 1001 Camelia St.
Berkeley, CA 94710
Telephone: 800-222-4222
415-527-2626

Publisher background

Date Founded: March 1982. *Number of Employees:* 100. *Annual Sales (Last FY):* $20 million. *Chief Executive Officer:* Buck Lindsey. *Applications Emphasis:* Communications, word processing, spreadsheets, and filing programs. *Intended Users:* Business and home users.

Package specifications

Package Name: Perfect Link. *Release Date:* December 1983. *Number Sold to Date:* Package introduced as of date of this writing. *How Sold:* Through retail stores and through distributors and OEMs (including KayPro and Columbia computers). *Published Reviews/Listings:* None. Package introduced as of date of this writing. *Warranties:* No. *Source Code Available:* No. *Program Updates Available:* Yes; cost, modest. *Special Modem Required:* No. *Size of User Manual:* 450 pages.

Systems available

Machines: IBM PC and various microcomputers that function under the specified operating systems. KayPro. *Operating Systems:* MS DOS, CP/M (for KayPro). *Distribution Medium:* 5¼-inch disk (other distribution mediums under development). *Minimum RAM Required:* 128K. *Other Special Requirements:* None specified. *Price:* $149.

Communications features

Communications to Public Databases: Yes. *Dedicated to a Particular Database Service:* No. Program facilitates "one-button" access to The Source, CompuServe, OAG, Knowledge Index, Dow Jones, NewsNet, Western Union EasyLink, and MCI Mail. *Communications to Other Microcomputers:* Yes. *Baud Rates for Communication:* 110 to 9600. *Variable Protocols for Communications:* Yes. *Auto Dial-up:* Yes (has a built-in file of Value-Added Network phone numbers). *Auto Log On:* Yes. *Uploading of Data:* Yes. *Downloading of Data:* Yes. *Alteration of Data Through Built-in Text Editor:* No. *RAM Buffer:* Yes. *Size of RAM Buffer:* 64K. *Automatically Writes to Disk When Buffer Full:* Yes. *On/Off Buffer Toggle Without Interrupting or Exiting the Program:* Yes. *Buffer On/Off Status Alert:* Yes (buffer always on when communicating). *Remaining Buffer Memory Status Alert:* No. *Character Redefinition:* Yes. *Printer Controls:* Yes. *Number of Columns in Screen Display:* 80. *Package Menu-driven:* Yes. *Break or Help Command Without Interrupting or Exiting the Program:* Yes.

Other features and comments

Disk-to-disk transfer utility. Can read and write to diskette of 20 different microcomputers despite data format incompatibility. Natural language commands. Integrates with Perfect Writer word-processing program.

Other communications packages by publisher

None.

Philadelphia Consulting Group, Inc.

Address: P.O. Box 102
Wynnewood, PA 19096
Telephone: 215-649-1598

Publisher background

Date Founded: 1980. *Number of Employees:* 5. *Annual Sales (Last FY):* Under $200,000. *President:* Dr. Wladimir M. Sachs. *Applications Emphasis:* Data communications. *Intended Users:* Professionals, small- and medium-sized businesses, and individual users in large corporations.

Package specifications

Package Name: ESL-Plus. *Release Date*: August 1983. *Number Sold to Date:* Over 50. *How Sold:* By mail direct from the publisher, and through retail stores. *Published Reviews/Listings:* International Software Directory. *Warranties:* Yes. Guaranteed to load; dysfunctions will be corrected. *Source Code Available:* No. *Program Updates Available:* Yes; cost, substantial reduction from retail. *Special Modem Required:* No. *Size of User Manual:* 140 pages, plus index.

Systems available

Machines: TRS 80 Models III, 4, II/12, 16; KayPro II, 4, 10; Access, Epson QX-10; and other CP/M Z-80 (CPU) machines. *Operating Systems:* TRS DOS, DOS PLUS, L DOS, TRS DOS 6.0, CP/M. *Distribution Medium:* 5¼-inch disk. *Minimum RAM Required:* 32K. *Other Special Requirements:* None specified. *Price:* $249.95.

Communications features

Communications to Public Databases: Yes. *Dedicated to a Particular Database Service:* No (but designed to facilitate use of Western Union's EasyLink). *Communications to Other Microcomputers:* Yes. *Baud Rates for Communication:* 110, 300, 1200. *Variable Protocols for Communications:* Yes. *Auto Dial-up:* Yes. *Auto Log On:* Yes. *Uploading of Data:* Yes. *Downloading of Data:* Yes. *Alteration of Data Through Built-in Text Editor:* Yes. *RAM Buffer:* Yes. *Size of RAM Buffer:* 1K to 2K. *Automatically Writes to Disk When Buffer Full:* Yes. *On/Off Buffer Toggle Without Interrupting or Exiting the Program:* Yes. *Buffer On/Off Status Alert:* Yes. *Remaining Buffer Memory Status Alert:* Yes. *Character Redefinition:* Yes. *Printer Controls:* Yes. *Number of Columns in Screen Display:* 80. *Package Menu-driven:* Yes. *Break or Help Command Without Interrupting or Exiting the Program:* Yes.

Other features and comments

Has been approved by Western Union for use with its system.

Other communications packages by publisher

Electronic Messenger for Radio Shack TRS 80 Models I, III ($149.95); ESL-Term for TRS-80 + CP/M ($149.95); T-Term for TRS-80 III ($49.95 to $64.95); POST Plus for same systems as ESL-Plus ($249.95); MCI Plus for same systems as ESL-Plus.

Radio Shack

Address: 300 One Tandy Center
 Fort Worth, TX 76102
Telephone: 817-390-2140

Publisher background

Division of: Tandy Corporation. *Date Founded:* 1921. *Number of Employees:* Information not available at time of publication. *Annual Sales (Last FY):* $2.5 billion. *President:* John Roach. *Applications Emphasis:* Accounting, word processing, communications, productivity tools, education, and home entertainment. *Intended Users:* Purchasers of Radio Shack computers, including both home and business users.

Package specifications

Package Name: Videotex Plus. *Release Date:* March 1983 (upgraded version of 2-year-old package). *Number Sold to Date:* Over 5,000. *How Sold:* Through retail stores (including dealers and franchise stores in 8,000 locations). *Published Reviews/Listings:* Information not available at time of publication. *Warranties:* Yes. Guaranteed to load. 90-day replacement guarantee. *Source Code Available:* No. *Program Updates Available:* Yes; cost, $10 to $25. *Special Modem Required:* No (but can utilize the features of a smart modem). *Size of User Manual:* Information not available at time of publication.

Systems available

Machines: Models I, II, III, 4, 12, 16. *Operating Systems:* TRS DOS 1.3 (Models I and III), TRS DOS 2.0 (Models II, 12 and 16), TRS DOS 6.0 (Model 4). *Distribution Medium:* 5¼-inch disk (Models I, III, 4), 8-inch disk (Models II, 12, 16). *Minimum RAM Required:* 32K (Models I and III), 64K (Models II, 4, 12, 16). *Other Special Requirements:* None specified. *Price:* $49.95.

Communications features

Communications to Public Databases: Yes. *Dedicated to a Particular Database Service:* No (but special features for running on CompuServe and Dow Jones). *Communications to Other Microcomputers:* Yes. *Baud Rates for Communication:* 110 to 9600. *Variable Protocols for Communications:* Yes. *Auto Dial-up:* Yes (with smart modem). *Auto Log On:* Yes. *Uploading of Data:* Yes. *Downloading of Data:* Yes. *Alteration of Data Through Built-in Text Editor:* Yes. *RAM Buffer:* Yes. *Size of RAM Buffer:* Uses balance of available RAM. *Automatically Writes to Disk When Buffer Full:* No. *On/Off Buffer Toggle Without Interrupting or Exiting the Program:* Yes. *Buffer On/Off Status Alert:* Yes. *Remaining Buffer Memory Status Alert:* Yes. *Character Redefinition:* Yes (user may define limited function keys). *Printer Controls:* Yes. *Number of Columns in Screen Display:* 64/80. There is line wrapping on 64-column display. *Package Menu-driven:* Yes. *Break or Help Command Without Interrupting or Exiting the Program:* Yes (limited capability).

Other features and comments

Supports Xon/Xoff protocol; package allows for remote controlling; graphics capabilities; cursor positioning; works in complement with Radio Shack's word-processing and spreadsheet programs.

Other communications packages by publisher

Videotex for all Radio Shack models except Model 4 ($29.95); Agristar for Models III and 4 (targeted to Agridata Resources System) ($199.95); Micro/Courier for Model III ($149.95).

Small Business Systems Group

Address: 6 Carlisle Rd.
Westford, MA 01886
Telephone: 617-692-3800

Publisher background

Date Founded: 1978. *Number of Employees:* 22. *Annual Sales (Last FY):* $1 million to $4.9 million. *President:* Peter O. Dion. *Applications Emphasis:* Accounting, data communications, media (publishing, etc.), medical and health care, payroll and personnel, and brokerage. *Intended Users:* Businesses, educational community, and "buffs."

Package specifications

Package Name: Smart Terminal 80-III (ST 80). *Release Date:* March 1979. *Number Sold to Date:* 300 (this version). *How Sold:* By mail directly from the publisher, through retail stores, and through dealer network. *Published Reviews/Listings:* International Software Database; *Datapro Directory of Microcomputer Software*; *80 MICRO*, September 1981. *Warranties:* Yes. Guaranteed to load; guaranteed to perform as documented. *Source Code Available:* No. *Program Updates Available:* Yes; cost, $25. *Special Modem Required:* No. *Size of User Manual:* 90 pages.

Systems available

Machines: TRS 80 models I, II, III, 4, 12, 16. *Operating Systems:* TRS DOS 2.0, TRS DOS 1.2, L DOS, NEW DOS-80, CP/M. *Distribution Medium:* 5¼-inch disk (TRS 80 4, III), 8-inch disk (for other TRS-80 machines). *Minimum RAM Required:* 32K. *Other Special Requirements:* None specified. *Price:* $150 (for Models 4, I, III), $250 (other models).

Communications features

Communications to Public Databases: Yes. *Dedicated to a Particular Database Service:* No. *Communications to Other Microcomputers:* Yes. *Baud Rates for Communication:* 110 to 9600. *Variable Protocols for Communications:* Yes. *Auto Dial-up:* Yes. *Auto Log On:* Yes.

Uploading of Data: Yes. *Downloading of Data:* Yes. *Alteration of Data Through Built-in Text Editor:* No. *RAM Buffer:* Yes. *Size of RAM Buffer:* 32K. *Automatically Writes to Disk When Buffer Full:* No. *On/Off Buffer Toggle Without Interrupting or Exiting the Program:* Yes. *Buffer On/Off Status Alert:* Yes. *Remaining Buffer Memory Status Alert:* Yes. *Character Redefinition:* Yes. *Printer Controls:* Yes. *Number of Columns in Screen Display:* 40/80. There is line wrapping on 40-column display. *Package Menu-driven:* Yes. *Break or Help Command Without Interrupting or Exiting the Program:* Yes.

Other features and comments

Compatible with word processor; simulates Lear Siegler, Televideo, and DEC terminals; The Source recommends this package for TRS 80 users.

Other communications packages by publisher

Produces 4 other versions of ST80; Forum-80 Electronic Mail ($350) for various TRS 80 machines.

Softronics, Inc.

Address: 6626 Prince Edward Pl.
Memphis, TN 38119
Telephone: 901-683-6850

Publisher background

Date Founded: January 1982. *Number of Employees:* 7. *Annual Sales (Last FY):* $300,000. *President:* A. M. Middleton. *Applications Emphasis:* Communications and utility software. *Intended Users:* Home and business users.

Package specifications

Package Name: Softerm II. *Release Date:* August 1982. *Number Sold to Date:* 2,500. *How Sold:* By mail direct from the publisher and through retail stores. *Published Reviews/Listings:* International Software Database; *List Magazine,* Summer 1983; *Microcomputing,* January 1983; *Microcomputer Software*, March 1983; *Desktop Computer*, April 1983; *InCider*, June 1983. *Warranties:* Yes. Guaranteed to load. *Source Code Available:* No. *Program Updates Available:* No. *Special Modem Required:* No. *Size of User Manual:* 400 pages.

Systems available

Machines: Apple II, II +, and IIE, and various microcomputers that function under the specified operating systems. *Operating Systems:* DOS 3.3, PASCAL, CP/M. *Distribution Medium:* 5¼-inch disk. *Minimum RAM Required:* 48K. *Other Special Requirements:* None specified. *Price:* $195.

Communications features

Communications to Public Databases: Yes. *Dedicated to a Particular Database Service:* No. *Communications to Other Microcomputers:* Yes. *Baud Rates for Communication:* 110 to 9600. *Variable Protocols for Communications:* Yes. *Auto Dial-up:* Yes. *Auto Log On:* Yes. *Uploading of Data:* Yes. *Downloading of Data:* Yes. *Alteration of Data Through Built-in Text Editor:* No. *RAM Buffer:* Yes. *Size of RAM Buffer:* 8K to 24K. *Automatically Writes to Disk When Buffer Full:* Yes. *On/Off Buffer Toggle Without Interrupting or Exiting the Program:* Yes. *Buffer On/Off Status Alert:* Yes. *Remaining Buffer Memory Status Alert:* No. *Character Redefinition:* Yes. *Printer Controls:* Yes. *Number of Columns in Screen Display:* 80. *Package Menu-driven:* Yes. *Break or Help Command Without Interrupting or Exiting the Program:* Yes.

Other features and comments

Provides exact terminal emulations of 20 popular CRT terminals; Xon/Xoff protocol supported.

Other communications packages by publisher

Softerm 1 for Apple II, II +, and IIE ($135).

Southwestern Data Systems

Address: 10761-E Woodside Ave.
Santee, CA 92071
Telephone: 619-562-3670

Publisher background

Date Founded: 1978. *Number of Employees:* 12. *Annual Sales (Last FY):* $500,000 to $1 million. *President:* Roger Wagner. *Applications Emphasis:* Data communications, utility programs, word processing, and text editing. *Intended Users:* Home and business users of Apple II and IIE computers.

Package specifications

Package Name: ASCII Express—The Professional. *Release Date:* July 1982. *Number Sold to Date:* 6,800. *How Sold:* By mail direct from the publisher and through retail stores and distributors. *Published Reviews/Listings:* International Software Database; *Datapro Directory of Microcomputer Software; List Magazine*, Summer 1983; *InfoWorld; Peelings*, November 1982; *Softalk*, December 1982; *Kilobaud Microcomputer; Creative Computer; InCider*. *Warranties:* Yes. Guaranteed to load. Unconditional 30-day warranty. *Source Code Available:* No. *Program Updates Available:* Yes; cost, $50. *Special Modem Required:* No. *Size of User Manual:* 320 pages.

Systems available

Machines: Apple II, II +, and IIE. *Operating Systems:* DOS 3.3. *Distribution Medium:* 5¼-inch disk. *Minimum RAM Required:* 48K. *Other Special Requirements:* None specified. *Price:* $129.95.

Communications features

Communications to Public Databases: Yes. *Dedicated to a Particular Database Service:* No. *Communications to Other Microcomputers:* Yes. *Baud Rates for Communication:* Up to 9600. *Variable Protocols for Communications:* Yes. *Auto Dial-up:* Yes. *Auto Log On:* Yes. *Uploading of Data:* Yes. *Downloading of Data:* Yes. *Alteration of Data Through Built-in Text Editor:* Yes. *RAM Buffer:* Yes. *Size of RAM Buffer:* 27K. *Automatically Writes to Disk When Buffer Full:* Yes. *On/Off Buffer Toggle Without Interrupting or Exiting the Program:* Yes. *Buffer On/Off Status Alert:* Yes. *Remaining Buffer Memory Status Alert:* Yes. *Character Redefinition:* Yes. *Printer Controls:* Yes. *Number of Columns in Screen Display:* 40/80. There is line wrapping on 40-column display. *Package Menu-driven:* Yes. *Break or Help Command Without Interrupting or Exiting the Program:* Yes.

Other features and comments

Supports Western Union TWX and TLX; supports Christensen protocol transfers; supports tone and pulse dialing; supports interactive and conditional macros; number-one selling Apple communications package according to *Softalk*.

Other communications packages by publisher

Online ($89.95); Z-Term ($149.95); Z-Term The Professional ($149.95); P-Term The Professional ($129.95); ASCII Express II ($79.95). All of these packages are for the Apple II and II + machines.

SuperSoft, Inc.

Address: P.O. Box 1628
Champaign, IL 61820
Telephone: 217-359-2112

Publisher background

Date Founded: 1978. *Number of Employees:* 25. *Annual Sales (Last FY):* $5 million. *President:* Herb Schildt. *Applications Emphasis:* SuperSoft publishes over 30 programs in the areas of languages, voice recognition, system maintenance, programmer utilities, financial planning, computer-aided instruction, word processing, and entertainment. *Intended Users:* Engineering, scientific, programming, and business users of CP/M-80, CP/M-86, IBM PC DOS, and MS DOS.

Package specifications

Package Name: Term II. *Release Date:* August 1981. *Number Sold to Date:* Information not available. *How Sold:* By mail direct from the publisher, through retail stores, and through distributors. *Published Reviews/Listings:* International Software Database; *Datapro Directory of Microcomputer Software; List Magazine*, Summer 1983; *Sofsearch. Warranties:* Yes. Guaranteed to load. 30-day replacement of defective media. *Source Code Available:* Yes. *Program Updates Available:* Yes; cost, $25 to $50. *Special Modem Required:* No. *Size of User Manual:* 200 pages.

Systems available

Machines: Various CP/M machines. *Operating Systems:* CP/M. *Distribution Medium:* 5¼-inch and 8-inch disks. *Minimum RAM Required:* 32K. *Other Special Requirements:* None specified. *Price:* $200.

Communications features

Communications to Public Databases: Yes. *Dedicated to a Particular Database Service:* No. *Communications to Other Microcomputers:* Yes. *Baud Rates for Communication:* Up to 19,200. *Variable Protocols for Communications:* Yes. *Auto Dial-up:* Yes. *Auto Log On:* Yes. *Uploading of Data:* Yes. *Downloading of Data:* Yes. *Alteration of Data Through Built-in Text Editor:* No. *RAM Buffer:* Yes. *Size of RAM Buffer:* 20K. *Automatically Writes to Disk When Buffer Full:* Yes. *On/Off Buffer Toggle Without Interrupting or Exiting the Program:* Yes. *Buffer On/Off Status Alert:* Yes. *Remaining Buffer Memory Status Alert:* Yes. *Character Redefinition:* Yes. *Printer Controls:* Yes. *Number of Columns in Screen Display:* 80. *Package Menu-driven:* No. *Break or Help Command Without Interrupting or Exiting the Program:* Yes.

Other communications packages by publisher

None.

Telephone Software Connection, Inc.

Address: P.O. Box 6548
Torrance, CA 90504
Telephone: 213-516-9430

Publisher background

Date Founded: 1979. *Number of Employees:* Information not available. *Annual Sales (Last FY):* Information not available (but estimated at under $500,000). *President:* Ed Magnin. *Applications Emphasis:* Data communications, education, entertainment, mathematics and statistics, programming aids, utility programs, business, and time management. *Intended Users:* Business and personal use.

Package specifications

Package Name: Terminal Program. *Release Date:* 1980. *Number Sold to Date:* Information not available. *How Sold:* By mail direct from the publisher and via modem teledelivery. *Published Reviews/Listings:* International Software Database; *Datapro Directory of Microcomputer Software.* *Warranties:* Yes. Guaranteed to load. *Source Code Available:* No. *Program Updates Available:* No. *Special Modem Required:* Yes. Hayes Micromodem or SSM Modem card. *Size of User Manual:* No hard-copy manual is supplied since software is usually delivered over the phone. Instead, help aids (user manual) are embedded within the program.

Systems available

Machines: Apple II, II +, and IIE computers. *Operating Systems:* DOS 3.3. *Distribution Medium:* Teledelivery transmission process (over the telephone) or via 5¼-inch disk. *Minimum RAM Required:* 48K. *Other Special Requirements:* None specified. *Price:* $35 (via teledelivery), $40 (via mail order).

Communications features

Communications to Public Databases: Yes. *Dedicated to a Particular Database Service:* No. *Communications to Other Microcomputers:* Yes. *Baud Rates for Communication:* 300. *Variable Protocols for Communications:* Yes. *Auto Dial-up:* Yes. *Auto Log On:* Yes. *Uploading of Data:* Yes. *Downloading of Data:* Yes. *Alteration of Data Through Built-in Text Editor:* Yes. *RAM Buffer:* Yes. *Size of RAM Buffer:* 10K to 16K. *Automatically Writes to Disk When Buffer Full:* No. *On/Off Buffer Toggle Without Interrupting or Exiting the Program:* No. *Buffer On/Off Status Alert:* No. *Remaining Buffer Memory Status Alert:* Yes. *Character Redefinition:* Yes. *Printer Controls:* Yes. *Number of Columns in Screen Display:* 40/80. There is line wrapping on 40-column display. *Package Menu-driven:* Yes. *Break or Help Command Without Interrupting or Exiting the Program:* Yes.

Other communications packages by publisher

Answering Machine ($35); Telephone Transfer II ($75); Phone Secretary II ($40); Picture Transfer Program ($35); GO-MOKN ($20); Chess Connection ($35); Tele-Gammon ($35). All of these packages are available for the Apple II, II +, and IIE computers.

Texas Instruments

Address: P.O. Box 402430
Dallas, TX 75240
Telephone: 800-527-3500

Publisher background

Date Founded: 1940. *Number of Employees:* 85,000. *Annual Sales (Last FY):* $50 million plus. *President:* J. Fred Bucy. *Applications Emphasis:* Electronic spreadsheet, business graphics, communications word processing, database management, accounting, industry specific software, operating systems, education, recreation, and entertainment. *Intended Users:* Manufactures mini- and microcomputers for business and home use, in addition to making terminals and other products.

Package specifications

Package Name: TTY Communications. *Release Date:* Early 1983. *Number Sold to Date:* Thousands. *How Sold:* Through retail stores. *Published Reviews/Listings:* International Software Database; *Datapro Directory of Microcomputer Software; Popular Computing,* October 1983. *Warranties:* Yes. Guaranteed to load. 90-day warranty on diskette, not on program. *Source Code Available:* No. *Program Updates Available:* No. *Special Modem Required:* No. *Size of User Manual:* 43 pages.

Systems available

Machines: TI Professional Computer. *Operating Systems:* MS DOS. *Distribution Medium:* 5¼-inch disk. *Minimum RAM Required:* 128K. *Other Special Requirements:* None specified. *Price:* $60.

Communications features

Communications to Public Databases: Yes. *Dedicated to a Particular Database Service:* No. *Communications to Other Microcomputers:* Yes. *Baud Rates for Communication:* 110 to 9600. *Variable Protocols for Communications:* Yes. *Auto Dial-up:* Yes. *Auto Log On:* Yes. *Uploading of Data:* Yes. *Downloading of Data:* Yes. *Alteration of Data Through Built-in Text Editor:* No. *RAM Buffer:* Yes. *Size of RAM Buffer:* 1.5K. *Automatically Writes to Disk When Buffer Full:* Yes. *On/Off Buffer Toggle Without Interrupting or Exiting the Program:* Yes. *Buffer On/Off Status Alert:* No. *Remaining Buffer Memory Status Alert:* No. *Character Redefinition:* Yes. *Printer Controls:* Yes. *Number of Columns in Screen Display:* 80. *Package Menu-driven:* Yes. *Break or Help Command Without Interrupting or Exiting the Program:* Yes.

Other features and comments

Auto answer/auto call (unattended operations). Supports Xon/Xoff and other protocols.

Other communications packages by publisher

Natural Link for TI Professional Computer ($150); Terminal Emulator II for TI Home Computer ($150).

VisiCorp

Address: 2895 Zanker Rd.
San Jose, CA 95134
Telephone: 408-946-9000

Publisher background

Date Founded: 1978. *Number of Employees:* 300. *Annual Sales (Last FY):* $30 million. *President:* Terry L. Opdendyk. *Applications Emphasis:* Financial planning, word processing, data management, business graphics, project and time management, and communications. *Intended Users:* Business managers and professionals in an office environment.

Package specifications

Package Name: VisiTerm. *Release Date:* 1982. *Number Sold to Date:* Information not available. *How Sold:* Through retail stores, dealers, and distributors. *Published Reviews/Listings: Datapro Directory of Microcomputer Software; List Magazine*, Summer 1983; *Softalk*, September 1981; *Infoworld*, January 25, 1982; *Creative Computing*, May 1982. *Warranties:* Yes. 90-day warranty on diskette but not on product performance. *Source Code Available:* No. *Program Updates Available:* Yes; cost variable, but charge is generally under $50. *Special Modem Required:* No. *Size of User Manual:* 200 pages.

Systems available

Machines: Apple II, II +, IIE. *Operating Systems:* Apple DOS. *Distribution Medium:* 5¼-inch disk. *Minimum RAM Required:* 48K. *Other Special Requirements:* None specified. *Price:* $100.

Communications features

Communications to Public Databases: Yes. *Dedicated to a Particular Database Service:* No. *Communications to Other Microcomputers:* Yes. *Baud Rates for Communication:* 110 to 1200. *Variable Protocols for Communications:* Yes. *Auto Dial-up:* No. *Auto Log On:*

No. *Uploading of Data:* Yes. *Downloading of Data:* Yes. *Alteration of Data Through Built-in Text Editor:* No. *RAM Buffer:* Yes. *Size of RAM Buffer:* Nominal (automatically writes to disk at user's request). *Automatically Writes to Disk When Buffer Full:* Yes. *On/Off Buffer Toggle Without Interrupting or Exiting the Program:* Yes. *Buffer On/Off Status Alert:* No. *Remaining Buffer Memory Status Alert:* No. *Character Redefinition:* Yes. *Printer Controls:* Yes (but cannot print while receiving). *Number of Columns in Screen Display:* 40/80. There is line wrapping on 40-column display. *Package Menu-driven:* Yes. *Break or Help Command Without Interrupting or Exiting the Program:* No.

Other features and comments

Supports Xon/Xoff and other standard protocols. Will send and receive DIF formats.

Other communications packages by publisher

VisiLink for Apple II, IIE, IBM PC ($250); Visi Answer for IBM PC (price not available).

E A Smorgasbord of Modems[1]

In this appendix we list many of the modems you can buy. We have tried to select a representative sample, but the market is changing rapidly and new products appear almost weekly.

The manufacturers listed have verified these details, but we haven't tested all the products. Thus a listing doesn't imply an endorsement, nor does absence imply any disapproval. Use the information for comparative purposes only.

In our discussion we have followed a single format to make it easier for you to compare and evaluate the modems. Before turning to the individual modems, we will explain our keys.

Application

Bell 103 compatibility—modems compatible with the Bell System (now AT&T Information Systems) 103 standard communicate in a range from 0 to 300 baud and are also compatible with Bell 113 originate-only/answer-only modems and Bell 108 private-line modems.

Bell 212A compatibility—modems compatible with the Bell System (now AT&T Information Systems) 212A standard communicate at 1200 baud and can also communicate with Bell 103-compatible modems at 0 to 300 baud.

Personal computer compatibility—designates specific personal computer(s) with which a modem is designed to work, if applicable. Modems without a specific personal computer appellation can work with any system, assuming proper interface connections and control signal designations.

Packaging

This section defines the physical packaging of the modem as a stand-alone, direct-connect unit for tabletop placement; as an acoustic coupler, which is also a stand-

---

[1]The basic material in this appendix and Chapter 30, All About Modems, was provided by Data Decisions, a research and consulting firm that publishes information services on computer systems, software, and communications. Additional information on the company's services is available from Data Decisions, 20 Brace Road, Cherry Hill, New Jersey 08034; telephone, 609-429-7100.

alone unit except with rubber "cups" for cradling a telephone handset; or as a plug-in board that would fit into a specific type of personal computer. Communications software for specific personal computers may also be supplied with either stand-alone or plug-in modems, as an extra-cost option or packaged with the basic modem; when provided, the software is noted as being supplied on diskette, cassette tape, or stored internally on ROM (read-only memory) or RAM (random access memory).

Operating parameters

Transmission mode—the direction that data is transmitted over a communications link is defined as simplex, half duplex, or full duplex. All modems in this survey are either half-duplex or full-duplex units.

Half duplex—defines two-way transmission between two points but in only one direction at a time.

Full duplex—defines two-way simultaneous transmission between two points.

Synchronization—data transmitted either asynchronously or synchronously. An online database service operates in asynchronous mode.

Asynchronous transmission (also referred to as start/stop transmission) frames each transmitted character with a start bit and one or two stop bits. The interval between successive characters can vary in time without affecting the transmission, but the interval between successive bits within a character is identical. Synchronization betweeen transmitting and receiving devices is achieved on a character-by-character basis by each character's start and stop bits, which define the beginning and end of data.

Synchronous transmission transmits data in a continuous stream; the time interval between successive bits within a character and successive characters is constant. Synchronization between transmitting and receiving devices is achieved through synchronization bits or characters at the beginning of each transmission.

Modulation—the method that the modem uses to alter its carrier frequency with respect to the data signal received from the data terminal equipment (personal computer). The modem industry uses several different modulation techniques. Some are simple such as FSK (Frequency Shift Keying), which is employed for asynchronous transmission up to 1800 baud; some are complex such as QAM (Quadrature Amplitude Modulation), which is used for synchronous transmission speeds up to 9600 baud. Each modulation technique is advantageous to a specific application. Communicating modems at each end of a data link must employ the identical modulation technique.

Data rate—the data rate, or speed, of a modem is measured in bits per second (baud). Ten bits per second is equivalent to one character per second; therefore, a 1200-baud modem can transmit and receive data at the rate of 120 characters (letters, digits) per second. The data rate of the modem must be matched to that of the personal computer, printer, and/or other attached equipment.

Originate/answer mode—modems covered in this survey are either originate only (they cannot accept a call) or originate/answer.

Electrical interface—the connection between data terminating equipment (DTE) and data circuit equipment (DCE); i.e., the personal computer and the modem. The interface passes digital data and control signals between devices but can differ electrically depending on the application. Modems in this survey are equipped with the following electrical interfaces: EIA Standard RS-232C (international version CCITT V24); current loop; TTL; and other special interfaces or adapters designed to fit the peculiarities of specific personal computers.

EIA Standard RS-232C—the most common electrical interface standard used throughout the industry; however, exact conformation to the standard is typically not followed by vendors. The RS-232C interface is a 25-pin connector that supports transmission at data rates up to 20K baud at distances up to 50 feet between DTE and DCE.

Current loop—an electrical interface that employs telegraph technology. Data is transferred in the form of current pulses of rates up to 150 baud. Two signaling standards exist: neutral, or unipolar, in which signaling is performed by switching DC current on or off; and polar, or bipolar, in which signaling is performed by positive or negative DC current pulses. Signal current standards are 20 or 60 milliamperes. Current-loop interfaces are most commonly associated with teletype machines and communicating terminals. They are rare among personal computers.

TTL (transistor-to-transistor logic)—an industry-standard, digital, noncommunication interface used to connect two digital devices. Often employed with plug-in modems, connecting the modem directly to the personal computer database.

Dialing

This section details the methods employed for dialing calls through a modem. All of the modems in this survey can be used to dial out; some require a regular telephone for calls to be manually placed, some contain an integral telephone key pad, and some allow dialing from the personal computer keyboard. Modems with an integral automatic dialer store telephone numbers for later dialing at the press of a button. Most of the features in this section are explanations of auto-dial functions and/or of the ability to alternate voice and data communications through the modem. Specific topics include the following:

Automatic dial—a modem feature that automatically dials a pre-stored number from modem memory. Auto dialers can store from one or up to dozens of telephone numbers, depending on the model, with varying or user-definable lengths. Modems may support pulse (rotary) and/or tone dialing.

Tandem dial—an auto-dialer feature that permits dialing through PBX (private branch exchange) or other in-house or on-campus switching systems. It requires dialing a specific digit to get into the public telephone network and the recognition of two separate dial tones. Some auto dialers, in addition to or instead of tandem dialing, provide blind dialing, which is designed for systems employing nonstandard dial tones. Blind dialers dial the first digit; pause for a predetermined length of time (usually five seconds); and then dial the telephone number.

Single keystroke dial—a convenience feature for auto dialing; allows dialing a complete telephone number with a single keystroke.

Multiple redial—some auto dialers will redial a busy or unanswered phone number for an established number of tries or until the call is answered. The number of retries may sometimes be programmable by the user, depending on the auto dialer.

Linked list dialing—sometimes called alternate dialing, this feature allows alternate numbers to be dialed in case the first number is busy or does not answer.

Alternate voice/data—some modems allow either voice or data to be alternately routed through the modem. This is usually accomplished by attaching a regular telephone to the modem and toggling a voice/data switch on the modem; by attaching a special telephone with an exclusion key on the handset cradle (when a talk/data switch is not supplied); or by attaching a regular telephone and entering keyboard commands to the personal computer (takes the place of a talk/data switch).

Call answering

The majority of modems represented in this survey support call answering, which may be in manual, and sometimes automatic, mode. Auto answer allows the user to accept messages on his personal computer unattended; the modem automatically responds to the ringing signal of an incoming call by generating an auto-answer tone (2025 Hz) and by connecting the personal computer.

Personal computer requirements

In this section we define the personal computer requirements to attach modems designed for those specific personal computers. Such requirements can include a minimum amount of main memory, a specific operating system, single or dual disk drives, a video monitor, or various (or all) of the preceding.

Software-supported menus/operator messages

Modems expressly designed for personal computers can often be configured from the user's keyboard. Some of these modems provide user-friendly screen menus or message prompting to assist in selecting basic modem communication parameters, auto-dialer functions, and other parameters outlined in this section. Most of these modems also provide screen messages to inform the user of call progress and/or list available commands, display modem status, or provide a "help" file for online instruction.

Diagnostics/indicators

Diagnostic test functions provided by a specific modem and visual indicators defining modem operating status are set forth in this section. Diagnostic testing for personal computer modems is usually implemented by a simple modem self-test, or local analog loopback. More complex requirements, such as testing a remote modem (requiring the same make and model at both ends) or testing private leased phone lines, require remote analog/digital tests or other end-to-end testing procedures.

Visual indicators are front-panel indicator lamps (LEDs, LCDs) that present a visual indication of operating status, including key interface signal status, such as Request-to-Send (RTS), Clear-to-Send (CTS), Carrier Detect (DCD), and Data Set Ready (DSR); test or error conditions; and high-speed mode.

Other features/options

Features and options associated with a specific modem are presented in this section. Topics include the following:

File transfers—includes software for sending and receiving disk files to and from a central computer. Unattended file transfers are sometimes referred to as store-and-forward.

Text editing—some communication software packages provide rudimentary text editing, allowing the user to alter online database retrievals and other text. These are usually not as comprehensive as separate word-processing software.

Error control—specifies the method by which some modems can detect and sometimes correct transmission errors generated over the phone line. The most sophisticated technique, cyclic redundancy checking (CRC l6), sends an error-detection algorithm along with the data stream and retransmits any errored blocks of data.

Cost/service

This features section provides single-unit pricing for a basic unit without options. Option pricing and quantity discounts are provided where applicable. Service is defined as provided by the vendor or third-party service organization for field or factory repairs.

Anchor Automation
6624 Valjean Ave.
Van Nuys, CA 91406

Signalman Mark I Modem

Application: Compatible with Bell 103 modems—FCC certified. *Packaging:* Stand-alone direct-connect modem. *Operating Parameters:* Full-duplex asynchronous at rates to 300 bps—originate/answer modes—FSK modulation—RS-232CD DTE interface. *Dialing:* Manual dial via telephone—supports alternate voice/data via talk/data switch plus regular telephone. *Call Answering:* Manual answer. *Personal Computer Requirements:* Not specified. *Software-Supported Menus/Operator Messages:* None supported. *Diagnostics/Indicators:* None supported. *Other Features/Options:* Operating power derived from 9-volt battery. *Cost/Service:* Basic price $99—quantity discounts to dealers only—1-year warranty—own service; factory service, 2-day turnaround from date received.

Signalman Mark VI Modem

Application: Compatible with Bell 103 modems—personal computer compatibility for IBM PC—FCC certified. *Packaging:* Plug-in board—communications software supplied on diskette. *Operating Parameters:* Full-duplex asynchronous at 300 bps—originate/answer modes—FSK modulation—IBM PC bus DTE interface. *Dialing:* Manual dial via telephone; terminal keyboard dial; automatic dial with storage for telephone numbers of 9 characters each—pulse dial—tone dial—tandem dial—single keystroke dial—multiple redial—supports alternate voice/data via talk/data switch plus regular telephone. *Call Answering:* Manual answer or automatic answer automatically connects the personal computer to the phone line. *Personal Computer Requirements:* Requires basic IBC PC; fits any address port (slot)—IBM A or B diskette. *Software-Supported Menus/Operator Messages:* Communications/other parameters established via screen menus—operator messages including help file, list commands/menu. *Diagnostics/Indicators:* None supported. *Other Features/Options:* File transfers—concurrent operations including data display/printer transfer; data display/disk transfer—operating power derived from the personal computer—supports options RS-232C digital interface for local printer or alternate communications line. *Cost/Service:* Basic price $279 suggested; option pricing not available—quantity discounts to dealers only—1-year warranty—own service; factory service, 2-day turnaround from date received.

Signalman Mark VII Modem

Application: Compatible with Bell 103 modems—FCC certified. *Packaging:* Stand-alone direct-connect modem. *Operating Parameters:* Full-duplex asynchronous at rates to 300 bps—originate/answer modes—FSK modulation—RS-232C DTE interface, with pin positions adaptable to any personal computer interface standard. *Dialing:* Manual dial via telephone; terminal keyboard dial; automatic dial with storage for 8 telephone numbers of 9 characters each—pulse dial—tone dial—tandem dial—single keystroke dial—multiple redial—supports alternate voice/data via talk/data switch plus regular telephone. *Call Answering:* Manual answer or automatic answer automatically connects the personal computer to the phone line. *Personal Computer Requirements:* Any personal computer with RS-232C interface and communications software installed. *Software-Supported Menus/Operator Messages:* Dialing parameters established via screen menus—operator messages including help file, list commands/menu. *Diagnostics/Indicators:* None supported. *Other Features/Options:* None supported. *Cost/Service:* Basic price $159 (suggested)—quantity discounts (to dealers only)—1-year warranty—own service; factory service, 2-day turnaround from date received.

Backus Data Systems, Inc.
1440 Koll Circle
San Jose, CA 95112

AC 312

Applications: Compatible with Bell 103; optional Bell 202 compatible. *Packaging:* Acoustic coupler. *Operating Parameters:* Half-/full-duplex asynchronous at 300 bps; optional half-duplex asynchronous at 1200 bps—originate only or originate/answer mode—FSK modulation—RS-232C DTE interface. *Dialing:* Manual dial via telephone. *Call Answering:* Manual answer optional. *Personal Computer Requirements:* Not specified. *Software-Supported Menus/Operator Messages:* None supported. *Diagnostics/Indicators:* Front-panel LEDs for power, carrier, DTR. *Other Features/Options:* Reverse channel for line turnaround commands, Bell 202 mode—local copy capability. *Cost/Service:* Basic price $199; option pricing $250 for answer/originate; $495 for Bell 202 mode—quantity discounts available—1-year warranty—factory service.

*Bizcomp Corp.
532 Weddell Drive
Sunnyvale, CA 94089

PC Intellimodem
Application: Compatible with Bell 212A modems—personal computer compatibility for the IBM PC—FCC certified. *Packaging:* Plug-in board—communications software supplied on diskette. *Operating Parameters:* Half- or full-duplex asynchronous at 110-1200 bps—originate/answer modes—FSK, PSK modulation—PC bus DTE interface. *Dialing:* Manual dial via telephone; terminal keyboard dial, automatic dial with storage for 99 telephone numbers of 32 characters each—pulse dial—tone dial—tandem dial—single keystroke dial—multiple redial, unlimited times—supports an indefinite number of linked phone numbers—supports alternate voice/data via keyboard-controlled talk/data function plus regular telephone. *Call Answering:* Manual answer or automatic answer automatically connects the personal computer to the phone line. *Personal Computer Requirements:* Requires 64K-byte main memory—DOS 1.1/1.0/2.0 operating system—single diskette drive—80-column display. *Software-Supported Menus/Operator Messages:* Communications/other parameters established via screen-labeled function keys—adjusts both modem and communications parameters—operator messages including no answer, ringing, busy, online, dial tone, help file, help prompts—targeted at the novice; full-status window display. *Diagnostics/Indicators:* Self-test of modem circuitry—analog loopback—1 back panel LED, programmable for different functions. *Other Features/Options:* File transfers—automatic database log on, programmable for any remote database—supports different terminal/modem data rates; modem/IBM computer communication at 1200 bps (fixed) independent of phone-line communication—automatic 300/1200 bps selection from directory—integral audible monitor—incoming call indication. *Cost/Service:* Basic price $499—quantity discounts available—2-year warranty—own service; factory service.

*Bytcom
2169 Francisco Blvd.
Suite H
San Rafael, CA 94901

*Bytcom 212AD
Application: Compatible with Bell 103, Bell 212A—FCC certified. *Packaging:* Stand-alone direct-connect modem. *Operating Parameters:* Full-duplex asynchronous at 300/1200 bps; synchronous at 300/1200 bps FSK, PSK modulation—RS232C DTE interface. *Dialing:* Manual dial via telephone; terminal keyboard dial; automatic dial with storage for 10 telephone numbers of 40 characters each—pulse dial—tone dial—tandem dial—single keystroke dial—multiple redial up to 15 times, supports a linked list of 9 telephone numbers—supports alternate voice/data via talk/data switch plus regular telephone—can change betwen tone and pulse dial within the same stored number features. *Call Answering:* Manual answer or automatic answer automatically connects the personal computer to the phone line. *Personal Computer Requirements:* Serial RS-232 interface. *Software-Supported Menus/Operator Messages:* Communications/other parameters established via screen menus—operator messages including no answer, busy, online, dialing, dead phone, invalid; single character or text response. *Diagnostics/Indicators:* Self-test of modem circuitry—local and remote analog loopback, digital loopback—front-panel LEDs for modem ready/check; modem busy; high speed; test mode; 3 key EIA interface signals. *Other Features/Options:* Compatible with popular communications software—

auto-parity, auto-data rate detection—reference stored numbers via a user-selected name—parameters stored in nonvolatile memory, battery backed—software disconnect capability—16-character answer-back capability—remote boot (for host CPU)—rack mount available. *Cost/ Service:* Basic price $595—quantity discount available—2-year swap-out warranty—own service; factory service.

Cermetek, Inc.
1308 Borregas Ave.
Sunnyvale, CA 94086

Info-Mate 212A
Application: Compatible with Bell 103, Bell 212A modems—FCC certified. *Packaging:* Stand-alone direct-connect modem. *Operating Parameters:* Full-duplex asynchronous at 110/300/ 1200 bps; synchronous at 1200 bps—FSK, PSK modulation—RS-232C DTE interface. *Dialing:* Manual dial via telephone; terminal keyboard dial; automatic dial with storage for 52 telephone numbers of 32 characters each—pulse dial—tone dial—tandem dial—single keystroke dial—multiple redial up to 15 times or alternate number up to 15 times; supports a linked list of 52 telephone numbers—supports alternate voice/data via keyboard commands plus regular telephone—during a data call, can put modem on "hold" and undertake voice communication and then reinitiate data call without redialing. *Call Answering:* Manual answer or automatic answer automatically connects the personal computer to the phone line. *Personal Computer Requirements:* Not specified. *Software-Supported Menus/Operator Messages:* Communications/other parameters established via screen prompts—operator messages including busy; electronic call progress tone detection; dial; ring back; human voice; answer tone. *Diagnostics/Indicators:* Self-test of modem circuitry—analog loopback; digital loopback—front-panel LEDs. *Other Features/Options:* Supports 5 auto-dialing procedures: dial last number, immediate, alternate, dial from memory, dial until answered—memory can store log-on message(s) instead of phone numbers—supports personal computers requiring EIA interface signal(s) to enable the keyboard. *Cost/Service:* Basic price $595—quantity discounts available—1-year warranty—own service; factory service.

Codex Corp.
20 Cabot Blvd.
Mansfield, MA 02048

5212R Data Modem
Application: Compatible with Bell 103, 113, Bell 212A modems—FCC certified. *Packaging:* Stand-alone direct-connect modem. *Operating Parameters:* Full-duplex asynchronous at rates of 300/1200 bps; synchronous at 1200 bps—originate/answer modes—FSK, PSK modulaton—RS-232C DTE interface. *Dialing:* Manual dial via telephone—supports alternate voice/ data via talk/data switch plus regular telephone. *Call Answering:* Manual answer or automatic answer automatically connects the personal computer to the phone line. *Personal Computer Requirements:* Not specified. *Software-Supported Menus/Operator Messages:* None supported. *Diagnostics/Indicators:* Self-test of modem circuitry—local and remote analog loopback, digital loopback—front-panel LEDs for 4 key EIA interface signals; high-speed mode; modem check; test mode; make busy. *Other Features/Options:* Automatically adjusts to speed of incoming call—integral abort timer automatically disconnects erroneous calls—rack-mount version available. *Cost/Service:* Basic price $595—quantity discounts available—1-year warranty—own service; field service; factory service—field service locations nationwide.

Concord Data Systems
303 Bear Hill Rd.
Waltham, MA 02154

CDS 224
Application: Compatible with CCITT V.22 bis and Bell 212A modems (in fallback mode)—FCC certified. *Packaging:* Stand-alone direct-connect modem. *Operating Parameters:* Full-du-

plex asynchronous or synchronous at 1200/2400 bps—QAM modulation—RS-232C DTE interface. *Dialing:* Manual dial via telephone, auto dial also available. *Call Answering:* Manual answer or automatic answer automatically connects the personal computer to the phone line. *Personal Computer Requirements:* Not specified. *Software-Supported Menus/Operator Messages:* None supported. *Diagnostics/Indicators:* Self-test of modem circuitry—analog loopback; digital loopback—front-panel LEDs for 10 EIA interface signals and operating modes. *Cost/Service:* CDS 224, $995; with auto dial, $1,195.

Datec, Inc.
200 Eastowne Drive
Chapel Hill, NC 27514

Datec 30
Application: Compatible with Bell 103 modems. *Packaging:* Acoustic coupler. *Operating Parameters:* Half-/full-duplex asynchronous at rates up to 300 bps—originate only mode—FSK modulation—RS-232C or 20-mA current-loop DTE interface. *Dialing:* Manual dial via telephone. *Call Answering:* None supported. *Personal Computer Requirements:* Not specified. *Software-Supported Menus/Operator Messages:* None supported. *Diagnostics/Indicators:* Front-panel LEDs for transmit and receive data. *Other Features/Options:* None supported. *Cost/Service:* Basic price $235—quantity discounts available—1-year warranty—own service; factory service.

Gandalf Data, Inc.
1019 South Noel
Wheeling, IL 60090

SAM 212A
Application: Compatible with Bell 103, Bell 212A modems—FCC certified. *Packaging:* Stand-alone direct-connect modem. *Operating Parameters:* Full-duplex asynchronous at 300/1200 bps; synchronous at 1200 bps—FSK, DPSK modulation—RS-232C DTE interface. *Dialing:* Manual dial via telephone; automatic dial with storage for 1 telephone number of 32 characters—pulse dial—tandem dial—supports alternate voice/data via talk/data switch plus regular telephone. *Call Answering:* Manual answer or automatic answer automatically connects the personal computer to the phone line. *Personal Computer Requirements:* Not specified. *Software-Supported Menus/Operator Messages:* Communications/other parameters established via screen prompts. *Diagnostics/Indicators:* Self-test of modem circuitry—analog loopback; digital loopback—front-panel LEDs for 6 key EIA interface signals, high-speed mode, and modem test. *Other Features/Options:* Adapts automatically to match the speed of incoming signal—enhanced auto dial available. *Cost/Service:* Basic price $618—quantity discounts available—1-year warranty—own service; field service or factory service—field service in 8 U.S. locations and 6 Canadian locations.

Hayes Microcomputer Products, Inc.
5923 Peachtree Industrial Blvd.
Norcross, GA 30092

Smartmodem 300 and Smartcom 1200
Application: Compatible with Bell 103 modems (300) or 212A modems (1200)—FCC certified. *Packaging:* Stand-alone direct-connect modem—optional Smartcom II communications software supplied on diskette. *Operating Parameters:* Half-/full-duplex asynchronous at rates up to 300 or 1200 bps—originate/answer modes—FSK modulation—RS-232C DTE interface—connects with single-line or multiline modular telephone jacks—40-character command buffer. *Dialing:* Terminal keyboard dial; pulse dial, tone dial, or mixed mode with a pause character. *Call Answering:* Manual answer or automatic answer automatically connects the personal computer to the phone line. *Personal Computer Requirements:* RS-232 interface. *Software-Sup-*

ported Menus/Operator Messages: None supported. *Diagnostics/Indicators:* Self-test of modem circuitry—front-panel LEDs for high-speed mode, auto answer and key EIA interface signals speaker with volume control to monitor calls. *Other Features/Options:* Optional Smartcom II communications software for the IBM PC, DEC Rainbow 100, KayPro II, Xerox 820-II, Wang and TI Professional, or optional terminal program for Apple computers. *Cost/Service:* Smartmodem 300, $289; Smartmodem 1200, $699; Smartcom II software or terminal program, $149—2-year limited warranty—90-day warranty, all software—own service; factory service.

Smartmodem 1200B

Application: Compatible with Bell 103, Bell 212A—personal computer compatibility for IBM PC or XT—FCC certified. *Packaging:* Plug-in board—sold alone or with communications software supplied on diskette. *Operating Parameters:* Half-/full-duplex asynchronous at 300/1200 bps—originate/answer modes—FSK, PSK modulation—IBM bus DTE interface, connects with single-line or multiline modular telephone jacks—40-character command buffer. *Dialing:* Terminal keyboard dial—pulse dial—tone dial—tandem dial (with a pause character)—redial of last number dial—supports alternate voice/data via keyboard command plus regular telephone. *Call Answering:* Manual answer or automatic answer automatically connects the personal computer to the phone line. *Personal Computer Requirements:* For IBM Smartcom II software, requires 96K-byte main memory—IBM DOS 1.10 or 1.00 operating system—1 diskette drive—80-column display. *Software-Supported Menus/Operator Messages:* Communications/other parameters established via screen menus—operator messages tell operator the modem status—helps messages give program instructions—stores 25 phone numbers—performs automatic log on. *Diagnostics/Indicators:* Self-test of modem circuitry—built-in speaker allows audible line monitoring. *Other Features/Options:* File transfers in 3 modes (store and forward)—error control CRC-16 (requires 2 1200Bs or any Hayes communications program)—concurrent operations including data display/printed transfer, data display/disk transfer, printing/disk transfer—programmable message/display parameters—backward screen scroll—remote access between two Smartcom II programs. *Cost/Service:* Basic price $539; with Smartcom II $599—2-year limited warranty—90-day software warranty, all software—own service; factory service.

Intelligent Technologies International Corp.
151 University Ave.
Palo Alto, CA 94301

PC Express

Application: Compatible with Bell 103 modems—personal computer compatibility for IBM Personal Computer—FCC certified. *Packaging:* Plug-in board—communications software supplied on diskette. *Operating Parameters:* Half-/full-duplex—asynchronous at rates up to 300 bps—FSK modulation—IBM bus DTE interface. *Dialing:* Terminal keyboard dial, automatic dial with user-programmable calling parameters—supports alternate voice/data via soft-key talk/data switch plus regular telephone. *Call Answering:* Manual answer or automatic answer automatically connects the personal computer to the phone line. *Personal Computer Requirements:* Requires 256K-byte main memory—PC DOS (MS-DOS) operating system—2 double-sided diskette drives—monochrome or color display. *Software-Supported Menus/Operator Messages:* Communications/other parameters established via screen menus or command-driven. *Diagnostics/Indicators:* None supported. *Other Features/Options:* Telephone management system with unattended file transfers (store and forward), programmable automatic database log on for remote databases, simple text editing, electronic mail, error control (ARQ), and remote terminal access using the PC as a host—DEC VT100/VT52 emulation—free membership to The Source—accommodates external modem up to 19.2K bps—optional IBM SNA 3270 emulation; emulates cluster controllers, 3770 RJE station—optional multiboard attaches to additional terminals—other user-programmable functions. *Cost/Service:* Basic price $895, option pricing $1,295 with SNA emulation—1-year warranty—own service; factory service.

*Lexicon Corp.
1541 N.W. 65th Ave.
Fort Lauderdale, FL 33313

LEX-10 modem
Application: Compatible with Bell 103 modems—FCC certified. *Packaging:* Stand-alone direct-connect modem. *Operating Parameters:* Full-duplex asynchronous at rates to 300 bps—originate/answer modes—FSK modulation—RS-232C DTE interface. *Dialing:* Manual dial via telephone. *Call Answering:* Manual answer, auto answer. *Personal Computer Requirements:* Not specified. *Software-Supported Menus/Operator Messages:* None supported. *Diagnostics/Indicators:* Front-panel LED for carrier detect. *Other Features/Options:* Optional Ni-Cad battery operation. *Cost/Service:* Basic price $119, option pricing $159 (battery operaton)—quantity discounts available at 10 to 35 percent, quantities of 10 to 500—90-day warranty—own service; factory service.

LEX-15 direct handset and acoustic modem
Application: Compatible with Bell 103 and Bell 202 standards—FCC certified. *Packaging:* Stand-alone direct-connect modem or acoustic coupler. *Operating Parameters:* Full-duplex asynchronous at rates to 300 bps or half-duplex asynchronous at 1200 bps—originate/answer modes—FSK modulation—RS-232C DTE interface. *Dialing:* Manual dial via telephone—supports alternate voice/data via talk/data switch plus regular telephone in direct-connect mode. *Call Answering:* Manual answer. *Personal Computer Requirements:* Not specified. *Software-Supported Menus/Operator Messages:* None supported. *Diagnostics/Indicators:* Front-panel LEDs for power-on, ready (carrier). *Other Features/Options:* Optional Ni-Cad battery option—5 bps reverse channel; "direct connect" is through handset, not wall jack. *Cost/Service:* Basic price $325, option pricing $395 (battery operation)—quantity discounts available at 10 to 35 percent, quantities of 10 to 500—90 day warranty—own service; factory service.

MFJ Enterprises
921 Louiville Rd.
Starksville, MS 39759

MFJ 1232 acoustic-coupled modem
Application: Compatible with Bell 103 modems. *Packaging:* Acoustic coupler—optional Apple II/II Plus communications software supplied on disk. *Operating Parameters:* Half-/full-duplex asynchronous at rates to 300 bps—originate/answer modes—FSK modulation—RS-232C, TTL, and CMOS DTE interface. *Dialing:* Manual dial via telephone. *Call Answering:* Manual answer. *Personal Computer Requirements:* Apple II or Apple II Plus. *Software-Supported Menus/Operator Messages:* None supported. *Diagnostics/Indicators:* Front-panel LEDs for power on, carrier detect. *Other Features/Options:* Cassette recorder port—can run on two 9-volt batteries. *Cost/Service:* Basic price $129.95, option pricing MFJ 1231 (Apple II terminal emulation software) $39.95—quantity discounts 35 to 40 percent for dealers only—1-year warranty—own service; factory service.

Micro-Baud Systems, Inc.
3393 De La Cruz Blvd.
Santa Clara, CA 95050

MB80514
Application: Compatible with Bell 212A modems—FCC certified. *Packaging:* Stand-alone direct-connect modem. *Operating Parameters:* Full-duplex asynchronous and synchronous at 300/1200 bps—PDK, FSK, PSK modulation—RS-232C DTE interface. *Dialing:* Manual dial via telephone; terminal keyboard dial; automatic dial with storage for 5 telephone numbers of 32 characters each—pulse dial—tone dial—tandem dial (blind dialing)—multiple redial up to 15 times; supports a link list of 2 telephone numbers. *Call Answering:* Manual answer or automatic answer automatically connects the personal computer to the phone line. *Personal Computer Requirements:* Any with RS-232 port and ASCII control characters. *Software-Sup-*

ported *Menus/Operator Messages:* Communications/other parameters established via screen menus—operator messages including no connect, nonline, ready, clear, idle, off line. *Diagnostics/Indicators:* Self-test of modem circuitry—1 front-panel LED for carrier detect. *Other Features/Options:* Integral speaker monitor, auto parity; auto data-rate detection—nonvolatile RAM; no need for battery backup. *Cost/Service:* Basic price $595—quantity discounts available; quantity of 100 or more, $375—1-year warranty—own service; factory service.

MICROCOM
1400A Providence Highway
Norwood, MA 02062

PCS/1200
Application: Compatible wtih Bel 103, Bell 212A modems—FCC certified. *Packaging:* Standalone direct-connect modem. *Operating Parameters:* Half-/full-duplex asynchronous at 0-300/1200 bps; synchronous at 1200 bps—RS-232C DTE interface. *Dialing:* Automatic dial with storage for 9 telephone numbers of 38 characters each—pulse dial—tone dial—tandem dial—single keystroke dial—multiple redial up to an infinite number of times. *Call Answering:* Automatic answer automatically connects the personal computer to the phone line. *Personal Computer Requirements:* Not specified. *Software-Supported Menus/Operator Messages:* Communications/other parameters established via command structures—operator messages including connect/no-connect modem status. *Diagnostics/Indicators:* Self-test of modem circuitry—digital loopback—front-panel LCDs for 2 key EIA interface signals; off hook; mail mode/mail-mode full. *Other Features/Options:* Unattended file transfers (store and forward)—error control (CRC-16; ARQ)—supports different terminal/modem data rates in a range up to 9600 bps (DTE to modem)—supports 2 additional digital interfaces for local printer, alternate communications line—integral flow control; includes an SDLC-like protocol—64K-byte battery-backed RAM—(32K for message creation) audio monitor for call monitoring—integral time-of-day clock. *Cost/Service:* Basic price $995, with 64K-byte RAM—quantity discounts available—1-year warranty—own service; factory service.

Microperipheral Corporation
2565 152nd Ave., N.E.
Richmond, WA 98052

P Connection
Application: Compatible with Bell 103 modems—personal computer compatibility for the IBM PC—FCC certified. *Packaging:* Plug-in board—communications software supplied on diskette. *Operating Parameters:* Half-/full-duplex asynchronous at rates to 300 bps—originate/answer modes—FSK modulation—PC bus DTE interface. *Dialing:* Terminal keyboard dial; automatic dial—pulse dial—tone dial—single keystroke dial. *Call Answering:* Manual answer or automatic answer automatically connects the personal computer to the phone line. *Personal Computer Requirements:* Requires 5.25-inch diskette. *Software-Supported Menus/Operator Messages:* None supported. *Diagnostics/Indicators:* None supported. *Other Features/Options:* Operating power derived from the personal computer. *Cost/Service:* Basic price $170—quantity discounts available—90-day warranty—own service; factory service.

Model Rl
Application: Compatible with Bell 103 modems—FCC certified. *Packaging:* Stand-alone direct-connect modem—communication software supplied for TRS-80 Model 1, 3 on diskette or cassette. *Operating Parameters:* Half-/full-duplex asynchronous at 300 bps—originate/answer modes—FSK modulation—RS-232C DTE interface. *Dialing:* Manual dial via telephone. *Call Answering:* Manual answer. *Personal Computer Requirements:* Requires single diskette or cassette drive. *Software-Supported Menus/Operator Messages:* Programmable operator messages. *Diagnostics/Indicators:* Front-panel LEDs for carrier, power. *Other Features/Options:* None supported. *Cost/Service:* Basic price $159—quantity discounts available—90-day warranty—own service; factory service.

Multi-Tech Systems, Inc.
82 Second Ave., S.E.
New Brighton, MN 55112

Multi-Modem PC
Application: Compatible with Bell 212A—personal computer compatibility for the IBM PC—FCC certified. *Packaging:* Plug-in board—communications software supplied on diskette. *Operating Parameters:* Half-/full-duplex asynchronous at 300/1200 bps—FSK, PSK modulation. *Dialing:* Keyboard dial; automatic dial with storage for 20 telephone numbers of up to 31 characters each—pulse dial—tone dial—tandem dial—single keystroke dial—multiple redial up to an infinite number of times; supports a linked list of 8 telephone numbers—supports alternate voice/data via keyboard command, automatic log on. *Call Answering:* Manual answer or automatic answer automatically connects the personal computer to the phone line. *Personal Computer Requirements:* Requires 64K-byte main memory—standard operating systems—5.25-inch diskette. *Software-Supported Menus/Operator Messages:* Operator messages including no answer; available with Crosstalk XVI Software. *Diagnostics/Indicators:* Analog loopback. *Other Features/Options:* File transfers—automatic database log on for on-line databases—data display/printer transfer; data display/disk transfer, operating power derived from the personal computer—second mode; built-in speaker; handset jack; Hayes Smartmodem 1200B compatible. *Cost/Service:* Basic price $595—quantity discounts available—2-year warranty—own service; factory service.

Multi-Modem
Application: Compatible with Bell 103 and 212A modems—FCC certified. *Packaging:* Stand-alone direct-connect modem. *Operating Parameters:* Full-duplex asynchronous at rates to 300 or 1200 bps—FSK and PSK modulation—RS-232C DTE interface. *Dialing:* Keyboard dial; software dial; automatic dial with storage for 6 telephone numbers of up to 31 characters each—pulse dial—tone dial—tandem dial—multiple redial up to an infinite number of times; supports a linked list of 8 telephone numbers—supports alternate voice/data via keyboard command. *Call Answering:* Automatic answer automatically connects the personal computer to the phone line, can answer on *n*th ring. *Personal Computer Requirements:* Many with RS-232 interface. *Software-Supported Menus/Operator Messages:* Operator messages including no answer, busy, connect, dial tone. *Diagnostics/Indicators:* Analog loopback—front-panel ELDs for 6 EIA interface signals. *Other Features/Options:* Hayes Smartmodem 1200 compatible, built-in speaker. *Cost/Service:* Basic price $549—quantity discounts available—2-year warranty—own service; factory service.

*Novation
20409 Prairie St.
Chatsworth, CA 91311

The 212 Auto-Cat Modem
Application: Compatible with Bell 212A modems—FCC certified. *Packaging:* Stand-alone direct-connect modem. *Operating Parameters:* Full-duplex asynchronous or synchronous at 1200 bps—FSK modulation—RS-232C DTE interface. *Dialing:* Manual dial via telephone, auto dial with appropriate software. *Call Answering:* Manual answer or automatic answer connects the personal computer to the phone line. *Personal Computer Requirements:* RS-232 compatible. *Software-Supported Menus/Operator Messages:* None supported. *Diagnostics/Indicators:* Self-test of modem circuitry—analog loopback; local and remote digital loopback—front-panel LEDs: transmit, receive, ready, answer, 1200, off hook, test, check. *Other Features/Options:* None supported. *Cost/Service:* Basic price $695—quantity discounts available—1-year warranty—own service; factory service.

*J-Cat
Application: Compatible with Bell 103/113 modems—FCC certified. *Packaging:* Stand-alone direct-connect modem. *Operating Parameters:* Full-duplex asynchronous at rates to 300 bps—FSK modulation—serial I/O interface compatible with RS-232. *Dialing:* Manual dial via telephone; terminal keyboard dial—pulse dial—tone dial. *Call Answering:* Manual answer or

automatic answer automatically connects the personal computer to the phone line. *Personal Computer Requirements:* RS-232 compatible. *Software-Supported Menus/Operator Messages:* None supported. *Diagnostics/Indicators:* Analog loopback—front-panel LEDs for off hook, ready. *Other Features/Options:* Auto search, auto status beeper, dial tone/busy status, 2 control keys, unique small size. *Cost/Service:* Basic price $149—quantity discounts 100 plus—1-year warranty—own service; factory service.

Penril/Data Communications Division
207 Perry Parkway
Gaithersburg, MD 20877

Model AD 300/1200

Application: Compatible with Bell 212A modems—FCC certified. *Packaging:* Stand-alone direct-connect modem—communications software supplied on RAM. *Operating Parameters:* Full-duplex asynchronous at 300 or 1200 bps—originate/answer modes—FSK, PSK modulation—RS-232C DTE interface. *Dialing:* Manual dial via telephone; terminal keyboard dial; automatic dial with storage for 10 telephone numbers of 20 characters each—pulse dial—tone dial—tandem dial (blind dialing)—single keystroke dial—multiple redial up to 15 times; supports an infinite linked list of telephone numbers—supports alternate voice/data plus regular telephone. *Call Answering:* Manual answer or automatic answer automatically connects the personal computer to the phone line. *Personal Computer Requirements:* Not specified. *Software-Supported Menus/Operator Messages:* Communications/other parameters established via screen menus for data rates, parity, command functions, full or half duplex, disconnect—operator messages including no answer, busy, online, help file. *Diagnostics/Indicators:* Self-test of modem circuitry—analog loopback; local and remote digital loopback—front-panel LEDs for make busy, high speed (for 1200 bps), modem check, test mode, and 4 key EIA interface signals. *Other Features/Options:* Programmable automatic database log on for online databases—electronic mail—rack mount available. *Cost/Service:* Basic price $650—quantity discounts available—1.5-year warranty—own service; factory service.

Racal-Vadic Inc.
1525 McCarthy Blvd.
Milpitas, CA 95035

VA103 Modemphone

Application: Compatible with Bell 103 modems—FCC certified. *Packaging:* Stand-alone direct-connect modem packaged inside a rotary- or tone-dial telephone. *Operating Parameters:* Full-duplex asynchronous at rates up to 300 bps—originate/answer modes—FSK modulation—RS-232C DTE interface. *Dialing:* Manual dial via (integral) telephone—supports alternate voice/data via talk/data switch. *Call Answering:* Manual answer or optional automatic answer automatically connects the personal computer to the phone line. *Personal Computer Requirements:* None supported. *Software-Supported Menus/Operator Messages:* None supported. *Diagnostics/Indicators:* Lights to indicate carrier on. *Other Features/Options:* Optional automatic answer mode; optional tone-dial telephone. *Cost/Service:* Basic price $250; option price $330 with auto answer; $300 with tone dial; $380 with tone dial and auto answer—quantity discounts available for 10 or more purchased units—1-year warranty—own service; factory service; field service provided by some distributors.

VA212LC

Application: Compatible with Bell 212A modems—FCC certified. *Packaging:* Stand-alone direct-connect modem. *Operating Parameters:* Full-duplex asynchronous at 300/1200 bps—originate/answer modes—FSK, PSK modulation—RS-232C DTE interface. *Dialing:* Manual dial via telephone—supports alternate voice/data via talk/data switch plus regular telephone. *Call Answering:* Manual answer or automatic answer automatically connects the personal computer to the phone line. *Personal Computer Requirements:* Not specified. *Software-Supported Menus/Operator Messages:* None supported. *Diagnostics/Indicators:* Self-test of modem circuitry—responds to remote test—front-panel LEDs for 3 key EIA interface signals; voice/data status; and high-speed mode. *Other Features/Options:* Automatically determines if calling modem is transmitting at 300 or 1200 bps—automatic detection algorithm and internal buffer accommodates 9- and 10-bit character codes. *Cost/Service:* Basic price $495—quantity discounts available for 10 or more purchased units—1-year warranty—own service; factory service; field service provided by some distributors.

*Rixon Inc.

Subsidiary of Sangamo Weston/Subsidiary of Schumberger Limited
2120 Industrial Parkway
Silver Spring, MD 20904

*Model PC212A

Application: Compatible with Bell 212A modems—FCC certified. *Packaging:* Card for IBM PC, COMPAQ, and PC compatible computers. *Operating Parameters:* Full-duplex asynchronous at rates to 300/1200 bps—FSK modulation (low speed) or PSK modulation (high speed)—RS-232C DTE interface. *Dialing:* Manual dial via telephone or auto dial from keyboard or program control. *Call Answering:* Manual answer or automatic answer automatically connects the personal computer to the phone line. *Personal Computer Requirements:* IBM PC, COMPAQ, or compatibles. *Software-Supported Menus/Operator Messages:* Help features, dial directory, options. *Diagnostics/Indicators:* Self-test of modem circuitry. *Other Features/Options:* Built-in abort timer for nondata calls—10-number (60 characters each) storage, linking, multiple re-dial, loss of carrier disconnect, etc. *Cost/Service:* Basic price $499—quantity discounts—2-year warranty—own service; field service, factory service—field service locations in 11 major U.S. cities and Ottawa, Canada.

Transend Corp.
2190 Paragon Drive
San Jose, CA 95131

PC Modem Card 300/1200

Application: Compatible with Bell 212A modems—personal computer compatibility for the IBM PC—FCC certified. *Packaging:* Plug-in board—communications software suplied on diskette. *Operating Parameters:* Full-duplex asynchronous at 300/1200 bps—originate/answer modes—FSK modulation. *Dialing:* Terminal keyboard dial—pulse dial—tone dial—blind dialing—multiple redial up to 8 times. *Call Answering:* Automatic answer automatically connects the personal computer to the phone line. *Personal Computer Requirements:* Requires IBM PC with 128K-byte main memory—5.25-inch diskette. *Software-Supported Menus/Operator Messages:* Communications/other parameters established via screen menus for data format, speed, character length, parity, redial—all can be set via menu or automatically—operator messages including busy, online, list commands, ready, dialing, option number, ringing, no dial tone, voice, failed call, time out, number of retries, answer tone. *Diagnostics/Indicators:* None supported. *Other Features/Options:* File transfer, programmable automatic database log on for online databases—text editing—electronic mail—error control—concurrent operations including data display/printer transfer; data display/disk transfer—operating power derived from the personal computer—includes handset jack. *Cost/Service:* Basic price $549 with terminal software, $649 with electronic mail software—2-year warranty—own service; factory service.

Universal Data Systems, Inc.
Motorola—Information Systems Group
5000 Bradford Drive
Huntsville, AL 35805

103 O/A LP

Application: Compatible with Bell 103 modems—FCC certified. *Packaging:* Stand-alone direct-connect modem. *Operating Parameters:* Full-duplex asynchronous at rates to 300 bps—

originate/answer modes—FSK modulation—RS-232C or current-loop DTE interface. *Dialing:* Manual dial via telephone—supported alternate voice/data via talk/data switch plus regular telephone. *Call Answering:* Manual answer. *Personal Computer Requirements:* Not specified. *Software-Supported Menus/Operator Messages:* None supported. *Diagnostics/Indicators:* Front-panel LED for data on. *Other Features/Options:* Operating power derived from the phone line. *Cost/Service:* Basic price $145—quantity discounts available—1-year warranty—own service; factory service.

212-LP

Application: Compatible with Bell 212A modems—FCC certified. *Packaging:* Stand-alone direct-connect modem. *Operating Parameters:* Full-duplex asynchronous at 1200 bps—DPSK modulation—RS-232C DTE interface. *Dialing:* Manual dial via telephone—supports alternate voice/data via talk/data switch plus regular telephone. *Call Answering:* Manual answer. *Personal Computer Requirements:* Not specified. *Software-Supported Menus/Operator Messages:* None supported. *Diagnostics/Indicators:* Front-panel LED for data on. *Other Features/Options:* Operating power derived from the phone line. *Cost/Service:* Basic price $445—quantity discounts available—1-year warranty—own service; factory service.

Ven-Tel, Inc.
2390 Walsh Ave.
Santa Clara, CA 95051

PC Modem Plus 300

Application: Compatible with Bell 103 modems—personal computer compatibility for IBM PC (and lookalikes)—FCC certified. *Packaging:* Plug-in board—communications software ("Cross-talk") supplied on diskette. *Operating Parameters:* Half-/full-duplex asynchronous at rates to 300 bps—originate mode—FSK modulation. *Dialing:* Manual dial via telephone; terminal keyboard dial; automatic dial with storage for 30 characters—pulse dial—tone dial—tandem dial—single keystroke dial—multiple redial to an infinite number of times—supports a linked list of telephone numbers. *Call Answering:* Manual answer or automatic answer automatically connects the personal computer to the phone line. *Personal Computer Requirements:* Requires IBM PC with 64K-byte main memory—5.25-inch diskette. *Software-Supported Menus/Operator Messages:* 100 plus communications/other parameters established via screen menus as provided by "Cross-talk" communications software—operator messages including no answer, busy, online, help file, list commands, various status indications. *Diagnostics/Indicators:* None supported. *Other Features/Options:* File transfers—automatic database log on for online databases—text editing (limited screen editing)—electronic mail—error control—concurrent operations including data display/printer transfer, data display/disk transfer—operating power derived from the personal computer—supports second digital interface for local printer. *Cost/Service:* Basic price $389, option pricing for speed adapter $300—price ranges from $389 to $689 depending on options—2-year warranty—own service; factory service.

Visionary Electronics
141 Parker Ave.
San Francisco, CA 94118

Visionary 1200

Application: Compatible with Bell 212 modem—FCC certification applied for. *Packaging:* Stand-alone direct-connect modem—internal file storage—internal real-time chronograph—communications software supplied on ROM. *Operating Parameters:* Half-/full-duplex asynchronous at 1200 or 300 bps rates—FSK modulation—2 RS-232C DTE interfaces. *Dialing:* Automatic dial with storage for thousands of telephone numbers (depending on optional size of memory)—pulse dial—tone dial—tandem dial—multiple redial until connection made—will dial a list of numbers and transmit internally stored files to each (with redial). *Call Answering:* Automatic answer will store incoming message internally (for later retrieval) or will automatically turn on personal computer and transfer incoming data. Supports answer back for Telex applications. *Personal Computer Requirements:* Any RS-232 machine and/or RS-232 printer.

Software-Supported Menus/Operator Messages: Communications/other parameters established via screen menus for half/full duplex, dialing mode, parity, error correction (on/off)—operator messages including current date and time, memory contents, memory remaining, help commands, status of outgoing calls, busy or no-answer conditions. *Diagnostics/Indicators:* Front-panel LCD clock display—LED indicators for off hood, carrier detect, sending, receiving, auto-answer active, messages waiting, memory full. *Other Features/Options:* Automatic file transfers—programmable automatic database log on for online database systems—text editing (delete characters only)—stand-alone electronic mail—error control (retransmit improperly echoed characters)—printer spooling—concurrent operations including data display/printer transfer, data display/disk transfer—contains integral nonvolatile RAM (expandable 2-48K); RJIIC jacks. *Cost/Service:* Basic price $795 (2K), option pricing $895 (16K), $995 (32K), $1,095 (48K)—quantity discounts available—120-day warranty—own service; factory service—distributor location.

INDEX

In the entries with multiple references, page numbers in bold face refer to a major discussion.

DATABASICS
Special Offer Section

SAVE $50–$150 ON BIZCOMP
1200 BAUD MODEM

BIZCOMP

The Bizcomp Corp. (see page 560) manufactures the Bizcomp 1012 modem. As a special offer for purchasers of this book, Bizcomp is making the 1012 modem available at a $50 discount when bought directly from Bizcomp (list price $549; special offer price $499). Or use the coupon to order two units for $474—a total savings of $150. For more information on this offer and a certificate for the special discounts, **circle offer number 1** on the reply coupon.

$56 DISCOUNT ON BYTCOM MODEM

Bytcom produces the Bytcom 212AD modem (see page 560). As a special offer to purchasers of this book, Bytcom will give a $56 discount off the normal price of $495 for the 212AD modem (final price after special discount: $439). For more information on the Bytcom modem and a certificate good for the $439 price, **circle offer number 2** on the reply coupon.

TWO FREE HOURS OF CONNECT TIME

CompuServe

CompuServe, Inc., is offering readers of this book two free hours of connect time on either of its diversified database and communications services, the Executive Information Service or Consumer Information Service (see page 307 for more information on CompuServe). **Circle offer number 3** on the reply coupon to receive a "Demopak" containing a certificate good for two free hours as well as an ID which allows access to CompuServe's demonstration system. To use the two hours, you must buy a CompuServe Subscription and Starter Kit, available at computer retailers across the United States and Canada. Then send back the certificate, indicating your subscription ID number, to be credited with two free hours. This offer expires December 31, 1984. Only one coupon per ID will be honored. The certificate is not transferable.

TRIAL MEMBERSHIP, FREE CONNECT HOUR, $10 GIFT CERTIFICATE

comp U store

Comp-U-Store is an online shopping service offering more than 50,000 name-brand products at up to 40% off manufacturers' suggested list prices (see page 304 for more information on Comp-U-Store). Comp-U-Store extends to purchasers of this book the following offer:

- A three-month free trial membership (normally $25 per year)
- One free hour of connect time, good during prime or nonprime time (worth $18 during prime time)
- A $10 gift certificate good toward any purchase of $150 or more

This offer is intended for new subscribers only. To enroll, customers must first charge a $25 fee to their Visa or MasterCard for a 15-month membership (three months free plus one year at normal price). The fee is refundable if membership is cancelled within the 15-month period. For full information and an application form, **circle offer number 4** on the reply coupon. This offer expires April 1, 1985.

10% DISCOUNT TOWARD PURCHASE OF EXECUPORT PORTABLE TELEPRINTER

Computer Transceiver Systems, Inc.

Computer Transceiver Systems, Inc., manufactures a variety of "Execuport" teleprinters and computers which are leased, sold, and serviced nationwide. The company offers to purchasers of this book a 10% discount on the Execuport 4120 portable teleprinter. The 4120 is normally priced at $3,495 (see page 505). For more information on this and other Execuport models (including the new Execuport XL microcomputer series), as well as a certificate good for 10% off the Execuport 4120, **circle offer number 5** on the reply coupon.

$50 REBATE ON CONTEXT MBA

Context
MANAGEMENT SYSTEMS

Context Management Systems is the developer of the Context MBA, the first fully-integrated decision support software program incorporating electronic spreadsheet, data management, business graphics, word processing, telecommunications, and custom forms (see page 534). Context offers purchasers of this book a $50 rebate on the Context MBA. For more information and a certificate entitling you to the rebate, **circle offer number 6** on the reply coupon.

10% DISCOUNT ON SUBSCRIPTIONS

Control Data Cybernet Technology Management Services (see page 407) provides four databases about business opportunities, technologies, and technology transfer mechanisms: TECHNOTEC, Develop, Renewable Energy, and Trade Opportunities. Control Data is offering purchasers of this book a 10% discount off the annual fee for subscriptions to any one of these services (subscriptions normally start at $500). For more information and a discount certificate, **circle offer number 7** on the reply coupon.

FREE ONE-YEAR TRIAL SUBSCRIPTION

Databasics Magazine

Databasics Magazine is a new periodical soon to be introduced by the authors of this book. Each month *Databasics Magazine* will keep its readers up-to-date regarding the practical business applications of electronic information services. As a special offer to purchasers of this book, you may receive a free 1-year trial subscription to *Databasics Magazine* (a $24 value). For more information and a free trial-subscription certificate, **circle offer number 8** on the reply coupon.

$60 DISCOUNT ON ANY SEMINAR ATTENDED

DATABASICS Seminars

DATABASICS Seminars are sponsored by the authors of this book. Each seminar explores the practical uses and applications of electronic information services. Topics covered include both online business databases as well as electronic mail. As a special offer to purchasers of this book, you may receive a $60 discount on the registration fee for any DATABASICS Seminar. For more information and a certificate good for the $60 discount, **circle offer number 9** on the reply coupon.

$250 WORTH OF DATAKITS

Data Resources, Inc.

Data Resources, Inc., produces DataKits, selections of financial and statistical data from DRI's many databases, in VisiCalc format (see pages 215 and 315). DRI offers purchasers of this book $250 worth of DataKits. (To use DataKits, you must have the VisiLink microcomputer program available for purchase from DRI for $250. Users who already own the VisiLink program may receive the $250 worth of DataKits at no further obligation.) For more information and a certificate good for $250 worth of DataKits, **circle offer number 10** on the reply coupon.

TWO HOURS OR ONE DAY FREE CONNECT TIME

Datasolve Ltd. produces the World Reporter database, which carries the Summary of World Broadcasts (information from 120 countries), transcripts of the BBC World Service News, and the full text of *The Economist* (see page 322). Datasolve offers new subscribers to Datasolve either unlimited free search time for one 24-hour period or two free hours of search time to be used up at the customer's discretion (search time normally costs $100/hour). There is a $200 prepayment required, applied toward the first $200 invoiced. This offer expires April 1, 1985. For more information and a certificate, **circle offer number 11** on the reply coupon.

FREE DAY OF CONNECT TIME

DELPHI™

DELPHI offers a wide variety of information and communications services, including electronic mail, an online encyclopedia, news wires, and gateways to other database vendors such as DIALOG and the Official Airline Guides (see page 411). DELPHI extends to purchasers of this book unlimited use of DELPHI for a day (worth $244). Individuals who take advantage of this offer may then, if they wish, register for continuing use at the special membership price of $29.95 (normally $49.95). There is no charge or obligation for the free day of use. The offer includes all standard DELPHI connect-charge services, though some premium priced services are not included. For more information and a certificate for a free day of use, **circle offer number 12** on the reply coupon.

$35 DISCOUNT ON DOCUMENTATION

DIALOG Information Services, Inc., is the world's largest online information retrieval service, with more than 180 databases online (see page 325 for more information on DIALOG). In addition to $100 free connect-time provided to new customers, DIALOG offers purchasers of this book $10 off the *DIALOG Guide to Searching* (normally $50) and free DIALOG documentation for 5 databases (worth $25). For more information on this offer and a discount certificate, **circle offer number 13** on the reply coupon.

$10 DISCOUNT OFF START-UP FEE

DIALOG
KNOWLEDGE-INDEX ^{SM}

Knowledge Index, the off-hours service from DIALOG, offers a selected group of databases at special low rates. Knowledge Index uses a simple command language which is easy to learn. A self-instructional manual and up to 2 hours free connect time are provided to new users. (See page 325 for more information on Knowledge Index.) Knowledge Index extends to purchasers of this book a $10 discount on the sign-up fee (normally $35). For more information and a certificate good for this $10 discount, **circle offer number 14** on the reply coupon.

FREE DAY OF USE

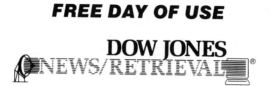

Dow Jones News/Retrieval, one of the major database services, offers a variety of online business news, information, and financial statistics, including text of *The Wall Street Journal,* a complete 20-volume encyclopedia, and foreign and national news. (See page 340 for more information on Dow Jones News/Retrieval.) Dow Jones News/Retrieval extends to purchasers of this book one free day of connect time at no obligation. This is good during the entire 22 hours a day that the service operates, and is worth as much as $1,380, depending on the specific databases used. This offer is available to new subscribers only. For more information and a certificate entitling you to a free day, **circle offer number 15** on the reply coupon.

$25 REFUND ON DOW JONES SOFTWARE

DOW JONES SOFTWARE™

Dow Jones News/Retrieval extends to purchasers of this book a $25 rebate on any Dow Jones Investment Series Software package: Market Analyzer (a technical analysis program), Market Microscope (a fundamental analysis program), or Market Manager (a portfolio management program) (see page 207). For information and a certificate worth $25 on any of these products, **circle offer number 16** on the reply coupon.

DISCOUNT ON USER MANUAL

Dun's Marketing Services
a company of
The Dun & Bradstreet Corporation

Dun's Marketing Services produces several databases available through DIALOG, including Dun's Market Identifiers and Million Dollar Directory (see pages 190 and 193). The user's manual covering these databases normally costs $50 (including updates for one year). Dun's Marketing Services offers purchasers of this book a 30% discount (worth $15) toward purchase of the user's manual. For further information and a certificate good for the 30% discount, **circle offer number 17** on the reply coupon.

ONE-HALF OFF THE RENTAL OF POPULAR TELECOMMUNICATIONS TERMINALS

Electro Rent Corporation

Electro Rent leases and services telecommunications terminals, microcomputers, modems, and electronic test equipment. As a special offer to purchasers of this book, Electro Rent will lease one of its terminals and modems at 50% off the one-month rental fee. This offer applies to popular models including the Televideo Personal Terminal and covers rental periods ranging from two months to one year. Service is included as part of this rental offer. To qualify, the Lessee must pass Electro Rent's usual credit check procedure. For more information and a certificate good toward the 50% rental discount, **circle offer number 18** on the reply coupon.

$200 FREE USE

SUBSCRIPTION AT 50% OFF COVER PRICE

Inc.

ONE-THIRD OFF REGULAR INITIATION FEE

INFO GLOBE

Info Globe is the online vendor for the full text of *The Globe and Mail* of Canada, as well as MARKETSCAN, a stock price database (see pages 139, 210, and 345). As a special offer to purchasers of this book, Info Globe will grant new customers one-third off the initiation fee for The Globe and Mail online database. The initiation fee (normally $100) includes a user's manual, password, and free half-hour of online time in the first month of use. For more information on Info Globe as well as a certificate entitling you to this special offer, **circle offer number 21** on the reply coupon.

$50 DISCOUNT ON REGISTRATION FEE FOR ANY IIA CONFERENCE

Information Industry Association

The Information Industry Association is the leading trade association for the online database industry. It sponsors numerous conferences and seminars of primary interest to individuals involved in the information industry. IIA offers to purchasers of this book a $50 discount on the registration fee for any IIA meeting. Upcoming meetings include:

• IIA Business Operations Council conference on marketing and downloading (September, 1984)
• Annual IIA convention, theme: "New Actors, New Factors" (San Francisco, November 11–14, 1984)
• Other meetings scheduled throughout the year

For more information and a certificate good for the $50 discount, **circle offer number 22** on the reply coupon.

$10 REBATE ON LEXICON LEX-II MODEM

LEXICON

Lexicon Corporation (see page 564) manufactures a line of inexpensive, U.S.-made modems, including the LEX-II acoustic-coupler 300 baud modem with a list price of $159.95. Their modems are available at various retail outlets around the country. Lexicon offers to purchasers of this book a special rebate of $10 on the LEX-II modem. To receive more information and a certificate valid for the $10 rebate, **circle offer number 25** on the reply coupon. This offer expires February 1, 1985. Offer limited to retail customers. Limit one modem per customer. Limit one rebate per customer.

33% DISCOUNT ON DATALINK SOFTWARE

Links Systems produces the Datalink telecommunications software (see page 540). As a special offer to purchasers of this book, Link offers a 33% discount on purchase of the Datalink package (normally $299 when purchased directly from Link). For more information on this offer and a certificate entitling you to the discount, **circle offer number 26** on the reply coupon.

FREE HOUR OF CONNECT-TIME AND FREE NEWSLETTER SUBSCRIPTION

NewsNet is the major full-text vendor of newsletters and other specialized publications (see page 364 for more information on NewsNet). As a special offer to purchasers of this book, NewsNet will give new users a $24 credit for connect-time. (Note: subscribers are obligated to use at least $15 a month in services.) In addition, NewsNet will give all respondents (even if they do not subscribe) a free one-year subscription to the monthly *News-Net Action Letter,* if they include their company, title, and phone on the reply card. To receive your newsletter subscription and more information about NewsNet, **circle offer number 29** on the reply coupon.

$10–$50 CASH REBATE ON MODEM PURCHASE

Novation Inc. makes the J-Cat modem (see page 566). Other products include the Smartcat, a 300/1200 baud stand-alone modem, and the Access 1-2-3, a 30/1200 baud modem card for the IBM PC and compatibles. As a special offer to purchasers of this book, Novation will give a $10 rebate on purchase of the J-Cat (normally $149) or a $50 rebate on either the Smartcat (normally $595) or the Access 1-2-3 (normally $595). For more information on these products and a rebate certificate, **circle offer number 30** on the reply coupon.

FREE SIGN-UP—SAVE $50

ELECTRONIC EDITION®

The Official Airline Guide Electronic Edition lets you find out up-to-date airline schedule and fare information through your terminal (see page 417 for more information on OAG). As a special offer to purchasers of the Electronic Edition, OAG will allow you to sign up and receive a password at no charge—saving the normal $50 sign-up fee. For more information and a certificate good for the free password, **circle offer number 31** on the reply coupon.

$100 DISCOUNT ON CUSTOM COMPUTER SEARCH

PAC Researchers publishes the PAC Directory, a database that tracks financial contributions to candidates for federal office. Information from the PAC Directory is also published in a set of reference books of the same name. Printed *PAC Directories* are available for the 1979–1980 and 1981–1982 election cycles. As a special offer to purchasers of this book, PAC Researchers will give a $100 discount off the price of a custom computer search, such as identifying PAC contributions to a particular federal candidate (typical cost $250 and up). For more information on PAC Researchers and this discount certificate, **circle offer number 32** on the reply coupon.

FREE SUBSCRIPTION TO PEACHTREE QUARTERLY

Peachtree Software, Inc., featured on page 543, manufactures a full line of software products including telecommunications, office productivity, accounting, business graphics, and educational packages. As a special offering to purchasers of this book, Peachtree offers a free subscription to *Peachtree Quarterly* ($12.00 value). Every issue includes technical briefs, a step-by-step approach for using software more efficiently, a question-and-answer section from Peachtree's technical staff, case histories, plus information and insights pertaining to the microcomputing world, and more! For your free subscription, **circle offer number 33** on the reply coupon. No purchase is necessary.

10% OFF PERFECT LINK COMMUNICATIONS PROGRAM

™ ■Perfect Software, Inc.

Perfect Software produces the Perfect Link communications software (see page 544). As a special offer to purchasers of this book, Perfect Software will give a 10% rebate on the purchase of Perfect Link ($149 suggested retail price). To receive more information and a certificate entitling you to the rebate, **circle offer number 34** on the reply coupon.

ONE HOUR FREE SEARCH TIME ON SELECTED INFOLINE DATABASES

Pergamon-InfoLine

Pergamon-InfoLine is a vendor of a variety of British and American databases (see pages 278 and 372 for more information on InfoLine). As a special offer to purchasers of this book, Pergamon will allow one-half hour of free search time on the PATSEARCH database of U.S. and PCT patents and one-half hour of free search time on Dun & Bradstreet's Key British Enterprises database. Both new users and current InfoLine customers may take advantage of this offer. There are no sign-up fees. For information and a certificate good for your free one hour of use, **circle offer number 35** on the reply coupon.

$10 DISCOUNT ON USER MANUAL

❑ QL Systems Limited

QL Systems Limited vends a range of databases with emphasis on Canadian legal topics and news (see page 419). As a special offer to purchasers of this book, the company will give a $10 discount on the *QL/Search User's Manual* (normally $35) or the *QL/Search Data Base Description Manual* (normally $40). No start-up costs are required to become a QL user. For more information and a $10 discount certificate, **circle offer number 36** on the reply coupon.

$25 DISCOUNT ON
QUIK-LINK 300 TERMINAL

Quazon Corp. makes the Quik-Link 300 terminal (see page 516). As a special offer to purchasers of this book, Quazon will give a $25 rebate on the Quik-Link 300 (normally $249.95). For more information on the terminal, as well as a rebate certificate, **circle offer number 37** on the reply coupon.

50% OFF CARRYING CASE

Radio ∫hack®

Two of Radio Shack's products are reviewed in this book: the TRS-80, Model 100 portable computer (page 518) and the PT-210 portable tele-printer (page 517). As a special offer for purchasers of this book, Radio Shack will take 50% off the price of a Model 100 System Briefcase (normally $49.95) or PT-210 Deluxe Carrying Case (normally $24.95). For coupons entitling you to this discount, **circle offer number 38** on the reply coupon.

TWO-THIRDS OFF THE REGULAR REGISTRATION FEE

THE SOURCE is one of the most popular consumer-oriented database and communication services (see page 399). THE SOURCE extends to purchasers of this book a special discount on new memberships: You may sign up for only $29.95, a two-thirds discount off the normal registration fee (major credit card required; $10 minimum monthly fee). This offer expires June 30, 1985. For more information and a certificate good for the special sign-up rate, **circle offer number 41** on the reply coupon.

FREE CASES FOR TELERAM PORTABLE TERMINALS AND COMPUTERS

Teleram makes a line of portable computers and terminals including the Portabubble/81 (see page 522). Teleram offers purchasers of this book a free carrying case worth $75 to $95 with purchase of a Teleram terminal or computer. For more information on Teleram products and a certificate good for your free case, **circle offer number 42** on the reply coupon.

*Be sure to fill out the reply card to claim
your DATABASICS Special Offer(s)* ⟹

MULTIPLE CHOICE OPTIONS FOR ANSWERING QUESTIONS 11, 16, AND 20 ON THE REPLY COUPON.

Choices for responding to *Question 11* on the Reply Coupon (you may select *up to 3* responses):

(a)	CEO/Owner/Partner/Chairman Director	(o)	Distribution/Warehousing
(b)	Other General Management	(p)	Customer Support
(c)	Office Management	(q)	Field Services
(d)	Librarian	(r)	Data Processing/MIS
(e)	Marketing	(s)	Data Communications/Networking
(f)	Sales	(t)	Accounting/Credit
(g)	Corporate Communications	(u)	Finance
(h)	Promotion/Public Relations	(v)	Personnel
(i)	Advertising	(w)	Training
(j)	Planning	(x)	Legal
(k)	R & D	(y)	Government Relations
(l)	Engineering	(z)	Consulting
(m)	Manufacturing/Operations	(aa)	Other
(n)	Purchasing		

Choices for responding to *Question 16* on the Reply Coupon (you may select *all* that apply):

(a)	ADP Network Service	(aa)	ITM
(b)	Agridata Resources	(bb)	Journal of Commerce
(c)	Bibliographic Retrieval Service (BRS)	(cc)	MCI Mail
(d)	Bunker Ramo Info Systems	(dd)	Mead Data Central—LEXIS
(e)	Chase Econometrics/Interactive Data	(ee)	Mead Data Central—NEXIS
(f)	Chemical Abstracts Service	(ff)	MEDLARS
(g)	Chilton Corp.	(gg)	NewsNet
(h)	Citishare	(hh)	OCLC, Inc.
(i)	Comp-U-Card	(ii)	Official Airline Guides (OAG)
(j)	CompuServe	(jj)	Pergamon-InfoLine
(k)	Control Data—Business Information Services	(kk)	Public Affairs Information
(l)	Control Data—Cybernet Technology Management Services	(ll)	Questel
		(mm)	Quotron Systems
(m)	Data Resources, Inc. (DRI)	(nn)	Reuters Ltd.
(n)	Datasolve	(oo)	SDC Information Services
(o)	Dialcom	(pp)	SOURCE Telecomputing
(p)	DIALOG Information Services	(qq)	Standard & Poor's Compustat Service
(q)	Dow Jones News/Retrieval	(rr)	Telerate
(r)	Dun & Bradstreet—Dunsprint	(ss)	TRW Information Services
(s)	Equifax	(tt)	Tymshare
(t)	European Space Agency—IRS	(uu)	VU/TEXT
(u)	G.E. Information Services (GEISCO)	(vv)	Warner Computer Systems
(v)	General Videotex—DELPHI	(ww)	Western Union—EASYLINK
(w)	Info Globe	(xx)	Westlaw
(x)	InnerLine	(yy)	Wharton Econometric Forecasting Associates
(y)	I.P. Sharp Associates	(zz)	Other
(z)	Institute for Scientific Information		

Choices for responding to *Question 20* (you may select *all* that apply):

(a)	Computers	(h)	Communications Software
(b)	Terminals	(i)	Other Business Software
(c)	Peripheral Equipment	(j)	Database Services
(d)	Modems	(k)	Electronic Mail Services
(e)	Printers	(l)	Office Systems and Equipment (other than computers)
(f)	Other Expendable Computer Supplies (like floppies)	(m)	All of the Above
(g)	Local Area Network Equipment and Software		